I0490049

CONTEMPORARY ART

FROM CRESCENT MOON PUBLISHING

Andy Goldsworthy: Touching Nature
by William Malpas

Andy Goldsworthy In Close-Up
by William Malpas

The Art of Richard Long
by William Malpas

Constantin Brancusi: Sculpting the Essence of Things
by James Pearson

Alison Wilding: The Embrace of Sculpture
by Susan Quinnell

Eric Gill: Nuptials of God
by Anthony Hoyland

*The Erotic Object: Sexuality in Sculpture
From Prehistory to the Present Day*
by Susan Quinnell

Minimal Art and Artists in the 1960s and After
by Laura Garrard

*Land Art: A Complete Guide to Landscape, Environmental,
Earthworks, Nature, Sculpture and Installation Art*
by William Malpas

Land Art In Close-Up
by William Malpas

*Colorfield Painting: Minimal, Cool, Hard Edge, Serial
and Post-Painterly Abstract Art From the Sixties to the Present*
by Laura Garrard

Mark Rothko: The Art of Transcendence
by Julia Davis

Jasper Johns
by L.M. Poole

Frank Stella: American Abstract Artist
by James Pearson

Maurice Sendak and the Art of Children's Book Illustration
by L.M. Poole

Sacred Gardens: The Garden in Myth, Religion and Art
by Jeremy Mark Robinson

Sex in Art: Pornography and Pleasure in Painting and Sculpture
by Cassidy Hughes

Postwar Art
by George Knighton

The Art of
Andy Goldsworthy

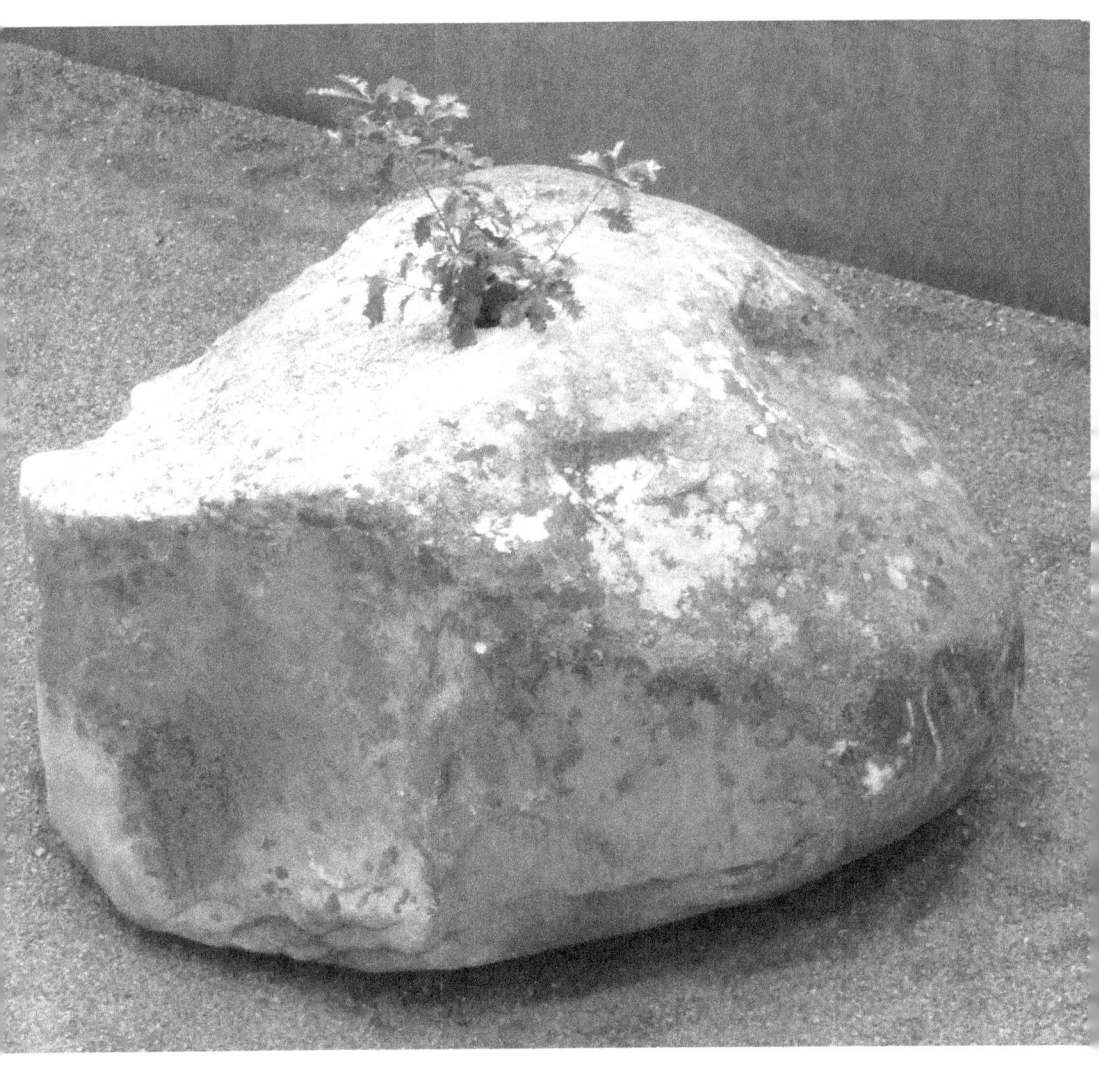

THE ART OF
ANDY GOLDSWORTHY

William Malpas

Crescent Moon

CRESCENT MOON PUBLISHING
P.O. Box 1312, Maidstone
Kent, ME14 5XU
Great Britain, www.crmoon.com

First published 1995. Second edition 1998. Third edition 2005. Fourth edition 2007.
Fifth edition 2013.
© William Malpas 1995, 1998, 2005, 2007, 2013.

Printed and bound in the U.S.A.
Set in Helvetica Neue Condensed 9 on 11pt.
Designed by Radiance Graphics.

British Library Cataloguing in Publication data

Malpas, William
The Art of Andy Goldsworthy. – 5th ed. – (Sculptors Series)
1. Goldsworthy, Andy, 1956 – Criticism and interpretation
2. Outdoor sculpture – Great Britain
I. Title

730. 9'2

ISBN-13 9781861714107 (Pbk)
ISBN-13 9781861714114 (Hbk)

Contents

Acknowledgements   *13*
Abbreviations   *15*
Introduction   *21*

1   **ANDY GOLDSWORTHY: LIFE AND WORK**   *25*

1 : Life • 2 : Works • 3: Critics of Andy Goldsworthy's Art

2   **ANDY GOLDSWORTHY AND SCULPTURE IN THE MODERN ERA**   *37*

1 : Andy Goldsworthy and Women Sculptors • 2 : Sixties Minimal and Postminimal Art • 3 : Constantin Brancusi, Andy Goldsworthy and Postwar Sculpture • 4 : Sugarman, Noguchi, Pomodoro, Samaras • 5 : Kinetic Sculpture • 6 : Light and Space

3   **ANDY GOLDSWORTHY AND LAND ART**   *53*

1 : The Spirit of Place • 2 : The Pollen Path: Art and Life • 3 : The Alchemy of Matter • 4 : The Economics of Land Art • 5 : The Object in Land Art and Minimal Art • 6 : Land Art and Conceptual Art • 7 : Land Art and Photography • 8 : Interior and Exterior Art • 9 : Land Art and Change • 10 : Land Art and Religion • 11 : Circles • 12 : Gender and Scale in Land Art • 13 : Land Art and British Sculpture • 14 : The British Landscape Tradition

4   **LAND ARTISTS IN BRITAIN, EUROPE AND AMERICA**   *97*

1 : Robert Smithson • 2 : Dennis Oppenheim • 3 : Robert Morris • 4 : Carl Andre • 5 : Michael Heizer • 6 : James Turrell • 7 : Nancy Holt • 8 : Alice Aycock • 9 : Mary Miss • 10 : Walter De Maria • 11 : Other American Earth Artists • 12 : Christo • 13 : Hans Haacke • 14 : Richard Long • 15 : David Nash • 16 : Chris Drury • 17 : Other British Land Artists

Illustrations   *156*

5   ANDY GOLDSWORTHY: WHOLE EARTH ARTIST   *203*

6   ANDY GOLDSWORTHY AND PHOTOGRAPHY   *211*

7   COLOUR AND DECORATION   *217*

1 : Andy Goldsworthy's Art and Decorative Art • 2 : Colour in Andy Goldsworthy's Art

8   TREES, TIDES, PLANTS AND HOLES   *229*

1 : Living Plants • 2 : Trees • 3 : The Black Hole • 4 : Tides

9   ANDY GOLDSWORTHY THE SNOW MAN   *239*

1 : Andy Goldsworthy and Snow • 2 : *Touching North* • 3 : *Snowballs In Summer*

10   ANDY GOLDSWORTHY THE GREEN MAN   *247*

11   INSTALLATIONS AND LARGE-SCALE WORKS   *255*

1 : *Stone* and *Herd of Arches* • 2 : The *Capenoch Tree* Series •
3 : Large-Scale Works and Installations • 4 : *Maze* • 5 : *Passage* •
6 : *Garden of Stone* • 7 : Cairns • 8 : *Three Cairns* • 9 : Walls •
10 : *Sheepfolds* • 11 : Arches • 12 : Digne

12   SPIRITUALITY AND SCULPTURE   *281*

13   TIME IN ANDY GOLDSWORTHY'S ART   *287*

List of Works   *299*
Notes   *305*
Bibliography   *323*

Acknowledgements

Thanks to Andy Goldsworthy; Ellie Hall; Viking Press, London; Penguin, London; Thames & Hudson, London; Cameron Books, Moffat; Harry N. Abrams, New York; Michael Hue-Williams Gallery/ Albion, London; Anthony d'Offay Gallery, London; Henry Moore Centre for Sculpture, Leeds; Storm King Art Center, New York; Old Museum of Transport, Glasgow; Common Ground, London; Fabian Carlsson, London; Galerie Lelong, New York; Galerie S65, Aalst; Galerie Aline Vidal, Paris; Haines Gallery, San Francisco; the British Museum, London; Yorkshire Sculpture Park.

Thanks to the authors quoted and their publishers.

Illustrations by Andy Goldsworthy © Andy Goldsworthy.

Thanks to the copyright holders of the illustrations:
Musée d'Art Moderne de la Ville de Paris. Tate Modern, London. Royal Mail Group. John Weber Gallery, New York. Chinati Foundation, Texas. Lisson Gallery, London. Howard Lipman, Connecticut. Chris Drury.

Andy Goldsworthy's art dealers: Fabian Carlsson, London; Galerie Lelong, New York; Galerie S65, Aalst; Haines Gallery, San Francisco; Springer und Winckler, Berlin; and Michael Hue-Williams (Albion) Gallery, London.

Abbreviations

ANDY GOLDSWORTHY

S	*Andy Goldsworthy: Stone*
AG	*Andy Goldsworthy,* 1990
HE	*Hand to Earth: Andy Goldsworthy, Sculpture, 1976-1990*
SS	*Snowballs in Summer Installation*
RSS	*Rain sun snow hail mist calm*
WH	*Winter Harvest*
MC	*Mountains and Coast, Autumn into Winter*
Sh	*Sheepfolds*
W	*Wood*
BS	*Black Stones*
TM	*Time Machine*
Wall	*Wall*
A	*Arch*
MS	*Midsummer Snowballs*
T	*Time*
RA	*Réfuges d'Art*
P	*Passage*

OTHERS

RS	Robert Smithson, *Writings*

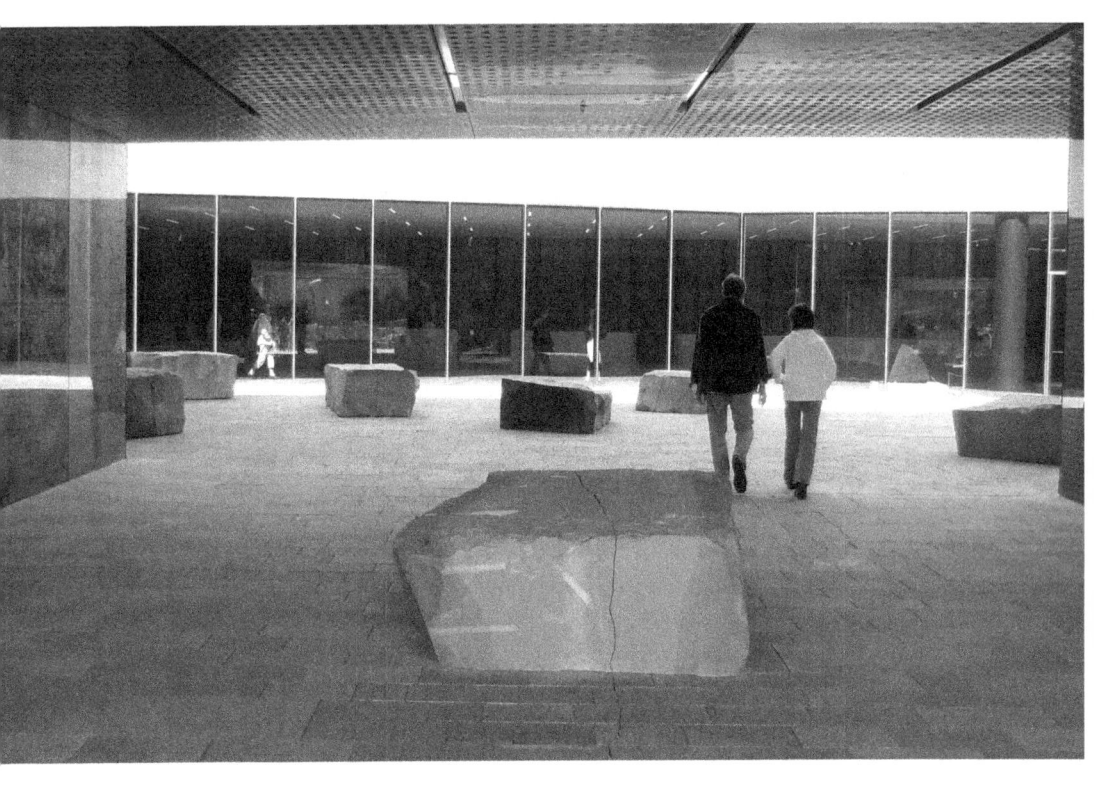

Some of Andy Goldsworthy's recent works in the United States of America
are shown on this page and the followng pages.

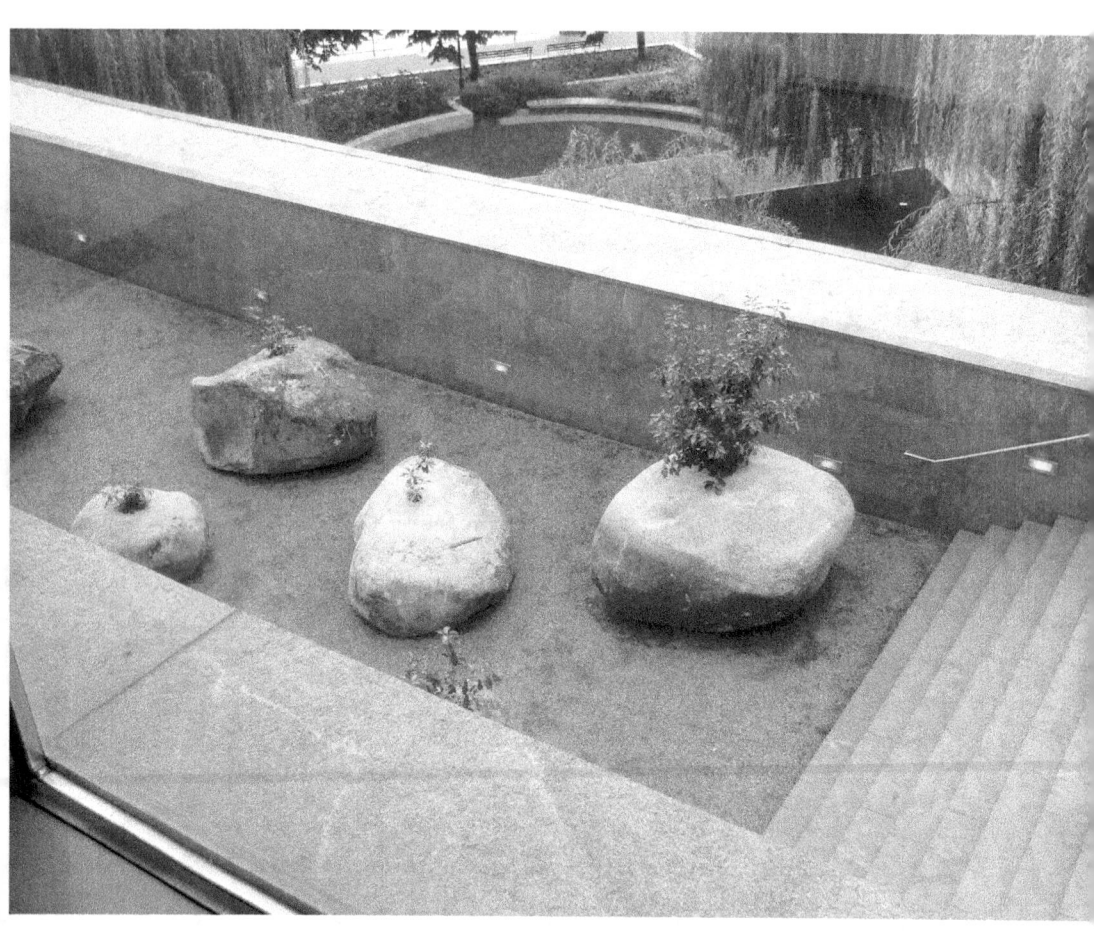

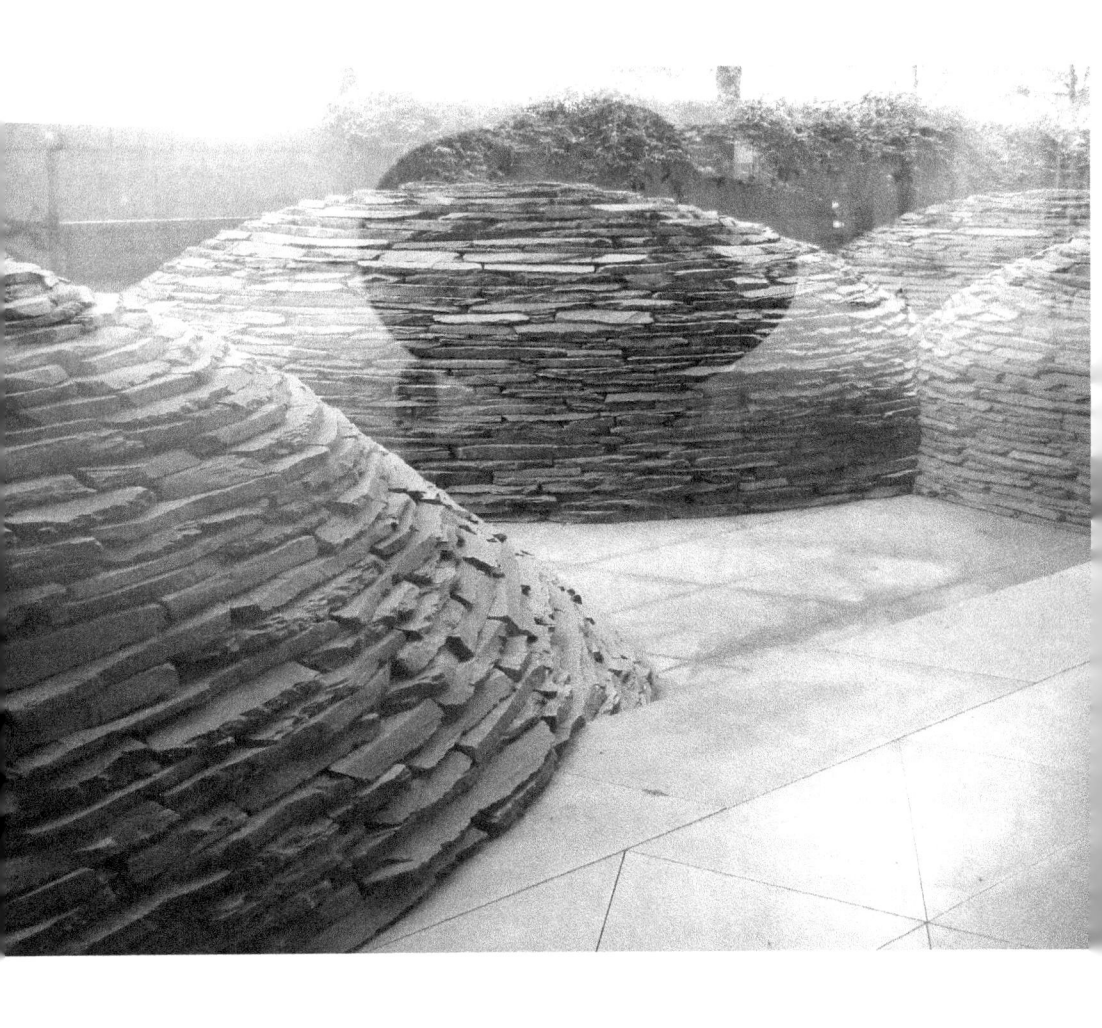

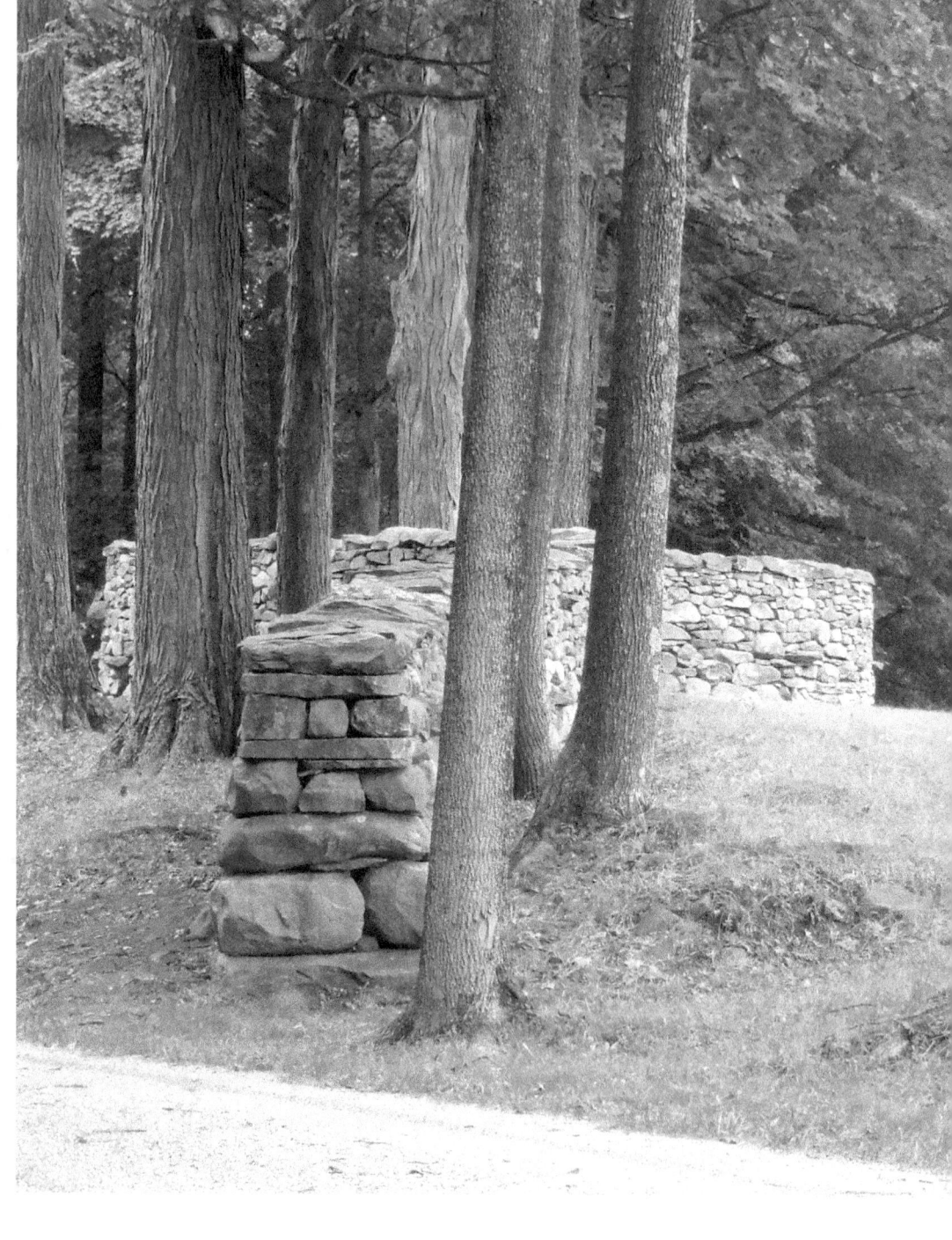

Introduction

This study looks at the contemporary British artist, Andy Goldsworthy.

This book is an updated and much expanded version of my previous book, *Andy Goldsworthy: Touching Nature* (Crescent Moon, 1995). The second edition of *The Art of Andy Goldsworthy* included more material (including new illustrations), many new elements, as well as correcting aspects of the first edition (1998) and second edition (2004).

This fifth edition is a revised edition of the third edition. The text has been corrected from previous editions, the bibliography has been brought up to date, and new passages have been added throughout the text. Some of the new additions to this fifth edition of *The Art of Andy Goldsworthy* are centred around the Andy Goldsworthy book, *Passage* (published in August, 2004), and others around exhibitions (such as London, 2005), and new works.

⁂

Before discussing Andy Goldsworthy's art, I look at sculpture in the modern era; at Goldsworthy's contemporaries (including fellow British sculptors); and at what is called 'land art'. The term 'land art' is used here as a shorthand to refer to many kinds of art, including landscape art, earth art, earthworks, nature art, green or ecological art, and installations.

Andy Goldsworthy's sculpture grew out of modernism and, in particular, 1960s art, the era of Henry Moore, Robert Morris, Robert Smithson, Yves Klein, Michael Heizer, Anthony Caro, William Tucker, Tony Smith and Phillip King. It was the 1960s-70s era of what Rosalind Krauss called 'expanded field' sculpture, the High Renaissance of land art. The whole planet became a site for art.[1] Krauss's 'expanded field' sculptors included Robert Irwin, Michael Heizer, Richard Serra, Walter de Maria, Sol LeWitt, Bruce Nauman, Alice Aycock, Mary Miss, Dennis Oppenheim, Nancy Holt, George Trakis, Richard Long, Hamish Fulton, Christo and Joel Shapiro.

The artists that impressed Andy Goldsworthy at art college included Gordon Matta-Clark, Mark Boyle, Ben Nicholson, Yves Klein and land artists the Christos. In his *Sheepfolds* book (1996), some of the artists that Goldsworthy cited as important included Ben Nicholson, Paul Nash, Joseph Beuys, David Nash and Constantin Brancusi (Katsushika Hokusai is also noted). Goldsworthy attended lectures by Richard Long and David Nash at Preston Polytechnic when they visited in 1978 (both Long and Goldsworthy have noted that it was more common in the mid-1970s to hear about new art and artists from Europe and the United States of America rather than from Britain).

Andy Goldsworthy admired Henry Moore and Barbara Hepworth, two of the biggest names in 20th century British sculpture (and both, like Goldsworthy, were associated with the North of England, and with Yorkshire). Goldsworthy exhibited at the Yorkshire Sculpture Park and the Henry Moore Centre. In *Passage* Goldsworthy describes visiting Hepworth's wonderful gallery and sculpture garden in St Ives, Cornwall, in 2003, and taking some friends to see Moore's *King and Queen* sculpture (1952-53), which's situated at Glenkiln in Scotland (P, 68).

Among the artists who are very close to Andy Goldsworthy's art in their works are Richard Long, Chris Drury, David Nash, Giuseppe Penone and Nils Udo. Some of those artists have fashioned sculptures that are so close to Goldsworthy's own, they can easily be mistaken for Goldsworthy's (Nash, Long and Udo). Some of Giuliano Mauri's woven sculptures, hanging from trees or sited in pools, recall Goldsworthy's art.

And a lot of amateurs have begun making Goldsworthyan art (I've seen some small stone cairns in the Rockies, and California, and a guy on the beach in Lyme Regis in Britain who balances stones exactly like Goldsworthy does).

✤

In this study I have concentrated on some of the more well-known land artists, such as Robert Smithson, Christo, Walter de Maria, Michael Heizer, Richard Long, Robert Morris, David Nash, Hamish Fulton, Nancy Holt, Alice Aycock, Mary Miss, Carl Andre, Dennis Oppenheim and James Turrell. There are, of course, many more artists working with place, site, landscape and the environment. They include Robert Adzema, Vijali, Ana Mendieta, Jan Norman, Jane Balsgaard, Jussi Heikkilä, Tom Van Sant, Sherry Wiggins, Charles Jencks, Roger Ackling, Gordon Matta-Clark, Kazuo Shiraga, Bonnie Sherk, Charles Simonds, Isamu Noguchi, Richard Serra, Tony Smith, Daniel Buren, Gutzon Borglum, Hans Haacke, Jørn Rønnau, Helge Røed, Lars Vilks, Andy Lipkis, Nils Udo, Giuliano Mauri, Bror Westman, Debbie Duffin, Gloria Carlos, Phyllidia Barlow, Richard Fleischner, Michelangelo Pistoletto, Hiroshi Teshigahara, Vong Phaephanit, Alighiero Boetti, Herman de Vries, Joseph Beuys, Betty Beaumont, Betsy Damon, Andy Lipkins, Keith Arnatt, Herbert Bayer, Ant Farm, Newton Harrison, Helen Myer Harrison, Charles Ross, Peter Erskine, Juan Geuer, Jody Pinto, John Baldessari, Donna Henes, Phyllis Yampolsky, William Furlong, Art & Language, Peter Fend, Christian Philip Müller, Cildo Meireles, Harriet Feigenbaum, Ian Hamilton Finlay, Meg Webster, Jan Dibbets, Toshikatsu Endo, Mark Dion, Guo-Qiang Cai, Peter Hutchinson, Lothar Baumgarten, Maya Lin, Douglas Huebler, Bruce McLean, Avital Geva, Barry Flanagan, Mierle Laderman Ukeles, Viet Ngo, Mel Chin, Agnes Denes,

William Jackson Maxwell, Constance DeJong, Doris Bloom, Reiko Goto, Michelle Oka Doner, Buster Simpson, Martha Schwartz, Peter Richards, Douglas Hollis, Patrick Zentz, Othello Anderson, Fern Shaffer, Lynne Hull, Patricia Johanson, Karen McCoy, Dominique Mazeaud and Alan Sonfist. What is written here about the more well-known land artists also applies to the other artists cited above, plus many others.

When it comes to performance art, the field is vast. Performance, live and action art has many links with land, environmental, nature and installation art. There isn't space in this study to consider them all (there are plenty of other studies). There are artists who talk to dead hares in their arms (Joseph Beuys), artists who carry out weird post-Catholic rituals or cut up sheep carcasses (Hermann Nitsch), artists who perform nude with film, video and installations (Carolee Schneemann), artists who draw on their bodies (while naked, of course), artists who sat in rooms and menstruated (Catherine Elwes), sculptors who stood and sang in suits (Gilbert & George), artists who replayed the physical martyrdom of saints (Ron Athey), groups who threw paint and food over each other while singing vaudeville songs (the Kipper Kids), artists who painted gallery floors with their long hair (Janine Antoni), artists who examined their genitals and masturbated before an audience (Annie Sprinkle), artists who had themselves bound and gagged in a gallery, holding a pig's heart (Tania Bruguera), artists who (while naked, of course) masturbate with cuddly toys (Mike Kelly), artists who meditate, chant, sing and play music (Caryle Reedy), groups who burn U.S.A. flags and protest against war while naked on Brooklyn Bridge (Yayoi Kusama), artists who re-enact car crashes at a happening (Jim Dine and Judy Tersch), artists who douse themselves in water (Nam June Paik), artists who shoot guns at paint-filled balloons (Niki de Sant Phalle), artists who burn books (John Latham), groups who stage a protest 'blood bath' in a New York street (Guerrilla Art Action Group), artists who sat on horses in galleries (Jannis Kounellis), performers who locked themselves in rooms for six days while covered in paint (Stuart Brisley), artists who hung themselves upside-down in galleries (Jill Orr), creative couples who walk and bump into each other for an hour (while naked, of course), artists who scrubbed cow bones (Marina Abramovic), artists who stand against trees (nude, of course), covered in mud and plants (Ana Mendieta), artists who set themselves on fire (Tomas Ruller), or ignite gunpowder charges (Roman Signer), groups who sit naked in healing baths (Cai Guo Qiang), performers who have their clothes cut off by the audience (Yoko Ono), artists who signed semi-nude women as 'living sculptures' (Piero Manzoni), artists who hid under wooden ramps in galleries and masturbated while speaking to visitors (Vito Acconci), artists who hung between bridges (Dennis Oppenheim), and artists who crucified themselves on the roof of a Volkswagen (Chris Burden).

There isn't space here to discuss many other contemporaries of Andy Goldsworthy's in sculpture. Other British sculptors of Goldsworthy's generation (all of these were born in the Fifties and early Sixties) include: Charlotte Baker, Jane Ackroyd, David Alesworth, Neale Andrew, Simon Allison, Janet Hedges, Stephen Hitchen, Rasheed Araeen, Lincoln Seligman, John Atkin, Daniel Harvey, Mandy Havers, David Begbie, Kate Blacker, Vincent Borghesi, Charles Quick, Kate Smith, Allan Sly, Michael Talbot, Colin Reid, Will Rogers, Mona Hatoum, Robert Persey, Tessa Pullan, Ian Rank-

Broadley, Barry Mason, Peter Erskine, Rob Olins, Michael Pegler, Tracey Emin, Ron Mueck, Renato Niemis, Julian Opie, Adam Kops, Jeffrey Lowe, Sarah Bradpiece, Philip Brown, David Hugo, Peter Mountain, Olivia Musgrave, Neil Jeffries, David Jacobson, Helen Chadwick, Emily Hoffnung, Hilary Cartmel, John Crossley, Timothy Crawley, Kate Denton, Micky Donnelly, Andrew Horsfall, Kate Whiteford, Richard Wilson, Peter Ellis, Mo Farquharson, Catherine Fenwick, Gareth Fisher, Nicola Godden, Rowan Gillespie, Brian McCann, Jock McFayden, Andrew Sabin, David Saxon, Mark Wallinger, Thompson Dagnall and Denise de Cordova.

It is worth looking at postwar and contemporary sculpture for a while, to see where Andy Goldsworthy's art fits in. British artists Goldsworthy, Richard Long, Hamish Fulton, David Nash, Anish Kapoor, Alison Wilding, Barry Flanagan, Tony Cragg, Richard Deacon and Stephen Cox (among others) are sometimes termed 'Romantic' sculptors, and part of this book relates their art to British Romanticism, as found in the work of William Wordsworth, J.M.W. Turner, Percy Bysshe Shelley, John Keats and others. The British novelist John Cowper Powys (1875-1963) and the British poet Peter Redgrove (1932-2003) are used as reference points for a poetic equivalent of land art and nature mysticism. Powys's and Redgrove's works evoke a sensitivity which is close to the sculpture and land art of Andy Goldsworthy.

Some of the artworks cited in the text are listed in the "List of Works".

William Malpas
London

1

Andy Goldsworthy

Life and Work

Andrew Charles Goldsworthy was born in Sale Moor (10, Delamere Avenue), Cheshire in England, on July 25, 1956. Goldsworthy and his three siblings grew up in Cheshire (at 10, Delamere Avenue, Sale Moor and, from 1961, Bowden Vale in Altrincham), and on a housing estate on the edge of Leeds (in Alwoodley, where his family moved in 1963, when he was 7). Goldsworthy worked on a farm part-time (Grove House Farm, Alwoodley) from age thirteen. Goldsworthy later said (in 2000) that working on the farm had been as important as attending art college. 'The farm and farming were to be as significant to my development as art school, especially as far as response to the land and the working of materials were concerned' (T, 180). Goldsworthy remained fond of farming and farmers throughout his life, often referring to that way of life and work. 'I like being amongst people who farm', he said in 2003 (P, 66), and in 2002 commented: '[m]any of my responses to sculpture have been formed by my experience of working on farms' (P, 118).

Andy Goldsworthy failed the 11-plus exam, for the English grammar school system, and went to Harrogate High School instead. Goldsworthy would subsequently fail to gain entrance to his chosen foundation and degree colleges. (Ironic, perhaps, because his father was Professor of Applied Mathematics at Leeds

University). The Goldsworthy family moved to Ilkley (Yorkshire) in 1975 (while Goldsworthy, now 19, remained in Alwoodley, living in a caravan with his brother at Grove House Farm and working part-time on the farm).

Andy Goldsworthy studied at Wigton Moor County Primary School, Wheatlands Secondary Modern and Harrogate High School (up to 1974). He attended Bradford College of Art (after being rejected from the Jacob Kramer College of Art, Leeds, his first choice), and Preston Polytechnic (based in Lancaster, not Preston), where he studied on the BA Fine Art course, graduating in 1978 (Preston Poly was tried at the last minute, because Goldsworthy hadn't got into Leeds, Nottingham and Hull Polytechnics, his preferences). The archetypal British art school ethics of liberalism, experimentation, art history discussions and the embrace of *avant garde* art prevailed at Bradford and Preston.[1]

As a young art student, Andy Goldsworthy spent much of his time outside college, working on the beaches at Morecambe and Heysham. Goldsworthy preferred to learn by direct experience, finding out about leaves, mud, stone, rivers and tides by living amongst them. Goldsworthy would go into college for one or two days a week, for the art history classes. This was not enough for the lecturers, who suggested that he spend more time in college, including attending life drawing classes. Little did Goldsworthy's lecturers know – that their truant student, who spent hours clambering around the muddy reaches of Heysham Head and Morecambe Bay instead of dutifully attending college classes, would one day become an artist of international renown, with exhibitions and commissions around the world. At the time (*circa* late-1970s), Andy Goldsworthy must have seemed just another crazy art student in jeans and long hair, pursuing his own wacky ideas (British art schools still contain plenty of kooky folk – not all of them students). Hearing of his beach-mud-stone-tide antics, Goldsworthy's tutors must have sighed heavily and put another stroke through the 'absent' column on his attendance record. Amazing to think that this artist-in-the-making would one day be exhibiting at the most prestigious museums in the world (the British Museum and the Metropolitan Museum of Art), designing Royal Mail stamps, and making a Holocaust memorial in New York.

For Andy Goldsworthy, the time spent working at Grove House Farm and the Lancashire beaches was as critical as his art education: '[t]he energy and unpredictability of art outside the studio and gallery were important to me. Going outside art college felt so much more raw, and that's what interested me' (T, 180). However, Goldsworthy did use some of his art school education – the artist's journal and workbook, for instance – the centrepiece of art training in Britain – has remained a significant tool for Goldsworthy (indeed, the accounts in his published books such as *Wood* and *Passage* derive from his notebooks).

Note, for instance, that in working outside, Andy Goldsworthy would be mainly working alone – not within a group of artists. Working without discussing the progress of his work with other artists. A non-urban art. He was also far from the social life of the city and the town, where artists gather to shoot the breeze (a famous group of contemporary (land) artists met in Gotham, for instance, with Robert Smithson at the centre). Or put it like this: there aren't any delis and bars on the

Yorkshire moors, and you can't get a decent cup of coffee in a remote valley in Scotland.

There's not a lot of anger, or angst, or suffering, or self-doubt, or lust, or violence, or propaganda, or neurosis, or disturbance in Andy Goldsworthy's art (again, non-urban) He's definitely not a haunted, tormented artist like Vincent van Gogh, or an aggressive, flamboyant self-publicist like Salvador Dali or Andy Warhol, or an ironic, fey commentator on the postmodern condition, like Jeff Koons or Robert Rauschenberg, or a stridently ideological combatant like Ana Mendieta or Karen Finley, or an in-your-face performance artist like Stuart Brisley or Annie Sprinkle, or a darling of the *avant garde* scene, like Yoko Ono or Matthew Barney. Goldsworthy is a much more modest artist, at least in his public persona, which may be one reason why he hasn't been fêted by the popular media in Britain like the YBAs (although he's had plenty of media exposure: there are now hundreds of articles and reviews of his work).

Andy Goldsworthy's wife, Judith Gregson (who died in a car crash in 2008, aged 48), was a ceramics teacher (she studied at Ilkley Teacher Training College in Yorkshire, and later taught at St Aidan's, Carlisle, Cumbria. Her father, Barry Gregson, ran the Lunesdale Pottery, which Goldsworthy used to make art). Goldsworthy met her at Ilkley in late 1979; they were married on July 17, 1982 (at Caton, Lancashire). Goldsworthy's children are Holly (b. 1990), Anna (b. 1993), Thomas (b. 1994) and Jamie. Goldsworthy's wife Judith occasionally accompanied the artist on his art-making trips into the wilds (though not as often as his assistants). Sometimes his children would come too (as in New Mexico in 1999), but one would expect that children might eventually get bored if their dad spent hours constructing ridges with sand or pinning leaves together.

Judith Gregson's influence on Andy Goldsworthy's art would probably include his use of ceramics (such as working with clay), and several collaborations. Gregson has probably had all manner of influences on the artist difficult to estimate exactly (lovers and spouses have an immense influence on many artists, but credit is seldom accorded. There are many famous cases, of course, of husbands, wives and lovers collaborating with their artist partners. I'd guess that Gregson's influence is substantial in many areas).

Andy Goldsworthy, however, seldom speaks of personal influences on his work. In fact, he rarely mentions other artists or writers in his writing or interviews (there are favourites, like Yves Klein, David Nash, Ben Nicholson and Christo, and the odd writer or poet, like D.H. Lawrence or Norman Nicholson. A lengthy extract from William Wordsworth's poem 'Michael' was quoted in the *Sheepfolds* book, as well as Virgil, from the *Georgics*). Rather than cultural matters, Goldsworthy's writings and interviews are more likely to contain discussions on the quality of stone in a wall or whether it rained or snowed today.

Apart from his wife and family, important people in Andy Goldsworthy's life include land artist David Nash, Steve Chettle (Public Arts Officer for Cumbria County Council), stone wallers Joe Smith and Steve Allen, the Earl of Dalkeith (Scottish land-owner), gallery owners Fabian Carlsson and Michael Hue-Williams, filmmaker Thomas Riedelsheimer, dance director Régina Chopinot, Simon Cutts (Coracle Press), photographer Julian Calder, assistants Ellie Hall and Andrew McKinna, Nadine Gomez (Digne museum), Guy Martini (director of Réserve Géologique in Haute-Provence), Jacob Ehrenberg (in the U.S.A.) and art critics Terry Friedman, Kenneth Baker, Clare Henry and Andrew Causey (one-time Chair of North West Arts).

'My art', Andy Goldsworthy noted in *Time*, 'is rooted in the British landscape, and this is the source to which I must return' (T, 7). Goldsworthy has lived mainly in the North of Great Britain: Cheshire, Leeds, Bentham and Ilkley (Yorkshire), Brough (Cumbria) and Penpont (Dumfriesshire). In Ilkley Goldsworthy created works in the River Wharfe valley and nearby woods.

> I understand best the places where I have worked most often. I have a large well to draw on when realising works in Britain and consequently most of my permanent sculpture has been made there. (*Wall*, 22)

Cumbria was 'very important for me during the two years I lived there', Andy Goldsworthy said.[2] Goldsworthy was a part-time gardener between 1981 and 1986, at Helbeck Hall, in Brough. Goldsworthy spoke nostalgically of the areas in Cumbria, Yorkshire and Lancashire that he knew well. At Clougha Pike, near Lancaster (a favourite Goldsworthy haunt), the artist ruminated in 1999 on places that had long been part of his art and personal life: the Lune valley, where he made sculptures along the river; Caton, where his wife was born; Brookhouse church, where he was married; Hutton Roof, where he worked in a lime kiln; Clapham Scar, where he made a sculpture; Heysham Head and Morecambe Bay, where many of his early works were made; and the Langdale Pikes and Lake District.

In 1986 Andy Goldsworthy moved from Yorkshire and Cumbria, where he'd spent most of his life, to Fernside, Penpont in Dumfriesshire, Scotland, where he has remained ever since. This's where Goldsworthy produces most of his work. Pretty much most of Goldsworthy's exhibitions (and books) feature something made around Penpont. A nearby 2 1/2 acre piece of land (dubbed Stone Wood by the artist) was leased from the Bucclech estate in the late 1980s. The River Scaur, one of Goldsworthy's most beloved spots, is on one side. Goldsworthy's first *Wall*, and many other works, were made at Stone Wood.

This area of Scotland is lowlands, not the famous Highlands of *Braveheart* and Celtic epics (it's hilly, but the hills are 300 or 400 yards high), and predominantly a rural region, a landscape of villages, tiny hamlets, country lanes and farms. It's a world away from the primary cultural centres of Scotland, Glasgow and Edinburgh (Carlisle, capital of Cumbria, down the A76 and A75 roads, is closer than Glasgow or Edinburgh). Penpont is a small village; nearby Thornhill is slightly larger; the main town in the area is Dumfries, 15 miles to the South.

If this part of Scotland is like other rural communities in the British Isles, then it will comprise little clusters of humanity amongst farming land; it'll be modest, provincial, small-scale, close-knit, politically and socially conservative, wary of 'outsiders', and everyone will seem to know everyone else. The American equivalent might be somewhere like rural Minnesota or Nebraska. Very little public transport (a car's pretty much essential). There'll be some locals who haven't been even the few miles to Dumfries, Annan or Ayr for years or decades. For those who like high culture and every amenity, as found in the modern, technological cities of the West, Dumfriesshire will appear as an isolated backwater. But for Andy Goldsworthy, it's perfect: it's Northern, it's rural (non-urban, non-industrial), with easy access to the natural world.

1 : 2   WORKS

Many of Andy Goldsworthy's site-specific works and commissions have been in (and about) the North of Britain: the giant maze and *Lambton Earthwork* (at County Durham, 1988-89), the Grizedale Forest site works (1984 onwards), residencies at Yorkshire Sculpture Park (1987-88), the Lake District National Park (1988), and St Louis Arts Festival (1986), *Penpont Cairn* (2000), *Sheepfolds* (1996-), and so on. Large Northern commissions included *Sidewinder* (1985) and *Seven Spires* (1984), *The Wall That Went For a Walk* (1991) at Grizedale, Cumbria, *Lambton Earthwork* and *Maze* in Durham (1988), *Stone Gathering* at Northumberland (1993), and *Enclosure* in Edinburgh (1990).

It's Andy Goldsworthy's contemporary, though, Anthony Gormley (b. 1950), who has made the sculpture in Northern Britain that has bedded itself in the public consciousness since the late Nineties: the *Angel of the North, a* 65 foot tall steel figure at Gateshead (1998). Goldsworthy has also created a work at Gateshead, a *Steel Cone* (1991) constructed on the site of a foundry (this was part of a proposal to build a group of cones, which was unrealized). It's kind of typical of how Goldsworthy is perceived in Britain that Gormley should have constructed a single work in the North which has entered the popular domain but Goldsworthy, though he has been working there far longer than Gormley, and his *Sheepfolds* project is potentially a much larger endeavour, is far less known.

Andy Goldsworthy has created land art in Grise Fiord, the North Pole, in Japan, upstate New York, California, the U.S. Mid-West, Castres, Digne, La Rochelle and Sidobre in France, the Australian Outback, and in Haarlem, Holland. The first work that Goldsworthy sold was a bunch of photographs to the Arts Council (via Andrew Causey at North West Arts). He has had one-man shows in France, Japan, Holland, the U.S.A. and Great Britain, and participated in groups shows in Italy, Germany, and the U.S.A.

Among his one-man exhibitions are the Serpentine Gallery (1981); *Evidence* (Coracle Press Gallery, 1985); *Rain sun snow hail mist calm* (1985, Henry Moore Centre for the Study of Sculpture, and touring); Kendall, Cumbria (1985); Lincoln (1986); Fabian Carlsson Gallery, London (1987); *Winter Harvest* (Scottish Arts Council, 1987); Gallery Takagi, Nagoya, Japan (1988); Yurakucho Asahi Gallery, Tokyo (1988); *Distant Thunder* (Liverpool, 1988); *Mountain and Coast, Autumn Into Winter* (Fabian Carlsson Gallery, 1988); *Touching North* (Edinburgh, 1989); *Black in Black* (1989);

Snowballs in Summer (Glasgow, 1989); Ayr (1989); *Leaves* (Natural History Museum, 1989); *Garden Mountain* (Paris, 1990); *Photography as Sculpture* (Cardiff, 1990); *Drawings* (Paris, 1990); *Leaves* (1990-91); *Sand Leaves* (Chicago Arts Club, 1991); *Attitudes to Nature* (Ile de Vassivière, 1991); *Mid Winter Muster* (Adelaide, 1992); *Lowther Snowballs* (Aaslt, Belgium, 1992); *Stone Sky* (Belgium, 1992); *Snow and Ice Drawings and Throws* (Edinburgh and Paris, 1992); *Flow of Earth* (1992); *Hard Earth* (London, 1992); *California Project* (San Francisco, 1992); *Morecambe Bay Works* (Lancaster, 1993); *Wood Land* (Galerie Lelong, New York, 1993); *Two Autumns* (Japan, 1993); *Stone* (London, Paris, Cardiff, St Louis, San Francisco); *Breath of Earth* (San Jose Museum of Art, 1995); *Four Stones* (Aasalt, Belgium, 1995); *Black Stones, Red Pools* (New York, 1995); *Earth Memory* (Musée de Digne les Baines, 1995); *For the Night* (Green on Red Gallery, Dublin, 1995); *Sheepfolds* (Carlisle and St Albans, 1996); *Wood* (London, New York, San Francisco, 1996); *Sheepfolds* (Cumbria, 1997); *Cairns* (Digne, 1997-98); *Sheepfolds Drawings* (Cumbria, 1998); *Arche* (Montréal, 1998); *Être Nature* (Paris, 1998); *Installation und Photographer* (Berlin, 1998); photographs (Michael-Hue Williams, London, 1999-2000); *Two Rivers* (Santa Fe, New Mexico, 2000); *Digne Works* (2000); an important show at Storm King in upstate New York and Galerie Lelong (2000); *Fall Creek* (Cornell University, 2000); *Snowballs In Summer* and *Time* (both London, 2000); Austin Museum of Art (2003); *Stone Houses* (New York, 2004); *Early Works* (touring exhibition, 2004-05); *Passage* (London, 2005); *Roof* (National Gallery of Art, Washington, DC, 2005); Yorkshire Sculpture Park in 2007; a Provence art trail in 2009; and a *Clay Dome* in Rio de Janiero in 2012.

Among Andy Goldsworthy's notable group shows are: *British Drawings* at the Hayward Gallery (1982); *Presence of Nature* (Carlisle, 1982); *Sculpture For a Garden* (Cheshire, 1982); *Art and the Land* (Rochdale, 1983); *Place* (London, 1983); *Photographs of Outdoor Work* (Altrincham, 1983); Yorkshire Sculpture Park (1983); *Discovery of the Lake District* (Victoria & Albert Museum, London, 1984); *Second Nature* (Newlyn Orion Gallery, Penzance, 1984); *A Sense of Place* (Sunderland, 1984); *City Thoughts* (Amsterdam, 1985); *Looking at Landscape* (Wigan, 1985); *Between Trains* (Leeds, 1986); *Land Matters* (1986); *The Unpainted Landscape* (Scottish Arts Council, 1987); *Landscape and Sculpture* (Cheltenham, 1987); *The Possibilities of Space: 50 Years of British Sculpture's Drawings* (Musée de Beaux Arts de Besancon, 1987-88); *Artists in National Parks* (at the V & A, 1988); Venice Biennale (1988); *With an Eye to the East* (Scottish Arts Council, 1988); *Camouflage* (Scottish Arts Council, 1988); *Touching On Nature* (Fife, 1988); *British Sculpture 1960-1988* (Antwerp, 1989); *Thomas Joshua Cooper, Andy Goldsworthy, David Nash* (Venice, California, 1989); *Through the Looking Glass: Photographic Art in Britain, 1945-1989* (Barbican Art Gallery, 1989); *Language of Landscape* (London, 1989); *Natural Art* (Dundee, 1989); *Out of the Wood* (Craft Council/ Common Ground, 1989); *Singular Visions* (University of Warwick, 1989); *Photo-Sculpture* (Bristol, 1989); *Landscape Now* (Stoke-on-Trent, 1989); *British Art Now* (Tokyo, 1990); *Shared Earth* (UK and Moscow, 1991); *Impermanence* (Alderich, 1993); *Trees* (Munich, 1993); *Time Machine* (British Museum, 1994, and Turin, 1995); *Northern Rock Art* (Durham, 1996); *Northern Exposure* (Preston, 1997); and *Northern Lights* (Harrogate, 1998). What's striking about the above list of Goldsworthy's group shows is the number that concentrate on landscape and nature art. It's also unsurprising that Goldsworthy has reduced the number of group shows he's participated in as his art has gained in reputation through the Nineties.

A major retrospective, *Hand to Earth: Andy Goldsworthy: Sculpture: 1976-1990*, was held at the Henry Moore Centre for the Study of Sculpture, Leeds City Art Gallery: the show also travelled to the Royal Botanic Gardens in Edinburgh, Stedelijke Musea, Gouda and Centre Regional d'Art Contemporain Midi-Pyrénées in Toulouse. This show also produced the most useful and detailed publication to date on Andy Goldsworthy's art, *Hand to Earth* (later reprinted – see bibliography). 2000's *Time* is a handy update.

Official websites are few on Andy Goldsworthy. There are 3 Sheepfolds sites: sheepfolds.org, sheepfoldscumbria.co.uk, and Striding Arches at stridingarches.com. Also: Andy Goldsworthy Digital Catalogue at goldsworthy.cc.gla.ac.uk, and the *Rivers and Tides* DVD info at: www.skyline.uk.com/riversandtides.

Also worth looking at are: The Artists: <www.the-artists.org>
Sculpture at Goodwood, CASS: <www.sculpture.org.uk>
and Crescent Moon Publishing: <www.crmoon.com>.

One of Andy Goldsworthy's first appearances in the U.S.A. was in the 1984 book *Earthworks and Beyond*, John Beardsley's survey of land art (one of the standard texts on the subject). Goldsworthy's first one-man show in the land of the free was in Chicago in 1991, at the Arts Club.

Andy Goldsworthy's work has appeared on TV in Great Britain in, as expected, Channel Four documentaries (*Alter Image*, 1987; *A Prospect of Rivers*, 1988; *Grizedale*, 1989); BBC 2's *The Late Show* (*Touching North*, 1989); an Arts Council film (*Two Autumns*, 1992, made with Borders TV, Channel 4 and Tyne Tees TV); *Flow of Earth* (1992) was produced for Granada TV's *Celebration* programme; regional current affairs programmes (London Plus in 1986; Tokai TV and NHK TV in 1988; Tyne Tees TV in 1989); a short French documentary (*Nature and Nature*, 1991); children's TV (*Blue Peter*, 1986); as well as a couple of Japanese broadcasts; a 2005 Crescent Moon TV documentary; also the ubiquitous appearances on Radio 4's arts show *Kaleidoscope* and Radio 3's arts interview slot, *Third Ear* (1989). In the late 1990s, Goldsworthy worked with German filmmaker Thomas Riedelsheimer (this resulted in the 2002 documentary *Rivers and Tides: Andy Goldsworthy Works With Time*, available on DVD).

A half-hour BBC TV programme on Andy Goldsworthy's *Sheepfolds* project was aired in 1997; short BBC films linked to *Sheepfolds* were shown in 1998; there was also a *Sheepfolds* exhibition at Michael Hue-Williams Gallery in London (1996). Goldsworthy was shown driving around the North of England in overalls, building stone walls and discoursing to the camera on art and the landscape. The *Sheepfolds* project was funded by Britain's National Lottery (a grant of £340,000/ $545,000) and overseen by Steve Chettle, Public Arts Officer for Cumbria County Council. It included exhibitions (Cumbria, St Albans, London), TV documentaries and books (*Sheepfolds*, *Arch*). It began in 1996 (Year of the Visual Arts) and extended to 2003 and beyond. Goldsworthy aimed to construct a hundred stone sheepfolds.

In the 1990s, Andy Goldsworthy's art began to rise in popularity: the glossy coffee table book *Stone* became a bestseller (bear in mind it was priced at 35 British pounds or about 55 U.S. dollars. 'Bestseller' in art book or hardback terms is not the same as trade paperback fiction. We're not talking about millions of copies sold.) Thames & Hudson, Goldsworthy's British publishers, announced that over 30,000 copies of *Time* had been sold by late 2004 (healthy sales for a hardback art book).

In 1994 Andy Goldsworthy took over some West End galleries with a large one-man show, *Stone* (this included *Herd of Arches*, also made for the Hathill Sculpture Foundation at Goodwood in Sussex, and ultimately finding a permanent home in Cornwall).[1] In 1995 he was part of an intriguing group show, *Time Machine: Ancient Egypt and Contemporary Art*, at the British Museum in London and Museo Egizio, Turin, creating sculptures, along with Richard Deacon, Peter Randall-Page and others, in amongst the monumental statuary of the famous Egyptian Hall. Also in 1995, Goldsworthy designed a set of Royal Mail stamps. As well as commissions, installations, TV and radio programmes, and books, Goldsworthy has also produced limited edition prints (the pictures of cairns were made with Eyestorm, in editions of 500, priced at $720 each).

Other Andy Goldsworthy shows and projects of the 1990s and after included *Mid Winter Muster* in Australia (1991), sand and mulga branchworks; *Seven Holes* (for Greenpeace, 1991); *Black Spring* in Adelaide (1992); a large gateway at Hooke Park in Dorset (1987); wall commissions (such as in New York, 1993, 1996 and 1997); *Cones* (New York and Oxford, 1995); *Four Corner Stones* (Nice, 1993); *Rockfold* (Northumberland, 1993); *Fieldgate* (New York, 1993); clay holes and throws at Runnymede Sculpture Farm, California (1992); *Two Autumns* in Japan (1994); *Breath of Earth* at San Jose Museum of Art (1995); a clay installation (a hole) in L.A. (at the Getty Center for the Arts, 1997; later destroyed by a burst pipe); 'ice houses' and stick lines made in Alaska (1995); a slate cone and chamber for British Airways at their West Drayton HQ in 1998; cairns and 'refuges' at Digne les Bains in 1998; new groups of work at the National Museum of Scotland in Edinburgh (1998); the new *Wall* at Storm King (1998); another wall at Storm King (*Folded Wall*, 1999); a large stone arch in Montréal (1998); *Snowballs in Summer* in London (2000); *Three Cairns* (Des Moines Art Center, Iowa, 2002); *Night Path* and *Chalk Stones Trail*, installed in Sussex in 2002-03; *Garden of Stone*, a memorial for victims and survivors of the Holocaust, sited in Manhattan (2003); the *Stones Houses* exhibited at Gotham's Met in 2004; London installations (2005); *Roof* (2005); Yorkshire Sculpture Park (2007); Provence (2009); and *Clay Dome* (2012).

Andy Goldsworthy's presence in North America grew steadily with a series of exhibitions beginning with the Storm King *Wall* and show at the end of the millennium onwards: Cornell University in 2000; the *Three Cairns* show and installations in 2002-03; Austin Museum in 2003; the *Garden of Stone* and *Stone Houses* in New York City in 2003-04; and *Roof* in Washington in 2005.

Andy Goldsworthy's private commission clients tend to opt for stone cairns/ cones, stone walls and stone arches. Goldsworthy has undertaken private commissions for clients such as British Airways, Royal Mail, Cirque du Soleil, Parnham Trust,

Greenpeace, Coracle Press, and many private houses and collectors (many of the commissions are for outdoor works – in Penpont, Oxford, Lancashire, Cumbria, Wiltshire, Nice, New York state, California, etc). While many public museums and galleries around the globe have bought and exhibited Andy Goldsworthy's work, in his home country, the premier public art gallery, the Tate Gallery, has tended to avoid it (up until 2005). While many Young British Artists have exhibited at the Tate Modern, as well as most of Goldsworthy's contemporaries (David Nash, Richard Long, Tony Cragg, Anthony Gormley, Barry Flanagan, Hamish Fulton *et al*), Goldsworthy has not. (However, Goldsworthy has had exhibitions at prestigious public sites such as the British Museum, the Barbican, the Victoria & Albert Museum, the Yorkshire Sculpture Park, and the Henry Moore Centre).[2]

Andy Goldsworthy has benefitted from a number of awards, bursaries and public arts funding: £300 ($480) from North West Arts Award in 1979 (when he was 23; Yorkshire Arts Award, 1980; Northern Arts Award, 1981; a £4,000 ($6,400) Northern Arts Bursary, in 1982; Scottish Arts Council Award, 1988; Northern Electricity Arts Award; Northern Arts Award, 1995; and National Lottery, 1996. At an early age, then, Goldsworthy was receiving arts funding. He was awarded the OBE in June, 2000.

Andy Goldsworthy's artist residencies include Yorkshire Sculpture Park (1987-88), the Lake District National Park (1988), St Louis Arts Festival (1986), Quay Arts Centre, Isle of Wight (1987) and Hampstead Heath (1985-86). In 1996 he taught for a year at the University of Hertfordshire (as Research Fellow in the art and design dept) and made *Jack's Fold*. Goldsworthy received an honorary BA degree from Bradford University in 1993 and an honorary fellowship from the University of Central Lancashire in 1995. Goldsworthy worked at TICKON (Tranekær Internationale Center for Kunst og Natur) in Denmark in 1993, Alfio Bonnaro's art park (other artists invited included David Nash, Nils Udo, Chris Drury, Karen McCoy and Alan Sonfist). In 1999 he was appointed Senior Lecturer/ Practitioner in Fine Art at the University of Hertfordshire. In June, 2000, he was selected as Visiting Professor at the University of Glasgow, and in July Andrew D. White Professor-at-Large at Cornell University.

Andy Goldsworthy has had many proposals which haven't been realized. One of Goldsworthy's propositions, which has been submitted a number of times, was for five hills along a road, twenty yards tall and planted with trees, which would change with the seasons and the light (T, 192). This work's concerns would have been 'travel, time and distance' (HE, 140). The Autumnal colours of the trees would be a central feature of the piece, and two of the hills would be positioned to catch the sun at dawn and twilight (ibid.).

Another proposal was for a line of rocks and a stone enclosure (S, 113) on a cliff in Toronto, Canada (1992), which would collapse as the cliff eroded. A row of trees growing out of circular openings in stone structures (1994) was unrealized. Many of the *Réfuges d'Art* (Digne) proposals were unrealized. In 1997 Goldsworthy proposed siting a group of fired boulders on the roof of the National Museum of Scotland in Edinburgh (abandoned because of technical problems [T, 199]). The *Snowballs In Summer* project had an American counterpart, which Goldsworthy proposed in Chicago in 1998 (this U.S. snowball project will probably resurface some time). Many of the *Sheepfolds* ideas have yet to be realized. A recurring Goldsworthy proposal is for a group of cones, in close formation: cones made from branches in *Woodland Cones* (1990), proposed for Vassivière in France; steel cones for Gateshead (1991); wooden cones for Grizedale; and stone cairns for Penpont and Grizedale (1987).

Andy Goldsworthy's publications often favour stark (one-word) titles: *Rain sun snow hail mist calm*, *Hand to Earth*, *Wood*, *Stone*, *Arch*, *Time*, *Passage*, *Leaves*, *Garden Mountain* and *Sheepfolds*. The book *Wood* is divided into chapters with single-word titles: "Earth", "Seed", "Leaf" and so on. These titles came from *Végétal*, the dance performance that Goldsworthy collaborated on in 1995. The title, *Wood*, continued Goldsworthy's preference for single-word titles, begun in *Stone* (and continued in *Arch*, *Wall*, *Time* and *Passage*). However, *Wood* might as easily be called *Snow* or *Ice* or, again, *Stone*, because there are many works based mainly on those elements.

Andy Goldsworthy continues to work in countries such as Japan, Australia, Canada, North America and France, but his home ground of Dumfriesshire in Scotland remains (at) the heart of his work. (From the mid-Nineties, Goldsworthy worked increasingly frequently at Digne in South France; it became one of the most valuable places for the sculptor outside of his home in Scotland, and was the site of a major commission, *Réfuges d'Art* [T, 82]). Digne became the focus of the biggest concentration of Goldsworthy art in the world.

It's significant, I think, that Andy Goldsworthy worked as a gardener (for the first half of the Eighties). Goldsworthy's art parallels developments and trends in gardening in Britain and elsewhere. For instance, the use of stones and pebbles in gardens as ornaments or sculptures (paralleling the increased interest in other garden forms, including oriental gardens, as with *feng shui* in New Age culture). The popularity of Goldsworthy's art, I would argue, is in tune with events such as: (1) the rise in gardening shows on TV (and those shows' links with house, food and interior design programmes); (2) the spread of household stores and gardening centres; (3) more gardens being open to the public (including many more private gardens in the *Yellow Book* scheme in Great Britain); (4) the interest in ecological and environmental politics, anti-pollution and recycling drives; (5) and the increase of New Age and mind/ body/ spirit pursuits (such as *feng shui* and Native American religion). Some of the things that fuel this revived (or new) interest in gardens, art and the environment include: (1) an increase in leisure time (and money for entertainment); (2) an ageing population (which also lives longer); (3) new technologies; and (4) new distribution and consumption networks.

Andy Goldsworthy has not created art everywhere. There are plenty of places Goldsworthy has not visited for making art. Even in the British Isles, Goldsworthy has not made much art in Cornwall or Devon or the South-West, or the East (Norfolk, Suffolk, the Fens), not much in the English Midlands, only a few works in Wales, and hardly any in Ireland. If Goldsworthy makes work in Britain, it's usually Scotland, Northern Britain (Cumbria and Yorkshire, but not so much the North-East), or London. (Sussex has been the site of one or two works, such as the *Night Path* and *Chalk Stones Trial*, or the sculptures at Goodwood). That's partly to do with the distribution of the major cultural centres in Britain: most art is exhibited in London and the South-East, and in some regional centres such as Liverpool, Bath, St Ives, Edinburgh and so on. But it's also Goldsworthy's preference for Northern Britain. Given the choice between making art in, say, Cumbria or Hampshire, Goldsworthy will plump for the former.

Around the world, Andy Goldsworthy has concentrated on Westernized territories: on America, of course (it's the centre of land art, and the international art market), Western Europe, Australia and Japan (with the odd excursion to exotic spots, such as the North Pole). Goldsworthy has not made much art in Eastern Europe, in Russia, in mainland China, in India, in Africa or South America. (Goldsworthy did visit Russia in 1991, but 'administration difficulties' prevented the intended work in Siberia [T, 193]). Visits to India, Africa, China and so on will probably come (a *Clay Dome* was shown in Rio in 2012).

.

1 : 3   CRITICS OF ANDY GOLDSWORTHY'S ART

Andy Goldsworthy's art has been discussed widely in the popular and scholarly media, including most of the major art journals (though an appearance in *Farmer's Weekly* – in 1988 – probably pleased Goldsworthy more than articles in *Art in America* or *Modern Painters*). Goldsworthy's supporters include Terry Friedman, Simon Schama, Andrew Causey, Kenneth Baker, Neil Hedges, Michael Hue-Williams, David Nash, Paul Oakes, Mary Beaumont, Paul Nesbitt, John Beardsley, Neil Sinden, and curators such as Hans Vogels, Susan Lubowsky Talbott, Nadine Gomez, Guy Martini, Stephanie Hanor and Chris Gilbert.

Andy Goldsworthy's art has been criticized on a number of levels. For example, its avoidance of political or 'important' or problematic issues, such as AIDS, poverty, 'Third World' debt, globalization, colonialism, war, terrorism, and so on. Its romanticizing of the natural world. Its conservatism. Its nostalgia (such as for a vanished agricultural, working-class past that never existed in the first place). Its escapism. Its self-indulgence. Its élitism. Its repetition and lack of imagination. Its lack of formal experimentation. Its over-simplification of its subjects.

For the nay-sayers, Andy Goldsworthy's art is a romantic retreat into escapist, nostalgic fantasies about nature, with nothing to say about the anxieties, problems and challenges of living in the contemporary, 21st century world. For the critics who deride Goldsworthy, he's a bearded hippy in jeans who panders to the middle class's nostalgia for nature, seen from the perspective of neurotic city dwellers who hanker for the peace and quiet of the countryside. It's also an art that flatters and assuages the bourgeoisie's liberal guilt over wrecking the natural world with its ceaseless, massive consumption and pollution. For detractors, Goldsworthy's art doesn't seem to say much about the particular world they valorize – a late capitalist world, a technological, post-industrial, consumer society.

A critic who dislikes Andy Goldsworthy's art, Jonathan Jones, is typical. In a newspaper article on Grizedale, where the director of the sculpture park, Adam Sutherland, was shifting the Grizedale Society and the park away from Goldsworthyan land art, Jones complained that 'Goldsworthy's art says nothing about the violence, hypocrisy and waste of our relationship to nature and is about as radical as the Body Shop'. While the U.S.A. had big, romantic works of (land) art, such as Robert Smithson's *Spiral Jetty* or Walter de Maria's *Lightning Field*, that were authentic attempts to grapple with the sublime in the natural world, Britain had tree huggers and Goldsworthy's 'twee arrangements of twigs and stones'.[1]

Andy Goldsworthy said that when he was working outside sometimes it was difficult to explain to the general public what he was doing there. Occasionally, he had 'to deal with the anger and bitterness that is sometimes shown towards contemporary art' (A, 74). There is a suspicion and distrust of contemporary art among parts of the population of Great Britain (*viz.*, the hostile reactions to 'Young British Art' or the Turner Prize). Americans, Goldsworthy remarked, were more sympathetic and welcoming (*Wall*, 12). In Digne in 2002 Goldsworthy encountered some resistance to his *Réfuges d'Art* sculptures (the cairns and monuments) – 'the usual dislike of contemporary art' – with some talk of locals sabotaging them. Goldsworthy attended a public meeting (as he has done from time to time) to defend his art (RA, 59). Goldsworthy's sculptures have occasionally been vandalized: for instance, the snowballs (which some folk can't resist kicking over), and the Gateshead *Cone* – the top part was stolen. Maybe some of the opposers of Goldsworthy's installations and sculptures grow to like them eventually. Some of the people who tried to block the Christos' *Running Fence* in California in 1976 got to appreciate it (and some missed it when it was taken down).

Andy Goldsworthy wasn't so sure about encouraging the general public to make their own sculptures, or add to his sculptures: of an idea to invite walkers to add to one of his sculptures on the Digne walking route in 2002, Goldsworthy had second thoughts: 'I'd feel uncomfortable if art released a frenzy of cairn, or sculpture-building' (RA, 97). That's unlikely. It would be more along the lines of some of the works of Richard Long: he has added one stone to an existing pile of stones or a cairn beside a route (cairns being way-markers for walkers).

However, there has definitely been an increase in people building small cairns recently, usually from stones and pebbles – on beaches and in wildernesses. Some of Goldsworthy's art isn't too difficult to replicate (compared with, say, creating a drawing as sublime as one by Leonardo da Vinci).

2

Andy Goldsworthy

and Sculpture in the Contemporary Era

2 : 1   ANDY GOLDSWORTHY AND WOMEN SCULPTORS

Sculpture is a three dimensional projection of primitive feeling: touch, texture, size and scale, hardness and warmth, evocation and compulsion to move, live and love.

Barbara Hepworth[1]

Andy Goldsworthy is one of the more 'feminine' of contemporary male sculptors (one thinks also of Peter Randall-Page, Tony Cragg, Stephen Cox and Richard Deacon among British sculptors). Goldsworthy employs feminine shapes and motifs, such as the vulva and the circle. Exhibited at his 1994 show *Stone* in London was a stone with a vulva-shape carved out of it (*Split sandstone*, 1990). The opening was in layers, receding into the stone, so that the effect was distinctly labial, suggesting the inner folds of the vagina and womb. The same form was used in an Australian sculpture in red sand in 1991 – a vulvic aperture straight into the earth. Goldsworthy also placed the vulva form using clay in a dead tree (1992), and fashioned a vaginal aperture from sticks in some rocks (1992), described by the artist as 'a hole within a hole' (P, 30).

For British rock musician Peter Gabriel's 1992 album *Us*, Goldsworthy created a labial shape out of twigs, set in some mossy rocks. *Slate hole* was a vaginal form made from slabs of slate arranged into a low mound. Richard Long spoke in gendered terms of his lines and circles: the lines are 'male things', while the circles and water are 'a sort of female'.2

As a footnote: Andy Goldsworthy has tended to avoid the vulvic shape since making the early 1990s works – perhaps the connotations are too explicit, or the form is linked to what feminist artists in the 1970s such as Judy Chicago termed 'cunt art'. (Vulvic forms have cropped up from time to time in Goldsworthy's later *œuvre* – such as the labial form fashioned out of mud and moss at the base of a beech tree in 1999, or the first Digne *Réfuge d'Art* [2002]).

Much of sculpture in the modern era in the West has been thoroughly traditional (conservative), and patriarchal, in its orientation and expression. Take Henry Moore (1898-1986), one of the most celebrated of Western sculptors, and one of the big names of modern British art (and admired by Andy Goldsworthy). Moore's nudes, though, are no different from the conventional female nude, found in so much of high art from the Renaissance onwards. Moore's polished wood surfaces, so softly rounded and enigmatic, seem so enchanting. But, despite his formal innovation, Moore is as sexist and reactionary a sculptor as Francis Bacon is as a painter (seen from a (second wave) feminist perspective: that is, Moore has not questioned received, stereotypical representations of women and femininity – which feminist artists have actively tackled).

Modern figurative sculpture (not only made by men) has rarely escaped the usual confines of patriarchal art (that is, pretty much all art continues to be ultimately patriarchal). David Smith's bronze sculpture *The Rape* depicted a woman being raped by a canon, a phallic gun which climbs over her. It is meant to be a savage and ironic comment on violation, but it isn't ironic enough, as with Aristide Maillol's relief of a man assaulting a woman, entitled – what else? – *Desire* (1903-05, Paris). Edward Kienholz's quasi-Surrealist *Back Seat of a '38 Dodge* (1964, the Kleiner Foundation, Los Angeles) is a reassembled car with all manner of bits added to it and inside it – what else? – two people make the beast with two backs.

The great works of contemporary sculpture – Richard Serra's props of metal (*Tilted Arc*, 1981, New York), John Chamberlain's squashed cars (1961, Art Institute, Chicago), David Smith's *Cubi XXVII* (1965, Guggenheim Museum, New York), Alexander Calder's mobiles (*Non-Objective*, 1947) – seem to eschew issues of gender and sexuality. Not much of mainstream (or 'malestream' as feminists dubbed it) modern sculpture concerns itself with eroticism without pain or violence (i.e., out of the Marquis de Sade and Sigmund Freud), and hardly ever feminism.

Important modern women sculptors include Nancy Graves, Eva Hesse, Niki de Sant-Phalle, Barbara Hepworth, Rebecca Horn and Louise Nevelson, and women land artists such as Mary Miss, Nancy Holt, Sherry Wiggins, Donna Henes, Ana Mendieta, Vijali, Betsy Damon, Phyllis Yampolsky, Jody Pinto, Viet Ngo, Helen Mayer Harrison, Mel Chin, Karen McCoy, Meg Webster, Maya Lin, Martha Schwartz, Dominique Mazeaud, Lynne Hull, Doris Bloom, Patricia Johanson, Constance DeJong, Harriet

Feigenbaum, Phyllidia Barlow, Debbie Duffin, Mierle Laderman Ukeles, Gloria Carlos, Agnes Denes and Alice Aycock.3

EVA HESSE is especially interesting; her works repay many visits. Hesse was part of the group that included Carl Andre, Robert Ryman, Sol LeWitt and Mel Bochner (and her art holds up beside any of those guys). Hesse worked in series, like other Process and Minimal artists. She called the repetitions 'sequels' and 'schemas'. Her artworks have an immediate, challenging impact: they are instantly memorable; there is nothing else quite like them. They hang from ceilings, in rows, made of rubber, latex, cloth, wire and fibreglass, evoking organic forms in ambivalent, sensual ways.4 Pieces such as *Ingeminate* (1965, Saatchi, London) offer up a mysterious affirmation of life in the form of two coils of cord connected by a long piece of surgical hose. *Accession II* (1967) was a steel cube filled with rubber tubing. *Several* (1965, London) comprised a bunch of rubbery, tubular forms hanging from a nail on a wall. *Sans II* (1968, Saatchi, London), meanwhile, was a dozen rectangular 'compartments' made from fibreglass which hinted at some obscure systematization of flesh and organic form.

Eva Hesse wrote: '[i]f I can name the content… it's the total absurdity of life'.5 As Anna Chave noted, Hesse's forms resemble abstract 'breasts, clitorises, vaginas, fetuses, uteruses, fallopian tubes', articulating a new feminine sexual subjectivity, utilizing the female, not the male gaze.6 In a 1968 statement, Hesse said (sounding like Ad Reinhardt):

> I remember I wanted to get to non-art, non connotive, non anthropomorphic, non geometric, non, nothing, everything, but of another kind, vision, sort. From a total other reference point. Is it possible? I have learned anything is possible.7

Sometimes loosely hanging, finding their own form (using gravity, like robert Morris's felt works), at other times Eva Hesse's sculptures were bound with wire, as if 'making psychic models', as Robert Smithson said.8 For Hesse, as for many artists, art and life were not separate things, but part of a continuum. Hesse said she didn't keep them apart: 'art is a total thing. A total person giving a contribution. It is an essence, a soul… in my inner soul art and life are inseparable' (C. Nemser, 1970, 59).

JACKIE WINSOR took the cube as one of her major forms, but she manufactured her cubes from natural materials, such as twine and wood. Winsor's cubes take the Minimal cube only as a starting point, because her series of cubes are explorations of the mysteries of ontology. Some of Winsor's works change or decay: the *Burnt Piece* (1977-78) cube burnt away, alchemically, when the artist fired its interior. As with the land artists, Winsor said: 'I was unable to see how the piece would look until the moment of completion'.9 As with many of Andy Goldsworthy's ephemeral sculptures, the process of transformation wasn't just the endpoint of the work, it was the foundation of it (Goldsworthy has also fired works, like Winsor – and David Nash).

LOUISE NEVELSON's signature works were huge reliefs or structures which were like Cubist or Constructivist altarpieces, full of objects, several articles made of wood, all painted in one colour, black, white or gold: chair legs, railings, door knobs. Her sculptures were like magical cupboards, vertical dreamscapes comprising boxes stacked on top of each other, irregular, yet unified by the single colour of the paint, and bound by the rectangle of the cupboard or frame. REBECCA HORN's sculptures are based, like Andy Goldsworthy's, on natural forms, but also on movement, dance, time and environments. Horn's wonderful *Peacock Machine* (1982) is an exuberant activator of space, one of those pieces that aims for the essence of a natural form (a peacock's magnificent tail) and captures it.10 Horn later ventured into some really unusual areas, especially effective when they took on the scale of an installation (as her show at Tate Britain demonstrated). Witty and ironic, but definitely in the black side of the humour spectrum, Horn's sculptures took a unique view of contemporary life.

BARBARA HEPWORTH is one of the great British sculptors of the modern era. Her organic forms, as with Constantin Brancusi's forms, hovered between subjectivity and objectivity, between natural form and æsthetic abstraction (as in her *Two Forms* [1937], for example). Like Brancusi, Hepworth maintained that she always returned to nature, and took her inspiration from nature. For her, nature meant the landscape (and the Cornish landscape in South-West Britain in particular), and the human body. 'We return always to the human form – the human form in landscape', she said. Her sculpture stems from emotion and expression: 'I rarely draw what I see – I draw what I feel in my body', she remarked.11 Hepworth's distinctive forms, with their smooth curves and holes, are clearly sensual objects. Hepworth acknowledged the sensuality of sculptural forms. Hepworth said that the natural setting was 'the most tremendously inspiring one to me'. Driving around Cornwall, Hepworth found that it was her personal (bodily) response to particular landscapes that mattered.12

Many women sculptors have explored 'feminine' imagery and issues. LOUISE BOURGEOIS (rightly one of the key female voices in the modernist era), explored the relations between form and eroticism, volume and psychology, shape and nature. Her forms usually deal with eroticism – her *Nature Study* (1984), for instance, featured the bulbous volumes which are practically her trademark, echoing breasts, clitorises, vulvas, buttocks, heads, hands, knees, tongues, all the parts of the sexualized body.

ALISON WILDING, a British sculptor (b. 1948) who has affinities with Andy Golds-worthy, directly embraced the potential for sculpture to be supremely sensual. Her abstract forms hint at alchemical transformations, intimate experiences, investig-ations of sexuality and the relations between space, imagination, fantasy and the body.13 Wilding's *Hemlock III* (1986), for example, was, like her *Blueblack* (1984), a wooden dish containing hemlock, lead, lime and beeswax, allusive of arcane experiments. The dish with its dangerous substances was a kind of womb, a motif or experience that appears in much of modern sculpture, from Judy Chicago's *Dinner Party* (1979) to the womb interiors of Louise Bourgeoise and others.

Alison Wilding's sculpture often featured two elements, one was usually large, the other, small. These two elements are luscious and mysterious, part way beyond interpretation, though some critics interpret them as masculine and feminine elements, the twin poles of heterosexuality, which are involved in some arcane dance or dalliance.14 Wilding herself stressed the enigmatic nature of her work: '[t]he obverse of making is looking, not telling'15 and she emphasized, as so many artists do, the creation of the sculpture: '[t]he making and doing processes…[are] always the mainspring of the work'.16 David Nash, Bill Woodrow and Andy Goldsworthy also iterate the making of sculpture.

The eroticism of Andy Goldsworthy's sculpture is of a different order from traditional, figurative sculpture, the sculpture of, say, Michelangelo Buonarroti and Gianlorenzo Bernini. Due to the 'abstract' nature of Goldsworthy's sculpture, his work generally escapes obvious sexism. The famous sexist and heterosexist depictions of people in modern sculpture include Alberto Giacometti's *Spoon Woman* (1926, Zurich), a view of woman as Earth Mother, a totemic figure; Gaston Lachaise's *Standing Woman* (1912-27, Whitney Museum of American Art), one of those smooth, curvy Goddess types, also favoured by Aristide Maillol; Hans Bellmer's bizarre *Dolls* (1936), where the slit of a vulva is where the head would be, and set amidst exaggerated, bulbous forms; Henri Gaudier-Brzeska's *Red Stone Dancer* (1914, Tate Gallery, London), though it attempts a new way of depicting gesture and posture in space, is still sexist; Elie Nodelman's *Dancer* (1918, New York), like Paul Manship's *Dancer and Gazelles* (1916, Smithsonian Institute, Washington, DC), and Edgar Degas' *Dancer* sculptures (Metropolitan Museum of Art, New York), is also sexist; and Ernst Ludwig Kirchner's *Standing Nude* (1908-12, Stedelijk Museum, Amsterdam) also affirms gender stereotypes.

French artist NIKI DE SANT-PHALLE produced exuberant Goddess sculptures, such as her *Black Venus* (1967, Whitney Museum, New York), or her marvellous *Pink Childbirth* (1964, Moderner Museet, Stockholm), a Great Mother Goddess constructed out of dolls, toys, tissues and several items collected together like a totem of the prehistoric world. Sant-Phalle's *Un Ensemble de "Les Nanas"* (1965, New York) was an effervescent – and multi-coloured – representation of female forms, dancing, cavorting, balancing.17 Among non-figurative, abstract or partially-figurative artists, women such as NANCY GRAVES are astonishing, with her superb multimedia constructions.18 Nancy Graves' skeletal, fossil-like works combine fantasy and natural forms in 'one exuberantly open-form, polychrome, free-standing construction after another'.19

The body features occasionally in the art of Andy Goldsworthy in a direct manner. The spectator sees the shape of Goldsworthy's body after a snowfall or rainfall (in his *Rain Shadows*), or 'printed' onto frosty ground by his shadow at sunrise. Goldsworthy sometimes appears in photographs, beside his work. Goldsworthy's hands are seen, and other parts of the sculptor, but there is nothing in Goldsworthy's work (or that of Hamish Fulton, Alison Wilding, Richard Deacon, Stephen Cox or Barry Flanagan) that is as ferocious as feminist and women's body and performance art (land artists are rarely as confrontational as feminist artists).

Feminist artists use the body to explore political, social, ideological, erotic, æsthetic and philosophical discourses. As Lisa Tickner wrote in "Body Politic": '[l]iving *in* a female body is different from looking *at* it, as a man. Even the Venus of Urbino menstruated, as women know and men forget'.20 The female nude, for so long the model and image (and object of desire) in so many high art paintings, has usurped the power relation between artist and art object, and between artwork and spectator.

The woman is no longer content to be looked at and lusted after: she is making her own art, employing her body in a radical, challenging way. The 'Old Master/ *Playboy* tradition', as Tickner called it, has been smashed.[21]

Some examples of performance and feminist artists include Carolee Schneemann, who pulled a scroll from her vagina and read from it; *Meat Joy*, dubbed 'lovemaking with brushes', is her most famous happening work, a classic piece of American 1960s performance art.[22] Karen Finley poured 'a can of yams over her naked buttocks' in a performance piece. She was called 'a frightening and rare presence'.[23] In her *Cut Off Balls* Finley 'castrated' Wall Street bankers.[24] Chila Kumari Burman made 'body prints'. Mary Duffy displayed her disabled body in performance and photographic sequences;[25] Jo Spence photographed the 'unhealthy and ageing female body'.[26]

Feminist body and performance art (particularly of the 1960s-1980s) was a way of repossessing the body, sexuality, identity and power; it was a way of 'rewriting the body' (in the terminology of French and postmodern feminism). It could be an act of transgression and subversion, which usurps the power relation between spectator and artwork, so that the (male) viewer's 'cloak of invisibility has been stripped away and his spectatorship becomes an issue within the work', as Catherine Elwes put it.[27]

One aspect of feminist or women's art was (and still is) embodied by the figure of the Goddess, the ancient and primæval Great Mother of all, celebrated then – and now – as Isis, Ishtar, Diana, Cerwidden, Demeter, Kali, and so on. The Goddess embodied aspects of the feminine – love, motherhood, purity, nobility, sacrifice, beauty, hunting, and so on. Since the 1960s, the Goddess has been variously interpreted as fact, experience, idea, æsthetic, cult, religion, pagan emblem and many other things by women artists and writers. (The rise of interest in witchcraft, the supernatural and paganism, in TV shows such as *Charmed, Hex* and *Buffy the Vampire Slayer,* especially among young women, are part of this. There are cross-overs in pop music, Goth culture, cinema, Neo-Romanticism, high street fashion, as well as contemporary art).

There are a host of artists who pursue what one might call 'Goddess art', art that employs the figure of the Goddess as an embodiment of female being or experience: Judy Chicago, Mary Beth Edelson, Miriam Schapiro, Carolee Schneemann, Niki de Sant-Phalle, Louis Bourgeois and Helen Chadwick are some of the famous ones. Menstruation, pregnancy, childbirth, child rearing, matriarchal families and societies, marriage, rape, violence against women, censorship, lesbian and queer identity, are some of the subjects addressed by feminist artists. Mary Beth Edelson engaged in the resurgence of interest in the Goddess in her *Great Goddess* series (1975). Edelson also produced a piece on menstruation, entitled, appropriately, *Blood Mysteries* (1973). In a performance, Catherine Elwes sat in an enclosed studio space and menstruated.[28] Judy Chicago looked to the flowers of Georgia O'Keeffe, which, she said, 'stand for femininity'.[29]

The spirals and circles of Andy Goldsworthy, Robert Smithson, Dennis Oppenheim, Richard Long and other land artists could be seen as Goddess art: circles so clearly evoke Goddess themes such as time, cycles, (Moon) phases, dance, transformation, ritual, initiation, astronomy, and so on. The circle is also a profound shape for

Renaissance alchemists. As the *Rosarium Philosophorum* has it: 'make a round circle and you will have the stone of the philosophers'.[30] Richard Long created, in Ireland, an ancient maze form out of small stones set on grass (*Connemara Sculpture*, 1971), and Robert Morris also constructed a labyrinth (*Labyrinth*, 1974). The shape of Long's and Morris's labyrinths directly recall the Cretan labyrinth of initiation and ritual, and the spirals at the entrance to Newgrange in Co. Meath, a huge passage grave some 4,500 years old. Richard Fleischner, Michelangelo Pistoletto, Hiroshi Teshigahara, and Vong Phaephanit have also created maze structures.

2 : 2   SIXTIES MINIMAL AND POSTMINIMAL ART

The world of Minimal art was clean, calm, devoid of unruliness, violence, dirt, even ambiguity (and for some, emotion). It was an art of new faceless, technological, advanced capitalist places like an airport: white, spotless, spacious, blank, anonymous. Or a new shopping mall. A row of pristine supermarket shelves, stacked high with new cans of fruit, and the labels all turned face-out (and all screenprinted *à la* Andy Warhol).

Minimal art was an art for the 1960s, an era of commodification and consumerism on a global scale, and the rising affluence in the West after the austerity of the 1950s and the catastrophes of the 1940s, an era when mass production created a uniformity to the appearances of so much of street, home, personal, medical, transport and educational furniture (especially in Western Europe and America). Minimal sculpture, critic Barbara Rose remarked in *Art International*, looks 'machine-made, industrial, standardized, materialized or stamped out as a whole'.[1] Other aspects of Minimal sculpture include the multiplicity of sculptural material, many of which were new media (fluorescent lights, Plexiglas, fibreglass, Formica, chrome, plastic), simplicity, surface, and the insistence on the environment and contextual space.

Minimal sculptures are (were) not set on pedestals, like Renaissance or Greek sculpture; they sit on the floor, or lean against walls (as in Robert Morris's *Floor Piece*, or Carl Andre's *Cedar Piece*). Richard Serra based his basic unit, the prop, around gravity, around one thing leaning on another. Minimal sculptures exist in the same space, on the same plane (the floor) as the viewer. They are, as Morris said, in an in-between cultural space, somewhere between being monuments and being ornaments, between being architecture and jewellery.[2] Andy Goldsworthy too does away with pedestals.

In Minimal sculpture, surfaces were, typically, utterly smooth and 'pure'. Simplicity was exalted, and repetition, seriality, process, flatness (as well as volume and space). The many materials were flattened out and depersonalized. Gestures, so important to certain kinds of sculpture (including Andy Goldsworthy's sculpture), such as the whole history of traditional figuration, were suppressed. Indeed, the flatness and smoothness of the surfaces, whether in the art of Robert Morris, Donald Judd, Dan

Flavin, Carl Andre, Ronald Bladen or Tony Smith, was crucial in Minimal art, and consequently some commentators called Minimal sculpture and the 'new sculpture' 'boring'.3 For Peter Fuller, there was nothing 'spiritual' about Minimal art: he spoke of 'the numbing vacuity of works by artists such as Carl Andre, Agnes Martin, Ellsworth Kelly or Brice Marden'.4 The boringness, though, becomes a part of the metaphysics of Minimal sculpture, so that Lucy Lippard wrote in "New York Letter: Recent Sculpture as Escape":

> the exciting thing about… the "cool" artists is their daring challenge of the concepts of boredom, monotony and repetition… their demonstration that intensity does not have to be melodramatic.5

Andy Warhol was a big fan of mundaneity. He said: 'I like boring things. I like things to be exactly the same over and over again'.6 And Donald Judd responded to the charge of reductionism, to those art critics who thought Minimal art was lessening or reduction:

> I object to the whole reduction idea. If my work is reductionist, it's because it doesn't have the elements that people thought should be there. But it has other elements that I like.7

Andy Goldsworthy's art maybe hasn't got enough in it for some people: it's certainly founded on many Minimal principles. But boring art for some is exhilarating art for others, just as erotic art for some is pornography for others. Critics tended to either love or loathe Minimal art: James Mellow wrote that a Donald Judd show was 'one of the most provocative of the season',8 while in "Looking at American Sculpture" Barbara Rose described Judd's art as 'our most radical sculpture, if not perhaps our fullest'.9 Certainly Judd's wall reliefs, hollow boxes and stacks are beautiful, sensuous, luscious, sexy – whether constructed from traditional materials such as brass or copper or newer materials such as Plexiglas and red automotive lacquer (a Judd favourite). Judd combined the eroticism of industrial materials with cool geometric patterns. Judd, like other Minimal sculptors, combined austerity with sensuality, producing 'minimal forms at the service of glamorous, hedonistic effects of light' (Hilton Kramer).10 As Barbara Haskell wrote in her book on Judd:

> By coupling these luxurious materials with spare forms, he exploited their inherent "language". The opposition between the inert and rigorous geometry of his forms, and the opulent hedonism and shimmering colour effects of his surfaces accounted for the unexpectedly exultant lyricism of his work.11

Although 'nothing' seems to be 'going on' in a Donald Judd sculpture, I'd says his art is far more compelling than thousands of other sculptors, including the ones who're brilliant with the human form, or social satire, or grand themes, or whatever. Indeed, one could make a case for Judd being not only among the two or three most important sculptors of the second half of the 20th century, but *the* most significant.

Only artists such as Robert Smithson, Henry Moore, David Smith, Tony Smith. Isamu Noguchi and Louise Bourgeois might be contenders.

Minimal artists such as Donald Judd, John McCracken, Carl Andre, Sol LeWitt and Robert Morris explored notions of 'boringness' and 'interestingness'. 'Boring art is interesting art', wrote Frances Colpitt in her excellent book on Minimalism (121). Donald Judd, the chief explicator of Minimal æsthetics, wrote: 'I can't see how any good work can be boring or monotonous in the usual sense of those words', adding: '[a]nd no one has developed an unusual sense of them'.[12] Clearly, the Minimal sculptors thought they were making 'interesting' art. Or at least, *they* were interested in it. If art's good, it can't be 'boring', said Judd, claiming that 'a work needs only to be interesting'. The discussion of discourses such as 'interesting', 'boring' and 'value' becomes a quagmire of semantics and the metaphysics of meaning. What *you* find interesting someone else might find dull as hell. Language soon fails to describe the kinds of intentions that artists have, and the kind of responses that critics and punters have to works. Robert Mangold commented, 'I certainly know whether I'm interested in the work or whether I'm not interested in the work'.[13]

One of the triumphs of Minimal art was to make seemingly dead and uninteresting materials such as steel and plastic sensual and appealing. On 'boringness', Robert Morris wrote that sculpture is found 'boring' by those who desire 'specialness':

Such work which has the feel and look of openness, extendibility, accessibility, publicness, repeatability, equanimity, directness, immediacy, and has been formed by clear decision rather than groping craft would seem to have a few social implications, none of which are negative. Such work would undoubtedly be boring to those who long for access to an exclusive specialness, the experience of which reassures their superior perception. (1967, 29)

Some might see this kind of Minimal, Conceptual or mathematical art as too abstract, too unreal, too dry and clinical. But critics such as Robert Rosenblum claimed that Conceptual art can be 'awesome'. Of Sol LeWitt's art, Rosenblum remarked that it

elicits…an immediate awe that… has to be translated by the same feeble words – beautiful, elegant, exhilarating – that we use to register similar experiences with earlier art.[14]

One might see Minimal sculpture as so 'cool' it's lifeless. Yet, despite the profusion of smooth white surfaces, which evoke clinics and hospitals, there is much sensuality in Minimal sculpture.

Some of sculpture in the decades after WW2 consisted of hard-edged cubes or rectangular slabs. Whether this use of such stark mathematical forms like cubes is rational or intuitive, it takes a scientific, numerical approach to art to extremes. The idea, Donald Judd wrote, is simply to do 'the next thing', to do 'one thing after another'. It is a strategy that is not called a strategy, a systemless system. Of Frank Stella's paintings, Judd wrote that the 'order is not rationalistic and underlying, but is simply order, like that of continuity, one thing after another'.[15]

The notions of Minimalism – seriality, succession, progression, repetition, permutation – have been around for a long time. Leonardo da Vinci, one might say, painted the same picture in different ways, often abandoning projects before completion, while J.M.W. Turner seemed to be painting the same sky, attacking it from thousands of different viewpoints and different locations, from every hilltop, riverbank and coastline of Britain, and in France, Switzerland, Italy and Germany. And many other artists seem to have one basic picture or form which they create time after time: Peter Paul Rubens, Eric Gill, Caspar David Friedrich, Wassily Kandinsky and Kenneth Noland.

But – whether the system is serial or modular, whether there is progression or simply repetition – the notion of Donald Judd's – 'doing the next thing', 'one thing after another' – explains so much of Minimal (and contemporary) art. It explains so much of Judd's work, for instance, those ladders or stacks of forms ascending to the ceiling in bronze or plastic, and those long lines of curved shapes set on a wall. It also describes how artists simply go on making work, as variations, or repetitions, or progressions, like Mark Rothko with his many canvases that explore different combinations of purple or yellow clouds floating on oceans of red or blue, or Ad Reinhardt's seemingly repetitious but actually methodical explorations of five foot square black canvases, or Andy Goldsworthy with his stone cairns, lines of leaves and walls. Minimal ethics can produce some extremes of mathematics and seriality.

Minimal sculpture is certainly austere – 'cool', as some critics call it. It is very ascetic, restrained, flat, exact, with its smooth surfaces and precise square edges and angles. The body seems to have been erased from this 'cool' Minimal art. There is no space for the body, and the spectator is also 'erased', in some way. The ruthless asceticism of Minimal art denies the body, like early Christian theology (although the body is always there finally).[16]

2 : 3   CONSTANTIN BRANCUSI, ANDY GOLDSWORTHY AND CONTEMPORARY SCULPTURE

It was Constantin Brancusi's (1876-1957) project to strip away the detritus that had accumulated around sculpture, Henry Moore said, and to offer the pure, simple form. What Brancusi did, Moore remarked, was 'to concentrate on very simple shapes, to keep his sculpture, as it were, one-cylindered, to refine and polish a single shape to a degree almost too precious.'[1] This is what many sculptors have done since 1945, keeping their shapes simple and purified: Andy Goldsworthy, Alison Wilding, Richard Deacon, Stephen Cox, David Nash, Richard Serra, Donald Judd and Robert Smithson. The influence of Brancusi's art is apparent in Minimal, Arte Povera and Postminimal sculpture. Robert Morris, Judd, Carl Andre, Dan Flavin, Chris Drury and Goldsworthy have acknowledged Brancusi's art as an inspiration. His *Endless Column* (1918) was cited by Minimalists. Andre's early work *Last Ladder* (1959, London) is something like Brancusi's *Endless Column* (putting Brancusi along the ground, as Andre said).

Quite a few artists (not all of them sculptors) have expressed admiration for Constantin Brancusi's photographs, and the way he would set up his sculptures in his studio and photograph them at particular times of day, when the lighting was just right. Andy Goldsworthy said he admired how Brancusi created the conditions in his studio so that his work 'comes alive at a particular time of day as the light momentarily touches it' (RA, 85). For Goldsworthy, Brancusi's works were at their best when they were arranged by the sculptor in his studio and photographed (Sh, 22-23). Somehow, it wasn't quite the same when they were displayed in modern art museums (such as the Pompidou Centre in Paris or the Museum of Modern Art in Gotham, which have important Brancusi pieces; in the Pompidou, for instance, you look into a central room of Brancusi's sculptures through plate glass, so you can't walk amongst them).

The Brancusian ethics, of simplicity, purity, smoothness, interiority and organic form, are found in the Minimal sculptors, as well as the Constructivist notion of working with materials in a 'natural' way, so that the material dictates the form one creates with it. Barry Flanagan commented that sculpture works directly with materials:

The convention of painting has always bothered me. There always seemed to be a *way* of painting. With sculpture, you seemed to be working directly, with materials and with the physical world inventing your own organisations.2

Andy Goldsworthy would agree with such views. For Goldsworthy, the Romanian sculptor

remains close both in his sculpture, his photography and the relationship between the two. His work explains much about the way I feel for sculpture, time, atmosphere and light. (Sh, 22)

For Andy Goldsworthy, it's not just sculpture on its own that's important, it's also how it's photographed and presented. Goldsworthy usually photographs his sculpture himself. Many artists hire someone else to do that, but Goldsworthy likes to choose the angles, the framing, the lighting and all the rest of it himself. He's not, as he acknowledges, a techno whizz, but he does have a Hasselblad (120mm) camera, a panoramic camera, lenses, tripods, etc. He also likes to choose the exact moment for photographing his work. He speaks of feeling anxious if he can't snap an ephemeral sculpture at the right time (for instance, with the cairns built for the incoing tide, Goldsworthy prefers to capture the precise moment of collapse, and worries when he's got to change the film over, in case he misses it). If a film doesn't come out, it's disappointing. When he was photographing his *Prairie Cairn* in Iowa in 2001, it was cold enough for his camera to slow down (P, 95).

Andy Goldsworthy's sheepfolds and stone walls are serpent-like forms, curving around trees, following the contours of the landscape, something akin to GEORGE SUGARMAN's (b. 1912) erotic, flowing sculptures. Like Lynda Benglis's or Gio Pomodoro's sculptures, Sugarman's works are twisting, entwined shapes painted in red, white, green and yellow. Sugarman created a series of objects, interlinked spatially and thematically, set end to end, a chain of mystery. Sugarman's seemingly disparate collections of objects were united in part by his use of colour. Taking his cue from Stuart Davis, Sugarman used colour spatially. In Sugarman's art, the flat colour – all-over red, or yellow, or green – tended to suppress the irregularity of his peculiar shapes (in, for example, *Bardana*, 1962-63, Zurich). Goldsworthy favours red as an all-over colour. This use of colour to flatten things gives a collection of objects a unity; it's found also in Tony Cragg's *New Stones* (1978), where all the kitchen utensils, household items, children's toys and miscellanea are painted with the colours of the spectrum in a uniform manner, going from red through yellow to blue.

When bright, primary colours are employed in sculpture, as in the grand scale of Minimal sculpture, such as on ISAMU NOGUCHI's huge *Red Cube* (or Andy Goldsworthy's poppy-covered stone), the result has a formal purity that borders on the child-like. How simple and 'right' seem these bold, sunny colours when combined with the simplicity, self-assurance and exactness of basic geometric shapes such as cubes, or spheres, cones or pyramids. One might see this indulgence in purity and precision combined with vivid colouration as an erotic pleasure. This simplicity of colour and formal purity is found in Philip King's orange and green painted blocks (*Call,* 1967, Juda Rowan Gallery, London), the powder colour on Anish Kapoor's semi-organic shapes (*Half*, 1984, Barbara Gladstone Gallery, New York), and the green lacquer on John McCracken's *Untitled* (1967, Saatchi Collection), although Minimal/Conceptual sculptors and painters such as Sol LeWitt and Robert Ryman only permitted themselves white. Isamu Noguchi spoke reverentially of the qualities of stone, like Goldsworthy: stone is 'the most physical involvement, to which I return with zest', Noguchi said (1968, 38).

GIO POMODORO's (b. 1930) sculptures comprised crumpled sheets of fibreglass which directly recall the fields of unbroken colour of the Abstract Expressionists, in particular Barnett Newman, Franz Kline and Mark Rothko (as in *Tensione*, 1959). LUCAS SAMARAS's (b. 1936) works were the flipside of George Sugarman's sensual forms. Samaras deliberately subverts the eroticism of sculpture by furnishing his sculptures and assemblages with pins, nails, razor blades, knives and scissors, as in his vicious *Book 4*, which is stuffed with knives, nails and razor blades. For Samaras, as for so many (male) artists from Dante Alighieri through the Marquis de Sade to Georges Bataille and William Burroughs, sex (pleasure) is intermixed with death. Or, as Samaras put it: 'I cannot separate beauty from pain.'[1]

Andy Goldsworthy's sculptures often move: the leaves shift in the breeze; the stalks bend in the wind; the snow melts; the tide crashes into the rocks and cairns; the arches collapse. They are real things set in the real world, which is always moving. Time extends outwards from Goldsworthy's sculptures, much as in Alexander Calder's mobiles, which, no matter what the scale, extend far beyond themselves, by virtue of their construction and motion. Like optical and light sculptures, Calder's mobiles create spaces around themselves which act on the viewer in a palpable manner, quite distinct from the relatively staid and stolid approach to sculpture of, say, Antonio Canova or Luca della Robbia. This is not to say that pre-20th century sculpture is immobile: far from it. Take Giovanni da Bologna's *Mercury* (1564, Florence) for instance: as the winged messenger of mythology, a 'static' depiction of Mercury or Hermes would be a mistake, and da Bologna's statue is full of movement. Gianlorenzo Bernini's *David* (1623, Rome) is similarly dynamic: the man's body is twisting, ready for battle, ready to carry out one of the most celebrated acts of murder in the history of art.

The kinetic dimension would be out of place in the sombre religiosity of Barnett Newman's or Constantin Brancusi's sculptures. There are some sculptor's work which just seems to be static and rock solid. Indeed if Michelangelo Buonarroti's statues of *Moses* (1513-16) or the *Pièta* (1498-99) were mobile, it would be utterly out of keeping with the tone and theme of these solemn, awe-inspiring sculptures. Gravitas demands solidity, mass, immobility. Other sculptors, though, actively developed motion in sculpture: Naum Gabo with his *Kinetic Construction* (1920), with its oscillating rod; Len Lye's magnetized steel *Loop* (1963) and *Fountain* (1959), which wafts from side to side; Marcel Duchamp with his *Roto-relief* (1920, Yale University Art Gallery), which span around, creating a circle; '*[m]ovement* is an important *dimension* in my art', Hamish Fulton said (1995); Andy Warhol created a room full of silver balloon-pillows, which drifted about (*Clouds*, 1966, Leo Castelli Gallery, New York); and George Rickey with his swaying rods of steel, as in *Peristyle III* (1966, Washington, DC). But the master of kinetic sculpture must be the rebellious Jean Tinguely, whose motorized sculptures gleefully and mischievously created chaos.

The affinities between Alexander Calder's (1898-1976) mobiles and Andy Goldsworthy's sculptures include a delicacy of touch, a love of thin, spindly shapes (stalks and leaves in Goldsworthy's art, wire and leaf shapes in Calder's art), and an actualization of time and motion. Calder's constructions are delicate filaments of wire, with the distinctive 'leaf' or circle forms at the end of each tendril. The facture of the mobiles is dazzling in itself. In *Thirteen Spines* (1940, Cologne), Calder fixed one wire to another, near the end, forming a chain of spines rather like the quills of some mechanical armadillo.

Andy Goldsworthy's sculptures dazzle with their sense of balance: Alexander Calder's mobiles mystify with their extraordinary balancing acts. The mobile is taken for granted now, so obvious does its construction seem. One sees mobiles everywhere, with teddy bears, whales, fairies, clowns, stars, moons, trains and Pierrots hanging from them. When an object balances it sets up an immediate, physical tension. Goldsworthy spoke in 1996 about how the 'precariousness of a balanced column is like the fine edge between success and failure – the tension of growth' (*Wood*, 23). What is most exciting about Alexander Calder's skeletal mobiles, though, as with Goldsworthy's precariously balanced rocks, is their motion, or their potential to move. Calder's mobiles drift slowly, each arm moving in a different manner from the others. They are powered by the random, natural energy of the breeze; thus, they could be seen as environmental artworks, because they are dependent for part of their impact on natural forces such as wind, temperature and air pressure. The balancing acts of Calder's mobiles are playful – the sculptures set alight the space around them with their gravity-shaping design and movement (as if in the act of moulding the space around them). Norbert Kricke created sculptures which looked like frozen lightning strikes, all spikey and angular, the thin rods of steel being set at different angles to each other.[1] Calder does not have a monopoly on thin, spindly sculptures made of steel: David Smith, Hans Uhlmann, Eduardo Chillida, Nancy Graves, Jean Tinguely, Alberto Giacometti and Kricke all produced sculptures in this manner.

2 : 6   LIGHT AND SPACE

Light: one recalls the reported dying words of Romantic artists like Johann Wolfgang von Goethe, who called for 'more light!', or J.M.W. Turner, who supposedly said 'the sun is god' on his deathbed. Numerous sculptors, installation artists and land artists have worked with light and lighting: Dan Flavin and his fluorescent tubes; Bruce Nauman, who made very narrow corridors lit by green fluorescents; James Turrell with his skyspaces; Robert Irwin's re-worked gallery spaces; Maria Nordman's extensions to studio exteriors; Nancy Holt's *Sun Tunnels*; Eric Orr's sound and light environments; and DeWain Valentine's acrylic tubes hanging alone from gallery ceilings. Other light artists include Douglas Wheeler, Hap Tivey, Susan Kaiser Vogel and Larry Bell.

Eric Orr (1939-98) constructed a *Silence and the Ion Wind* installation (1980), a series of dark rooms culminating in the *Golden Room*, 'an allusive structure for an elusive experience', approached through an ion wind.[1] In *Wall Shadow, Sky Lights, Sound Tunnel, Zero Mass, Sunrise, Blood Shadow, The Stone Snake, Prime Matter* and *Blue Void*, Orr deployed sound, light, wind, sand, ice and shadow. In *Prime Matter* (1981), Orr created fog and flames from a twenty foot tall metal column (a larger version was constructed outside the Mitsui Fudosan Building in L.A. in 1991). Orr has fired xenon lasers up into the sky on top of skyscrapers in Long Beach, CA (a permanent installation, *Landmark Lumière*, 1991).

Many artists have taken gallery spaces and reworked them, adding walls or scrims, or curtains, or false ceilings, or doorways, or new windows. Often these light and sound spaces look like empty gallery rooms: Eric Orr (*Light Space*, 1985), Hap Tivey's *Sodium Exchange* (1976), Susan Kaiser Vogel's *Point Conception* (1980), DeWain Valentine's *Curved Wall Spectrum* (1974), Larry Bell's *Leaning Room II* (1988), Bruce Nauman's *Yellow Triangular Room* (1973), Douglas Wheeler's *All Gray Graduating Light* (1976), Maria Nordman's *6/ 21/ 79 One Day Only* (1979), James Turrell's *Second Meeting* (1988), and Robert Irwin's Kansas *Installation* (1979).

The forerunners of these light spaces includes Yves Klein's *Le Vide*. Some artists made the reconstituted gallery interior one of their trademarks. For example, Robert Irwin has constructed *Fractured Light – Partial Scrim Ceiling – Eye-level Wire* (1971), *Acrylic Column* (1970), *Eye-level Room Division* (1973), *Soft Wall* (1973), *Scrim Veil* (1975), *Wall Division – Portal* (1974), *Window Room* (1973), *Black-Line Volume* (1976), *Scrim Veil – Black Rectangle – Natural Light* (1977) and *Untitled (Three Triangulated Light Planes)* (1979).

Andy Goldsworthy has created many works specifically for particular lighting conditions, for moonlight, for sunrises, or the sunlight shining through a forest canopy. Working in Virginia in October, 2003, for instance, on leaf and clay sculptures in a wood, Goldsworthy made light one of the elements he'd explored. He spoke of the light as 'extraordinary, at times hypnotic, even nauseating' (P, 75). As he worked in the Government Island location, Goldsworthy said that he had learnt about 'what I find the most difficult of lights – sunlight through trees' (ib.). Goldsworthy said he had achieved 'a great lesson in time, colour and light' by creating a pointed stone edged with red leaves (*Red Leaves,* 2003). It was the way the sunlight created shadows on the floor of the copse, and over his sculpture, that intrigued Goldsworthy. It was also the *changes* in the light, from sunlight to deep shadow: to illustrate this, Goldsworthy printed a series of photographs in his book *Passage* (76-79). (And not only of *Red Leaves*, but also of other works created in Virginia: a group of pictures depicting a serpentine line of clay placed in a cut in a rock at different times during the day [P, 80-82], and a clay chevron [83-85]).

3

Andy Goldsworthy

and Land Art

3 : 1   *SPIRIT OF PLACE: LAND ART*

…it is an intensely spiritual affair I have with nature: a relationship.

Andy Goldsworthy[1]

For the land artist, the whole planet can be an artist's studio. The land artist ranges over the whole globe (and into the sky, too). A desert, a beach, a field, and a forest can become a studio, a place of creative activity. The landscape itself is crucial in land art: every aspect of a landscape. The weather. The light. The wind. The very texture and colour and shape and dampness and springiness and strength and size of moss, for instance. Or a stone. Or a crevice in a rock formation. The way the light falls on a patch of grass, with little bits of dead, yellowish grass on top of newer, green grass. Redwood tree cones, closed-up. Icicles forming on a wall. Flowers turning sunward in the late afternoon. The sound of water.

I have always paid great attention to natural forms, such as bones, shells, and pebbles, etc [wrote Henry Moore in the 1930s]. Sometimes for several years running I have been to the same part of the seashore – but each year a new shape of pebble has caught my eye, which the year before, though it was there in hundreds, I never saw. Out of the millions of pebbles passed in walking along the shore, I choose out to see with excitement only those which fit in with my existing form-interest at the time.[2]

These are the things land artists deal with in making art. These are the actualities that artists employ when they create artworks. To fully appreciate land art, then, the spectator has to look really closely, to grasp the details, as well as the overall conception and the distant view. This is true of Andy Goldsworthy's sculptures, as well as the larger American earthworks.

David Nash asserted that 'land art' was 'close-up', not distanced.[3] For Nash, land art is about getting as near as possible to nature: the land artist does not paint nature, from way off, with a paintbrush or watercolour block in front of her/ him. The sketchpad or easel is a wall between artist and world. The land artist, rather, dives in, 'gets right in there', as Nash put it. The land artist does not use oil or pastel or ink to 'represent' nature. Rather, s/he works directly with nature, getting her/ his fingers dirty with mud, snow, sheep shit, stone, ferns, wood.

It is exactly the same with poetry. Poets have long written of nature in close-up, of the minutiæ that go to make up an accurate description of the natural world. Land art can be seen as the sculptural equivalent, in one sense, of nature poetry, so that Robert Irwin, Hamish Fulton, James Pierce, Alan Sonfist and Alice Aycock are the inheritors of William Wordsworth, Matsuo Basho, Francesco Petrarch, Robert Frost, Emily Dickinson and Aleksandr Pushkin. The nature poem itself is a piece of land art, a work evoking or representing or describing or situated in particular places. ('The sculpture that I do,' said David Nash, 'is appropriate to a particular place and it stays in that place. It is made from and for that place.')[4]

'Land art' is a term that includes a wide variety of artistic forms, like the term 'garden'. Gardens are not a single form with a single set of characteristics. Gardens can be so various that some critics have suggested that the word 'garden' is as broad and vague as words such as 'art'.[5] If art can be just about anything in modern times, then perhaps a garden can also be anything.[6] Gardens can be very small or very large; they can be flat or terraced on a hill; they can be organized around a 'natural' plan or a strictly geometric plan; they can be 'wild' or 'tamed'; they can be enclosed or open; they can be surrounded by walls or fences or hedges or trees; they can contain lakes, ponds, streams, fountains, statues, trees, lawns, shrubs, rocks, walls, fences, benches, flowers, stones, follies, ruins, grottoes, temples, paths, boardwalks, arches and many kinds of environmental art.

A Japanese Zen garden, for instance, with its stones and sand raked into patterns, and its very minim al use of plants and colour, is quite different from an Iowa kitchen garden, or a mediæval herb garden within the walls of a monastery. Gardens can be vast displays of state and regal power, such as the gardens at Versailles or Tivoli, or modest attempts at cultivating food in a yard. Gardens have been made for many reasons: in the pursuit of decoration, finance, medicine, religion, contemplation, play, sport and food. Isamu Noguchi thought of gardens as the sculpturing of space: a beginning, and a groping to another level of sculptural experience and use: a total sculpture space experience beyond individual sculptures. A man may enter such a space: it is in scale with him; it is real. (1968)

For some critics, the most interesting aspect of land art is its connection with gardening and landscape design.[7]

If there can be 'found art', can there be a 'found garden'? Perhaps an artist, working in the Conceptual and environmental art mode, could simply claim any piece of land as their 'found garden', just as artists such as Marcel Duchamp, Kurt Schwitters and Robert Rauschenberg took found objects and exhibited them as art. American artist Gordon Matta-Clark bought tiny pieces of land and incorporated them in an artwork. Andy Goldsworthy said that even farming could be regarded as a 'very sculptural activity', so that an act like making haystacks could be 'one of the biggest acts of Minimalism you've ever seen', and planting a row of potatoes could be (seen as) an installation (*Wall*, 14-15). Land art's premier artist – Robert Smithson – took a dim view of gardening: art degenerates as it approaches gardening, he said.[8]

When does a garden start becoming a garden? Is a blade of grass a garden? Is two plants on a window ledge a garden? Or five plants, or ten plants, clustered together in pots? Is an overgrown path a garden? Or an allotment dedicated to growing tomatoes and runner beans? Is a patch of grass behind an abandoned gas station a garden? Is a municipal park, consisting only of children's swings and slides on grass a garden? Is a farmer's field a garden? And when does a garden stop being a garden? Is a garden of a hundred years ago that can barely be seen amidst piles of refuse still a garden? How much of the human touch is required to make a piece of land a garden? If sand raked into a pattern can be a garden for the Japanese Zen Buddhist, is any piece of raked sand a garden? Are the patterns made in the sand by the receding tide a garden? Is the sea making gardens with every tide? Or the wind, or erosion, or earthquakes or other natural forces?

Environmental or land or garden art can include American earthworks (such as those by James Turrell and Mel Chin); ephemeral interventions in the environment (such as those by Andy Goldsworthy, Hans Haacke and Michael Singer); architectural installations (such as those by Mary Miss, Alice Aycock, and Nancy Holt); land art as performance art (Richard Long, Hamish Fulton, Christo), even if the artist is the only audience; land art that involves landscaping and garden art (such as Alan Sonfist, Patricia Johanson, Robert Irwin and Ian Hamilton Finlay); and sculpture or art parks. There are 'video gardens', too, such as Matthew McCaslin's *Bloomer* installation: 12 TV monitors played tapes of flowers blooming in time-lapse. The TV sets were arranged in groups like plants, with the cables tangled on the floor (St Louis Art Museum).

Key land art shows include *Earth Art* (Andrew Dickson White Museum of Art, Cornell University, 1969), which showed Dibbets, Long, Smithson, Oppenheim and Morris, *Land Art* (Hanover, 1970), *Earthworks* (Dwan Gallery, 1968), *The New Sculpture, 1965-75* (Whitney, 1990), *Qu'est-ce que la sculpture moderne?* (Paris, 1986), *Virginia Dwan, Art Minimal, Art Conceptuel, Earthworks* (Paris, 1991), *Earthworks* (Seattle, 1979), *Conceptual Art, Arte Povera, Land Art* (Turin, 1971), and many of the

Documenta exhibitions at Kassel. At *Earth, Air, Fire, Water* (Boston, 1971), Haacke, Christo, Smithson, Oppenheim, Long, Sonfist, Huebler, Hutchinson, Warhol and Heizer showed works. Some of the key writers on land art include Rosalind Krauss, Lucy Lippard, Michael Fried, Kenneth Baker, John Beardsley, Lawrence Alloway, John Coplans, Diane Waldman, Harold Rosenberg, Stephanie Ross, Robert Hobbs, David Bourdon, Mel Gooding, Germano Celant, Alan Sonfist, Baile Oakes, Jeffrey Kastner, Andrew Causey and Gilles Tiberghien.

3 : 2   THE POLLEN PATH: ART AND LIFE

Land artists, like nature poets and nature mystics, are inspired by particular places. Nature poets, like religious mystics or land artists (or all artists), can be described as 'following their bliss' (Joseph Campbell's term). When you follow your bliss 'you come to bliss'.[1] Campbell used the model or metaphor of following the 'pollen path' of the Navaho Indians. As Campbell defined it:

> The Navaho have that wonderful image of what they call the pollen path. Pollen is the life source. The pollen path is the path to the centre. The Navaho say, "Oh, beauty before me, beauty behind me, beauty to the right of me, beauty to the left of me, beauty above me, beauty below me, I'm on the pollen path".[2]

This is one way of imagining the creative journey – towards the centre, the life source. Paradise, the Golden Age, Eden, was not back there then, but it is now. 'Eden *is*…this is it, this is Eden', insists Campbell (ib.). It's *now*, and can only be 'now'. There is no other time it could possibly be (and here, too: where else could it be?). The journey, whether physical, psychic, spiritual or imaginary, is along the *feng shui*, the 'dragon lines', or along the 'lines of song' or 'dream tracks' of the Australian aborigines, or the 'pollen paths' of the Navaho Indians.[3]

Like Chris Drury, Hamish Fulton and Richard Long, British author Bruce Chatwin spoke lovingly of walking, of wandering, of nomads and wildernesses. In *The Songlines*, Chatwin made notes upon Australian dreamtime and 'songlines', the lines that crisscross the landscape. Britain has its own version of this *feng shui* or earth magic: ley lines ('discovered' by Alfred Watkins).[4] Richard Long's maps often look like those of a New Age ley line hunter, crisscrossed with ink lines. Andy Goldsworthy, Dennis Oppenheim, Hamish Fulton and Long produced their own versions of 'songlines', whether in powdered snow, drips of water, lines of maple leaves, or words. As in the books of Bruce Chatwin, Paul Theroux, Jonathan Raban, Colin Thubron and other travel writers, there is a deep sense of motion and travelling in the art of Fulton, Drury and Long. Theirs is an art born out of travels, even if the journeys are nothing more than morning walks out from the studio. These journeys don't have to be weeks long, crossing the Sahara on foot or over the Poles by sled; they can be made on an afternoon stroll.

Andy Goldsworthy has also constructed works based around walking: his *Réfuges d'Art*, sculptures sited along a walking trail, the *Chalk Stones Trail* and *Night Path* in Sussex, the more recent Provence art trail, a work that is a journey in itself – i.e., it's not the chalk and the path in the Petworth (Sussex) wood that's important, but the act of walking along it. It's a walk, an experience, not just an installation of materials in the landscape.

Where people live is both local and universal, both particular to the individual and particular to everyone. The path snaking around the hill outside that town in Peru or India, where one walked in childhood, say, is both a very particular place, with its own kinds of shadows, stones, twists, humps, slopes and plants, and also a universal path, like all other paths. (Art, for Goldsworthy, was 'one of the few ways of looking at the world in a very local, personal and individual way which at the same time can communicate internationally' [P. 133]).

Mircea Eliade, who was another Jungian, like Joseph Campbell, wrote of regaining what he called the 'mythic centre', which is the spiritual core of one's life. For Eliade, the recovery of this mythic centre is spatial. That is, it pivots around certain places: in *Ordeal By Labyrinth*, Eliade wrote:

> Wherever one is, there is a center of the world. As long as you are in that center, you are at home, you are truly in the real self and at the center of the cosmos. Exile helps you to understand that the world is never foreign to you once you have a central stance in it... (100)

For Mircea Eliade, sacred acts create a 'mythic centre'. As art is a sacred act, the creation of an artwork can be seen as the creation of a sacred place or mythic centre. A piece of land art (the boulder, hole, pillar, stone circle) is an obvious form of a mythic centre. Making land art (or any art) can be seen as a sacramental experience – essentially one of a sacralization of life and living things. It is like the Australian Bushmen's *alchuringa* experience, mythic dreamtime and mystical participation with the earth and with life. In the *alchuringa* of the Australian aborigines the world is sung into existence (a notion also found in Western occultism, in the 'music of the spheres' of hermetic philosophy).[5] As the poet Rainer Maria Rilke put it, 'song is existence' (*Gesang ist Dasein*), where art is life itself, and making art is not a commentary 'about' life, but *is life itself*.[6]

This notion of art equals life is certainly the foundation of Andy Goldsworthy's art. As Barry Flanagan put it: '[m]y work isn't centred in experience. The making of it is itself the experience'.[7] James Turrell said, in 1987, the goal was not to turn an experience into art, but 'to set up a situation to which I take you and let you see. It becomes your experience... not taking from nature as much as placing you in contact with it'.[8]

Germano Celant, one of the key theorists of Arte Povera, likened the sculptor and land artist to an alchemist:

> The artist-alchemist organizes living and vegetable matter into magic things,

working to discover the root of things, in order to re-find them and extol them...
What interests him... is the discovery, the exposition, the insurrection of the magic
and marvellous value of natural elements.[9]

The Arte Povera-type artist-alchemist uses simple, natural elements, said Germano
Celant: copper, zinc, earth, water, snow, fire, grass, air, stone, gravity, growth. S/he
rediscovers the magic of the world, its composition, growth, precariousness,
falseness, reality (1969).

At the same time he rediscovers his interest in himself. He abandons linguistic
intervention in order to live hazardously in an uncertain space... his availability to
all is total. He accumulates continuously desire and lack of desire, choice and lack
of choice. (1969)

The Arte Povera artist works with life, within life, Germano Celant asserted,
discovering the 'finite and infinite moments of life', art as life, 'the explosion of the
individual dimension as an æsthetic and feeling communion with nature'; making art
becomes identical with living: '[t]o create art, then, one identifies with life and to exist
takes on the meaning of reinventing at every moment a new fantasy, pattern of
behavior, æstheticism, etc. of one's own life'. Celant quoted from John Cage (another
acknowledged influence on land artists such as Richard Long): '[a]rt comes from a
kind of experimental condition in which one experiments with the living'. What counts
is to live the work, Celant said, to be open to the world, 'to be available to all the facts
of life (death, illogic, madness, casualness, nature, infinite, real, unreal, symbiosis)'
(1969).

The 'sacred' or 'mythic' does not have to be extraordinary. Ordinary things can be
the sources of sacrality, the mythical and the ecstatic. Things such as moss on a wall,
or the feel of wood, or the colour of a particular patch of sky. Artists such as Leonardo
da Vinci show the viewer that the 'ordinary' is really extraordinary (think of Leonardo's
fabulous drawings of a sprig of oak, a lily, a rain storm). The Cornish poet Peter
Redgrove told me:

....this 'strangeness' is 'strange' because reality is so fucking extraordinary, and
strange too because most of us try to live without strangeness, and construct
something called the 'ordinary' which never existed. Actually, the strangeness is so
ordinary as to be quite natural. The strangeness is wonder and what is wondered at
is so wonderful that it is strange we do not wonder more.[10]

What happens is that these tiny sensations and feelings are sidelined, displaced,
buried, forgotten, suppressed and ignored by society, by the media. Hardly anyone
speaks of such minute feelings, because they seem to be 'unimportant'. Poets such
as Marina Tsvetayeva, Louise Labé, Novalis, John Skelton and Bernard de Ventadour
show that these sensualities are important. They don't seem to add up to much, as
John Cowper Powys says in his *Autobiography,* yet they are crucial to poetic living.
Maybe it's not just that 'God's in the detail', but that everything is detail.

Marcel Proust knew that a ray of sunshine could lift the spirits, and for John Cowper Powys, simply by seeing the sun on a wall one could have a 'Beatific Vision'.11 Yes, a real, proper, fully authentically mystical Beatific Vision. Nature poetry (and similarly land art) veers between the sensualism of the pastoral view of life, as created in the bucolic poetry of Theocritus and Virgil, and a more intense pantheism as found in mystics such as Meister Eckhart, Jacob Boehme and Jala al-Din Rumi. The British Elizabethan and Renaissance poets (Edmund Spenser, William Shake-speare, Michael Drayton, Samuel Daniel, Thomas Campion and others) were partic-ularly fervent about nature. Sir Philip Sidney wrote: 'O sweet woods, the delight of solitariness!'12 Unlike the world of ancient bucolic verse, land art is not populated with images of satyrs, sylphs, Pan-figures, shepherds, shepherdesses and magicians.

Land art gains much of its power from particular places. Many land artists, for instance, work away from built-up areas (too much to compete with). Some, like Michael Heizer, Nancy Holt and Walter de Maria, operate in what are regarded as 'exotic' locations – deserts and mountains. The 'glamour' of the locations aids the sculptures. Some land art is over-powered by the Romantic settings. Some of Richard Long's stone circles, for instance, look feeble in their desert or snowscape locations.

The fiction of Lawrence Durrell, V.S. Naipaul, Bruce Chatwin and Toni Morrison is set in – and is an expression of – what is now called by theorists the 'post-colonial' world, a diaspora world. It's an epoch in which 'ethnic', 'national' and racial bound-aries are dissolving, producing uncertainty and anxiety. The upside of this post-colonial world is the ease with which land artists such as Andy Goldsworthy, Hamish Fulton, Christo, Carl Andre and others jet around the world. Land art is very much the product of the privileged, relatively wealthy First World, a world in which the Northern hemisphere is dominant over the Southern; American-Eurocentric ethics prevail; bourgeois/ 'imperialist' politics predominate; and the racial 'colour' of the art is not 'black', 'brown', 'red' or 'yellow', but definitely 'white'. Though 'post-colonial', land art is distinctly not 'politically correct' when it comes to issues of ethnicity or economy (although there is a strain of land art that engages with political, financial and ecological issues. but it's quite a small proportion of land art).

In a key text, the essay "Landscape and Character", Lawrence Durrell spoke of being a 'residence writer', that is, someone who lives in a place not as a tourist or visitor.13 This is the opposite of Richard Long's desire, which is to pass through the world 'invisibly'. Andy Goldsworthy likes both philosophies – to create ephemeral artworks, and not make a lasting mark on the world, but also to be an artist in residence, getting to know an environment over many years. Thus, Goldsworthy likes visiting new areas to make art, but just as important is coming home to Dumfriesshire and making work on his home turf. Creating art is Goldsworthy's way of 'arriving': 'I do not feel that I have arrived in a place until I have made a work', he remarked in 2001 (P, 94).

Any number of (travel) writers (Bruce Chatwin, Paul Theroux, Julia Kristeva, V.S. Naipaul, Colin Thubron) have explored the dislocation of a postwar, post-colonial world. The narrators of their fictions, like land artists themselves, are exiles, ex-pats, 'castaways', 'displaced persons', colonials, 'migrants'. While land art is about 'centring' oneself in a particular place, in postwar fiction the sense of displacement continues to be paramount.

3 : 3   THE ALCHEMY OF MATTER

There is no habitation between our road and the Schroon river four miles cross country. I enjoy the phenomenon of nature, the sounds, the Northern lights, stars, animal calls, as I did the harbor lights, tugboat whistles, buoy clanks, the yelling of men on barges around the T.I.W. in Brooklyn. I sit up there and dream of the city as I used to dream of the mountains when I sat on the dock in Brooklyn. I like my solitude, black coffee, and daydreams. I like the changes of nature; no two days or nights are the same.

David Smith (1951)[1]

Nature poetry is an ancient form of poetry: from Greek bucolic verse and Classical mythology onwards, poets have written of nature. Land art and land artists seem to have much in common in literature with Romantic art and Romantic artists. The marks of late 18th / early 19th century European Romanticism included: exalting nature, going to extremes, infinity, the sublime, the cult of solitude, the predominance of subjectivity, and so on. Thousands of modern artists (such as Mark Rothko, Robert Smithson, David Inshaw, Anish Kapoor and Thérèse Oulton), express some of the marks of Romanticism cited above. The cult of solitude, for instance – as found in the works of 19th century writers like Ralph Waldo Emerson, Johann Wolfgang von Goethe, Henry Thoreau, Jean-Jacques Rousseau and Friedrich Hölderlin – is a part of modern art. Modern art exalts the subjectivity and sovereignty of the artist creating on her/ his own. R.W. Emerson wrote of the ecstasy of being alone in nature:

The lover of nature is he whose inward and outward senses are still truly adjusted to each other... His intercourse with heaven and earth becomes part of his daily food. In the presence of nature a wild delight runs through the man in spite of real sorrows.[2]

Land art in its grander moments echoes the gestures of High Romanticism (the Blakean, Hölderlinian, Goethean, Turnerian gestures) which have become so familiar in Western art. One of the apotheoses of High Romanticism is Johann Wolfgang von Goethe's novel *The Sorrows of Young Werther,* where the soul alone actualizes the myriad aspects of nature. In this passage from Goethe one can see similarities with the more opulent (sublime) moments in the art of Andy Goldsworthy, Robert Smithson and James Turrell:

Ah, to view this vast landscape from there! Oh, distance is like the future: before our souls lies an entire and dusky vastness which overwhelms our feelings as it overwhelms our eyes, and ah! we long to surrender the whole of our being, and be filled with all the joy of one single, immense, magnificent emotion.[3]

The 'Land Art Sublime' (*pace* Robert Rosenblum's coining of the term 'Abstract Sublime' to describe Barnett Newman's and Mark Rothko's Abstract Expressionist paintings) might include the snow and stone circles made in the wildernesses of Scotland, Ladakh and Peru of Richard Long; the stone circles of Nancy Holt; the Christos' islands surrounded with pink polypropylene; and of course Smithson's *Spiral Jetty*. The 'Goldsworthy Sublime' would include works such as *Touching North* at the North Pole, the Durham maze, *Montréal Arch, Garden of Stones* and the stone walls (such as the *Storm King Wall*).

There are links between land art and the theory of the sublime in the history of art. These are useful to consider. In 1927, art critic Christopher Hussey defined seven aspects of the sublime, derived from the philosopher Edmund Burke's *Philosophical Enquiry Into the Origin of Our Ideas of the Sublime and Beautiful* (1757):

(1) obscurity (physical and intellectual);
(2) power;
(3) privations (such as darkness, solitude, silence);
(4) vastness (vertical or horizontal);
(5) infinity;
(6) succession;
(7) uniformity.

(The last two suggest limitless progression).[4] These tenets can be applied to land art, especially that of Jameses Turrell and Pierce, Roberts Irwin and Smithson *et al*, and to Andy Goldsworthy's art (again linking the art of Goldsworthy to the British Romantic nature tradition).

The nature poet uses the same emotional/ cultural stuff as the land artist: the human relationship with nature. Whatever the poet writes about or the land artist sculpts, it is the *feeling* for nature that is important, the *relation* between self and nature, that is employed by both poet and land artist. As Clement Greenberg, the foremost critic of postwar art in America, wrote: '[a]rt is a matter strictly of experience, not of principles', a statement which chimes with the views of Andy Goldsworthy, Chris Drury, James Turrell and other land artists, for whom experience is primary.[5] The Arte Povera artist, said Germano Celant, has 'chosen to live within direct experience, no longer the representative... he aspires to live, not to see' (1969).

The sheer *scale* of some of the works of land artists is of itself visceral and erotic (Michael Heizer's *Complex 1,* the Christos' *Running Fence,* and Andy Goldsworthy's *Lambton Earthwork*).[6] Among novelists, it is British author John Cowper Powys who has captured most poignantly the synæsthetic experiences of life, where so many tiny and seemingly ordinary and inconsequential sensations fuse into illumination. Powys writes about landscape in a way wholly in tune with land artists such as Goldsworthy, David Nash, Hamish Fulton, James Turrell and Alice Aycock. One extract from Powys's

Autobiography, which is one long record of ecstasies and sensations, serves to introduce his highly charged, eidetic, pellucid way of seeing. The author has been out walking and is returning to Cambridge:

> What I am revealing to you now is the deepest and most essential secret of my life. My thoughts were lost in my sensations; and my sensations were of a kind so difficult to describe that I could write a volume upon them and still not really have put them down. But the field-dung upon my boots, the ditch-mud plastered thick, with little bits of dead grass in it, against the turned-up ends of my trousers, the feel of my oak-stick "Sacred" whose every indentation and corrugation and curve I knew as well as those on my hand, the salty taste of half-dried sweat upon my lips, the delicious swollenness of my fingers, the sullen sweet weariness of my legs, the indescribable happiness of my calm, dazed, lulled, wind-drugged, air-drunk spirit, were all, after their kind, a sort of thinking, though of exactly what, it would be very hard for me to explain. (1967, 168-9)

What John Cowper Powys is discussing here is *extremely* close to the world of Andy Goldsworthy's art – closer in fact than most other writers and poets. It's a world of seemingly unimportant and mundane details: sunlight on a boulder, the yellow of an Autumnal beech or elm leaf, the sound of a brook over stones in the still mid-afternoon.

Constantin Brancusi, Bill Woodrow, Shirazeh Houshiary, Andy Goldsworthy and many sculptors have spoken of the importance of materials in their work, how they learn from their materials, and 'follow' their materials. Tony Cragg spoke of 'works in which I learnt from the materials'.[7] A stone is not merely a stone for land artists: it has its own essence, its own form and presence.

> Nothing could convince Brancusi that a rock was only a fragment of inert matter [commented Mircea Eliade]; like his Carpathian ancestors, like all neolithic men, he sensed a presence in the rock, a power, an "intention" that one can only call "sacred."[8]

The land artist has a special, fetishistic relation with her/ his materials: they are not simply bits of matter to be wielded in a particular way. They are treated with respect. Wolfgang Laib dusted the ground with pollen, to form an enormous square layer of brilliant yellow. The delicacy – and potency – of the sculpture is immediately apparent. This is the sort of sculpture that exerts a synæsthetic power over the gallery-goer: the pollen affects not only the visual sense with its incandescent hues, but also affects smell, taste and touch. 'I believe that the impossible, the invisible and visions can become reality if one really wants to make the effort' said Laib.[9] Another of Laib's installations is *The Passageway* (1988-93), comprising huge panels of beeswax.

Anya Gallaccio made large installations using flowers: thousands of red roses in *Red On Green* (1992), 101 sunflowers in *Preserve Sunflower* (1991) and 1,600 zinnias in *Untitled* (1992). Gallaccio's flower-pieces emphasized beauty and decay, sensuality and death. Andy Goldsworthy, Wolfgang Laib, Nils Udo and Chris Drury collect leaves, berries, pollen, honey and other natural elements and weave sensuous artifacts that are ephemeral and intricate.

Dennis Oppenheim worked with snow and circles in his *Annual Rings*, a series of concentric circles made by cutting ot shifting snow and ice, that straddled the Canadian/ American border, and with burning circles onto grass in his *Branded Mountain*. In fact, Oppenheim was the first land artist to work with snow on a grand scale. Oppenheim was making snow works in the late Sixties, years before Goldsworthy (when Goldsworthy was only twelve).

3 : 4   THE ECONOMICS OF LAND ART

Not all of land but quite a bit of land art is very expensive. That is, it is expensive moving tons of earth around. Taking a motorbike out into the desert and drawing lines with it is one thing (as Michael Heizer had done in *Circular Surface Displacement* [1968], North of Las Vegas), or pinning leaves together, as Andy Goldsworthy regularly does, but making a 40 mile 18 foot high fence (by the Christos) is another. Much of land art requires patrons, sponsors, co-ordination with galleries, lawyers, public administrators, helpers and industry. (The costliness of land art may explain why much of it is American).[1] Land art requires investment with no immediate return. Patrons are crucial to land art. In heyday of American earthworks the key patrons were the Dia Art Foundation, Robert C. Scull and Virginia Dwan, director of the Dwan Gallery between 1966 and 1971.

Richard Long voiced a common view (perhaps) among many British (and maybe European) sculptors when he wrote of his aversion to American earthwork art:

> In the sixties there was a feeling that art need not be a production line of more objects to fill the world. My interest was in a more thoughtful view of art and nature, making art both visible and invisible, using ideas, walking, stones, tracks, water, time, etc, in a flexible way… It was the anti-thesis of so-called American "Land Art," where an artist needed money to be an artist, to buy real estate to claim possession of the land, and to wield machinery. True capitalist art.[2]

Although Richard Long (and other Brits) may despise the amounts of money spent by the American earthwork artists, aren't they also part of 'true capitalist art'? Of course they are: don't they also live off their art? Doesn't Long just wander around the planet on his sacred 'walks', putting a few stones into a pile, and taking a photo of his efforts? Aren't Richard Long, Andy Goldsworthy, David Nash, Shirazeh Houshiary, Rachel Whiteread, Richard Wentworth, Bill Woodrow, Helen Chadwick, Alison Wilding, Hamish Fulton and Richard Deacon (among British artists), also a part of the capitalist art world? Don't their artworks sell for lots of money, a lot more money than the materials (plus a little profit) cost? Aren't (British) artists being hypocritical when they criticize the bombastic aspects of American land art when they too benefit from the hugely over-priced art gallery system, where even mundane art it seems (such as artists' prints) are sold for 'silly prices'?[3] Long (like Goldsworthy) produces artists' books, postcards, and posters (many of these items are limited editions, sold on websites, via catalogues, or telesales, or bookstores, by publishers, distributors, and museums).

If he'd been American, Andy Goldsworthy mused, his art would have probably developed differently. American earth art for Goldsworthy tended towards conflict, division, and the pioneering spirit (W, 11). It's easy to view the Christos' wrapped buildings or Walter de Maria's $500,000 *Vertical Earth Kilometer* as expensive, pointless art. This sort of land art may be 'true capitalist art', an art of excessive cost and excessive waste, but then, art has been full of silly amounts of money for ages.

What about the Christos' wrappings? They cost a bomb, for sure, but, as Christo says, he pays for it himself, with money made from selling smaller works. The Christos' *Running Fence* cost $2.5 million; *The Umbrellas* in Japan and California cost $26, 000,000. Christo says his art 'has to do with things that are very simple'.[4] This definition can also apply to other land artists, including Andy Goldsworthy: they, too, transform ordinary things.

When these transformations of the ordinary cost so much, and require 200 rock climbers, as the Christos' covering of the Reichstag building in Berlin needed, then commentators wonder about the 'importance' of such artistic productions. There is something right and homely about Andy Goldsworthy and his couple of stonewall helpers building a wall in the Northern wildernesses of Britain. They toil away in true grimy, stalwart, craftsman style. But there's something cynical and obscene, perhaps, about Michael Heizer or Walter de Maria carving great gashes in the American desert, or the Christos making artworks that cost 26 million dollars yet only last for two weeks. Surely that money would be better spent on a hospital? Or on feeding needy communities? Surely artworks that cost millions of dollars but only 'benefit' a (relatively) tiny amount of people are wasteful? Isn't famine relief a better alternative? Perhaps one could make famine relief/ earthquake relief/ medical supply/ housing, and other 'charity' and 'aid' projects, an art event? Perhaps if the Christos spent $26 million on providing food for the needy instead of wrapping a building in Berlin in a bit of plastic, people would not be so angry? When artists spend such vast amounts of money on art, it's no wonder some people find this gross. But then, if spending millions of dollars on art were outlawed, there'd be no Hollywood, no music industry, no television, no entertainment industry, no leisure industry, no grand projects (for some, that might be a good thing). These are the hypocrisies and ambiguities that surround art. How can one 'justify' a $26,000,000 Christo wrapping? Or a typical Hollywood feature film (cost: $45 million, with a typical advertizing budget of $5-15 million)?[5]

Although it may appear that land artists tour the whole globe making art, they actually stick to a small number of countries (tending towards the Northern hemisphere, and the Western world). For instance, there are few major land artists who have made significant work in Africa, or large parts of South America, or mainland China, or Russia. There are few Western land artworks in Egypt, for instance (perhaps because the competition is pretty fierce there from some of the most wonderful structures humans have ever made – the tombs, temples, cities and pyramids of ancient Egyptians. Of course, there are also social, political, cultural and ideological reasons for the lack of major land art in Islamic and Middle Eastern territories).

Europe's a favourite location for land art, but not Eastern Europe. Favoured places tend to be North America and Europe, obviously, and Japan, and occasionally Australia. Once in a while also India (if it's India, it's usually the scenic parts to the North, or Nepal or the Himalayas). But even in North America, birthplace and primary centre of land art, artworks tend to be clustered around the East (New York, Washington, DC, Chicago), the South-West (New Mexico, Arizona), the Mid-West (Colorado), or California.

3 : 5   THE OBJECT IN LAND ART AND MINIMAL ART

With the rise of Minimal, Process and Conceptual sculpture, in the 1960s, sculpture became all 'object'.[1] 'Objecthood', the 'objectness' or 'thingness', became crucial; the 'thing-in-itself', as the Existentialist philosophy of Jean-Paul Sartre and Edmund Husserl put it.[2] Inner and outer space became one: objects were simply what they are, without referring to anything outside themselves. Critic Barbara Rose wrote that in the new Sixties art the 'thing…is not supposed to be suggestive of anything other than itself'.[3] It was Frank Stella who had emphasized the object-in-itself of art, and the objecthood of his paintings in particular. His paintings are objects which display openly their 'objecthood' (such as his *Ophir*, one of his shaped canvases, a zigzag shape with striped paint [1960-61, private collection]). 'What you see is what you get' he said.

Frank Stella influenced many of the key artists of the 1960s: Donald Judd, Carl Andre, Sol LeWitt and Robert Morris. Stella was an important artist in the world of 1960s Minimal sculpture: '[t]he idea that a painting is primarily a thing-in-itself has been around for a long time,' wrote artist and critic Mel Bochner, 'But before Frank Stella not much was done about it'.[4] Stella developed the notion of Barnett Newman's – of the unity or 'all-overness' of an artwork, so that it strikes the viewer all at once, every part at the same time. Stella said of his 'black paintings':

I had to do something about relational painting, i.e. the balancing of the various parts of the painting with and against each other. The obvious answer was symmetry – make it the same all over.[5]

This certainly applies to Andy Goldsworthy's clefts of rock or snow cairns: the viewer sees them all at once, without frames, without being 'led', illusionistically, into the work (however, Goldsworthy uses plenty of pictorial devices which have been around since Renaissance art, and earlier: frontality, perspective, musical proportion, geometry, symmetry, *chiaroscuro*, and so on, as well as illusion and artifice).

Frontality is the foundation of Andy Goldsworthy's art in pictorial terms: many of his sculptures are designed to be viewed from one angle (with a built-in proscenium arch, to to speak, which is invisible). Like a traditional painter, Goldsworthy arranges the layers and space in his works to move back from the frontal plane into the distance, paying particular attention to the relation between the object and the background, and the relation between foreground and background. Later works, such as the Scottish leaf sculptures of 2002 supported by sticks from behind, play around with foreground and background relationships.

In Minimal and Sixties sculpture, the object and its 'objecthood' is primary. As William Tucker wrote: '[it] is the matter-of-fact 'objectness' of sculpture that has become in recent years its prime feature'.6 Sculptures of the time were objects *as much as* sculptures (and sometimes they were objects much more than sculptures). The notion of 'objecthood' is problematic, theoretically and artistically, because the world is full of objects, it is a continuum of objects. As critics have noted, much of what makes sculpture sculpture is that the object is contextualized, physically as well as æsthetically and psychologically, as a sculpture. Context is crucial, as the philosopher Julia Kristeva said, for context carries so much meaning. The *response*, affected by so much of culture, socialization, physical context, education, and so on, makes objects sculptures. In 1970, Michael Heizer said that the old kind of sculpture had been replaced – 'destroyed, subverted, put down' (170).

One can see the body written into, say, Andy Goldsworthy's delicate leaf sculptures, or Constantin Brancusi's extraordinary egg shapes, but not, perhaps, in the giganticism of Michael Heizer's *Double Negative*. Yet, even here, the human body is present – if only by the way it is dwarfed by the scale of Heizer's earthwork (and the best way to see Heizer's *Double Negative* is visiting it and walking around it, including down the ramps (as also with Goldsworthy's walkworks. Thus, to experience land art fully or properly, it is best to see it in person – bodily).

Much of land art is vast. As Carl Andre said:

> I once described the change in sculpture in the 20th century as moving in its concerns from form to structure and now having a concern with place... I believe now you can make sculpture you can enter.7

Minimal sculptures are not set on pedestals, like Renaissance or ancient Greek sculpture; they sit on the floor, or lean against walls (as in Robert Morris's *Floor Piece*, or Carl Andre's *Cedar Piece*). The new sculptural space must have 'three, not two coordinates', said Morris. 'The ground plane, not the wall, is the necessary support for the maximum awareness of the object' (though of course sculptors such as Richard Serra employed walls and gravity, but in a new way).8 Minimal sculptures exist in the same space, on the same plane (the floor) as the viewer. They are, as Morris said, in an in-between cultural space, somewhere between being monuments and being ornaments, between being architecture and jewellery.9

Minimal art had its limits, argued Dennis Oppenheim, which was why artists wanted to go beyond it, using phenomenology. 'We know that Minimalism quickly lifted off into phenomenology via the work of Bruce Nauman and Turrell and the writings of Robert Morris'.10

3 : 6   LAND ART AND CONCEPTUAL ART

Land art is related to, and a part of, Conceptual art. Much of land art exists only in photographs, memories, words, and different cultural texts which are not the land art itself. Works that can be seen and those that are hidden or 'invisible' have the same importance for the artist. One of the hallmarks of the 'ideal Conceptual work', as Mel Bochner pointed out, is 'an exact linguistic correlative, that is, it could be described and experienced in its data and it could be infinitely repeatable'.1 Land art is often Conceptual art: Dennis Oppenheim's *Whirlpool Eye of Storm* (a jet trail in the sky), Hans Haacke's balloons floating over Central Park, Robert Morris's steam pieces, and many of Andy Goldsworthy's leaf, stone, snow, mud and clay sculptures exist now only as photographs, memories and criticism.

By contrast, James Turrell wanted to place the viewer right in the midst of his artworks, so they could experience directly the subject of his art (light, the sky, celestial events) for themselves. It was important for Turrell that his art wasn't a record or a photograph of something that happened elsewhere, that the viewer hadn't seen or couldn't see for themselves. Thus, at Roden Crater in Arizona, Turrell constructed spaces that the spectator could enter physically, to experience light and the sky directly.

The pictorial or visual aspect of land art was over-emphasized by critics and viewers, Dennis Oppenheim argued in 1992. It was 'basically the *idea* of earthworks, the idea of the salt flats' that was important, not the visual element; '[t]he visual quotient is not as strenuous as you think'. Many land artworks were conceptual, mental, not visual or even physical. 'In other words,' said Oppenheim, talking about Bob Smithson's *Spiral Jetty*, 'it's about the salt, submersions, the jetty, what is around the salt flats. In the end it's about mental configurations' (1992). This presents a problem, because most land artworks are known primarily in a visual form – in photographs. It'd be great if all land artworks were visited or directly experienced, as Oppenheim and others intended, but they aren't (how many land artworks have you visited this year?). For Richard Serra, the 'focus of art for me is the experience of living through the pieces', but the actual work itself, the physical object, was not the whole point, or the whole pleasure, of making art: 'that experience may have very little to do with the physical facts of the work of art'.2 (Once again, it seems that the best way to appreciate or experience land art would be to become a land artist yourself).

One of pluses of Conceptual art was that art could be just ideas, and the artist wouldn't have to carry around masses of materials. Dennis Oppenheim wrote:

In 1968 and 1969 I lived in an apartment. I didn't need a studio. Everything that I had done as an artist was contained in one small case of slides. And it accounted for two of the most strenuous years of work in my whole life.3

Land art is meta-art, art about art, art that relies on other art to 'exist'. Land art exists for a brief moment, then becomes myth, gossip, photography and words (and most often criticism and journalism). Many of Richard Long's works are simply collections of words, printed in capitals, in Eric Gill's font, Gill Sans, a favourite with typographers, on large pieces of paper. The text of one of Long's works can be printed here, and this text here will be very close to being a Richard Long artwork in itself (although he likes them printed larger). Thus:

A LINE OF GROUND 226 MILES LONG

ROAD COAL TIP ROAD ROMAN MOUNTAIN ROAD ROAD WOODLAND RIVERBED ROAD STONY TRACK ROAD MUD TRACK ROAD GRASS LANE ROAD PEBBLE RIDGE ROAD BARE ROCK LANE ROAD SLURRY ROAD

A 7 DAY WALK
WALES 1980

Well, that's a Richard Long artwork. Is that it? Yes. This Richard Long work has no picture, no map, no funny little arrows dotted around to indicate wind direction, no 'SPLASHES' phrases, no squiggly lines for routes or rivers, and no reference to anything other than itself. It's not a painting *of* something, a sculpture *of* something (a place, perhaps, or a walk), or an object brought back from the making of the work. This textwork is simply these words (reproduced in *Richard Long* [1986, 164]). At the same time, Long's textworks have all sorts of possible readings. He chooses particular words, often seemingly plain words (*road, lane, rock, mud*), or words used in simple phrases and clauses (*a line of ground, the lark in the morning, ashes blowing in the wind, 120 miles in 4 days*). The vocabulary Long employs – *night, place, clouds, ground, sea, river, grass* – is simple and direct, with few embellishments (one might call it 'plain English', an unadorned vernacular that prefers words with roots in Anglo-Saxon rather than Latin or Romance languages).

It seems as if Richard Long has nothing much to 'say'. Well, he is a sculptor, so he wouldn't have to be so good at writing or speaking. Wrong. He's a land artist (though he dislikes the term 'land art'), and land artists are always much concerned with writing and written texts. An Andy Goldsworthy exhibition, for instance, features written texts on display, and photographs, as well as installation works and sculptures.

The texts of land artists also draw on poetry, on concrete poetry (also known as 'visual poetry' or typewriter art). Richard Long, for instance, prints his brief texts in circles (*Full Moon Circle of Ground*, Dartmoor, 1983), in concentric circles (*Three Moors, Three Circles*, Liskeard to Porlock, 1982), in vertical lines, as in trendy style magazines (*The Isle of Wight as Six Walks*, 1982), and in curved swathes of text (*A Moved Line in Japan*, 1983).

1960s Conceptual U.S. artist Lawrence Weiner (b. 1942) produced text works, capital letters on a wall or in a book (Barbara Kruger, the Art & Language group and Michael Craig-Martin have also made post-Conceptual wall-works of words). Weiner's solution to making sculpture was that a sculpture on a plinth has to be 'translated' into language, so that people can understand it. Sculpture is language, and words are language, therefore, Weiner reckons, words can be sculpture:

> when you see a piece of wood lying on the ground with a piece of stone on top of it, you must translate that in your own head into language. What I try to do is present language itself as a key to what sculpture is about... It is a presentation of a piece of sculpture in language.4

Like John Baldessari and Sophie Calle, Lawrence Weiner fashions capital letters in short phrases which are about a viewer's relationship with an object. The words are a means or the expression of a relationship with something.

This is a typical Lawrence Weiner artwork. This is another one, shown at Leo Castelli's gallery in 1974:

UP ON (IN) THE AIR
DOWN ON [IN] THE GROUND
BEING WITHIN THE CONTEXT OF [A]
REACTION

BEING WITHIN THE CONTEXT OF
REACTION.
UP ON (IN) THE AIR
DOWN ON [IN] THE GROUND

This is a characteristic Lawrence Weiner artwork. Richard Long commented that '[t]he discovery [Weiner] made that art does not necessarily have to be made, that was a great breakthrough'.5 Weiner is right, of course: words alone can be sculpture, for poets have long known that language is an *experience*, not simply abstractions or concepts. Language really does affect people – otherwise why would they spend so much time consuming language? That is, they consume 25-40 hours of broadcasting per week (in Europa) – that's over a day and a half spent consuming television and radio per week.

So the words on a gallery wall of Lawrence Weiner, Sophie Calle, John Baldessari, Hans Haacke and Hamish Fulton don't seem at first to be 'art'. They are not sensual and graspable in the physical realm, like a marble statue. Yet those words, whether photocopied on cheap paper or printed in high quality typography on deluxe paper, or painted onto the wall, are 'art', they are communication, language – even sculpture.

Laid over Richard Long's walks is the grid of the map: the maps in Conceptual art constitute a new landscape of the soul, as Robert Smithson wrote in 1968:

A cartography of uninhabitable places seems to be developing – complete with decoy diagrams, abstract grid systems made of stone and tape (Carl Andre and Sol LeWitt), and electronic "mosaic" photomaps from NASA. (1968, 26)

Just about every land artist used maps in their work. Not just in the obvious sense of mapping (and finding) future sites for artworks, but as key elements in the artworks themselves. Jan Dibbets chose places on a map at random, visited them and took a photograph. Dennis Oppenheim made maps a central ingredient in his 2-D Conceptual works, which combined maps, text, photos and sketches. Richard Long based many walks around maps, such as a circle or straight line drawn on a map, then followed in the landscape. John Baldessari spelt out 'California' using maps in *The California Map Project* (1969). Charles Ross made star maps (1975-86). Jasper Johns painted a large map collage painting (1966-71). Chris Drury cut up and wove maps together (a development of his love of basket-weaving). Robert Smithson made many mapworks, including map games, folded maps, aerial maps, and cut-up circular maps (*Untitled Circular Map* [*c.* 1968-70] and *Entropic Pole* [1967]). Tom Van Sant collaged satellite maps. Nancy Holt buried poems (the poems were dedicated to Carl Andre, John Perrault, Robert Smithson, Michael Heizer and Philip Leider) in remote locations, with a map marking the burial sites (1969-71).

3 : 7   LAND ART AND PHOTOGRAPHY

In land art photographs, the spectator is often not offered a *range* of viewpoints of a work, although land artists clearly take more than one shot of each work they make. No artist takes just *one* photo out of a 36 exposure 35mm film, or one frame out of a twelve shot 120mm format film, or one digital shot out of hundreds on a digital still camera. No, an artist, like an photographer, takes a range of shots, at different, bracketed exposures (as Andy Goldsworthy does [P, 95, 101]), from different viewpoints (much as the trendy commercials film director of today shoots twelve hours of footage for just one thirty second advert).[1] Even with bracketing exposures, though, still meant that only one or two shots might be properly exposed (this made Goldsworthy anxious when he used his panoramic camera, because it only had four shots per roll of film).

Andy Goldsworthy also spoke of not being able to capture the collapse of a sculpture (such as a *Sea Cairn*) because he was re-loading the camera, or winding on the film, or taking another light reading. Of the California *Sea Cairn* (2001), for instance, Goldsworthy remarked: 'changing film was a nervous business, and I always held a finger on the shutter release, just in case' (P, 106). Goldsworthy said he could have a photographic assistant, or more cameras, but he didn't want to get too deeply involved with the photographic side of his art (P, 101). At the same time, of course, Goldsworthy is always very reliant on photography, and photography is absolutely central to his art.

Andy Goldsworthy, for example, typically takes two viewpoints or shots: a close-up, which is about the artist's subjective relationship with his work – taken from just a few feet away. Then there is a second, more 'objective' view, showing the sculpture as the independent observer might see it. This second photograph shows the work in its environment, which is crucial. Goldsworthy's photos are a mix of these two viewpoints, the subjective and the objective, close-up and distance: often the most powerful shots are not the near-side images, showing the detail in the sculpture, but the distant views.

Each land artist, then, must select this or that viewpoint, behind this bush or next to that tree. The land artist is therefore also a photographer, selecting views, reframing their works, making choices about lighting, angles, lenses, film stock, etc. Land artists will make decisions about exactly *when* to photograph their work. Some works are ephemeral, and last only moments, so the photograph must be taken immediately (but even when a work lasts only a few seconds or minutes, there are still choices about which moment to capture).

Other artworks, such as the *Storm King Wall* or *Leadgate Maze* of Andy Goldsworthy or Nancy Holt's *Star-Crossed* (1981), last longer. The land artist as photographer can therefore wait for a certain combination of sunlight and clouds. This is particularly crucial in cloudy places like Britain, where light can vary so dramatically over a few minutes. As anyone will know who has been in, say, Dartmoor or the Lake District during low pressure, the sunlight can burst through the clouds at one moment, then a moment later there'll be dark, sombre clouds, looking as if it's going to rain. A moment later, it *will* rain, and afterwards, facing away from the sun, one might see a rainbow. Much of the world's weather is this changeable, so every land art photograph is a highly selective and subjective view of a particular place. Thus, there can never be a totally objective, totally detached and totally comprehensive photograph of a land artwork.

Another critical aspect of photographing land art is not only deciding what to *include*, but choosing what to *exclude* from the composition. Visiting a land artwork in the flesh, one can see it from all sorts of angles, with all sorts of backgrounds, in all sorts of conditions. Knowing a land artwork only from a photograph, one knows only *that* particular viewpoint, under *those* particular weather and lighting conditions, and no others. The land artist will take great care in framing the images, to show the artwork from the best vantage points. Many aspects of the surroundings might be elided from the final published photographs – an apartment block, a row of cars, trash, people, power lines, and so on.

Land artists must also oversee the journey of the images they've shot from development through printing to framing. As anyone who has taken a photo and processed and printed it (or manipulated it on a computer) will know, all manner of details can affect how a photograph is interpreted: how it is printed, light, dark, soft, hard, cropped, full frame, more red, more blue, burnt in, dodged, touched up, glossy or matt paper, and so on. The size of the photo affects it very much, as does the frame. Go into any framer's store and one'll see a plethora of different types of frame. All these things the viewer might take in at one glance in a gallery, but the artist has to make decisions all the time about all of these matters, and many more. Land artists/ sculptors, then, must be accomplished photographers. Their work must be high standard, if it is exhibited in high art locations, such as the city gallery, or glossy coffee table art books.

In land art, the commentary, the written records, the obsessive documentation, is just as important as the artwork itself. Often, it *is* the artwork. The land artist's life becomes part of the artwork. The American sculptor David Smith spoke of this consuming aspect of sculpture, where the artist lives and breathes art. In a series of questions to students, Smith described the committed artist's stance:

> Do you make art your life, that which always comes first and occupies every moment, the last problem before sleep and the first awaking vision? ...How do you spend your time? More talking about art than making it? How do you spend your money? On art materials first – or do you start to pinch here? ...How much of the work day or the work week do you devote to your profession – that which will be your identity for life?2

Andy Goldsworthy said '[m]y art will always be a reflection of my way of life.'3 Brilliant late 1960s sculptor Eva Hesse spoke in Romantic, emotional terms of her art, employing words such as 'essence' and 'soul'. She talked about wanting to emphasize 'soul or presence or whatever you want to call it.' Although Goldsworthy is not as openly emotional in his descriptions of his art, these words of Hesse's could apply, with some minor revisions, to Goldsworthy's (and other land artist's) art: 'I think art is a total thing. A total person giving a contribution. It is an essence, a soul... In my soul art and life are inseparable.'4

Jan Dibbets said that documenting the work wasn't important: 'I've done lots of works without taking photographs'.5 But most land artists record their activities (e.g.: 'walk this morning; made a snow sculpture; it wasn't successful; back home for lunch'). Ultimately, *any* activity can be land art. Going to the stores can be a piece of art. One might drop a stone on the path as one goes, or perhaps not. Either way, you've just made a work of art. Is, then, walking to Gilmor's corner store for a pint of milk and a pack of cigarettes a fully accomplished and thoroughly authentic work of art? Where does authenticity end and artifice begin? Or, rather, where does life end and art begin? Clearly, they are a continuum in land art.

Richard Long told me that '[n]ot all walking is art'; that is, a walk becomes art when it is conceived as art. The conception of the walk, made before the walk, is crucial, even if there is no 'reason' at all for the walk. 'A walk, and place, can be chosen for any reason'.6 Long also said, though, that '[a]nything an artist makes, is art', but adds cautiously: '[n]ot everyone is an artist.'7

The relation between outdoor and indoor works, between stone cairns in some remote zone and a stone cairn in a Western gallery, is resolved simply in Andy

Goldsworthy's art by being regarded by the artist as a continuum. One can see how for Goldsworthy both indoor and outdoor works are one, i.e., part of the same thing. But the viewer might see them as separate, because the viewer (usually) can't see Goldsworthy's outdoor pieces (Richard Long likes to keep his locations secret and anonymous).8 The viewer only knows Goldsworthy's outdoor pieces from his photos. So it's always an odd relationship with Goldsworthy's work for the viewer. For the artist, it's great, because the big photos and writings relate to his own experiences, of working outdoors. He knows the work inside out: *he lived it*. The viewer, though, gets a different experience: s/he sees odd phrases, titles, dates, measurements. Odd snippets of info. Or photos.

So people love Andy Goldsworthy's work not because they love the photographs, or his writing. They love it, perhaps, because of *what it suggests*. Goldsworthy's work persuades people to look outwards, away from cities, towards the landscape, towards stones and water and all the rest of it. Perhaps that's why people love it, and other land art, and nature poetry, and all things to do with nature, from gardening to walking the dog to vacations in wildernesses. As Hamish Fulton put it, 'I walk on the land to be woven into nature' (1995).

The outdoor work itself isn't present in Andy Goldsworthy's text pieces or photos. The work isn't 'in' the gallery. No, the work is *elsewhere*, and it is to that Elsewhere Place that people want to go. Land art creates *desire* in people, as the work of J.M.W. Turner or Aleksandr Blok creates desire – for travel, for other places. Richard Long spoke in a Santa Fe interview of feeling refreshed and renewed after a good walk: that's the experience, perhaps, that viewers wish to gain from land art, from all art.

Land art, then, whether by Alice Aycock, Kazuo Shiraga, Chris Drury, the Christos or Andy Goldsworthy, is part of a postmodern trend in self-reflexivity, the *mise-en-âbyme* commentary so familiar now. Art about (the artist's) life. It's found not only in the postmodern literature of the 1960s and 1970s, but also in the fiction of, say, André Gide. The novel *The Counterfeiters* (1925) by Gide is a key text in this respect: the main character Edouard is, of course, a novelist. But Edouard is more interested not in the novel he's trying to write, but in his book about the writing of his novel. Thus, the diary/ journal of the work becomes more important than the work itself; and the act of *writing about* the art becomes more important than *making* the artwork itself. Indeed, so crucial was the 'making of' the book *The Counterfeiters* to Gide that he published a book after *The Counterfeiters*, called precisely that, *The Journal of The Counterfeiters* (although he swore he'd never do that, despising artists 'explaining' their works). Land artists, like Conceptual and Process artists, steer clear of 'explaining' their works.

The 'deep-lying' subject of the novel-within-a-novel in *The Counterfeiters* is, Edouard muses in his journal:

the rivalry between the real world and the representation of it which we make to ourselves. The manner in which the world of appearances imposes itself upon us, and the manner in which we try to impose on the outside world our own interpretation – this is the drama of our lives. The resistance of facts invites us to transport our ideal construction into the realm of dreams, of hope, of belief in a future life, which is fed by all the disappointments and disillusions of our present one. (183)

Andy Goldsworthy keeps diaries, journals, notebooks and sketchbooks, which record his working days, ideas for future works, and sketches of sculptures he's completed. Much of Goldsworthy's published writing is derived from his diaries.

André Gide's modernist, self-reflexive concerns are also those of land artists. For, as he lived his life, Gide was conscious of *how he would write it up later*. When something extraordinary occurred, Gide would be thinking about it as an account in his journal. After living, for Gide, comes making art. Life is continually being fictionalized: life is food for art. Like the ready-mades of Marcel Duchamp, Gide's *The Counterfeiters* thoughtfully and elegantly destroys the diegetic effect of fiction, its naturalism and suspension of disbelief. Like Jean-Luc Godard's movies and Jasper Johns's paintings, Gide's art is self-reflexive art, a Pop Art æsthetic forty years before Pop Art.

When Marcel Duchamp and Kurt Schwitters put 'real' objects into the gallery and into their paintings, they did so because it seemed a logical thing to do. It's the same with land artists: why not, they say, have an art made out of found objects, stones found on a remote path, or leaves, or household bricks. The use of ordinary objects in (land) art ushers in a new sense of the object in sculpture, a new way of looking at art.

The 'real' objects and readymades of Marcel Duchamp and Kurt Schwitters were developed by Robert Rauschenberg and Jasper Johns, among others. As with Rauschenberg, the stuck-on objects set alight Johns' paintings.[9] Easy to see how Johns' idea of turning a painting into an *object*, as a 'real thing in itself', as he put it, applies directly to land art: David Nash, Roberts Smithson and Morris, and Andy Goldsworthy also like what they see to be real, to be the object in and of itself (the 'thing-in-itself' of Existentialism, or Rainer Maria Rilke's *Kunstding*, or 'thing of art'). They too dislike illusionism. For Goldsworthy and other land artists, their sculpture doesn't 'symbolize' or 'represent' nature, it *is* nature, a part of nature. Goldsworthy said he tried to damp down the aspects of his art which could be seen as sculpture, preferring to see his art as something 'organic' (*Wall*, 15).

As Jasper Johns remarked: 'I find it more interesting to use a real fork as painting than it is to use painting as a real fork.' Similarly, one can see how, for Andy Goldsworthy, Patricia Johanson, James Pierce, Michelle Stuart and other land artists, it's much more interesting to use a stone as a stone, a leaf as leaf, a tree as a tree, rather than as a representation of something else. Robert Smithson's definition of an earthwork is pertinent here: 'instead of putting a work of art on some land, some land is put into a work of art'.[10] Smithson's ethic can be applied directly to Goldsworthy's art.

I love the land… My sculptures were mostly intended to be seen outside. The sky is the perfect background. It's space with no dimensions. I like working in the open air and seeing my things in the open.

Henry Moore (in C. Chandler, 184)

Sometimes it's odd to see land art in a gallery, because the mound of soil, the cairn of stones, the wooden beams, demands the viewer to look outwards, to nature, to the wildernesses from whence this art came. Andy Goldsworthy's leafworks and stalks are familiar now, having been seen in galleries and museums, but one is always aware of the place of their origin, and how odd they look.[1] The leaves and stalks are tiny parts of nature, bits extracted, rearranged, as all art is nature chopped up and reformed according to the artist's æsthetics. Land art creates an ambiguous continuity with the world of nature that exists outside the gallery (but also inside). Sometimes this ambiguity works against the art on show in the gallery space.

Land art sites, in the first wave of land (late 1960s/ early 1970s – land art's 'golden age'), tended to be wildernesses, deserts, post-industrial spaces, waste grounds, quarries and dumps. One of the reasons for going far from the gallery, the city and the pretty countryside spots was because land artists wanted to avoid the cultural modes of the 'pastoral' and the 'picturesque' at all costs.[2] Land artists, asserted Dennis Oppenheim, wished to go beyond the picturesque, beyond the history of art (while British land artists, such as Richard Long, had some relationship with the picturesque [ibid.]).

David Nash, a key influence on Andy Goldsworthy, discussed this indoor/ outdoor problem in a 1978 interview (a couple of years before Goldsworthy came to work for him):

> An object made indoors diminishes in scale and stature when placed outside. The reverse happens when an object made outside is brought inside, it seems to grow in stature and presence. It brings the outside in with it. The object outside has to contend with unlimited space, uneven ground and the weather. The sculpture I show inside is meant to be seen inside, it relates to the limited space, the peculiar scale, and the still air.[3]

The indoor-outdoor dialectic much concerned Robert Smithson, who said: 'I don't think you're freer artistically in the desert than you are inside a room'.[4] In fact, Smithson said he 'liked the artificial limits that the gallery presents'.[5] For David Nash, artistic work was simply more engaged and more interesting out of doors. In interior spaces, elements were

> neutralised, passive, controlled, time is paused. Outside, on and in and over the land, they are active, making space alive and potent with the movement of time. I look for ways of engaging with the life of this space.[6]

Ephemeral, land art aims for an eternity in one place: the soul. As Lawrence Weiner, the Conceptual/ Process artist who exhibited 'statements' (texts on a wall), said: '[o]nce you know about a work of mine, you own it. There's no way I can climb into somebody's head and remove it.'7 Thus, much of land art exists in that socio-cultural space (the 'cultural imaginary') which is actually inside people's heads. Thus, anyone can 'own' land art: simply by thinking about it. Once thought about, land art, Conceptual art or Process art is 'possessed' by the viewer, in Weiner's system. Indeed, some Conceptual art requires the existence of the viewer to make the work work at all. The viewer brings the piece alive.

Working inside was problematic for Andy Goldsworthy, he confessed, because he was disconnected from the natural world outside, with its changes, its seasons, animals, people and history. The outside world was alive, while the gallery or public space could all too easily begin to feel dead after a while. 'I am not sustained by working indoors. I have too much control inside, and after a while I am drained of reasons for being there' (T, 11). That's a significant point Goldsworthy makes, about having too much control inside a gallery or indoor space. It's the opposite of what many artists are after – control over creation. Clearly, for Goldsworthy, the sense of the unpredictable, the random, the chance and the spontaneous is vital.

3 : 9   LAND ART AND CHANGE

Crucial in land art is the concept and reality of change, because these works in wood, snow, ice, leaves, water, slate, grass, and so on, do not stay. They are not 'permanent', in the way that, say, bronze, marble, steel or stone sculptures can be (and the *concept* of change is as significant as the reality). The soil in Walter de Maria's *Earth Room* dries out and alters (requiring maintenance); Robert Morris's steam works and Hans Haacke's fog and ice sculptures are blown away by the wind; the Christos' plastic wraps stay on for two weeks only.

Joseph Beuys emphasized process, evolution and change in his art: his sculpture, he said, was not

> fixed and finished. Processes continue in most of them: chemical reactions, fermentations, colour changes, decay, drying up. Everything is in a *state of change*.1

Some land artists enjoy the impermanence of (their) art, and exploit it. As politicians know, words such as 'permanent' are difficult to define, and even more difficult to maintain. Artists with a large vision of life know that nothing on Earth will be truly 'permanent'. After all, 'civilized' humanity is only 10,000 years old, or 40,000, or two or three million (depending on how one views 'civilized'). And the planet itself will not last forever: millions more years, but not forever.

Some environmental/ performance/ Conceptual artworks had a built-in impermanence, such as Allan Kaprow's *Fluids* (1967, Pasadena, California), large structures
made from blocks of ice, which were left to melt. Barry Flanagan's *Hole in the Sea*
(1969) was a cylinder embedded in a beach: Flanagan filmed the water covering the
hole as the tide came in (another forerunner of Andy Goldsworthy's tidal works). Hans
Haacke produced impermanent works with a Goldsworthyan flavour, such as ice
freezing around a heating element.[2] Haacke wrote of an artwork which would be as
majestic and as transient as birds gathering in the sky: 'I would like to lure 1000
seagulls to a certain spot (in the air) by some delicious food so as to construct an air
sculpture from this combined mass.'

In "Natural Phenomena as Public Monuments" (1968), land artist Alan Sonfist
suggested building 'museums of air' in cities, which would 'recapture the smells of
earth, trees and vegetation different seasons and at different historical times, so that
people would be able to experience what has been lost' (1978). Sonfist also suggested
monumentalizing the natural world with sounds: '[c]ontinuous loops of natural
sounds at the natural level of volume can be placed on historic sites' (ibid.). (This
already happens in natural history and science museums, which create sensory
environments of sound, touch, smell and taste, as well as cabinets and displays to
look at. And in *son et lumière* shows, sounds, music and lights are employed to
explore historical sites).

There are bronze and marble sculptures still looking remarkable from the Græco-
Roman period, and stone figurines from the Palæolithic period (i.e., sculptures with a
40,000-year permanence). Michael Heizer's scars in remote deserts will endure, but
not Hans Haacke's *Grass Grows* (1969), a mound of grass. Indeed, ephemerality,
transiency and change are key components in land art. As Barry Flanagan wrote:

> Truly sculpture is always going on. With proper physical circumstances and the
> visual invitation, one simply joins in and makes the work…there is a never-ending
> stream of materials and configurations to be seen, both natural and man-made,
> that have visual strength but not object or function apart from this. It is as if they
> existed for just this physical, visual purpose – to be seen.[3]

Andy Goldsworthy builds transience into many of his sculptures; indeed, the
subject matter of some works is their ephemerality (with the form as secondary).
They are about the fact that they won't last very long. In fact, the bulk of
Goldsworthy's art is ephemeral, with 'permanent' works – such as the Storm King
Wall, the Montréal *Arch,* the New York *Garden of Stones*, the Cumbrian *Sheepfolds* and
the Digne *Water Cairns* – in the minority. Making permanent works was restrictive for
Goldsworthy, because his art was an art founded on ephemerality (RA, 111).

It's no surprise that the American form of earth art should be sympathetic to Oriental mysticism, as Zen Buddhism, Hinduism, Shinto, Confucianism and Taoism were particularly popular in 1960s culture (in the Beats and 'dharma bums', or the West Coast hippies, or the graduates of Western universities, or rock musicians, for example). It was a logical cultural development, it seems, from Parisian Existentialism to Californian Zen Buddhism, from the Old World philosophies based on Classical ideals to the New World's appropriation of the even older Oriental philosophies. Many of the chief precepts of Taoism, Confucianism, Hinduism, Shinto and Zen Buddhism chime with those of land art, not only the American earthworks, but also the British form of land art of Andy Goldsworthy, Richard Long, Chris Drury, Hamish Fulton, David Nash and others. Matsuo Basho, an important Oriental poet, wrote:

> Go to the pine if you want to learn about the pine, or to the bamboo if you want to learn about the bamboo. And in doing so, you must leave your subjective preoccupation with yourself.[1]

And Makoto Ueda glossed Matsuo Basho thus: '[f]or learn means to enter into the object, perceive its delicate life and feel its feelings.'[2] These notions of searching for the 'essence' are absolutely in tune with the æsthetics of Andy Goldsworthy, Constantin Brancusi, Carl Andre, and Donald Judd. Goldsworthy spoke in exactly the same terms of trying to find the 'essence' of nature, of going out into the natural world in order to learn about it. Goldsworthy followed Basho's Taoist precepts of going to nature to study it to the letter.

Minimal art pursued the oft-used tenet that 'less is more', a radical reductionism and simplification, which is Oriental. Or as Carl Andre put it, ''minimal' means to me only the greatest economy in attaining the greatest ends'.[3] Michael Heizer confessed he preferred to see art more as a religion than a recreational activity: 'if you consider art as activity then it becomes like recreation. I guess I'd like to see art become more of a religion'.[4] In other words, artistic activity as a way of being-in-the-world, a spiritual or religious stance, not just something that artists 'do'. In short: *being* not *doing* (or being *as well as* doing).

The Chinese Taoist mystic, Chuang-tzu, the 'Groucho Marx of Taoism' as Lawrence Durrell calls him, wrote: '[l]eap into the boundless and make it your home.'[5] This statement perfectly describes the artist's act of faith and risk, which is so essential for good artistic creations. As the Existential philosopher Søren Kirkegaard said, without risk, life is not worth living. Again, these quasi-Existential and Taoist notions of risk are perfectly in tune with 1960s earthworks art and Goldsworthy's art. John White, discussing Oriental art, made points which can apply to land art:

> In Chinese art the surface emphasis is negative rather than positive. It is in close accordance with the calm acceptance, the contemplative natural mysticism, which reached its highest flowering in Taoism. The surface is left undisturbed. Colours are few, and soft. Ink, and delicate monotone washes are the characteristic media.

Spiritual and decorative qualities are valued high above imitative naturalism, the evocative above the representational... The unmarked silk, or paper, is at once the atmosphere, the space, and the inviolate decorative surface.[6]

The great philosophers of the Far East, some mythical, some historical, provide numerous points of contact with contemporary Western art since the 1950s: Mencius (371-289 BC), Confucius (551-479 BC), Chuang-tzu (c. 369-286 BC), Lao-tzu (6th century BC), author of the Tao Te Ching, Bodhidharma (c. 470-543), one of the founders of Zen Buddhism, the Zen Buddhist monk Hui-Neng (638-713), Zen masters Fa-yen (885-958), Lin-chi (10th century), Hui Hai (8th century AD), known as the 'great Pearl', and Chao-chou (778-897), Kuo Hsiang (d. 312), Japanese Zen master Dogen (1200-53), author of the Shebogenzo, Shoichi Kokushi (1202-80), Tao-hsin (580-651), Tao-Sheng (c. 360-434), Hui Shih (4th century BC), and Tibetan mystic Jetsun Milarepa (1052-1135). The great books of Far Eastern mysticism – Tibetan Book of the Dead, Chuang-tzu, the I Ching (Book of Changes) and the Tao Te Ching – have many correspondences with land art.

Among Western mystics and philosophers, one could cite, in connection with land artists, Heraclitus (everything's in flux), Empedocles, Paracelsus, Plato, and several Neoplatonists (such as Philo and Plotinus – Platonism and Neoplatonism is everywhere in Western philosophy). Maybe some Quietism, some alchemy (in Andy Goldsworthy's transmutation of materials, such as heating, melting and cracking stones), and bits of occultism and hermeticism. Pantheism (= nature mysticism) is Goldsworthy's basic religious outlook, of course. Native American spirituality is another reference point, as well as Australian aborigine religion, with their profound reverence for the land.

Andy Goldsworthy doesn't have much to do with the repressive aspects of Western religion, with sin, with guilt, with body-denial, or with repentance. You won't find many conscious references in Goldsworthy's art to Catholicism, Anglicanism, Protestantism, Calvinism, Judaism, Qabbalism, or Zorasterianism. Goldsworthy's art doesn't employ any conscious Christian iconography – no Crosses, no Virgin Marys, no Pietàs, no Jesuses or saints in his art.

However, there is undeniably a utopian aspect in Andy Goldsworthy's art, a nostalgia for an earlier, apparently better time. Goldsworthy identifies it with rural, agricultural economies, with farmers and farming. It's a pre-Industrial Revolution period, up to, say, the 1800s (in Europe). In Western religion, that period is much further back in time. Christianity, for example, is haunted by the idea of Paradise, some earlier Eden or 'pure land', before the Fall of Man.

The relation between Western land art and Oriental mysticism – in particular, Taoism, Shinto and Zen Buddhism – has been noted by many commentators. Zen and Taoism, for instance, speak of (1) the 'here and now', (2) spontaneity, (3) satori or enlightenment, (4) intuition, (5) nature, (6) emptiness and the void, (7) change, (8) meditation, (9) cosmic unity. All these qualities (there are others) can be applied to land art, and are sometimes elucidated by land artists.

(1) For example, the Zen Buddhist notion of the 'eternal now' or 'now-streaming' (nunc fluens) as Alan Watts called it. Zen philosophy makes the present moment

primary, the only true reality, and land artists too work in the present. Sculptors continually evoke the transient nature of sculpture: Hans Haacke's fog pieces; Chris Drury's fires; Ana Mendieta's snow and mud body prints; Wolfgang Laib's pollen. Andy Goldsworthy's poppy lines are only there for an instant, then they are blown away by the wind.

(2) Spontaneity: this is as crucial in land art as it is in Zen Buddhism and Taoism. The land artist works with whatever materials are to hand, reacting spontaneously to the environment (Andy Goldsworthy does not (often) use tools or machines); changes in weather must be accommodated into the artwork.

(3) The experience of viewing land art is not quite Zen *satori*, in the strict definition of *satori* or enlightenment, but certainly land artists aim for an 'epiphany', as James Joyce called the æsthetic shock, however brief it may be. In land art as object, there are 'no strings attached', i.e., 'what you see is what you get', as Frank Stella put it. The viewer sees the whole thing there, and that is everything you get. This instantaneous aspect of land art, as also in contemporary painting, is a Zen-like notion.

Satori also has affinities with the descriptions of land art/ sculpture that some land artists have given (Robert Morris's objecthood, for example). Hui-Neng, the 8th century mystic, said that *satori* was 'seeing into one's own nature'. Some land artists have written of art as a journey towards some inner essence. D.T. Suzuki termed Zen *satori* an 'insight into the Unconscious'. Andy Goldsworthy has said that the relation between sculpture and photography is about 'seeing and time itself' (Sh, 23).

(4) Most land artists value intuition highly, as do most poets and artists. The land artist trusts her/ his instincts, and works grow organically. Systems are adhered to, but land artists often veer off into intuitive areas.

(5) Nature dominates Zen Buddhism and Taoism, as it does in land art. One is always encouraged in Taoism and Zen Buddhism to 'follow one's nature', and to co-operate with the universe. Nature is the teacher in Zen and Taoism, as it is in land art.

(6) Its easy to see the lure of the void of religions in land art, in those wildernesses beloved of Michael Heizer, Walter de Maria, Andy Goldsworthy and Dennis Oppenheim. Evocations of voids are found in much of postwar and contemporary culture, from Samuel Beckett's sparse texts and 'fizzles', which painstakingly describe near-nothingnesses (the stone circle, so like a piece of land sculpture, in *Ill Seen Ill Said*, the sun setting over the hills in *Still* and the ruthless white 'inscape' of *Ping*), to Ad Reinhardt, Jo Baer and Robert Ryman painting all-black or all-white canvases.

In the paradoxical bliss of Oriental mysticism, emptiness is also fullness, and to 'have' nothing is to 'have' everything. Zen and Taoism thrive on paradox, on the 'not-this-not-that' dialectic of philosophy, as a way of getting at the unsayableness of the essence. Similarly, Goldsworthy, in a paradoxical manner, speaks of the monumental aspect of sculptures made from leaves: the very small can also be very big, he says:

some of the largest works I've ever made have been of leaves; the surface of a leaf when I am working with it, bending, folding, shaping, pinning together, has a scale which is enormous. True scale is determined by the material I'm working with.[7]

In the manner of Eastern philosophy, Andy Goldsworthy acknowledges that the very small contains the very large, another take on the cosmic unification of Oriental mysticism, where the macrocosm and microcosm are interrelated.

The imagery of Zen Buddhism, Shinto and Taoism is also that of land art: stones, mountains, rivers, water, flowers. China has a long tradition of landscape painting (called 'the floating world'), and it is easy to see the many connections between the contemplative aspects of Chinese landscape painting and land art.

(7) Change is central to land art (and underpins a good deal of contemporary art): all land art occurs within a changing landscape, whether it be the artificial (human-made) changes in the gallery, or the natural transformations of erosion, weather, water, light, season, and so on. Land art thrives on change and transformations, and many land artists have deliberately exploited time and change in their works, from Nancy Holt with her *Sun Tunnels*, which alter as the sunlight pours through the holes in the concrete tubes, to the transience of Andy Goldsworthy's *Leaf/ River/ Stone* sculpture of 1999, a 'serpent' of leaves on a rock, which the elements will swiftly erase.

In Taoism, everything changes, the *yin* and *yang* energies or principles create change, yet the Great Whole remains the same. In nature, everything is changing, transforming into something else, yet the Earth remains whole. Flow is crucial – so land art steps away from Western art, which stops life in snapshots or 'still life' paintings, and produces transmuting art, art which has change built into its design. In the West, there is much anxiety when artworks change (when paintings decay, for instance). On the one hand, there is the desire to keep everything 'natural' and 'hands off', without being interferred with; on the other hand, museums and galleries constantly intervene with art – 'restoring' paintings, putting things behind glass, behind ropes, continually re-hanging it, and so on. The very nature of 'preserving' art is controversial – witness the anger surrounding the 'restoration' of Michelangelo Buonarroti's Sistine Chapel and Leonardo da Vinci's *Last Supper*.

Land artists, though, relish such changes and decay in artworks. Andy Goldsworthy loves it when his sculptures collapse. They are designed to disintegrate. He spends much of his time waiting around for the fall, so that he can photograph it (or, in the case of the ice arch on Hampstead Heath, Goldsworthy's wife, Judith, photographed the collapse. Judith Goldsworthy contributes much to Goldsworthy's art, not only in helping to photograph it).

(8) Meditation is clearly not a goal of land artists – they make no pompous claims concerning mysticism and meditation (it may be an aim of an artist like James Turrell and his skyspaces, however). Yet, clearly, contemplation is a part of their work, as it is a part of all artists' work. Making land art often involves a mild form of meditation. Richard Long's walks, for instance, are meditations of a kind. 'A journey in the wilderness becomes a fantastic focus of concentration. I can get totally absorbed in the place and totally absorbed in my work', Long said.[8] Andy Goldsworthy too speaks of an intense relationship with his subject as he works (it's the typical trance state of the artist, which many creative people have talked about. Other people would call it concentration, or focus, or being in the moment, in the zone, or whatever). The Cornish poet Peter Redgrove told me that 'the ideal state for ordinary going about is

the first stage of orgasmic arousal'.9 This is 'walking' in the Taoist sense; that is, walking in Taoist religion is another name for feeling ecstatic.

The very activity of walking releases chemicals in the brain that promote pleasure.10 Joggers and atheletes get hooked on them sometimes. The physical action of walking is soothing. Since time immemorial people have 'walked off' their problems, babies can be calmed by the motion of walking, and many artists were famous for their walks: Arthur Schopenhauer and Immanuel Kant took twilit walks; Thomas Hardy tramped through Dorset; William Wordsworth and Samuel Taylor Coleridge walked in the Lake District; John Cowper Powys always took a morning walk from his home in rainy North Wales; Henry Miller was in ecstasy simply by walking around the backstreets of New York and Paris (as described in the *Tropic* trilogy and *The Rosy Crucifixion*); and Bruce Chatwin made walking and nomadic existence his central theme – in his life as in his art.

(9) Land art is close to Taoism in its worldview: like Taoists, land artists believe in a holistic view of things, where each part affects the rest. This interconnected worldview (sometimes called 'Gaia-consciousness') is also the philosophy of ecology and the offshoots of the ecological/ green movement: eco-feminism, Goddess religion, animal rights, eco-paganism, direct action, road activism, anti-hunting lobbies, and so on. Art now has a world consciousness, said sculptor Isamu Noguchi (1968). In the Taoist view, inner and outer commingle, the individual and the mass interconnect.

Andy Goldsworthy is very much concerned with ecological issues, and like many earth artists is careful to make sure his artworks do not scar the landscape. There is no trash in the land artists' photographs of their artworks. They are ecologically and societally conscientious artists, and thus Goldsworthy has been hailed as Britain's primary ecological artist. Richard Long said, and Goldsworthy would agree with him, that his art is about finding a harmony between the human and the natural world, between the abstractions of humanity and the reality of nature. As Long put it, his work is 'a balance between the patterns of nature and the formalism of human abstract ideas like lines and circles.'11 (Actually, I think the ecological aspect of both Goldsworthy and Long has been overdone by some critics; in fact, there are other artists who discuss green issues far more than either Goldsworthy or Long).

In *Being and Circumstance,* Robert Irwin proposed four types of land art: 'site dominant', such as monuments and murals; 'site adjusted', in which some considerations are made towards the site, but it's still studio-made; 'site specific', in which steps are made towards integrating the work into the site; and 'site conditioned', work which responds to its surroundings. The 'site determined' category is the one Irwin preferred, and it's also the type of sculpture favoured by Andy Goldsworthy. Irwin defined 'site conditioned' work as an 'intimate, hands-on reading of the site', which results from 'sitting, watching, and walking through the site'; it means being aware of water, weather, sound, surface, movement, history, and so on. Such considerations determine whether the response 'should be monumental or ephemeral, aggressive or gentle, useful or useless, sculptural, architectural, or simply the planting of a tree, or maybe even doing nothing at all' (1985).

The land artist orients her/ himself in terms of post-Renaissance space and time.

The Neoplatonic, magical, neo-pagan view of the world in the Renaissance saw humanity at the centre of the cosmos, and humans were the microcosm reflecting the make-up of the macrocosm, the 'as above, so below' philosophy of Hermes Trismegistus, occultists and the alchemists. In the view of Christianity, however, God was at the centre (as in Dante Alighieri's extraordinary vision of a mechanical universe in which God is at the centre of the surrounding nine hierarchies of angels, with the rest of humanity around the edges). During the Renaissance, one sees so clearly the crumbling of the hegemony of mediæval culture, where there was an unambiguous system of good and evil, God and 'man', us and them. In the Renaissance, this worldview falls apart, moving towards an emphasis on the individual, on the Existential sense of beingness and being alone in the universe.

> Because his body exists in space, any man orients himself by the four horizons and stands between above and below [wrote Mircea Eliade]. He is naturally the center. Any culture is always built on existential experience.[12]

This is what the land artist does: s/he orients her/ himself to the four horizons, and to post-Renaissance time. The human level becomes the spiritual centre. Land art – in the work of Andy Goldsworthy, David Nash, Peter Erskine, Andy Lipkis, Nancy Holt – puts people, not God or deities, at the centre of the cosmos. Goldsworthy speaks of feeling 'at home' in a particular landscape, of regarding a place as his 'home'. Land art, then, can be seen on one level as the reaffirmation of 'home', a re-instatement of the notion of 'homeland'. The 'homeland', though, is not primarily a physical place, but a cultural and spiritual space. Homeland is a state of mind as much as a landscape. Land art may be the manifestation of a spiritual re-orientation. In land art, the 'mythic centre' of one's life is reaffirmed.

Andy Goldsworthy always affirms the 'livingness' of his art, that he *lives* his art. His art is not to be intellectually discussed first or made at a critical distance. Rather, the artist is right in the middle of her/ his art, living it. There is no separation of art and life. Land art is a way of mythicizing one's sense of being-in-the-world, a way of making presence visible, tactile, *there*. 'Presentness is grace', wrote Michael Fried in his influential essay "Art and Objecthood".[13] Making land art is a religious activity because simply being in the world is religious. Land art, like all art, replays the primordial myth of Creation: each earthwork or land sculpture reaffirms the Creation. 'Once the center has been reached, we are enriched, our consciousness is broadened and deepened, so that everything becomes clear, meaningful,' wrote Mircea Eliade.[14]

In archaic societies, through symbol and ritual, sites would become 'sacred'. For postwar, postmodern, post-everything people, any site can become 'sacred' if one thinks of it as sacred. If one thinks of this junk yard next to the car lot as a sacred space, why, then it is a sacred space. All that sacred spaces need is human consciousness. It is the level of *desire* that makes a place sacred. In olden times, one might have required a god or a government or a priesthood to have the 'authority' to make something sacred. In the postwar, post-everything world, the individual is her/ his own government, priest and God. If s/he says a place is holy, then it's holy.

Consecration of a sacred space may include any number of rituals. The simple fact of drawing out a circle in the sand on a beach isolates a sacred space in amongst profane space. By drawing the circle, one marks out a sanctuary or sacred zone. Magicians add to the glamour of creating a magic circle by drawing it with a special knife, making it nine feet in diameter, and placing candles or some ritual object at the four cardinal points. The magician's circle is simply a stylized, ritualized version of the land artist's circle (well, magicians are certainly have a sense of theatre). The religionist or magician has the weight of religion or hermetic magic behind her/ him; the modern artist has the weight of art (culture) behind her/ him. One can't say that a church or a magic circle is 'holier' than a circle made with a stick by an artist on a sandy beach. Cathedrals simply have the 'authority' of paternal figures (priests, kings, gods) behind them. The artist making a sand circle doesn't seem to have the same 'authority', the same tradition of sombre theology and religious *gravitas*. Yet the artist on a beach, or in a forest, or a desert, is making a sacred space out of profane space.

Land artists do not think in these terms: or they may do, but they rarely admit it publicly. For the land artist, as for any artist, it is perhaps embarrassing to admit that much of art is about 'child-like' feelings; that is, the 'simple' pleasures of making a line out of stones, or walking at dawn, or filling a room with soil. These are the basic pleasures of art, which both artist and viewer enjoy. They are, on one level, 'child-like', even 'infantile', psychologically. Sure. But many other grave, time-honoured institutions are founded on childish impulses: marriage, Catholicism, pop music, cinema, tourism, the insurance industry.

The land artwork, then, remakes the sacred in a profane world: 'the manifestation of the Sacred in any space whatsoever implies for one who believes in the authenticity of this hierophany the presence of transcendent reality', remarked Mircea Eliade.[15] Not only, then, do land artists make sacred spaces, as all artists do, they also create a sense of the 'real', a sense of beingness, a reaffirmation of the transcendent. Eliade again:

> The Sacred is that something altogether other to the Profane. Consequently, it does not belong to the profane world, it comes from somewhere else, it transcends this world. It is for this reason that the Sacred is the real par excellence. A manifestation of the Sacred is always a revelation of being.[16]

For the land artist, most, if not all, of the world is not just potential art material, but beautiful. Land artists, declining to admit to being romantic or emotional, nevertheless create art that is Earth-loving, nature-loving, ecologically-friendly, that is, in short, full of emotion.

Not every critic exalts land art as spiritual. British art critic Peter Fuller, who advocated a distinctly *British* form of modern painting, sees spiritual bankruptcy in land art. Of Richard Long (and his fulmination might apply also to Andy Goldsworthy), Fuller intoned:

> It is, I believe, a tragedy that consideration was given to inviting an artist such as Richard Long to create a piece within Lincoln Cathedral. His work, for me, is

symptomatic of the loss of both the æsthetic and the spiritual dimensions of art. He shows little trace of imagination, of skill, of the transformation of materials. Seen in contrast to the greatest achievements of the British tradition in art, Long's relationship to the world of nature is simply regressive. His work is sentimental and fetishistic... claims that his work is worthy of 'spiritual' attention are preposterous...[17]

One sees clearly Peter Fuller's outrage that Richard Long might sully the building beloved of John Ruskin, Nikolaus Pevsner and D.H. Lawrence, one of the finest English cathedrals. But surely Fuller is missing the point with Richard Long, who is clearly as mystical, as in awe, as deep in his feeling for nature as Fuller's cherished Cecil Collins, Henry Moore, J.M.W. Turner or Patrick Heron.

Uncomfortable as they are with notions of 'spirituality' or 'mysticism', land artists such as Andy Goldsworthy, David Nash, Chris Drury and Robert Smithson are religious artists, sensitive to the emanations of particular places. Art has been deeply associated with magic and religion for at least 40,000 years, and probably millennia more. Land art, like all art, is full of deep emotions. These emotions collect in clusters around certain places. It is understandable, then, that critics and the public see these emotions as potentially religious.

3 : 11   CIRCLES

The circle motif, one of the primæval symbols of eternity, cycles, time, rebirth, and so on, is employed throughout the work of Andy Goldsworthy and much of land art (Goldsworthy realizes that it's virtually impossible to do away with the circle). Circles in land art are made from slate, timber, snow, salt, grass or by walking in a circle; they seem to be gentler, more eco-friendly kinds of sculpture. The circle shape itself speaks of organic forms, and, in some religions, evokes the 'feminine' and the Goddess. Not a few sculptors and land artists have made the circle crucial to their works: Alison Wilding, Richard Deacon, Stephen Cox, Mary Miss, Anish Kapoor, Peter Randall-Page, Robert Morris and Dennis Oppenheim (and most land artists employ the circle at some point or another).

In *Sheepfolds*, Andy Goldsworthy remarked that he didn't think of his circular forms as circles or geometric shapes, but as containers, something that concentrates or contains a space. As expected, Goldsworthy wasn't a fan of perfect circles – his circles were always hand-drawn, 'organic', irregular (rather than land artists such as Richard Long, who draws his circles with string). Goldsworthy also said he liked the idea of circles that were in the process of becoming squares (and vice versa [Sh, 13]).

Land art based on circles includes Vijali's *World Wheel* (1987), Alan Sonfist's *Circles of Life* (1987) and *Pool of Virgin Earth* (1975), Adam Purple's *The Garden of*

Eden (1975), Charles Jencks' *Snail Mound* (1992-94), Michael Heizer's *Circular Surface Planar Displacement Drawing* (1970), Stan Herd's *The Circle* (1992), and Mel Chin's *Revival Field* (1993). Many of Nancy Holt's works are circular: *Annual Ring* (1981), *30 Below* (1980), and *Sun Tunnels* (1976).

Donald Judd produced two circular steel bands, 180 inches in diameter, as well as a concrete circular 'wall'. Robert Morris made gigantic circular works, such as his *Observatory* (1971), which was a huge earthwork recalling the megalithic structures of ancient times, such as Avebury stone circle in Great Britain. Morris's *Labyrinth* (1974) was a maze-size sculpture, the kind of maze one finds in theme parks and country houses, except that Morris's *Labyrinth* used the ancient pattern of the Cretan labyrinth, itself a motif some see as distinctly feminine, speaking of Goddess mysteries. Herbert Bayer's *Mill Creek Canyon Earthworks* (1979-82) was a series of earthworks recalling ancient monuments. Robert Smithson's *Closed Mirror Square* was like an Aztec ziggurat, while his *Amarillo Ramp* recalled the massive embankments found at Neolithic earthworks such as Maiden Castle in Britain, or the serpent mound in Ohio.[1]

Some artists have produced stone circles which look very much like Stonehenge, such as Nancy Holt's monumental *Stone Enclosure: Rock Rings* or Alan Wood's *Ranchenge* (1983), a wooden Mid-West American version of Stonehenge. Vida Freeman's *Installation* (1981) in an L.A. gallery comprised white porcelain and stoneware stones with white pillars emerging from them. Michelle Stuart constructed cairns and circles in *Stone Alignments/ Solstice Cairns* (1979). Margaret Hicks fashioned three concentric circles from oak and sandstone in Texas (*Hicks Mandala*, 1975), intended for a 'Ritual of Giving'. David Harding cast his *Henge* (1972) from nine foot tall slabs of concrete, while Donna Myars' *Dream Stones* (1979) were cast and carved from cement. Michael McCafferty built his *Stone Circles* (1977) on a beach in Oregon, where they were flooded at high tide. Marlene Creates' interventions on prehistoric earthworks included laying rows of paper over them (*Paper Over the Turlough Hill Cairn*, 1981).

Many land artists have made mounds which recall prehistoric burial mounds (apart from the works cited above) including Charles Jencks (*Snail Mound*, 1992-94), Judy Varga's *Geometry of Echoes Converge* (1980), Maya Lin's *Wave Field* (1995), Peter Walker's *Turf Mountain* (1993) and James Pierce (*Burial Mound*). These (Minimal) sculptures are ambivalently related to ancient monuments, however, as Samuel Wagstaff remarked of Tony Smith's works: '[t]hey are related to early cultures intentionally or through sympathy – menhirs, earth mounds, cairns… [and] to this culture with equal sympathy – smokestacks, gas tanks, dump trucks, poured concrete ramps.'[2]

Land artists, then, consciously or slyly invoke ancient, prehistoric monuments. Michael Heizer, Robert Smithson, Anthony Gormley, Robert Morris and Nancy Holt make references to ancient earthworks. Gormley likened the *Angel of the North* site to a burial mound. (What separated Hans Haacke's earth mound from gardening? By its *intent*, Haacke replied.) The famous *Serpent Mound* in Adams County, Ohio, dating from the 10th century AD, is an obvious ancestor of Andy Goldsworthy's *Lambton*

Earthwork and landscaped art by Heizer, Herbert Bayer, Morris and others.

Some land artists work in landscapes dense with megalithic structures (such as Richard Long in the South-West of Britain). There are over nine hundred stone circles in the British Isles. Long too makes connections with prehistoric art in terms of manufacture: the cave paintings at Lascaux, Long said, were made by people's hands on the rock. Long has made references to some of the key sacred/ religious/ prehistoric sites of Britain: to Silbury Hill, the largest human-made mound in Europe, so the textbooks say; to the ithyphallic Cerne Giant in Dorset; to Offa's Dyke; to Glastonbury Tor (mecca for hippies, occultists and New Age travellers); to Windmill Hill, and so on. Long put a picture of himself with a rucksack in Africa right next to one of the famous ancient hill figures of England, the so-called 'Long Man of Wilmington', 231 foot tall, in Sussex. This is one of those prehistoric sites that some see as being an alien, or St Paul, or a Roman emperor, or King Harold. Long ironically compared himself with another 'Long' Man.[3]

Locations such as Silbury Hill and Glastonbury in Britain, or Luxor and the Pyramids in Egypt, have long been revered by people as holy sites, 'places of power' as they are called. Land artists capitalize on the mystery of such places. One of Richard Long's works is a walk between two prime magical centres of Britain, Stonehenge and Glastonbury, both deeply associated with prehistoric astronomy, ancient priesthoods, Arthurian legend, Merlin the Magician, the Age of Aquarius, ley lines, Druids, geomancy, and so on:

ON MIDSUMMER'S DAY
A WESTWARD WALK
FROM STONEHENGE AT SUNRISE
TO GLASTONBURY BY SUNSET
FORTY FIVE MILES FOLLOWING THE DAY[4]

The photograph that goes with this text is the sort of picture postcard view one finds in newsagents and heritage centres around Great Britain: Glastonbury Tor at sunset. Like St Paul's, the Tower of London, Big Ben, Buckingham Palace, Beefeaters, the changing of the guard, red buses and telephone boxes, this is one of the archetypal images of Britain. And, typically, it is Glastonbury Tor that Long chooses to photograph, not the stores nearby, the electricity poles, the junk yard behind the highways, the rows of garages, the housing estates.

Land artists' stone circles often recall prehistoric stone circles. While they may deny it verbally, Nancy Holt's *Stone Enclosure*, Robert Morris's *Observatory* and Richard Long's circle sculptures evoke the great circles of Britain: the Rollright Stones in Oxfordshire, Boscawen-Ûn and the Merry Maidens in West Penwith, Cornwall, Castlerigg in Cumberland, Stanton Drew in Somerset and of course the mother of all British stone circles, Avebury in Wiltshire.

Some land artists, such as Richard Long, maintain that their stone rings are subjective, private, individual works, quite different from the public, social art of the prehistoric stones circles. Andy Goldsworthy would probably make similar assertions of secular, non-religious individuality of his artworks (Goldsworthy's artistic state-ments assert spirituality, but of a personal, vaguely pantheistic, non-institutional kind, though Goldsworthy was aware that some spectators could read his sculptures in terms of religion. A screen of thorns and stalks which Goldsworthy proposed for a church (as part of the *Réfuges d'Art* project) might be interpreted as Christ's crown of thorns, Goldsworthy acknowledged, especially in a country like France, where Catholicism still has a hold [RA, 67]). Goldsworthy has referred to Stonehenge occasionally, but tends to avoid direct contact with prehistoric sites. It would be easy in Scotland for Goldsworthy to build sculptures next to or in relation to burial mounds or stone circles, but Goldsworthy doesn't. He has, though, built sculptures near or in relation to the Nine Standards rock formations in Cumbria.

The ancient stone rings were made by a group of people, a society, constructed, perhaps, according to the plans of a priestly élite. Land art circles are the work of one person, but a major contemporary artist is no less a member of the cultural, æsthetic élite. Prehistoric stone circles may have been made for religious rituals, perhaps connected with the position of celestial bodies. The circles in stone, snow, dandelions, trees and concrete of land art are made for private consumption, for the artist alone, or for an onlooker who wanders into a gallery or a space then out again, back into the chaos of the city. Yet the ancient sacred sites and land art/ Postminimal/ Arte Povera earthworks have much in common, because art and religion join at so many points. Andy Goldsworthy says that the circle in his works is not a design, not something imposed externally, but a 'concentration of space' (Sh, 13). 'It's what's contained within that interests me, it's not the 'circle' as such' (ibid.). A circle of leaves is not a circle of leaves, for Goldsworthy, but a 'concentration of colour' (ibid.). (This's certainly true of a sculpture like *Elm Patch* (2002), a small circle of bright yellow elm leaves laid on top of dark brown leaves in Dumfriesshire).

Land artists benefit from the allusions to ancient monuments, because the atmosphere and magic of prehistoric stones rubs off on their own work. In stressing the importance of megaliths, the land artists not-so-subtly imply a continuity between themselves and these prehistoric relics. The æsthetic continuity that's emphasized also implies religious affinities. Thus, the land artist is the contemporary equivalent of the priests and hieratic sects who created Stonehenge, the lines in Peru, the Pyramids, and Australian aborigine 'songlines'. A spirituality is affirmed in land art, which only a few land artists actually speak about. But this religious feeling is definitely there, definitely a part of the discourse of Andy Goldsworthy, James Turrell, Robert Smithson, Hamish Fulton, Robert Morris and Nancy Holt.

3 : 12   GENDER AND SCALE IN LAND ART

The awareness of scale is a function of the comparison made between that constant, one's body size, and the object. Space between the subject and the object is implied in such a comparison.

Robert Morris (1966, 21)

However exciting a painting by, say, A.R. Penck, Georg Baselitz, Francesco Clemente or Philip Taaffe may be, sculptures by artists such as Nancy Graves, Rebecca Horn, Tony Smith, Mark di Suvero, Eva Hesse, Louise Nevelson and Andy Goldsworthy outdazzle the painters. While Renaissance painting may represent the apotheosis of high art in the Western world, and Greek sculpture may be the height of 'high sculpture', contemporary sculpture really is startling. Part of the reason is, of course, *scale*. Contemporary artists, of all kinds, have made massive art. David Smith's *Wagon I* (1963-64, National Gallery of Scotland) and his *Cubi* sculptures are huge, heavy, chunky, truly colossal pieces which dominate their surroundings.

In sculpture [noted Carl Andre], there's quite a concrete relationship between one's size as a person and/ or mass as a person and the mass of a piece of sculpture. (1970, 57)

Donald Judd commented that '[t]his scale is one of the most important developments in twentieth century art'.[1] One of the largest earthwork projects is James Turrell's *Roden Crater Project,* a series of tunnels and chambers in an Arizonan extinct volcano, begun in 1974 and funded by the DIA Foundation. Andy Goldsworthy's art is not monolithic in scale – usually: his pieces are, typically, small-scale; although the walls and one or two other pieces are large. The Abstract Expressionists, such as Helen Frankenthaler, Mark Rothko, Franz Kline and Barnett Newman, fabricated huge paintings, which swallow up the spectator when s/he moves close to them. One can get up close to a Morris Louis canvas and be enveloped by it (creating a sense of intimacy was one of the chief motives for large-scale, as Rothko asserted).[2] Similarly, contemporary sculptors have made massive works. Artists such as the Christos built pieces that were 24 miles long. Even medium-sized pieces, such as Donald Judd's wooden boxes, are sometimes seen as monumental. A critic on *The New York Times* called Judd's 1977 installation at the Heiner Friedrich Gallery a 'majestic and finely measured presence'.[3]

Lucy Lippard described scale not just as something mathematical, optical, *seen*:

Most discussions of scale consider it a strictly optical experience... But a sense of scale is also a *sense* proper. Scale is *felt* and cannot be communicated either by photographic reproduction or by description.[4]

The bombastic, monumental, massive and brash 3-D art of contemporary sculpture was not made exclusively by male artists. Land artists Mary Miss, Nancy

Holt, Sherry Wiggins, Donna Henes, Lynne Hull, Patricia Johanson, Alice Aycock and Agnes Denes have all made very large works (other female architectural sculptors included Jackie Ferrara, Donna Dennis and Elyn Zimmerman). For feminist critics, these women artists were drawn to shelter imagery: the origins of 'shelter sculpture', as Lucy Lippard called it, were in female biology and the female body.[5] Mary Miss created a 5 acre scale work in Illinois,[6] Patricia Johanson designed a large lagoon park in Dallas (1981-86), while Nancy Holt produced gigantic *Sun Tunnels*, 18 foot long pipes that were 9 feet high, with many holes punched in the side, to let light in.[7]

Helen Escobedo built some huge concrete and steel sculptures which 'attempt to fuse hard-edge geometric forms with nature's organic manifestations', as she put it. Works such as *Snake* (1980-81) rise impressively from the Earth, celebrating the flux and movement of organic forms. Beverly Pepper's large, curving mirrored slabs of wood buried in sandy beaches (*Sand Dunes*, 1985), might be seen as a type of 'Earth Mother art', art which worships and works with the Earth, rather than, as in so much of male land art, cutting or penetrating it, phallically (like Michael Heizer, Robert Smithson and Walter de Maria).

Many of the celebrated products of contemporary sculpture since 1945, however, have been made by male artists: Donald Judd's 'specific objects', blocks or stacks or ladders of aluminium, steel and Plexiglas that 'climb' gallery walls;[8] Tony Smith's monumental hollow black cubes with their *thereness* (celebrating the primacy of presence, not effect);[9] Dan Flavin's mesmeric fluorescent tubes, a sculpture of light and space;[10] Sol LeWitt's Conceptual cubes and wall drawings like enormous graphs; Richard Serra's huge props or slabs of steel leaning together;[11] and Carl Andre's tiles of steel, copper and zinc laid on the floor.[12]

One of the most exciting developments of contemporary sculpture and art is the installation, the taking over of a whole space or environment – the floor, walls and ceiling of a gallery, as in Rebecca Horn's *Ballet of the Woodpecker* (1986-87), a room full of mirrors, or Sylvia Stone's *Crystal Palace*. Andy Goldsworthy's art, like many land artists' works, is clearly related to the art installation: it is an art of environments, where the relatively small addition of a stack of stones forming a cairn sets alive the surrounding landscape. One sees the landscape in a new way: context is all-important. (Sometimes, Goldsworthy has created installations, such as *Snowballs in Summer* on the streets of London in 2000. *Garden of Stones* (2003) and *Stone Houses* (2004), both in Gotham, can be regarded as installations).

Sixties British sculpture was connected with the art schools (St Martin's, Slade, Chelsea, RCA); with teachers and modernists such as Anthony Caro, Philip King, Hans Haacke, Lawrence Weiner, Joseph Beuys and Henry Moore; with American Minimalism and Conceptual Art; with New Realism; and with Italian Arte Povera. The student days of artists such as Bruce McLean, Jan Dibbets and Richard Long at St Martin's were summarized by critic David Lee:

> [at] St Martin's School of Art... the definition of sculpture was all-inclusively expanded to embrace a hike in the Hindu Kush, a sing song, an OS map with felt tip graffiti, a collection of empty bottles or a stack of horse blankets. Anything, in fact, providing it did not resemble in the smallest particular anything that sculpture had either used or made before.1

The new British sculpture (when it was still 'new') was loved and loathed passionately. Amazingly, art critic David Sylvester reckoned that Richard Long 'has too many admirers' (a backlash against Andy Goldsworthy may be developing also). What did Sylvester mean? That people uncritically adore Richard Long's works? Or that there is too much criticism about him? Peter Fuller targeted Bill Woodrow's work as an example of what he hated most in (postmodern) New Art.2 Fuller loved artists who make 'beautiful' things, things that may be difficult or challenging, but which are also 'beautiful' (his favourites included Maggie Hambling, Eric Gill, J.M.W. Turner and Paul Nash). But Bill Woodrow's sculpture, like Tony Cragg's, Jean-Luc Vilmouth's and David Mach's, destroys the traditional notions of the 'beauty' of an art object. Stable (modernist) notions of 'purity' or 'meaning' in art are refuted by sculptors such as Cragg, Mach, Woodrow et al. Fuller's critique of such (post-Conceptual) sculptors argued that their work lacked craft skills, that it was gimmicky.3 This is often the way certain pop groups are criticized: 'they can't play their own instruments' pundits often carp. But it doesn't matter if a pop musician can or can't play or sing, writes their own material or not: what counts, in the postmodern era, is the text itself, the effect, the experience. What counts is the song, the sound, the image. The question in postmodern, post-Conceptual art (or culture) is not: 'what does it mean?', but 'what does it feel like?'... 'what is the experience?'

It doesn't matter if there is no 'craft skill' or special techniques used in sculpture if there are a host of other things going on in it. As Donald Judd said, a work only has to be interesting. Richard Long claimed his photographs are not made with great skill, but it doesn't affect the value they have as artworks. Similarly, Andy Warhol showed an artist didn't have to be as skilled as a Leonardo da Vinci to be able to produce 'great art'. One needed to be a good publicist, good with mass mechanical production techniques, good at organizing other people. (Though Warhol was of course highly skilled, a canny media manipulator as well as a highly sophisticated artist).

Tony Cragg was known for his coloured spreads of found objects arranged in lines on the floor (such as his New Stones, 1978). Cragg's sculptures were constructed from all manner of found objects, each given the same status, in a non-hierarchical fashion, laid out on the floor (anti-hierarchical structures being one of the marks of postmodernism). Cragg's 1980 sculpture *Black and White Stack* contained bicycle tyres, tin cans, car radiator grills, the side of a child's crib and an ironing board.

Tony Cragg's sculptures, like Bill Woodrow's and David Mach's, are not simply sensual modernist objects but ironic, postmodernist commentaries on the social and political uses of commodities (their work is sometimes dubbed 'post-industrial'). In the art of Cragg, Mach and Woodrow familiar consumer durables and industrial materials are represented in an ironic, metaphoric and parodying manner.4 Cragg, and other sculptors who trawl the dumpsters and junk yards of urban landscapes (Nicholas Pope, Anthony Gormley, Woodrow), make ironic comments on scavenging and ecological recycling. Cragg was not interested, he said, 'in romanticizing an epoch in the distant past', but questioning the massive amount of commodity consumption in a late capitalist epoch:

> We consume, populating our environment with more and more objects, with no chance of understanding the making processes because we specialize in the production, but not in the consumption.5

The humour, scepticism, pathos and irony in the art of Brits Tony Cragg, Bill Woodrow, David Mach, Anthony Gormley *et al* makes their post-industrial, post-Conceptualist sculpture automatically disruptive. They evade categorization and easy definitions. It is this sense of shifting meanings and ambiguity in flux that makes much of New Sculpture and late modernist art disliked by some critics, because the work won't *keep still*. It won't be nailed down as an object of High Modernism, such as a family group bronze by Henry Moore or a Pablo Picasso nude statue.

The vehemence that much of postmodern or Conceptual or post-Conceptual art engenders is understandable. Walking into one of the big, white-walled brightly-lit modern gallery spaces in the Western hemisphere (in Barcelona, Frisco, Amsterdam, Milan, Gotham), the viewer is often confronted by a series of baffling photographs, or 'found objects' placed in a line against a wall, or photocopies. These shows seem full of worthless, everyday objects, things anyone can find. There seems to be nothing *special* about the objects in Tony Cragg's *New Stones* or Bill Woodrow's dumpster works, or Lawrence Weiner's printed 'wall statements' or the deconstructionist projects of the Art and Language group. Why, the exasperated art lover fresh from a blockbuster show of older art (Pierre Renoir or Peter Paul Rubens, say) at the Met in NYC or the Kunsthalle in Hamburg might complain, 'there's no *skill* here, no *talent'*. How many times have we heard that most common criticism of contemporary art: *anyone could do that!* Yes, it does seem, at first, as if 'anyone could make' Andy Warhol's screenprints, Tony Cragg's spreads of found objects or Tim Head's vibrators and tape recorders (*State of the Art*, 1984). But no, art's not like that, it doesn't work that way. The argument that 'anyone could do that', such a common complaint, also lies behind Peter Fuller's 'high art' criticism. But it is such a simplistic view, revealing such a naïve understanding of what art is, what it does, and how and why it is produced.

Postmodern and post-Conceptual art ignites many important questions, such as:

how does one gauge the 'authenticity' or 'originality' of something when it is mediated by the mass media? How does one know something is 'the real thing', when all that's known of it is through images and sounds on radio, television, online and the press? Does it matter if the 'original' artwork is fake when the mediated product has such 'truth'? Is an artwork that consists of photographs that refer to an idea or object or experience that exists elsewhere (Lawrence Weiner's printed words 'wall statement' *Sometimes Found,* or any of Andy Goldsworthy's sculptures) as 'authentic' as a marble sculpture by Auguste Rodin? Is an artwork that is an 'idea' as sensual or compelling as one made out of marble or oil? The 'new' British sculpture of the 1960s-1980s and 1980s to the present day, with its scavenged objects and seemingly 'ordinary' objects displayed on the floor, disrupts modernist and traditional notions of 'beauty', 'purity', 'tradition', 'objecthood', 'presence', 'value' and 'meaning'.

A typical exhibition of Conceptual art was held at the Kunsthalle in Bern, curated by Harald Szeemann: *When Attitudes Become Form* (1969); some key land artists were involved: Walter de Maria installed a telephone, with a message beside it saying the visitor could talk to him; Richard Long walked in the mountains and recorded his walk in a gallery statement; Jannis Kounellis put bags of grain on a stairway; Michael Heizer created *Berne Depression*, smashing the pavement near the Kunsthalle with a wrecking ball; Joseph Beuys smeared fat along the walls.

3: 14   THE BRITISH LANDSCAPE TRADITION

> *I actually believe in Modernism, in the excitement of new ideas. Art is anyway*
> *beautiful if the idea is beautiful, if it has clarity and truth. A lot of the history of*
> *landscape art has been to reveal the beauty of nature, a sort of religious celebration.*
> *All that beauty is still there and can be overwhelming, but I was always interested to*
> *develop landscape art in new ways.*
>
> Richard Long (interview, April, 1985)[1]

The American/ New York/ Abstract Expressionist/ Minimal/ Arte Povera influence is one strand of influences in British sculpture, but another is the British art tradition, and another still is the British landscape itself. Landscape art in Albion is bound up with notions of Romanticism. For Robert Rosenblum, the Abstract Expressionists (in particular Mark Rothko) were the last in a long line of Romantic artists. Speaking of his important book *Modern Painting and the Northern Romantic Tradition*, Rosenblum said

> were I to write a supplementary chapter to it – I stopped with Rothko and Abstract Expressionism – I would probably include earthworks of the late 1960s and 1970s. Those seem in some way to be the last gasp of that tradition of trying to find some sort of connection with the Great Beyond or the Void.[2]

Certainly the works of Andy Goldsworthy, Hamish Fulton, Chris Drury, David Nash *et al*, are part of this Romantic tradition, as expressed in British landscape art. Associated with land art was the group of British artists, the 'New Arcadians', 'New Romantics' or 'New Ruralists'.

The influence of the landscape in the Great Britain on British sculpture is apparent in many, but by no means all, of British sculptors. Specifically *British* landscape, as opposed to other kinds of landscape, occur in the art of David Nash, Hamish Fulton, David Tremlett, Chris Drury, Roger Ackling and Goldsworthy, as one might expect. It was Carl Andre who noted, quite rightly, that the British landscape is 'one vast earthwork'.[3] Fulton, Nash, Drury and Goldsworthy, in particular, evoke the British landscape tradition in art, the tradition of the pastoral, the sublime, the Arcadian. Fulton, Goldsworthy, Drury and Nash are Romantic, in the sense of British Romantic poetry (Williams Blake and Wordsworth, John Keats, Percy Bysshe Shelley, Samuel Taylor Coleridge); in the sense of the British Romantic painters (J.M.W. Turner, John Constable, Thomas Girtin, John Sell Cotman, Philip Wilson); and in the sense of the Romantic attitudes and aspirations of infinity, nostalgia, mythology, soul, magic, nature and the Gothic.

In sculptors such as Tony Cragg, Hamish Fulton, Rachel Whiteread, Shirazeh Houshiary, Anish Kapoor, Richard Wentworth, David Nash, Bill Woodrow, Barry Flanagan, Ian Hamilton Finlay, Anthony Caro and William Tucker one can see the elements of British Romantic literature (as well as the Neo-Romanticism of the 1930s and 1940s): the anarchic idealism of Shelley, the luscious sensuality of Keats, the epic nature poetry of Wordsworth, the angelic visions of Blake and the synæsthetic poesie of Coleridge. The Romantic ethics of taking things to extremes, of going to the infinite and the eternal, are very much to the fore in land art, which is an art which quite definitely sustains Romantic myths and tenets.[4]

Land art is the sculptural companion of nature poetry. The connections between poetry and painting are ancient: Chinese landscape painters produced the voids found in *haiku* poetry; J.M.W. Turner and John Martin drew on Romantic poetry for their imagery; Renaissance painters drew on Classical poetry (such as Ovid) in their depictions of myths such as Diana and Actæon, or Leda and the Swan (Jupiter). While poetry and painting are often aligned in art history, poetry and sculpture are rarely mentioned. The importance of British landscape in both poetry and painting has long been noted. Its significance in sculpture is not as often acknowledged by art critics. The relation between poetry and landscape is vividly described by Ted Hughes in his book *Poetry in the Making*. Hughes's poetry has many affinities with land artists, particularly the British ones: Hughes, and other British nature poets (Tony Harrison, Seamus Heaney, Alan Bold), celebrate rainy, grim, Northern landscapes, as beloved of William Wordsworth, John Clare and Samuel Coleridge.[5] Hughes used Gerard Manley Hopkins as an example of first-rate, visionary British landscape:

In this...poem there is much more of what we might call straightforward description, but the vivid details are all aiming one way: it is a scene in sharp focus: all gloom and brilliance, the exhilaration and uneasy sunniness of a bleak, rather lonely place. It is the closest thing to a conventional beauty spot that I know of in poetry. And it is so clean and right that whenever I see anything like it in actual scenery I think – "It's almost as good as Inversnaid" which is the title of this poem by Gerald Manly Hopkins:

This darksome burn, horseback brown,
His rollrock highroad roaring down,
In coop and in comb the fleece of his foam
Flutes and low to the lake falls home.

A windpuff-bonnet of fawn-froth
Turns and twindles over the broth
Of a pool so pitchblack, fell-frowning,
It rounds and rounds Despair to drowning.

Degged with dew, dappled with dew
Are the groins of the braes that the brook treads through,
Wiry heathpacks, flitches of fern,
And the beadbonny ash that sits over the burn.

What would the world be, once bereft
Of wet and of wildness? Let them be left,
O let them be left, wildness and wet;
Long live the weeds and the wilderness yet.[6]

4

Land Artists in Britain,

Europe and America

4 : 1   *ROBERT SMITHSON*

Instead of putting a work of art on some land, some land is put into a work of art.

Robert Smithson[1]

Robert Smithson (1938-1973) was the chief mouthpiece of American earth/ site æsthetics, and is probably the most important theoretician among all land artists; and Smithson is also the premier land artist. When you look at land art, you have to start with Smithson first. Smithson's theoretical statements were published in three essays. In "The Crystal Land" Smithson recounted a trip he made to a quarry with Donald Judd, the key Minimal artist. Smithson evoked the decayed nature of the quarry, those aspects of entropy which would feature in his own work ('cracked broken shattered earth, of fragmentation, corrosion, decomposition, disintegration, rock crisis, debris slides, mud flow avalanche' [RS, 20]).

In the second article, "Entropy and the New Monuments" (1966), Robert Smithson discussed the important Minimal show *Primary Structures* at the Jewish Museum. Smithson's themes were entropy in nature and art; he used the science of crystals and minerals as paradigms of the new art. Smithson had collected crystals and rocks as a child. Crystallography, for Smithson, offered 'a way of dealing with nature without falling into the old trap of the biological metaphor'.2 No wonder, then, that when Smithson saw Donald Judd's pink plastic boxes he compared them to 'giant crystals from another planet' (RS, 19). The dissolution of crystals also provided Smithson with another analogy for his theory of natural entropy. The third theoretical piece, "A Sedimentation of the Mind: Earth Projects" (1968), concerned notions of time and place. While sculptors such as Anthony Caro and his ilk still clung to the old-fashioned ideas of beauty, Smithson spoke warmly of artists such as Walter de Maria, Carl Andre, Michael Heizer, Dennis Oppenheim, Tony Smith and Douglas Huebler (RS, 85). A group of artists were grouped around Smithson socially, too; they used to meet in New York (Andy Goldsworthy hasn't been associated with social groups of artist in the same way).

Robert Smithson was also interested in science fiction: the poetic elements of his art thus form a continuum: between the industrial wastelands he visited for his 'non-site' sculptures and the desolate planets of science fiction; between chaos theory in the New Physics and its exploration in postmodern science fiction; between the forms of crystals and those of Minimal sculptures, and so on.

Robert Smithson's exaltation of lonely post-industrial sites was echoed in the speculative fictions of writers who evoked post- or near-holocaust worlds. J.G. Ballard, for example, wrote of post-industrial desert lands and run-down townscapes (in The Drought, Vermilion Sands, High-Rise and Low-Flying Aircraft). J.G. Ballard, as one would expect, took an eccentric view of Smithson's earthworks: Ballard mused on what kind of cargo might have been berthed at Smithson's Spiral Jetty and Broken Circle. Ballard wondered if the cargo was a 'very special kind of clock... so many of Smithson's monuments seem to be a potent amalgam of clock, labyrinth and cargo terminal'.3

In the essay "Tour of the Monuments of Passaic", itself a sci-fi sort of title, Robert Smithson wrote about 'great pipes, sand boxes, bridges with wooden sidewalks, all standing for the irreversibility of eternity. Under the dead light of the Passaic after-noon, the desert becomes a land of infinite disintegration and forgetfulness' (RS, 56). This sort of apocalyptic imagery is echoed in William Burroughs, J.G. Ballard, Tom Disch and other speculative fiction writers. It's the desolate wasteland imagery of Andrei Tarkovsky's film Stalker (1979) and other post-apocalyptic visions.4

J.G. Ballard wrote of Robert Smithson:

The Amarillo Ramp I take to be both jetty and runway, a proto-labyrinth that Smith-son hoped would launch him from the cramping limits of time and space into a richer and more complex realm... I see Smithson's monuments [as] artifacts intended to serve as machines that will suddenly switch themselves on and begin to generate a more complex time and space. All his structures seem to be anal-ogues of advanced neurological processes that have yet to articulate themselves.5

Andy Goldsworthy remarked that he got to know the American earth artists first (at art college), and found out about Richard Long and the British land art tradition later

(*Wall*, 14). For Robert Smithson, Carl Andre, Walter de Maria, Michael Heizer, Dennis Oppenheim and Tony Smith were 'the more compelling artists today, concerned with 'Place' or 'Site''.[6] Smithson was impressed by Tony Smith's vision of the mysterious aspects of a dark unfinished road (see below) and called Smith 'the agent of endlessness'. Smith's æsthetic became part of Smithson's view of art as a complete 'site', not simply an æsthetic of sculptural objects. Smithson was not inspired by ancient religious sculpture, by burial mounds for example, so much as by decayed industrial sites. He visited some in the mid-1960s that were 'in some way disrupted or pulverized'. He said he was looking for a 'denaturalization rather than built up scenic beauty.'[7] Andy Goldsworthy said he had always been attracted to the waste ground in urban areas, where he can work 'so long as some growth exists'.[8]

Robert Smithson explained he was concerned, like many land (and postwar) artists with the thing in itself, not its image, its effect, or its critical significance: 'I am for an art that takes into account the direct effect of the elements as they exist from day to day apart from representation' (RS, 133). Smithson's theory of the 'non-site' was based on 'absence, a very ponderous, weighty absence'.[9] Smithson proposed a theory of a dialectic between absence and presence, in which the 'non-site' and 'site' are both interacting. In the 'non-site' work, presence and absence are there simultaneously. 'The land or ground from the Site is placed in the art (Non-Site) rather than the art is placed on the ground. The Non-Site is a container within another container – the room' (RS, 115).

Robert Smithson proposed a schema for 'non-site' art in his essay "Dialectic of Site and Non-Site" which ran thus:

Site	Non-Site
1. Open limits	Closed limits
2. A series of points	An array of Matter
3. Outer coordinates	Inner coordinates
4. Subtraction	Addition
5. Indeterminate certainty	Dominate uncertainty
6. Scattered information	Contained information
7. Reflection	Mirror
8. Edge	Center
9. Some place (physical)	No place (abstract)
10. Many	One (RS, 115)

The 'non-site' works were permanent, gallery works. Robert Smithson's *Mirror Displacements* (1968) consisted of putting some mirrors in several settings and taking photographs of them before moving them somewhere else. *Mirror Displacements* was documented in Smithson's *Artforum* article "Incidents of Mirror Travel in the Yucatan" (1969). Sometimes Smithson put soil on top of the mirrors, to dirty them up, to sabotage 'the perfect reflections of the sky'. Smithson, like Michael Heizer, liked dirt, gravel, sand, sludge and sediment – indeterminate, malleable substances. Land artists often sabotaged the clinical nature of much of art – putting soil or grass or slate or horses in the clean, white gallery space. Of his Italian horse piece, where he stabled horses in a gallery, Jannis Kounellis said the aim was to increase awareness of the 'basic nature of a gallery, of its bourgeois origin', its economic and ideological aspects.[10]

Robert Smithson's other projects of the time included putting raw, natural materials into Minimal spaces, creating a tension of dialectic between 'site and non-site', as he called it. *Ziggurat Mirror* was completed by the use of mirrors. The sculpture needed the mirrors to work properly. Using the mirrors to create repetition, Smithson pointed to the delimited nature of the sculpture: with the right use of mirrors, a sculpture could be extended infinitely. Endless repetition was central to Minimal and 1960s art (Andy Warhol, Sol LeWitt, Carl Andre, Robert Morris, Donald Judd, Frank Stella and others took a simple unit and endlessly repeated it).

Before he made the famous *Spiral Jetty,* Robert Smithson had already been considering the scientific notions of rotation and equilibrium. His sculpture *Gyrostasis* (1968) was a 75 by 57 by 40 inch painted steel structure based on the spiral. Smithson explained that *Gyrostasis*, as the title implied, was about how rotating bodies maintain their equilibrium. 'The work is a standing triangulated spiral. When I made the sculpture I was thinking of mapping procedures that refer to the planet Earth' (RS, 37).

Robert Smithson's famous *Spiral Jetty* is a 'monumental' earthwork, though the use of the spiral motif has connotations with the ancient symbols of the Goddess.[11] Of his *Spiral Jetty*, Smithson wrote:

> As I looked at the site, it reverberated out to the horizons only to suggest an immobile cyclone while flickering light made the entire landscape appear to quake. A dormant earthquake spread into an immense roundness. From that gyrating space emerged the possibility of the Spiral Jetty. No idea, no concepts, no systems, no structures, no abstractions could hold themselves together in the actuality of that phenomenological evidence.[12]

Robert Smithson was impressed by the characteristics of the Great Salt Lake site, the pinkish mud, the faintly violet water surrounded by limestone hills, and the 'crushing light' of the sun. He had been reading about salt lakes in Bolivia, where bacteria turned the water red to match the colour of the flamingos. Smithson found out that the Utah salt lakes were also red and pink due to algæ and mineral waste. Smithson and his wife, Nancy Holt, surveyed the area and chose a lake at Rozel Point in Utah, which had a number of cracks in the mud under the shallow water. Smithson began building it in April, 1970, excavating 6,650 tons. *Spiral Jetty* was made from rocks, water, mud and precipitated salt crystals. It was 1,500 ft long and 15 ft wide. Smithson was aided by Virginia Dwan and the Ace Gallery of Vancouver. As with many other projects of the time a film was made of the construction of *Spiral Jetty*. Smithson related the work to spiral nebulæ, to salt crystals and microscopic organisms. Smithson thought in terms of eons of time, and mused on how entropy would overtake the site.[13]

Robert Smithson used one of the primary forms of land art, the circle, in many works, combining it with ideas taken from science (such as *Gyrostasis*, which, said Smithson, 'refers to a branch of physics that deals with rotating bodies' [ib., 37]). Smithson was not adverse to religious feelings about art: when he visited the site of his *Spiral Jetty*, in the Utah salt flats, he experienced a feeling of 'a rotary that enclosed itself in an immense roundness' (ib., 111). The two elements – rational, mathematical, scientific precision and intuitive, emotional, religious feeling – are two of the chief characteristics of land art. On the one hand, land artists talk about measurements, practical details, materials, maps and spatial data. On the other hand, they hint at religious awe, spiritual feelings, prehistoric art and the influx of the numinous into modern art. As Andy Goldsworthy says, '[a]lthough it is often a practical and physical art, it is also an intensely spiritual affair that I have with nature: a relationship.'[14]

Robert Smithson also identified his *Spiral Jetty* with a mythic whirlpool that sprang up from a tunnel connected to the Pacific Ocean. His *Spiral Jetty* was an 'immobile cyclone', it spiralled inwards from the outside: the track leaves the shore and twists round and round to the centre. *Spiral Jetty* was also linked with notions of decay in nature. In "A Sedimentation of the Mind: Earth Projects", Smithson had written '[e]very object, if it is art, is charged with the rush of time, even though it is static' (RS, 90). Ironically, Smithson's *Spiral Jetty* was itself subject to natural entropy: the water level rose and *Spiral Jetty* was submerged under water (in Summer it is usually exposed). It was ironic too that Smithson died in a plane crash while he was flying over and inspecting a site in Texas (one of the biggest losses in contemporary art).

Robert Smithson's 1971 *Broken Circle* was another large earthwork using circular motifs that was set adjacent to the land and extended out into a lake. Smithson chose a quarry site near Emmen, Holland. Again, the site had an interesting geological aspect, which was in keeping with Smithson's love of rocks and minerals. Glacial action had formed unusual layers of soil. Unlike *Spiral Jetty*, which was often submerged, *Broken Circle* remains close to Smithson's conception. It is maintained by local funds. It is a 140 foot circle comprising one half of soil and one half of water, with a twelve foot wide canal cutting round the earth section of the circle, forming a semi-circle. At the centre of *Broken Circle* is a very large glacial boulder. It was supposedly one of the largest in the Netherlands. Significantly, Smithson allowed nothing at the centre of *Spiral Jetty*: the spectator walked round the inward-turning spiral to find nothing. Smithson was exasperated by the prehistoric stone at the centre of his *Broken Circle*, but he let this 'accidental center' stay there, commenting 'it became a dark spot of exasperation, a geological gangrene on the sandy expanse'.[15]

Robert Smithson's last major work, before his untimely death, was *Amarillo Ramp*, one of many land artworks conceived as an observation structure. Nancy Holt worked with one of the major American sculptors of the era, Richard Serra, to complete Smithson's plans. *Amarillo Ramp,* 15 miles North-west of Amarillo in the Texas Panhandle, is a huge inclined ramp or road, made from quarried rocks. The summit of *Amarillo Ramp* is a viewing point.[16]

Taken together, Robert Smithson's three large-scale earthworks, *Spiral Jetty*,

Broken Circle and *Amarillo Ramp,* all revolve around circular or spiral motifs, a sense of temporality, of decay and transience and each uses primitive, mythic forms and gestures in a monumental manner. Two of them are set in wilderness spaces, where the marks of humanity are at their weakest. Yet each earthwork of course speaks acutely of the mark of humanity upon the Earth, and a very particular kind of mark: that of late twentieth century American urbanized art-making. Robert Smithson's influence on land art has been immense (for Smithson's influence on Andy Goldsworthy, see the section on Goldsworthy's large-scale works).

4 : 2   DENNIS OPPENHEIM

Like Robert Smithson and James Turrell, Dennis Oppenheim (1938-2011) was one of the most interesting of U.S. earth artists, an artist who produced an amazing body of work which has many affinities with Andy Goldsworthy's art. It's significant, for instance, that Dennis Oppenheim was the first American land artist to work with snow on a grand scale. Oppenheim began making snow works in the late Sixties, many years before Goldsworthy (when Goldsworthy was only ten). The only other important environmental artist who regularly used snow and ice, really, was Hans Haacke. But, more than any of the other first generation land artists, Oppenheim made snow one of his primary media.

Dennis Oppenheim's *Annual Rings* (1968), a series of concentric circles that straddled the Canadian/ American border, was created with snow (one of Oppenheim's recurring motifs was the border zone; margins and thresholds in time and space and concept). Oppenheim has drawn a number of snow works with a snowmobile: *One Hour Run* (1968) was a continuous track made in the snow in Maine. Two tracks, side by side, were carved in the snow between Fort Kent, Maine and Clair, New Brunswick, Canada, in 1968, for *Time Line,* a work which explored the different time zones. Oppenheim's *Negative Board* (1968) was a dark cut in the snow and ice in Maine.

Dennis Oppenheim burnt circles onto grass in *Branded Mountain. Accumulation Cut* (1969) was made at Cornell University: a hundred foot long cut made in the ice, running away from a waterfall. Also at Cornell, Oppenheim took the floor outline of gallery 4 of the Andrew Dickson White Museum of Art and drew it into the snow and ice outside (1969). Another *Gallery Transplant* was made in 1969, transplanting the floor plan of a gallery in the Stedelijk Museum in Amsterdam to a snowy hillside in New Jersey.

Dennis Oppenheim's *Whirlpool Eye of Storm* (1973) was an ephemeral piece of land art in the Hans Haacke vein: a jet trail created in the sky by a plane flying above the desert at El Mirage Dry Lake in California. *Directed Seeding* (1969) parodied Action Painting by harvesting a wheat field. In *Cancelled Crop* (1969), Oppenheim cut a giant

'X' in a field in the Netherlands, and kept the grain, as if he were preventing the material he'd cultivated for his art from becoming the raw material for other (illusionistic) art: 'isolating this grain from further processing becomes like stopping raw pigment from becoming an illusionistic force on canvas'.[1] Another 'X' was laid onto the landscape at El Mirage Dry Lake California out of asphalt primer (covering an area 610 yards square), entitled *Relocated Burial Ground* (1978). (The 'X' shape, as Lucy Lippard noted, was a favourite motif with male land artists – Chris Burden, Richard Long and Robert Smithson also created 'Xs' – and also with Minimalists).[2]

Many of Dennis Oppenheim's artworks are conceptual pieces in the tradition of Sixties Conceptualism. That is, many are works made to be exhibited in galleries, on walls. They comprise photographs, drawings and maps, with Oppenheim's type-written captions and explanations: *Three Downward Blows* (1977), *Salt Flat* (1969), *Boundary Split* (1968), and *Negative Board* (1968) (maps were central to Oppenheim's art). Many of Oppenheim's land artworks also existed as these framed photo-text-sketch-map works. One of Oppenheim's specialities was to impose human-made geometries, symbols and ideas onto the landscape: to transpose map contours, for instance, or the rings of a tree trunk onto snow (in *Annual Rings*), or the International Date Line in snow (*Time Pocket*). Robert Smithson remarked that Oppenheim was 'transforming a terrestrial site into a map'.[3] Generally, Oppenheim tended to enlarge symbols or ideas or images, and recreate them on a colossal scale in the landscape.

In *Time Pocket* (1968), Dennis Oppenheim 'drew' the International Date Line with a diesel-powered skidder in snow in Maine. In *Boundary Split* (1968), Oppenheim carved lines perpendicular to the Time Boundary between Canada and the U.S.A. *Star Skid* (1977) was Oppenheim's proposal for a series of concrete and glass stars that would look from the air as if they had landed on Earth and skidded to a halt.

In *Salt Flat* (1969) Oppenheim created a 'salt flat' (a favourite place for land artists to make work in the U.S.A.) in New York City, with a thousand pounds of salt. The rectangle of salt was recreated in the sea in the Bahamas, and in the Salt Lake Desert. In *Directed Harvest* (1969), Oppenheim carved up fields of crops. Oppenheim set off underground explosions in *Three Downward Blows (Knuckle Marks)* in Montana in 1977.

In *Ground Mutations – Shoe Prints* (1969), Dennis Oppenheim created shoe print works over the course of three Winter months (by wearing shoes with a 1/4 inch groove cut in the sole and heel): 'I was connecting the patterns of thousands of individuals... My thoughts were filled with marching diagrams'. The use of shoes and prints links with Goldsworthy's direct use of the body (and Richard Long's walks).

Speaking in 1970, Dennis Oppenheim opined that art was now 'more concerned with the location of material and with speculation' (i.e., locations or ideas). Now, art was meant to be visited (location) or 'abstracted from a photograph' (concept-ualized).[4] Oppenheim moved towards a kind of art that would be discovered or visited by the spectator, rather than 'made' in the old, traditional manner (this was part of the 'dematerialization' of the art object in Sixties art). Oppenheim moved away from the idea of the special, unique art object, towards found objects, and utilizing existing sites. Oppenheim was replacing objects with locations.

The *Site Markers* series (1967) comprised posts in locations which were documented with texts, maps and photos. The maps and photos explained where the posts were situated, so that the location, rather than the object, became the centre of the piece. As Oppenheim explained, the *Site Markers* works were intended to be about the sites themselves, rather than the manipulation or replication of an object: 'beginning with the site-markers started in a sense a journey: art is travel'.5

One of Dennis Oppenheim's more Conceptual pieces (*Sound Enclosed Land Area*, 1969) comprised four tape recorders buried in cages in Paris enclosing an area 500 by 800 yards. Each machine played a tape loop which had a voice repeating its position (North, South, East or West). *Contour Lines Scribed in Swamp Grass* (1968) transposed contour lines on a map in two different locations (a swamp and a mountain). The use of aluminium filings poured onto grass in concentric circles recalled Long's stone circles.

The contours of Dennis Oppenheim's own thumbprints were the basis for *Identity Stretch* (1970-75), where a truck sprayed white paint on the ground, using the thumbprint (which Oppenheim had elongated) as a guide, within a grid. In 1970 Oppenheim created a performance piece, entitled *Parallel Stress*, performed between a collapsed concrete pier and a wall at Manhattan and Brooklyn bridges. Oppenheim stretched his body between the wall and the pier, echoing the New York bridges nearby. The same body position was recreated at an abandoned sump in Long Island.

Like many land artists, Dennis Oppenheim produced a maze (in 1970). But Oppenheim's *Maze* was just a little different: it was the design of a maze used in a scientific laboratory for rats transposed onto a large field, with cows now the rats, lured around the maze by the promise of food.

4 : 3   ROBERT MORRIS

Robert Morris (b. 1931) was one of the most eloquent theorists of Sixties, Minimal and Postminimal sculpture (along with Donald Judd and Carl Andre). Morris had, like Judd, begun working in painting, but moved on to sculpture. He was part of the Fluxus school, alongside Yoko Ono, Simone Forte, Walter de Maria and Henry Flynt.

Robert Morris is the genius of negative presence and the perversity of odd proportions that are subliminal in their aggressiveness [wrote John Perreault]. Works of art can in some sense be defined as those man-made objects that are designed solely to call attention to themselves. In this age of bombast, chatter, and random activity, that which does not move and that which is silent is often that which compels our attention and stimulates our awareness most effectively. Donald Judd, too, appears to have this "anti-art," pro-silence bias, and his works, although scrupulously elegant, are a well-formulated attack on "artistic" cliché.1

Robert Morris wrote many artistic statements, the most famous probably being the articles published in *Artforum* entitled "Notes on Sculpture". For Morris, one of the things that was new about 1960s sculpture was the object's relationship with the viewer. Before then, Morris argued, the viewer related to the object as something separate; the new æsthetic put the viewer into the same space as the object. 'One is more aware than before that he himself is establishing relationships as he apprehends the object from different positions and under varying conditions of light and spatial context.'[2] This is a crucial concept in Minimal art, which is nearly always viewed in an object-spectator continuous space.

Robert Morris's concept of 'objecthood' was central to his notion of sculpture. 'Morris wants to achieve presence through objecthood, which requires a certain largeness of scale, rather than through size alone', wrote Michael Fried (1967). Just as important as the object itself was the sense of space around it, the spatial context in which it was displayed. Morris wanted to emphasize that 'things are in a space with oneself', rather than the notion that 'one is in a space surrounded by things' (ib., 127). The whole context of the object in its space ('the entire situation') was important to Morris's notion of the new sculpture. One might say the new, 1960s sculpture, like land art, was about the 'thing-in-itself', a notion borrowed from Existentialism, but also about the 'thing in its space'. Although Morris denied being an 'environmental' artist, the context was important to his art.[3] For one critic, Morris's sculpture 'redirect[s] the entire environmental experience'.[4] Referring to Donald Judd's "Specific Objects" article, Morris said he did not separate the two, he did not think that something must be either an object or an environment.[5] As he moved towards Postminimalism, Morris advocated doing away with a figure-ground relationship; instead, heterogeneous 'stuff' should be used, an 'accumulation of things or stuff'.[6] In 1975, Morris wrote "Aligned with Nazca", an article in one of the key magazines of the period (*Artforum*) which related earthwork art with ancient art such as the Nazca lines. However, such connections with ancient art had already been made by artists and critics of land art.

Robert Morris's sculptures were often simple polyhedrons, such as cubes, circles, ovals and beams. They were modular and serial. 'Unitary Objects' he termed them, recalling Donald Judd's 'Specific Objects'. They appeared to be 'simple'; as with Judd's or Sol LeWitt's sculptures, Morris's did not seem to be hiding anything. Yet just because they appeared 'simple' did not mean that their effects were simple: 'simplicity of shape does not necessarily equate with simplicity of experience', wrote Morris,[7] and Minimal art proved him right. Morris's art was by turns ironic, blank, unambiguously clear and frustratingly amorphous. Morris's *Battered Cubes* (1965/88, Margo Leaven Gallery, Los Angeles) were four boxes of painted steel that were set near each other. Each unit had a gently sloping outside face. His Unitary Objects were made in materials such as wood, concrete, wire mesh, aluminium and granite. Morris also made felt works which could not be arranged the same each time, which determinedly refused to be locked into the Minimal æsthetic of straight edges and regularity. The felt was partly haphazard, relying on gravity, but it was also stiff enough to stay roughly where it was put. It was not final, but malleable.

Among Robert Morris's stranger concepts was his 'mobile' mausoleum: in an aluminium tunnel 3 miles long a coffin made from iron and suspended from pulleys would be moved intermittently. An attendant with a magnet would shift the coffin from above. By the entrance to the tube would be swooning maidens in marble, carved in the style of Antonio Canova (B. Rose, 1965). 'If something is still capable of moving, is it dead?' Morris wondered.8

In *Pace and Progress*, Robert Morris made a work by walking a horse back and forth over a piece of grass until a path had been worn. The action of walking the horse rubbed down the grass. One of Morris's largest commissions was the *Grand Rapids Project*, in Michigan (1973-74), consisting of huge ramps leading up to a plateau. Another large Morris sitework was created in King County, Washington (1979), a series of oval terraces recalling Iron Age hillforts.

Robert Morris produced some works of a highly 'ephemeral' nature, such as his 'steam piece' (*Untitled*, 1968-69), which was made out of doors on a patch of grass. How the work turned out was dependent upon physicalities such as humidity, air pressure, wind speed and direction, and temperature. Clouds of steam drifted over the grass. A number of (land) artists have worked with clouds: Chris Drury, James Turrell, Alice Aycock, Dennis Oppenheim, Hans Haacke and Peter Hutchinson.

British artist Rose Finn-Kelcey has produced a steam work: her *Untitled* (1992, London) comprised water placed on a sheet metal base, with an extractor hood hung above it. In between the two was a cloud of steam, made dramatic by the lighting. Some of Hans Haacke's most intriguing works were with ephemeral natural events such as steam, ice, condensation, fog and flooding. Peter Hutchinson made a cloud piece (*Dissolving Clouds*, 1970) using Hatha yoga meditation techniques, trying to dissolve clouds through thought. The work consisted of a sequence of 6 photographs of clouds. Alice Aycock also made a *Cloud Piece* (1971), photographs of cumulus clouds which melted after a few minutes.

Robert Morris's *Box With the Sound of Its Own Making* (1961) was precisely that: inside the box was a tape lasting 3 hours which replayed the sound of the box being constructed. The past history of the box and the processes which went towards its construction became available to the viewer – a new way of displaying self-reflexivity. Morris's *Box With the Sound of Its Own Making* combined the personal touch valued by modernism (the sound of the carpentry and hand saw); an emphasis on the process of manufacture, important for Sixties art (process, materiality); and the use of technology (the tape recorder), valued by Pop Art. *Box With the Sound of Its Own Making* was also a kind of performance art, and it was also the primary structure of Minimal art, the cube.

For Frank Stella, the artist was a privileged participant in the making of art: the 'audience' or viewer is always one step away, was always 'after the fact': '[t]he sensation is one that the artist experiences as the first and only necessary viewer' (1986, 127). Robert Morris's *I-Box* (1962) was a jokey comment on Sixties art, on Constructivism and Minimalism. Morris's *I-Box* featured an I-shaped door which revealed a photo of Morris in the nude, smiling. The Duchampian nature of Morris's *I-Box* recalled those paintings of Jasper Johns' which included bits of human anatomy (an arm, a pair of testicles) in amongst otherwise abstract works. The *I-Box* also recalled Johns' *Target* which put male genitals in a little niche above the target.

Robert Morris's *Untitled* (1968) was a pile of cotton waste and mirrors. The mirrors were seen sticking up in the cotton. An *Untitled* of 1969 comprised of little trees in soil set in rectangular boxes of steel; above the trees hung fluorescent 'grow' lamps. These works interfused the human or 'artificial' (the lamps and mirrors) with the 'natural' or organic (the cotton and trees). A number of Morris's works were what appeared to be piles of concrete and wool, large oblong blocks piled up on top of each other. Morris produced both indoor and outdoor versions of these sprawls of oblong blocks. Sometimes they looked like the stacks of timber at a wood merchant's yard on the outskirts of a town, or the detritus that's thrown into heaps beside sidings at railroad stations. Morris's later works (in the Nineties) included wall drawings made blindfolded, and felt works, where an element of randomness and chance dictated how the felt strips would hang.

Robert Morris preferred not to give titles to many of his works (in common with many contemporary artists, though not Andy Goldsworthy). Morris explained:

> I think that the reason I don't title them is that I don't think the work is about allusions. And I think titles always are. And I think the work is very much about that thing there in space, quite literally. And titles seem to me to have some allusion to what the thing isn't, and that's why I avoid titles.[9]

The links between art of Robert Morris and Andy Goldsworthy would include an emphasis on spontaneity, materiality, chance, randomness, change and ephemerality. 'I have an art that understands decay and change, an art that welcomes that change', remarked Goldsworthy (RA, 107).

4 : 4   CARL ANDRE

Since the 1960s the statements of a handful of artists have proved to be the most illuminating about 1960s art, and Minimalism in particular. Robert Smithson, Donald Judd, Robert Morris and Carl Andre have been among the most lucid of Sixties theorists among artists.[1] Andre has many pertinent things to say about sculpture. Andre also forged links with British land art (such as his friendship with Richard Long). His mid-1960s summary of the history of sculpture applies directly to land art:

> The course of development
> > Sculpture as form
> > Sculpture as structure
> > Sculpture as place.[2]

Carl Andre's (b. 1935) biography is often cited in accounts of his art. He worked on the railways, as a freight conductor and brakeman (in Newark, at the Pennsylvania Railroad) from 1960 to 1964, and this is used to explain Andre's use of modules and units which join together to form a work. Like Sol LeWitt and Donald Judd, Andre took one unit and multiplied them until he had a line or a square. Before working on the railroad, Andre was 'a wood-carving disciple of Brancusi', carving chunks out of wood beams. For a long time the shadow of Brancusi lay over Andre's art. When he came to explain his floor-standing works, such as *Lever*, a line of firebricks, he said he was

> putting Brancusi's *Endless Column* on the ground instead of in the sky... Most sculpture is priapic with the male organ in the air. In my work, Priapus is down on the floor. The engaged position is to run along the earth.[3]

The sexualization of sculpture in Carrl Andre's remark is no accident: Andre has spoken in interviews that the best creative work is erotic. In a 1970 radio discussion (with Lucy Lippard, Douglas Huebler, Dan Graham and Jan Dibbets on WBAI FM), Andre said desires, not ideas, were important. 'I have very few ideas, but I have strong desires.... I agree with Dr Guillotine that all ideas are the same except in execution... You can't cut off desires except painfully'.[4] Nature was also crucial: Andre said he disliked Conceptual art because it was cut off from nature – a view Andy Goldsworthy would endorse (ibid.). Andre said his art 'has never been conceptual in any way'.[5]

While he was in New Hampshire in 1965, canoeing on a lake, Carl Andre (so the story goes) realized that sculpture ought to be level, like water. After this moment of insight, most of his sculpture was floor-standing and flat. Lines of bricks or squares made from plates of metal were typical Andre works. Andre's use of materials was not 'poetic' or 'spiritual' in the usual sense of the word. In works such as *Cedar Piece* (1959/ 64), *Pyre* (1971, S. & C. Gilman), *Herm* (1976, Guggenheim), *Stile* (1975) and *Well* (1964), which were made out of wood, Andre was using materials as themselves, but 'not to evoke nature'.[6] Andre did not intend his materials to refer to other things, to be allusive in the art historical or lyrical sense. His Styrofoam planks were not alluding to marble, as some viewers mistakenly thought.[7]

Carl Andre's notion of the 'dematerialization' of sculpture was central to his art, and also to land art. When they were not being exhibited, Andre's sculptures simply disappeared. They were not objects on permanent display, but were made specially for each occasion and space. Most land art is like this. Andre's works outside of shows exist as ideas, photographs, descriptions, memories, and so on, but not as actual works. Much of land art is also this ephemeral, made for a particular occasion then dismantled (the Christos, Andy Goldsworthy, Robert Morris). This emphasis on the materiality and dematerialization of his works led Andre to regard his art as non-spiritual. He said:

> My work is atheistic, materialistic, and communistic. It's atheistic because it's without transcendent form, without spiritual or intellectual quality. Materialistic because it's made out of its own materials without pretension to other materials. And communistic because the form is equally accessible to all men. (in ib., 107)

This is a humble, self-effacing view of his own art. It is this aspect of his art that annoyed people when the Tate Gallery in Great Britain bought, with public money, one of his piles of bricks. The form (a low oblong shape) and the material of the work (brick) seemed available to anyone who visited a household supply store and bought a few hundred bricks and arranged them in a certain way. Yet Carl Andre's art is of course not as simple as that, and not as easy to produce as that.

Carl Andre's *37 Pieces of Work* is a good example of Minimal æsthetic permutations taken to extremes. It is a sculpture that is typical of Andre's art, as David Bourdon wrote in *Carl Andre: Sculpture, 1959-1977*:

> Taken as a whole 37 Pieces of Work consists of 1,296 plates, 216 each of aluminium, copper, steel, magnesium, lead and zinc. Each metal appears alone in individual six-foot square plains. Then alternates with another, checkerboard fashion, in every possible permutation. Since each of the six metals in the large piece was laid out in the alphabetical order of its chemical symbol, alternating successively with the others, there are two versions of each combination.[8]

Many of Carl Andre's floor-pieces are similar: the spectator is aware of the material first and foremost: the colour, mass, weight, size and texture of the metals. *37 Pieces of Work* is a 432 inch wide floor-hugging square, in which the colours of the copper, aluminium, lead, steel, zinc and magnesium is beautifully foregrounded.

Carl Andre's *Element* series consisted of wood-carved beams that recalled Constantin Brancusi; Andre's *Equivalents* were floor-standing sculptures shown in 1966. The magnet pieces, which preceded the metal squares, also hugged the floor, so much so that the third dimension was nearly expunged. The floor-pieces neatly rid the sculptor of dealing with pedestals. They became 'place-markers'.[9] They have no space, according to one critic; they have 'no appearance of inside or center. Rather they seem to be co-extensive with the very floor on which the viewer stands'.[10] Place, not space or sky, became what matters for Andre. Andre's floor-pieces are viewer-friendly, too: the viewer is invited to (or allowed to) walk over them. Like Donald Judd, Andre wanted his sculptures to be seen from a variety of viewpoints. Instead of a single viewpoint, one could have a number of angles; he compared viewing his sculptures to walking on roads: '[t]hey cause you to make your way along them or around them or to move...over them' (1970, 57). Andre's works seem to be slight, almost insubstantial, but, simultaneously, 'their matter-of-factness that makes them in a multiple sense *present*'.[11]

Carl Andre's works are extremely sensuous, with their shiny or dull surfaces of copper, zinc, steel or aluminium. Andre's *Sixteenth Copper Cardinal*, sixteen square copper slabs, is a work that could be described as luscious. People are used to marble and stone being beautiful, and also certain metals – bronze, silver and gold in particular have been central to sculpture for millennia. Why not zinc and copper, too? Andre, like other Minimal sculptors, introduces the viewer to the sensuality of copper, bronze and zinc shaped into nothing more than... a simple shape, like a slab, put on the floor. Andre's slabs are not 'narrative', allusive, literal or anthropomorphic; they do not 'depict' animals or gods or people; but they are no less beautiful, as objects in their own right. Spectators are invited to walk on his sculptures, offering a new relation with the work (there are fewer sculptors than one might think who let punters walk over their sculpture in a gallery. although it is a hallmark of sculpture since the 1960s that viewers are invited to experience it firsthand).

Carl Andre commented:

> The materiality, the presence of the work of sculpture in the world, essentially independent of any single individual, but rather the residue of many individuals and the dream, the experience of the sea, the trees and the stones – I'm interested in that kind of essential thing. [12]

('I will try to have in my work only what is necessary to it', Carl Andre said (1984).) Andre's *Stone Field* (1977) was one of his site-specific works of the 1970s, consisting of 26 very large glacial boulders. It was an imposing piece, introducing the idiosyncratic, organic shapes of nature into the 'geometric wilderness' (D.M. Thomas's term) of the city (Hartford, Connecticut). Andre created a line of hay bales, placed end to end, in a field in Vermont (*Joint*, 1968). [13] It was a line like Richard Long's stone rows, or Tony Cragg's floor spreads.

> Many of the activities in farm work are sculptural [remarked Goldsworthy]: stacking the hay bales, ploughing fields, feeding animals; also the marks left behind by the animals or made by farmworkers, tractors… the texture of the land. (T, 180).

Carl Andre made one of his floor-pieces of slabs of metal deliberately so it would be altered by being outside. It was called *Small Weathering Piece* (1971), and contained a large number of metals (large for an Andre sculpture): lead, zinc, aluminium, copper, steel and magnesium.

One of Carl Andre's most intriguing theoretical statements is this: 'my ideal piece of sculpture is a road'. [14] This applies not only to Andre's lines of bricks or hay bales, but to Richard Long's lines of stones and walks along roads, to the Christos' *Running Fence*, to Andy Goldsworthy's stone walls, and to other land artworks. Andre's notion of the ultimate earthwork as a road has a parallel with the famous anecdote of U.S. artist Tony Smith who, when driving along the New Jersey turnpike, was impressed by the 'dark pavements moving through the landscape of the flats, rimmed in the distance, but punctuated by stacks, towers, fumes, and coloured lights'. [15] Something in such a long stretch of empty roads, as with airstrips (and, more dubiously, a drill ground at Nuremberg) impressed Tony Smith, who wrote '[i]t seemed that there had been a reality there that had not had any expression in art' (ib., 131). Roads are not 'art', and not wholly functional either – they have an aura or mystery which Smith tried to explain. Richard Long emphasized the functional or workaday aspect of his walks. He saw his walks as hard work; roads, in the Smith view, are also for and about labour and functionality. The road, for the Minimal or Process artist, in the Carl Andre manner, embody materially the sense of a sequence or process. One unit (the foot or brick or slab of tarmac or concrete) is placed next to another, forming a road. Artists such as Carl Andre (and Bladen, LeWitt and Judd) did exactly the same, putting one unit next to another, creating a line or sequence of units.

The road also may have no obvious end: endlessness was crucial to Minimal, Process and Conceptual art, as it is to land art. Many land artists emphasize art that goes on and on. The Christos' fence, for example, goes on and on for 26 miles. One imagines that the Christos would love a fence that could run across a whole country, or, even better, a whole continent. Similarly, Long's walks could extend far beyond their limits, and the modular art of Donald Judd, Robert Morris, Ronald Bladen and Sol LeWitt could expand indefinitely, once the basic pattern had been established. The seriality or endless process of art was identified by Judd as the idea of 'one thing after another'. [16]

Carl Andre's concept of the road as the ideal artwork fits in with this urge towards endless process and seriality. The road motif also fits in well with stereotypical American culture, with its love of the 'open road', in photography (Robert Frank), road movies (*Easy Rider, Duel, Natural Born Killers, Thelma and Louise*), the frontier spirit (in the Western movie genre), in hippy and beatnik culture (Jack Kerouac's *On the Road*, Allen Ginsberg and the 'dharma bums') and drifter, outsider, Existential literature.

4 : 5   MICHAEL HEIZER

Land art or earthworks have proved to be among the most authoritarian, phallic and patriarchal of contemporary artistic productions.[1] The Christos work on a gigantic scale, wrapping buildings or stretching curtains across valleys or surrounding islands. Some of the most phallic, domineering works of land art are by Michael Heizer (b. 1944). In his *Double Negative* (1969-70), his most famous work, a team took two chunks out of the earth, a gigantic 'violation' of the planet, in ecological terms.[2] (Heizer claimed *Double Negative* is 'the smallest piece I've done in relation to the size of the site' – because the desert in Utah is built on a colossal scale).[3] Heizer gouged out 240,000 tons of earth from the site at Mormon Mesa in Nevada with bulldozers. The cuts are ramps, going down 50 feet through the cliff of the canyon. The spectator can walk down them. The overall dimensions of *Double Negative* are 1,500 x 42 feet. Heizer is very much concerned with *scale*, as well as other formal characteristics of a work. Heizer said he liked working outside because of the scale; he could work large. He also said that '[m]an will never really create anything large in relation to the world.'[4]

Michael Heizer's *Double Negative* is a widely celebrated example of land art. Photographs of it have been reproduced in many art history books. *Double Negative* appeals to trendy 1960s notions of Zen Buddhism, Existentialism, negativity and emptiness. The point about *Double Negative* was its sense of symmetry and relationship, the one cut reflecting the other across the Nevada canyon. Some viewers

saw Heizer's enterprise as combining the sublime grandeur of Abstract Expressionism with the emblematic forms of Minimalism. American earthworks art rejuven-
ated the myth of the sublime West.5 Mary Miss was not convinced. When she looked
at the work of Heizer or Smithson, 'there's always been an aspect which impedes my
relating to it... It's like a mark on the earth' (1981, 6-7). For Heizer it wasn't about
violation or disruption, it was actually based on sound æsthetic principles.

Michael Heizer went on archæological digs as a child with his father. He started out
with the ambition to be a painter (like many sculptors and land artists), which he
studied in San Francisco. He made his first earthwork in 1967, and accompanied
Robert Smithson on geological expeditions. In 1968, Heizer collaborated with Smithson and Nancy Holt on a Super-8 film, *Mono-Lake*. (Heizer had invited Holt and
Smithson to his parents' house at Lake Tahoe). Heizer's motorbike earthwork was
entitled *Circular Surface Displacement*; it was made at Mono Lake. 'My work is closely
tied up with my own experiences; for instance, my personal associations with dirt are
very real. I really like it, I really like to lie in the dirt'.6 While Andy Goldsworthy hasn't
said exactly the same thing, he certainly is an artist who lies to get his hands dirty,
who likes the physical aspects of making sculptures out of doors.

Michael Heizer's other works include excavating huge holes in the ground and
putting great chunks of rock in them (one form nestling inside another is a recurring
motif in land art, and in Andy Goldsworthy's art – his stone houses, for example). *Nine
Nevada Depressions* (1968) comprised five cuts in the Blackrock desert, each one
twelve feet long in an area 50 by 50 feet. *Munich Depression* (1969) was another cut,
a line 15 feet deep. Heizer's *Complex One* (1972) was a huge bunker-like mass of
earth built with the aid of two assistants in Nevada. It was 23.5 feet high and 140 feet
long. Each end of the hill had a cut-off triangle of reinforced concrete like giant book-
ends. Over the work were cantilevered concrete beams. '*Complex One* is a
magnificent spectacle. Even its minatory look, suggesting a bunker, seems proper to
the site – the edge of the Nevada nuclear proving-ground', commented Robert
Hughes.7

4 : 6   JAMES TURRELL

One of the largest earthwork projects of all is James Turrell's *Roden Crater Project,* a
series of tunnels and chambers in an extinct volcano near Flagstaff, Arizona. Begun in
1974, it was funded by many different sources and administered by the Skystone
Foundation.1 The first stage of Turrell's on-going, life-work *Roden Crater* project
involved bulldozing 200,000 cubic yards of earth from the volcano's rim, 'so as to
shape the sky'. Turrell (b. 1943) planned tunnels, pools and viewing chambers at
Roden Crater. There were spaces where clouds were projected onto the floor during
the day, which at night were related to the procession of equinoxes. Many of the

spaces planned at *Roden Crater* were built around celestial events, such as full moons, solstices, equinoxes, the movement of the sun, or just being able to the view stars and some planets. The connection with the heavens was important for Turrell: most of his works have openings to the sky, and the relationship with the sky is the centrepiece of the works. It's important for Turrell, in short, to see the stars.

The *Roden Crater* work was about the relationship between the viewer and the elements, in particular the sky, celestial events, and light. James Turrell said:

> My art is made for one person. I like the solitary experience. Standing alone at night, perceiving the Roden Crater and the moon and stars, you really feel the vastness of the universe and yourself entering into it.[2]

The environment was a volcano, relating to geological time. 'The work I do intensifies the experience of light by isolating it and occluding all other light. Each space essentially looks to a different portion of sky and accepts a limited number of events', James Turrell explained (1995, 67). Thus, each space at *Roden Crater* was designed to highlight some celestial event. The subject of some spaces was the vaulting of the sky, and the curvature of the Earth. Some were about daily events, such as sunrises and sunsets, or the movement of the stars.

The North section of *Roden Crater* is about looking North, the North Star, the rotation of the Earth, changing light, and includes a *camera obscura* (which projects whatever is overhead onto a white sand floor), and a seat for viewing Polaris. The Eastern space is for witnessing sunrise, and a 'skyspace' overhead. *Bath Space* projects a magnified image of the sky above onto a white sand floor, using a water bath above a large sphere as a lens. The *Sun and Moon Room* was constructed around the furthest South moonset (every 18.61 years), the furthest North sunrise and the Summer solstice. *Tso Kiva* is a hemispherical space in the centre of the volcano, for observing light, shadows, shapes and the horizon. The *South Space* is an astronomical observatory and star chart. The *West Space*, as one would expect, is for the sunset, and the 'twilight arch', the projection of the Earth's shadow into the atmosphere at nightfall. James Turrell said he didn't want Roden Crater to be 'a mark upon Nature, but to be enfolded in Nature in such a way that light from the Sun, Moon, and stars empowered the spaces' (1995, 66).

James Turrell's creative task, as he saw it, was not to impose *his* own vision or æsthetics *on* the viewer, but to encourage *them* to see things for *themselves*, to create the situation in which they could have their *own* experience. These were æsthetics common in much of land art. As he said in 1987, the goal was not to turn an experience into art, but 'to set up a situation to which I take you and let you see. It becomes your experience… not taking from nature as much as placing you in contact with it'.[3] Turrell regarded his art as a 'seeing aid', as showing the observer something that was already there but that they might not have noticed (one of the most laudable and enduring goals of all art).

On the indoor-outdoor debate, which exercised so many land artists (dn still does), James Turrell said that, instead of bringing nature into the museum, he wanted to 'bring culture to the natural surround as if designing a garden or tending a landscape'

(1995, 66). The artwork became something to visit in itself, rather than one of many artworks in a museum to see. The viewer travelled specially to see the artwork, as they visited Michael Heizer's *Double Negative,* or Donald Judd's Marfa in Texas, or Robert Smithson's earthworks.

James Turrell's primary material was not earth or stone or the usual stuff of land art, but light itself, what he called 'light in the space itself'. Turrell wanted to use light as a thing-in-itself, which had presence, just as the sculptor used a physical object which had presence. He achieved this, he said, by setting limits on the space in which light manifested itself: 'I give light thingness by putting limits on it in a formal manner. I do not create an object, only objectified perception' (1995, 65). Turrell was attempting to create spaces in which viewers could perceive the subject of his works, light itself, and celestial events. It was important also for Turrell that the viewer was able to enter those spaces physically, not virtually. Turrell's art was not about creating illusions or artificial scenarios or a record of the artwork. Turrell called it 'non-vicarious seeing': '[t]he subject of my work is *your* nonvicarious seeing. You are not looking at a record of *my* seeing' (1995, 64; my italics). Thus, Turrell's art was not about recording some event that took place elsewhere, or taking photographs of his art, or writing down what happened, as in some land art. Rather, Turrell wanted to place the viewer right into the artwork, to have them able to walk into and around the artwork, and to experience the artwork for themselves.

Many of James Turrell's artworks were about working with not just light, but with the sky. The archetypal Turrell space was an enclosed area (a 'skyspace') which had an opening above onto the sky. Turrell spoke of the vaulting of the sky, how the sky looked when the viewer was standing up, or sitting down, or lying down.

Some of James Turrell's 'skyspaces' – indoor rooms or spaces which are open to the sky above – include *Space That Sees* (1992) in Jerusalem, *Heavy Water* (1992, Poitier) and *Razor* (1991, London). *Razor* was an empty blue room, using a mix of artificial and natural light. Turrell said he was influenced by painters such as Mark Rothko, Claude Monet and Paul Cézanne, who explored light.

Kielder Skyspace is open to the public, situated outside the village of Kielder near the Scottish border (not too far from Andy Goldsworthy's home). Turrell has also constructed pools of water which combine water and light: in these works (at *Roden Crater*, and Poitier, France), the viewer is invited to dive under the water to reach a space beyond which's open to the sky.

James Turrell emphasized the spiritual aspects of light in his land art.

> I am interested in light because of my interest in our spiritual nature and the things that empower us. My art deals with light itself, the bearer of revelation, but as revelation itself. (1995, 64)

The kind of effect that James Turrell was after in his light works he compared to staring into a fire, a kind of meditation or daydreaming. Turrell encouraged the viewer to sit or lie down and contemplate light itself, and the effects of light in a particular space. Thus, the spaces that Turrell constructed were furnished with viewing platforms, or benches, or places to lie down and look up at the sky. Situating the spectator in relation to the subject of the artwork (light itself) was Turrell's goal.

As well as drifting off by looking at a fire, James Turrell also often spoke of the experience of flight, of being in a plane and rising into new zones of light, different kinds of light. Turrell also spoke of the curvature of the Earth when seen from a plane (and how, between 600 and 3,000 feet, the Earth seems to curve the wrong way). The Roden volcano was chosen partly because of its relation at that particular place in the Painted Desert to the curvature of the Earth. The low mound of the volcano and its relation to the curvature of the Earth and the sky above had the right mixture of components Turrell was seeking.

4 : 7   NANCY HOLT

Nancy Holt (b. 1938) married the key earthwork artist, Robert Smithson, in 1963. She worked with him on his non-site projects, including the famous *Spiral Jetty* and *Amarillo Ramp*. Nancy Holt's art, with its large, heavy landscaping gestures (such as her *Dark Star Park*) is comparable with the male land artists. The globes and pools of water, though, are traditional 'feminine' volumes, here given a new, monumental turn. Holt's art concerned the movements of the heavens. Her sculptures focus the viewer on the motions of the earth, moon, sun and stars. Holt's art is about time, in particular geological time, the relation between time and the Earth. Holt was impressed by the desert when she visited it in the late 1960s with Robert Smithson and Michael Heizer.

> Time is not just a mental concept or a mathematical abstraction in the desert. The rocks in the distance are ageless; they have been deposited in layers over hundreds of thousands of years. Time takes on a physical presence.[1]

Nancy Holt said she was interested in 'conjuring up a sense of time that is longer than the built-in obsolescence we have all around us.' Hence she used long-lasting materials, such as steel and rocks. Using enduring materials does not stem from a sense of vanity, of wanting one's works to last forever, but rather because Holt wanted to create a sense of time that extends beyond the human lifespan.[2]

While working on Robert Smithson's enormous *Amarillo Ramp* after his death in a plane crash, Nancy Holt developed the idea for the gigantic *Sun Tunnels*, 18 foot long pipes that were 9 feet high with many holes punched in the side, to let light in.[3] She searched for a suitable site – a desert floor surrounded by low hills. The site she chose (and bought) was in the Great Basin Desert of Utah. *Sun Tunnels* was finished in 1976, with holes in the side of each concrete tube 7, 8, 9 and 10 inches diameter. The holes corresponded with star constellations (Capricorn, Draco, Columba and Perseus), as with *Hydra's Head*. During the day the sun creates points of light on the bottom of the tunnels that move. The moon also shines through the holes by night.

Sun Tunnels links together the movements of celestial objects and the viewer on the planet. Holt said she had the idea for *Sun Tunnels* while being out in the desert and watching the sun rising and setting. The flat desert area evoked 'a sense of being on this planet, rotating in space, in universal time' (1977). It is a cosmological piece of land art, a form of an observatory, like the Bronze Age stone circles of Europe. 'I wanted to bring the vast space of desert back to human scale' (1977). The astronomical observatory has been an enduring theme in land art. Robert Morris, Michael Dan Archer and Julia Barton have also made viewing sites, as has Andy Goldsworthy.

Nancy Holt's *Hydra's Head* (1975) also concerned the relation between the heavens and earth. Next to the Niagara River at Art Park, Lewiston, New York, Holt sank 6 concrete tubes into the soil. Each three foot pipe was filled with water, so they formed circular mirrors flush with the ground. Again, Holt based the position of the concrete pits on a constellation (Hydra). *Hydra's Head* combined the presence and noise of the rushing Niagara River with the reflections of the sky, stars and moon. Holt's concrete pipe sculptures used the prime symbol of change and all things cosmic, the circle. The *Sun Tunnels* were like enormous telescopes or astrolabes, while *Hydra's Head* evoked six fallen stars, the circles of water reflecting the sky and stars.

Nancy Holt's romantic evocations of stellar, cosmological themes in concrete and soil flourished again with *Stone Enclosure: Rock Rings* (1977-78), constructed at Western Washington University, Bellingham. Holt's *Stone Enclosure* directly recalled, even emulated, prehistoric stone circles, in particular Stonehenge. Holt used ancient schist rocks, between 200 and 230 million years old (known as brown mountain stone) to construct two concentric rings 10 feet high. In each wall of stone Holt made 4 arches, each 8 feet high, and 12 'portholes'. It was not a large stone ring, in terms of diameter (the outer diameter was 40 feet), but being ten feet high it was much taller than most Bronze Age stone circles (in Great Britain). The arches and holes provided views to the cardinal points, and to NE, SW, EW, NW-SE.

Nancy Holt's *Stone Enclosure* made the connections with ancient astronomy and stone circle building explicit, not slyly implied, as in much of land art. Holt was clear that she was dealing with the ancient astronomical realities of weather, seasons, cycles, stars and time. Another work, *30 Below* (1980), a tower with arches facing the points of the compass, was positioned around the North Star. The still point in the heavens, the Pole Star, was also one of the keys to *Stone Enclosure*, which, Holt said, related to a true North, a dead centre.4 (The North Star was the land artists' favourite star, appearing in works by James Turrell and Charles Ross, among others. It links to the Cosmic Tree, the centre of the world, of shamanism; the tent pole in some cultures is related to the Pole Star and is called the Pillar of the Sky).5

Annual Ring (1981) was an 'open hemi-dome' of steel bars, 30 feet in diameter and 15 feet high, constructed in Saginaw, Michigan. Again, Holt built the dome to highlight celestial events: the sun at the Summer solstice, the equinoxes, and the North Star. One of Nancy Holt's biggest projects was the *Sky Mound*, begun in the late 1980s (the first phase cost $11 million). Situated in amongst Amtrack and NJ Transit train tracks, highways, bridges, the Pulaski Skyway, the New Jersey turnpike, and metropolitan

New Jersey and New York, with views over Newark and Manhattan, *Sky Mound* was a converted landfill which Holt turned into an observatory to mark solstices, equinoxes, and the stars Vega and Sirius.

4 : 8   ALICE AYCOCK

Alice Aycock's (b. 1946) sculptures are much more ambiguous and deliberately problematic than Nancy Holt's or Carl Andre's constructions. Many of Aycock's land artworks involve underground passages and spaces. In 1972 she fabricated a series of underground spaces in *Low Building Made with Dirt Roof (For Mary)* in Pennsylvania. The visitor entered the 20 feet by 12 feet work through a doorway thirty inches high. The work was experienced by crawling through it. Aycock's intention was to evoke an experience of claustrophia, of being in a cellar. Aycock's works have titles such as *The Machine That Makes the World* (1979), *A Theory of Universal Causality* (1983) and *How to Catch and Manufacture Ghosts* (1979). (Aycock is great with titles). Aycock's sculpture explored the rationality of machines and technology and the irrationality of ghosts and magic.[1]

Alice Aycock's 1972 *Maze* had direct parallels with the observatories and labyrinths of Robert Morris, Nancy Holt, Julia Barton and Michael Dan Archer. *Maze* consisted of 5 concentric wooden rings, each six feet high, forming a 12-sided labyrinth. Essentially it was a fence maze, the kind that can be seen at theme parks, zoos and country houses around the globe. However, Aycock's New Kingston, Pennsylvania *Maze* was intended to be a labyrinth of the ancient type, a structure in which one is meant to get lost. Aycock stated that she wanted 'to create a moment of absolute panic – when the only thing that mattered was to get out.'[2] Aycock's intentions, then, were quite different from, say, Nancy Holt's, who wished to infuse a sense of celestial contemplation, or James Turrell's, who wanted to instill awe at light, the sky and revelation. Aycock wanted viewers to be confused, even frightened, by her underground passages and mazes. Aycock did not want the viewer to be able to get out of her labyrinth easily (it was partially based on a circular Egyptian labyrinth (designed as a prison), the Zulu *kraal* and the Amerindian stockade. Aycock also cited a circular Greek temple at Epidarus, a 'Place of Sacrifice').

Alice Aycock has spoken of the relations between her art and her own childhood dreams and fears. Her works recreate disturbing moments from her childhood, such as when she was trapped in a revolving barrel at an amusement park. Aycock's works deal with such moments of fear, confusion, strangeness and risk.

Aycock's *A Simple Network of Underground Walls and Tunnels* (1975) was made in a corn field at Far Hills, New Jersey. It consisted of six square wells in two rows of three excavated out of a 20 by 50 foot area. Two of the wells had seven foot ladders that enabled the spectator to climb down and explore the dark connecting tunnels.

Some of the wells were capped, others were open. The effect was a series of spaces that recalled 'ominous historical precedents, caves, catacombs, dungeons and beehive tombs', wrote critic Roberta Smith).3 Aycock's 1974's *Walled-Trench/ Earth Platform/ Center Pit* was a series of three concentric walls built from concrete blocks. A platform of earth was made between the inner two walls: it was possible to jump onto this platform over the outer pit. Only when the spectator is standing on the inner platform does another aspect of *Walled-Trench/ Earth Platform/ Center Pit* become visible: a tunnel which leads into a dark inner chamber.

The fear and fantasy elements in Alice Aycock's land and site work found a new level of ambiguity in her 1976 *Circular Building with Narrow Ledge for Walking*. Again, the spectator was invited to explore this artwork physically (and psychologically). *Circular Building with Narrow Ledge for Walking* was a round structure thirteen feet high. Inside the well were three concentric ledges, only 8 inches wide. The wall went 7 feet into the ground, and was 'no more perilous or threatening than a treacherous cliff', the artist said, reassuringly.4 Again, the spectator was invited to investigate the work by climbing a ladder outside the building, then edging her/ his way along the ledges. Indeed, the only way to fully appreciate *Circular Building with Narrow Ledge for Walking,* as with Aycock's other works, was to experience it directly by entering it. With Aycock's bewildering and unsettling catacombs and mazes one had to move 'one's body through them', a process which also involved descending back through time and memory.5

Confronted with the subterranean passage or the *Circular Building with Narrow Ledge for Walking* it is soon apparent to the spectator that one is not dealing simply with an art object to be admired for its formal characteristics alone. Alice Aycock wanted the spectator to become physically involved in the sculpture: the physical actions of climbing and scrabbling over and through the sculpture trigger an exploration of one's own psychology and memory.6 The physicality of the body as a tool for exploration in Aycock's works soon becomes a pretext or an inspiration for an exploration of personal psychology. Spectators are invited to risk themselves in exploring her works. Her land/ site art offers seductive as well as potentially dangerous spaces. Aycock encouraged the spectator to enter, but then confronted her/ him with a door that opened onto a wall, or a tiny passage to crawl through, or a ledge over a precipice, or a pit to vault over. Such devices go straight back to childhood, to acts of dare and bravado (such as walking along a high brick wall, egged on by other children).

Mary Miss (b. 1944) attended the University of California at Santa Barbara, Colorado College, and the University of California. After graduating, Miss studied at the Rhinehardt School of Sculpture at the Maryland Art Institute until 1968. Early works included a 'waterline': at Fountain Creek in Colorado, Miss suspended a double knot of hemp rope 100 feet over a dry riverbed; every twenty feet were lines of rope. At War's Island in New York, Miss threw 15 foot long wooden stakes into the water which were weighted with rocks. In the middle of a wood in Connecticut in 1974 Miss made *Sunken Pool*: it was a circular wooden structure, 10 feet tall, filled with one foot of water in a galvanized steel interior. *Sunken Pool* was sunken because Miss set it in a hole three feet deep and twenty feet across. As with the large site work of Alice Aycock and Robert Smithson, the spectator was invited to explore Miss's *Sunken Pool* physically, either by stepping into the water, or by climbing up the outer part of the wooden structure and looking over the top. Like Aycock's underground caverns, Miss's *Sunken Pool* was secretive, hiding away in a dense wood, with tall wooden sides. It seemed to speak, like Aycock's works, of childhood memories and half-remembered spaces.

Mary Miss's 1978 *Perimeters/ Pavilion/ Decoys* was created in Roslyn, New York state, in a field that was part of the Nassau County Museum's ground. *Perimeters/ Pavilion/ Decoys* consisted of three wooden towers, which looked like tree houses with four platforms on stilts, two mounds of earth, and an underground space which was accessed by a ladder. The wooden towers were not for climbing on, but for viewing. The tallest was 18 by 10 by 10 feet. The subterranean atrium was for exploring. It was a pit sixteen feet square with a seven foot hole acting as an entrance; visitors climbed down a ladder to explore the different underground spaces, some with wooden walls, others with soil walls. *Perimeters/ Pavilion/ Decoys* was related to Pueblo Indian structures, Pompeiian and Mexican courtyards, and Mesopotamian brick complexes. The site explored the physical and psychological aspects of 'inside/ outside, above/ below, light/ dark, open/ closed, nature/ artifice'.[1] Miss's works were often large, spreading over a wide area of ground (in Illinois, for instance, she created a 5-acre scale work.[2]

Walter de Maria (b. 1935) made a dramatic land art gesture when he cut a 4.5 mile-long 6 foot-wide drawing in the desert in Nevada with a bulldozer (*Las Vegas Piece*, 1969). Detractors have spoken of this cut as a 'wound' on the Earth. The ultimate in ithyphallic, male land art must be de Maria's *Vertical Earth Kilometer*. At a cost of $500,000, de Maria & a team sunk a one kilometre-long brass rod into the planet.

Nothing can be seen of it now except a two inch wide brass disc on the ground. The making of de Maria's piece is perhaps far more interesting than the artwork itself. It must be the ultimate art statement/ non-statement. De Maria's *Vertical Earth Kilometer* remains practically invisible. It neatly melds two Sixties æsthetic movements: Conceptualism (wow, what an idea, sticking a kilometre of solid brass into the Earth!), and Minimalism (there's nothing to see of it except... a two-inch brass disc!). Yeah, that's *real art*, a kilometre-long piece of metal stuck into the ground with nothing of it showing except a tiny disc. This is, in Richard Long's words, '[t]rue capitalist art', an art of excessive cost, and maybe excessive waste (it took 79 days to bore the shaft).[1] Shown at Kassel Documenta 6 in 1977, de Maria's *Vertical Earth Kilometer* annoyed British artist Stuart Brisley so much he made *Survival in Alien Circumstances*. This was a hole in the earth dug with his bare hands, which Brisley lived in for 2 weeks, intending to mock de Maria's overblown American earthwork. But then, art has been full of idiotic amounts of money and out-size projects for eons.

Walter de Maria started out as a musician rather than, like many land artists, as a painter or sculptor. He played drums with *avant garde* rockers the Velvet Underground. One of his early ideas (1962) for an earthwork was a mile-long pair of walls that would be 12 feet high and 12 feet apart. De Maria said that 'when you walk between, you can look up and see the sky'.[2] After the bulldozer square cut in the Earth, de Maria made a chalk drawing in the desert.

Walter de Maria's *Earth Room* was a gallery full of dark earth made in 1968 in Munich and later in New York (*The New York Earth Room*, SoHo Gallery, 1977). This was a vivid (and aromatic) example of bringing the outside inside, one of land art's key projects. The contrasts were immediate, between the flat, clean, white, controlled gallery space and the 1,600 cubic feet of uneven, 'dirty', dark, organic soil. Roberta Smith said it was a 'shock' to see the soil taking up the interior space usually reserved for things such as furniture and people. 'The dirt carried its own absence, was somehow a living substance'.[3] A related work, *5 Continents Sculpture* (1987-88), comprised white rocks filling an area 42 by 77 feet in a Stuttgart gallery.

Walter de Maria's *Bed of Spikes* (1969) was called 'a piece of Dadaist Sadism' by Harold Rosenberg.[4] *Bed of Spikes*, an installation at the Dwan Gallery, comprised 153 metal spikes set in five planks on the floor. Spectators were asked to sign a release form that exempted the gallery for being responsible for any accidents on viewing the installation. *Bed of Spikes* looked forward to *Lightning Field*.

Art critic Kenneth Baker called Walter de Maria's most famous work, the *Lightning Field*, the 'grandest Minimal work of the 1970s' and 'the closest thing to a masterpiece to come out of Minimalism'.[5] De Maria's first *Lightning Field* was sited 40 miles from Flagstaff in Arizona, consisting of 2 inch diameter steel poles, 18 feet tall, 30 feet apart, in five rows of seven. The second, larger *Lightning Field* was a grid of 400 stainless steel poles, each about 20 feet high, 16 along the width, 25 along the length, each about 20 feet high, set in the New Mexico desert.[6] The site was chosen for its flatness, isolation and lightning activity. The most lightning activity occurs during May-September; there are about 60 days when thunder and lightning can be seen from *Lightning Field*.[7] *Lightning Field* is about a mile by a 0.6 mile in size. The poles were set in concrete, one foot below ground, able to withstand winds of 110 mph. The poles in *Lightning Field* stand alone, about 220 feet apart. Nothing remains on the ground of the work needed to set them there. The tips of the poles define a plane in space parallel to sea level: the length of each pole varies according to the contours of the landscape. The *Lightning Field* is an exact, mathematically-precise human site laid onto nature, where the poles are tiny mirrors which mark out and calibrate the landscape. The site looks like a scientific or industrial project – like a radio telescope site, say, or a military communications centre. *Lightning Field* is spectacular, with masculine and phallic connotations (lightning is related in symbolism to male creativity, sperm, fire, power and shamanism).

Lightning Field is ambiguously associated with the Dia Art Foundation, which financed its construction. The site recalls technological experiments, while the poles themselves evoke Brancusi's *Birds in Space*, and his *Endless Column*. Kenneth Baker related de Maria's *Lightning Field* to issues of philosophy and politics:

> The piece also serves as an instrument for intensifying one's grasp of the beauty of the earth… The Lightning Field acquaints the visitor with the possibility that beauty may be the only conscionable and feasible refuge from history. That is, the apprehension of reality as everywhere radiant with its being may be the only bearable consciousness of life that does not entail repressing awareness of the horrors of our time. Beauty in this sense is just what the Lightning Field makes available… (1988, 127)

Walter de Maria's *Lightning Field* attracts lightning, and a storm is one of the most jaw-dropping phenomena in nature.[8] And during the peak season for great storms in the area, sometimes 'two or three a week cross this field of poles'.[9] Joseph Beuys produced a startling piece entitled *Lightning* (1982-85, Tate, London) a gigantic chunk of bronze, narrow at the top, splaying out towards the bottom, as if he was trying to make manifest the bolt of energy leaping down to the Earth. Justin Holland too used lightning in artworks; he collaborated with Westinghouse Electric, making human-made lightning, and 'seeded' clouds to produce storms.

Incredible as Walter de Maria's *Lightning Field* is, or the Christos' wrapped coasts and islands, far stranger and wilder are the constructions of modern science. The gigantic particle accelerators, for instance, where quarks, strangeness and charms are examined, are truly mind-boggling structures.[10] 'Only by battering streams of other particles together in giant underground accelerators has it been possible to generate the energies necessary to create these elusive entities,' wrote Robin McKie.[11] Andy Goldsworthy has not thus far come anywhere near the mega-budget earthworks of de Maria, Heizer or the Christos (although the Durham earthworks and the *Storm King Wall* are pretty big, and the *Garden of Stones* was fairly costly). However, given the right project, the right context, the right timing, a sufficient budget and the right team, Goldsworthy may produce something at the same spectacular, enormous scale.

Some other American earth artists include JAMES PIERCE, who created a series of earthworks at Pratt Farm in central Maine in the 1970s: there was a triangular turf maze; a small earth *Observatory*; a *Serpent* made from large rocks; a *Stone Ship*; a *Burial Mound*; a stone *Altar* (in the shape of male genitals); and several figures built out of grass and soil: *Earthwoman* and *Suntreeman*. Pierce's *Earthwoman* (1976-77) was a recumbent female shape, with prominent buttocks, evoking the erotic gardens of the 18th century, and the links between prehistoric earth mounds, fertility and femininity.

HERBERT BAYER (1900-85) created earthworks which directly evoked prehistoric structures: Bayer's *Earth Mound* (1955) in Aspen, Colorado, contained the familiar motifs of ancient religions and cultures: a circular rampart enclosing a small mound; a standing stone and a hollow were placed beside the mound. In Kent, Washington, Bayer built a series of earthworks (*Mill Creek Canyon Earthworks*, 1979-82) which featured circular ramparts, circular moats, mounds surmounted by walkways, and circular ramparts split by a path. At a quarry in upstate New York William Bennett fashioned a *Wedge (Stone Boat)* (1976), an 80 foot long smooth-sided channel in the limestone.

DONNA DENNIS (b. 1942) took the vernacular architecture of New York City as her starting-point in her 1970s works: *Tunnel Tower* was based on the entrance building to the Holland Tunnel. Later, nostalgic works, such as *Deep Station* (1981-85), recreated the shadowy recesses of subway stations. Christine Oatman lit a fire on a frozen lake in the centre of a circle of tall icicles in *Icicle Circle and Fire* (1973). Elyn Zimmerman constructed large-scale ecological land art, such as her *Keystone Island* (1989), a 50-foot wide artificial island built on a lagoon in a mangrove swamp. PATRICIA JOHANSON's best known work is probably the large water park she fashioned in Dallas, Texas, between 1981 and 1986. *Fair Park Lagoon* comprised a series of interlacing walkways above the pool in an 'organic', Gaudiesque manner, and cost over $2 million.

GORDON MATTA-CLARK (1943-78), one of Andy Goldsworthy's favourite artists, transformed buildings by knocking enormous holes in them (*Conical Intersect*, 1975), or cutting a house in New Jersey in half (*Splitting*, 1974). But these were not sculpted spaces or physical gestures so much as Conceptual reorganizations of a structure. It's easy to discern the influence of Matta-Clark's interventions in houses and buildings (which he called 'unbuilding') on Goldsworthy's holes (and Rachel Whiteread's works).

Gordon Matta-Clark bought up pieces of land in the borough of Queens (in 1973), in another Conceptual piece; none of them were big enough for housing or much else (some were only 2 by 3 feet). *Reality Positions, Fake Estates* explored the notion of land ownership. Matta-Clark explained:

> One or two of the prize ones were a foot strip down somebody's driveway and a square foot of sidewalk. And the others were kerbstone and gutter-space. What I basically wanted to do was to designate spaces that wouldn't be seen and certainly

not occupied. Buying them was my own take on the strangeness of existing property demarcation lines. Property is so all-pervasive.[1]

CHARLES ROSS (b. 1937) constructed a large observatory, *Star Axis* (1989), which recalled the celestial viewing spaces of James Turrell, Nancy Holt and Robert Morris. It was designed for viewing the North Star, the land artists' favourite star. Charles Simonds made an *Abandoned Observatory* (1976), in model form. Juan Geuer has also worked with the sky: he mounted four pairs of large mirrors in the National Gallery of Canada in order to reflect the sky in the glass cupola above (*Karonhia*, 1989).

DOUGLAS HOLLIS (b. 1948) constructed 'sound gardens' – a series of wind organ pipes mounted on towers beside the shore in Seattle, WA (1980). Hollis's *Field of Vision* (1980) comprised 900 wind vanes at Lake Placid, NY, to 'explore the choreography between windscape and landscape'.[4] In the Seventies Hollis experimented with sending up kites that emitted sound (*Sky Soundings*, 1975).

Most of ANA MENDIETA's (1948-85) art was based around her body and its shape and form. She covered herself in mud (while nude, of course) and stood against a tree, and left the outline of her body in leaves on a tree trunk for *The Tree of Life* series (1977, made in Old Man's Creek, Iowa), a combination of Goddess art, body art, performance art and environmental art. Some of Mendieta's performance works directly recall Andy Goldsworthy's: in the *Silueta* series (1979), Mendieta imprinted her body in the snow in Amana, Iowa, and in mud on a riverbank, or set the form on fire in the earth, or made a silhouette from flowers. These pieces echo Goldsworthy's rain and snow 'body prints' (however, Mendieta's art has an undisguised ideological, spiritual and ecological agenda; some of Mendieta's works are explicit performance explorations of rapes, and Mendieta was also exploring her Cuban and Latin American heritage. Goldsworthy has very rarely taken on political issues, and especially not explosive issues).

In some pieces Ana Mendieta remodelled the entrance of a cave and a ravine into her Goddess shape. She also buried herself under turf – a literal Earth-Goddess mound, and had herself photographed in an ancient Mexican stone grave.[2] Mendieta also lit fires in sculptures (such as *Volcano*, 1979), like Chris Drury and David Nash, and lit candles and fireworks in the shape of a woman. Teresa Murak covered her naked body with cress seeds, while lying in a bath (*Seed*, 1989). 'They sprout, swell and begin after a few hours to grow right on my body'.[3]

Christo makes huge, very public gestures: tarpaulin and plastic shrouded buildings, the wrapped Pont Neuf and Reichstag, and curtains hanging across Colorado valleys. His art is not 'invisible' like Walter de Maria's kilometre-long brass rod which only reveals a brass disc on the ground, or created in a secluded vale, like Andy Goldsworthy's leaf sculptures. Christo often works with his wife, Jeanne-Claude, so his work is often referred to as by the Christos.

Born in 1935, in Bulgaria, Christo (Christo Javacheff) attended the Fine Arts Academy in Sofia. One of his early activities as a student involved tidying up the Orient Express train route through Bulgaria by covering old farm machinery and haystacks with tarpaulin. At Prague Christo studied set design, and one of his mid-1960s works in New York was making replicas of storefronts, like a stage set, but the windows were covered with cloth or paper. In his early works, Christo wrapped up items such as books, bottles, tins and boxes. Other assemblages or *empaquetages* (assemblages as packages) included nude models, cars, chairs and motorbikes.

Christo's most famous assemblage, though, was on a larger scale, the *Wall of Oil Barrels – Iron Curtain* (1962). This was a pile of barrels stacked across and blocking one of Paris's oldest streets, Rue Visconti. *Wall of Oil Barrels – Iron Curtain* parodied the Berlin Wall, which had recently been constructed. The sculpture annoyed the locals, and the Christos' large-scale works have been upsetting neighbours (and bureaucrats and politicians) ever since.

The Christos' first large-scale wrapping was to cover the Museum of Contemporary Art in Chicago with 10,000 ft2 of brown tarpaulin. The Christos' wrapping of the museum made it the focus of attention in the neighbourhood – some people hadn't realized the museum was there until it had been wrapped. The museum's director reckoned the Christos had parodied 'all the associations a museum evokes: a mausoleum, a repository for precious contents, an intent to wrap up all of art history'.1 Inside the museum was the *Wrapped Floor*, consisting of 2,000 square feet of rented drop cloths.

In 1969 the Christos wrapped a mile-long section of the Australian coastline. The use of open weave cloth (one million square feet) meant that wildlife would not be affected. *Wrapped Coast*, at Little Bay near Sydney, stayed up for 4 weeks. It was a dramatic land art gesture, difficult to ignore.

Valley Curtain (1972), at Rifle Pass in Colorado, did not last so long. It was blown down. The huge bright orange curtain hung across the valley, providing a passage-way as well as a visual block to what was beyond. Christo explained:

When I was doing Valley Curtain everybody knew that this is a huge curtain cross-ing a valley. Now everybody knew what it is that is behind the valley. The thing that is behind is not so important... only that motion, the passing through.2

The use of orange, as with the pink in *Surrounded Islands*, gave *Valley Curtain* a new æsthetic, more attuned to Henri Matisse and Claude Monet, quite different from the dull brown tarpaulin of the *Wrapped Museum*.

Many of the Christos' large-scale wrappings took place next to water: *Running Fence* plunged into the sea; *Wrapped Coast* was submerged by the tides; *Surrounded Islands* floated on the ocean; *Pont-Neuf* stretched over the Seine. *Surrounded Islands* (1980-83) was one of the Christos' largest works. Not a wrapping this time, but still involving masses of fabric (6 million square feet of it). With a budget of $3.5 million, 4 engineers, 2 ornithologists, a marine biologist, 2 attorneys and 430 helpers, the Christos surrounded 11 little islands for 2 weeks in May, 1983. The choice of brilliant pink meant the enclosed islands stood out vividly against the green sea at Biscayne Bay in Florida. The pink-enclosed islands looked like flowers floating on the sea, recalling the Japanese Buddhist ceremony of setting flowers afloat. Or, more in tune with Western art history, evoking Claude Monet's waterlilies.

Running Fence (1972-76) consisted of 2,050 18 foot panels of white nylon attached to steel poles, running across Marin and Sonoma counties in California. As with the Christos' other mammoth projects, there was much opposition to *Running Fence*. A committee designed to 'stop *Running Fence*' brought the subject to the Superior Court of the State of California 3 times. The subsequent report on the environmental impact of the *Running Fence* project found that there were no endangered species in the region, except for the Brown Pelican, and virtually no wildlife would be affected by it. *Running Fence* went ahead, and stayed up for two weeks.[3] When it was taken down, nothing remained of it in the area: the holes were filled in, and bare parts of soil were reseeded. As with other Christos projects, when it was taken away some locals were dismayed: the work had helped them realize the beauty of the area.

Christo said his art was

about displacement. Basically even today I am a displaced person. And this is why I make art that does not last. Of course, it will stay for ever in the minds of people.[4]

Christo here espouses the fundamental Romanticism in land art: that it will live on in the memories of people. The Christos' large-scale projects – *Running Fence, Surrounded Islands, Wrapped Coast, Umbrellas* – were spectacular works, part of the land art tradition which moved towards the sublime in landscape art (which has affinities with the Abstract Expressionism of Mark Rothko, Barnett Newman and Robert Motherwell). The ocean end of *Running Fence* was particularly impressive: at Bodega Bay the *Fence* extended gracefully into the Pacific, 558 feet, descending from a height of 18 feet on land to 2 feet at the section which was anchored to the bottom of the sea. The *Umbrellas* stretched for 12 miles in Japan and 18 miles in California.

The Christos' large-scale works are expensive: *Running Fence* cost over $3 million, *Surrounded Islands* cost $3.5 million, and *The Umbrellas* in Japan and California cost $26 million. Denigrators of the Christos' work have noted the expense of the projects, but the Christos pay for them himself, by selling photos, drawings, lithographs, collages, models and plans and other works, and by collaborating with industry. But the Christos were keen to remind viewers that their sculptures were not funded by sponsors.

The German artist Hans Haacke (b. 1936) has produced some of the most intriguing land artworks (although Haacke is more usually linked with Arte Povera, Conceptual and Process art, than land art). Many of Haacke's early works explored natural or organic systems. Later, Haacke moved on to social, economic and political systems (what Haacke called 'real-time systems'). Haacke's 1965 artistic statements included: 'make something that lives in time and makes the "spectator" experience time... articulate something natural'.[1] One of Haacke's tenets was 'the simpler the better'.

Grass Grows (1966 and 1969) was a mound of soil with grass growing out of it. Hans Haacke later fashioned a row of beans growing along string suspended at an angle, in soil mounted on glass on the gallery floor (*Directed Growth*, 1972), and in tropical plants growing on a circular area of soil, *Rye in the Tropics* (1972). *Condensation Cube* (1963-65) was a Plexiglas cube (a yard on each side) with water inside which condensed on the clear sides of the box, an exploration of process. 'It is changing freely, bound only by statistical limits', remarked Haacke of his 'Weather Box'.

In *Sky Line* (1967), Hans Haacke released white helium balloons over Central Park. Haacke commented that

> in spite of my environmental and monumental thinking I am still fascinated by the nearly magic, self-contained quality of objects. My water levels, waves and condensation boxes are unthinkable without this physical separation from their surroundings.[2]

Many of Hans Haacke's most compelling artworks were made to explore the ephemeral qualities of ice, snow, fog, steam, smoke and water. *Fog, Flooding, Erosion* (1969) employed a sprinkler system to turn a lawn in Seattle (WA) into mud. *Fog Dripping From or Freezing On Exposed Surfaces* (Boston, 1971) and *Spray of Ithaca: Falls Freezing and Melting On Rope* (1969) explored water and fog freezing on waterfalls and trees.

One of Hans Haacke's air and wind constructions comprised a fan blowing a seven by seven foot chiffon sail hung parallel to the gallery floor. Another air sculpture was a balloon balanced above an air jet (a favourite with science and natural history museums). He had proposals for monumental-sized windmills and sails, all naturally powered by the winds. Haacke preferred to use unmechanical sources of energy.

In *Rhine-Water Purification Plant* (1972), the process of purifying polluted river water was examined. Via a series of acrylic containers, filters, hoses and pools, the spectator could follow the process of the purification of the contaminated Krefeld sewage water. The final destination of the water flow was a square pool containing goldfish. *Rhine-Water Purification Plant* recalled the 3-D displays in science and natural history museums that explained the processes of nature and science.

In Hans Haacke's piece *Ten Turtles Set Free* (1970), the animals were released in a forest near St Paul-de-Vence (France), a symbolic gesture about humanity's relationship with the natural world and its inhabitants. Haacke photographed seagulls feeding on bread scattered on a lake in *Live Airborne System* (1965/ 68).

Hans Haacke later considered economic systems in works such as *Shapolsky et al, Manhattan Real Estate Holdings, a Real-Time Social System* (1971). For the *Information* show at Gotham's MOMA (in 1971), Haacke exhibited a poll about Governor Rockerfeller running for election, inviting visitors to vote. Haacke took on cultural institutions such as museums, landlords, and politicians such as President Reagan and British Prime Minister Margaret Thatcher. On a few occasions Haacke's proposals were negated by the authorities of the Guggenheim, Wallraf-Richartz and Metropolitan museums, with works and shows being cancelled as a result. Other artists (such as Daniel Buren) protested in support of Haacke. Such direct, confrontational approaches to art, and to social, ideological and political issues too, is something Andy Goldsworthy is not interested in pursuing (Goldsworthy tackling the issue of the Holocaust is a very rare occurrence in his art – but his *Garden of Stones* has oblique, somewhat abstract allusions to the Holocaust).

4 : 14   RICHARD LONG

The central fact and act of Richard Long's art is *walking*. His work is founded entirely on the art of walking, the act of walking, and on walking as art, as act, as experience. His walks become 'artwalks', Art Walks which become artworks. For Long, (art)walking is (art)working. As he walks he works. Art-walking and art-working become interchangeable. 'I have met with but one or two persons in the course of my life who understood the art of Walking, that is, of taking walks – who had a genius, so to speak, for *sauntering*', noted Henry David Thoreau.[1]

Born in 1945, the same year as David Nash, Richard Long studied at the West of England College of Art (Bristol) and St Martin's (1966-68). In 1967 Long made his first important walk-work, *A Line Made By Walking*. Like most land artists, Long makes indoor (gallery) works and outdoor works (not intended for public consumption). He also produces art books, which are not typical exhibition catalogues, but artworks in their own right, usually with text works, photo works, and sometimes map works (and limited edition books and artists' books).

Richard Long is associated with the American land, Minimal, Process, Conceptual and postmodern artists (such as Lawrence Weiner, Michael Heizer, Dennis Oppenheim, Nancy Holt, Alice Aycock, Judy Pfaff, Donald Judd, Robert Smithson, Sol LeWitt, and especially Carl Andre, with whom he's had many shows), and with European Arte Povera and Minimal/ Conceptual artists (Hans Haacke, Christo, Jannis Kounellis, Lucio Fontana, Piero Manzoni, Daniel Buren, Giovanni Anselmo, Mario Merz). Other key names one might link with Richard Long include Joseph Beuys, Yves Klein, Constantin Brancusi, Isamu Noguchi, Mel Ramsden, Joseph Kosuth, Bruce Nauman, Barnett Newman, Anthony Caro and Henry Moore. As Andy Goldsworthy's stature in

British contemporary art increases, he is often compared with Richard Long (though Long is more 'establishment' than Goldsworthy, or seems to have been accepted by the establishment's institutions, such as the Tate Modern, more than Goldsworthy).

Key exhibitions of the new British/ international sculpture included *The New Art* (Hayward, 1972), *Objects & Sculpture* (ICA/ Arnolfini, 1981), *British Sculpture in the 20th Century* (Whitechapel, 1981), *Figures and Objects* (Southampton, 1983), *New Art* (Tate, 1983), *The British Art Show* (Arts Council, 1984), *The British Show* (Australia, 1985), *The Poetic Object* (Dublin, 1985), *Entre el Objeto* (Madrid, 1986), *A Quiet Revolution: British Sculpture Since 1965* (Chicago, 1987), *About Landscape* (Otterlo, 1993), *Gravity and Grace* (Hayward, 1993), *Land Marks* (New York, 1998), *Live In Your Head: Concept and Experiment in Britain, 1965-75* (Whitechapel, 1999) and *Paysages* (Amiens, 2001). Long contributed to many of these shows. He still lives in Bristol, and is very active, travelling the world, making art, and having exhibitions.

Richard Long appears as a late British Romantic landscape artist, someone who fuses Sixties Conceptualism with 1800s pantheism; he's something of both a High Modernist and a postmodernist Conceptualist. He has been described a 'traveller, explorer, pilgrim, shaman, magician, peripatetic poet, hill-walker' as well as an artist.[2] He says it is not enough for him to have an idea or concept: he has to make it.[3] His stone circles espouse the sensuality and beauty of the post-Romantic and modernist art object (as in sculpture by Auguste Rodin, Pablo Picasso, Aristide Maillol, Henry Moore, Käthe Kollwitz), while his photographs and text works exhibit the cool, philosophic distantiation and ideations of Process, Serial, ABC, Conceptual and Minimal art. Long's mud and stone and terracotta works are real, sensual objects, which satisfy the modernist critics who exalt the art object. The text and photographic pieces, however, 'feed the imagination', as Long puts it.[4] They are only understandable, like television shows or traffic signals, by a heavily enculturated imagination. The text pieces are lingual structures, dependent for their effect on what the viewer brings to them.

Like Hamish Fulton and Andy Goldsworthy, Richard Long has travelled to some wild places in pursuit of interesting spaces: Lappland, Africa, Australia, Peru, Alaska and the Himalayas. It's easy to see Long's and Goldsworthy's art as simply pure Romanticism, a 'back to the land' art that utterly ignores political, societal, ideological, racial, economic and gender issues. True. Their art does not seem to be concerned with the urban 'real world' at all. And it looks odd to see their work in galleries in cities, to see the stones and stalks in a setting quite different from the wilderness. Rather, the art of Goldsworthy, Long, Chris Drury and David Nash comes across as deeply poetic, personal, subjective and romantic. It is *all* about a response to nature, about getting into connection with nature.

Richard Long's art mixes postwar, (post)modernist and Romantic (traditional) æsthetics. For critic Anne Seymour, Long 'has not only penetrated more deeply into the world of natural landscape than anyone since Turner, he has taken abstract art with him, creating a new art which allows all parties to retain their full identities'.[5] Mary Rose Beaumont also placed Long within a British Romantic tradition. This was a tendency of art criticism of the 1980s, as espoused by fine art gurus such as Peter

Fuller and Robert Rosenblum. There was much talk in the 1980s of New Romantics/ Neo-Romantics/ New Ruralists, and so on. Whether High Modernism or post-modernism, Long's art is certainly a romance with nature, but always in an ecologically-friendly fashion.

Like Andy Goldsworthy, Chris Drury and Hamish Fulton, Richard Long uses his hands and feet to make his art, and not an array of machines and tools. The aim is to be unobtrusive, 'invisible', in tune with the Earth. So Long acts like many walkers and hikers: he covers his tracks, does not leave behind trash, does not harm nature. So fierce is the 'right on', politically correct eco-friendly tendency of some walkers and campers, they worry about leaving even a footprint in grass as they pass by. Fulton declines to make any mark on the world as he moves through it, except footprints. 'The natural environment was not built by man and for this reason it is to me deeply mysterious and religious'.6

For Richard Long, walking itself is the primary act of his art. Walking is mainly what he does, as an artist. His talent, he said, is to be able to walk. Walking clears the mind, it is a process and experience of simplification and purification. It purges the soul, Long remarked, it forces the self to concentrate on simple things such as air, sky, earth, rock.

> Like art itself, it [walking] is like a focus. It gets rid of a lot of things and you can actually concentrate. So getting myself into these solitary days of repetitive walking or in empty landscapes is just a certain way of emptying out or simplifying my life, just for those few days or weeks, into a fairly simple but concentrated activity which, as you say, is really quite different from the way that people normally live their lives, which is very complicated. So my art is a simplification.7

For Richard Long, as for many people, walking is a way of simplifying life, of cutting through the clutter. When walking, one moves into a different space, a space set quite apart from the rest of life. The time of walking is not the everyday, day-in-day-out time of the working world. It is not the profane, boring time of working at a check-out in a supermarket, or slaving away in an Argentinian factory. Walking takes one right away from that sort of everyday time. Walking takes one into a non-profane time and space. Walking in fact sacralizes space and time. As the walk takes places, sacred time is reinstated. Walking therefore has a religious or philosophical dimension, which sounds odd only if terms such as religion or art sound odd to the ear. In walking, in travelling, in holidays or other escapes and escapades, people put themselves back together. Walking in wildernesses, people say, is invigorating and refreshing: walking returns people to themselves, and of course renews their contact with nature. These things can sound stupid – 'renewing one's contact with nature'. Wow, *maaan*, it sounds hippy-dippy, doesn't it? But one can't avoid nature in the wilderness anywhere – it surrounds the self entirely. It *is* the self.

> I do the things that have a deep meaning for me. I have the most sublime or profound feelings when I am walking, or touching materials in natural places. That is what I've decided to do and that is what I am showing you in my art.8

Perhaps Richard Long should move into multi-media, interactive and technological presentations (the sound of recorded atmospherics and wind from his walks in the gallery, or more of the multi-sensory experience of a walk in the gallery space). Or perhaps he ought to encourage someone to spend a proportion of the next exhibition budget on employing some museum designers and curators to create a multi-media *Walk Show*. Sounds tacky? But isn't having a framed Ordnance Survey map on a wall and calling it an artwork tacky? One knows it doesn't cost much to produce a map work (ten bucks for the map, 150 for the frame, a few cents for the pen to mark on the map). The stone circles 'cost' nothing, it seems, like the River Avon mud. Long's main 'materials' for his sculpture seem to be 'free' – the walk itself is 'free'.

Art possesses nature and yet does not possess nature: something always remains elusive. What's there, in nature, is no longer there in the artwork. As David Reason noted of Hamish Fulton's work, and this applies to Richard Long's text pieces: '[i]n the work, everything derives from what cannot be shown and shared – walking and camping in close relationship to a specific patch of the natural world.'[9] The viewer does not experience the real subject of the work, which is the walk. Instead, the viewer has to place her/ himself into the role played by the artist, as s/he walks in the landscape. Land art text pieces can be seen as sophisticated forms of holiday snaps, those little coloured slips of plastic, pixels and photochemicals which record two weeks' escape from labour.

Richard Long's text works do not 'describe' the landscape, in the usual manner. Short phrases, and sometimes (as in Hamish Fulton's work), single words stand in for (a description of) the landscape (Andy Goldsworthy too favours short phrases and single words). Long's text works do not claim 'this is the world', but record tiny parts of the world seen from a particular subjective perspective on a particular day in a particular season and frame of mind. The particularity of each work is emphasized in the art of Long and Goldsworthy by the artists' placing of the time and place in the final sentence of each text piece. Sometimes, as in the art of Long, Fulton and Goldsworthy, a distinct date is mentioned; at other times, just the year. The duration of each of Long's walk is also critical: thus the viewer can get an idea of when and where the walk took place, how much mileage was covered in a certain amount of time.

Instead of trying to depict or describe nature, then, Richard Long's art (like Hamish Fulton's) may be about the impossibility of representing landscape in art. At the same time (here's the paradox again) both Long and Fulton (and David Nash, Andy Goldsworthy, Walter de Maria, Michael Heizer *et al*), are consciously making art in or about the landscape. Even though the impossibility of the project is stressed, they are still making art. That is, still indulging in a particular kind of Western, bourgeois, intellectual, creative activity.

Whether presented as a map (*Low Water Circle Walk*, 1980) or text (*A Circle of Middays*, 1997), Richard Long's circular walks are designed as fascinating artworks. While some people might organize a circular route in a town (bank to post office, then to the grocery store then home), Long makes the circular walk a matter of Conceptual art and geometry. The casual circular walk of everyday life (once along the boardwalk and back through the mall, or once round the power plant) becomes in Long's art a living sculpture founded on 'universal and common' principles. 'My work has become a simple metaphor of life… I am content with the vocabulary of universal and common means,' writes Long, 'walking, placing, stones, sticks, water, circles, lines, days, nights, roads'.10 And Andy Goldsworthy said, '[m]y art will always be a reflection of my way of life'.11

Richard Long, who is not a poet of the stature or talent of John Cowper Powys or Arthur Rimbaud, is not adept at communicating the experience of a walk in words. Why, then, is Richard Long's work so popular? It may be that before he made the text pieces he made very sensual works to which people could relate instantly. Long's (relative) fame or popularity must stem (partly) from his stone and slate circles, which people can see and touch and walk on and discuss. If Long had never made a stone circle, would he be as popular as he is today? That is, has a painter or sculptor become successful simply by sending words to a typesetter to be printed and framed and put on gallery walls? No images, no photographs of works outside the gallery, and no objects. Just printed words. It's an interesting question. Of course, Long was making the text works *as well as* the slate rings. Even Conceptual artists such as Gilbert & George had actual objects people could see. They might have been 'living sculptures', but they also made colourful images. There are few artists, it seems, who have become famous merely by manipulating and exhibiting words in frames.

The other factor explaining Richard Long's success, as with Andy Goldsworthy, is his use of the Great Outdoors, the wilderness landscape which is so dear to Anglo-American-European art audiences (the photos depict gorgeous wild zones in Bolivia, Iceland, Scotland, the Sahara, Nepal). In the grey and drab cities of the Western world, Long's works suggest wide open spaces, vast cloudscapes, cycles of growth and decay which have been long obliterated from the Western city.

One knows about Richard Long's walks from the maps, text and photos, as one knows about Andy Goldsworthy's ephemeral stone towers or leaf walls from his books. So, as he walks, Long is making art. It is not quite the same with Joseph Beuys or Gilbert & George, who were performing, who were 'living sculptures'. Long's absence from his photos and texts is part of his ecologically-friendly, non-destructive stance (Long is much more absent from his works than Goldsworthy – Goldsworthy is a more familiar figure than Long). Long's walks, though, are not a 'performance'.12 The walk is not 'performing' something, a performance *of* something, a representation. It is about movement in space, a lived experience.13 The walk is the walk. To call it art is also to call it life, in Long's view. The two things are continuous. The central thing to grasp with Richard Long's art, as also with other land artists, such as Goldsworthy, Heizer, de Maria, Nash, Fulton, Aycock and Holt, is the essence of their work, the mythic centre, which may be an idea, an essence, a structure or an experience.14

Richard Long, though, does polarize critics and art consumers (as Andy Goldsworthy does). People seem to love him or loathe him. For fans, Long's a New Age, eco-friendly mystic, making cool, Conceptual art that doesn't harm the environment. For sceptical critics, Long's pretentious, shallow, repetitive and unoriginal. Modernist critics moan that there's no object to grasp in Long's art – for them it's a series of empty Conceptual gestures. Postmodernist fans can admire how Long plays the art market, trouncing conventional views of the art object. For Long, a sculpture can be two hundred and thirty miles long if he wishes. If a sculptor wants to make a 'real', physical object 230 miles long, s/he has to have a lot of money (like the Christos with their *Running Fence*). Long, however, retorts that his 230 mile-long sculpture really is a physical thing: he walked those 230 miles, physically. He might record sensual aspects of the walk: wind direction, incidents along the way, weather, and so on. So, 'conceptual' though it seems, Long's sculptures are 'real', physical objects. A walk, after all, is one of the most physical, and fundamental, activities for humans (but very few humans make art out of it).

Not all of Richard Long's works are circles – there are always the lines. Long continued to make lines in the shape of a cross from time to time, such as in *Two Places* (Bolivia, 1972), where a small cross is made on marshland in a pile of stalks. Another cross was made in Iceland from some stones (*Stopping Place Stones*, 1974). The crosses are very much like geometric marks 'drawn' onto the landscape, as if to mark a place. Most of the single straight lines are short, like the crosses, such as *Walking Without Travelling* (Sahara, 1988). Occasionally, Long makes a square zigzag line: short right angles are marked upon bare soil, as in *Campfire Ash* (Bolivia, 1972 – all these works are from *Mountains and Waters*). Another zigzag line sculpture, in Antwerp in 1973, extends outwards to take over the gallery: each Long sculpture is made for a particular space, and expands to consume the gallery floor. The zigzag lines recall the Peruvian Nazca animals and symbols drawn on the lava plain (Long had walked along one of the desert lines in 1972: he also made sculptures which employed symbols such as the puma, condor, falcon, moon, sun and rain). Like Andy Goldsworthy, Long has his visual motifs which he returns to time and again (circles, lines, rows, and, lately, ellipses and arcs). Goldsworthy's recurring icons include circles, lines, ovals, cairns, snakes, shields, arches and mounds.

Richard Long spoke warmly of Carl Andre and Lawrence Weiner, important Sixties Minimal and Conceptual artists.[15] It is significant, too, that Long felt he was working on his own in Britain, that there was nobody else doing his kind of art. When he stepped out of Britain he realized there was 'a whole new world of ideas going on'. Long noted, perhaps wryly, that '[t]here was an immediate interest and under-standing of my work as soon as I stepped outside England'.[16] Similarly, the first land art that Andy Goldsworthy encountered was American earthworks. Long himself declined being described as a Conceptual artist ('[m]y work is real, not illusory or conceptual. It's about real stones, real time, real actions').[17] He spoke sympathetically of Arte Povera, the use of 'simple, modest means and procedures'.[18]

Some commentators have negated the tendency to view Richard Long's art in Romantic terms. 'Richard Long's landscape is... as modern (in feeling) as the city of Bristol from which he sets out for a walk', claimed critic R.H. Fuchs (1986, 43). Long, Fuchs opined, tries to play down 'as much as he can the romantic/ Romantic, poetic connotations' of his locations (ib.). Yet, surely wildernesses such as Dartmoor, Mexico, Nepal, Canada and Lappland, where Long makes his art, have been inscribed with connotations of Romanticism. They are places now described in terms of 'spirit' and 'soul', spaces that in contemporary romantic, nostalgic culture imbue one with a sense of infinity, solitude, pantheism, awe, eternity and all the rest of the Romantic æsthetic baggage. 'A walk is also the means of discovering places in which to make sculpture in 'remote' areas, places of nature, places of great power and contemplation' remarked Long, speaking in Romantic terms of his walks.[19] In a walk such as *Straight Miles and Meandering Miles* (1985), Long walked some 'straight miles' along the way, between Land's End and Bristol. As expected, these 'straight miles' were walked in wilderness or countryside or 'Romantic' locations, such as Bodmin Moor, Exmoor and the Mendip Hills. The starting points and the end points of the *Four Walks* (1977) sound like a list of destinations a landscape painter might make for a 1790s Grand Tour of Britain: the source of the River Severn, Snowdon, Chesil Beach, Sherwood Forest and Carantouhil peak.

Although he may downplay the Romantic associations with the art made in or about landscape, Richard Long described landscape in romantic, emotional terms. He reacted to landscape directly, facing it straight on, as is apparent in all his interviews and writings. He spoke of the need for transcribing landscapes purely and clearly. So, for instance, his photographs are simply taken, without too much trickery, and they are printed in a straightforward manner.[20] At the same time, Long described 'places of great power and contemplation', terms which William Wordsworth might have used a hundred and fifty years before Long, or Henry Vaughan, the Metaphysical poet born on the Welsh borders, before that.

Stressing the Romantic heritage/ tradition of Richard Long's art though, only makes up part of the picture. Like other artists of the Sixties (whether Pop, Conceptual, Minimal, Process, ABC, Cool, Arte Povera, body, performance or other art), Long suppressed notions of poetry and Romanticism. 'My art is not urban, nor is it romantic', Long said.[21] Looking at *A Line in Iceland* (1982), a line of boulders in a wilderness space, shot against a brooding sky and a backdrop of snowbound mountains, one can see the affinities with the High Romanticism of William Wordsworth's poeticizing of the Lake District, J.M.W. Turner and his watercolours of Snowdonia or the Alps, or John Ruskin and his evocation of the Sublime. 'Working out there in nature, then, Long is a performer in the open-air theatre of the sublime', wrote David Sylvester. True, *Red Slate Circle* (1980) in the Fogg Art Museum in Cambridge (MA), or *Sandstone Spiral* (1983) in the National Gallery of Canada, or the *Puget Sound Driftwood Circle* (1996) in Houston, or *Forte de Vinadio Circle* (Italy, 2001), are set on museum floors, in the clean, sparse gallery environment, and look Minimal. What concerns Richard Long is that '[e]ach work is appropriate to its place and context', and the wilderness works and the museum pieces are 'equal and complementary'. What counts, Long asserted, is the feelings that the work, whether inside or outside, aroused: 'my ambition is basically with the emotional power of the work, in both idea and image.'[22] Walking, nature and the landscape are at the heart of Long's work,[23] but Long knows, as any professional artist must know, that the art world conducts its business indoors.

Richard Long's slate, stick and wood circles look like late 20th century artworks, not 'Romantic', but Minimal, Conceptual and Arte Povera, like Carl Andre's copper and zinc plates. They have a coolness and clarity that one associates with Dan Flavin, Robert Morris, Tony Smith and Sol LeWitt. Long's stone circles make sense partly because of the viewer's grounding in the discourses of postwar and contemporary art. Without a knowledge of the myriad discourses, analyses and signs that flow around contemporary art, one might not know how to make full sense of Long's circles. True, the circle as a shape has been around for eons, but only in the contemporary era have circles been made out of bits of the landscape, in galleries and in landscape settings in this particular way.

The *Tarahumara Circle* (Mexico, 1987), a typical Richard Long work, is what seems at first to be a simple shape. But it's not 'simple'. It's a 'negative circle', a circle made into a circle by the ring of rocks around it. The line of rocks marks out the circle, but not evenly. Some of the rocks are piled deeper on one side of the circle. Hardly anyone will have seen this circle intact, in its situation, so one knows it only from a photograph. The seemingly straightforward approach of Long's photography has made a few æsthetic decisions, which shape spectators' perception of this artwork. For instance, one sees the stone circle in the centre of the frame, in the lower third, in the sort of classical composition that was taught in the fine art academies of yore. Behind the circle one sees the trees and hills of Mexico. Long's photograph thus 'captures' the stone ring amidst the Mexican landscape, placing it firmly within a wilderness landscape. The setting is impressive and it is meant to be. With its wooded slopes and hills receding into the blue haze, the photograph is worthy of the ærial effects described by Leonardo da Vinci in his treatise of Renaissance painting. The composition of *Tarahumara Circle*, the more one studies it, becomes increasingly 'classical': there are even two small trees either side of the stone circle, in the foreground, framing the circle, a compositional device favoured by J.M.W. Turner, Thomas Girtin, John Sell Cotman and other late 18th century landscapists.

Richard Long's *Brough of Birsay Circle* (Orkney, 1994) is a large open circle which relies on plants and their blooming in Summer to make it work. Like his late 1960s lines made by walking, Long has walked in a large circle on a field of flowers. The flowers have been pressed flat, leaving a circular mark, recalling Andy Goldsworthy's works, such as his body prints. The largest of Long's circles are of course the circular walks he makes, which could be many miles in diameter. Some of these are on maps, some are suggested through words. These are 'imaginary' circles but no less significant than the tactile stone circles. It's the same with science: the largest scientific experiment in the world is not the particle accelerator buried underground in Switzerland, it's those astronomical observations which use radio telescopes on either side of the Earth to correlate data from deep space. The diameter of the planet is the size of the experiment. The telescope is as large as the Earth. There are even larger astronomic experiments: the journeys to Mars and Venus, for instance, or the grand tours of the Solar System of the Voyager spacecraft. But even larger than these million-mile space voyages are the radio telescope investigations, which cross interstellar space at the speed of light. Conceptually, then, humans have made experiments – or art – that stretch away from Earth at light speed. That is, if radio waves have been beamed into the cosmos for, say, ninety years, then the extent of the human touch in the universe is something like 5.3 x 10^{14}, or 530,000,000,000,000 miles. It is a reach that is expanding 186,000 miles every second.

Some of Richard Long's stone circles are small – *Circle of Standing Stones* (1983), which is 26 stones arranged in a circle of a half yard in diameter, *Cornwall Slate Circle* (1982), 34 stones in a 2 yard circle, and *Standing Stone Circle* (1982), 36 stones in a similar size circle. The small stone circles are often made of standing stones, and many of the outdoor circles are of this type (*Evening Camp Stones,* 1995, for instance). Long's use of standing stones, rather than ones laid flat, echoes prehistoric stone circles – for instance, the Scottish stone circle *Stones and Stac Pollaidh* (1981), or *Sincholagua Summit Shadow Stones* (1998). Long's small stone circles are intimate works compared to the broad, large pieces. In Britain there are a number of small stone circles which produce similar atmospheres of human-scale and intimacy (such as the small circles on the ridges of hills in Dorset). 'I like simple, emotional, quiet, vigorous art' remarked Long.[24] While the large circles in the galleries of Western cities spoke of polished, upmarket art, the small, 1.5 yard stone circles evoked small wayside shrines. The large gallery circles are planned and organized months in advance, but still look spontaneous. Long's small outdoor stone circles, though, are direct and spontaneous responses to a landscape. (Some of Andy Goldsworthy's sculptures are very close to Long's in form and conception: Goldsworthy's *Flat-topped Stones* (2001), for instance, recalls Long's lines and rows of stones. In *Flat-topped Stones*, Goldsworthy laid stones in a line along a rock scree in Idaho specifically to reflect the noonday sun).

Some of Richard Long's techniques echo Andy Goldsworthy's: Long sprinkles snow in a circle, or smears mud, often from the River Avon near his home in England, in huge circles or arcs or lines on walls, or he makes marks on grass using his feet. The use of hands, feet, the body, mud, soil, stones, snow and sand chime with many of Goldsworthy's practical methods.

> I like the idea that I can make a show anywhere [commented Long] by just going down to the river taking a few handfuls of mud… and literally get on a plane and go anywhere and make a big show with the mud from my bag.[25]

Richard Long's art ethic – *have mud, will travel* – fits in with the notion of a pared-down, simplified, 'essential' æsthetic that was current in the 1960s and 1970s. The great thing is not so much that Long can splatter mud on a wall and call it art (he does the former, not the latter), but that people around the world accept mud splattered on a wall as art.

Richard Long – one of the success stories of the British art school system (along with David Hockney, Patrick Caulfield, Peter Blake, Barry Flanagan, Shirazeh Houshiary and Andy Goldsworthy) – knows only too well from his days at St Martin's College of Art that he is lucky to be able to travel the world with a bit of Avon river mud in his bag, and have gallery audiences lap it up, because for every major (successful) artist there are thousands of students pouring out of the art colleges each year. And these art students are often producing work just as rich and challenging as that of

Inshaw, Blake, Houshiary, Kapoor, Gormley, Vilmouth, Cragg, Woodrow, Hockney and Flanagan.

One of the most intriguing of land artists working in Great Britain is David Nash (born in the same year as Richard Long, 1945), with whom Andy Goldsworthy worked early in his career. David Nash was (is) an important artist for Goldsworthy. Goldsworthy had first encountered Nash when the sculptor visited Preston Polytechnic (with Richard Long) in 1978. Nash invited Goldsworthy to look after his studio, Capel Rhiw, in Blaenau Ffestiniog, while he was away for a while in 1980. Nash would become one of the few artists with whom Goldsworthy formed a friendship. Nash helped Goldsworthy gain his first one-man show (at LYC Museum and Art Gallery, Banks, Cumbria, in July, 1980).

David Nash's æsthetics chime with those of Richard Long and Andy Goldsworthy among British artists.[1] Hugh Adams saw David Nash as a kind of 'fixed abode Richard Long', working from one place (North Wales), while Long travels the globe, regarding the whole world as his studio, as material for making art. Hugh Adams wrote:

Nash is Long in microcosm: the sensibility is the same but, whereas Long travels the world, making, marking, and recording, in distant places, Nash is more sedentary, and content to do the same thing where he has made his home.[2]

David Nash built a number of 'stoves' and 'hearths', out of natural materials – snow, slate, wood. These structures burn away – fire as 'living' sculpture (like Chris Drury's cairns or Ana Mendieta's *Volcano*). *Snow Stove,* made in Japan in 1982, burnt beautifully – a snow pyramid, fusing those two eternal mysteries – fire and snow, fire and ice. Nash also made a *Wood Stove* (1979), a *Slate Stove* (1981) and also a *Sea Hearth*.[3] Anyone who's lit a fire right next to the ocean will know what a magical experience it can be, and Nash's *Sea Hearth* is certainly rich in magic. Nash set his fire built of large stones inches from the waves, to accentuate the contrast between the two elements. Nash's stoves and hearths are thick with alchemical and elemental allusions: they are a poetry of elements, the basic elements out of which everything is made. (William Jackson Maxwell has made burnt tree stumps, like Nash).[4]

David Nash loves working with wood: his *Wooden Boulder* (1978) was exactly that – a huge, near-spherical chunk of oak. Nash tipped the boulder into a stream near his studio at Blaenau Ffestiniog, North Wales. His idea was for the sculpture to make its way to the ocean. Instead, it stayed put in a pool (for a long time), and interacted continually with the environment (Nash later recorded that the boulder moved about seven times in 22 years, making it to an estuary, and looked 'more and more like a stone').

Welsh streams, with their chilly, clear water, mossy boulders and constant noise, are one of the most poetic environments Britain possesses. Ramblers are aware of streams and rivers, not only because they have to cross them somehow, but also because they are crucial sources of drinking and washing water. David Nash's art, like Robert Smithson's, is respectful of water and the landscape. His art is gentle and based firmly in a reverence for nature.

In the Forest of Dean (in Western England), David Nash made a circular mound of larch poles charred at the end. He spent two weeks charring nine hundred pieces of wood, which were then stuck together in a 'wide circular hole in the ground'.5 Nash wanted to have his *Black Dome* as a mound of nothing but charcoal, but realized it would not last long enough for the public to see it. He wanted to use charcoal because it was a part of the industry of the forest; Andy Goldsworthy has made many similar links with local industry and rural economies. It was important too that Nash's large sculpture would decay away and become integrated into the forest again. Nash envisaged his *Black Dome* 'gradually reintegrating with its environment, rotting down gradually – fungus, leaf-mould, plants adding to its process of 'return'' (ib., 66).

David Nash constructs fascinating pieces, works which are instantly appealing (the viewer 'gets' a Nash sculpture immediately), partly because of the materials, the natural materials which urban-based cultures are so thirsty for: wood, stone, water, fire. These are the elements not found in cities. Well, one sees trees, stones, skies and wood in cities, but it's not the same somehow: land artists wake the viewer, making them aware, again, of nature, of natural materials. One of Herman de Vries's aims was to 'make visible that which people don't see anymore', to draw attention to things happening in the 'primary reality' (nature) that people have forgotten about.6

It's refreshing, after being encased in grey concrete and a maze of straight or manmade lines in the city, to imbibe these works of artists such as David Nash, Andy Goldsworthy, Chris Drury and Nicholas Pope. For instance, David Nash's marvellous *Fletched Over Ash Dome*.7 This is a circular group of trees in Wales which Nash planted in 1977: it is a 'living' sculpture, which, over thirty years, will be trained into a dome. It will be not only a circle of trees, but a dome of trees. Nash wrote:

> A circle of young ash trees fletched and woven into a thirty foot dome fletched three times at ten year intervals then left alone. A silver sculpture in winter, a green canopy space in summer, a volcano of growing energy. (1978)

While Robert Morris and Hans Haacke used steam, and Nancy Holt assembled stone, David Nash's deployment of living trees (such as in his *Fire Engine Sweep*, planted in 1980) created, as with Andy Goldsworthy's art, a new form of sculpture, a sculpture which is alive, which changes over decades, rather than seconds. Morris's and Haacke's steam and fog works last mere moments, while Nash's, Jackie Winsor's and Drury's fires last a few hours. *Fletched Over Ash Trees*, though, is a sculpture that will endure for decades, and will change year in year out. Nash's trees will grow and develop for a long time before they decay, which will make them a particularly exciting type of sculpture.

David Nash explained:

Earlier, I used sawmill wood, regular standard units; later, greenwood, fresh from the tree; now the tree itself. The more I look at the tree, the more I see the tree; it's space and location, its volume and structure, its engineering and balance. More than that, I see the uniqueness of each simple tree, and beyond that still I see it as a great emblem of life. A potent vibrant tower, a whirling prayer wheel of natural energy.[8]

David Nash spoke of 'observing trees: how they enter and survive in the particular space of their location. Their form being the balance of continual change in the elements and the seasons'.[9]

Some more of David Nash's works include: *Vessel and Volume II* (1988, General Mills), a hollow boat form in black, next to a similarly-shaped boat, as if one could fit inside the other. *Serpentine Vessels* were also boat shapes (1989, collection: the artist), but their prows and sterns were tilted up, away from the floor. These were large objects, basically two slabs of wood fixed together. *Three Longboats* (1986, in oak) were hollow boat-forms, set on pieces of wood (Chris Drury has also made groups of boat forms). These are not boats that will float; they are bottomless. *Descending Vessel* (1988, collection: the artist) was another boat-form, again hollow, set upright on top of a wooden plinth-wall, more like a tower. The end of the vessel was slid into a crack in the top of the tower.

Quite a few of David Nash's sculptures consisted of two objects seen in tandem, one above the other. Like *Descending Vessel, Comet Ball* (1989, Trans Art, Cologne) was one object above the other – a tall curving piece of wood was stuck into a near-spherical globe of wood. Like *Descending Vessel, Comet Ball* recalled Constantin Brancusi – *Descending Vessel* was particularly reminiscent of *Birds in Space*. To emphasize the inspiration for the 1990 *Comet Ball*, Nash built a fire under it. Nash has also made waterfalls and streams from hollowed-out tree trunks, entitled *Wooden Waterways* (1978, Grizedale, and 1982, Japan), in which water from a stream was diverted along the trunks of a fallen oak tree, an ash, a sycamore, and onto more troughs.

Other vertical or tower-like works include *Oak Spoon* (1988, collection: the artist), and *Red Throne* (1989, collection: the artist). *Started Beech* (1989, collection: Eric Franck, Switzerland) was a tree trunk split into a series of thin planks, still connected at one end to the end of the beech tree trunk. The ends of the planks fanned outward slightly, creating the 'skirt effect'. At Grizedale Forest David Nash's *Horned Tripod* (1977) was a tall tripod made from straight trees, a large-scale work. *Crack and Warp Column* (1989, collection: the artist) was a tower made from thin squares of wood, piled on top of each other, recalling Andy Goldsworthy's cairns of slate. Like Goldsworthy's slate towers, Nash's *Crack and Warp Column* was irregular; each slab of wood bends slightly. In *Crack and Warp Column,* the warped slabs were more severely bent, but the size and shape of each slab was still controlled. The now-destroyed column of 1970 was one of the most Brancusi-like of Nash's sculptures (many sculptors have their Constantin Brancusi phase): it was fashioned in sections, one tapering into the next. The tall, vertical Nash sculptures recalled not only Brancusi's *Endless Column* but also Barnett Newman's *Broken Obelisk* (1963, MOMA,

New York), and notions of growing upwards, skywards, verticality, and are related to Nash's idea of a tree as a fountain of energy.

David Nash has produced giant-size versions of common, domestic forms, such as *Ancient Table, Table with Cubes, Oak Spoon, Branch Chair* and *Bowl and Platter*. *Ancient Table* (1983, collection: Capel Rhiw), which has huge weathered trunks for the table's legs; *Table with Cubes* (1971, Cardiff) has a variety of sizes of cubes on it; *Elm Bowl* (1988, collection: the artist) was a large, thin bowl, irregular, the outside smooth, the inside showing the marks of a chisel on top of a chunky wooden pedestal; *Bowl and Platter* (1988, collection: the artist) set the oversize objects on a large, thick table. Other large-scale versions of everyday objects included *Big Ladder* (1984, Japan), *Branch Chair* (1976) and *Standing Frame* (1987, Walker Arts Center).

David Nash took a common form, put it into wood, roughed up the outlines and textures, and enlarged the forms. Some of his most intriguing works were spindly, expanded versions of household items. *Branch Chair*, for example, was a recognizable chair, but with twigs and branches poking out of it; *Branch Cube* (1982, private collection) was recognisably a cube, but with twigs and branches sprouting out of it, making it a much larger sculpture than it would be if it was just a cube.

Some of David Nash's sculptures were slotted together, extended forms, one form expanding outwards to produce a series of forms, as in *Extended Cube* (1986, collection: the artist), where the cube spilled out over the floor, in ever-decreasing sizes. *Slot Table* (1979, collection: the artist) was a tree trunk with a large slot cut in it, and displaced slightly. *Extended Length* (1980, Rijksmuseum Kröller Müller) was a large oblong which was dissected, so that the inner part slides out, showing its internal perspectives. *Nature to Nature* (1987, Walker Arts Center) took three simple forms – globe, cube and pyramid – and made them out of solid wood. Nash put the three solids together in a row and built a fire under them. The blackened solids were shown in a gallery, with charcoal drawings of them on the wall behind.

In *Sod Swap* (1983), David Nash took sods of grass from Caen-y-Coed in North Wales to Kensington Gardens in London (and vice versa), planting the grass in a circle. Later Nash works included charred wooden sculptures based on the yew hedge 'twmps' which Nash had seen at Powis Castle garden in mid-Wales (such as *Beak Twmp*, 2000).

4 : 16   CHRIS DRURY

Of all the land artists, in Britain and elsewhere, who have affinities with Andy Goldsworthy, there is one who appears very close to Goldsworthy: Chris Drury. Born in 1948 (in Sri Lanka) and educated at Camberwell School of Art in London in the late Sixties, Drury is a British artist who has made works with numerous links with those of Andy Goldsworthy. Drury is 8 years older than Goldsworthy and belongs to the generation of Alan Sonfist, Charles Simonds, Michael Heizer, William Furlong, Alice Aycock and Richard Long (all born between 1944 and 1946).

Chris Drury began to make land art at about the same time as Andy Goldsworthy (in the mid-Seventies); he had begun with figurative sculpture. Among the artists that Drury admired were Roger Ackling and Constantin Brancusi (Drury said he found Joseph Beuys 'immensely irritating' and 'too self-obsessed' [2002, 91]). Drury has exhibited in many solo shows, including some of the same places as Goldsworthy (such as the Henry Moore Centre in Leeds, Royal Botanic Gardens in Edinburgh, and London's Serpentine Gallery).

The art of Chris Drury and Andy Goldsworthy share so many elements: they are both British land artists, both emphasize spirituality, both use similar forms (cairns, shelters, globes, spirals, circles), use similar materials (boulders, grass, willowherb stalks, wood, snow, clay), and both have worked and exhibited in similar territories: Japan, the U.S.A. and Scotland (Drury has made works, though, in places Goldsworthy has not been associated with, such as Ireland, Italy, Denmark and Spain, and Drury has created many works near his home in Lewes, Sussex). They also share the same book publishers (Thames & Hudson and Cameron Books), the same art critics who've written about their art (Paul Nesbitt and Terry Friedman), and have worked with the same institutions (such as the British Council, Common Ground, the Henry Moore Foundation, Sustrans, the Scottish Arts Council and the Arts Council).

Like Andy Goldsworthy, one of Chris Drury's concerns was human history, the relation between people and the land (British land art is acutely conscious of history, maybe because it infuses every single square foot of Britain): his artworks re-use dew ponds and stone walls, draw attention to tumuli by building domes over them, and alter maps, one of the most elegant manifestations of human history. *A Dense History of Place* (1996) was one of Drury's map works which combined maps with written text (a common motif in land and Conceptual art). Dense lines of text spread outwards in a circular pattern from an area near the coast in Sussex depicted in an Ordnance Survey map, an area which has many personal associations for Drury.

Another distinctly Goldsworthyan form of Chris Drury's is the globe set on the ground. Drury has created spheres from pine cones (1984), deer bones and deer scats (*Four Spheres,* 1984), and bamboo, ginkgo, vines, moss and seeds (*Shimanto River Spheres,* 1997, Japan). In *Bound Oak* (1990), made in Sherwood Forest, Drury wrapped a rope of grass around an old oak tree, recalling some of Goldsworthy's interventions with trees.

Chris Drury's art departs from Andy Goldsworthy's art at many points, however: the use of materials such as animal bones, antlers, horns, and feathers, the basket weaving, the spherical 'baskets' like pots, the kayaks, and the cloud chambers. Drury is much more inclined than Goldsworthy to use in his sculpture material from animals, such as whale bones, or reindeer antlers, or ram's horns, or elk bones, or gull's feathers, or cow dung. In the *Adharc* pieces (1991-92), Drury took the form of a ram's horn and multiplied it in peat and bronze. Drury affirms the community aspect of his art more than Goldsworthy, and the spiritual dimension (he speaks of meditation and the Buddhist void, for instance).

A key sculpture in Chris Drury's *œuvre* was his *Medicine Wheel* (made in 1983), a calendar work which collected 365 found objects strung on bamboo stalks mounted around the edge of plant papers and a mushroom spore at the centre. Drury wrote his diary in lines spreading outwards from the centre (a recurring motif in his work). Among the objects were hen feathers, wheat, runner beans, snail shells, pebbles, twigs, bark, berries, acorns, flowers, seeds, fish bones, grass, grapefruit, cherry blossom, hawthorn, crab, mussels, sheep bone, mistletoe, seaweed, cork, walnuts, quinces, rabbit skin, figs, and a cat's skull. The *Medicine Wheel* inspired many new forms in Drury's art:

> out of that came different categories of work [Drury explained]. It started me off on making shelters and baskets, and then the shelters led to cloud chambers, and the baskets and the large, woven works I've made outside led me to the dewpond works. I've made woven maps, weaving ideas of landscape. And then there are the found objects.[1]

Like many land artists and sculptors, Chris Drury has made many works near his home in Lewes, Sussex (like Andy Goldsworthy in Penpont, Nash in Blaenau-Ffestiniog and Richard Long in Bristol and the South-West). Drury's works in Sussex include *Vortex* (Lewes Castle), *Cuckoo Dome*, *Beehive Shelter* (Goodwood), *Holding Light* (Brighton), *Guardian Shelter* (Sheffield Forest), *Chalk Chamber* (a barn in Sussex), *Rhythms of the Heart* (Hastings), *Heart of Reeds* (Lewes), Towner Art Gallery, Eastbourne, *Seven Sisters Bundles* (near Eastbourne), and the dew ponds.

Chris Drury stated that his work was not self-referential, that it referred to things outside of itself. However, there was plenty of self-referentiality in Drury's art: the *Medicine Wheels*, for example, comprised diary entries for every day of the year. Another work also heavy with thousands of closely written words, *A Dense History of Place*, was full of autobiographical associations. The emphasis on cataloguing also had a biographical element, as did the penchant for works linked to Drury's home-ground of Lewes in Sussex. Then there's the emphasis on community projects, where the artist interacts with a local community. Those personal interactions, which Drury cherishes, also contain a strong biographical element.

Basket weaving is one of Chris Drury's passions, and he has created many forms using weaving, including a large open dome from hazel branches (*Cuckoo Dome*, 1992), kayak forms (*Kayak Bundles,* 1994), globular forms (*Basket For the Forest Deer*, 1987), and small vessels (*Basket For the Trees*, 1988, *Hollow Vessel*, 1989). Many of Drury's baskets are recognisable traditional baskets: *Five Sisters* (1994), *Basket For the Moment Between Life and Death* (1985) and *Dream Basket* (1985). In *Basket For the Crows* (1986), the distinctive black crow feathers are employed to weave a basket, placed on the floor, with a long row of feathers suspended above it.

Linked with the basket woven pieces are the small bundles of found objects (such as *Cholla Bundles* [1993], *Beaver Sticks* [1991], and *Stick Bundle* [1992]). *Seven Sisters Bundles* (1994), for instance, comprises objects found at the famous Sussex Seven Sisters chalk cliffs (driftwood, flint, chalk and fishing twine). The bundles, for Chris Drury, were 'talismans of time and place, souvenirs, made simply at a campsite, or alternatively created at a later date as an act of remembering' (1998, 58).

An off-shoot of Chris Drury's penchant for weaving is the interlacing of maps (maps being one of the key components of land art). Thus, Drury has interwoven a map of Manhattan with one of the Hebrides (1996) and West Cork with New Mexico (1995). Like Tony Cragg, Drury has collated found objects into patterns (such as *Tidelines*, 1985, made from pieces of plastic, metal, rubber, driftwood and feathers).

Some of Chris Drury's vessels have been woven from willow (1994), or bamboo (1997), some have been covered with cow dung (1992), and some have been made with turf (1991). Some of Drury's wall drawings, fashioned with river mud (*River Vortex*, 1998), recall Richard Long's mud wall drawings.

Chris Drury's art tended to be interconnected: the baskets and woven vessels were linked to the woven maps, and the woven globes, and also some of the larger shelters. The dew ponds were patterned after baskets.

On occasion I have taken a basket weave, enlarged it, and turned it upside down to act as a shelter or as a valve between inner and outer... basket to shelter, shelter to basket... A web of interconnections links all these works. (1998, 22-23)

One of Chris Drury's most striking sculptures was *Stone Whirlpool* (1996), built from river stones arranged into a spiral in a Japanese river (in Okawa-mura), near a waterfall. It was one of Drury's works which explored vortexes and spirals. An associated piece which took on currents of energy was *Edge of Chaos* (2000), a large paper work covered with handwritten texts describing the world's ocean currents and winds. One of Drury's largest vortex sculptures was *Heart of Reeds* (2000).

Chris Drury has reclaimed and reworked dew ponds, mainly in Sussex (*Basket Dewpond,* 1997, and 1999), some of which are quite ancient. In these shallow dips in the landscape Drury has fashioned his favourite motifs of spirals and vortexes from grass and snow. *Snow Vortex* (1999) was a labyrinth with paths dug out of snow on Firle Downs in Sussex. Drury has also made a dry stone vortex maze and a 'wave garden'. (Like Andy Goldsworthy with his serpentine curves, Drury has his favourite motifs: the mushroom gill form, the dome, and the spiral or vortex, which recur in so many sculptures.)

Boats, kayaks and 'vessels' are another recurring form in Chris Drury's art. Some of the vessels are enormous cannibalized stone walls (such as *Long Vessel*, 1995) or heaps of stones, willow and reeds woven on top of them (such as *Shelter Vessel*, 1988, made in County Galway). (Some of Andy Goldsworthy's key works are stone walls). Some of the vessels are basket woven (such as *Connemara Vessels*, 1988). *Air Vessel* (1994), woven from willow, is one of Drury's most intriguing sculptures: in the form of a kayak, a skeletal form of woven twigs, it was exhibited hanging in space in the gallery, evoking all sorts of associations (with boats as flying transports, or the rich symbolism of flight, or shamanic flight). For Drury, *Air Vessel* was about journeying, the 'moments of exhilaration on mountains where I have experienced a feeling akin to flying'.[2] Some of the shelters, Drury said, were 'like overturned boats and denote journey, movement' (1998, 20).

Chris Drury has treated his cairns in different ways: many of the stone cairns have had fires lit inside them, such as *Midsummer Fire Cairn* (1989), *Falling Water Fire Cairn* (1997, Norway), *Fire Cairn* (1993, Ireland), *Fire Mountain Cairn* (1996, Japan), and *Fire Cairn* (1989, Colorado). Some cairns have been enclosed with basket weaving, such as *Basket Cairn* (1991) and *Covered Cairn* (1993, Denmark). Like Andy Goldsworthy's cairns, Drury's stone cairns are usually erected in wilderness or spectacular scenery: Norway (1988), New Mexico (1993), De Lank River, Cornwall (1990), Lappland (1988), Wester Ross, Scotland (1992), Kintail, Scotland (1994), Ladakh (1997) and Colorado (1989). For Drury, the cairns are about commemorating a particular moment in a special place: 'they're just saying, 'this is an extraordinary place'. Grab a few rocks, put them up before the moment's gone and photograph it'' (2002, 79). If the shelters were the stopping-places on a journey, the cairns were the 'markers of highpoints/ moments of exhilaration along the way' (1998, 58).

Another favourite Chris Drury motif is the shelter: low, squat structures, some like teepees or witches' hats, some like prehistoric beehive huts. The shelters were often made from stone (but also in chalk, turf, ice, wood, plants and coal. Some of these materials, such as turf, coal and chalk, are unexpected, and give Drury's shelters a very particular quality). The shelters are usually (but not always) constructed at human scale. That is, in the correct scale for someone to enter them. *Beara Shelter* (1995), in West Cork, Ireland, was a squat, square, stone structure, with views of the sea and Bulls Rock. 'The intention was to provide a space for being and con- templation' (1998, 20). Some of the shelters, such as *Shelter For the Winds That Blow From Siberia*, made near Drury's home in Lewes in 1986, have a distinctly Golds- worthyan flavour: blocks of ice mounted on a hazel frame, looking like an igloo. *Shelter For the Northern Glaciers* (1988) was constructed in the spectacular coastal setting of Seiland island, in Norway, surrounded by snow-capped mountains. Geoffrey Harris has also constructed wooden shelters in forests (*Hollow Spruce*, 1988).

Some of the shelters, as with the cairns, have had fires lit inside them (*Shelter For Dreaming*, 1985). Some of the shelters are open structures, without a covering (rather like a frame tent before the canvas is pulled on top). Others are a frame which's wrapped with ice, or turf, or reeds (such as *Shelter For Herbs and Healing*, 1986). *Tree Mountain Shelter* (1994, Italy) was a stone cairn enclosed with a cone of hazel branches. *Turf Chamber* (1992) comprised sections of turf laid on top of a hazel branch frame. *Wave Chamber* (1996) was constructed beside a flooded valley in Northumberland, and contained a mirror and lens in a steel periscope mounted atop the structure so that the image of the waves could be projected inside, onto the floor.

Chris Drury's shelters have all sorts of connotations, stretching back thousands of years (shelters must have been one of the first structures that humans ever built – shelter being one of the primal human needs). 'Shelter is a basic human need and a manifestation of human presence', remarked Drury (1998, 20). Drury's shelters have obvious affinities (with Celtic and Bronze Age huts and houses in Britain, for example), but they are also about 'organic' forms, forms which repeat endlessly, and geometrically, like crystals. They are stopping and resting places, and also enclosing spaces. 'I like the way this interior space draws you inside yourself, enclosing, pro- tecting, just as mountains pull you outside yourself, pushing mind and body beyond their usual confines' said Drury (ibid.).

The shelters are also about the landscapes in which they are constructed, like land art in general. They tend to be built in rural or wilderness zones, and are the only structures of that kind in the area (they stand out as artworks, not as part of the agricultural machinery, for instance, like Andy Goldsworthy's sculptures). The shelters are thus also free-standing sculptures, artworks which draw attention to themselves. The shelters are also about land art concerns, such as the tensions between what's inside and what's outside, between the humanmade structure and a 'natural' context (the landscape), about the relation between form and function, æsthetics and use. The shelters draw attention to the landscape around them.

One of Chris Drury's shelters, *Covered Tumulus* (1997), took on the theme of human history directly, and the sense of revealing what's there: Drury built a dome of hazel branches over a prehistoric mound on the South Downs in Sussex. The *Hut of the Shadow* (1997) was sited in North Uist in the Scottish Western Isles with the local community in mind. In *Covered Cairn* (1993), made at TICKON in Denmark, Drury placed a hazel and willow twig frame dome over a stone cairn, an approach that combined the Druryan motif of the open, woven frame, with the Goldsworthyan motif, of the stone cairn created by balancing rocks atop each other.

The woven dome is a division between outside and in [commented Chris Drury], 'which nevertheless allows a transition from one to the other, a free flow of inner to outer. The experience inside it is different from the experience outside. (1998, 80)

One of Chris Drury's more unusual shelters was *Mind Wave* (1996), made in the Botanic Gardens in Copenhagen: Drury combined a couple of his favourite forms: the mushroom-shaped text drawing, and the dome. In *Mind Wave*, Drury opted to adapt a geodesic dome greenhouse, which he painted blue and scratched the words 'mind' and 'wave' in the paint, spreading outwards from the centre of the dome, in the pattern of the gills of a mushroom.

Some of Chris Drury's most appealing sculptures are 'cloud chambers', developments of his shelter form: these are basically circular stone or wooden shelters with holes and mirrors in the roof which act as lenses and reflectors. In these *camera obscuras*, the spectator can observe the sky above projected onto the floor below. The cloud chambers (constructed in many areas) articulate classic land art concerns: the dialectic between inner and outer, indoor and outdoor, stillness and movement, nature and culture. Drury's cloud chambers include *Coppice Cloud Chamber* (1998, Kent), *Cloud Chamber* (Piccadilly, London, 1993), *Cloud Chamber* (1994, Aberdeen), *Eden Cloud Chamber* (2002, Cornwall), *Reed Chamber* (2002, Arundel), *Cedar Log Sky Chamber* (1996, Japan), *Hut of the Shadow* (1997, Western Isles), *Clohan Cloud Chamber* (1992, Dublin), *Cloud Chamber* (1990, Belgium), *Cloud Chamber For the Trees and Sky* (2003, North Carolina) and *Wicklow Cloud Chamber* (1990, Glencree, Ireland). The cloud chambers are 'still, silent, meditative and mysterious places' Chris Drury wrote on his website.

Some of Chris Drury's larger works, such as *Vortex* (an enormous hollow cone of woven hazel and willow made at Lewes Castle in 1994), have more in common with artists such as Tony Cragg or Richard Deacon than Andy Goldsworthy. Another large work, *Heart of Reeds* (2000), was a proposal for a spiral vortex on five acres of reclaimed land in Lewes, Sussex (built in the mid-2000s).

A later development of Chris Drury's art was to see the (human) body as 'landscape', to explore the processes of the body, and the relationships between the body and the Earth. Manifestations of this development in Drury's interests were the Lewes *Heart of Reeds* project (which was based on the human heart), *Heart River* (1999), a pattern on paper from a cross-section of the heart, and several works Drury has made in conjunction with hospitals (such as *Rhythms of the Heart*, 2000, created in Hastings). In these works, Drury has explored the flow of blood and water in the body, wave patterns from echocardiograms, and the formations in rocks, trees and the landscape.

For Chris Drury, there wasn't a separation between humans and nature, no 'us and them' (or, rather, 'us and it'): nature was all around, inside as well as outside: '[w]e ourselves are nature... '[w]e're a part of nature'.[3] Drury was interested in exploring the relation between inside and outside, nature and culture, and how 'nature is really culture' (2002, 76). For Drury, the natural world could never be 'natural', on its own, completely distinct from humanity – at least as far as humans were concerned. The natural world was always totally enculturated. In other words, if humans were looking at nature, they could only ever see nature in human terms.

> When you're out in the countryside, culture, or our view of nature, determines how you see what's in front of you. So you never see a thing as it is, you always see it in the way that you've been programmed to see it. And you can't get away from that, ever... We are nature, we have to touch nature, we touch it every single second of the day, we breathe it.[4]

Chris Drury said he went out into the countryside (into the 'natural' world) to make art because it was inspirational, it was away from telephones, people, cars, etc, and it was different from humanmade environments (like cities). Also, work made outside tended to be less self-conscious (2002, 72). Andy Goldsworthy has said similar things – that he has to work outside, because it's more inspiring and nourishing, and because when he's indoors he starts to run out of reasons for being there.

> I work directly with the land because it nourishes me. It is full of energy and change and growth and I feed on that. I need that. I see myself as the next layer on the many that have made the landscape so rich [Andy Goldsworthy said in 1999].[5]

A work being 'site-specific' was important for Chris Drury: it was about the place, the uses of the place, the history of the place, and the people who lived in the place.

> It's made there, it's made out of the material that's there and it's made by people who live there. All those elements come into it and it has to find its place with the landscape but also within the culture relative to what those people are. (2002, 73)

Chris Drury saw the spaces he made that people entered as 'meditative spaces'. They were direct experiences. The cloud chambers, for example, were 'very still, meditative places' where visitors would not sit and think but sit and experience the place directly. The effect the cloud chambers had depended upon the person. They worked best when they encouraged the viewer to sit still for a moment and reflect (2002, 76). The idea of the *Beara Shelter* was 'a space for being and contemplation' (1998, 20).

One of the developments of 1960s land art was to put the artist *inside* the art. In the traditional manner of painting the landscape, the artist was viewing the landscape from a distance, standing back; but 'since the 1960s artists have been putting themselves into it', Chris Drury observed (2002, 76). For Drury, the photograph is a poor substitute for the work itself. Drury said he had taken photographs of ephemeral works (such as the cairns), but was more interested in working 'with people in the real world' (ib., 81).

Unlike some of his British contemporaries (Andy Goldsworthy, Richard Long, Hamish Fulton), Chris Drury encouraged people to visit the sites of his works. He published a website and postcards with instructions on how to find them.

In no way could that work communicate itself through a photograph because it's an experience, and nothing you could bring to a gallery would get anywhere near what the thing is about. (2002, 81)

In this respect, Chris Drury has more in common with American earth artists, such as Dennis Oppenheim or Robert Smithson, who exalted site and location.

Going out and walking or making work from time to time is important for Chris Drury – especially if he hasn't done any travelling or walking for a while. 'I'm really fortunate to be invited to extraordinary places to go and make work' (ib., 79). However, it wasn't the object itself that was the really valuable aspect of travelling or working on commissions for Drury, but the process and experience of making it, interacting with people, living in particular environments. 'The main thing you bring back is how the experience has changed you inside' (ibid.). So some of the pieces Drury makes are not about specific places or times, but 'the whole activity of being out there in those places'.

In a sense you can't not be a conceptual artist these days [said Drury], because you have to think about the world and if you don't you're not contributing to the debate in any useful way. But at the same time, in order to make art that's really interesting you have to stop thinking. (2002, 90)

Chris Drury said he didn't think of himself as really fitting into the land art or art and nature genre. 'As soon as you say 'art and nature', it makes people think of fiddling about with sticks, which is really not what I'm interested in' (2002, 90). Although labelled as a land artist, Drury preferred to see himself as an artist who 'explores nature and culture, inner and outer'.[6] There was no division between art, nature and humanity, for Drury: the artist – and art – was always part of nature ('there is no division between man, art and nature').[7] Drury did not think of himself, either, as the kind of artist who had something to express, who wished to make statements about issues or the world.

> Personally I have nothing to communicate, consciously or unconsciously; the work simply reflects the moving from moment to moment in the world as it is, and so it is nature itself that communicates. (ibid.)

In this view, Chris Drury saw himself as a shamanic translator of nature and the world, a creative interface between the world and the viewer. As well as shamanism, critics have also linked Drury's art (as with Andy Goldsworthy) to Buddhism. Rather than an 'creator' of art, or an 'expresser' of emotions or statements or views, then, Drury would be seen as a 'reflector' of nature and the world, someone who does not 'create' art but reflects what is already in the world and in nature (and in himself and in other people). In this view, Drury's output is a manifestation of his being-in-the-world, so to speak. It's an art of ontology, of beingness, of being in the moment, of reflecting the moment (or the passing of moments), rather than the traditional (Western) view of art as being about personal expression, about crises of subjectivity, about angst and suffering, about visionary creativity, and all the rest of the Freudian, Nietzschean, psychological baggage. It's not an art of putting a personal stamp on the world (such as making the big earthworks gestures in the American desert), or promoting ego and self (and celebrity and fame), or advertizing a set of philosophical or ideological views. 'Making art, for me, is never the means of finding insight. It is rather the reflection of a growing consciousness'. Drury spoke in Zen Buddhist terms of his artistic process: 'I go to 'outer nature', which is thoughtless, void, in order to see the whole. From the void comes insight, which makes art'.[8]

4 : 17   HAMISH FULTON

For Hamish Fulton, as for Richard Long, the walk is central to art. If there is no walk, there is no work: 'no walk, no work', as Fulton put it. 'First the walk second the artwork', Fulton asserted.[1] Most of his walks have been made alone, Fulton said (though Fulton has also walked in groups, which Long hasn't really done, such as with C.A.S.K. in Japan). But not every walk needed to be be made into a work of art. They were sufficient unto themselves.[2] On the other hand, Fulton said he had to walk to be able to make a work of art. The artwork came out of the work, and if he didn't walk, there couldn't be any art.

Hamish Fulton has conducted walkworks without sleeping, such as walking through a day and a night without sleep. And Fulton has gone much further than Richard Long in testing himself by walking for long distances without sleep (such as his walk along the Pilgrims' Way in Southern England between December 21st and 23rd, in 1991, a 125 mile continuous walk without sleep. Or his *Seven Walk Without Sleep* (the *Winter Solstice Full Moon* walk of 1991 being one of them). Fulton likes to toy with the hallucinations and altered states that sleep deprivation brings (i.e., it can be a walk along a familiar route, but it's a completely different experience because the artist-walker's gone without sleep).)

Many of Hamish Fulton's artworks are very similar to Richard Long's – textworks, photo-works, photographs of mountain tops or hillsides or country lanes or lakes or snowfields. And both Fulton and Long opt for irregular snaking lines on gallery walls to indicate the routes they undertook. And they both quote words in Japanese and Chinese ideograms. Like Long's textworks, Fulton photoworks and textworks recall concrete or visual poetry, word sculpture, *haiku,* diaries and journals, and Conceptual art.

Hamish Fulton's art differs from Richard Long's in terms of the appearance of the text-works and wall works. Fulton loves to set text in a variety of typefaces, so that his exhibitions and books look a little like a typographer has gone nuts. While Long usually sticks to trusty old Gill Sans font, Fulton happily indulges in shadowed capitals, white out of black, vertical type, extra bold fonts. Fulton, like Barbara Kruger, also loves very large and very bold (and coloured) lettering (such as in *Sweet Grass Hills* [1999], and *Warm Dead Bird* [1999]). (Fulton did not, though, make the wall works in his exhibitions himself. Unlike Long with his handmade mud drawings, Fulton gave the job of putting up his texts and photoworks to others.)

Both Hamish Fulton and Richard Long employ short phrases which aim to capture some of the experience or remind the viewer of something of their walks. In a seven day walk in Scotland, Fulton filled a work with lines and lines of descriptions of the walk which recall many of Long's works: 'sound of the small stream / pale grey pale blue yellow sky in the late afternoon / small herd of deer one rubbing a branch stop look turn and run'. In a 1987 walkwork made in Mexico, Fulton wrote: 'shooting star – dark night – grey morning – snowflakes – snow covered ground' and so on. Short phrases which sometimes evoke a *haiku* approach to the evoking the experience of the walk (*less* may be *more*, but Fulton certainly likes to fill some of his walkworks with hundreds of words). While Long counts hours or days or miles, Fulton has sometimes counted footsteps as a way of measuring a walk (as in *Counting 6234 Barefoot Paces* [1994-97], or the barefoot paces counted in Kent between 1999 and 2001).

Hamish Fulton had more a philosophical and ascetic view of walking-as-art than Richard Long.[3] Walking was not, Fulton asserted, for recreation or leisure or for studying nature, or for taking photographs or making sculptures along the way.

> It is about an attempt at being 'broken down' mentally and physically – with the *desire* to 'flow inside' a rhythm of walking – to experience a temporary state of euphoria, a blending of my mind with the outside world of nature.[4]

Despite the monk-like austerity, Hamish Fulton also said he loved walking, and 'lived for it. I compare everything to my walks. I've enjoyed all the walks and some were more challenging than others, therefore more rewarding' (2002, 108).

As well as the numerous similarities between the art of Hamish Fulton and Richard Long, there are plenty of key differences: no sculptures in Fulton's work, like Long's stone and mud circles, rows, or ellipses, on the wall or the floor. No sculptures made out of doors on walks and photographed. No water splashes or waterlines. No lines made by kicking away stones or flattening grass. No marks made by sleeping places or tents. No fingerprint marks on pieces of wood or hand-made Korean paper. No walks within imaginary circles or along imaginary lines. No mapworks (or very few). No walks carrying stones (or throwing stones, or adding them to cairns).

As with Richard Long and Andy Goldsworthy, Hamish Fulton rarely included images of people in his art, but he said his art 'should not be thought of as anti-people' (1995). Instead, Fulton's photographs are of wildernesses (mountains, lakes, forests, fields and country lanes). Fulton separated the walk from the artwork. 'The artwork cannot represent the experience of a walk', Fulton affirmed (1995). The walk was always elsewhere, always only for the walker-artist. 'The *location* of the walk is not in the gallery – and the walk itself is a past event'.[5] Aspects of the work could remind the artist of making the work, but could not communicate the experience of the work to the viewer. 'The texts are facts for the walker and fiction for everyone else' (1995). The artworks, instead, were pointers towards the experience of the walk, reminders perhaps, or dim correlations. Fulton hoped that the viewer 'will create a feeling, an impression in his or her own mind based on whatever my art can provide' (2002, 108). Fulton said he preferred experiences to objects (ib., 108). For Fulton, 'an object cannot compete with an experience' (ib., 27). Some artists, however, did not separate the two: since the 1960s, the object *is* the experience, and the experience *is* the object.

Hamish Fulton said he preferred to walk rather than sit in a train or plane or car. Travelling (sitting) was of 'little interest' to him (1995). And when he embarked on a walk, Fulton said he walked directly from his home, rather than use transport. The walk was the thing, always. 'I am an artist who walks, not a walker who makes art', Fulton said (1995). Fulton complained that he seemed to spend more time on organizing exhibitions, on admin and paperwork, than walking (1995). Like Long, Fulton said that his walks were not performances.

Hamish Fulton's artistic inspirations came from mountaineering and the exploits of mountaineers such as Reinhold Messner, Peter Boardman and Doug Scott (Fulton, like Richard Long, has travelled many times in mountain regions, but neither would call themselves professional climbers; Fulton has climbed some high peaks, but says he's an 'armchair mountaineer'). It was the mind-set that mountaineering created in the individual that interested Fulton (some mountaineers have written in spiritual terms of their experiences). Fulton had been impressed by Doug Scott's light, independent ascent of Kangchenjunga in 1979 (Scott had helped to pioneer the newer, lighter climbs, instead of the big funded expeditions involving hundreds of people). 'The story of [Scott's] ascent of Kangchenjunga in 1979 became for me a symbol for combining a lightness of touch with a genuinely great experience – two qualities I strive for myself, but not without considerable difficulty', Fulton explained (2002, 110).

Another influence was Native American culture (Hamish Fulton had visited the sites of Sioux, Cheyenne and Plains Indians in the late 1960s). Yet another was ecology and ecologists (Fulton voiced ecological concerns more often than Richard Long or Andy Goldsworthy, and is a more politicized artist). Fulton also drew on pilgrims and pilgrimages (he has walked a number of pilgrim routes, including Pilgrims' Way, near his home in Canterbury in Kent). Tibetan religious art, *haiku* poetry from Japan (Santoka Teneda and Basho), and 'the walking peoples of the world from all periods of history' were also cited by the artist (1995).

Among artists, Hamish Fulton has referred to Marina Abramovic, Nancy Wilson, Roger Ackling and Richard Long as influences. He also cited *Monsters From the Deep* (1997), a CD by Lawrence Weiner, Bruce Nauman's video *Good Boy Bad Boy* (1985), and native cultures as some of the art he admired (such as the Huichol of Mexico). The Marathon Monks of Mount Hiel (Tendai Buddhist monks in Japan) were also inspirations for Fulton (in particular their repeat walks, walking around a hill for seven years until they had travelled the same distance as the circumference of the Earth).

Hamish Fulton resisted being categorized as an artist related to the British Romantic tradition or landscape tradition. He wanted to work, like Richard Long, in an international mode, and not be tied down to the provincial British view of landscape art. He said he was not part of the outdoor sculpture tradition, either. He also preferred, like Long, to walk in landscapes wilder and more extreme than those found in dear old England. Fulton said he respected and was a devotee of countryside walking, but he needed extreme conditions too, like the Himalayas or Alaska. Fulton was happy that his work had 'never been fashionable', that he had survived so long in the art world, and that he could continue to make a variety of work (2002, 107).

The typical Hamish Fulton artwork is a large black-and-white photograph in a frame with a short piece of text in capitals underneath (the look of Fulton's text and photo pieces recalls Richard Long's and Dennis Oppenheim's art). Fulton's works include *Rock Fall Echo Dust* (1988), recording a walk made on Baffin Island; *The Crossing Place of Two Walks at Ringdom Gompa* (1984), *Grims Ditch* (1969-70), *Rock Path, Switzerland* (1986), *Night Changing Shapes* (1991) and *Gazing At the Horizon Line, Sky Horizon Ground* (Australia, 1982). Some of Fulton's works consist only of text in capitals painted on a wall in a gallery: *No Talking For Seven Days* (1993) and *Rock Fall Echo Dust* (1988).

In King's Wood, near Challock in Kent, Britain (a modest but appealing woodland sculpture park), Hamish Fulton walked back and forth along the same route for seven days. The results were published in a book (*Walking Through*, 1999). Like Richard Long, Fulton has published books about particular walking trips, and the books can be counted as artworks in themselves (though Andy Goldsworthty's books cannot usually be considered as artworks). As well as wallworks and photo and textworks, Fulton also produced postcards (the postcards were a part of his art as much as the larger works).

Like many British land artists, Hamish Fulton didn't want to make massive and long-lasting marks on the landscape. It was, rather, absolutely the opposite. Fulton said his art was not aggressive or technological: 'I do not directly rearrange, remove, sell and not return, dig into, wrap or cut up with loud machinery any elements of the natural environment, Fulton asserted, clearly having several well-known land artists in mind (1995). Fulton was acutely conscious of the ecological aspects of his work. It was ironic, for instance, that putting on an exhibition could actually do more damage to the environment in terms of pollution (such as jet travel and transportation) than if the artist had stayed at home and conserved energy.

4 : 18   OTHER LAND ARTISTS IN BRITAIN AND EUROPE

Other British and European land and site artists of Andy Goldsworthy's generation whose art has some affinity with Goldsworthy's art include GRAHAM MOORE, whose works include three circles of mown grass, entitled *Herbe Garden* (1989, Christchurch Park). This work echoed Long's early turf circles. Gwen Heney made a 30 yard long snake out of bricks at the Garden Festival Wales show (1992). Also at 1992 Welsh show was Mick Petts' *Mother Earth*, created out of a huge pile of slag which was required to be disguised. Valerie Pragnelli made a spiral from rocks in a stream (*Langslie Spiral*, Milepoint). Ron Haselden produced a dance of lights, called *Fete* (1992), out of strings of lights hung from a group of willow trees. One of the largest of contemporary garden and landscape design projects was Giuliano Gori's Parco di Celle.

RICHARD HARRIS (b. 1954) has produced a wall sculpture, *Dry Stone Passage* (1982), which is similar to Andy Goldsworthy's walls. Harris wrote: 'I want the sculpture to become a living and working part of the existing environment'.[1] Harris made a *Willow Walk* (1990), a walk lined with willow branches. Harris's works at Grizedale, apart from the Goldsworthyan *Dry Stone Passage*, included *Cliff Structure* (1978), slate slabs set on split oak, and *Quarry Structure* (1977), a 'bridge' of slate and oak sticks.

Another British sculptor, PAUL RUSSELL COOPER (b. 1949), has built a distinctly Goldsworthyan sculpture, *Two Circles in a Stone Bridge*. This is a large dry stone work at Portland in Dorset (1983). Two circles were created with the stones, one 'positive', the other 'negative': the 'negative' circle was a large hole like an archway. Other works by Cooper include *Quincunx*, a series of five globes in concrete set in an open space at Rufford Country Park (near Newark, 1983). The globes sit open partially to display something different in each globe: water, rocks, burning detritus from the garden and a sundial. Cooper's *Quincunx* is based on natural forms – in this case, five-petalled plants.

MICHAEL DAN ARCHER's *Observatory* (1994) recalled Robert Morris's *Observatory*: it was basically a low circular embankment, the kind seen in Iron Age hillforts or in some Bronze Age stone circles in the United Kingdom (Archer's *Observatory* in particular recalled Avebury stone circle). A stone shaped like a post and lintel (as at Stonehenge) marked the entrance, and two broken circular stones did for benches in the centre of *Observatory*.

Patricia Leighton reworked the earth at the side of the M8 freeway, turning it into a series of *Sawtooth Ramps*, which recalled Andy Goldsworthy's *Lambton Earthwork*. Julia Barton created *A Rural Landmark: Viewing Platform* (1994) in Yorkshire stone at Kirklees Way: the circular platform was cut into a hillside, backed by a low wall and clad in stone. There were no signs to indicate what to look at, as in municipal viewing sites (the sort of tourist brass discs found on hilltops that state '25 miles to Mesa Verde').

PETER RANDALL-PAGE (b. 1954), one of the most appealing of British sculptors (certainly one of the most accomplished of the members of the Royal Society of British Sculptors), created an interaction between modern sculpture and mediæval architecture when he sited some of his boulders made from Finnish glacial granite at Wenlock Priory in rural Shropshire. *Boulders and Banner Boulders: Secret Life I, II, III, IV* (1994) contained sculptures that were split open like gigantic seeds. Randall-Page's sculptures were suitably monumental (and abstract) for the architectural space of the ruined Priory.

At Grizedale forest, HELEN STYLIANIDES produced a tree sculpture that looked like a tree with the branches cut off, about five feet from the trunk – a tree with no leaves, but stumps for branches (*Tree Sculpture*, 1984). Alyson Brien fashioned *A Curve Around a Lime Tree* (1987) which looked like a low fence of stripped wood. Eric Geddes bent two young trees over and tied them to a central tree, so they formed a semi-circular arch, with the tree in the centre standing upright.

In the Forest of Dean a number of interesting commissions took place in the late 1980s. YVETTE MARTIN's *Four Seasons* was an environmental, 'land' sculpture. The first work, *Spring* (1986), was an oval-shaped pond with copper coloured water, a marshy space surrounded by webs of twigs and branches. It was a womb-like space, with a sense of being closed-in.[2] The branches on the trees growing on the bank of the small pond were bent down to add to the feeling of enclosure. Martin's *Spring* was the sort of space novelists such as Thomas Hardy and John Cowper Powys would enjoy, for secluded pools recur in their fictions (Rushy Pond in *The Return of the Native*, and the haunting Lenty Pond in Powys's great novel of nature mysticism, *Wolf Solent*). Like other land artists, Martin spoke in terms of 'growth cycles', the 'cycle of life from conception, emergence, growth, reproduction, maturity, decay and death' (ib., 75). The pond or pool is a recurring favourite in land art (it's found in the art of Chris Drury, Patricia Johanson, Mary Miss, James Turrell, Evelyn Zimmerman and Jim Sanborn, among many others).

The most exciting sculpture in the Forest of Dean at this time was CORNELIA PARKER's (b. 1956) *Hanging Fire*, a large ring of iron hung 25 or so feet above the forest floor. Parker created a ring of iron flames, which were rusted overnight in salt water (partly for the colour). They hung upside down from the ring. Parker wanted to portray the idea of a perpetual flame, a 'flame that would perpetually burn because it was cast in iron' (ib., 89). Hanging sculptures, as Alexander Calder showed time after time, are often intriguing, and Parker's *Hanging Fire*, though made of heavy materials, floated in the trees. She also wanted to incorporate the notion of a 'circle or fairy ring', and a crown, and to use iron because iron was mined in the Forest of Dean.

Cornelia Parker's most famous work was probably *Cold Dark Matter: An Exploded View* (1991), an installation of a garden shed that Parker had blown up by Army experts, exhibiting the debris hung from wires in the gallery (it became a favourite at London's Tate Modern). Parker's installation concerned cosmological themes of opposites, inhaling and exhaling, centripetal and centrifugal motion.

PETER HUTCHINSON was born in England (in 1930), but spent most of his artistic career in the U.S.A. (based in Massachusetts). He collaborated with Dennis Oppenheim on a series of underwater works: fruit, vegetables and bread were packed in plastic bags and suspended from a fishing line in the West Indies (1969). Hutchinson also planted flowers in the sand underwater, and made a dam from sand bags in Tobago (*Underwater Dam*, 1969). Along the rim of a volcano (Paricutin, 1970), Hutchinson sited a 76 yard line of white bread wrapped in plastic. Hutchinson recorded the growth of mould and decomposition. Later works include *Ice Sandwich* (1994), a Brancusi-like tower of slabs of wood interlaced with blocks of ice, and 'thrown ropes' of flowers planted in the ground in the shape of a rope that Hutchinson threw (1996). Hutchinson preferred works that combined his love of horticulture, science, art and botany.[3]

NICHOLAS POPE (b. 1949) is a British artist whose works recall Barbara Hepworth's and Stephen Cox's sculptures – in particular Pope's outdoor works, such as *The Arch* (1985). Made from oak, the arch is large (18 feet long). It is the arch itself that fascinates Pope, as with Andy Goldsworthy, the arch being such an elegant structure (ancient Roman architecture, such as the Pont du Gard or Colosseum, is a good example). Pope's *Arch* was dovetailed and pegged together, made from two young trees and one mature tree. Pope was consciously trying to make a work with oak, not just with any wood. 'I wanted to make an oak-wood arch not an arch made from wood.'[4]

Like Carl Andre, Nicholas Pope has placed large stones in an urban environment. Pope's *Three Wilderness Stones* (1980, Southampton) and *Five Amorphous Shapes* are huge boulders of Forest of Dean stone in human-made environments. Pope's stones spread out across parkland or the forecourts of modern business complexes, bringing the individual, irregular forms of nature into the angular, linear environment of the city.

Like Barbara Hepworth and Constantin Brancusi, Nicholas Pope was fascinated by stones. Hepworth loved the white granite rounded stones of of the tableland of West Penwith, and scattered them around her studio in St Ives. It's easy to see how some of Hepworth's sculptures took some of their inspiration from the beautiful granite boulders of Cornwall. David Nash made a large wooden boulder, while Anthony Gormley emulated a large granite glacial boulder in 1981. Each of Gormley's *Two Stones* is nine feet high, one made of granite, the other of bronze. Set beside an artificial lake in Kent, the 'natural' granite stone was already contextualized as a work of art by its placement in such a setting, just as Carl Andre's boulders on the city street are made into art by their context (ditto with Andre's infamous bricks). One of Andy Goldsworthy's most important commissions consisted of granite boulders (*Garden of Stones*, in Gotham).

Another British sculpture venture, the New Milestones Project in Dorset, set up by Common Ground (which Andy Goldsworthy contributed towards), turned up some accomplished works. For instance, Simon Thomas's *Seed Forms* (1988), oak shapes placed on the Dorsetshire downs; or Peter Randall-Page's *Wayside Carving* (1988), a large spiralling cone in blue Purbeck marble, a response to Dorset's richness in fossils. Nigel Lloyd's *Red Deer Wallow* (1983, Grizedale) was a Goldsworthyan horseshoe-shaped stone wall enclosure. Keir Smith's works at Grizedale included *The Realm of Taurus*, linking the constellations of stars with animals in enclosures. Gabriel Orozco also worked like Goldsworthy with snowballs – in *Planets of the Volcano* (1992) he placed small snowballs on top of some posts near Popocatepetl volcano.

Anish Kapoor's *Void Field* (1990) had a Goldsworthyan flavour: each of twenty large pieces of sandstone had small holes bored in the top, which were painted black inside. Chris Jenning's *Vault* (1992) reacted to the Museum of Installation's space by filling it with curving metal rods which connected the walls and floor together. The thin rods curving through space recalling Goldsworthy's wall drawings. Bill Viola brought a whole tree into the Newport Harbor Art Museum in California for his *Theatre of Memory* (1985), the branches were hung with bells blown by electric fans. The tinkling tree faced a giant video image of hissing static.

Recalling Wolfgang Laib's pollen floor-pieces, Shelagh Wakely covered the marble floor of the British School at Rome with a layer of tumeric spice (*Curcuma sul Travertino*, 1991). Anthony Gormley covered the entire area of a gallery floor in his *Field* installation (1991) with over 35,000 small humanoid figures. Giovanni Anselmo used stone like painted canvases, mounting thin slabs of granite on a Paris gallery wall like paintings (*Meeting of Two Works*, 1990).

Some installation artists used liquid to cover the floor area: in Glen Onwin's alchemical installations in Halifax (1991), water, wax and black brine were poured into a large concrete pool. Richard Wilson's *20/ 50* (1987) was a steel pool of sump oil with a walkway in the middle of it. Per Barclay also used pools of oil: in *Old Boathouse* (1990) an oil pool was set in a Norwegian boat-house beside the sea; in *The Jaguar's Cage* (1991), made at Turin Zoo, a large oil pool was set behind bars. Rasheed Araeen spoofed Richard Long's art in his 1988 London installation: a Longian floor circle was made with empty wine bottles, and a Long-like row was made with bones. Eve Laramee spread a rectangular mound of cobalt glass on the gallery floor in her *Requiem For a Blue Fluid* (1991).

SJOERD BUISMAN (b. 1948) constructed a floating mound of willow sticks on a wooden frame in the moat of the Old Castle at Jeemstede (Netherlands, 1995-98). In 1975 Buisman knotted a willow tree stem which the tree absorbed into itself as it grew (*Knotted Willow Branch*). In 1991 Buisman constructed an 'arch' of lime trees (at Haarlemmerhout, Netherlands, where Andy Goldsworthy has worked), which formed a low curve along a road (a work with affinities with a long-running proposal of

Goldsworthy's for a series of trees on mounds beside a road). Using petals and berries, some of NILS UDO's sculptures are uncannily like Goldsworthy's use of the same materials. Udo has, for instance, pressed berries into the bark of an old tree, just as Goldsworthy has done with leaves and sand.

NIKOLAJ RECKE (b. 1969) planted a field of clover in a gallery (1999) covering the whole floor in a carpet of green plants. Although the result recalled land art gestures such as Walter de Maria's *Earth Room* or Andy Goldsworthy's *Stone Sky*, the aim, according to Recke, was to explore the folklore of four-leaf clovers. Other pieces with a Goldsworthyan flavour included Giuseppe Penone's *To Breathe Shade* (1997-99), a human shape made from bronze bay leaves installed in five bay trees, and his *Skins of Leaves* (2000), a 'skin' of bronze leaves in humanoid form.

Illustrations

Works by Andy Goldsworthy • some of the forms in Goldsworthy's art • some of Goldsworthy's contemporaries, • and some of Goldsworthy's influences.

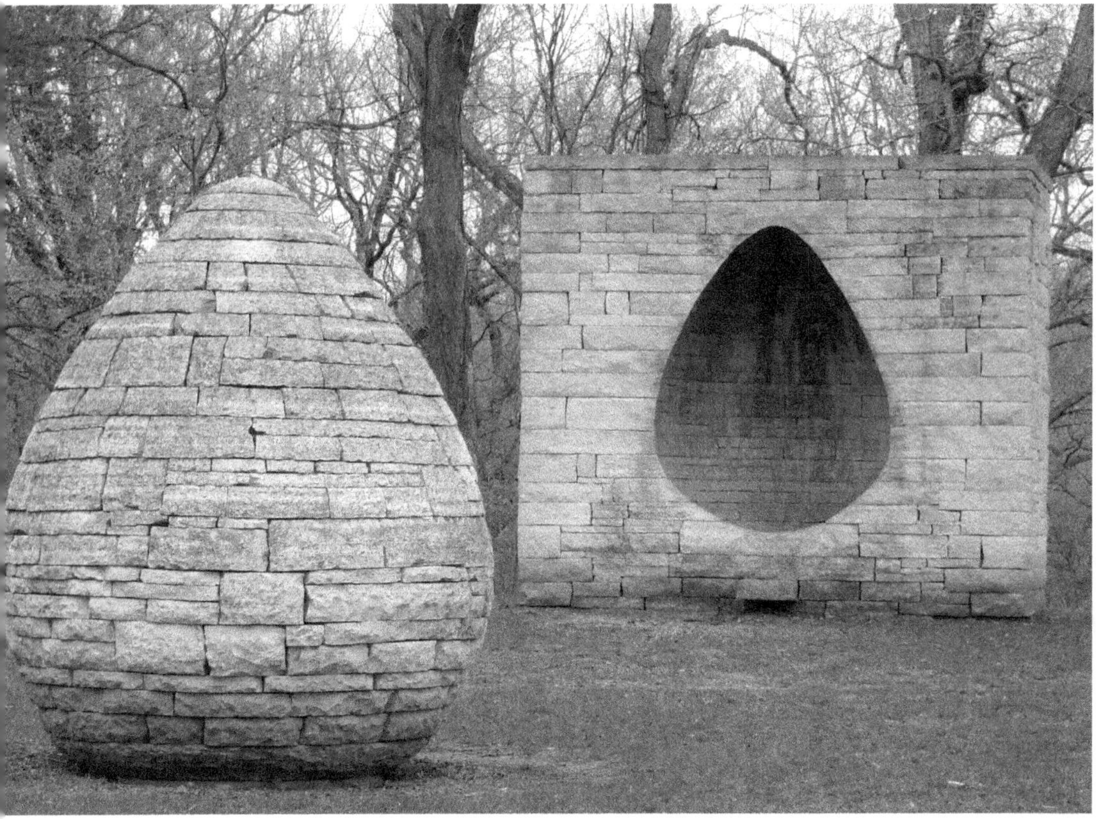

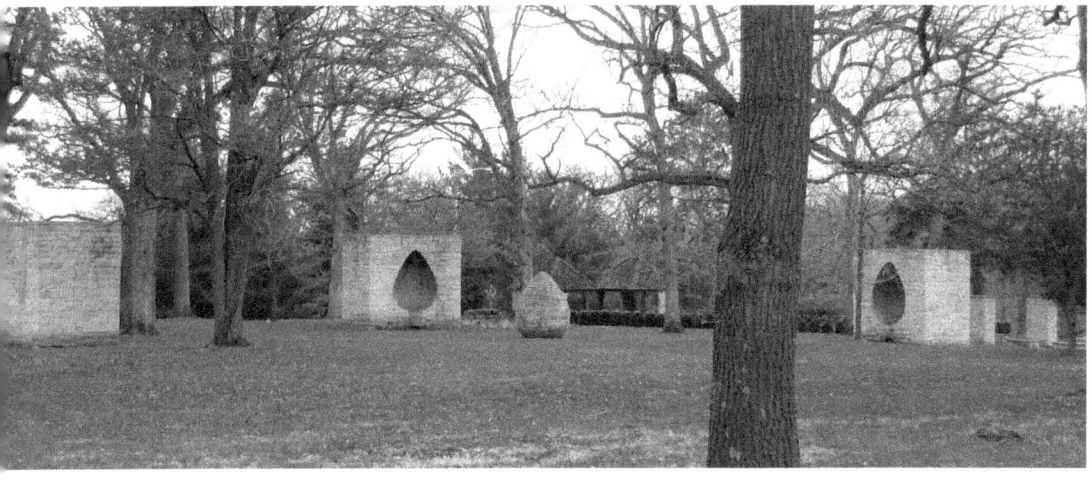

Andy Goldsworthy, Three Cairns, 2002, Des Moines, Iowa
(this page and over. Photos: author)

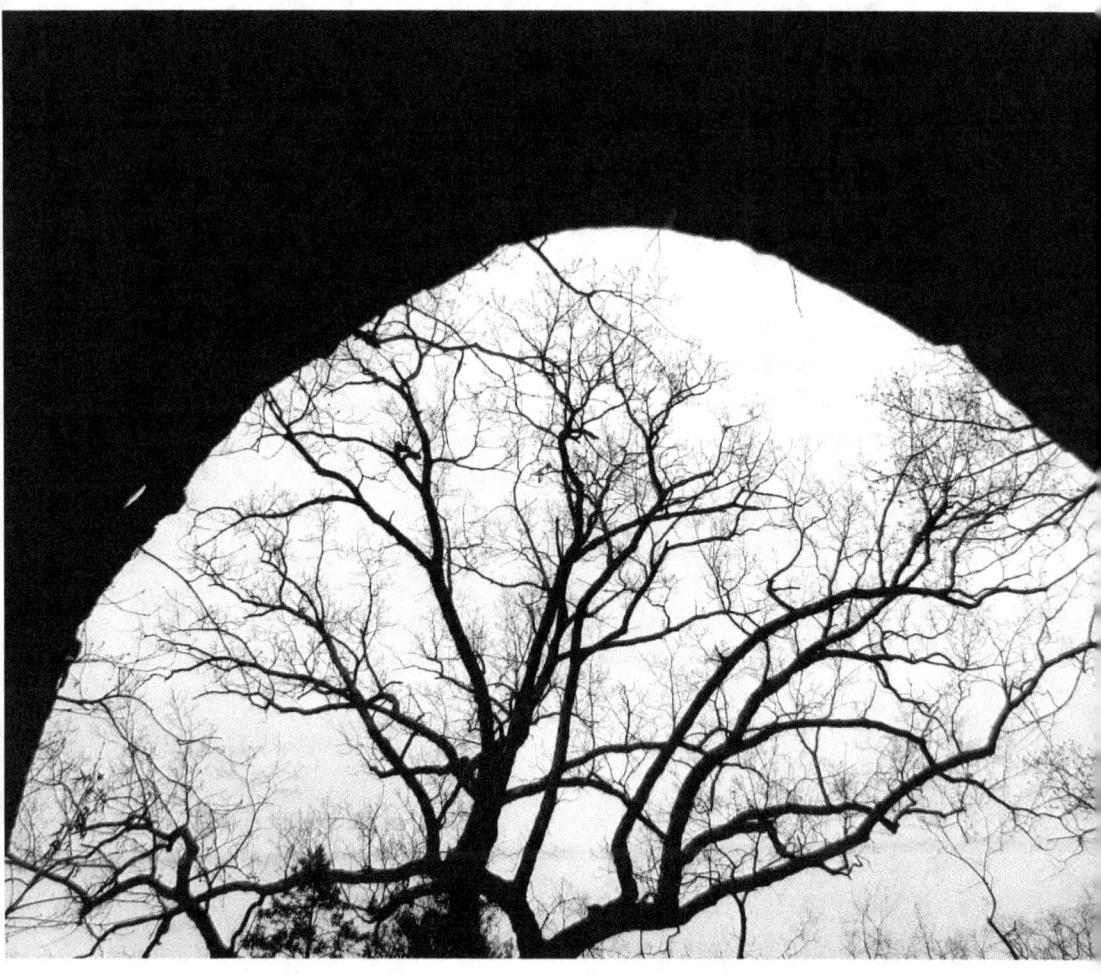

Three Cairns (2000-02) was an important large-scale commission to construct three cairns in the United States of America: one on the West Coast (in California), one on the East Coast (in New York state), and one in the Mid-West (at Des Moines, Iowa). Three Cairns was a collaboration with three cultural institutions: Des Moines Art Center, Neuberger Museum of Art, Purchase, New York, and La Jolla Museum in San Diego. In the event, Andy Goldsworthy built six cairns: apart from the three permanent pieces, there were three ephemeral sculptures: two were tidal, on the East and West coasts, and the third, in Iowa, was built on the prairie, which was set alight (with fire replacing water as the natural force which engulfed the sculpture. However, the stone cairn survived the fire).

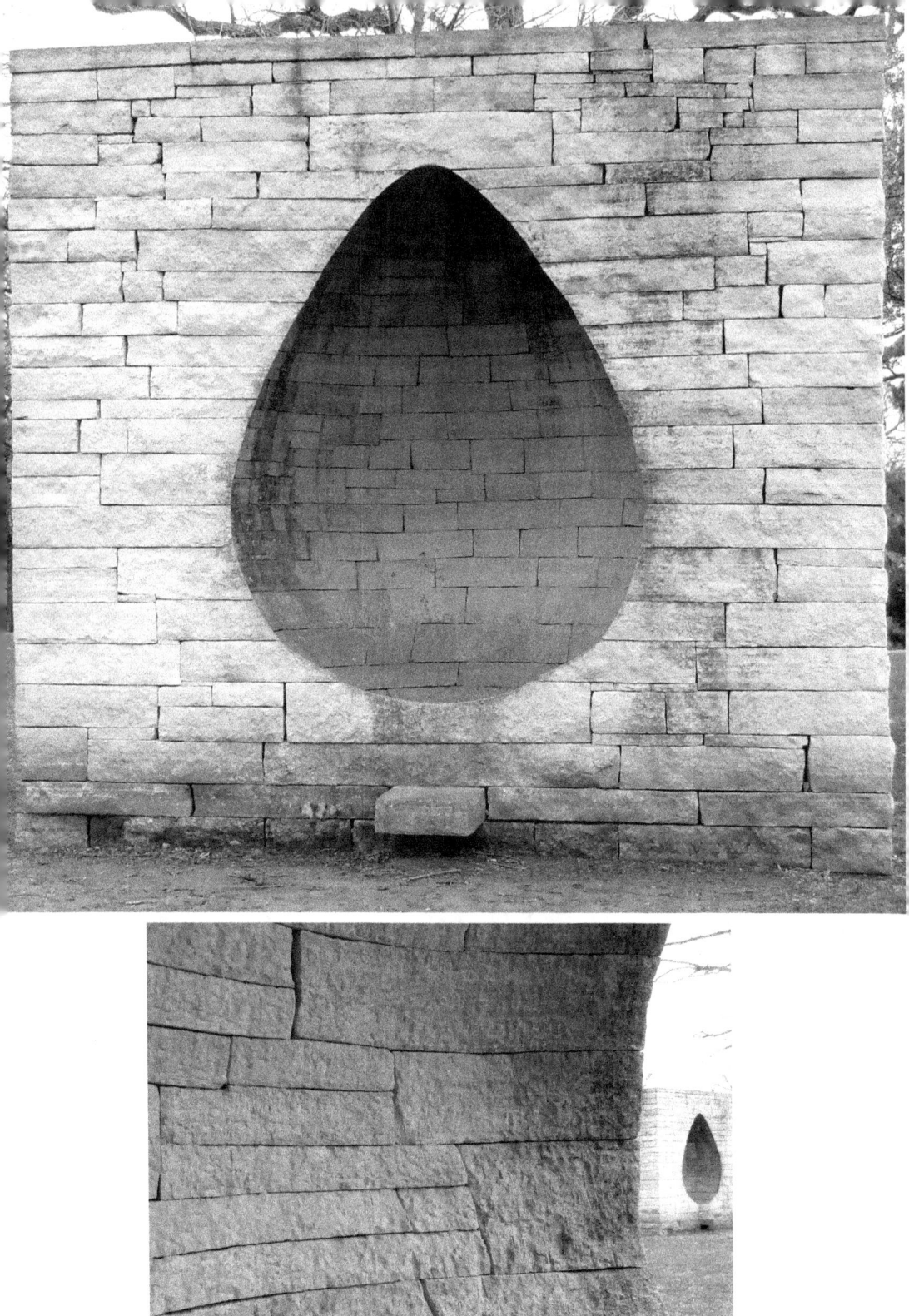

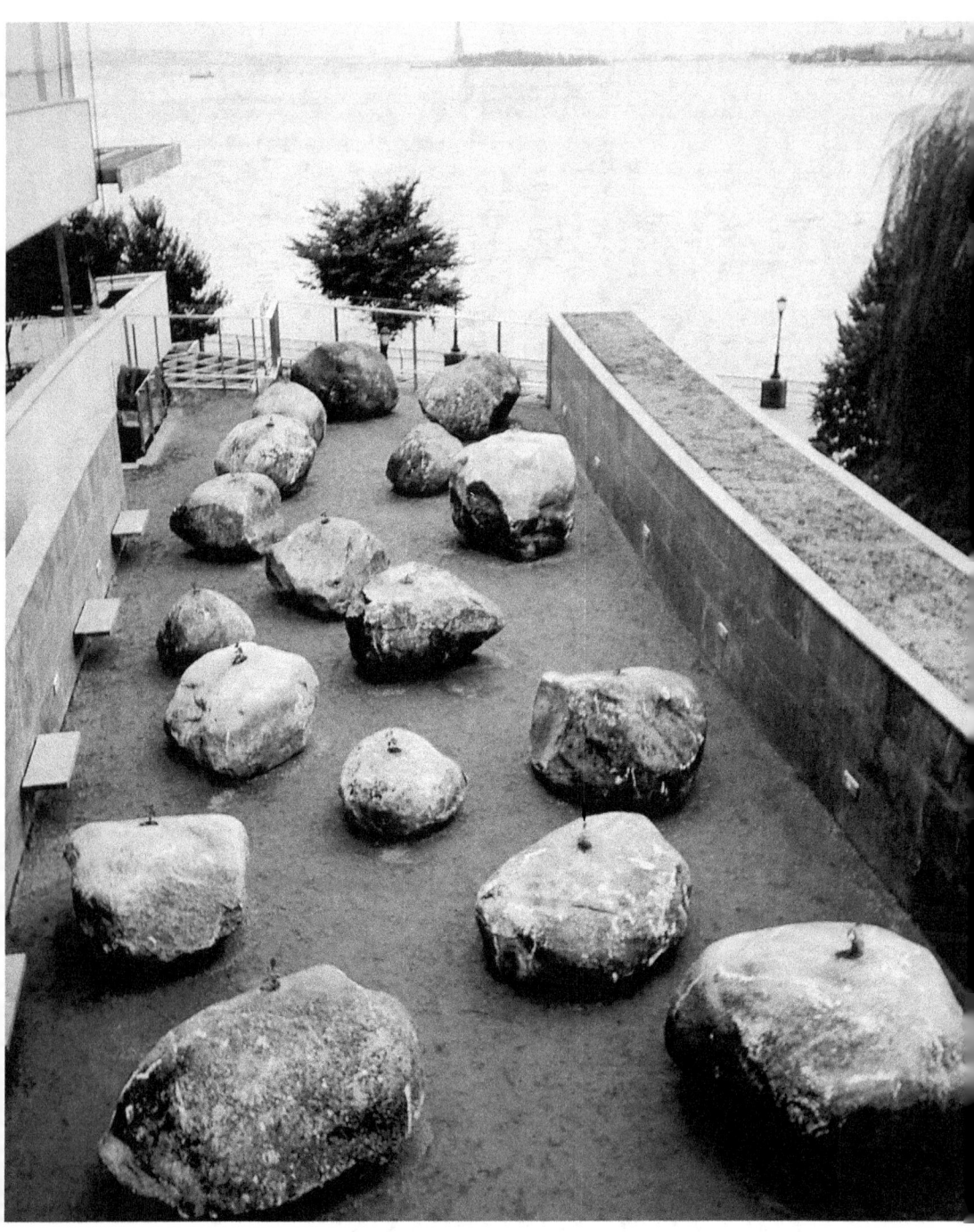

Andy Goldsworthy, Garden of Stones, New York City, 2003
(this page and over. Photos: author)

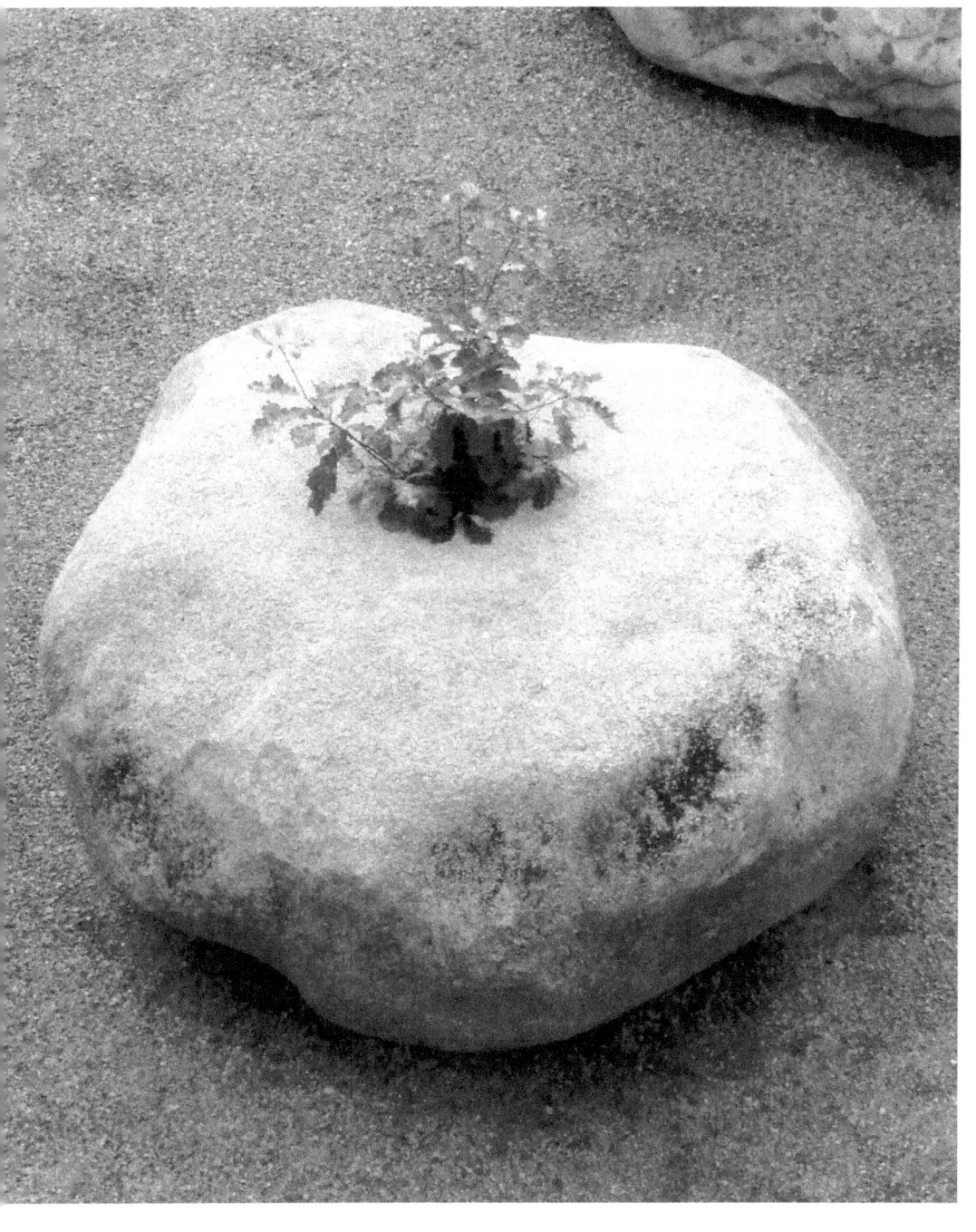

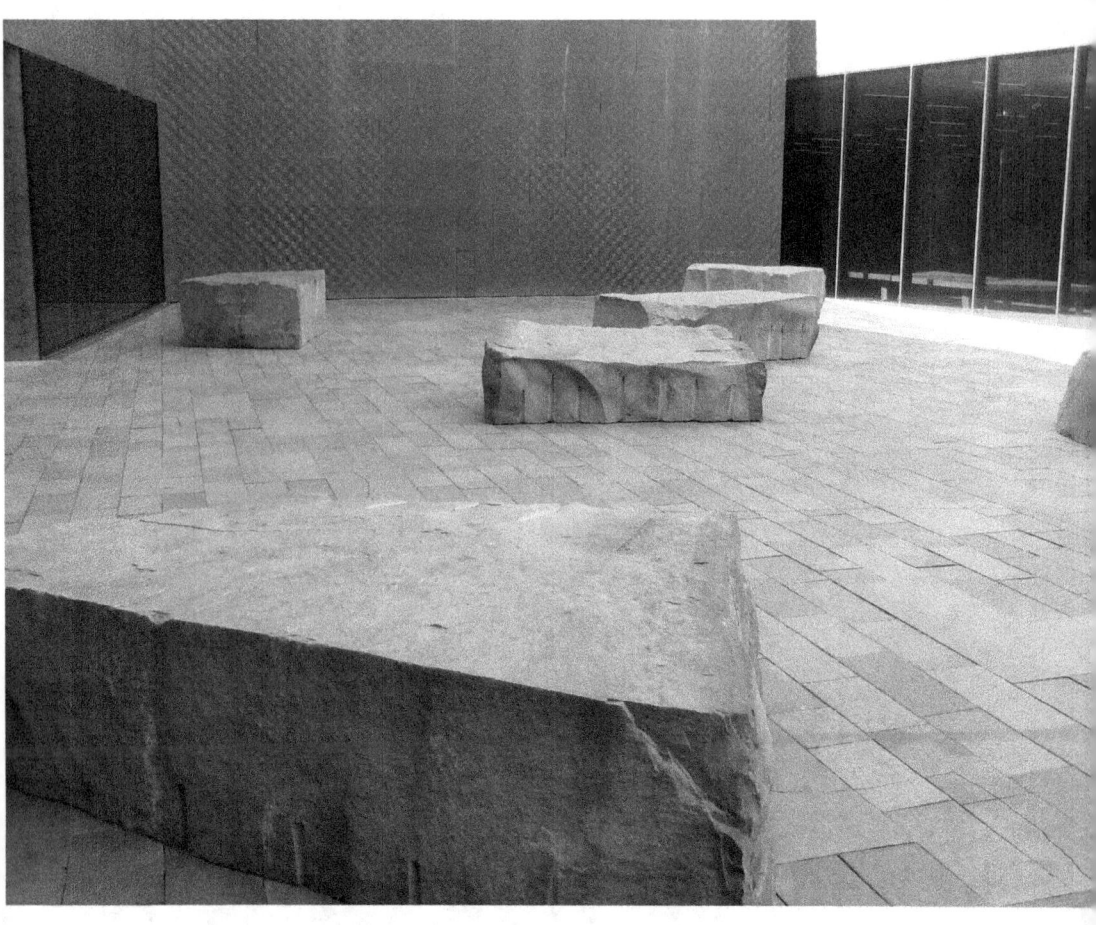

Andy Goldsworthy, Drawn Stone, 2005, San Francisco
(this page and over. Photos: author)

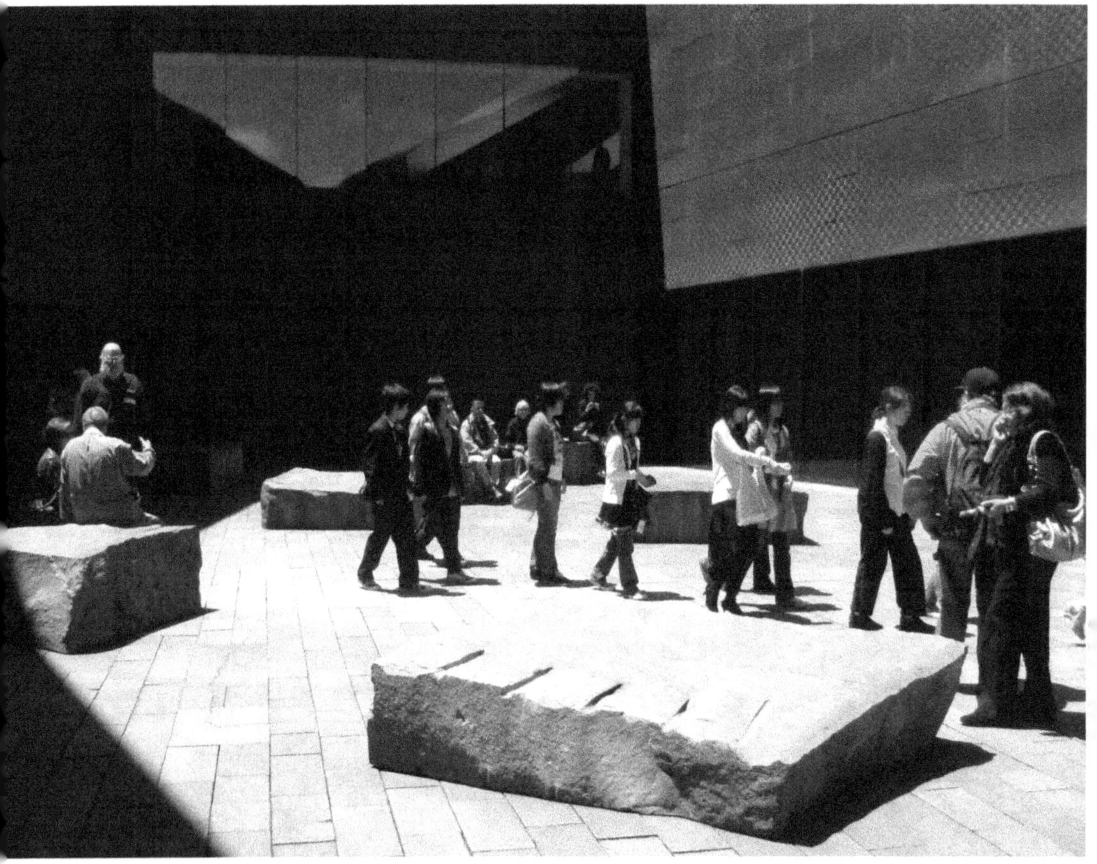

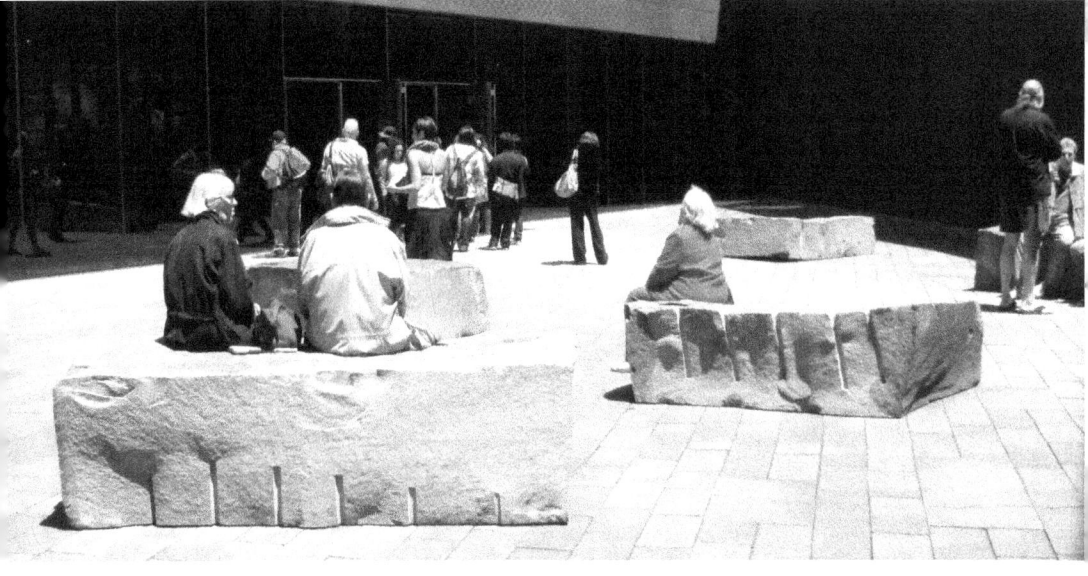

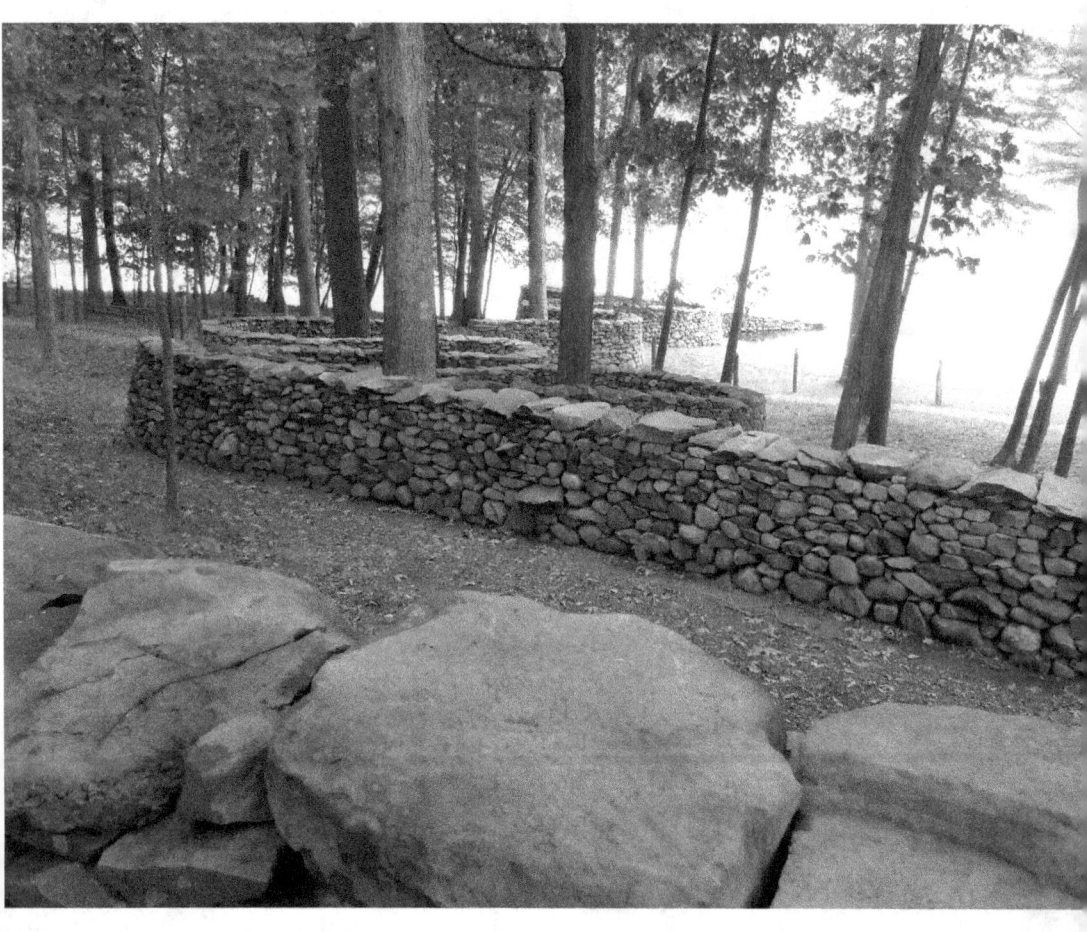

Andy Goldsworthy, Storm King Wall, 1998, New York State
(this page and over. Photos: author)

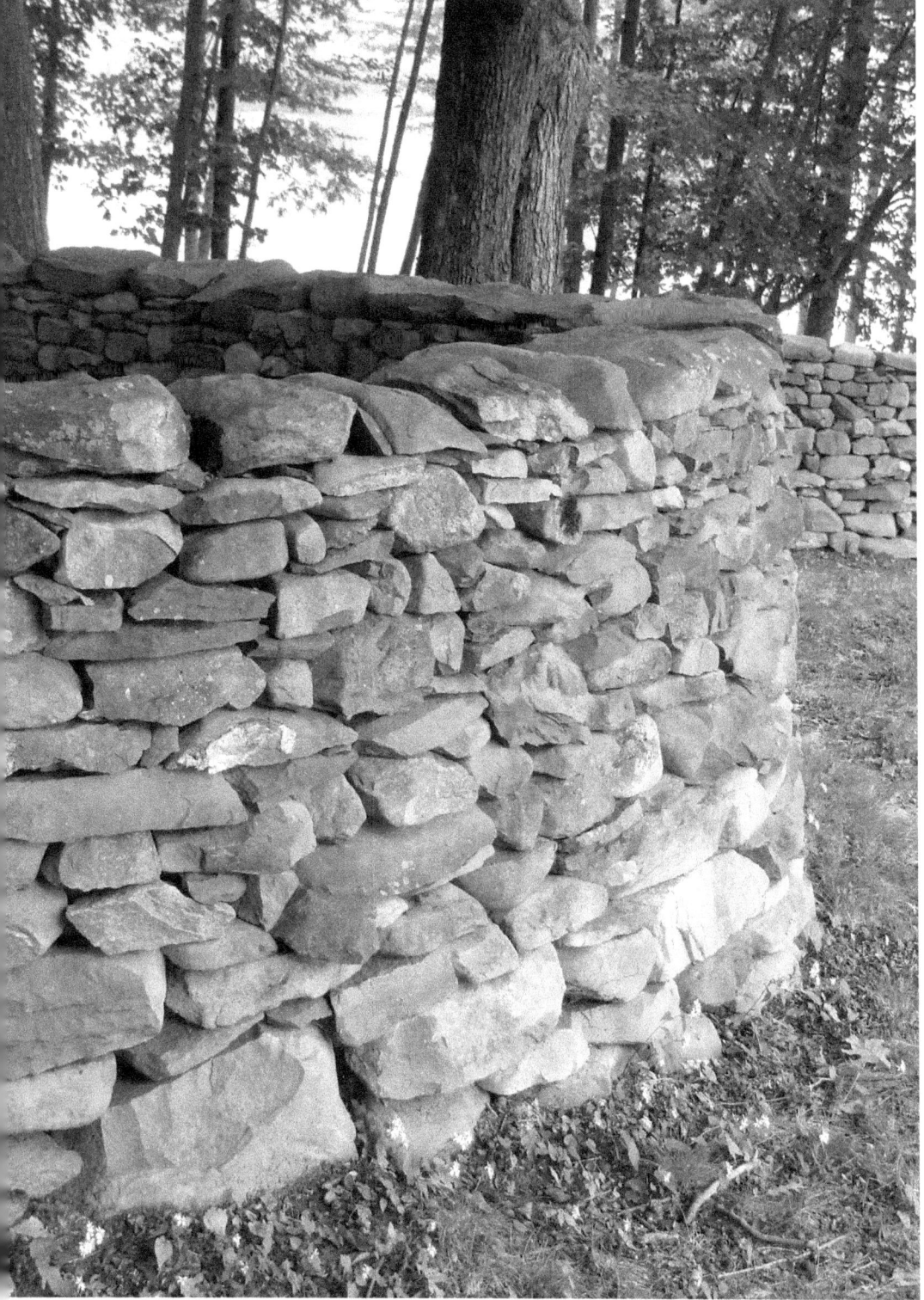

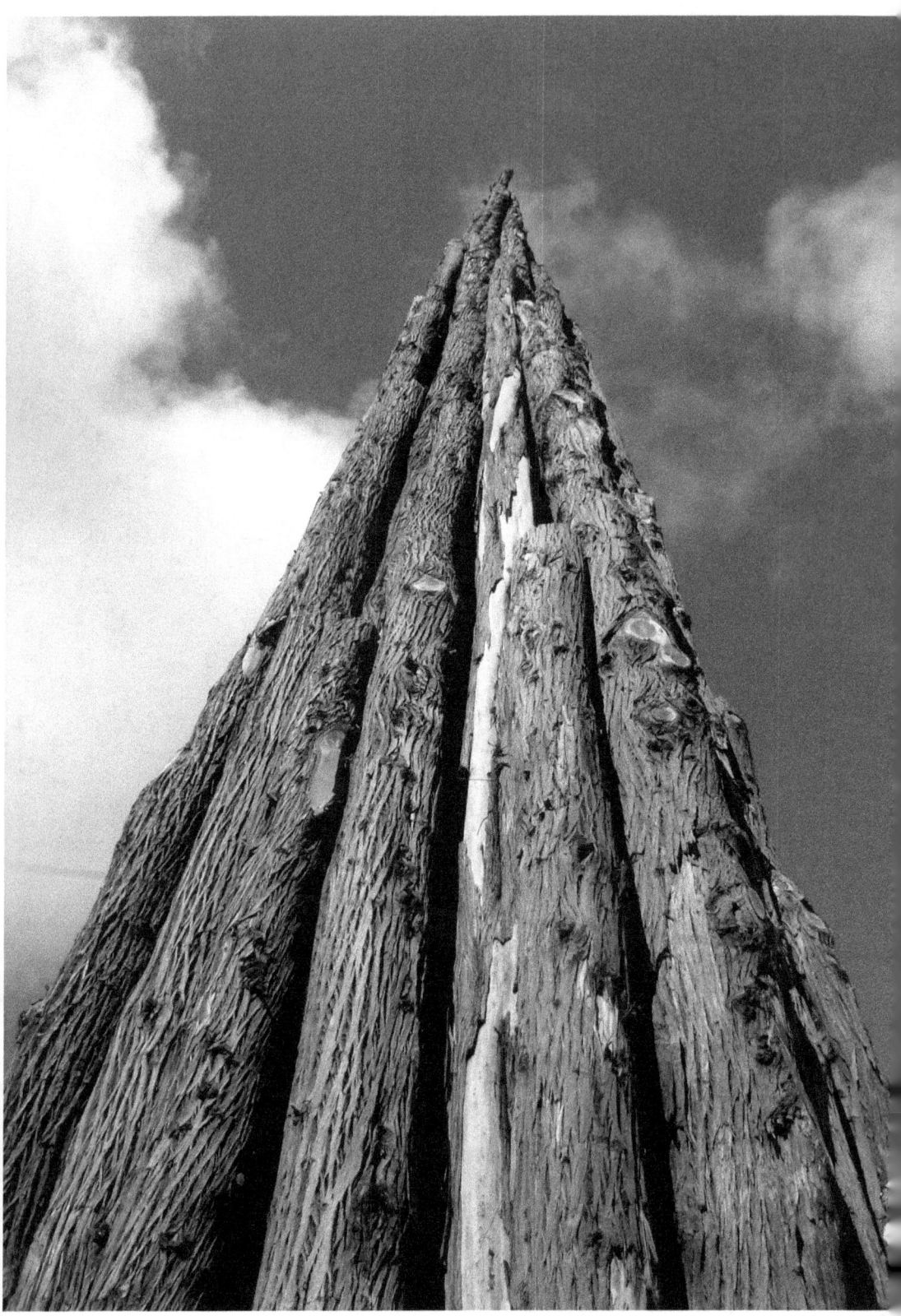

Andy Goldsworthy, Spire, 2008, San Francisco
(this page and over. Photos: author)

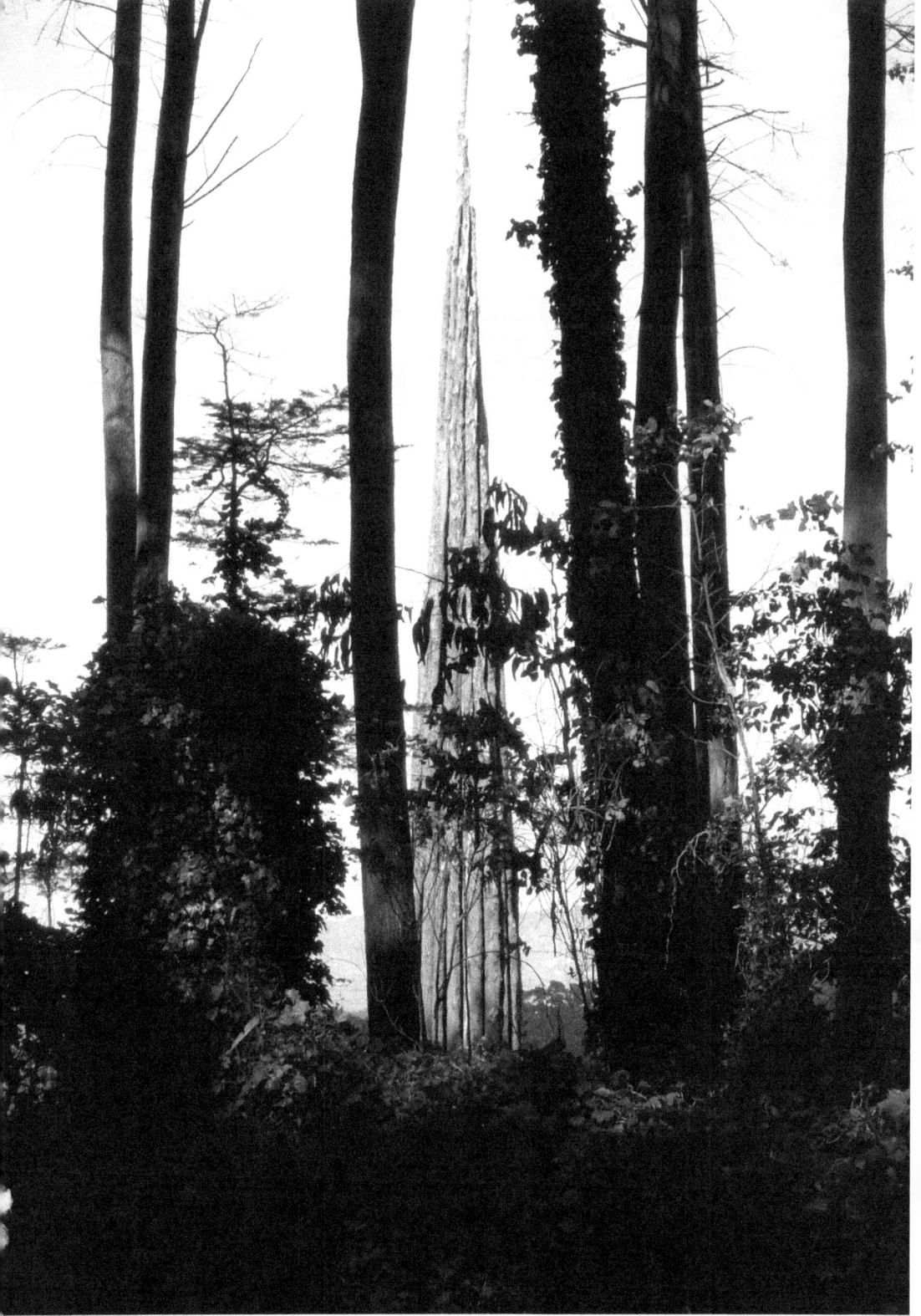

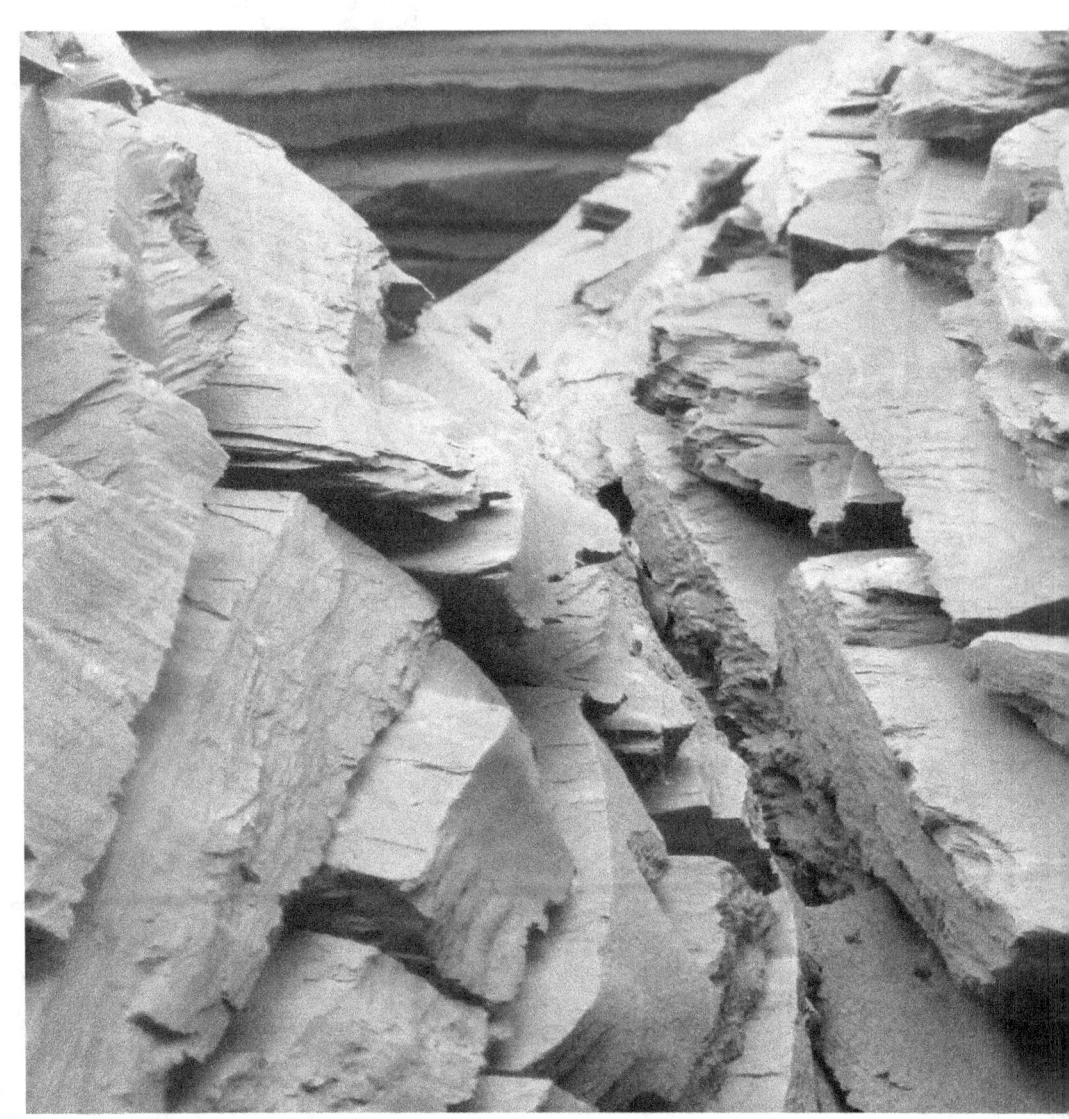

Andy Goldsworthy, Roof, 2005, Washington, DC
(this page and over. Photos: author)

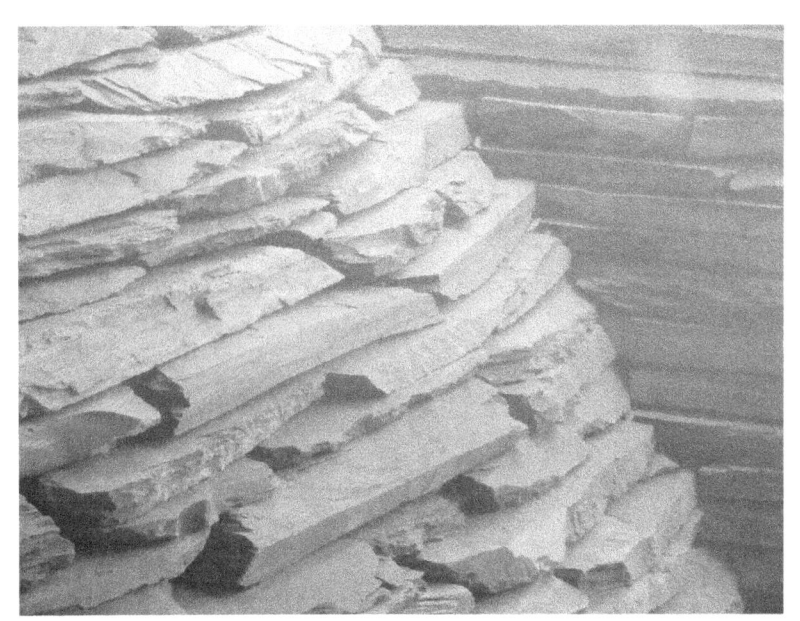

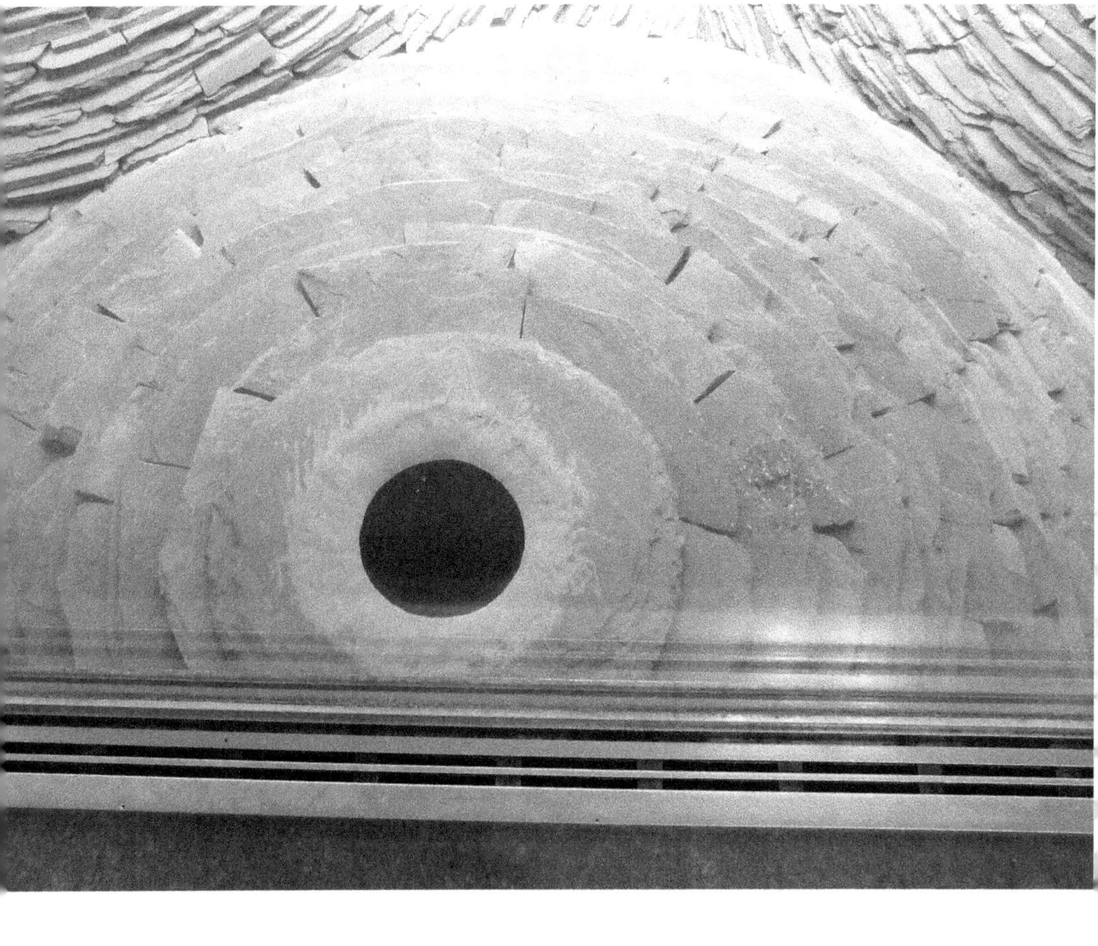

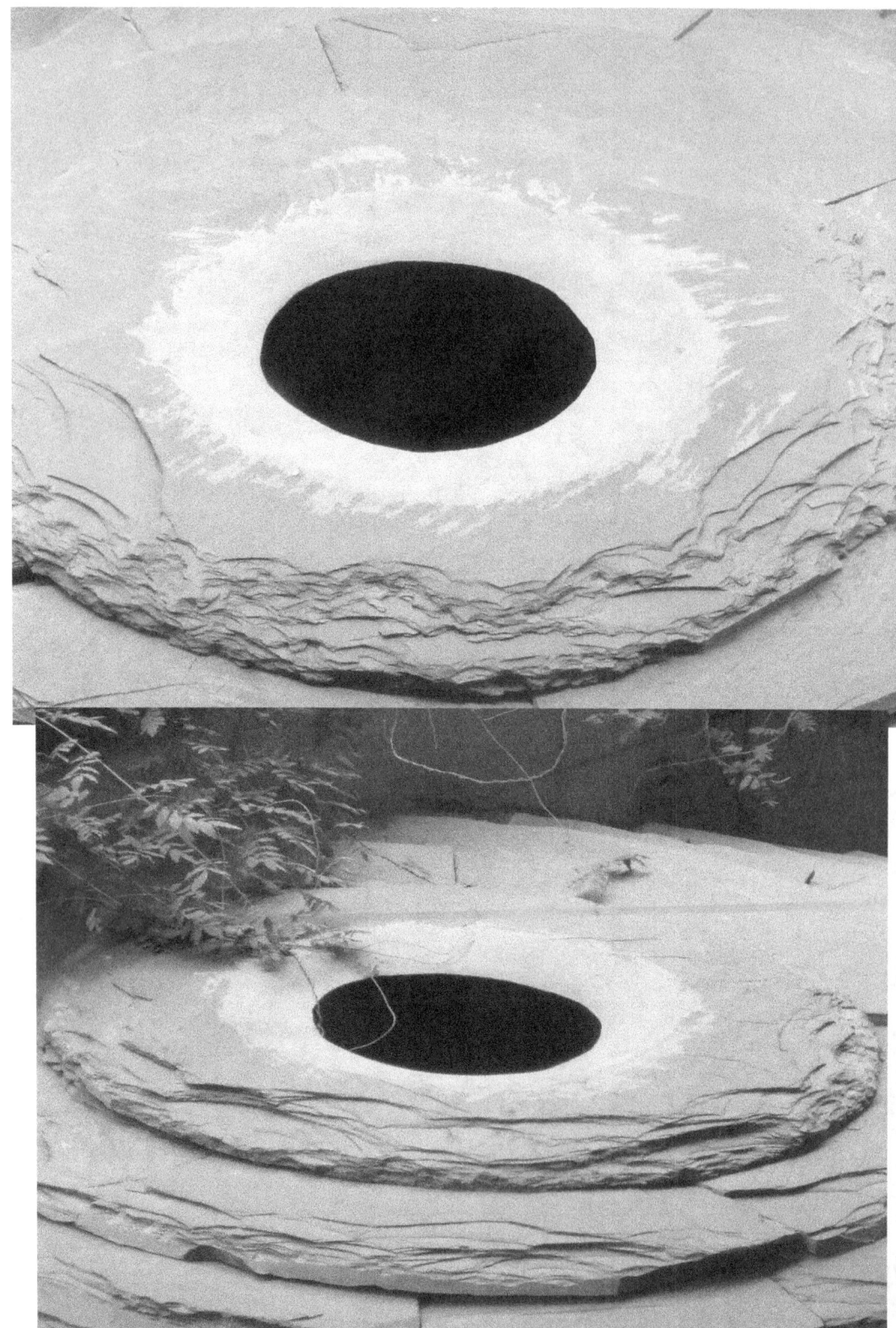

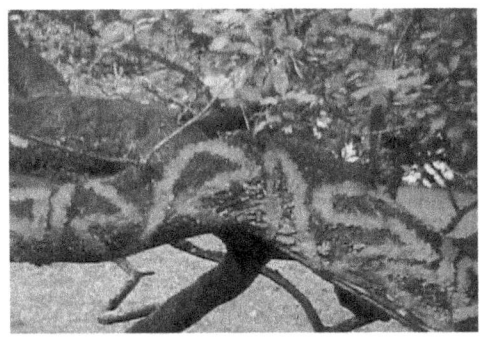

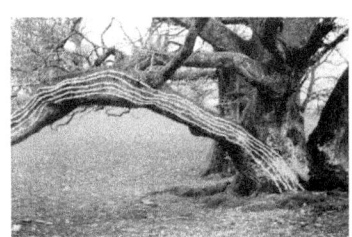

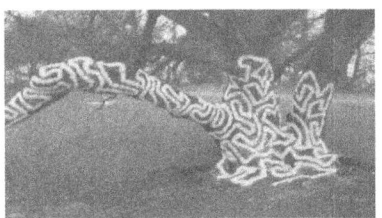

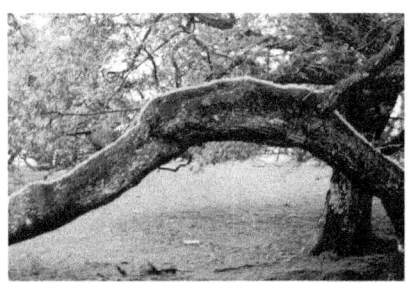

Andy Goldsworthy, from the Capenoch Tree series, 1994-96

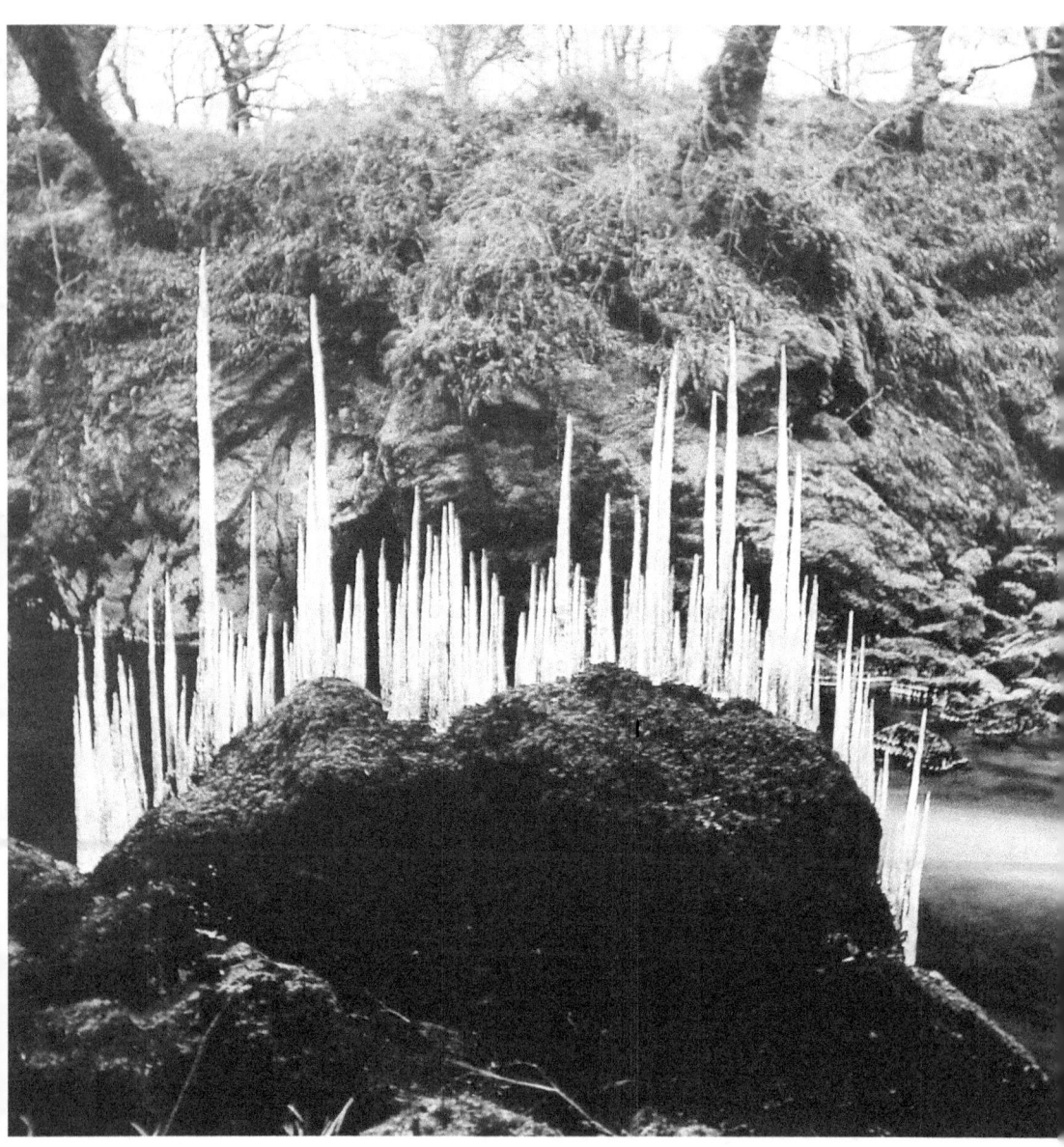

Andy Goldsworthy, Icicles, 2003

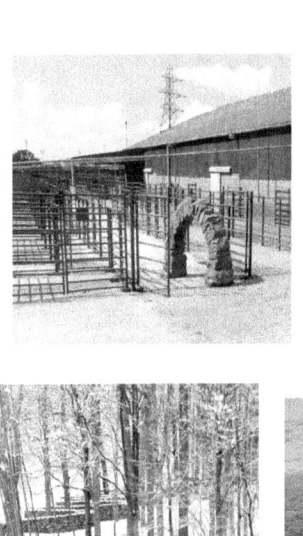
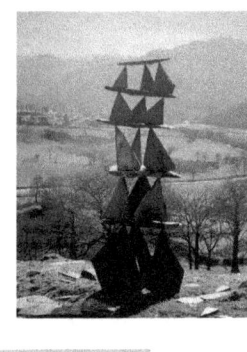
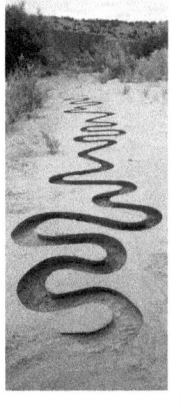
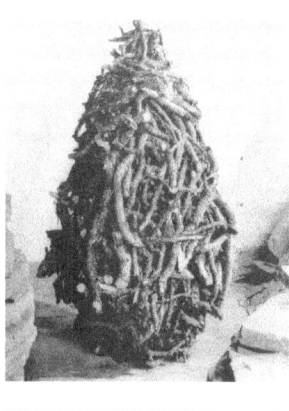
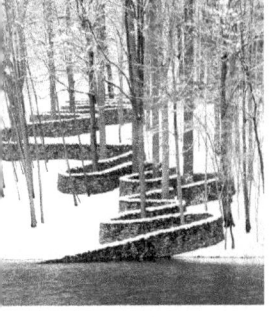
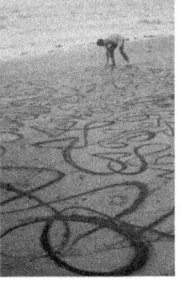
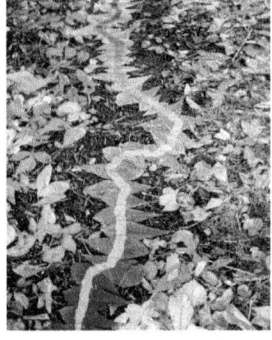
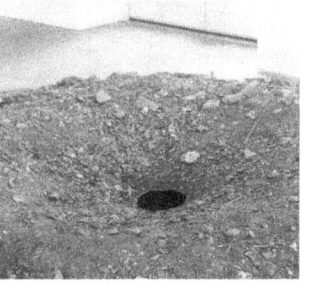
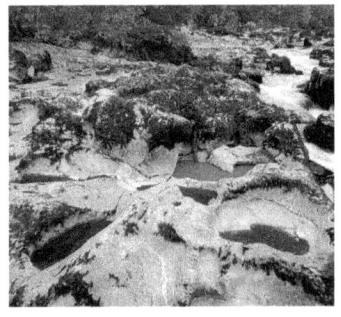
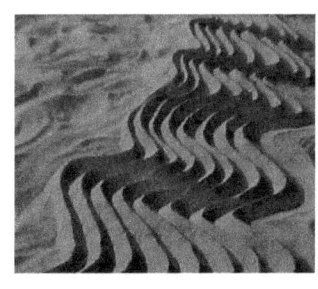
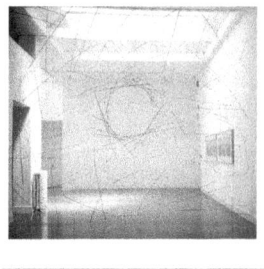
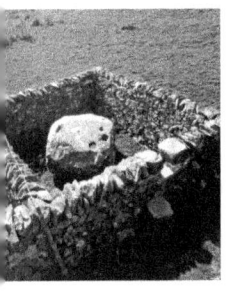
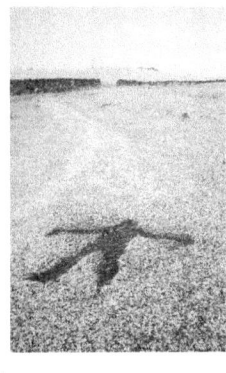
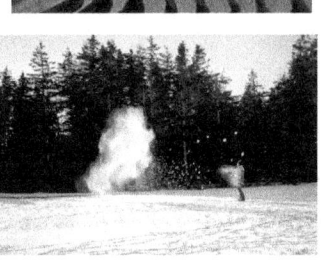
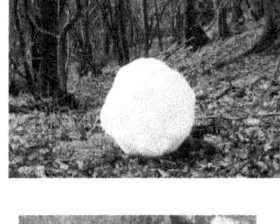
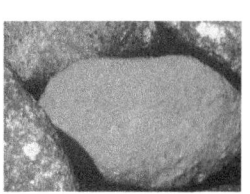
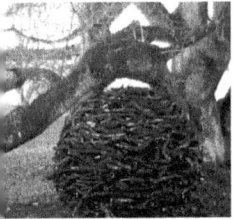

Goldsworthy's forms

The recurring forms in Andy Goldsworthy's include:

Lines. Cairns. Walls. Snowballs. Holes. Cracked lines.
Screens. Sheepfolds. Arches. Shadow prints. Throws.
Leafshields. Globes. Stained pools. Wrapped rocks.
Broken stones. Ridged sand. Sand drawings. Balanced rocks.

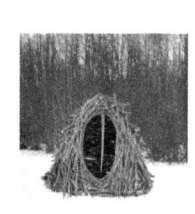

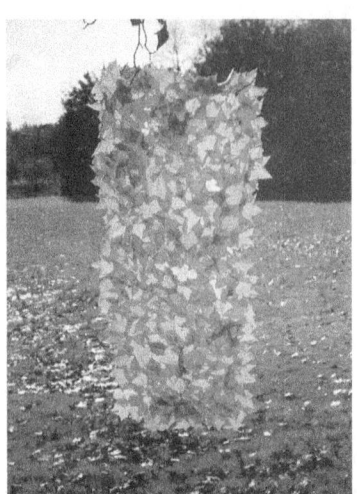

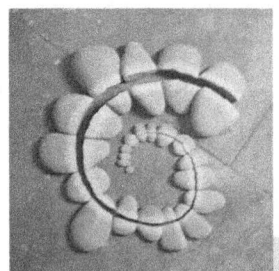

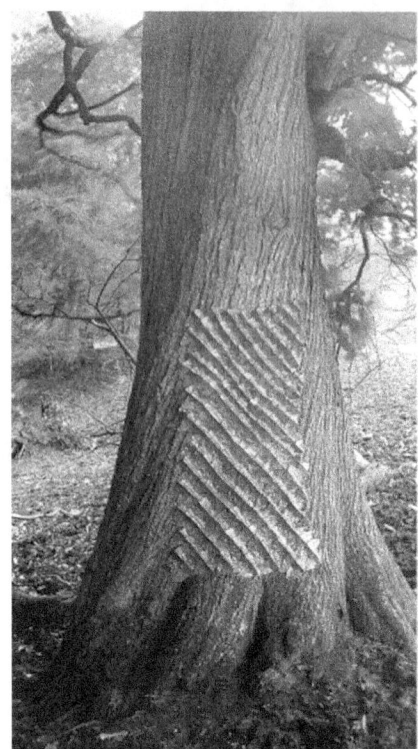

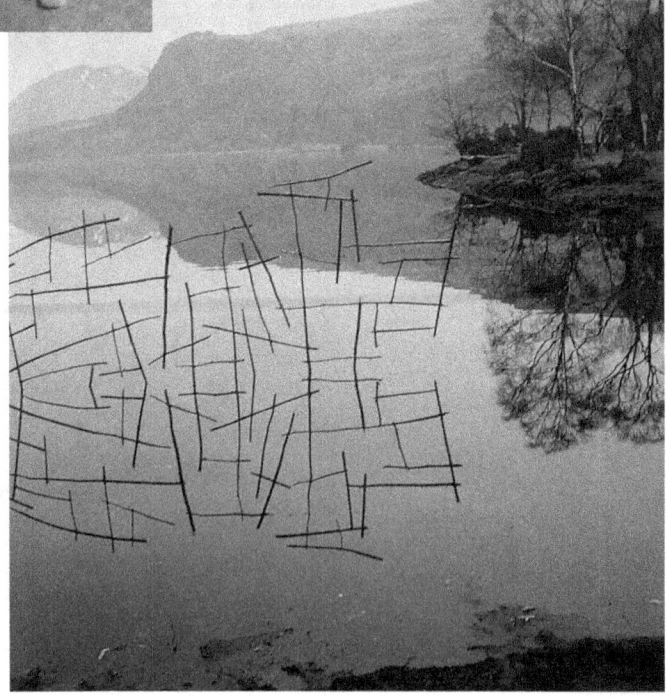

Frontality

Goldsworthy usually employs classic Renaissance space (like most
Western art since the 1300s). He often emphasizes the frontality of his
sculpture, as in the examples above: leaves pressed into the bark
of a tree; a leafshield; sticks in a lake; and broken pebbles.

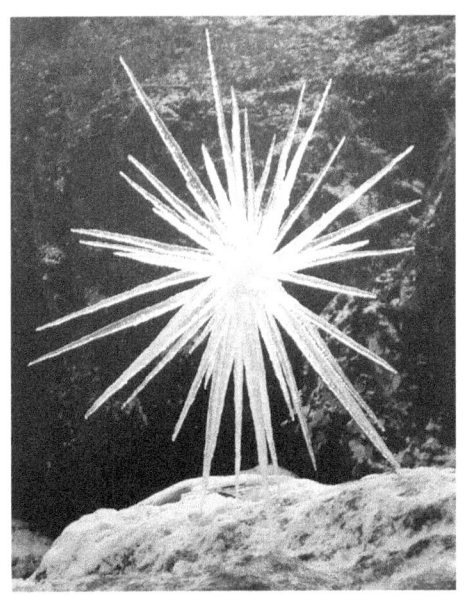
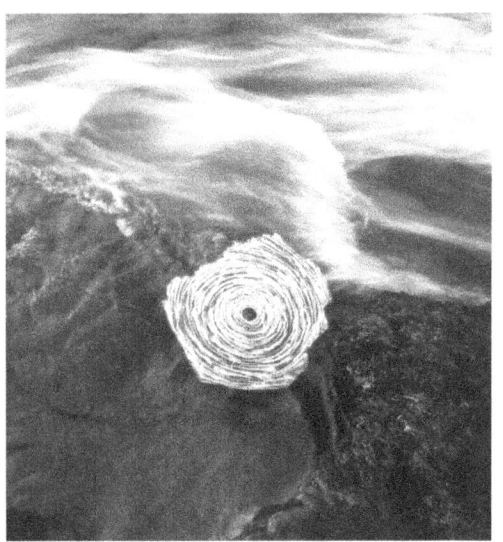

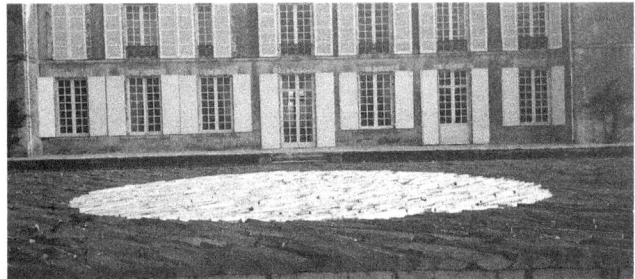

Light, shadow, contrast

Goldsworthy is often working with light as a central element
in his artworks: cloudy, shadowy light is often favoured,
as in the Roof installation; Pool of Light uses the direction
of sunlight; high contrast is deployed in the wool pieces;
and the ice pieces use backlight.

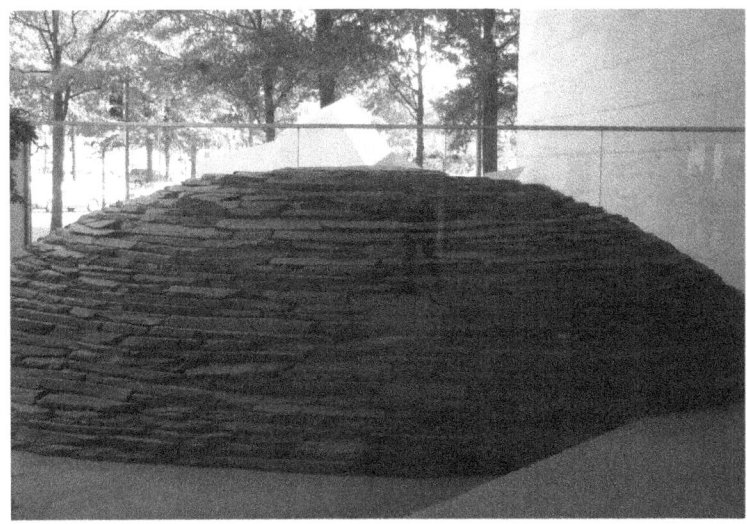

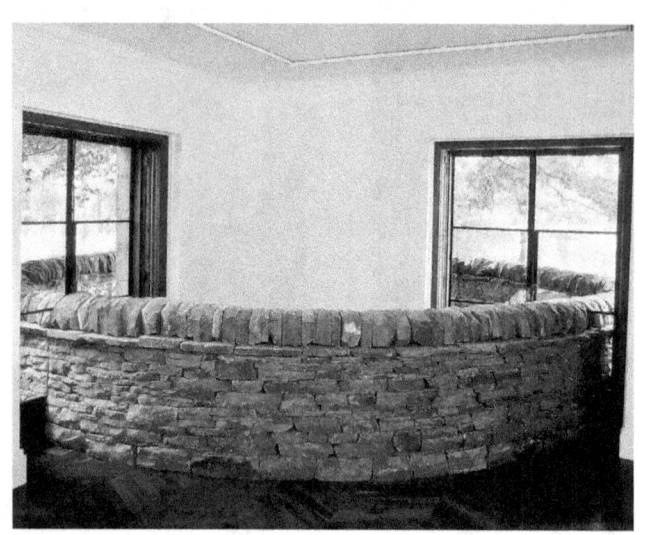

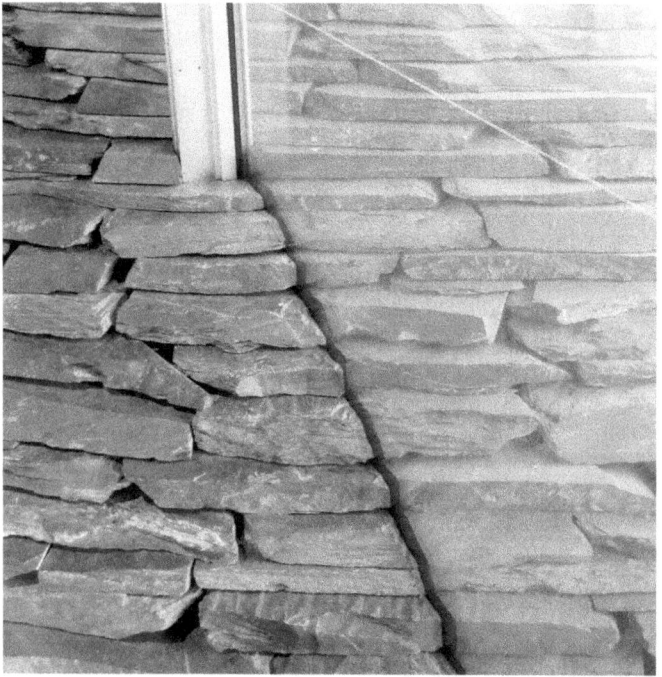

Optical illusions

Goldsworthy likes to play optical tricks from time to time:
for instance, to continue a shape or form through barriers,
as in these examples in New York state (Storm King Fold)
and the National Gallery of Art in Washington (Roof).

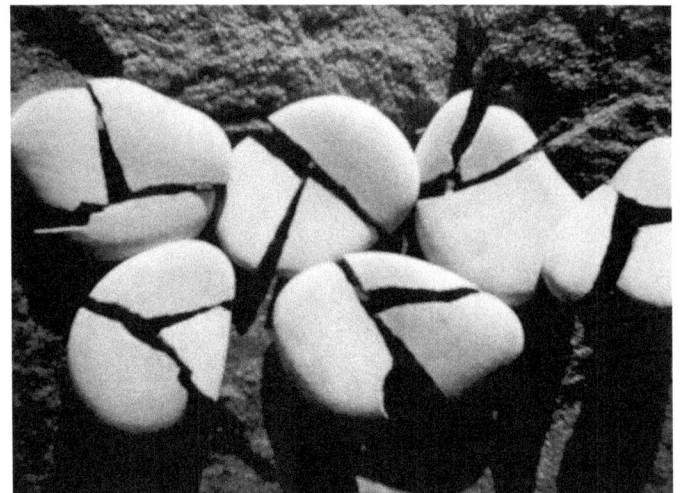

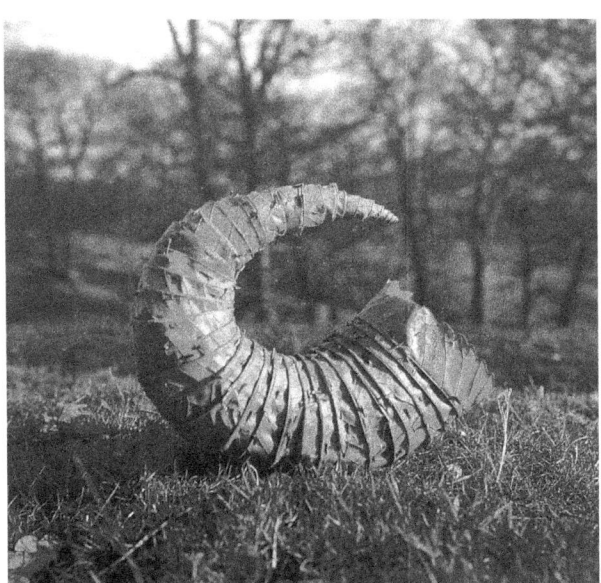

Single material

A large proportion of Goldsworthy's artworks are created from a single material: one type of stone, as in the broken pebbles; a collection of one kind of leaf, as in Autumn Horn; a Clay Wall installation; and a throw of red soil.

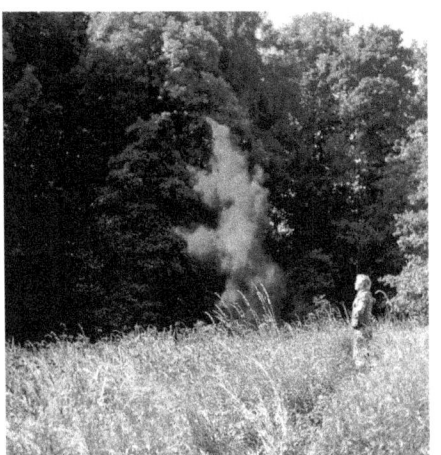

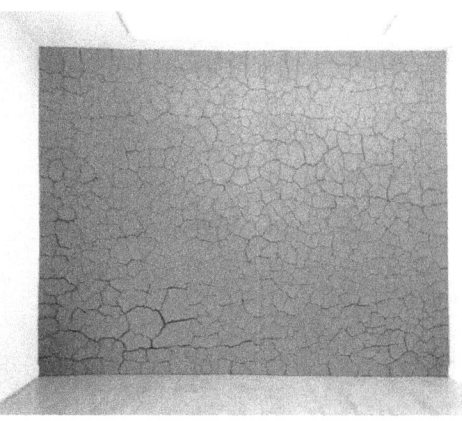

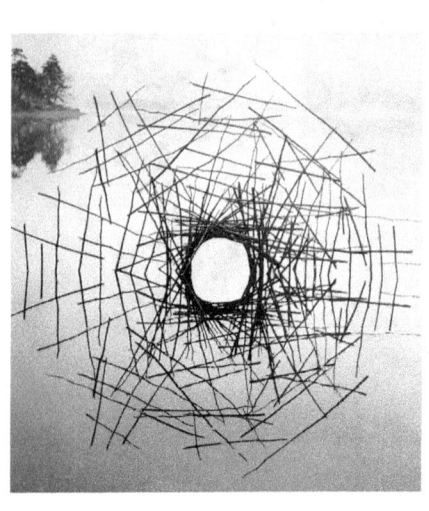

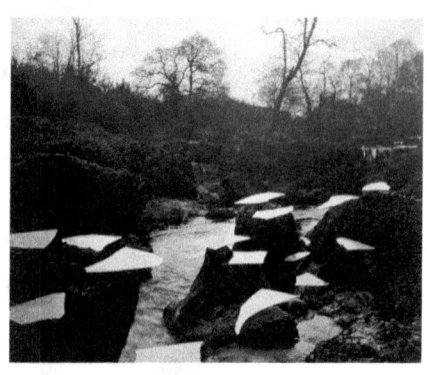

Wilderness setting

Without a doubt a central ingredient in Andy Goldworthy's art is his choice of settings, and primary among these is a wilderness setting, as in these works from Alaska; the Lake District's lakes; and Goldsworthy's homeground of Scaur Water in Scotland.

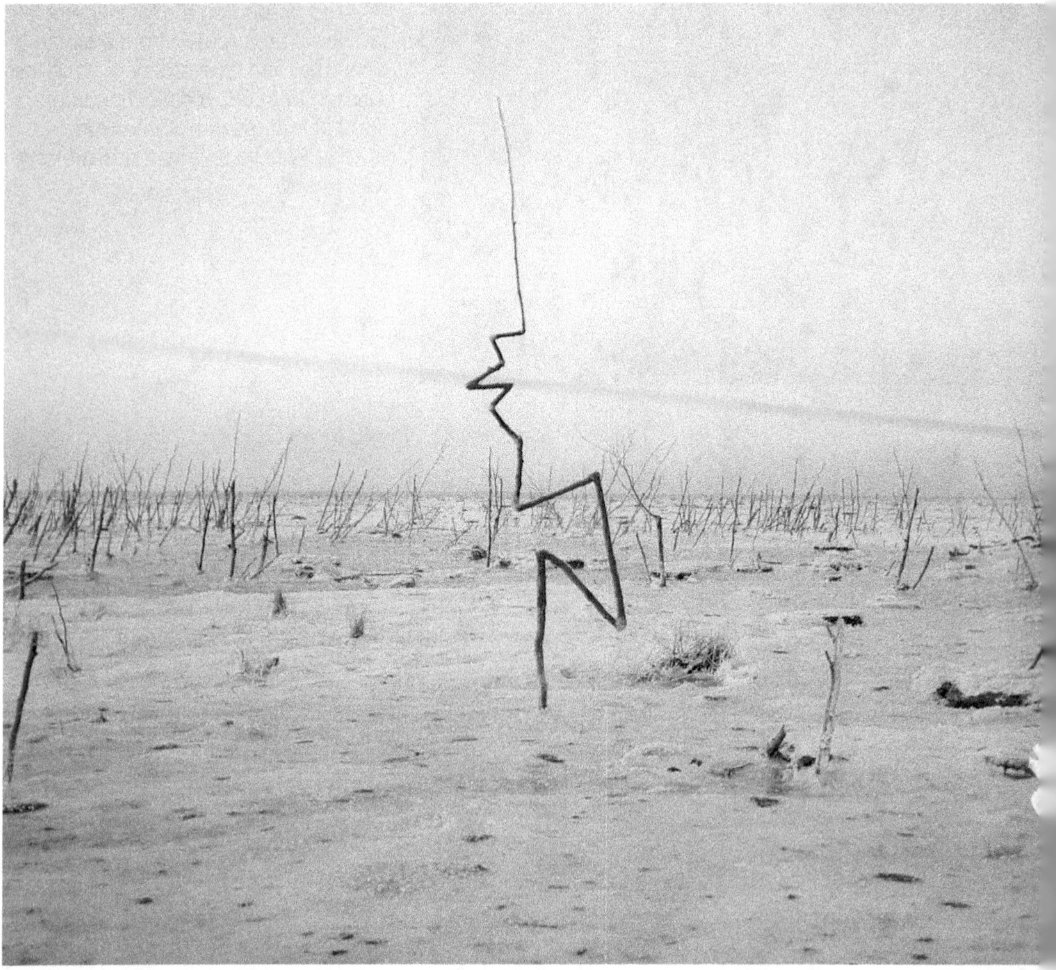

Wrapping

Goldsworthy has made an art of wrapping objects, though not yet on the scale of the king of wrap art, Christo. Goldsworthy has wrapped rocks, trees, branches, and other objects with leaves, wool, sticks, feathers and flower petals.

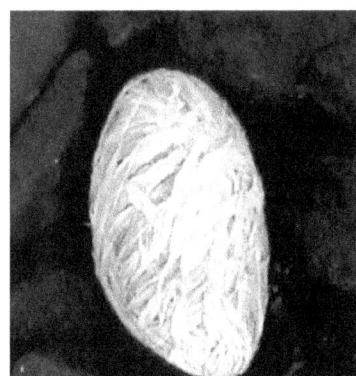

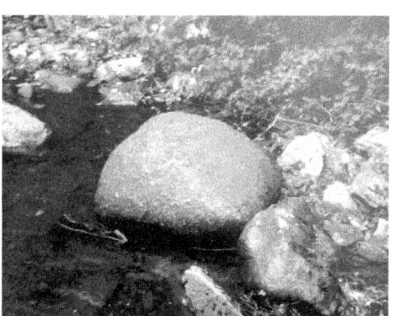

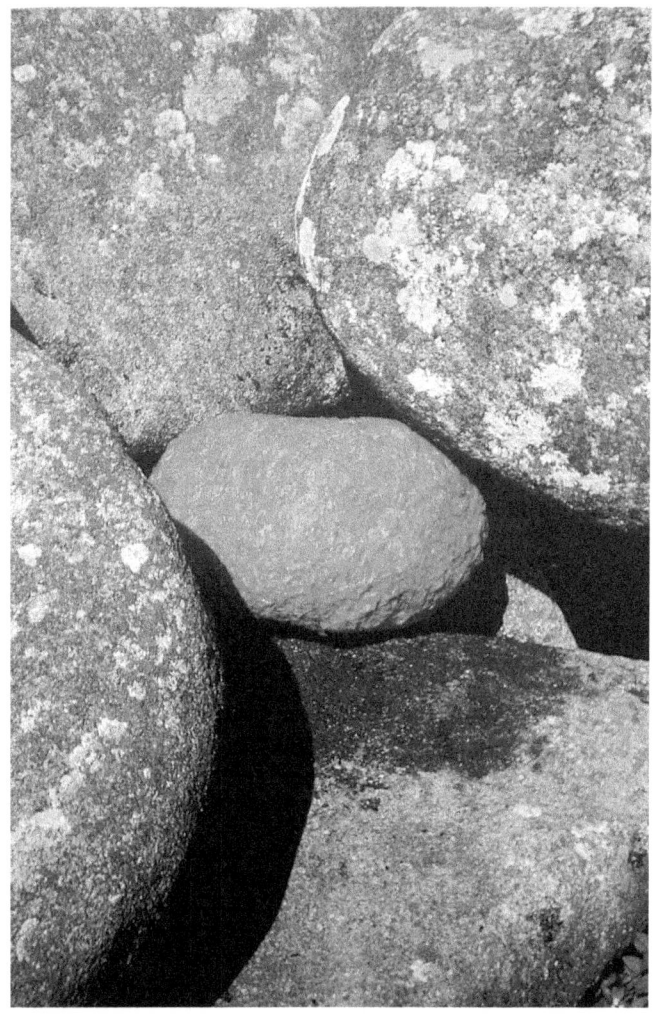

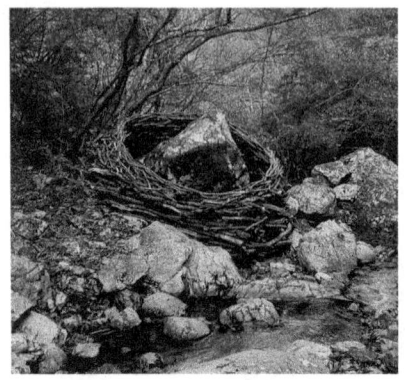
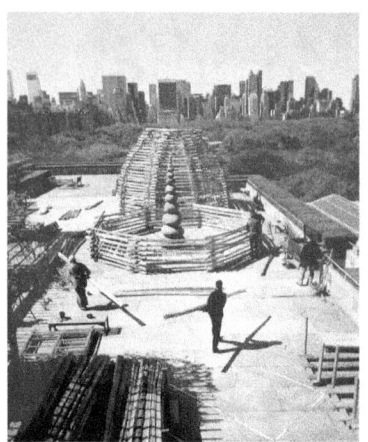
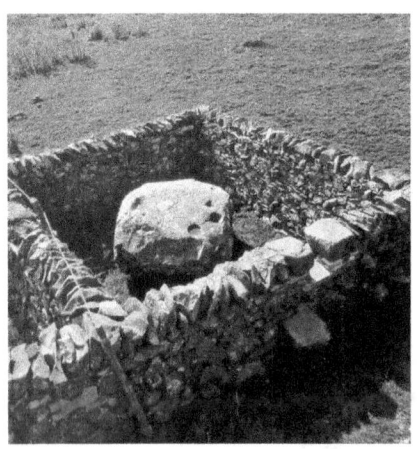
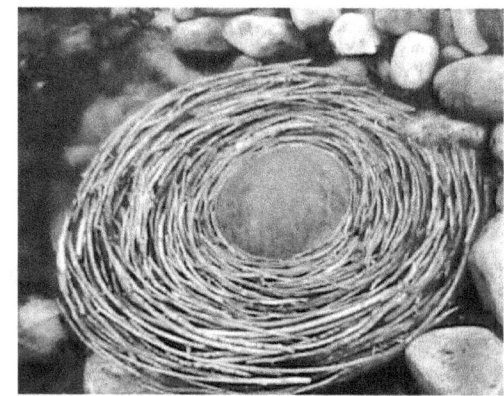

Enclosure

Enclosing an object or putting an object inside another
is a key Goldsworthy motif, occurring more and more
in his later works: such as the sheepfolds; or putting towers
of rocks inside wooden cairns, as in New York City;
or enveloping boulders with sticks.

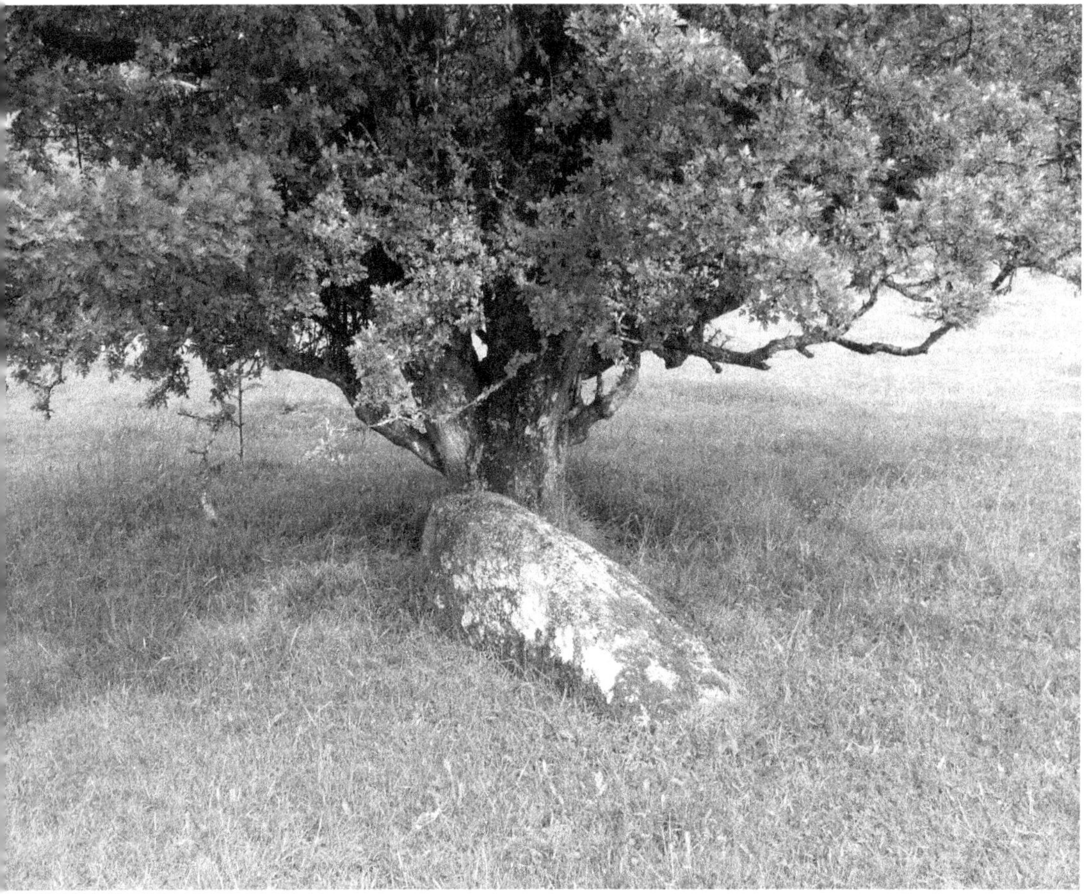

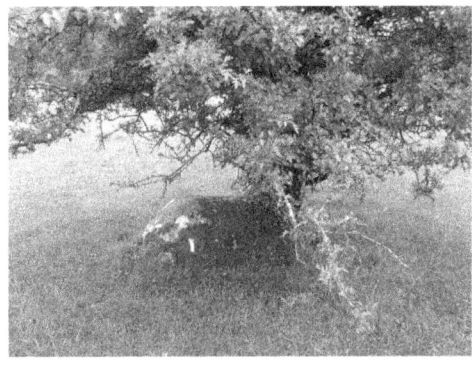

Andy Goldsworthy changes the way you see the world. For instance, I start to see Goldsworthy sculptures round and about – what you might call 'found Goldsworthy' works, like this boulder and tree I passed on a walk in Dartmoor, near Newbridge.

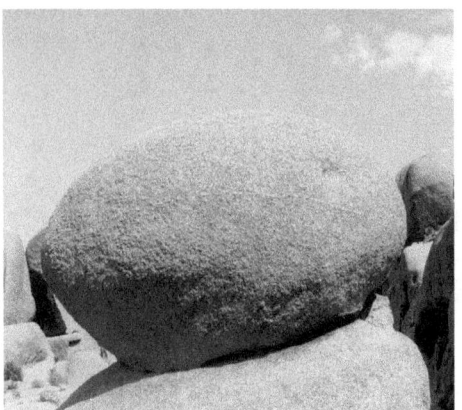

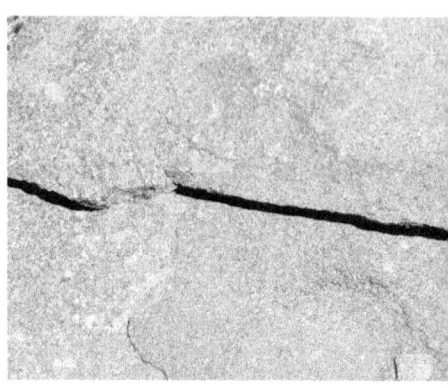

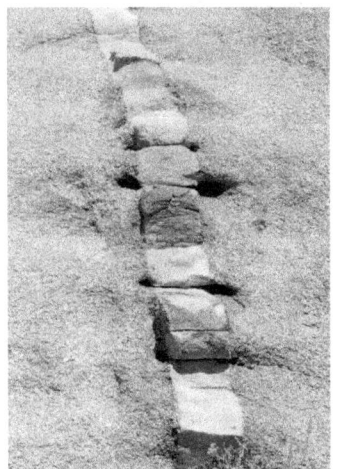

Joshua Tree National Park in the Sunshine State is a great place for finding 'found Goldworthys' – in balanced rocks, or cracked rocks, or rocks wedged into stone walls (above and left).

Sometimes you come across little sculptures made by people, like these stones in the Rocky Mountains near Estes Park, Colorado (below right).

I don't know who built the stone cairn (bottom) that I saw driving through the Rockies in Lyons, Colorado, but it must be inspired by Andy Goldsworthy.

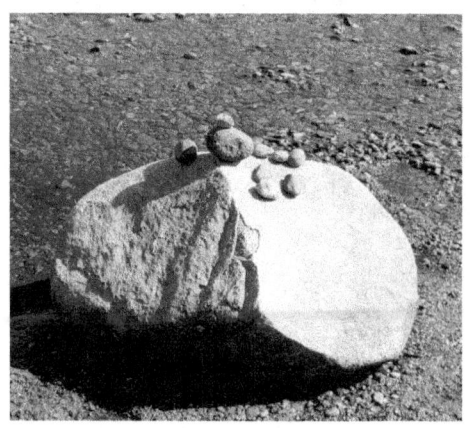

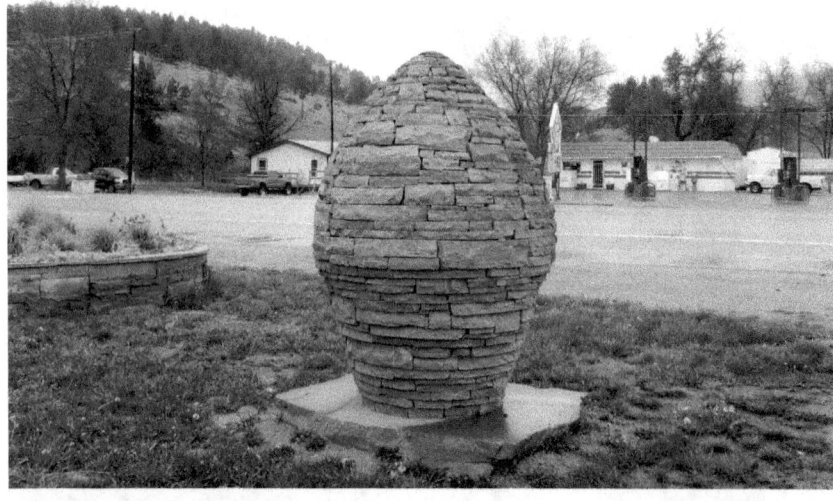

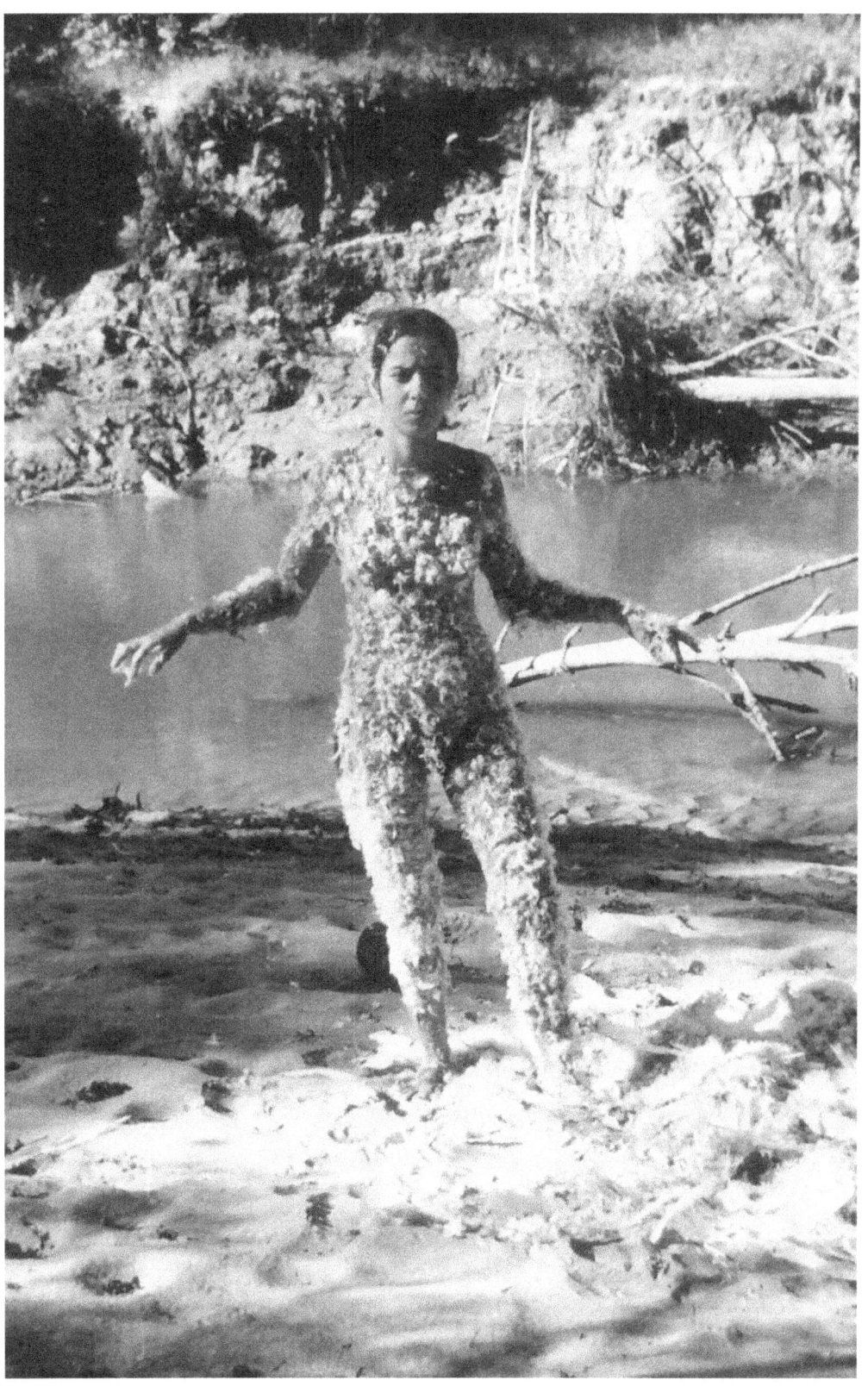

Ana Mendieta, Blood and Feathers, 1974

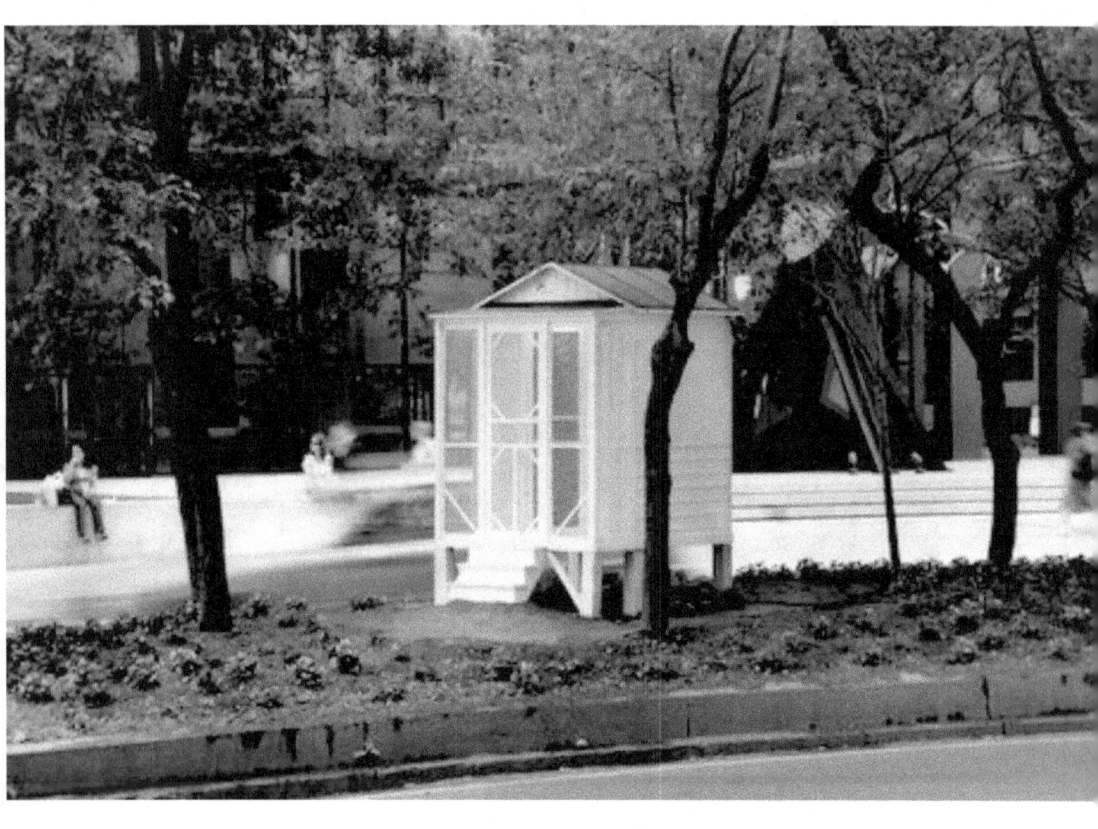

Donna Dennis, Tourist Cabins On Park Avenue, 2007

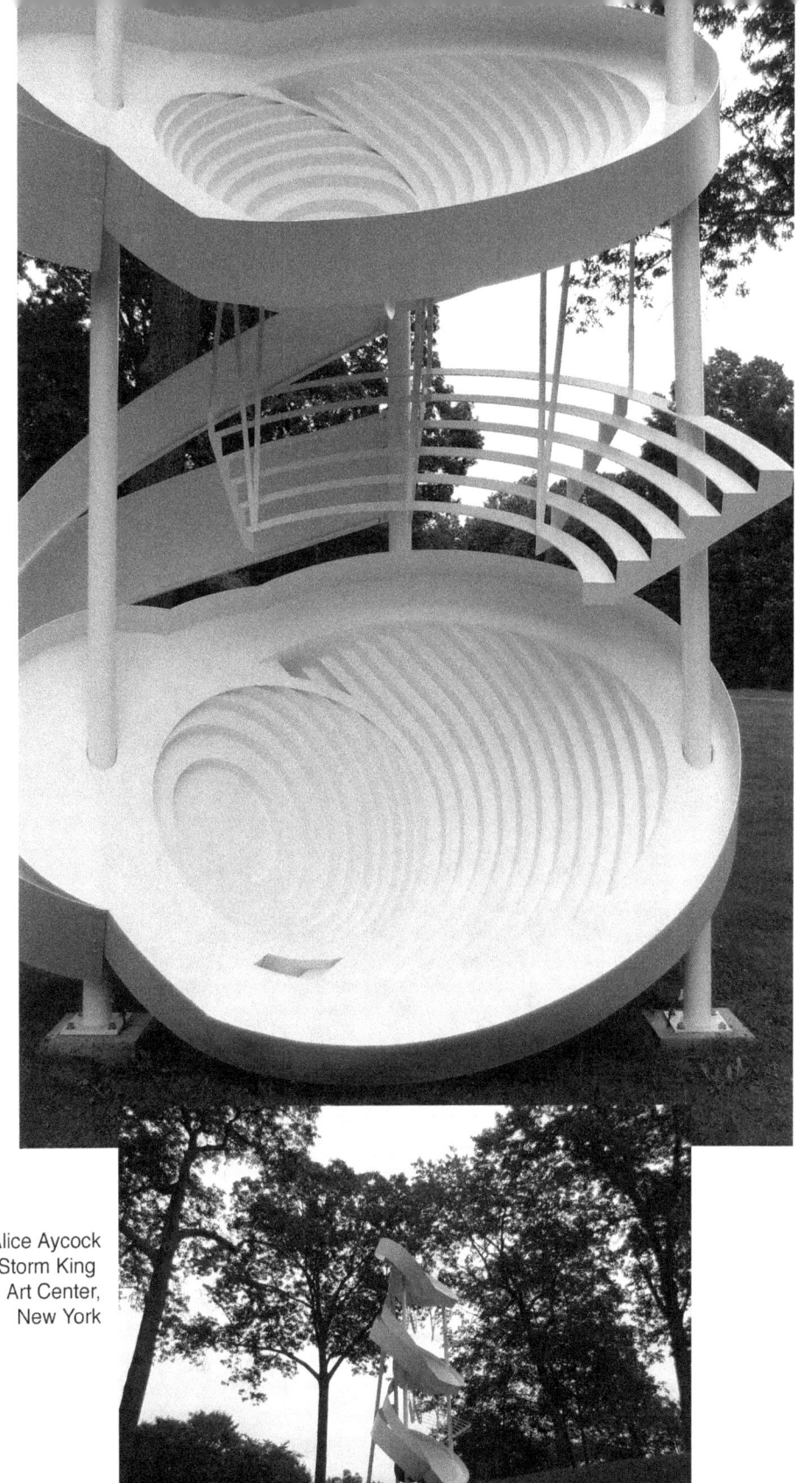

Alice Aycock
at Storm King
Art Center,
New York

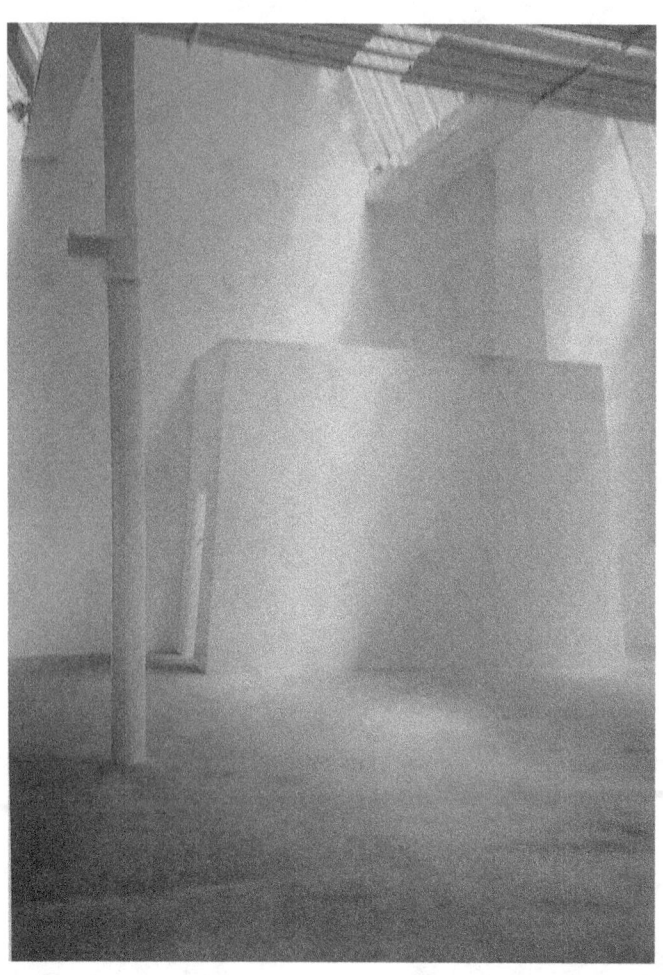

Alison Wilding, Pulse, 1991

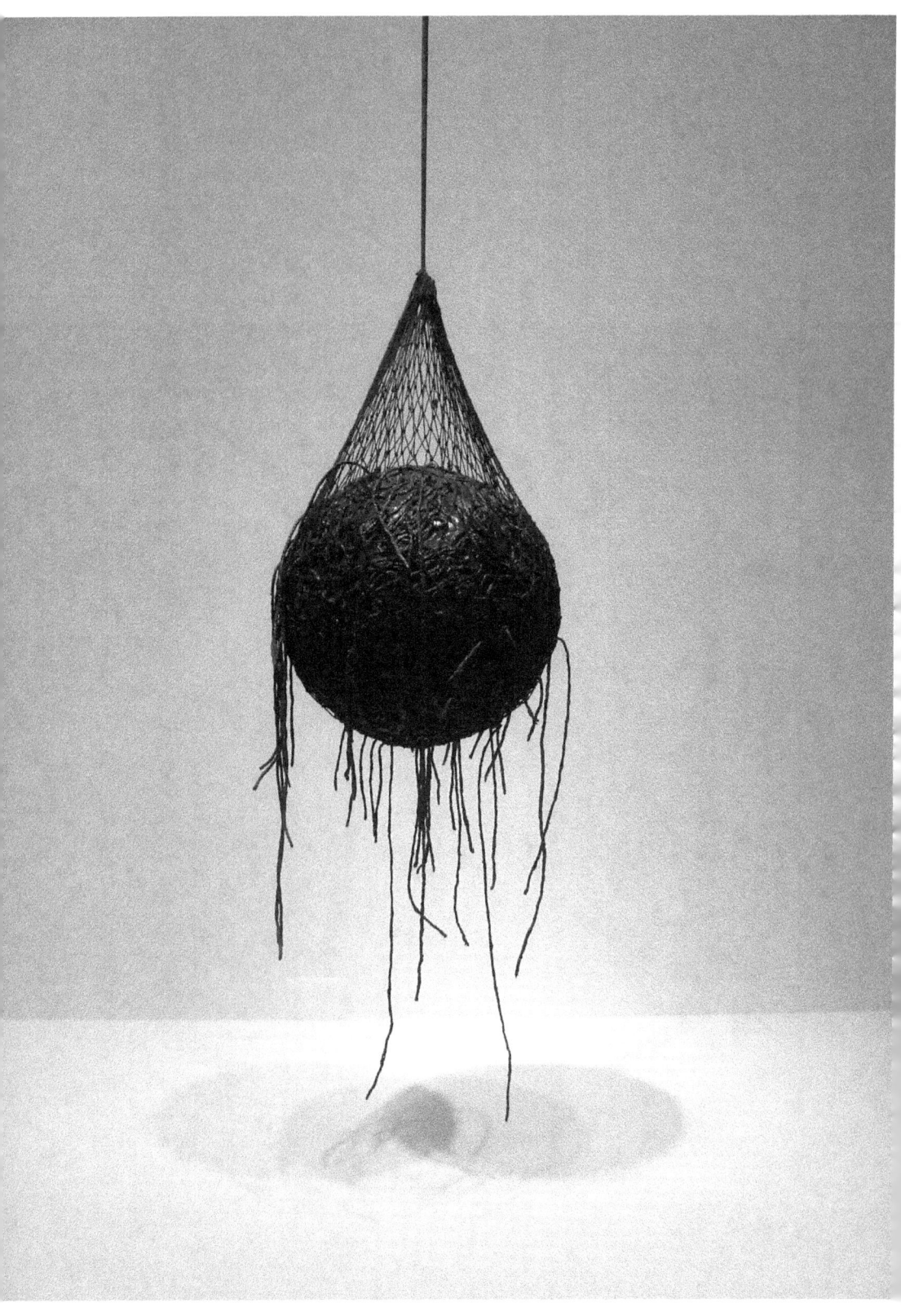

Eva Hesse, National Gallery of Washington, DC

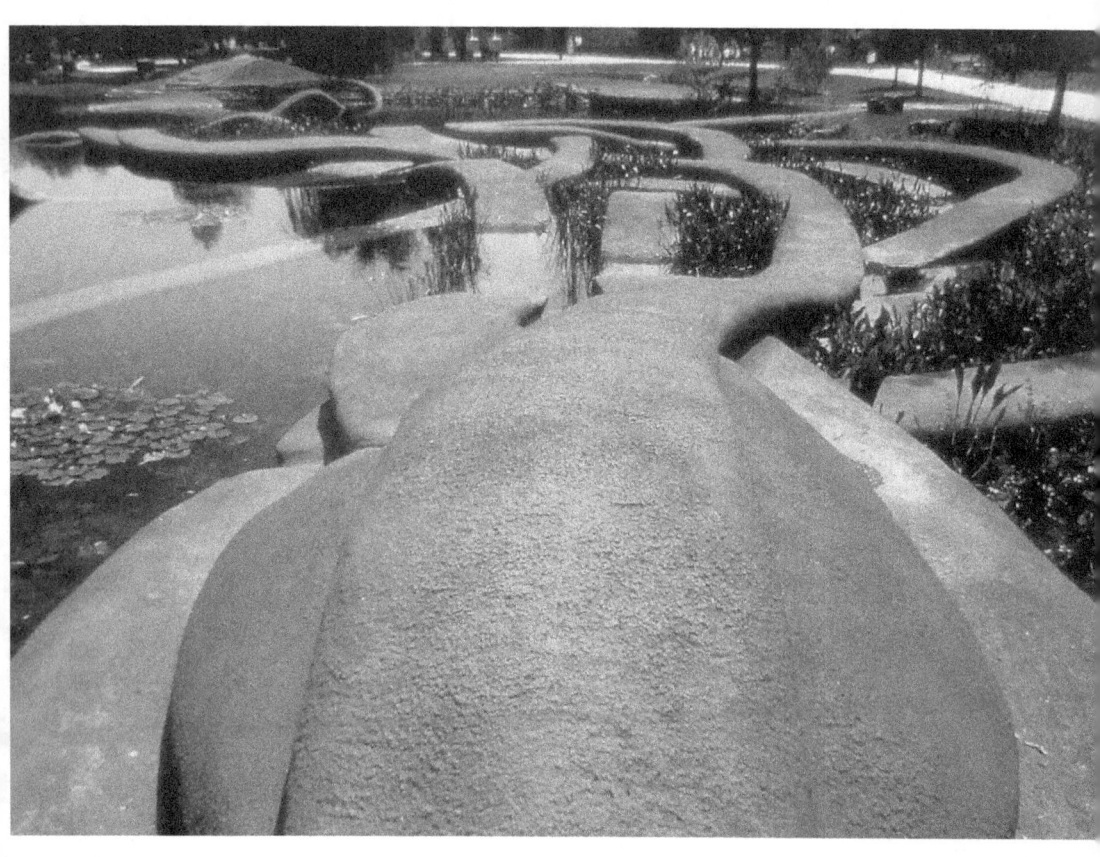

Patricia Johanson, Fair Park Lagoon, 1981-86

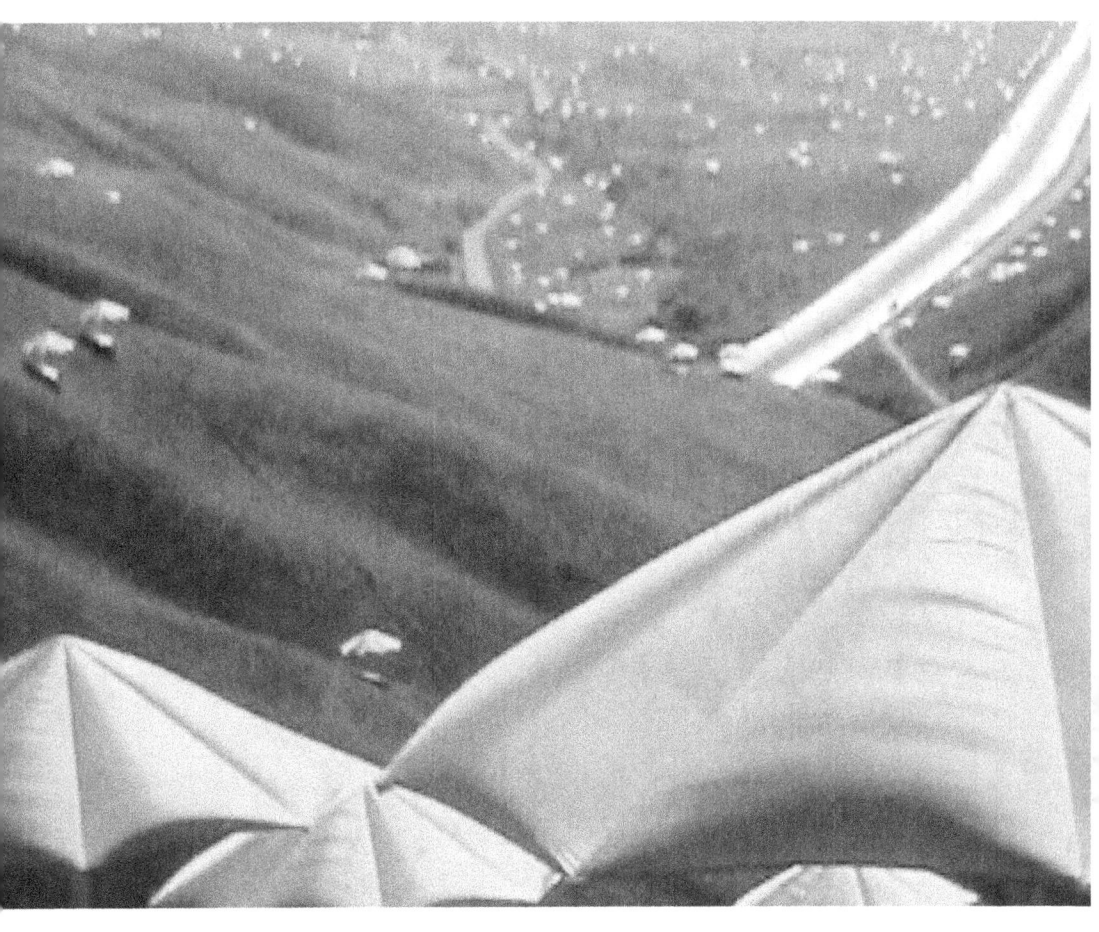

Christo, Umbrellas, 1976

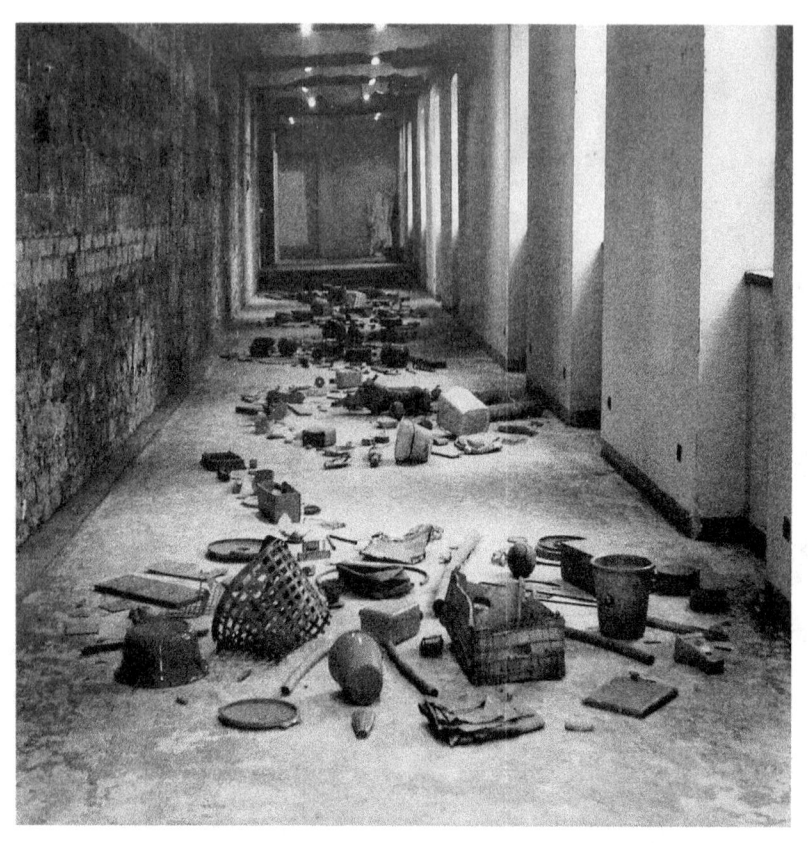

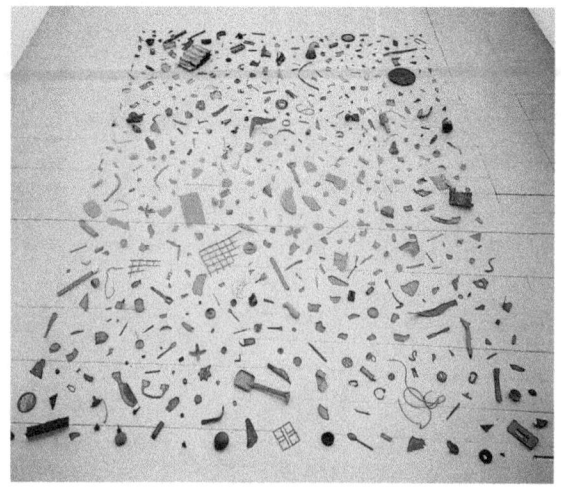

Tony Cragg

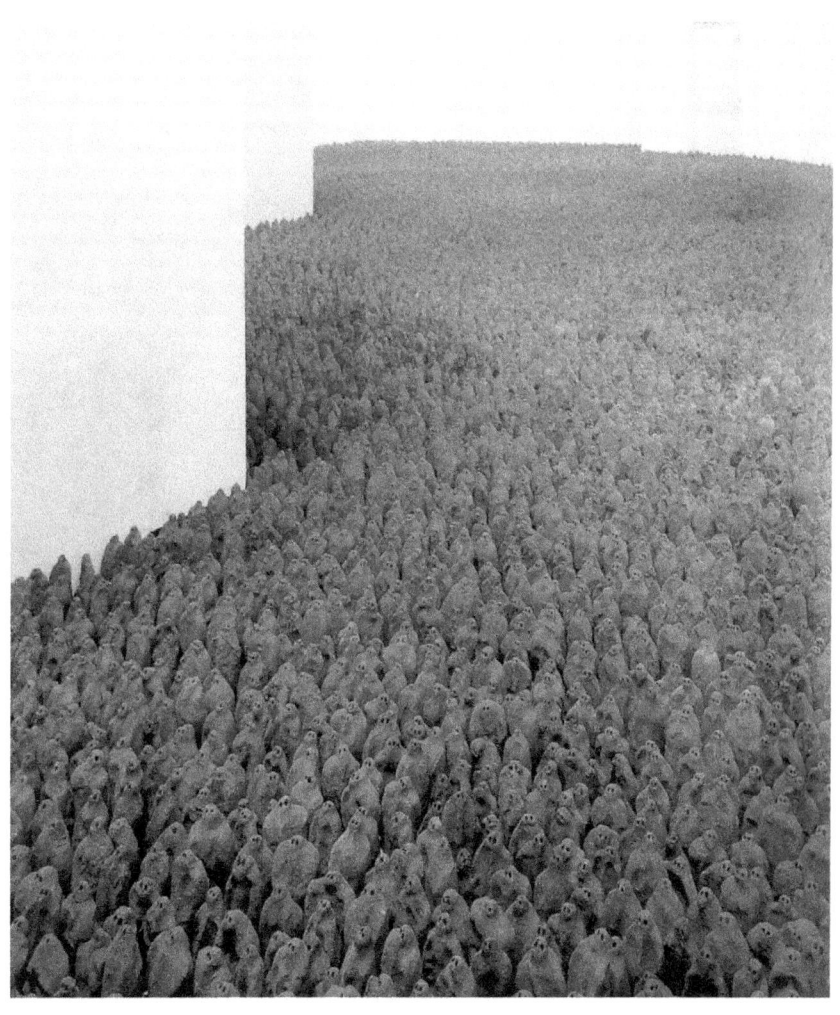

Anthony Gormley

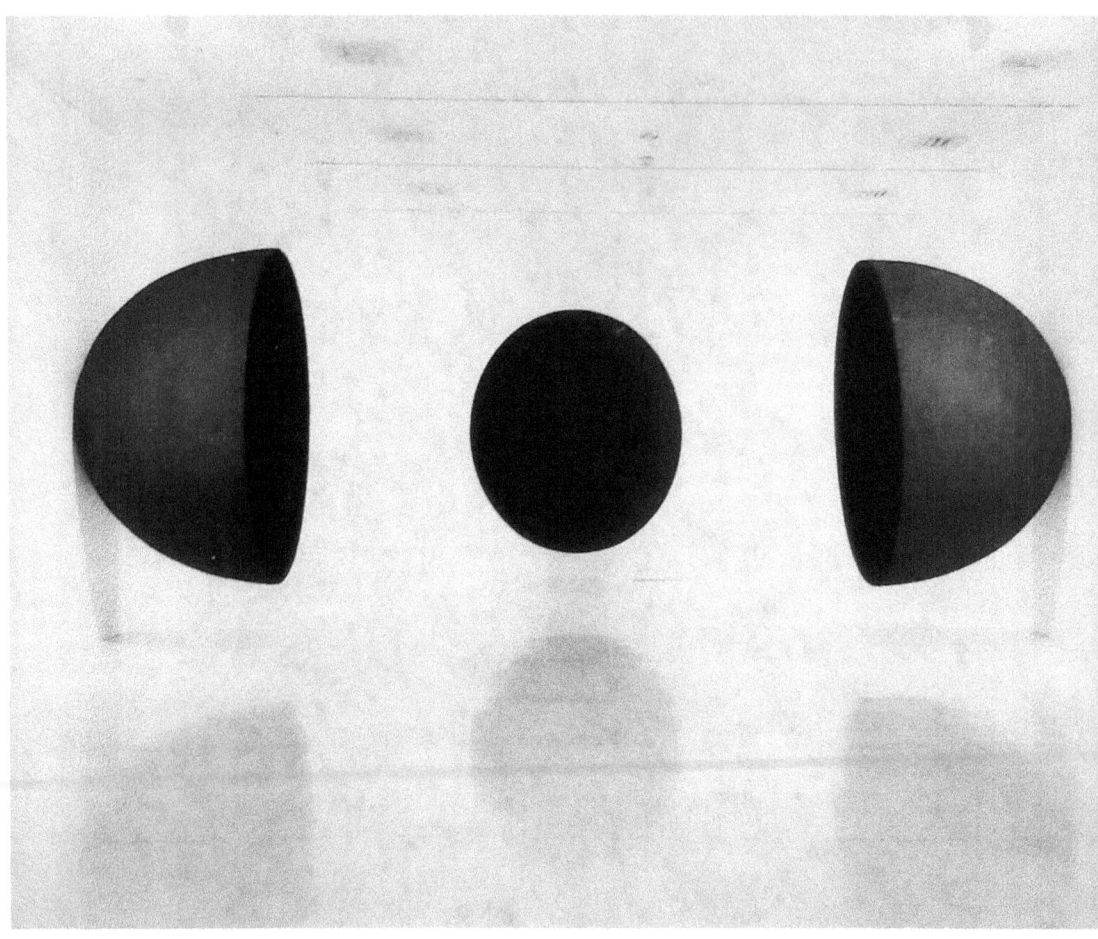

Anish Kapoor

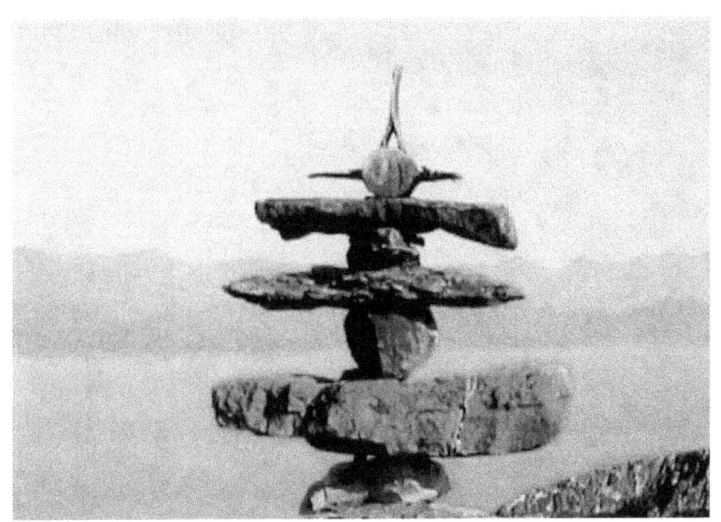

Chris Drury, Whale Bone Cairn, 1993

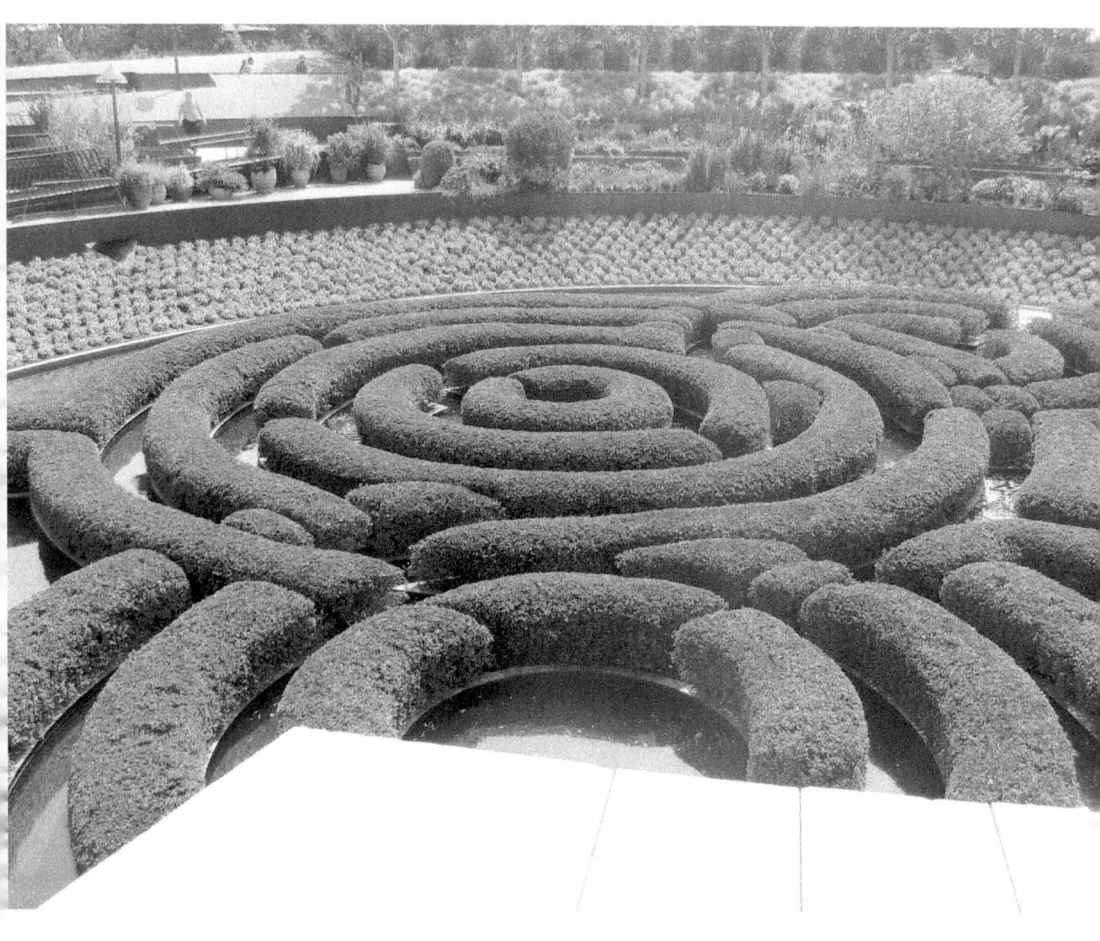

Robert Irwin's garden at the Getty in L.A.

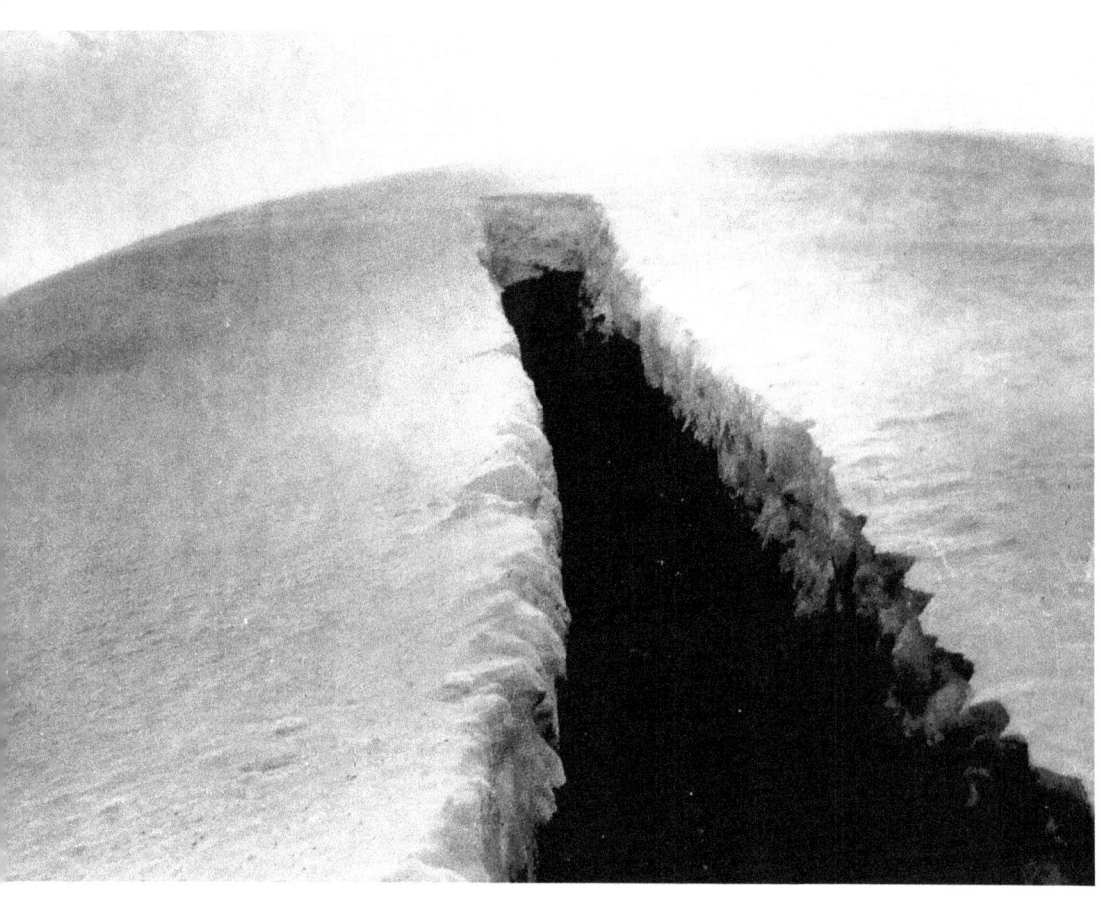

Dennis Oppenheim, Negative Board, 1968

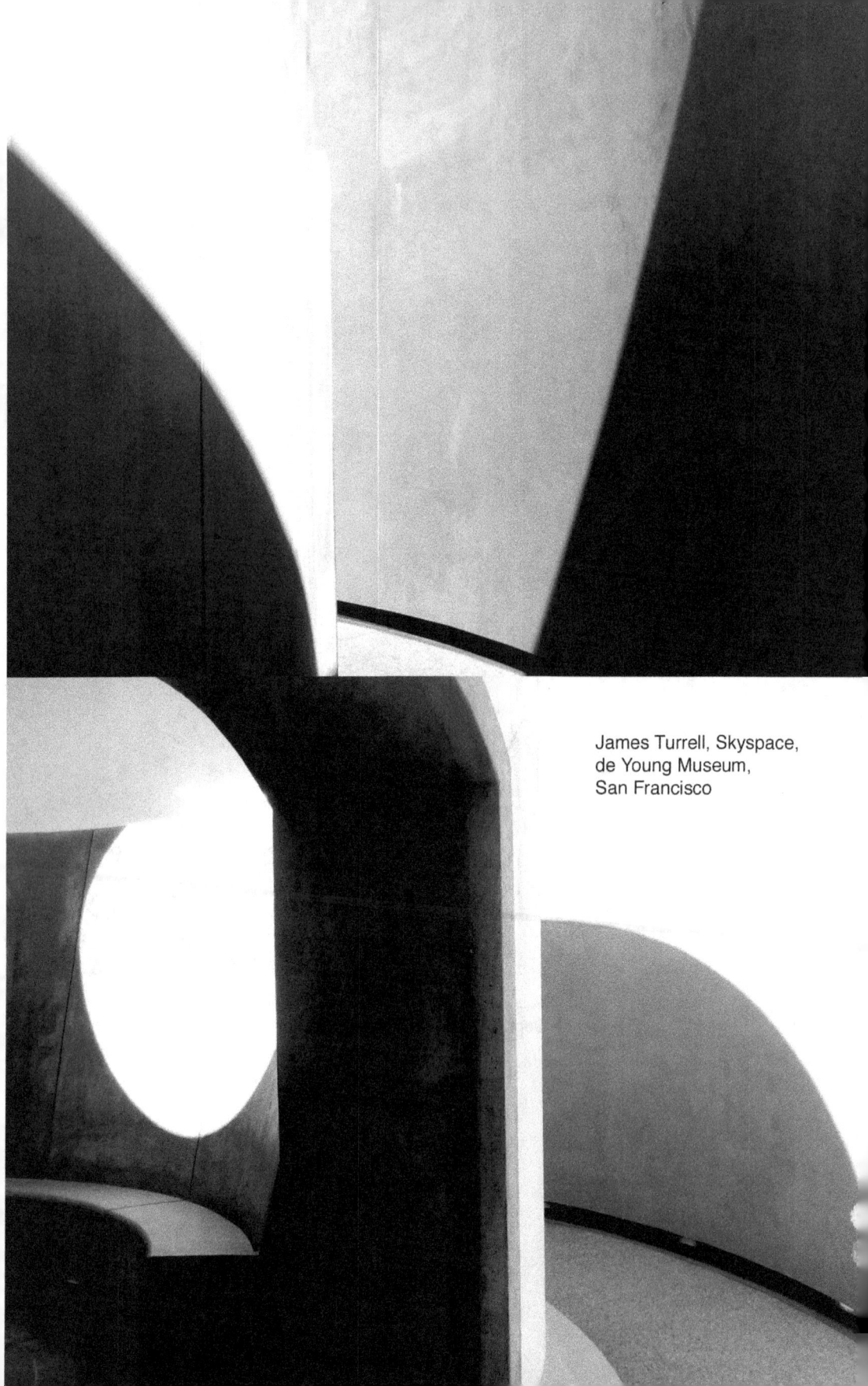

James Turrell, Skyspace,
de Young Museum,
San Francisco

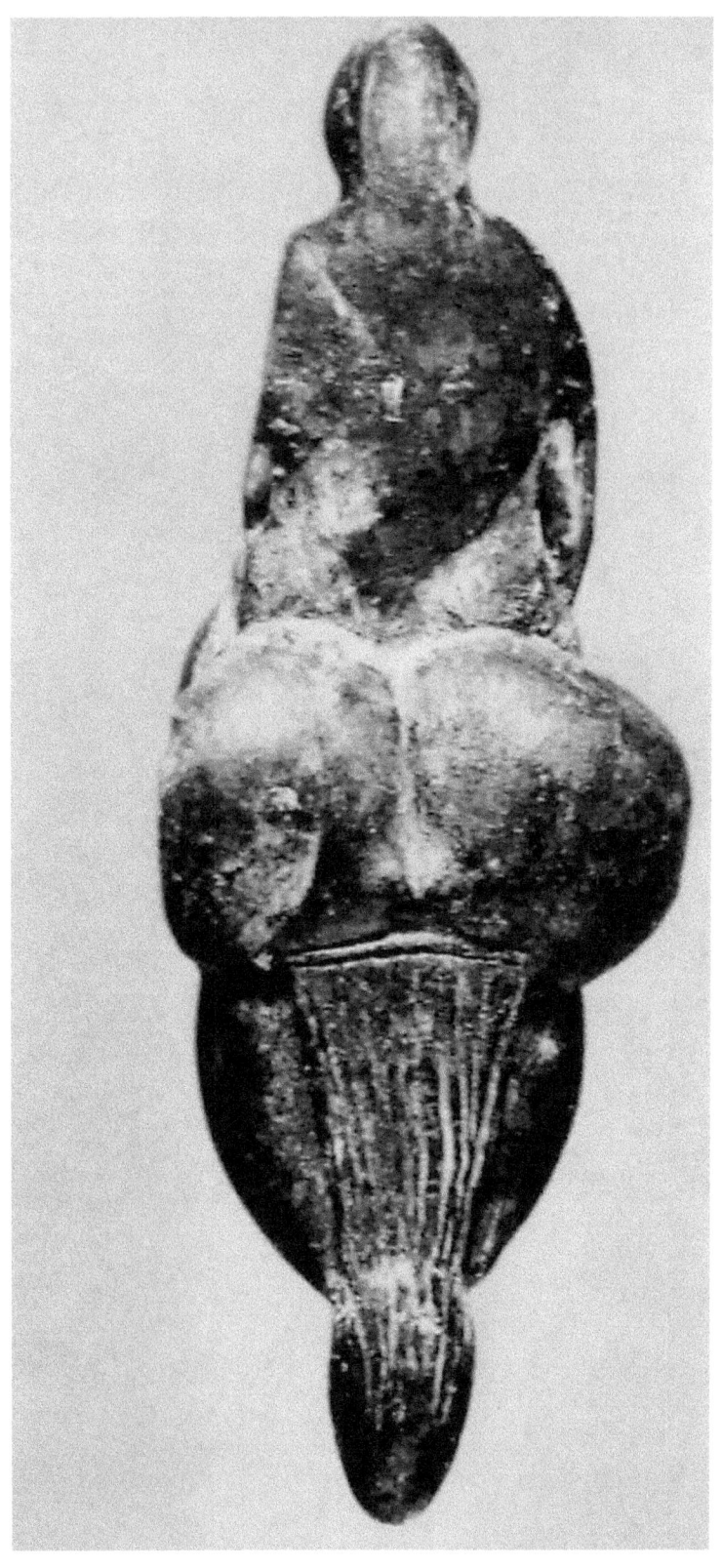

Venus of Willendorf, prehistoric, Vienna

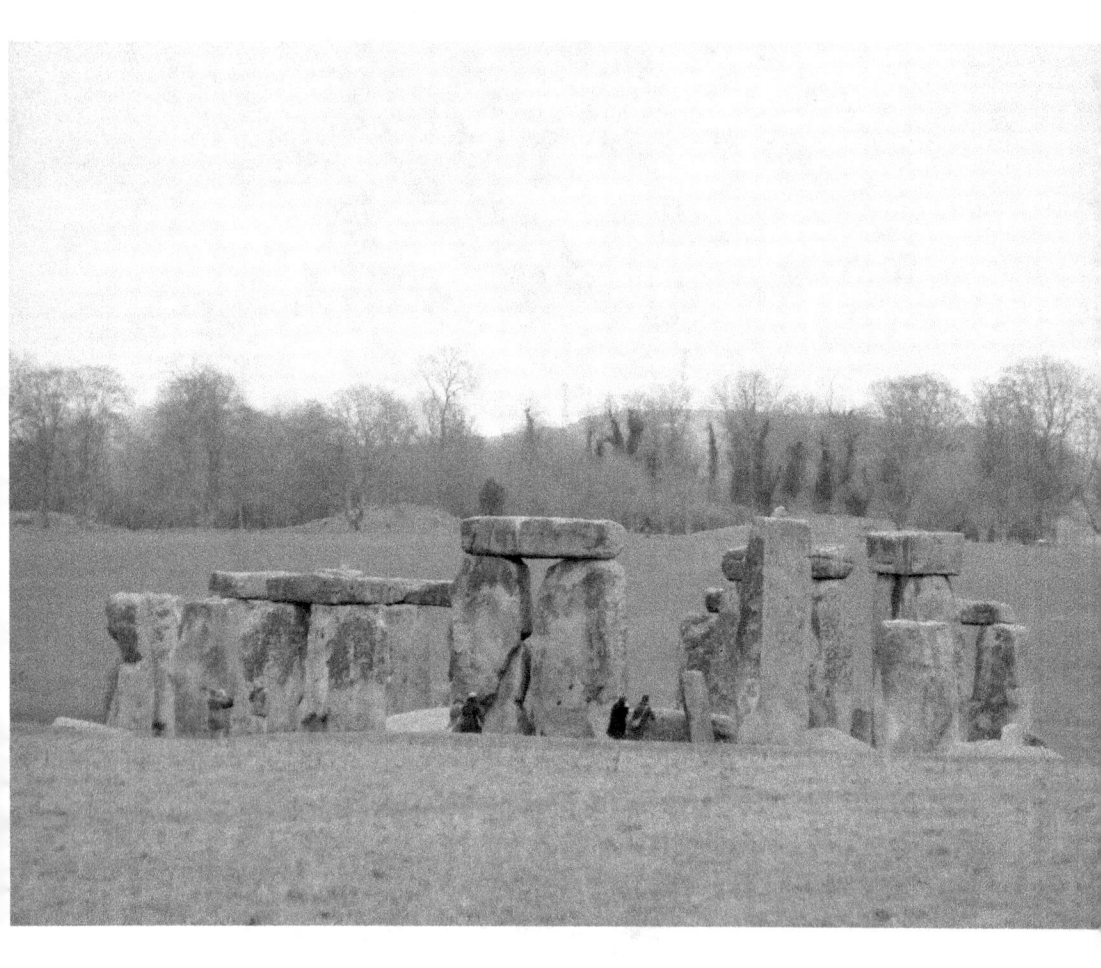

Stonehenge, Wiltshire

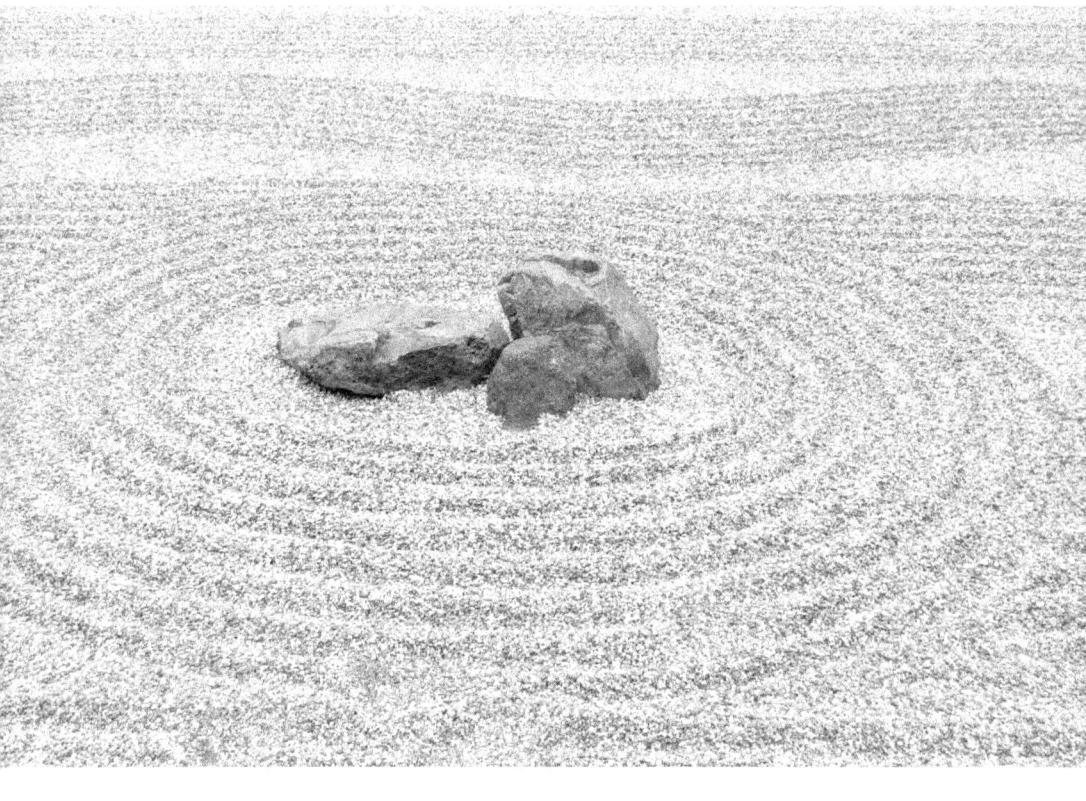

A modern version of the traditional Japanese Zen Garden,
in Pasadena, California

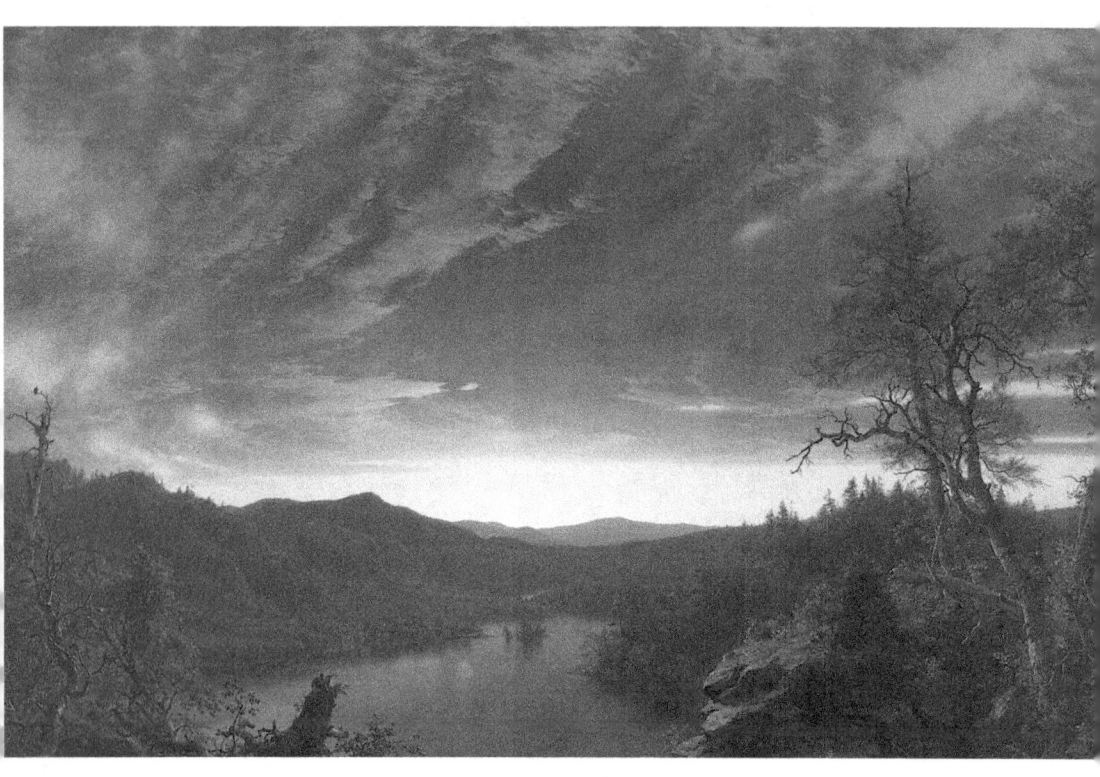

Frederic Edwin Church, Twilight In the Wildnerness, 1860,
Cleveland Museum of Art

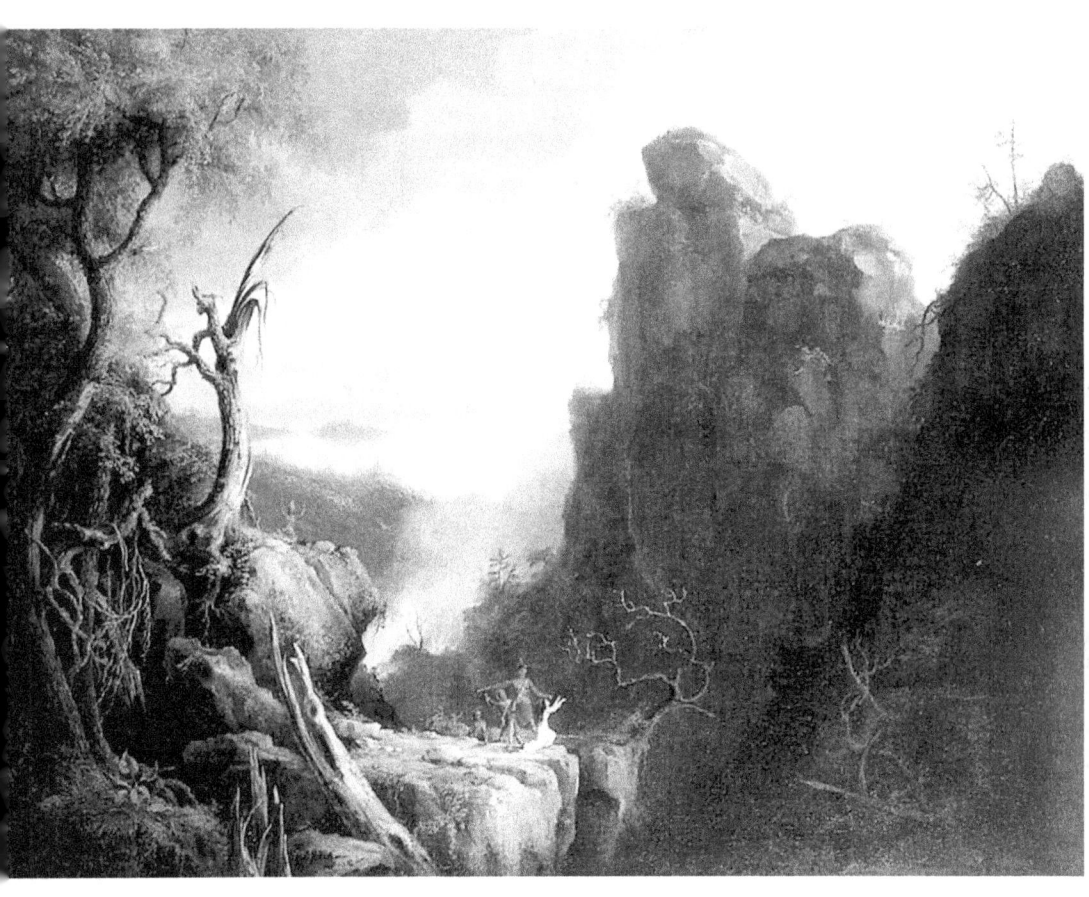

Thomas Cole, Indian Sacrifice, 1826

John Constable, Cloud Study

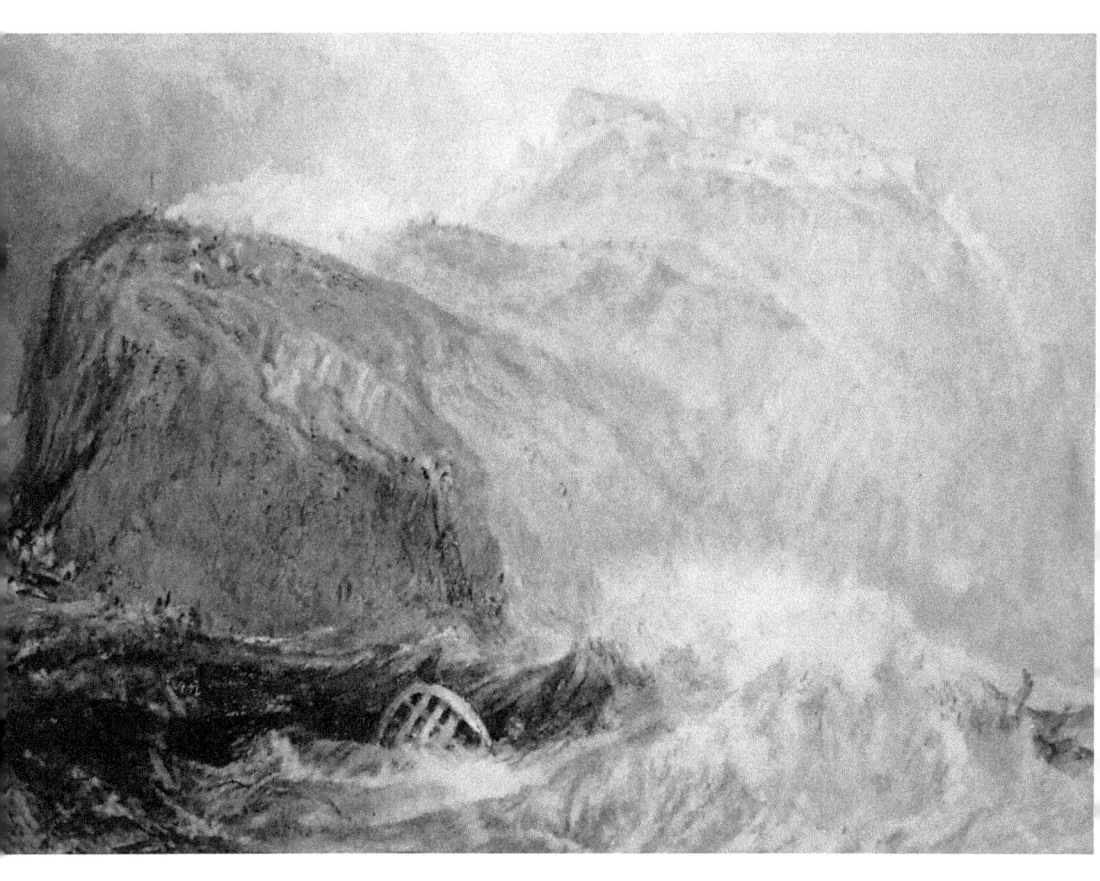

J.M.W. Turner, Tintagel Castle, 1815, Boston

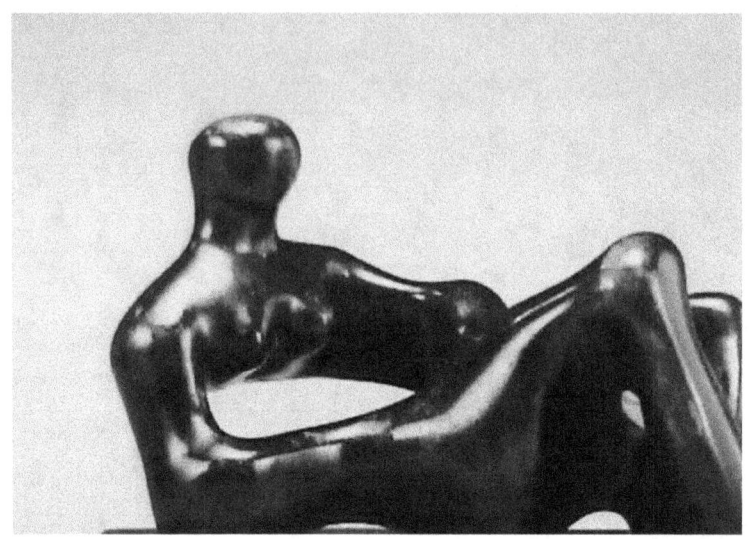

Henry Moore, Maquette For Recumbent Figure, 1938

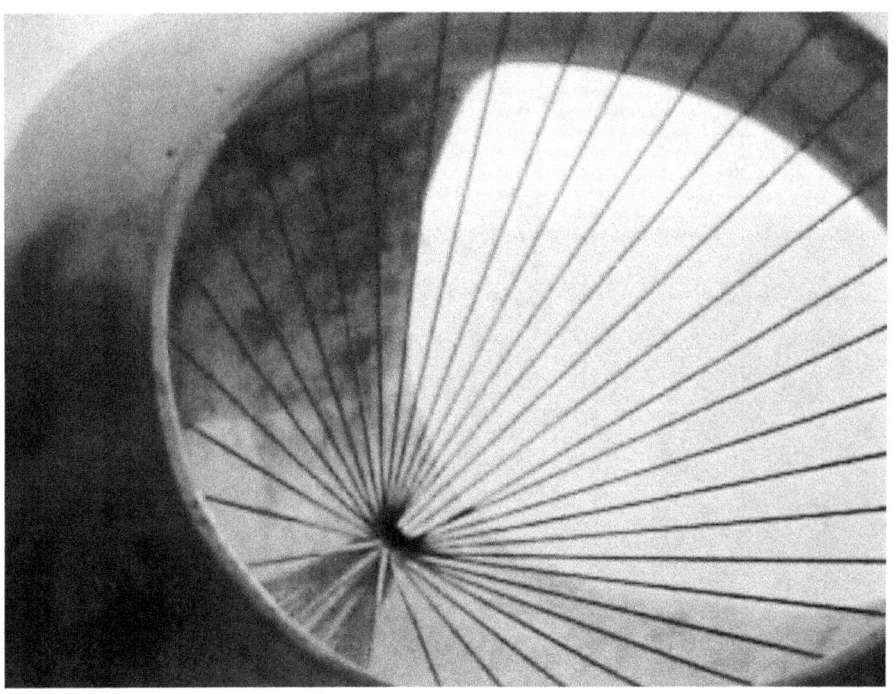

Barbara Hepworth, Sculpture with Colour and String, 1939-61

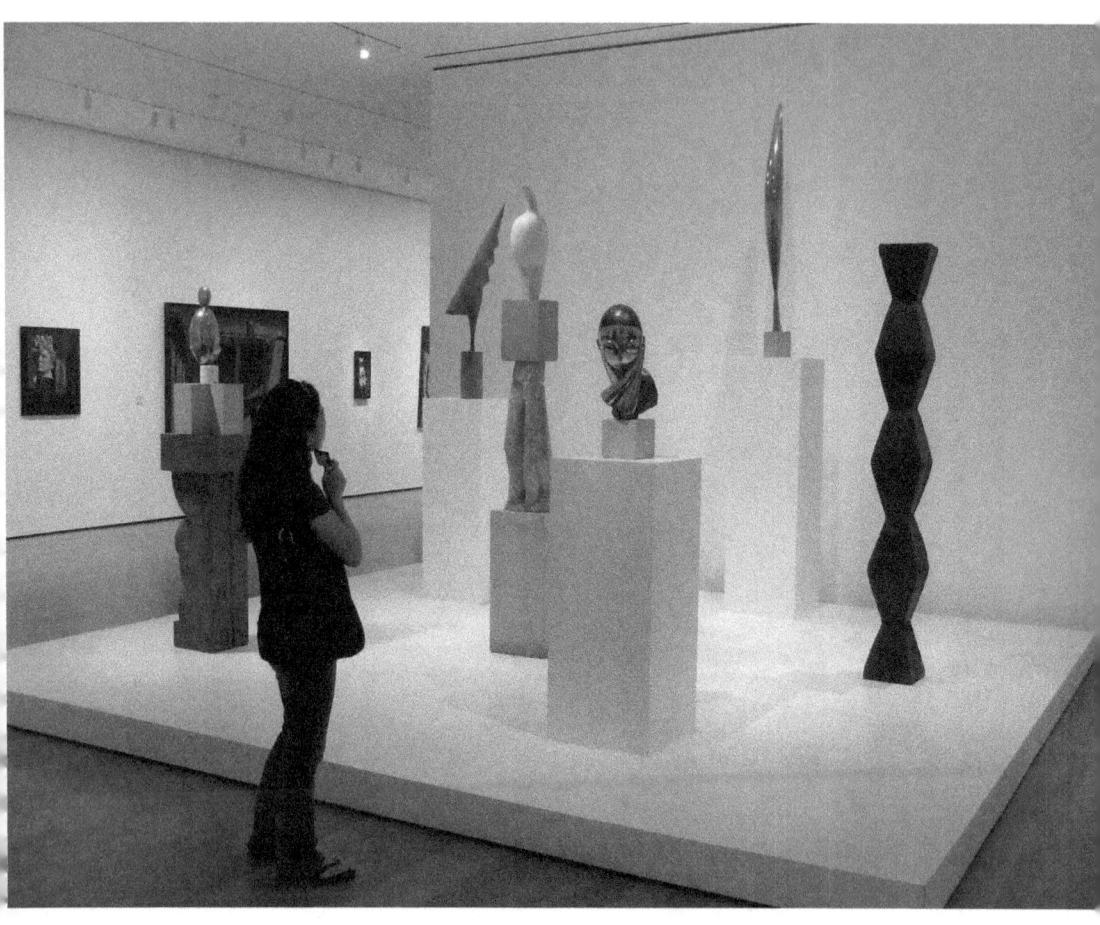

Constantin Brancusi display, Museum of Modern Art, Gotham

5

Andy Goldsworthy

Whole Earth Artist

Andy Goldsworthy works with the natural world, and within nature, like most (but not all) land artists. Goldsworthy uses natural materials in natural shapes and forms set in natural contexts. Goldsworthy takes his cue from nature: as Jan Dibbets put it in 1969: 'I realized that if you want to use nature, you have to derive the appropriate structure from nature too'.[1] Nature may be the starting-point but, as we'll see, the end-point – art – is entirely cultural and not something you'll ever find in the natural world.

Andy Goldsworthy seems to be a particularly gentle and sensitive artist, compared to many sculptors and land artists: he stitches together leaves to form lines (which're often placed in water, or over branches), or makes circular slabs of snow, or entwines twigs in an arc. He creates a delicate spiral of chestnut leaves, called *Autumn Horn* (1986); he pins bright yellow dandelions on willowherb stalks in a circle, on bluebells (1987); he makes lines and cairns of pebbles; a horizontal line of red sumach leaves was pinned to a willow (at Storm King Art Center in 1998); he rubs red stones to stain rockpools; he pins leaves to tree trunks; he fashions a zigzag line of hogweed stalks along a fallen elm tree (2002); he makes hollow, circular structures, recalling igloos, from slate, leaves, driftwood and bracken; he fashions long wavy ridges in Arizonan and Australian desert sand; he throws sand and sticks in the air and photographs the moment; he makes arches, globes, hollow spheres, slabs, spires, spirals and star-shapes out of snow and ice. Very impressive it all is. The sculptures made of sticks, for instance, stuck together in an arch, or a line, reflected in the mirror-like water of Derwent Water in Cumbria in 1988, are indeed wonderful. The sculptures exude tranquillity, an early morning calm (quite the opposite of another water work, Klaus Rinke's *Water Sculpture*, where a water canon blasted water over visitors as they approached a gallery, or Jim Sanborn's 1995 *Coastline*, which employed a wave generator to simulate waves in a Maryland garden).

Then there's the globe Andy Goldsworthy made from oak leaves in different states of autumnal decay, superb (Dumfriesshire, 1985). Or the sphere of sticks made in Fairfax, California (1995), set next to a sheltering tree. Or the sand serpent in the British Museum (1994). Or the globe made out of snow, and perched amidst some young trees (1980), or the slabs of snow, set up in a line with slits cut in them (1988).

Andy Goldsworthy has stated: 'I want an intimate physical involvement with the earth. I must touch'.[2] Touching is 'deeply important' for Goldsworthy.[3] Only touching gives the artist the deep understanding of his materials and nature, he asserted.[4] Goldsworthy's *Forked branch and twig* is exactly that: a forked branch with a twig suspended between the two parts of the branch. The photograph of this 1978 work shows a space enclosed by the twig and branch, a rough circle of air and sky enclosed by the twig and branch. Goldsworthy rarely uses animals in his art; stones and vegetation are his usual materials. Some sculptures refer to animals (such as sheep and cows). One or two pieces were made from feathers (*Goose feathers* [1983], *Wood pigeon wing feathers* [1977], *Feathers plucked from a dead heron* [1982], and *Wet feathers wrapped around a stone* [1999]). And some from wool (*Wool line*, 1995).

The sense of touch is supremely important to sculptors, as it is to most artists. Sculptors often describe the qualities of materials in terms of texture, surface, flexibility, malleability, viscosity, colour, strength, smell, associations, difficulty, and so on. Sculptors know that granite is quite a different material from steel, and certain woods – oak and holly, say – are different from pine, willow or walnut. Sculptors have a heightened haptic sense, a sense of touch which involves the whole body, not just the hands. Viewers of sculptures also react to them with all the senses, not just sight. One reacts to a sculpture with the whole body. This haptic sense, wrote K. Bloomert, is

> the means of touch reconsidered to include the entire body rather than merely the instruments of touch, such as the hands… It includes all those aspects of sensual detection which involve physical contact both inside and outsider the body.[5]

The sexuality of sculpture is everywhere affirmed in 'high art', and in 'high art' cultural criticism. This has to do partly with the eroticism of the nude human form, which thousands of sculptors have explored and exploited. Renaissance sculptors – Luca della Robbia, Lorenzo Ghiberti, Andrea del Verrocchio, Pietro Lombardo, Michel Colombe – systematically exaggerated the sexuality of the body. Donatello's famous *David*, for instance, is a highly camp, homoerotic boy, an icon of stylized homo-eroticism. (A similar eroticization occurs in Verrocchio's *David*, Benvenuto Cellini's

Perseus and Giovanni da Bologna's *Mercury*). This Renaissance sexualizaton of the human form finds its apotheosis in, of course, the art of Michelangelo Buonarroti – his *Dawn*, *David*, early and late *Pietàs*, and the most voluptuous of all figurative statues, the *Dying Slaves*. The heroic, homoerotic style of Michelangelo's sculpture continued throughout post-Renaissance sculpture. In, for instance, the bombast and masculine power of Antonio Canova's *Hercules and Lichas*, or Gianlorenzo Bernini's *David*. It's not just the body, though, or touch itself, that's eroticized in sculpture: it's the art object as erotic object, the ultimate fetish object (there isn't space here to go into the history of the art object seen through the eyes of psychoanalysis: the art-work as fetish, as lost maternal phallus, and so on).

The eroticism of Andy Goldsworthy's sculpture is readily apparent (and one of the reasons for his art's popularity), but the sensuality of Goldsworthy's art is non-human; there are no 'human' figures in his work, though there are vaginal openings, phallic rocks, mounds like breasts, cairns bulging outwards like pregnant bellies, and stalks that bend gracefully like ballet dancers: if one wants to anthropomorphize and sexualize Goldsworthy's art, it's easy. Goldsworthy himself anthropomorphizes his work. He says the cones on a hillside are like sentinels or a group of people (Sh, 17). Goldsworthy spoke of stones and seeds in terms of phallic tumescence and orgasmic release: 'I found an energy in stone that can best be described as a seed that becomes taut as it ripens – often needing only the slightest of touch to make it explode and scatter its parts' (W, 23).

Andy Goldsworthy has made more traditional forms of art in galleries: his bracken, fern and horse chestnut stalk works, for instance, were created by pinning the materials onto white gallery walls. These works – *Bracken fronds* (Ecology Centre, London, 1985), *Reeds, bracken and horse chestnut stalks* (Centre d'Art Contemporain, Castres, and Galerie Aline Vidal, Paris, 1989), and *Reed line drawing* (Paris, 1990) – were essentially free, open wall drawings, often employing basic motifs such as the circle and open curve. Hanging screens of plants that Goldsworthy made in galleries include the *Susuki grass* and *Horse chestnut leaf stalks* (both produced in Japan in 1993), *Horse chestnut leaf stalks* (1994, Japan), *Yucca blades* (New Mexico, 2000), and *Rushes thorns* (1992, San Francisco). *Rosebay willowherb* (1990) was crafted in Goldsworthy's studio.

In a 1992 Scaur Water sculpture, Andy Goldsworthy took up rosebay willow-herb stalks, one of his favourite media, and fashioned them into three curved, intertwining lines which moved down from a waterfall over mossy rocks. It was a variant of the many lines of leaves Goldsworthy has constructed. Goldsworthy called it 'drawing a waterfall' (P, 38). *Rush Line Drawing* (1999) employed linked rush stalks in a continuous, serpentine line, looping across the front of a group of butterbur plants. The stalks were held in place by piercing the edges of the large leaves.

In the course of his work outdoors, Andy Goldsworthy must have been bitten and stung by insects, stung, scratched and cut by plants, rained on millions of times (zillions!), frozen by cold, burnt by the sun, blown about by the wind, deafened by thunder, snowed on, and bruised by rocks and branches. Interrupted by people (and animals) many times. Mud, freezing water, birds and traffic would be frequent problems. And one of the biggest challenges in working out of doors is invisible: the wind (Goldsworthy often mentions it).

Although he has carved stone from time to time, in the traditional sculptural manner, and also modelled clay, Andy Goldsworthy disliked both processes. Although both methods have been central to sculpture for centuries, Goldsworthy rarely used them. 'I dislike the malleability of modelling and the imposition of carving as processes. Carving is a process that relies upon the integral strength of the block of stone' (RA, 105). Instead, Goldsworthy preferred to employ drawings or shaping with his hands, or weaving stalks or plants or leaves, or rubbing stone to make powder, or splitting stone to make walls or cairns, or piling up snow, or throwing stalks in the air, or balancing rocks.

Rather than modelling with clay, dabbing on a bit here and there, Andy Goldsworthy preferred to add one layer after another, until the work was complete. The form emerged partly from the process, then – a notion very much in keeping with 1960s art practice, with its emphasis on process and the *experience* of making an artwork. Goldsworthy spoke of forms that were 'integral' or 'rooted internally' in the materials (RA, 105). Many other contemporary sculptors have emphasized following the dictates of the material, and the actualities of making the work. It's a sculptural process that incorporates spontaneity, accident, mistakes, and external forces such as weather.

In 1995 Andy Goldsworthy was invited to have his art appear on British Royal Mail stamps (the national mail service), as part of their 'Springtime' Royal Mail Mint stamps (a stamp commission is one of the signs of becoming 'establishment'). Significantly, the Royal Mail chose Goldsworthy's leafworks for the stamps (some of his most approachable and appealing sculptures). The stamps comprised photographs of five leafworks, printed in landscape format, with the Queen's head and the price of the stamp printed in silver. The artist's name did not appear on the stamps: instead, the word 'Springtime' was printed in silver. The 19 pence stamp was an open circle of dandelions, with the ubiquitous black Goldsworthy hole at the centre. The first class (25 pence) stamp was a leaf horn made from sweet chestnut leaves.

Andy Goldsworthy's British mail stamps were marketed as small, delicate but ecologically-friendly expressions of the pastoral sublime. In the information card that went with the presentation pack, the blurb, in a flamboyant green script, waxed lyrical about the changing of the seasons, the coming of Spring and Maypole dancing (clichés of Spring in British culture), before introducing Goldsworthy as an artist of the ephemeral and pastoral, a poet who catches the spirit of nature as it changes and grows. The sensitivity, fragility and empathy of Goldsworthy's art were emphasized. 'Andy has celebrated *springtime* in a language that is all his own', purred the Royal Mail brochure. Pull quotes were placed around the text, with colour photographs of Goldsworthy's sculptures.

The Royal Mail commission was another example of the widespread acceptance of Andy Goldsworthy's art. Stamps are a prestigious assignment. Simply in terms of numbers, millions of postal stamps will be printed. Goldsworthy's sculptures appeared on all manner of letters and parcels. The 'transient' nature of Goldsworthy's art was made 'permanent' on a massive scale. A further set of stamps, featuring Goldsworthy's ice works, appeared in 2003.6 The icework stamps appeared in Winter, making them suitably seasonal.

Andy Goldsworthy has always spoken of the significance of the surrounding environment in his works. His sculptures are as much about the surroundings in which they are situated, as they are about the sculptures themselves. An exhibition inside, under a roof, in a gallery, is always going to be a problem, then. The contemporary gallery, with its sparse settings, white-washed walls and trendy magazines and postcards, is a powerfully *cultural* environment (and commercial – a gallery is a store selling art). The contemporary gallery is not 'natural' at all, it is not 'nature', it is not a place of mist, wind, skies and soil. No wonder, then, that earth artists such as Walter de Maria wanted to fill a whole gallery with dark soil, to bring nature into the contemporary art gallery in a big way.

Andy Goldsworthy's shows are something of a disappointment, in one sense, because the works have to breathe without their usual natural surroundings. Goldsworthy emulated Walter de Maria in a direct manner: in November, 1992, he covered the interior of the London gallery of his art agent with clay (*Hard earth – Dorset clay smoothed out, left to dry*). The exhibit began as a smooth creamy-white expanse of wet clay/ earth on the floor. It looked as if the gallery was empty, said Goldsworthy (S, 64), recalling Yves Klein's gallery showing nothingness, *Le Vide*, of 1958. *Hard earth* directly re-echoed de Maria's *New York Earth Room* (1977): the natural world was present in the gallery in both works in force: in de Maria's *New York Earth Room* the dark soil had a solemn, weighty, fecund presence; in Goldsworthy's *Hard earth* time and transformation played a part: gradually, the clay dried and cracked, allowing the Goldsworthyan vision of the dark energies of nature to well up: nature was erupting in the gallery space.

❀

Andy Goldsworthy tended to add a few pages of his own writing to his published art books, drawn from his artist's journals. The books mainly consisted of colour photo-graphs of his artworks. In one or two books, such as *Time, Passage, Midsummer Snowballs* and *Arch*, Goldsworthy wrote considerably longer pieces. In *Time*, for instance, there are about 50 pages of writing by Goldsworthy.

Andy Goldsworthy's writings are sometimes simple, sometimes blunt and always matter-of-fact – in an indomitable, Northern British fashion. Goldsworthy's persona in the texts is a rugged man of the wild, a 'whole earth man', ecologically sensitive, someone 'in touch' with nature, working with his bare hands, in boots, hat and an anorak, often in Winter. A modern-day Henry David Thoreau living off the land at Walden. There is a macho posturing to this (no doubt unintentional), in which the relationship with nature is 'fundamental', 'raw', 'violent', 'intense'. Goldsworthy sees working in the hard conditions of Winter a challenge, a 'test of my commitment to the landscape'.7 Goldsworthy has spoken about being 'shocked' by small-scale natural events, about work suddenly becoming 'intense', about the 'raw energy' of colours (he doesn't mean 'shock' in the usual sense, though). Goldsworthy's writings are marked by words such as 'powerful', 'wildness', 'deeper', 'rooted', 'flesh and bone', 'feeling', 'essential', 'sense', 'energy', 'touching' and 'essence' (these words are taken from a single page of Goldsworthyan philosophy, in *Stone* [6]).

All this talk of raw, powerful essence in nature suggests one British poet in particular – Ted Hughes, the stolid Yorkshireman and former British Poet Laureate whose books (*River, Hawk in the Rain, Lupercal, Wodwo* and *Elmet*) are full of post-Gerard Manley Hopkinsian evocations of wild shingle beaches, desolate moorland, ancient forests and craggy heights. If ever there was a poetic equivalent of Goldsworthy's boulders, melting snowballs, slate cairns and red mud 'throws', it is Ted Hughes' verse.

Another link is nature-man Oliver Mellors in *Lady Chatterley's Lover* (1928), the no-nonsense outdoor man and ganekeeper who is in fact a New Man, painfully sensitive and alive (an amazing lover, too, and he lives alone in the woods; macho, self-sufficient, a 'man's man'). The D.H. Lawrence connection with Andy Goldsworthy has been emphasized by Goldsworthy himself: in *Stone* he quoted from Lawrence's *The Rainbow* (1916), one of those euphoric, ithyphallic passages about the ecstasy of consummation in an arch. Here's an extract from Nottinghamshire's greatest artist, from a scene where Will Brangwen visits Lincoln cathedral:

Here the stone leapt up from the plain earth, leapt up in a manifold, clustered
desire each time, away from the horizontal earth, through twilight and dusk and the
whole range of desire, through the swerving, the declination, ah, to the ecstasy, the
touch, to the meeting and the consummation, the meeting, the clasp, the close
embrace, the neutrality, the perfect swooning consummation, the timeless ecstasy.
There his soul remained, at the apex of the arch, clinched in the timeless ecstasy,
consummated.[8]

Hardly anyone writes like that these days; Andy Goldsworthy can't be the only artist who'd love it if critics wrote about their art like that. D.H. Lawrence's intensely poetic novel *The Rainbow*, about three generations of a Midlands family (his 'Brangwen-saga'), is a strident inrush of energy into Goldsworthy's otherwise pedestrian prose in the book *Stone*. Goldsworthy's own pontifications can be banal, and the quotes from John Locke and Lawrence (as in *Stone*) highlight that.

The arrogance which Andy Goldsworthy occasionally voices is inescapable: for all his humble sensitivity, he is a proud and confident artist. For example, of a 12 foot high cairn sculpture made beside a river in Illinois, Goldsworthy said that the work 'gives a feeling of the weight, power and volume of a river in flood in a way that a marked pole never could' (S, 37). He was so sure of the effect his sculpture will have on the viewer. But this interpretation of the cairn only makes sense if the viewer is primed first about the 1954 flood, and regards a pile of stones as more powerful as a measurer of a river's flood than a marked pole. After all, the dumb punter might remark, one can stand right under a 12 foot pole (if it's in the same place), and see it towering over one's head. A pole may be just as impressive as a stone mound (it has measurements and dates painted on it, for instance, of the floods in, say, 1858, or 1916). Goldsworthy was cautious about appearing too self-confident. In an interview in *Sheepfolds* (1996) he said '[m]y monuments do not sit arrogantly on top of the hill,

[but] that doesn't mean that they don't have a power' (Sh, 17). Of course: no artist wants their sculptures to be overwhelmed by the landscape; they have to assert themselves within the environment.

'At its most successful, my 'touch' looks into the heart of nature', Andy Goldsworthy affirmed in the late Eighties (WH and AG). This is a pretty self-confident statement. It's like a Hollywood movie director saying 'my films touch the heart of contemporary society • war-torn Vietnam • life on a Mid-West farm' or whatever. Goldsworthy does not say my art *tries* to look at or explore nature, but 'my 'touch' looks into the heart of nature'. It's a formidable æsthetic, one with a self-assurance right-wing philosophers like Friedrich Nietzsche or Plato would be proud of.

Of a cairn made out of scrap steel which was placed next to an old foundry, Andy Goldsworthy claimed that the cairn 'touches the nature of an urban environment' (S, 35). Does it 'touch the nature' of the place? What is the nature of the place? How can a human 'touch the nature' of the place? What is the quality of this touching? What kind of touching is it? And what is the nature of 'the nature of an urban environment'? How does the artist know he's touched it? Simple: he believes wholeheartedly in his subjective, intuitive feelings. He just *knows*, like a mystic.

Of steel, for example, the artist stated: 'I can feel its source' (ibid.). Huh? What does this 'source' 'feel' like? And what is the 'source' of steel? The planet itself? The energies that formed it? The people that dug the original material out of the ground and shaped it? How, too, does the viewer know about this feeling for the source of a material? Is it expressed in the work? How can the audience test the authenticity of the artist's feelings? These are questions which one can (and should) fire at any artist. Andy Goldsworthy's art is often unsure about the answers. It knows it is about nature, ecology, place, organic form, and so on, but its views on these matters, and its relation to them can be often confused, ambiguous, banal or simplistic.

A dandelion work such as *Dandelions* (1993 [S, 21]) highlights the recurring problems with Andy Goldsworthy's sculpture: it has instant appeal: brilliant yellow dandelions are set in a mossy, pitted rock next to a stream (how can you not enjoy that colour?). The work seems to emphasize the relative beauty of both the flowers and the setting: the 'organic', individual shape of the rock pool (this shape, and no other), the contrasts in brightness and colour in the natural world (grey and green rock, yellow dandelions), the transience of nature (the dandelions' colour will fade; the flowers will be pummelled by the next rain, or wind, or swept away when the river rises). Yet the sceptical viewer might also say, well *anyone* could make that work (or many other Goldsworthy sculptures). There is little 'technique' (art) or skill (craft) involved: it seems that one simply places dandelions in a pool (or rocks on top of each other, or wraps boulders in clay, or rubs the bark off twigs, or cracks open pebbles, and so on).

Dandelions seems so simple, so easy, like so many of Andy Goldsworthy's sculptures (*Beech leaves, Balanced stone, Balanced rocks, Two Scaur Water snowballs, Red river rock pools, River rock, Peat, Clay-covered rocks, Torn stones, Red sand thrown into a blue sky, Orange stones* and *Yellow elm leaves*, to cite some works from the book *Stone*). Hang on, the sceptic might claim, the fraud has simply stuck some flowers in a pool! That can't be 'art'! Easy to see how Goldsworthy's art can seem a sham, like Carl Andre's bricks, or Yves Klein's leap, or Andy Warhol's six hour film of someone sleeping. *Come on*, the sceptic'll say, this can't be *serious*.

Some artists make a virtue of simplicity and ease: Jan Dibbets said he liked projects that anyone could do. For example, he chose four sites at random on a Netherlands map and went to each place and took a photo. It was '[q]uite stupid. Anybody can do that', Dibbets admitted. But Dibbets said he enjoyed searching for the places and photographing what was there. It was also silly for people to buy such works: 'it's stupid for other people to do it, or to buy it from me. What matters is the feeling'. And the feeling of the artist was something that couldn't be bought (1970). Similarly with Goldsworthy's art: the audience with the best view, the deepest connection to the sculptures, and the richest experience of the artworks is the artist himself.

6

Andy Goldsworthy

and Photography

Andy Goldsworthy's sculptures such as *Yellow elm leaves, Red maple leaves, Beech leaves, Red river rock pools* and other riverside works seem so simple, so easily put together. But Constantin Brancusi's eggs and fish and heads are also very 'simple' shapes and forms: the Romanian sculptor reduced and rationalized natural forms until he reduced them to an 'essence' (the 'essence' of a fish, of a head, of a bird in flight). Yet Brancusi does not get accusations of superficially and banality thrown at him. Indeed, his sculpture is really powerful (and celebrated) precisely because he radically simplified it. (What the viewer doesn't see in the gallery, of course, are the hundreds of failed attempts, the mistakes, and the years of research and refinement to get to that stage. Simplicity is achieved at great cost and after years of refinement).

With Andy Goldsworthy's art, though, the simplicity is of a different order: is the confusion over and criticism of Goldsworthy's work because he is using the *actual* material of nature? An actual leaf, rock, petal or ice sheet, not an imitation or image of them? Is it that anti-Goldsworthy critics see a rock covered with real leaves, not a mock-up made in an artist's studio, or a bronze or marble interpretation? Is it that Goldsworthy is getting so 'close' to nature that he is using the very material of nature itself, without altering it much at all? Goldsworthy doesn't seem to *do* much with his materials: he wraps them round a rock, sticks them in a pool, builds a mini tower out of 'em, takes a photo, and then it's 'art'. Is it that his art does not do anything more than this?

Andy Goldsworthy does not, for example, spend hours painting flowers in a meticulous, painstaking fashion, like Leonardo da Vinci. Leonardo also thought of himself as investigating nature: he drew lilies and oak tree sprigs so beautifully, but the beauty was partly in the 'faithfulness' of Leonardo's recording of the plant; that is, the 'beauty' was in the plant (in nature) itself. Leonardo was perhaps revealing again to the viewer what was already there in the world (one of art's noblest and most important functions). Goldsworthy too does this: it is one of his aims. But Leonardo da Vinci made an *image* out of the flower, while Goldsworthy uses the flower itself: he puts the flower into a pool, or takes the petals and wraps them around a boulder. There isn't that same distance between subject and representation that there is in Leonardo's drawings: the traditional way is to draw, paint, sculpt, film, sing or act the thing. Goldsworthy uses the thing-in-itself, by itself.

This is how the art of postwar (postmodern) artists such as Andy Goldsworthy, Yves Klein, Andy Warhol, Joseph Beuys and Carl Andre differs from traditional Western art. They use the *actual object*, a process begun by Marcel Duchamp with his *Urinal* and umbrella stand and developed by Kurt Schwitters. Schwitters' reasoning was along the lines of: why not stick some real objects into an artwork? Jasper Johns reasoned the same way: he preferred the real object itself to a representation of it. Instead of using a replica or an imitation or an image of a rock or an icicle or a leaf, Goldsworthy uses the rock and icicle and leaf themselves.

The confusions of this relationship between reality and illusion, object and image, life and art in Andy Goldsworthy's art are compounded by his use of photography, which instantly renders everything an image, a mode of representation, a text, a simulation, a copy, subject to all the strictures and structures of art, politics, ideology and representation. Goldsworthy's photographs are plainly *not* the object in itself, but a *representation,* a simulation, an equivalent of it, which is very different, and much more complicated.

Andy Goldsworthy has written two short statements on the relation between photography and his art (both entitled "The Photograph" – in *Hand to Earth* [9], and *Stone* [120]). Both mini-essays reveal a confusion and ambiguity regarding photography and art. Firstly, Goldsworthy states that the photograph simply records the work, in a direct, clear, routine fashion. His idea is to 'capture' (document) the work of art, which may change at every minute or moment. The photograph, Goldsworthy said, is the *outcome* of his art, not the initial reason for it. He quoted Yves Klein, one of his gurus, discussing Klein's monochrome pictures:

They are the leftovers from the creative process, the ashes. My pictures, after all, are only the title deeds to my property which I have to produce when I am asked to prove that I am a proprietor. (HE, 9)

A photograph is necessary for Andy Goldsworthy because it brings an outdoor experience into the context of the indoor gallery. The photograph, Goldsworthy says, is necessary to communicate something of the outdoor work in an indoor context, even though '[m]uch of the energy is lost' (HE, 9).

This is all very well, this view that Andy Goldsworthy propounds of the photograph as a necessary record of the outdoor work. In *Stone*'s "The Photograph" essay, the urge to 'capture' the sculpture out of doors becomes much more anxious (it was published in 1994). For example, if the film goes wrong, Goldsworthy says he feels disappointed – the photograph is needed to 'confirm the success or failure' of the work. He's dismayed if he misses photographing the collapse of his sea cairns. Goldsworthy acknowledged in *Wood* that in making balanced columns of stones there were 'inevitably more failures than successes' (23). Throughout his career Goldsworthy must have known hundreds of failed artworks, and must have plenty of photographs of sculptures that didn't work. If the film doesn't come out, Goldsworthy continued, then the sculpture becomes 'dislocated – like a half-forgotten memory' (i.e, it becomes memory, memory being one of the most mysterious of all human phenomena).

These statements demonstrate just how important photography is for Andy Goldsworthy. He is not only a sculptor or land artist: he is also very much a photographer. The photograph is needed by Goldsworthy to keep the work alive – for himself, in his memory: it 'completes' the work, rounds it off. And, crucially, photography shows the work to others. Photography is Goldsworthy's main means of displaying his outdoor work. Rarely are the general public invited to see Goldsworthy making a work of art: 'I am not a performer', he says (S, 120). The ephemeral, outdoor sculpture 'lies at the core of my art and its making must be kept private' (ib.).

Further confusions arise when Andy Goldsworthy discusses the conceptual aspects of photography: it is appropriate, he says, to use a time-sensitive medium such as photography. Why not, then, move into video and film? Why not record the red mud splashes on film? Why not take out stills from the movie of a collapsing arch, and exhibit those? Why not employ time-lapse photography, over a period of a year, to record changes in season, hue, form? In fact, Goldsworthy already has done just that: he has returned to a stone over a year; he has taken motor-wind shots of collapsing stone sculptures; he has made works on the sites of former works. Video was part of the *Time* exhibition (2000) in London, where footage of the snowballs installation of June 21, 2000 was featured. The documentary *Rivers and Tides*, in which Goldsworthy collaborated with filmmaker Thomas Riedelsheimer, appeared in 2002 (and on DVD in 2004).

Future developments in Andy Goldsworthy's art over the next decades will include, one imagines, more use of video and film technology. Instead of using large Cibachrome framed photographs, maybe slides will be projected onto gallery walls, *à la* installation art. Then 'the visual smell and detail of the work' might be even better expressed than in a Cibachrome print. Or maybe the artist will experiment with Quantel paintbox video technology, or Photoshop, or digital technology, like Peter Greenaway and David Hockney, and produce sequences of kinetic sculpture. Surely Yves Klein, Goldsworthy's guru, would have leapt into these new computer/ digital/ video/ film technologies just as vigorously as he 'leapt' into space in his faked *Leap Into the Void.*

Andy Goldsworthy's biggest confusion concerning photography, however, is about that age-old philosophical chestnut, the 'reality' of the image, photography's troubled relationship with 'the real'. Ever since photography was invented, in the early/ mid-19th century, critics have pondered on how 'real' photography is (famous explorations of the thorny subject include those by Roland Barthes, Susan Sontag and John Berger). Goldsworthy's confusion on this point is illustrated by his last words in *Stone*: '[i]f the photograph were to become so real that it overpowered and replaced the work outside, then it would have no purpose or meaning in my art' (S, 120). Aren't photographs already 'real' then? Or are they mere 'illusions'? Surely the photograph is 'real' already, because Goldsworthy admits it is a 'record' of the work, needed to 'confirm' the work? What does he mean, about photography becoming 'so real'? Isn't photography or the image already 'so real', like film and television are 'so real'? Film/ TV/ photo images are 'so real', in fact, they are consumed as 'real', believed as 'true': the average Westerner, for instance, spends 25-40 hours a week watching TV. That's 50-80 continuous days per year of watching television. Is that not 'real' too, in Goldsworthy's æsthetics? What about other forms of technological recording; are these, too, not yet 'so real'? What about virtual reality, or the 'cyberspace' of the internet, or the 'hyper-space' of telephone conversations? Are these, too, still lodged in an archaic argument of being mere 'illusion'? No.

One way of estimating how far things have changed since before mass communication is to consider how people how consume art generally nowadays. Many people will have seen an Andy Goldsworthy artwork in person, but far, far more will have read about his work, seen it in newspapers and magazines, seen it in books, or on the internet, or in TV documentaries, or posters, or stamps.

Andy Goldsworthy has to face up to the fact that most people know about his art (and love his art) from photographs. Most people who know of Goldsworthy have *not* seen a Goldsworthy exhibition; have *not* seen his art in its outdoor environment; have *not* seen Goldsworthy making a work. They have bought the books *Time* and *Wood,* or seen photos of his art in magazines and books. For the punter who consumes art in books and printed material (or on TV or radio or the web), the 'real' art object doesn't need to exist: what counts is the media representation or simulation of it. But this would upset a realist and sensualist (a modernist) like Goldsworthy, who so passionately needs 'to touch' ('I must touch', as he puts it), who needs the real object. A world of computerized virtual reality would be abhorrent to him, where experience is only simulations and images. Yet that is how his art is mainly consumed. Punters have bought the books, seen the photos in magazines and that, for them, is Andy Goldsworthy art. Thus, the *photographs* of Goldsworthy's sculptures are *already* 'so real' that they have, for the consumer, replaced his art.

Andy Goldsworthy has said that it is important for the viewer of his art to fill in the gap between the photograph of the sculpture and the real sculpture that he made someplace else. The photographs are incomplete on their own, as artworks: they require the spectator to create the rest of the artwork by using their imagination and memory, by remembering what it was like to be cold or wet or in a wood. To recall what it was like to be a child, touching leaves or snow or ice (S, 120).

The viewer, then, supplies the 'reality', the 'real' experience, the effect, which the photographs suggest but cannot complete. This could be another reason for Andy Goldsworthy's popularity: that his art leaves some part of the sculptures incomplete, and the viewer can supply the rest from their many memories of the real world. There's a space for the viewer included in the work. A kind of art of interactivity, fed by nature photography. It's also a not insignificant fact that by the time the photographs are published in books or on the net or exhibited in a gallery, most of Goldsworthy's sculptures have already ceased to exist (they've been blown away, collapsed, eroded, dissolved, etc).

Of course, art consumers would probably like to know that the stones *really were* balanced on top of each other on the Welsh coast, or the icicles *really were* stuck to a stone wall in Dumfriesshire. It's probably essential, in fact, for many spectators to think that Andy Goldsworthy really made those works. But Yves Klein faked his *Leap*, and invited people to see an empty gallery. In the age of art impresarios and art gangsters (such as Yves Klein, Andy Warhol, Claes Oldenburg, Jeff Koons, Bruce Nauman, Piero Manzoni, Gilbert & George, and the KLF), when artworks are only known through radio, TV, the web and the press, Goldsworthy could have faked everything. (There are numerous techniques to fake images – not just with modern computers, digital manipulation and Photoshop software, but older methods such as montage, airbrushing and printing separate negatives. Consider masters of photographic superimposition such as Oscar Rejlander, Henry Peach Robinson, Alexander Rodchenko, Max Ernst or John Heartfield).

7

Colour and Decoration

7 : 1   ANDY GOLDSWORTHY'S ART AND DECORATIVE ART

For Richard Long, Andy Goldsworthy is a 'second generation' artist, and is 'decorative (!)' ('decorative' being a put-down).[1] Many (but not most) critics, though, have been extremely praiseworthy of Goldsworthy's art. Neil Hedges wrote: '[t]he artist always achieves his goal, establishing and stimulating our own senses to view or touch conversant shapes and materials with much delight' (73).

Andy Goldsworthy uses modes of art-making dubbed 'feminine': *weaving* stalks or *stitching* leaves together. Weaving, sewing and stitching are regarded as 'feminine' means of production, linked with art and craft, and denigrated by masculinist criticism. Artist Miriam Schapiro took up materials branded 'feminine' by patriarchal culture (cotton, taffeta, burlap, wool, sequins, buttons, thread), and fashioned art-works (she calls them 'femmages') that dealt with notions of the home, feminist iconography, abstraction and the æsthetics of 'Pattern and Decoration'. Schapiro said: 'I wanted to explore and express a part of my life which I had always dismissed – my homemaking, my nesting'.[2] A number of male artists have explored traditionally 'feminine' notions of pattern, decoration and colour, among them Robert Zakanitch, Lucas Samaras, Robert Kushner, Rodney Ripps, Kim MacConnel, Frank Stella and Ned Smyth. But it is women artists who make the most flamboyant and intricate artworks in these areas, such as Joyce Kozloff or Valerie Jaudon.

The 'traditional' 'women's' arts and crafts of textiles, pattern, sewing, decoration, pottery, and so on, are (consciously) bound up with the economies of labour, race, class, identity, patriarchy, politics and money. They are modes of production and art that are regarded as secondary by patriarchal culture, not as high art, such as painting or sculpture. The economics of artistic production are embedded with patriarchal slants, just as much as the images themselves. The piece of textiles, the decorative tile, the pot, are objects that in the patriarchal system speak of their second-rate mode of production. As Catherine King wrote, '[m]edia associated with 'malestream' codes, like bronze, marble, or oil, have been regarded with suspicion' by women artists.3 Although Andy Goldsworthy uses impermanent materials such as leaves and snow, he also employs traditional, 'masculine' media such as stone. This helps his art to be regarded by the art establishment as 'high', 'serious' art.

The beech leaves Andy Goldsworthy placed in a rock pool at Scaur Water in Dumfriesshire (in October, 1992) are certainly pretty and decorative. The next Spring, Goldsworthy put dandelions in the same pool. The two works were printed in the art book *Stone*, and look like a diptych of the seasons Autumn and Spring. They were an obvious exploration of time and seasons, a reading emphasized by the use of the same viewpoint for each photograph. Handfuls of more dandelions were set on top of a large rock in the midst of Scaur Water. A different yellow, of elm leaves, was the colour component in another Scaur Water rock work, *Yellow elm leaves* (1991). In a 2000 sculpture at Townhead Burn in Dumfriesshire Goldsworthy placed yellow elm leaves around a mossy boulder. And another waterbound boulder sculpture was covered with red Japanese maple leaves; the colours, yellow and red, stood out dramatically from the subdued greys and greens of the water and surrounding rocks of the rivers. These works were also about the fact that the intense colours will one day fade and die. 'The intensity and beauty of the yellow are heightened by the know-ledge of the decay that will inevitably follow', Goldsworthy remarked in *Passage* (128).

Andy Goldsworthy's art is 'decorative', definitely, but the colours and patterns are taken from nature: the seemingly 'pretty' colours of bluebells and dandelions, of maple leaves and the Australian Outback, are colours already present in the natural world: they've been there for millions of years. Rather than finding colour 'decorative', for Goldsworthy it is 'raw with energy' (S, 6). The published books might have contributed towards the impression of the artist as decorative, Goldsworthy admitted, but he would carry on using colour anyway, because it was part of the natural world (P, 61).

When Andy Goldsworthy placed red Japanese maple leaves in water their colour 'becomes so intense' he said.4 Many of his works are built on the 'patterns' found in nature. For example, there are many sculptures of Goldsworthy's which create patterns from leaves or stones which have changed colour. He makes lines of bramble leaves which have changed colour, becoming yellowed and browned (1985, AG). He aligns the coloured sections of the leaves together. There are lines made of cherry leaves, poplar leaves and rosebay willowherb leaves (1981-86, reproduced in *Andy Goldsworthy*). The colours of the cherry leaves (Cumbria, 1984) turn from green through yellow to red then brown. Some lines fuse different coloured pebbles together (*Line*, at St Abbs, 1985), going from grey through yellow to white to red. Red, yellow and green beech leaves were laid in a pool in 1999, their colours blended. These are

Autumnal works, rejoicing in the incredible colours of the season. Even in clogged-up, noisome, foggy cities the changing colours of Autumnal leaves may be noticed. In the countryside settings of (most of) Goldsworthy's sculpture, the colours are really rich. They really stand out, when the visual clutter of the modern, technological city is left behind. The 'shield' of sycamore leaves made on Hallowe'en, 1986, in Glasgow, for instance, glowed bright gold. Goldsworthy was excited by the colours of this particular Fall:

> I arrived during a week of the most intense autumn weather I have experienced and the most extraordinary range of colours in the leaves scattered everywhere – sycamore, elm, chestnut...5

The suspended leafshield turned out to be 'one of the best pieces I have ever made', as Andy Goldsworthy put it. The hanging leafworks enable light to become a key element in the sculpture: the translucence of the leaves was highlighted (Goldsworthy usually photographed the leafsheilds back-lit, i.e. with the leafshield in between the artist and the sun). The sun completed the sculpture, making the leafwork as 'extraordinary as going to the Arctic' (HE, 167).

Light is one of the key formal elements that Andy Goldsworthy explores in his sculpture. Critics have spoken of Goldsworthy's 'stunning effects of light and atmosphere'.6 The two leafworks of October, 1997, at the Storm King Art Center in New York state (orange and yellow leaves stuck onto a rock), were made specifically to catch the morning sunlight.7 Another shield, *Horse chestnut leaves* (Yorkshire, 1987), was deliberately created for darkness, hanging in amongst some rhodo- dendron bushes. The Getty Institute clay hole was positioned so that the sun would shine on it once a year, at Midsummer (using solstices or equinoxes or full moons or other celestial events is common in land art). Some of Goldsworthy's *Réfuges d'Art* were constructed to take advantage of certain lighting effects (such as the rising sun at certain times of the year [RA, 85]). *Pool of Light* (2000) was a wooden installation in France built to reveal the changing light (but throughout each day, not over a year). One of the key decisions with regard to light is whether to photograph a sculpture against or with the sun – with the sun backlighting the work, or illuminating it frontally (the leafshields were often photographed from both sides, with Goldsworthy preferring the backlit side).

Another favourite Andy Goldsworthy motif was the rectangle of leaves pinned together (usually measuring a foot and a bit by a couple of feet, but sometimes much smaller, as in *Elm Leaves*, 2000 [P, 133]). Sometimes these leaf oblongs were shields hung from trees (Glasgow, 1986); sometimes they were leaves pressed into the bole of a tree (Dumfriesshire [1998], New York state [1998]), or a rock (New York state, 1997); and sometimes they were set afloat on rivers (*Leaf sheet*, Digne, 1998). Goldsworthy has also covered solitary branches with poppy petals and leaves in many locations, including Yorkshire (1981), TICKON (1993), Stonewood (1992) and Cornell (1999).

A form Andy Goldsworthy has occasionally explored is the serpentine extension of the roots and base of trees, so the roots appear to spread across the ground outwards from the base of the tree in the form of snake-shaped tubes a few inches thick (at Drumlanrig, Dumfriesshire [1999], and Holland [1999]). These tree extensions are usually made from sand or mud (and sometimes snow). Goldsworthy has also carved hump-backed tubular forms, from ice and snow, the loops and humps recalling the Loch Ness monster (Holland, 1984).

Another favourite Andy Goldsworthy sculpture is the serpentine hole (or 'river') carved out of sand, usually on a beach (Holland, 1999), but sometimes inland (Goldsworthy dug quite a few in New Mexico in 1999). Another snake form on the ground was *Woven windfallen ash* (1983), fashioned from branches. Goldsworthy has also made many upright drawings on tree trunks and walls in his customary serpentine form, out of sand, clay and water (in Holland [1999], and Digne [1998]).

Because place is so important,[8] light (and colour) becomes a primary tool. Some Andy Goldsworthy works pivot very much on luminosity and opacity, not just the leafshields, but some of the snow walls, the holes in sand, and so on; so that without the right sort of lighting, they do not work properly. Some sculptures are created in response to certain lighting conditions – the stick sculpture in the Lake District (1988), made in the pale, liquid light of dawn, for example, or the red leaves on the tip of a rock in Government Island in 2003. 'When I work with the land I work with the sky. When I work with water I am working with the clouds', Goldsworthy stated (HE, 167). The branches from a mulga tree in Australia (in 1991) were edged with red sand in order to catch the light of the setting sun: set end to end, the red-edged branches looked like a snake (appropriate for the Australian Outback). Some of Goldsworthy's weakest works were made in Australia in 1991: *Mulga branches* had the branches laid on the red sand in two directions; they changed colour as the light changed.

Other sculptures are seen in a variety of lighting conditions – stormlight, snowlight, misty skies (the snow wall of 1988 at Blencathra in Cumbria is an obvious instance). Some of the brightest of Andy Goldsworthy's leafworks have been made in Japan, where the maple leaves are dazzling in October and November (in, for example, *Maple patch*, November 22, 1987, or *Japanese maple*, November 21-22, 1987).

Andy Goldsworthy's flower pieces are inevitably 'pretty'. It's difficult to use flowers, in poetry, sculpture, painting or performance, without appearing 'pretty' (Goldsworthy realizes this [S, 6]). Think of Rainer Maria Rilke's many flower poems (to roses, irises, lilies), or the beautiful, sonorous flower watercolours of the German Expressionist Emil Nolde. Like Nolde's radiant flowerpieces, like the flowerworks of 17th century Flemish and Dutch art, Goldsworthy's flower sculptures are luminous. The dandelion piece (April 28, 1987), which is a spread of flowers forming a hole in the middle, is striking not because of the shape the artist's made, but because of the vibrant yellow of the flowers.

Flowers are amazing, some of the most exquisite creations on Earth. All Andy Goldsworthy seems to have to do is to arrange them in a simple structure and the beauty of the flowers does the rest. What's also noteworthy about *Dandelions newly flowered* is that the sculpture is set on 'a grass verge between dual carriageways' (highways), so the title informs the viewer. If this is so, then this sculpture and photograph is very noisy: there will be cars roaring up and down the roads on either side of the sculpture. Goldsworthy's art reveals, as good poetry does, the incredible beauty of nature, even amongst the smelly, grey environment of a busy highway. Even at the verges of roads, in hedges beside ugly freeways, on empty intersections, there are amazing things growing.

Sometimes Andy Goldsworthy goes too far in evoking the beauty of nature. In another dandelion piece, *Dandelion flowers pinned with thorns to wind-bent willow-herb stalks laid in a ring held above bluebells with forked sticks* (May 1, 1987), Goldsworthy fashioned a large open circle of dandelions and ranges them above a field of bluebells (S, 11). But it's too much: the incandescent yellow of the dandelions set against the equally rich blue of the bluebells. Bluebells in a wood don't require anything to make them look beautiful. Thus, *Dandelion flowers* (May 1, 1987), is a powerful image, but does nothing to explore nature, Goldsworthy's avowed artistic aim. Other dandelion works include a line of dandelions laid on grass growing in a pool (Yorkshire, 1987), dandelion petals edging mud slits (Yorkshire, 1987), a line of dandelions following the outline a rock (Dumfriesshire, 1994), a line of dandelions pressed into the edge of a village lane (Cahors, France, 1996), and dandelions laid along the Capenoch tree (1994). (Note that Goldsworthy hasn't used dandelions so much since the 1990s, along with all other flowers).

It's noteworthy that Andy Goldsworthy has only used a very small selection of flowers in his sculptures: poppy, foxglove, dandelion. He's far more inclined to use leaves or grass or stalks (such as hogweed or willowherb). Also, when Goldsworthy does use flowers, he avoids the hugely symbolic flowers of the Western tradition, such as the rose, lily or iris. And the flowers of Britain are also side-stepped: the daffodil, the primrose, the snowdrop, the carnation, the gladioli, the tulip, the forget-me-not, and so on. In addition, Goldsworthy has not made many flowerpieces in his later work.

Notice also that Andy Goldsworthy tends to produce work outdoors with a very small number of plants: he has his favourite materials, such as willowherb stalks, or yellow beech or elm leaves, or green sycamore leaves. He has not fashioned many sculptures from nettles or brambles (for obvious reasons, perhaps). Or thistles. Or ferns and bracken. Cowslips, gorse bushes, ivy, pine cones and mistletoe are other plants Goldsworthy doesn't use much (although he has put some of these elements in his snowballs). And among trees, Goldsworthy hasn't employed the following trees much: yew, pine, laurel, willow, hawthorn, holly, and the vine. Goldsworthy may avoid certain plants and flowers for all sorts of reasons, some practical, some æsthetic, some social, and some symbolic. Some of the plants noted above are loaded with thousands of years of symbolism: rose, lily, willow, laurel, hawthorn, mistletoe. Goldsworthy really likes the colour red, for instance, and it would be so easy for him to employ rose petals: instead, he opts for the poppy.

Some of the most popular flowers, like tulips, roses, irises and carnations, come in many different hues and types, and are cultivated on an industrial scale. That may be another reason (a social one) why Goldsworthy prefers not to use those flowers. Maybe they've lost their wildness, their individuality, their magic, and now they've become commercial, mass-produced products, just another part of the natural world that humans have 'tamed' and turned into commodities.

The attention to the minute, detailed qualities of nature that Andy Goldsworthy's art rejoices in is mirrored in Romantic poetry and nature poetry. John Cowper Powys, for instance, could get excited by nothing more 'spectacular' than a patch of moss on a wall. Goldsworthy's sculpture has the same delight in the small, seemingly unimportant aspects of the natural world, stuff that would be overlooked by most all of contemporary culture. In his *Autobiography* (1934), John Cowper Powys wrote: 'I am looking at a patch of moss on a greenish marbly rock and I am aware of a deep sensual pleasure' (41). And in Cambridge, on one of his many walks around the outskirts of the city, Powys remarked that 'certain patches of grass and green moss transported me into a sort of Seventh Heaven' (199). (Like land artists such as Robert Smithson and Dennis Oppenheim, Powys liked the outer areas of towns, border zones and abandoned realms).

In his fiction (still criminally neglected by the literary establishment), John Cowper Powys described the ecstasies that (land) artists have when interacting with nature. Powys's characters, like those in the work of William Wordsworth, Johann Wolfgang von Goethe, George Seferis, and Maria Tsvetayeva, are nature mystics, just as land artists such as Andy Goldsworthy, David Nash, Peter Randall-Page, Nancy Holt, Chris Drury and Robert Smithson are in part nature mystics. Sam Dekker, in Powys's massive nature mysticism novel *A Glastonbury Romance* (1932), experiences a *participation mystique* with the Earth: '[w]hat he felt was a strange and singular reciprocity between his soul and every little fragment of masonry, of stony ground, of mossy ground...'9 And Dud No-Man in the last of Powys's Wessex quartet books, *Maiden Castle* (1936), when he comes to 'a patch of green moss on a grey wall' gets 'a sensation that's more important than what you call 'love', or anything else, nearer the secret of things too!'10

7 : 2   COLOUR IN ANDY GOLDSWORTHY'S ART

Colour is an expression of life.

Andy Goldsworthy (*Passage*, 127)

Andy Goldsworthy has spoken of the significance of using the colour red: in Japan, he remarked, he learnt about a 'deeply disturbing' red (W, 15), a 'heightened awareness of red. A bright red maple tree in the middle of a green forest, like an open wound' (in ib.). It is the *colour* of the 'red splashes' or 'throws' that contributes much in making them powerful. Goldsworthy often uses red in his art – in the boulders covered in red maple leaves (1991) or the poppy-leaved covered stones (1989), or poppy petal-covered branches (1992), or the ridged holes made on the beach at the Isle of Wight with red edges (1987, AG). Red maple leaves climb up rocks or are layered on top of little rockpools (1993). Goldsworthy relates red to the iron in human blood.

The Harrlemmerhout, Holland work, *Poppy petals* (1984), was a seven-foot long line of poppy petals held together with spit which was hung from an elderberry. It was, a critic said, 'one of the most impressive and poetic works' that Andy Goldsworthy made during his time at Haarlem.[1] At Hampstead Heath (in London) an associated work, a line of beech leaves, was floated over a pool.[2] Red-tinted water spread like blood over the floor of the Barbican Centre in London, melted from inside a snowball (2000). In Australia the colour red did not arrive in Goldsworthy's work, as one might expect, from flower petals or red stones, but from red sand: Goldsworthy rubbed the sand into the bark of a mulga tree (1991). Gathering rain clouds and a brilliant, low sun created the right lighting conditions to bring out the red tree against the brooding grey sky (S, 54-55). Goldsworthy said that the red of the Australian Outback was 'deeply moving spiritually'. 'I have tried to touch that colour not just with my hands, but also with light' he added (W, 15).

Andy Goldsworthy is using a standard observation of natural science: the colour red really stands out in a landscape. In the historical Japanese Zen garden, colours are carefully orchestrated, so that a single leaf can set off a vast acreage of predominantly green or ochre. In the Oriental garden, notions of *feng shui* and *yin* and *yang* control how a landscape is shaped by humans. In the system of *feng shui*, the elements of a garden or a building must be in harmony with the natural forces of air, water and earth. Get it wrong and one messes up the creation. The Zen or Taoist harmonizing approach is very much that of Goldsworthy's art. In the manner of the ecologically-friendly follower, Goldsworthy speaks of wanting to be in harmony with nature. Goldsworthy, like other artists, can be seen as an ecological artist, artists committed to ecological issues.[3] (Although other artists foreground political concerns far more often).

Chinese gardens were designed by balancing the principles of *yin* (feminine) and *yang* (masculine), water and mountain. Andy Goldsworthy's art, like other land art, can be seen as a kind of modern *feng shui,* a Westerner's (secular) way of harmonizing the *yin* and *yang* elements. Land artists reorganize the landscape, building mountains, digging holes, creating pools, as in *feng shui.*

Oriental gardens were asymmetrical – in that single æsthetic element they differ greatly from Western formal gardens with their patterns, squares, crosses, parallel paths, and mathematically exact *parterres*. Oriental gardens were founded on stone, sand, water, flowers, moss and trees, an elementalism that chimes with land art concerns (compare with the materials Andy Goldsworthy favours: ice, water, petals, leaves, stone). If sand was used, it could evoke water by being raked into wave-like shapes. Stones could be mountains, but also, via abstraction, other natural forms. In the 'dry garden' of Zen Buddhism (the *karesanui*), stone could be water, or cascades. Stones were valued highly for gardens, and were bought and sold. Many kinds of stone were used in Oriental gardens, including schist, volcanic rock, granite, limestone, slate and jasper.

Perhaps the most famous of the Japanese Zen gardens is at Ryoanji, Kyoto (made in the 1480s). It is 30 by 70 feet with white gravel raked parallel to the longer side. There are 15 rocks placed in it, and a verandah surrounds it. The Ryoanji garden is garden design reduced to its simplest elements, an ultimate in reduction and purification. There are no trees, flowers or plants in the garden. In Andy Goldsworthy's art there is a similar emphasis on asymmetry, on keeping forms as they appear in nature, on contemplation, on valuing objects such as stones as sacred in their own right, with nothing needing to be added to them.

Contemplation was clearly a key purpose of the Oriental garden. 'Contemplation gardens' were meant to be consumed from one viewpoint (from the noble's house, for example). The 'contemplation garden' was often a 'dry garden', with several islands in its midst having particular meanings. Some of Andy Goldsworthy's sculptures recall the 'islands' in Oriental gardens; like contemplation gardens, Goldsworthy's works are usually designed to be viewed from one point (Goldsworthy endorses the single-viewpoint in his work in his use of photography, with its monoscopic vision. Artworks are built to be seen from one viewpoint – unless they are public sculptures, which visitors can explore from a variety of angles). Goldsworthy can thus be seen as creating Western versions of Oriental and Zen gardens, in which contemplation is the primary activity for the art consumer.

J.M.W. Turner, England's greatest artist, also knew the impact and beauty of the colour red. Turner's artistic rival, John Constable, recounted an incident where he, John Constable, had painted a famous river scene which he was sure would be the pride of the Royal Academy show. Not to be outdone, Turner came in ot the gallery when Constable was away and added a smudge of red to an otherwise grey seascape. The red blob was intended to be a buoy, and it lifted up Turner's painting a few notches. Constable was enraged. It's a nice story of a great artist knowing exactly how to wield colour.

In a similar way, Andy Goldsworthy puts in a red object in amongst the soft, muted colours of green moss and grey, wet rocks of South-West Scotland. The colour red stands out even more on wintry, overcast days, when there is hardly any deep colour in the surroundings. In 1993 Goldsworthy fashioned a number of sculptures in small pools of water he found on the rocks at his beloved Scaur Water in Dumfriesshire. He stained the pools with the powder from some red stones. The manufacture of these sculptures consisted of nothing more elaborate than rubbing some stones together to stain some water (other, later pools had red maple leaves or poppy petals laid in them, as at Storm King in New York in 1995). The results, though (photographed in *Stone* and *Black Stones, Red Pools*), are dramatic: as Goldsworthy says, often a good sculpture needs only a delicate or small-scale touch in the right place to make it work (S, 95). In amongst the weather-worn and water-worn boulders of Scottish streams the mid-red stands out vividly. It reveals the contours of the surrounding rock; the relation between the pool of water in its isolation from the rest of the river (which formed it); and the elegant ovals and circular shapes of each pool. These are the landscapes of Goldsworthy's art, these bleak, grey, wintry scenes, beside a lake, or the sea, or a river, or halfway up a mountain. Next to a mound of grey slate, the colour red stands out, like 'a wound', as Goldsworthy says, emphasizing the flesh-and-blood nature of his art.

It is the leafworks that are the most colourful of Andy Goldsworthy's sculptures. What the leaf sculptures demonstrate is how beautiful the colours of nature can be: Goldsworthy shows the viewer these subtle colours by contrasting one leaf with another. *Maple patch* (1987, Japan) grouped the red/ orange/ yellow of Japanese maple leaves together; *Poppy leaves* (1984, Netherlands) set the red poppy leaves against the mid-green of an elderberry bush; a Stone Wood sculpture of 1992 (*Poppy petals*) consisted of poppy leaves wrapped around a hazel branch, the red contrasting vividly with the wet green leaves of late Summer; *Dock Leaves* (1978, Morecambe) interwove red leaves in green grass stalks. Two sycamore leafworks of 1980 and 1981 (in Yorkshire) were very simple: a leaf black from cow shit was placed against pale Autumn leaves; another leaf, bleached white, was set down on a bed of dark leaves. Goldsworthy pinned together two colours of sycamore leaves (sycamore is a favourite Goldsworthy medium) in *Sycamore leaf sections* (1988), and hung the line of leaves from a tree. Shot with the sun behind them, the photograph of the leaves showed them glowing green and gold, the two classic colours of poetry and alchemy. The Fall colours of course connote nostalgia, decadence, sensuality, Romanticism, time passing, the decay of the year, and so on, all those things John Keats wrote about in his 'Ode: To Autumn', and in a billion other poets in a billion poems about Autumn.

Other lines of leaves laid on water include Digne (1998), *Japanese maple* (Japan, 1987), *Horse chestnut leaves* (Leicestershire, 1987), *Hazel leaves* (Dumfriesshire, 1991), *Elm leaves* (1994, Dumfriesshire), and *Beech leaves* (London, 1985). Some of Andy Goldsworthy's leafworks were created with Tom Lang, in St Louis (1987), where Goldsworthy explored pulping plants.

A group of works made in Andy Goldsworthy's stamping ground of Dumfriesshire in Scotland in the Fall of 2002 explored the bright yellow of elm leaves. In amongst the browns and greys of autumnal landscape and the dull, overcast light, the yellowy elm leaves stood out vividly (these leaf-works, and the later ones using dark brown leaves, were made for 'the transition from autumn into winter and the damp, grey short days that are so common at this time of year in Scotland', Goldsworthy remarked [P, 134]). Goldsworthy fashioned a ring of leaves around a mossy rock; wrapped in a band around a branch (an 'old style' Goldsworthy sculpture); a square shape of leaves placed on a rock, with lines torn through them; *Elm Sticks* was a border of leaves around some elm branches supported by bark, over a stream; *Elm Leaves* was a row of leaves moving from brown through yellow to green, laid on bark over a stream. (Goldsworthy was also making work in Townhead Burn, a different stream and valley not far from his favourite spot of Scaur Water).

A new form appeared in Andy Goldsworthy's *œuvre* in late 2002: leafworks which employed a new play with spatial illusions, in particular the relation between foreground and background (which was heightened by the use of bright-hued leaves against predominantly dark backgrounds), and the idea of an invisible support for a sculpture. These new works took the form of: leaves laid on top of bark over a stream (*Elm Leaves*, 2002), so it looked as if the leaf row was floating above the water; and the image that formed the cover of *Passage*: four rows of yellow elm leaves laid on top of bark over a stream. These leafworks (like the other works exploring elm leaves made from Fall, 2000 onwards) were all very small in scale, and used the brightness of the leaves against the dark hues of the autumnal landscape as the visual hook.

Andy Goldsworthy's aim in the leaf pieces, though, drew attention to the fragility and delicacy of leaves, as well as their strength and function. A leaf, after all, is a complex biological factory, so the natural scientists suggest. 'There is a whole world in a single leaf', commented Goldsworthy.[4] Goldsworthy's leafworks do not have a scientific agenda. Rather, they celebrate the presence of leaves, the being-in-the-world of leaves, so to speak. In his sketchbook of August 17, 1984, Goldsworthy wrote:

> I am beginning to get more structure into leaf work – forced to find structure in leaves – No rocks or branches. The key is in the leaf veins – The leaf architecture. Amazing how geometric the structure is. (HE, 100)

Andy Goldsworthy's leaf sculptures are, like all land art, specific to particular places. The brilliant oranges and reds and yellows in *Maple patch* (1987) or *Line to explore colours in leaves, calm, overcast* (1987) could only occur in Japan, it seems. Place and work are one for Goldsworthy: he does not distinguish between elements in a work: '[l]ooking, touching, material, place, making the form and resulting work are totally integral'.[5]

The forms Andy Goldsworthy explored in his 1989 *Leaves* show in Britain's capital included boxes of sycamore and plane leaves (with the stalks sticking out); a 16 inch cube; cones and pyramids; beech shields; seed pods; hollow globes of sweet chestnut; spiral bands; a lengthy serpent form (51 inches long); and probably the most distinctive shape of Goldsworthy's leafworks, the horn.[6]

Andy Goldsworthy weaved in brown leaves with yellow leaves, forming a contrast between the two colours, as in *Yellow and ruddy leaves* (1986). As with so many of Goldsworthy's sculptures, *Yellow and ruddy leaves* includes in its title the mode of its making:

> [The] Yellow and ruddy leaves[:]
> [I] made [the] edge [of the line] by finding [a] ruddy and yellow leaf [which were] the same size[.]
> [I] tore [the] yellow leaf in two, [and] spat underneath one half [of it,]
> [then] pressed it on to the ruddy leaf[.] (HE, 64)

Andy Goldsworthy's leaf sculptures are often at their most effective in Fall, not surprisingly, as the dates for many of the leaf pieces demonstrate (November 1, 1986, November 22, 1987, November, 1977, October 22, 1992, November, 2003, and so on). Works such as *Line to follow colours in maple leaves* (1992) use the changing colour of leaves in Autumn as their basic structure: the leaves pinned to the fallen tree change from green through yellow to orange, red and damson. One of Goldsworthy's finest leafworks was made in Illinois in 1992. It comprised of a shield of red maple leaves set in the 'V' of two tree trunks. The importance of light was emphasized in *Maple leaves* in the book *Wood* by the decision to include a photograph of the sculpture from both sides, showing the sun shining on the leaves from one side, and shining through the leaves from the other.

Sometimes the wind is a problem, blowing away works which Andy Goldsworthy has painstakingly constructed (Goldsworthy often chooses valleys or woods or more sheltered spots for his leafworks – there are few leaf pieces on an open mountainside in the Goldsworthy *œuvre*, for instance.) Making the leafworks enables Goldsworthy to learn about leaves – leaves blown from trees, or cold, brittle leaves, or 'wet frost-fallen' leaves, or freshly grown leaves. He is careful to take only a 'few leaves from each tree.'[7] He follows the seasonal development of leaves closely, most especially in and around his studio in Scotland. Leaves, like stones or snow, teach the artist much.

> The sycamore has taught me most [Goldsworthy said]. The biggest lesson being that so much can be found in something common and ordinary. Its leaf can turn all colours; its stalks can go bright red and within its leaf structure I realised my first leaf construction.[8]

Andy Goldsworthy's art might not work in richly coloured gardens, such as British gardens like Sissinghurst Garden in Kent, or Powis Castle in Wales. In amongst the beautiful white lilies and roses, the brilliant yellow daffodils and primroses, the succulent blue of irises and pansies, Goldsworthy's poppy-red stones would not stand out so much (indeed, they would be totally lost in a rose garden). Goldsworthy's artworks are compelling partly because they are sited in wildernesses, not in the projects, not on the trash-strewn verges of highways, not in the bleak streets of dreary towns. Set amongst the green grass and slate-grey rocks, Goldsworthy's blocks of snow or stitched sycamore leaves hollow out their space and influence. They could not compete with most urban environments, or with freeways or out-of-town shopping malls. (For instance, when Goldsworthy installed snowballs on the streets of London in 2000, they were large snowballs, not small snowballs. Works in the same scale as the leafworks, for example, would be lost in the cityscape).

Andy Goldsworthy's sculptures require specific (and controlled) contexts and environments in order to work. The foxglove petal sculpture, with its delicate pink tones (Leeds, 1977), needs to be set in amongst the grey rocks to work properly. Similarly, pieces such as the russet-coloured dock leaves, woven into bright green grass stems (Morecambe, 1978), are small sculptures, requiring close-up photography to make them live. In the case of the dark soil or peat-covered rocks, made in Japan, Lancashire and the Isle of Skye, the close-up photograph does not work so well: it is the context of these large boulders in their wild landscapes that makes them stand out: thus Goldsworthy includes the rural surroundings in the composition.

Andy Goldsworthy's photographs, too, are carefully framed so that they miss out the electricity poles, the trash heaps, the kicked-in fences, the smashed bottles, the abandoned cars, the supermarket carts, that are a feature of every landscape everywhere in the British Isles (and many other places Goldsworthy visits), no matter how far from the throbbing centres of humanity. However far one goes, one confronts the marks of humans. Go wandering in the wildernesses of central Wales, say – one of the least densely populated places in Great Britain – and one'll find trash. One may be able to purchase a few miles between oneself and the nearest road, so that the sound of cars will fade into the susurrus of the wind. Sky above, grass underfoot, and nothing but the 1,500 foot high system of mountains.[9]

Andy Goldsworthy's photographs present an idealized world, veritably the pastoral world of ancient times. Goldsworthy's Arcadia, though, is definitely a Northern European pastoral realm, not the Southern, Mediterranean paradise of satyrs, shepherdesses, gods and wild animals. Goldsworthy's 'pastoral sublime', to use the phrase applied to a category of J.M.W. Turner's works, is a Northern European realm, very much in the tradition of Turner's paintings of the Alps, with lowering, gloomy skies, raging wind, snow-capped mountains and mossy riverbanks. John Martin, Thomas Girtin, John Sell Cotman, John Constable and J.M.W. Turner made many paintings of the landscapes Goldsworthy works in. Apart from Australia and Japan, Goldsworthy's art centres around cold, rain-sodden, Northern landscapes (he has made many works in Southern France, though, since the mid-1990s). True, there is much sunlight in his photographs of Australia, photographs that evoke the stereotypical colonial view of the out-back as a rugged, inhospitable place where the white people sit around camp fires. Goldsworthy's Japan is a more sublime, rarefied place, though it is still rough and distinctly non-human.

Andy Goldsworthy photographs his sculptures often looking down on them, so the surrounding landscape is not seen. He edits out unsightly buildings or roads, but art has always involved much more editing than many artists would admit. Goldsworthy knows that what one leaves out of a work is as important as what one puts in. Goldsworthy said that photographs were 'very important to me as a working record', and that he had a record of nearly everything he'd made, which he could look on and use.[10] 'A good work is the result of being in the right place at the right time with the right material', said Goldsworthy.[11]

8

Trees, Tides, Plants and Holes

Andy Goldsworthy is by no means the only contemporary artist who uses living plants. Hundreds have. Some artists have installed trees upside-down (Vito Acconci) and plants upside-down in galleries (Michael Blazy, Henrik Håkansson, Sam Kunce). Some artists have trained plants to grow at odd angles (Hans Haacke, Cartsen Höller). Some artists have forced plants into vacu-formed moulds (Laura Stein) and rubber foam (Ingo Vetter, Annette Weisser). Some artists have lined rooms with cages of bay leaves to produce an aromatic environment (Giuseppe Penone). Some artists have planted seeds on their naked bodies (Teresa Murak). Some artists have planted clover fields in galleries (Nikolaj Recke) and made couches from grass (Daniel Spoerri). Some artists have built parks running up the sides of buildings, complete with benches and steps (Vito Acconci); some have made enclosed indoor gardens (Knut Åsdam). Other artists have created portable orchards (the Harrisons); portable indoor vegetable gardens (N55); and crammed hothouses (Lothar Baumgarten). And some have let roses run riot over cars (Silvie Fleury). Herman de Vries is a close competitor with Goldsworthy for the artist who's created the most works with living plants.

Plenty of land artists and sculptors have used real flowers as well as Andy Goldsworthy: Anya Gallaccio took up roses (1992), sunflowers (1991) and zinnias (1992) (she's become more associated with flowers than Goldsworthy); Herman de Vries (who spread thousands of lavender flowers on a gallery floor in 1998); Wolfgang Laib with his pollen floor spreads; Richard Long, who pressed flowers flat in a field in

Brough of Birsay Circle (1994); Jenny Holzer's *Black Garden*, a war memorial garden of very dark plants and flowers (1994); Gary Rieveschl, who planted *Heart Wave,* a line of 12,000 red tulips, in 1980; Daniel Buren also made a row of tulips, *11,000 Tulips* (1987, Holland); and Peter Hutchinson, who planted 'thrown ropes' of flowers (1996). And also Annette Wehrmann, Shelagh Wakely, Mark Dion, Meg Webster, Carsten Höller, Paula Hayes, Peter Fischl, David Weiss, Tobias Rehberger, Lothar Baumgarten, Brigitte Raabe, and Olaf Nicolai.

One of the most famous of contemporary sculptures using living flowers was Jeff Koons' giant dog sculpture (*Puppy*, 1992), constructed in Arolsen with 17,000 flowers, and standing 11.5 yards tall. 'I decided I wanted to make an image that communicated warmth and love to people. A very spiritual piece. It just came to me to make the *Puppy* out of live flowers'.[1] Although Koons' art was known for its postmodern, camp, trashy chic, Koons likened the interior of the *Puppy* to a church: 'I wanted the piece to deal with the human condition, and this condition in relation to God. I wanted it to be a contemporary Sacred Heart of Jesus' (ibid.).

8 : 2   TREES

Many sculptors and land artists have worked with trees as well as Andy Goldsworthy: David Nash, Giuseppi Penone, William Jackson Maxwell, Robert Irwin, Jackie Winsor, Daniel Buren, Alan Sonfist, Harvey Fite, Peter Walker, Giuliano Mauri, Nils Udo, Luc Wolff, Maria Nordman, Sjoerd Buisman, Cosima von Bonin, Stefan Banz, Vito Acconci, Jørn Rønnau, Buster Simpson, Jan Dibbets, Helge Røed, Lars Vilks, Andy Lipkis, Herman de Vries and Mel Chin.

Using trees means working within a long and celebrated religious and cultural tradition.[1] For example, trees have since time immemorial been associated with spirits and religions. The Greeks believed that trees had spirits; there were the apples of immortality and trees of eternal life; Daphne turned into a tree when pursued by Zeus; Actæon was transformed into a stag in the forest when he spied Diana bathing nude; deities such as Athena, Artemis, Dionysus, Apollo, Orpheus and Cybele are associated with trees and woods. The Celts worshipped trees, and the Germanic tribes had mystical relations with trees. The Druids revered the oak, the royal tree of ancient England, and had rituals that involved oaks and mistletoe. The oak (a favourite Andy Goldsworthy tree) was sacred to Jupiter, Hercules, the Dagda, Thor, Jehovah, Allah and other gods in their 'thunder-god' mode. Trees were associated with secret languages and religious symbolism. Fire festivals are in particular linked with trees – burning wood is central to many land artworks: there were the bonfires at the Celtic fire festivals (such as Samhain, or Hallowe'en, a fire festival inaugurating the beginning of the Celtic year which transferred in Britain to Bonfire Night); on Midsummer Day fires are lit, traditionally with oakwood; Midsummer was also the time of the sacrifice of the oak-king of Nemi. The willow is deeply associated with witchcraft (the words 'witch' and 'wicked' are derived from the same ancient word for 'willow'); the laurel is linked with poetry – the reward for great poetic endeavour was the laurel ('Daphne', in Greek, is associated with Apollo's pursuit of the Goddess Daphne); laurel was also an intoxicant – the leaves were chewed to induce a frenzy – and the Italian poet Francesco Petrarch revered the laurel tree, linking it with his beloved Laura and the longed-for notion of poetic immortality which the laurel symbolized. Particular trees have been mythologized: there was the 'holy thorn' that, as legend has it, sprang from Joseph of Arimathea's staff as he planted it in the sacred ground of Glastonbury; the wood of the Sacred Tree of Creevna, at Killura, had healing properties; naked children were passed through gaps in pollard ashes before dawn as a cure for rupture; Yygdrasill was the sacred ash tree of the Viking god Woden – he used it as his steed; in secular times trees still play a mythic role: there are the trees that hid figures such as Robin Hood and Charles I from their foes.

In fairy and folk tales, forests are places of enchantment, initiation and trial, where strange beasts and beings are encountered, spells are undertaken. The 'dark forest' or *selva oscura* occurs at the opening of the great poem of European culture, Dante's *Divine Comedy*, where the first thing the poet-pilgrim does is enter the 'dark forest'.

When land artists pick up a bit of wood, then, or use a branch in their work, they are activating a mass of associations in the fields of symbolism, legend, myth, magic and religion. Every tree and type of wood has its symbolic associations: oak, beech, laurel, willow, sycamore, ash, larch, hawthorn, holly, vine, hazel, ivy, rowan, alder and birch.

One of the most ancient religious functions of the tree was the World Tree of shamanism, the oldest of all religions. The World Tree was the mythic centre of the world of the community, it was the *axis mundi*, the pivot of time and space. The archaic shaman had many tasks: one of them was to travel to the Other World, to bring back news of what happened there, and to guide the souls of the departed to the Land of the Dead. The shaman did this by climbing up the Cosmic Tree: the shaman's magical flight to the Other World was linked with climbing the World Tree.

What has all this to do with contemporary land art? A lot. Constantin Brancusi, more influential on land art than Pablo Picasso, Jean Arp, Alberto Giacometti, Auguste Rodin, Henri Matisse or Aristide Maillol, worked notions of shamanic flight into his *Birds in Space* sculptures, and most especially in his *Endless Column*, which is cited by many key sculptors (Donald Judd, Carl Andre, Robert Morris) as an important inspiration. Brancusi's *Birds in Space* aimed to express the essence of flight, the moment when a quivering verticality is released from the chains of gravity and flies upward. One only has to look at David Nash's *Tripods*, Andy Goldsworthy's tower of rocks, Barnett Newman's *Broken Obelisk*, or Donald Judd's stacks, to see how important Brancusi's sculptures were, with their shamanic, World Tree associations.

Planting trees has become a favourite with land and environmental artists: Andy Goldsworthy has planted dwarf oak saplings in his Holocaust memorial in New York; Alan Sonfist created several solid circles and rings of trees (*Circles of Life* [1986], *Circles of Time* [1987]); Mel Chin planted trees and plants on a landfill site in St Paul, MN (*Revival Field*); Joseph Beuys led the planting of oak trees at Documenta 7 in

Kassel in 1982; Andy Lipkis planted trees in urban areas (such as L.A.), and organized fund-raising marathon runs for trees (1979); Giuseppe Penone placed a long white crystal in tree trunks, a very Goldsworthyan piece (*Light Traps*, 1994); Vito Acconci constructed a tower of trees (1996), one above the other, all of them upside-down; Robert Irwin installed nine plum trees in Seattle, WA (1983), separated by blue screens; and Buster Simpson planted willow trees in drinking fountains (1993).

Daniel Buren constructed one of the most compelling of all treeworks: an olive tree standing atop a huge cube of soil in a gallery (*Untitled*, 1999), a truly spectacular (and enigmatic) work, with the tree and earth in proportion, quietly dominating the ornate room at Castello di Rivoli. *Pace* his *Sheepfolds* project, Goldsworthy remarked in 2001 that the

> planting of any tree is a gesture of optimism and renewal – growing out of stone in the protective embrace of a sheepfold will, I hope, give that gesture a potent mixture of feelings – hardship, struggle, fragility, precariousness and strength.[2]

Andy Goldsworthy has worked intimately with trees since the beginning of his career as a sculptor and land artist. He has his favourite trees (oak, beech, elm), with sycamore trees favoured for their broad, flat leaves (for building objects such as the leaf boxes). Elm trees, for example, are Goldsworthy's chief source of yellow in the Fall (P, 127). Some of Goldsworthy's most important works have used trees as their focal point, such as the *Capenoch Tree* series, and *Sidewinder* and *Seven Spires* at Grizedale forest. Goldsworthy has employed trees in countless works, using leaves and branches as materials in hundreds of sculptures, or trunks as easels or scaffolding. He's hung many works from trees: snowballs, shields, and lines of leaves. He's decorated trees with dandelions and snow. He's pressed leaves and sand into boles. He's extended trees with sand and clay. He's wrapped branches with petals and leaves. He's created footpaths winding between trees. He's used trees as backgrounds for carved sand drawings. He's built branches into stone walls. He's let trees define the path of his major works, such as the stone walls. He's worked in many, many forests and woods.

Indeed, if you took trees out of Andy Goldsworthy's art, there would be a huge gap. In Goldsworthy's art, trees embody time, change, beauty, mystery, and place. Trees are, in short, the 'architecture of the planet'.[3]

Andy Goldsworthy's anxious, ambivalent attitude towards holes in the ground recall the views of (usually male) philosophers on the negativity of holes and voids, which are associated with the sexual identity of women. These fears and ambiguities are found in much of Western culture: in Sigmund Freud's castration myth; in the bilious misogynist Christian theology of St Augustine, Tertullian, St Paul and Origen; or the sadomasochistic literature of the Marquis de Sade and Georges Bataille. In this view, women are vampires and witches, preying mantises and carnivorous spiders sucking up male desire and energy. Another religious view sees women as Mother Goddesses, identified with nature, the seasons, vegetation and the powers of the Earth. A deity which some feminists and British poets (such as Robert Graves and Peter Redgrove) have worshipped (though they would not use that term) is the 'Black Goddess', a divinity of darkness, night, the unknown and the supernatural.

The psychologist Jacques Lacan's notion of the 'lack' or loss, which subsequent feminists (such as Hélène Cixous, Julia Kristeva and Luce Irigaray) have critiqued, is another obvious reference to the hole. What women lack (for Lacan) is the phallus, the 'transcendent signifier' as cultural theorists call it. The art object is thus (in Julia Kristeva's interpretation) a fetish, a stand-in for the imaginary maternal phallus. Friedrich Nietzsche had similar views of the 'feminine': it was not menstruation or lactation that scandalized Nietzsche so much as the lack or absence of a visible (sexual) organ. 'What Mother Nature needs so urgently to hide from view is not so much what she has as what she lacks. Nietzsche suspects a void at the center of the body of nature.'[1] In French feminist Luce Irigaray's reading of Lacan's philosophy, what women lack is the ability to speak from/ with the phallus: the genital lack suggests an ideological or æsthetic lack, an absence which becomes cultural silence.

This masculinist fear of the black hole or void at the heart of nature is very apparent in Andy Goldsworthy's statements: 'looking into a deep hole unnerves me' he wrote; the black holes of his sculptures are openings into the 'deep insecurity in nature – a fragile, unpredictable and violent energy' (S, 64). Goldsworthy is fascinated by holes: 'I enjoy the seductiveness of a hole', he said, 'which always makes me want to explore the spaces inside or beyond' (HE, 61). Goldsworthy admitted to being frightened as well as fascinated by the powers of nature. He spoke of the blackness under the Earth rising up and buckling the rim of the holes he makes in the ground and in the floors of art galleries. He made a hole in a gallery floor (in London) to remind the spectator that just below the building is the unpredictable and immense energy of nature and the Earth.

Andy Goldsworthy dug holes at the Serpentine Gallery (London) in 1982 and 1984, at Coracle Press, London (in 1985), and at the Frans Hals Museum (in 1984). Sculptures such as the Greenpeace office commission – *Seven Holes* (1991) – are obviously about the Earth's energies (planetary as well as local forces). The sculpture *Black Water Stone* (1993) made explicit the identification between the Earth and 'feminine' discourses: the low cairn with the small hole at the summit was placed under water: the presence of the 'feminine' element, water, added another layer of connotation to the already symbolically rich sculpture (the cairn or mound; the circle; blackness; the hole; the submerged or partially out of sight setting).

The hole is also associated, of course, with death and the grave. In a portentous moment, Andy Goldsworthy said that '[i]t is possible that the last work I make will be a hole' (HE, 24). Of course the last sculpture he'll make will be a hole: then he will disappear down it, like the White Rabbit in *Alice's Adventures In Wonderland*. The body is returned to the Earth after death, in one way or another. After all, there's nowhere else for it to go (unless one can afford fifty million dollars for a burial in outer space).

Like a gravedigger, then, Andy Goldsworthy scrabbles about in the soil, producing a hole in Hyde Park (1982); a hole in peat in Blaenau Ffestiniog (1980); a double hole in Cumbria (1980); and a hole just under a tree trunk in the Yorkshire Sculpture Park (1983). The sculpture *Sumach leaves* (1998), made at the Storm King Art Center, combined three Goldsworthyan motifs: leaves blended for hue, concentric layers around a circular hole, and a hole in the ground. Goldsworthy occasionally returned to hole sculptures, such as in a hole carved out of sand between two stones on the beach at Collieston (2000).

Andy Goldsworthy regarded his hole made at the London's Serpentine Gallery in the 1980s as 'perhaps the best work I ever made in a building', because he claimed he 'touched the nature of the building'.2 The Goldsworthy hole is also a key element of many of his cairns: the holed cairns are usually low circular structures with a circular aperture on the small flat summit, as in *Black water hole,* or another water hole, in the Thames (1987), or *Slate hole* (1983) and *Stick hole* (1999). Sometimes the holed slate cairns recall hearths or alchemical vessels in which the energies of nature are being harnessed. One thinks of David Nash's 'hearths' and stoves (*Sea Hearth, Snow Stove, Wood Stove, Slate Stove*, etc), and Chris Drury's shelters. (Goldsworthy has fired stones in a kiln, in order to release the stone's essence, exactly as mediæval alchemists did. It is not the spectacular nature of fire and flames that intrigues him, though, but 'the slow intense powerful heat that is at the core of nature' [S, 65]). The rounded dome with a hole at the top is also a shape that humans *live in*: one thinks not only of Eskimo igloos, Central Asian *yurts* and prehistoric 'beehive' and Iron Age huts, but also modern astrodomes and even camping tents. Other holed cairns include ones made from rowan leaves (Yorkshire, 1987) and pebbles (Japan, 1987). Goldsworthy planted a hawthorn tree in a holed stone cairn (*Dunesslin Cairn*, 1999), a work which looked forward to the key recent work, *Garden of Stone* (2003).

Andy Goldsworthy made a line of circular holes in Runnymede, California (1992) in dry weather. When it rained a few days later green shoots of grass started growing up through the holes. 'For me, there is something deeply interesting about a bright green grass blade growing out of a black hole', he noted (W, 15). Another hole, *Branch and hole*, also at Runnymede (1992), looked like the shadow of the branch as it lay on the earth, or the image of the branch if projected onto the ground. *Torn Hole* (Cambridge, England, 1986) was a simple piece: horse chestnut leaves stitched together on a tree in full leaf with a small circular hole torn into them. In Mallorca, Goldsworthy made a stone cairn around an olive tree with a circular opening for the tree (1994). The effect was of a monument to the tree, or of a form enclosing and protecting the tree. In Central Park in the Big Apple, Goldsworthy constructed a base of stacked sticks around three trees (1993). Also at Mallorca, Goldsworthy created a series of stone columns next to or on top of olive trees (1994), but these are not particularly distinctive works.

The most 'violent' of Andy Goldsworthy's sculptures are not the holes in floors and cairns, though they are related to them: Goldsworthy's trenches or cracks are made directly into the soil (at Yorkshire Sculpture Park [in August, 1987], and Little Langdale [1988], for example). Significantly, Goldsworthy did not pretty up these cracks by making them into spiral, circle or gentle serpentine shapes. They were jagged cracks, which resembled the fissures earthquakes make, or the trace of a lightning strike in the sky. The energy of these trenches does not flow smoothly out of the planet but comes out in ragged pulses. Like the torn stones, Goldsworthy was opening a window in the trenches into the energies of the Earth. Opening up a huge gaping hole may be too simple (as Michael Heizer has done): the zigzag lightning form is more suited to the unpredictable form Goldsworthy's version of the Earth's energies takes.

Andy Goldsworthy says he is unsettled by holes, by stones cracking open ('a deeply unnerving but beautiful expression of change' [S, 65]), by the potential in nature for destruction as well as birth. What is striking about Goldsworthy's writings, which are sometimes portentous or banal, is the number of times the word 'shock' appears. Goldsworthy is 'shocked' when a landscape is altered by a manmade lake (at Vassivière [S, 106]); he is 'deeply shocked' when a stone he was working on was smashed by another one falling from a cliff above (S, 94); he is 'shocked' when a pool of water is turned to red by rubbing two stones together (S, 83); he is 'deeply unnerved' by a heated stone splitting open (S, 65). The 'shock' of such natural events presumably derives from Goldsworthy's 'sensitivity' (he is portrayed a 'sensitive' artist in the pro-Goldsworthy criticism and media). Only someone with an exquisitely, breathlessly delicate sensitivity could be *shocked* by a little pool of water turning red, or *shocked* when a stone falls off a cliff. The jaded casual onlooker, seeing the tiny pool turn red might then say, 'well, like, *duh, so what?'* But artists often work on an incredibly small and enclosed scale, in which the tiniest changes can be startling. Goldsworthy's project is to show the casual observer that a crack in the ground can be startling, to show that the 'fragile, unpredictable and violent energy' in nature can be discovered even in the smallest areas of nature. Even the little holes in the flattened domes can be windows onto the 'deep insecurity in nature' (S, 64). The world-weary viewer yawns and says, yeah, but Los Angeles, India, Russia, Iran and Japan have *real* cracks opening in the planet, earthquakes that can kill two thousand people in one day.

Some of Andy Goldsworthy's earliest works (of the 1970s) were tidal, beachbound sculptures which relied very much on the power and majesty of the sea to make them work. Some were sculptures which required the action of the tide to complete them. They were fabricated specifically so that the sea would cover them up. They involved Goldsworthy working very fast, usually arriving at a beach site at lowest tide, to give him the most time to complete a sculpture (it was thus best when low tide coincided with early morning). Beaches were often good places for materials, too (always an important consideration for an artist): sand and stones aplenty, and wood, and flotsam and jetsam. Building the sculpture was only half of the work, though: Golds-worthy always stayed around for the moment when the tide came in, photographing the sculpture throughout its immersion. The moment of collapse was particularly important for Goldsworthy, and he was disappointed if he didn't witness it.

Although the tidal works are dealing with big themes, of time, change, decay, the sea, nature, lunar power, and so on, there is also something undeniably child-like about such sculptures. They're reminiscent of children (and adults) who build castles, boats and walls from sand below the high tideline, so they can watch them (or stand in them) when the waves approach. Thus, Andy Goldsworthy's tidal works are some of his most fun art: they can be regarded as serious explorations of nature and time, or larking about on a beach, building stuff then watching it disintegrate.

At Morecambe Bay in Lancashire, England, in October, 1976, Andy Goldsworthy buried a serpentine line of stones and photographed them as the tide came in. Another work, at Heysham Head, comprised the now-familiar Goldsworthy motif: a series of rocks on a tidal pedestal: as the water rose, the sculpture altered. Golds-worthy's later sea sculptures of balanced rocks are essentially no different from these early Lancashire works. The early works, like the latest sea pieces, employ the formal elements of the littoral environment: the presence of the sea, the changing levels in water, the reflectivity of the water, the colour of the sea, and sky, the movement of the water, the constantly changing light, and so on. These environmental elements are incorporated into Goldsworthy's sea sculptures.

Later tidal works included *Eleven Arches* (1992, Carrick Bay); *Sand Stones* (1992, California); *Beach Holes* (1990, Morecambe); *Balanced Rocks* (1993, Porth Ceiriad, Wales); *Sand Holes* (1997, Rockcliffe); *Cairn* and *Stick Dome Hole* (both 1999, Nova Scotia); and the *Three Cairns* project on the East and West coasts of the U.S.A. (2001-02). In Collieston (Aberdeenshire) in 2000, Andy Goldsworthy produced a group of ephemeral beachworks: a rock covered with smooth sand, or ridges of sand, or a negative circle of sand. Each sand work was washed away by the tide. Goldsworthy's very early works were consciously irregular and 'organic' in shape and form, rather than the more geometric forms he later adopted (such as circles, spirals and lines).

Many (land) artists have worked with the tide apart from Andy Goldsworthy: Barry Flanagan, the Christos, Dennis Oppenheim, Michael McCafferty, Michelle Oka Doner, Chris Drury and Jan Dibbets. Dibbets had a tractor plough the sand on a beach which would then be covered by the tide, in a film made for television (in 1969), for a *Land*

Art exhibition.

Andy Goldsworthy's Welsh *Sea Cairn* (1993) was a 'feminine' cairn built on a pile of barnacled rocks right next to the ocean: when the tide came in, it surrounded the cairn. The sculpture was another 'before and after' work, and could hardly fail: like the cover of *Stone* (*Balanced rocks*), *Sea Cairn* was seen against and beside the ocean. The presence of the surging waves gives the stone sculptures a grandeur they certainly would not possess if they were sited in a slate quarry (although Welsh slate quarries, such as those around Blaenau Ffestiniog in Snowdonia, have their own special atmosphere). When a cairn made on the beach in Nova Scotia in 1999 didn't collapse when the tide came in (as was usual), Goldsworthy said he found the event 'profoundly altered the way I see things. My art has shown me so many things that were hidden to me' (T, 104).

In going out to work in the landscape everyday, Andy Goldsworthy said he was learning, bit by bit, about the natural world, creating 'an intensely personal know-ledge' (the pedagogical aspect is emphasized in many of Goldsworthy's writings). He didn't feel he was 'breaking new ground', but neither did he feel 'the weight of history'.[3] Goldsworthy said that if possible 'I make a work every day' (T, 7). Golds-worthy said he didn't want to be seen as 'some sort of romantic in the landscape, escaping from the city', and that he enjoyed working on 'patches of waste ground' in cities (ibid.).

9

Andy Goldsworthy

the Snowman

9 : 1   ANDY GOLDSWORTHY AND SNOW

When I work with winter, I work with the North. For me, north is an integral part of the land.

Andy Goldsworthy[1]

Much of Andy Goldsworthy's art is about and made from ice and snow (which also means, in the Great Britain, working mainly in Winter). Other artists who have worked with snow include Dennis Oppenheim above all, and Joseph Beuys and Hans Haacke. Goldsworthy is distinctly a 'Northern' artist, who makes work in landscapes that come out of the 'Celtic fringe', out of the sort of landscapes that Celtic culture exalts: misty, rocky hillscapes; sodden Autumnal forest floors knee-deep with leaves; wild snowscapes; overgrown paths through woods; perpetual 'magic hour' light; cold, clear streams banked with large mossy boulders; and still lakes at dawn. Goldsworthy's landscapes could have mythical figures such as the Lady of Shallot, Lancelot or King Arthur or Gandalf riding through them without altering anything. They are the landscapes of Merlin, Taleissin and Morgan Le Fay, of Welsh legends such as *The Mabinogion*, of historical events shrouded in mists, of historical figures such as Robert the

Bruce, Owen Glendower, King Edward and Boadiccea. The places associated with Goldsworthy – his studio at Penpont, Scaur Water in Dumfriesshire, Carlisle, Yorkshire Sculpture Park, Grizedale in Cumbria, Leeds, Leadgate in Durham – are all Northern British sites. And the cultural stereotypes of Britain's North – grimy towns, rain, bleak moors, gloomy skies, deadpan humour, heavy industry, terraced houses, down-to-earth and no-nonsense attitudes – all chime with Goldsworthy's sculpture.

One wonders whether Andy Goldsworthy would like to work in snow and ice more than in any other medium; some of his best and most interesting works are ice and snow. His notes and titles record many frustrations stemming from working with snow. In temperate snowlands, though, one feels Goldsworthy is very much at home. Snow has the right sort of qualities Goldsworthy looks for in a material: it is malleable, it melts and changes, its whiteness makes for good, contrasty imagery, and it seasonally alters the landscape, and later dissolves into it. (And it's free, and it's sometimes found in abundance).

In Andy Goldsworthy's snowworks one senses also the sheer fun of working with snow. For people in most of Britain, snow is not a definite event each year, as it is in, say, Northern Russia or Alaska. For children, snow can be an exciting occurrence (while British adults *always* gripe about it). Snow was a perennial delight and 'shock' for Goldsworthy. In *Midsummer Snowballs* he wrote that '[e]ven in winter each snowfall is a shock, unpredictable and unexpected' (MS, 31). Goldsworthy retained the child-like enjoyment of snow falling in Britain throughout his life. While much of Great Britain grinds to a halt at the sight of a snowflake, Goldsworthy has the child's joy when it snows (school's cancelled, snowball fights, ice skating, sledging, and making snowmen and snowballs).

Andy Goldsworthy speaks in wonder and awe of 'the effect, the excitement' of the first snowfall (HE, 165). Some of this excitement comes across in Goldsworthy's snowworks. He has made, for example, patterns in the snow by rolling a snowball around a field, exactly as kids (and adults) do when it snows (*Snowball trail* [Brough, Cumbria, 1982], and Yorkshire Sculpture Park [1987]). So thousands of people make Goldsworthyan sculptures every time it snows, without realizing it. Linked to the snowball trail was a rectangular wall of snow built on the hills in Penpont in March, 1998.

Some of Andy Goldsworthy's earliest pieces with snow were large snowballs. In some of these early snow works, Goldsworthy placed snowballs in areas such as woods or fields which didn't have any snow, so the snowballs stood out against the trees and grass (as in Ilkley, Yorkshire, 1981). The snowballs were sometimes carried down from higher slopes. Into some snowballs Goldsworthy inserted branches and other material (at Clapham, Yorkshire [1979], Bentham [1980], and London [1985]).

In some sculptures, Andy Goldsworthy's snowballs are small and look like seeds placed inside the trunks of broken trees (as in the 1993 piece in *Wood*, 24). Other snowball-in-tree works include *Oak tree snowball* and *Beech tree snowball* (both Dumfriesshire, both 1994). Goldsworthy photographed these sculptures from a distance, to include the whole tree and its snowy surroundings (and also carefully composed the pictures so that the snowballs were contrasted with the dark tree trunks or walls). These are atmospheric pieces, with the white of the sky and the snow predominating. Goldsworthy has been lucky in that there were some good, cold, snowy Winters in Britain around the late 1970s and early 1980s. 1977-78 and 1981-82 I remember were good – his art might have developed differently if he had made work during milder, snowless Winters.

Other Andy Goldsworthy iceworks include icicles stuck onto a wall (made on New Year's Eve, 1992) and *Icicles frozen to a rock* (1991). In these works, the icicles are clustered together, like a mini forest of trees. The icicle works, like the mound of stones which were dipped in water then frozen onto a rockface (S, 44-45), are testaments of endurance: the artist had to keep returning to the same place to pull the work off. *Icicles,* made on the last day of 2003 at Goldsworthy's favourite Scaur Water spot, was a row of icicles, some a few feet long, frozen to a rock (P, 18). *Ice 'fish'* was a flat curve made from little sheets of ice; *Ice column* was also constructed from sheets of ice refrozen together: the result looked like a Naum Gabo Constructivist tower (both 1991, Dumfriesshire). There was also an *Ice star*, two icicles aimed at each other ('pointing their frozen energies towards each other'),[5] small slabs of thin ice frozen to rocks in a stream and photographed to catch the rising sun (2004), an icicle that appeared to pierce an oak branch (2002), an *Ice hole* made in Yorkshire Sculpture Park, *Ice Spires* (2003), a cluster of icicle spikes frozen together, and a hollow *Ice ball* (1987).

An icicle work was made in Winter 1995-96, which Andy Goldsworthy called '[t]he coldest I have ever known in Britain' (W, 67). This work has a privileged position in the *Wood* book, having three photographs to itself: two close-up, showing the spiral icicle in cloudy and sunny conditions, and one long shot showing its location at Glen Marlin Falls in Dumfriesshire. Goldsworthy spoke of the intensity of the sun shining onto the icicle: 'it was as if the icicle was both absorbing and generating light. This was the moment when the work came alive' (W, 10). Goldsworthy likened the moment when the icicle was illuminated to when Constantin Brancusi photographed his *Bird in Space* sculpture in his Paris studio.

To enhance the grandeur of some of his snow pieces, Andy Goldsworthy's publishers printed them in a large, double page spread format in the book *Andy Goldsworthy* (1990). To evoke the beauty of the setting and the changeability of the weather,[6] Goldsworthy reproduced (in the same book) three double page spreads of a snow wall made at a favourite spot, Blencathra in Cumbria. The full title of the work explains some of it:

Slits cut into frozen snow
stormy
strong wind
weather and light rapidly changing

The title reads like a *haiku*, like many of Andy Goldsworthy's titles. The title, however, does not convey the Romantic power of these photographs which directly recall the oil paintings of J.M.W. Turner. Behind the slitted snow wall the viewer sees brooding cloudscapes, with the sun burning through in the second shot. In the third picture, the wall, in the foreground, is in shadow, while the sun shines onto a portion of a distant hill. Above roam clouds with softened edges, as out of Mark Rothko's abstract panels or Emil Nolde's watercolours of North Friesland.

In Anchorage, Alaska, in 1995, Andy Goldsworthy built a series of lines from branches frozen together. The forms – curving and zigzagging columns – were familiar Goldsworthyan motifs. Later, Goldsworthy took down the stick towers and used them to form a long line of 114 sticks which stretched out over the Alaskan snow. Goldsworthy related the line of sticks to the tree line, the line of distant mountains, and the line of the estuary.

> I want the line to be made up of wood, ice, wood, ice, wood, ice. Winter, summer, winter, summer, winter, summer [Goldsworthy wrote]. I like the idea of many pieces being joined together in a continuous line, just as the seasons are. (W, 49).

This series of works culminated in a stick house in which Andy Goldsworthy hung a 3 foot icicle made by dripping water. In his journal Goldsworthy said that the icicle was meant to be like a knife with the surrounding wood as a sheath. He also related the vertical icicle to the spine of the dancers in the *Végétal* performance, and to the stone columns (W, 10). The ice house was about the relationship between trees, water and the cold. 'The tree needs water, yet water makes it vulnerable to the cold. Water at its core, its spine: delicate, fragile and vulnerable' (W, 49). Goldsworthy spoke of the relation between stone and wood, stone and trees. 'It is no accident that I called the piece of land near to where I live 'Stone Wood'. I've always been aware of the relationship between these two materials' (Sh, 22). Note that two of Goldsworthy's major art books are entitled *Stone* and *Wood*.

The biting cold maybe gives Andy Goldsworthy a sense of heroism, for suffering invariably enhances a work (as in, 'this work was difficult, made under adverse conditions'). After all, Goldsworthy is not an artist who makes work in the 'comfort' of a home or studio (working indoors doesn't feel 'real' to him). No: he goes out into the natural world, where it can be uncomfortable and challenging. He claims to know the landscape around his studio in Penpont, Scotland, very well, so that a snowfall does not hide the world: 'I know what lies under the snow – I know the earth beneath' (HE). Always Goldsworthy stresses the intimate relationship he has with nature. Part of this intimacy comes from returning to the same patch of land again and again. Through successive visits, layers of touch and meaning in the landscape are uncovered by the artist. The artist returning to the same space always works in time as well as space, for s/he creates a personal history of that place. S/he works with her former selves, as well as in the present – with the artist and ideas she had two years ago, ten years ago, twenty years ago. 'Some places I return to over and over again, going deeper – a relationship, made in layers over a long time' (AG). Sometimes, as he wanders round familiar spots, Goldsworthy comes upon old works (and occasionally photographs them).

The personal dimension is important in Andy Goldsworthy's work. His work is not 'impersonal' in the sense that it could be made 'anywhere'. It is, like most land art, always a product of a relationship between an artist and a particular place. Making the art itself, the doing of it, is important for Goldsworthy. So that when people ask the eternal question, *but is it art?*, he retorts, well, he doesn't know and doesn't care, but 'it is important and necessary for me as a person.'[2] (Artists always leave it up to others to define their works).

Sceptics can claim that many of Andy Goldsworthy's sculptures gain much of their fire from their situation in wilderness landscapes. They would be right. Although Goldsworthy states that many of his sculptures are made in built-up areas, areas of dense population and human activity, a glance through any Goldsworthy book or a visit to a Goldsworthy show will reveal the large proportion of wilderness or rural landscapes in his art. He expunges all the trash, houses, cables, aerials, bullboards, signs, telephone poles, apartment blocks, cars and roads from his photographs, and presents lush streams, moorland, forests and hillsides (if his art is often made in cities, where are the buses, the graffiti, the signage, the mail boxes, the phone booths, the dumpsters?). There are no people at all in his art, except Goldsworthy himself, who is sometimes seen, with his beard, sweater and jeans (often a hat, sometimes gloves), making a piece of art.

In this sense, Andy Goldsworthy's work is not at all figurative – but neither is it wholly 'abstract', in the Mark Rothko or Piet Mondrian sense, because real, recognizable objects appear in his work. This is one of the reasons for the growing popularity of his work: apart from the Eighties ecological/ green movement, and the accessible, decorative quality of his work, it is thoroughly countrified and rural, quite in keeping with primæval desires for escape into the country, that nostalgia for nature that lies behind the pastoral and landscape tradition in the West.

Andy Goldsworthy speaks as poets do of the spirit of place, where the place itself becomes as important as the object: 'the work is the place', Goldsworthy has stated (S, 6). Any number of artworks gain much from their setting, from Greek temples to a Michelangelo Merisi da Caravaggio discovered in a dark, incense-smoky church in a backstreet in Rome. For the land or earth artist, of course the place becomes (identical with) the work. In the typical Goldsworthy piece, though, there is usually some object at the centre of the landscape or the photograph. Usually a rock covered in leaves, a red pool, a slate cairn is at the centre. At first glance, the object seems to be the subject of the artwork and the focus for the eye. Not so: the surroundings are just as important, and these pastoral landscapes help to sell Goldsworthy's art just as much as the woven grass stalks or the sticks wrapped around a boulder.

Andy Goldsworthy's skill is not just to 'touch nature' (whatever that means), but to touch the chords of desire for nature in people. Goldsworthy's art is popular partly because of this powerful desire among Western audiences for contact with the natural world, an appetite which is manifested in natural history programmes on television, in jaunts to zoos, gardens and wind-swept hillside car lots and beauty spots, in Edward Hopper, Norman Rockwell and Claude Monet posters and prints, in gardening magazines and gardening centres and plants in the house, and in the popularity of English rural novels by George Eliot, Thomas Hardy and the Brontës.

The eco/ green movement (and its associated movements in pagan/ New Age/ road, anti-capitalist, anarchist and animal activism), taps into this nostalgic love of an urban-centric culture for all things 'natural'.3 The natural world seems to be green and life-giving and untarnished by the complexities of modern life. The natural world, which is Andy Goldsworthy's preferred world, is a place of leaves, rivers, animals and stones, a place seemingly devoid of people, the ones who mess things up, who complicate things, who introduce the concepts and realities of neurosis, confusion, waste, violence, consumption and politics into the 'pure' natural world.4

It's not like that at all, but these eco, green, pastoral feelings are powerful. Andy Goldsworthy's art, like the pastoral novels of George Eliot and Thomas Hardy, like green politics or the money-spinning popularity of Vincent van Gogh and Claude Monet, trades on the desires for an earlier, ancient Paradise, a time when things seemed to be simpler, richer, deeper. This is the 'green world' of childhood, a time of playfulness and living close to the Earth, enjoying the seasons passionately but also freely, in a relaxed manner. In mythology, it is the 'Golden Age', *il illo tempore, ab origine*, in the Creation era, at the origin of the world, before the Fall of Adam and Eve into sin, a time before œdipal anxiety and patriarchal psychosis, a Gaia time, a whole earth time, all 'natural' and recycled and vegetarian, a holistic time, a time of social unity, when everyone felt as one in communities and loved each other, a time of maternal bliss, when women were nurturing Mother Goddesses and men could be sweetly dreaming babies without feeling embarrassed.

Andy Goldsworthy's art books, commissions and shows trade on this pastoral imagery and desire: they allow stressed, overworked and neurotic city dwellers time out from staring at the control screens (TV, computers, cel phones, ATMs) of the megavisual world, encouraging a little day-dreaming into the soft greens and greys of wild moorlands. Goldsworthy's art may be increasingly successful because it reminds people that, yes, one does love nature after all: one came from it, one'll go back into it, in the end, in death.

Andy Goldsworthy's art may hit home because it does *not* bombard people with telephones, computers, cars, factories, radios, TVs, microwaves, washing machines, hoovers, irons, faxes, and all those machines that connote *labour*, that are the symbols and mechanisms of working life. In Goldsworthy's green world, all is natural, untechnological, with artifacts that evoke a return to basics: stone, wood, leaves, ice.

9 : 2   *TOUCHING NORTH (1989)*

Andrew Goldsworthy's most dramatic work to date is probably *Touching North* (1989), four circular arches made of snow. It is dramatic mainly due to its location, that space so thoroughly a masculine 'wild zone', the place of macho adventures, colonization and courage: the North Pole. The *Touching North* project was organized by the Fabian Carlsson Gallery, London (one of Goldsworthy's dealers at the time), and overseen by Fabian Carlsson. In March and April, 1989, the expedition visited Montréal, Resolute,

Grise Fjord, Camp Hazen and the North Pole, and the show travelled to London, Edinburgh and L.A. through 1989.

Andy Goldsworthy's intention with the grandeur of *Touching North* was 'to follow North to its source'. He had already encountered 'North' in 'the cold shadow of a mountain', he said, meaning he had already found the extreme cold associated with the North Pole in Scotland or Northern Britain. But there was a practical reason for going all the way North to the North Pole, and that was so that Goldsworthy could enjoy 'the luxury of constant freezing' (in Britain, snow comes and goes: it does not stay for months on end as it does in the North Pole). As Goldsworthy wrote: 'so much that I have made in ice has been frustrated by a rise in temperature. I have held ice seemingly for ages waiting for it to freeze only to let go and see it drop off.'[1] Yeah, we all know that feeling.

Although the four circular walls were the centrepiece of the *Touching North* project, Andy Goldsworthy made other snowworks at the time. *Snow Spires* was two little groups of pyramid forms between five and seven feet tall (1989, Ellesmere Island), while *Snow Slabs* was a long line of slabs, recalling the lines of prehistoric stones at Carnac in France. Other works in *Touching North* included a wall constructed from narrow slabs of snow balanced on top of each other; flat wedges of snow piled on top of each other to form a low bridge; a series of free-standing arches placed in a row, recalling the nave of a Gothic cathedral; a cairn made from circular slabs of snow; a low wall of snow with arrow-shaped slits carved in it; another wall consisting of chevrons placed end-to-end. There were also several narrow walls of snow with slits carved in them: one in the shape of a star; another in a Goldsworthyan serpent; another with parallel zigzag lines.

9 : 3   SNOWBALLS IN SUMMER (2000)

Snowballs In Summer (a.k.a. *Midsummer Snowballs,* 2000) was one of Andy Goldsworthy's larger, more complex installations. Fourteen snowballs were gathered from the snowfields of Scotland's Dumfriesshire and Perthshire in 1999 and 2000, kept in storage, transported to London and exhibited on the streets of the City of London (the oldest part of London, and now the financial district). This, coupled with the show *Time*, at the Barbican Centre in the area (in August-October), made 2000 the most prominent display of Goldsworthyania for some years in the British Isles. Goldsworthy liked the idea of the snowballs appearing in the middle of Summer in an urban setting (a variation on his early works of carrying snowballs down hills to place them among snowless woods). The snowballs were not 'made for people. They are about people' (MS, 33).

Sites for the London *Snowballs* show were explored on foot, with Andy Goldsworthy planning where to position the snowballs by painting white typing correction fluid (Tippex) on photographs. Installing the snowballs between midnight and dawn on

June 21st required a carefully organized effort involving helpers, forklift trucks, cranes and lorries. The snowballs were placed in the Barbican area of central London, including the Barbican Centre, Silk Street, Moorgate, St John Street, Long Lane, Smithfield Market, London Wall, Bunhill Fields cemetery and Charterhouse Square.

Andy Goldsworthy wanted the snowballs to be *in situ* by dawn, so for the public they would just seem to have appeared from nowhere. Surprise was important. Goldsworthy said he aimed the snowball installation at the workers in the City who'd be travelling to work in the morning, popping out for lunch, and going home later (it is mainly a business, not residential area). At that time, at five or six in the evening, the contents of the snowballs would be gradually emerging (MS, 34). The melt would be integrated into the working day of the City. The centrepiece of the *Time* show was a large wall of mud, which dried gradually, and *Red Stone*, the last of the London *Snowballs*, which had been packed with red stone powder and allowed to melt in the Barbican Centre's Curve gallery, spreading red-stained water over the floor.

Time, change and the millennium was another aspect Goldsworthy wanted to explore in the London *Snowballs* installation: the snow would be gathered at the end of the 20th century and exhibited at the beginning of the 21st century. (Remember what a big deal the Millennium was?). Goldsworthy made other sculptures, such as arches and cairns, which were completed either side of New Year's Eve, 1999. Thus, for Goldsworthy, it was important that the sculptures bridged two centuries and two millennia (T, 12). For *Snowballs In Summer*, Goldsworthy also employed a link up on the web to images of the snowballs on the streets.

The materials set inside the London *Snowballs* included pebbles, sheep's wool, cow hair, crow feathers, horse chestnuts, Scots pine cones, beech branches, barley, elderberries, barbed wire, chalk and ash keys. (The contents in the snowballs in the Glasgow, 1989 show included willowherb stalks, daffodils, pine cones, pebbles, horse chestnut stalks, stones, dog-wood, reeds, oak and birch twigs, slate, chestnut leaves, chalk, soil, ash keys and pine needles.) Andy Goldsworthy also placed scraps of farming machinery he'd gathered from near his home in Penpont. Some of the snowballs melted quickly, some stayed for a day or so (June 21st was a dry, cool day, but the wind eroded the snowballs quicker than anticipated). Some snowballs were vandalized, others were moved. Some of the materials contained in each snowball related to where they were situated (cow hair, for example, in the snowball outside Smithfield market). Goldsworthy remarked that he could have easily included sensational materials in the snowballs, to give the project a higher profile (though the TV and press were there anyway).

10

Andy Goldsworthy

the Green Man

All forms are to be found in nature, and there are many qualities within any material. By exploring them I hope to understand the whole.

Andy Goldsworthy, *Winter Harvest*[1]

One of the problems Andy Goldsworthy's art addresses head on is the age-old tension between the 'real world' and art, between objects as they are in the everyday world, and objects as they are represented in art. Goldsworthy encourages the viewer to look again at the natural world: not just at the beauty of it, but at the multitudinous variety of forms in nature. His sculpture is a poetry of natural forms (but notions of representation and simulation are not sidestepped, because although Goldsworthy's art is based on things 'as themselves', the use of photography sees a swift return of confusions over the politics of representation). The snowball in the *Snowballs* install-ations (1989 and 2000) is not plastic or concrete masquerading as a snowball, but a real snowball. Similarly, the twigs and stalks and needles and pebbles folded into the snowballs are real (but the snowballs are also art objects).

What's amazing is the actuality of nature: the variety of forms (the way the branches twist, for instance). Paul Nesbitt wrote of Andy Goldsworthy's art:

Throughout these works the dominant theme is one of working with nature, to reveal nature itself – physical, chemical and biological. Goldsworthy uses nature's materials – rock, water (snow and ice, rain and mist), earth and the plants and animals which inhabit these; he uses nature's properties – structure, shape, form and colour; he uses nature's forces which together create, alter and animate those materials and properties – forces of light, heat, wind and gravity.2

Andy Goldsworthy likes to encourage the viewer to look closely at nature again. By using 'real' objects, Goldsworthy aims to demolish notions of representation and mediation. Instead of a picture of snow, one has in Goldsworthy's art snow itself; rather than paint pebbles, or sculpt them in bronze, Goldsworthy uses real pebbles.

Of course, there are problems with using objects as objects – Marcel Duchamp with his readymades confronted this problem. The dilemma is partly one of context: because, placed in a museum or art gallery, as items to be studied, enjoyed, critiqued, natural forms become art (as contemporary art has demonstrated, you can place *anything* in an art gallery and it is contextualized as art). Andy Goldsworthy's snowballs may not be on pedestals, but they are perceived as art objects (and intended and presented as such). The leaf sculptures are more obviously works of art, set on shelves, or photographed against paper backdrops, as bottles of perfume or Swiss watches are photographed for adverts. If one is looking at a Goldsworthy sculpture in a book or a gallery, one is a already anchored in a gallery/ art/ æsthetic mode of viewing. If Goldsworthy's sculptures are in a gallery, one sees them as art (and a particular kind of Western, bourgeois art, the sort of art that is exhibited in Western, bourgeois galleries).

Carl Andre explored the relation between real and represented objects with his controversial pile of bricks. The sculpture was 'controversial' (a journo's inaccurate shorthand for something that's really a mild argument) because the general public (whoever they are) perceived, via the media, that Andre had simply stuck some bricks into a gallery. Or rather, that British taxpayers' money had been used to purchase Andre's bricks (in the 1970s, the Tate Gallery was partly funded by public money). A pile of bricks on a building site is… a pile of bricks. A pile of bricks in an art gallery is… sculpture. Context is everything here. This is what Andre explored, whether consciously or not: the *response*, affected by so much of culture, socialization, physical context, education, and so on, makes objects sculptures. People make art. A leaf simply exists, but if someone puts it in a gallery or an art book, it becomes art (as well as remaining a leaf; but being an artwork takes precedence). If people think something is art, then it's art, as Donald Judd said. As Garth Evans wrote in "Sculpture and Reality" (1969):

What happens to a sculpture is determined largely by factors outside of itself. The fact of its being thought of as a sculpture is more critical to its existence, its life, than any other facts about it. This is a fundamental distinction between objects and sculpture.3

Obviously, Andy Goldsworthy's leafworks – the sycamore boxes, the sweet chestnut horns, the maple circles – are sculptures, seen and described (and sold) as sculptures. That's easy, to see the leafworks as sculptures. The petal-covered rocks, those too, are clearly sculptures. There is no mistaking the carefully crafted pieces as anything other than high art. Every artwork creates a multitude of readings, but one of the dominant readings of Goldsworthy's 'real' objects is that they are high art sculptures.

One of the most beautiful of Andy Goldsworthy's works is *Rosebay willowherb* (1990), a web of willowherb stalks woven together into a circle. At the centre was an open circle made by the stalks: Goldsworthy wove the stalks together so that they expanded in gentle curves. *Susuki Grass* (1993), made in Japan, was a similar work, a wall or curtain of stalks. Related to *Rosebay willowherb* was *Woven silver birch* (fabricated at Langholm in Dumfriesshire, 1986): again the sticks were woven together to form an open circle at the centre. On the outside of the sculpture, the sticks moved off in every direction. It looked like a catherine wheel firework, with the sparks frozen in the air.

Andy Goldsworthy produced a few of these 'drawings in air', free-standing sculptures which were practically two-dimensional. They were drawings in space, where Goldsworthy employed the fine bendy stalks to delineate elegant curves in the air. These works – *Knotwood stalks* (Holbeck Triangle, 1986), *Rosebay willowherb* and the stalks stuck in the lake bottom in the Lake District (*Early morning calm*, 1988) – were wholly dependent on Renaissance notions of perspective, space and illusion. They were flat works, best seen from one particular direction, and preferably with contrasty lighting, set against a sky, for instance. One or two stick works, though, broke out in all directions, such as *Hazel sticks* (1980), made in Cumbria, where a group of straight sticks, some six or more feet long, were bound together on a pole.

Andy Goldsworthy's sculptures used all the tricks and devices of post-Renaissance illusion and representation, including figure-ground relationships, negative space, perspective, selective viewpoint, *chiaroscuro*, silhouettes, outlines, and so on. A good example of the strong pictorial element in Goldsworthy's art are the sculptures that use negative space to create the illusion of continuous form: these sculptures typically have loops of ice or sand on two sides of a rock or a tree. In, for instance, *Reconstructed refrozen icicles* (1999 [T, 112]),

Andy Goldsworthy's ethics are those of Chris Drury, Hamish Fulton, Richard Long, David Nash (he has worked at Nash's Blaenau-Ffestiniog studio) and other British land artists: a mystical feeling for the landscape, expressed by an exquisite sensitivity of *touch*, that all-important component in the eroticism of sculpture:

> Movement, change, light, growth and decay are the lifeblood of nature, the energies that I try to tap through my work [said Goldsworthy]. I need the shock of touch, the resistance of place, materials and weather, the earth as my source.[4]

As Andy Goldsworthy affirmed, he *must* touch. A world in which he would not be allowed to touch would be hateful. A world in which the trees had 'DO NOT TOUCH' signs on them would be horrendous. Significantly, Goldsworthy works mainly in areas in which the ownership of the land is not contested. He operates in landscapes where he has been given permission to work, invited (and paid) to work. No 'DO NOT TOUCH' signs for him.

For Andy Goldsworthy, as for any number of sculptors, the personal touch, of hands on materials, is crucial:

> The work itself determines the nature of its making. I enjoy the freedom of just using my hands and 'found' tools – a sharp stone, the quill of a feather, thorns. I am not playing the primitive. I use my hands because this is the best way to do most of my work.

Indeed, when it comes to drawing on the sand on a beach, Andy Goldsworthy will not take up a stick, as many folks would. Instead, he uses his hands, kneeling or crouching on the sand. His *Dark dry sand drawing* is worked by hand, dribbled onto the sand on the Isle of Wight (1987). The result, all swirls and curves, comes directly from Jackson Pollock (the beach drawing has the sense of harmony, of each part balanced with the rest, not part having precedence over any other, of Oriental landscape painting). Goldsworthy has also drawn lines on frozen water (Nova Scotia, 1999). A lot of work Goldsworthy has done in deserts has been with carved sand (in New Mexico, Arizona, California and Australia). In a way, these drawings and sculptures of sand (in the shape of spirals, snakes, zigzags and boulders) are basically developments of the work with sand on the beaches of Northern England that Goldsworthy undertook in the late 1970s.

Many sculptors have spoken of the importance of the *making* of the sculpture, its actual construction, with real (and sometimes organic, living) materials. In some artists, the material employed also has a symbolic or added meaning, as in Joseph Beuys' *Fettecke* or 'fat corner', a sculpture with powerful autobiographical and semiotic associations.

Land artists such as Andy Goldsworthy use their hands, primarily, as their means of making art. Goldsworthy does not go out into the landscape with anything, except a knife.[5] Perhaps he should, to be really purist, make do without even a knife? Anyway, he *does* go out into the landscape with 'tools' – the camera not least among them (also spare film too, maybe a lens filter or two, batteries, and a tripod, and probably two cameras). Without that camera, the viewer wouldn't know about many of his works. Ditto with all land artists. Without the camera (or notebook), their work is 'lost'. That is, not really 'lost', but the camera means the viewer too can share in the work. Without the camera, the viewer would have to rely on written texts, perhaps, as a means of 'recording' artworks. Photography is also 'a way of communicating', Goldsworthy told an interviewer, 'and we wouldn't be sitting here if I didn't take the photographs.'[6] Here Goldsworthy admits that without the photographs there would be not much communicating going on with his art: it needs photography to work.

But, as one can readily see, Andy Goldsworthy and other land artists are not writers. Indeed, their writings are, well, often in note form, designed as a 'record' for themselves, or as notes towards some artwork. While there have been some painters and sculptors who were also good writers who provided many insights – Leonardo da Vinci, Ad Reinhardt, Vincent van Gogh, Donald Judd – Goldsworthy is not among them. So, relying on photographs, the viewer gets to find out about many works of land art that might otherwise have never known. The camera is thus an essential tool for the land artist (Goldsworthy could go out without a knife, or gloves, but he needs a camera and film).

Andy Goldsworthy also works outdoors with many other invisible tools of his craft – his awareness of land art, his education, his knowledge of other sculptors and art history, his memory of previous works, and so on. No artist works alone, culturally. Goldsworthy's art, like all land art, like all art, works within a culture and tradition and history of postwar and contemporary art. Tracing the links with Minimalism, Arte Povera and Conceptualism, for instance, is only one way of looking at Goldsworthy's art.

Spontaneity is the key to Andy Goldsworthy's working method – but an intentional kind of spontaneity. Just going out for a walk, with no intention in mind, is not the thing to do. In Goldsworthy's methodology, one goes out with a sense of direction, of going somewhere in particular, with the intention of making something. Intentionality, a direction or drive, a desire (the Western, Schopenhauerian or Nietzschean Will) is crucial. 'It is *very important* that I have a direction', says Goldsworthy.[7] The sense of intention or direction primes the artist, encouraging him to look attentively.

> For me, looking, touching, material, place and form are all inseparable from the resulting work [commented Goldsworthy]. It is difficult to say where one stops and another begins. Place is found by walking, direction determined by weather and season. I take the opportunities each day offers...[8]

Like many land artists, Andy Goldsworthy waxed lyrical about particular places, which are special for him. The Lake District, an inspiration for many British artists, was lovingly described in 1988 by Goldsworthy in the *Artists in National Parks* show:

> I have lived for most of the time within sight of the Lake District... The mountains have become important to me not only to visit and work but as a place by which I orientate myself. It has taken on the significance that all mountains, hills, mounds and single trees have to people living nearby. It has become a landmark which creates a sense of presence and location, defining the surrounding landscape... When I first visited the Lake District I was impressed by the mass and space – and the things that made that space active. It offered new experiences on a massive scale, being able to walk up into the clouds and touching snow when I thought winter was over.[9]

Andy Goldsworthy's sculptures are 'simple', in that there doesn't seem to be much going on. But, as Donald Judd wrote in his influential essay "Specific Objects":

> it isn't necessary for a work to have a lot of things to look at, to compare, to analyze one by one, to contemplate. The thing as a whole, its qualities as a whole, is what is interesting.[10]

Andy Goldsworthy's sculptures are marked by a number of elements familiar in land art: transience, domination, penetration, circular forms (globes, circles, spirals, snakes, cones), and nature mysticism. The ephemerality of the pieces, for instance, is a key component. Snow and ice will melt away, leaves will disintegrate, stones will be blown over.

Each Andy Goldsworthy sculpture has a date printed with its title. Not just a year, as in the usual artwork, but a specific day (we can't be sure even what year a masterpiece by Giotto or Duccio was painted, but we know the exact day, even hour, when land artworks were created).

Thus, one of Andy Goldsworthy's best pieces, the delicious poppy covered boulder, has the title: *Poppy petals wrapped around a boulder held with water*, with the time and place inscribed as: Sibobre, France, June 6, 1989. The petal-covered rock, with its brilliant red colour, nestled in some mossy boulders, looking very much like one of Constantin Brancusi's 'cosmic eggs' (egg-shaped sculptures which Brancusi titled *The Beginning of the World*). The red colour revealed the rock's shape, size and form, its position amongst and relation to other rocks. Not wishing to disturb or move the rock (it's not that small really), Goldsworthy's act of covering it in wet poppy petals drew attention to this particular egg-shaped rock, *this* one and *not* the others (although the surrounding boulders also became the subject of the sculpture: attention was drawn to them as well as to the red rock). In *Poppy petals wrapped around a boulder held with water,* then, the place becomes as crucial as the centre-piece, the red rock.

Another red-covered rock, again linked with water and a river, was made at Scaur Water in 1992: *River rock* was made by rubbing a soft red stone over a small rock which was then lowered into the shallow river. Before the sculpture settled it released a cloud of red colour which was slowly washed away. Again, it was the situation of the rock, as much as the reddening of the rock itself, that did the expressive work in this sculpture. Andy Goldsworthy used red stone ground down as the filling of the final snowball of 2000, causing red water to spread over the floor of the Barbican Centre. Goldsworthy has also released red stone powder above a waterfall (at Scaur Water, 1997), so the pool below turns ochre.

When working with rivers, Andy Goldsworthy said, it was not the water itself that was the really interesting element, but everything that used the river, the flow of life and change around it: 'a river of wind, animals, birds, insects, people, seasons, climate, stone, earth, colour' (T, 10). Goldsworthy spoke of '[r]hythms, cycles, seasons in nature working at different speeds'.[11] Each date records a particular day (September 24, 1982, December 30, 1987, February 9, 1981, March 11, 1984, October 19, 1988); each day has its own weather, atmosphere and events, which are important for the artist. Goldsworthy records personal details sometimes in his titles:

Fine dry sand
edges and ridges
softened by the breeze
[...]
Eleven arches
made between tides

followed the sea out
working quickly
waited for its return
sun, wind, clouds, rain

11

Installations and

Large-Scale Works

11 : 1   STONE AND HERD OF ARCHES (1994)

Andy Goldsworthy's 1994 London shows (entitled *Stone*) provided 'a one-man invasion on the West End', as critic Richard Cork put it. The exhibitions were very impressive. The stone arches in *Herd of Arches* at 27, Old Bond Street in the West End loomed out of the semi-darkness. There was no lighting on the ground floor, and even in the bright morning light the interior was dark. The arches were all of the same size and height and type. Each one was different in details only. Goldsworthy had fitted together masses of small slabs of stone, with tiny pebbles and wafer-thin stones wedged in, to hold the arch tightly together. Roger Partridge has made an arch out of stone (1983, private collection) which recalls Goldsworthy's *Herd of Arches*. Alan Sonfist's *Rock Monument of Rocky Mountains*, very much an ancestor of Goldsworthy's arches, was produced in 1971.

The London Bond Street location was not a white-on-white pristine central London gallery space. Nor was it the even whiter, even more pristine interior of Charles Saatchi's London galleries. Andy Goldsworthy's *Herd of Arches* were indeed like living things. The title used the word 'herd', and Goldsworthy's arches, evenly spaced throughout the ground floor of the gallery, evoked a herd of animals. In the course of doing so much work out of doors, Goldsworthy must encounter many sorts of animals

– sheep and cows most often, one supposes (but also very likely plenty of rabbits, foxes, voles, mice, birds, worms, bees, flies, spiders, bugs, etc). They appear in the background to his photographs. In *Herd of Arches* Goldsworthy makes the connection between seemingly inert stone and living animals, between the human-shaped artwork and the nature-shaped organism. In the book *Arch*, Goldsworthy remarked that the stone arch itself was not an animal, but it did have 'interesting rhythms and movements that can be interpreted sculpturally in response to the energy, reactions and movements of an animal' (*Arch*, 16).

Upstairs at 27, Old Bond Street, London, were photographs and snowball prints. The latter were smears of ochre-coloured stone dust and water on large sheets of paper. Like other land artists, Andy Goldsworthy works in the landscape, so there are numerous problems when he shows work in a city. The city is definitely *not* the obvious Goldsworthy place. The photographs and prints, then, point always towards the outdoors, towards the ideal Goldsworthy space, which is some wilderness – Scotland above all, and the North Pole, Japan, France, Iowa, Cumbria, and so on.

The forerunners of Andy Goldsworthy's snow prints are Conceptual pieces like Bruce McLean's *Seascape* and *Treescape* (both 1969), where the artist wrapped paper around trees and put photo-sensitive paper on the ocean. A variation on the snowball prints were the 'sheep paintings' which Goldsworthy embarked upon in 1998, part also of Goldsworthy's fondness for the agriculture industry (sheep footprints were recorded on pieces of white canvas, with feed containers situated in the centre of the canvas). Artists such as Stephen Turner have also taken painter's canvas into the countryside and used mud and other materials to make art. (Goldsworthy had also combined elements of seal and caribou on the Arctic expedition).

The snowball prints (which Andy Goldsworthy produces by allowing snowballs to melt onto big pieces of paper) are disappointing, really. A snowball melting on a sheet of paper is too random and easy, perhaps. The combination of a natural act of melting and the framed piece of paper in a gallery, with the gallery's art historical context, is problematic. The viewer might prefer to see Goldsworthy making these prints, or combining them with other forms. Then they would make more sense (on their own, they're a little lean). Perhaps a photograph of the artist making the print would suffice. As it is, the snowball prints are full of suggestions of things they cannot deliver. They are, like Goldsworthy's photographs, a record of something that occurred elsewhere. And what occurred elsewhere is of course what *really* interests Goldsworthy.

No land artist can be satisfied with written accounts of art made in the landscape, just as no painter would be satisfied with photographs or written accounts of their paintings. No, they must have the paintings themselves, the actual flesh and blood of the painting, so to speak, the very feel of the oil on canvas, the shape and size and texture and reflectivity and proportion and tactile qualities of the actual painting. Photographs of paintings only disappoint the artist. Ditto with the land artist. Goldsworthy's photographs and prints are not what they're really interested in: the work is elsewhere, in the landscape (note that Goldsworthy has participated – in London and Bristol, for instance – in group shows which focus on photography as sculpture).

11 : 2   THE CAPENOCH TREE SERIES (1994-96)

The largest section of Andy Goldsworthy's book *Wood* (1996) is devoted to the *Capenoch Tree* series of works, made between 1994 and 1996 in Dumfriesshire in Great Britain. The 'Capenoch tree' was an old oak tree standing slightly apart from other trees on private land. Goldsworthy concentrated not on the whole tree, its trunk or its branches (as he often did), but on one particular branch that grew sideways out from the tree, horizontally, a few feet above the grass. As Goldsworthy explained, '[t]he long branch that has grown horizontal to the ground has taught me that the tree is the land. The branch is like the landscape' (T, 195). So Goldsworthy treated the branch as a landscape in miniature, a small-scale setting for a range of sculptures which represent all of Goldsworthy's work in microcosm.

The *Capenoch Tree* series was unified by its location: every work was centred on the same tree and its long branch. The unity of the series was enhanced by Andy Goldsworthy publishing only photographs of each piece taken from the same angle, the same side of the tree. In nearly all of the photographic records of the *Capenoch Tree* series in *Wood* the same elements are present: the trunk on the right, the branch extending across the picture plane from right to left, the ground underneath and the background of trees. Goldsworthy returned to the Capenoch tree in all seasons, but favoured Fall and Winter – the best works in the *Capenoch Tree* series are those made in Winter. Goldsworthy wrote somewhat portentously of the Capenoch tree and of trees in general in *Wood*:

> The stone grows within the tree – the seed. The column is a growth form, pro-
> gressive. Tree is stone expressed in wood... The long branch that has grown
> horizontal to the ground has taught me that the tree is the land. The branch is like
> the landscape. It is the earth, it is stone... (W, 23, 85)

In a way, the *Capenoch Tree* series offered a summary of all of Andy Goldsworthy's land art techniques: there were leaves pinned along the branch; wood and snow cairns and globes placed next to the tree; snowballs set in the tree; arches made out of ice and stone on the branch; screens of willowherb and rosebay; walls of snow (some serpentine, some holed); lines of dandelions; and holes in the ground.

One of the earlier *Capenoch Tree* works was a cluster of lines of oak leaves pinned together and hanging from the branch (July, 1994). Andy Goldsworthy admitted that he found it difficult to make successful works in high Summer, when trees are loaded with leaves. 'I hope one day to make work that touches and understands better that time in the tree's life', he wrote in *Wood* (85). Not only leafful trees but also bright sunlight can make it hard to produce a good work: bright light doesn't always bring out the best in a work, Goldsworthy said. 'Bright sunlight makes the form too much about surfaces' (W, 23). Shadowy light, or the softer light of sunrise or sunset, was favoured.

In May, 1994, Andy Goldsworthy made one of his characteristic lines of dand-elions, which ran along the Capenoch tree's long branch, emphasizing its undulating form (another work designed to be viewed from one spot, to catch the shape of the branch, and the light). Sculptures which also drew attention to the shape of the branch included a line of orange oak leaves pinned to the branch (October, 1994); a group of five lines of oak wood pinned along the branch (April, 1995); and a serpentine line of snow pressed into the bark (*Snow line*, 1996). The snow wall of February, 1996, followed the curves of the Capenoch branch, sometimes mirroring it. The wall was narrow, culminating in a top edge which Goldsworthy smeared with mud. This work was made after Goldsworthy had built a wall of snow underneath the branch, which stretched unbroken from the ground to the branch. In the wall Goldsworthy made a large hole which he photographed from different angles and in different lighting conditions. Another hole made in a wall beneath the tree occurred in *Rosebay willowherb stalks thorns* (February, 1995), a sculptural form that Goldsworthy favours for gallery installations.

A sculpture which pleased Andy Goldsworthy greatly was the arch of ice created overnight in February, 1996. The structure incorporated the tree by having the branch move directly through the arch. Goldsworthy worked throughout a moonlit night, 'an extraordinary night, so intense' (W, 85). The arch consisted of slabs of ice stacked on top of each other from the ground to the branch. 'This is a very good piece, I am very happy with it… Works like this are what I live for', said Goldsworthy (W, 85). An earlier, more basic ice arch had been constructed at Brough, Cumbria, in 1982.

Apart from the hanging oak leaf lines, some of the less successful works in the *Capenoch Tree* series were the cairns and towers. The branches stacked against the tree trunk with a large circular opening (January 16, 1996), for example, looked out of place, as did the *Five Stone Arches* (March, 1994), a 'herd of arches', fashioned from thick slabs of stone. The line of seven snowballs, meanwhile, balanced along the length of the horizontal branch in decreasing sizes, worked well: this was one of the most adaptable of Andy Goldsworthy's forms. The large hollowed snowball made in March, 1995, when the snow was thawing also suited the location and its place in the *Capenoch Tree* series. The two 'stone houses' made in August, 1995, consisted of a stack of branches leaning against the tree with a large oval opening. Inside the 'house' was placed a column of balanced stones in decreasing sizes. This Goldsworthyan form is complex and difficult to harmonize satisfactorily with its environment. The simpler structures, such as the lines of leaves pinned to the branch, were finer realizations of Goldsworthy's explorations of the tree-in-the-landscape and tree-as-landscape theme.

Of the other stacks of sticks placed next to the Capenoch tree, the simpler forms worked best: not the cone with a hole through which the branch was glimpsed, but the globe of sticks next to the trunk, and the tower of sticks through which the branch passed (Nov, 1994). *Two holes* (1995), one made with leaves, attached to the branch, and one dug in the ground, was a weak work. *Oak tree snow cairn* (1996) was a simple but effective form: a shallow cone located underneath the upward curve of the long branch. Andy Goldsworthy capped the snow cairn with mud, then covered it with mud.

11 : 3 LARGE-SCALE WORKS AND INSTALLATIONS

Andy Goldsworthy has stated that he is not against long-term art:

That art should be permanent or impermanent is not the issue. Transience in my work reflects what I find in nature and should not be confused with an attitude towards art generally. I have never been against the well-made or long-lasting.

Domination and *penetration*. These are familiar terms describing patriarchal actions or constructions or ideologies used by feminists. Is Andy Goldsworthy, seemingly so delicate in his touches, dominating nature? He insists he isn't:

By working large, I am not trying to dominate nature. If people feel small in relation to a work, they should not assume that there is an intention to make nature itself small. (AG)

Yet, clearly, Andy Goldsworthy, and the American land artists (Michael Heizer, Walter de Maria, Robert Smithson, Charles Simonds, Alice Aycock), do dominate nature. James Turrell's *Roden Crater* or Heizer's gigantic *Double Negative* will clearly be around for a long time, unless someone or something destroys them (an earthquake could destroy any land artwork in the blink of an eye). Goldsworthy's stone pieces, too, may stay around for a while. There is a sense of gloating when Goldsworthy says:

Fourteen years ago I made a line of stones in Morecambe Bay. It is still there, buried under the sand, unseen. All my work still exists, in some form.

Daring not to change or affect the natural world, land artists do just that, all the time. They 'interact' with nature, but their 'interactions', however small scale, can't help changing nature (all artists change nature if they work in it). 'I like the idea of using the land without possessing it', said Richard Long, ever the idealist.[1] Andy Goldsworthy's aim is to 'touch' something in nature, the essence of nature itself, to understand it, and the identification of himself within nature.[2] Thus, about the 'lake pieces', the stick and stalk sculptures he was commissioned to do in England's Lake District in 1988, he remarked: 'I felt I really got through in the lake pieces. I had touched it, and understood it'.[3]

Andy Goldsworthy, like James Turrell, Alice Aycock and Herman de Vries, has made some huge pieces, such as the long 'snake' and the 'pool' or maze, in Country Durham, large works which take up a lot of space, and certainly *dominate* the surrounding landscape. Goldsworthy's large-scale outdoor works often use the serpent coil as a fundamental form. Goldsworthy maintained, however, that his 'snake-like' or serpent-shaped sculptures does not refer directly to snakes.[4] Instead, he preferred to call one of his favourite motifs a 'river of earth', or a tree root, or a river (RA, 113).

Whatever the artistic intention, however, it is impossible to limit readings of sculptures such as *Sidewinder, Lambton Earthwork,* the *Storm King Wall* or the serpentine shapes in the British Museum's Egyptian Hall to responses to the environment.

The serpent as symbol connotes time, change, seasons, cycles of birth-and-death-and-rebirth, eternity, sexuality, evil, the cosmos, and so on. Andy Goldsworthy might wish to determine how viewers read his serpent-shaped forms, and emphasize the response he makes to the natural environment, but consumers of art will make any interpretation they like, and some artists might wish to suppress (snakes also connote dirt – they slide on the dust; and excrement; the alimentary canal; eating and defecating; poison; reptile life, and so on). In 1998, Goldsworthy confessed:

> after working for many years, I have to admit that I have a fascination for the snake. For me it is perfect sculpture. It's so simple. The way it moves on the ground or in the water, it draws the place. It's so expressive of the place it moves through. It's not like any other animal. It actually moves with the surface of the land. (RA, 113).

While Andy Goldsworthy insisted that he wasn't interested in the symbolic associations of the snake, or in the snake as an animal, he did link his use of the snake to Constantin Brancusi's birds and fish (Brancusi sculpted radically simplified, abstract versions of birds and fish). For Goldsworthy, the serpent wasn't a totemic or symbolic creature, but a form that expressed 'the energy of movement' (RA, 113).

One of Andy Goldsworthy's recurring artistic ideas is the walk or journey: the *Drove Arch* project of the late 1990s followed an agricultural route across Cumbria; the Digne cairns of around the same time were connected by a walking route; the *Night Path* (2002) wound through a Sussex wood; the unmade proposal for five tree-lined mounds were set beside a road; in the late 1980s Goldsworthy planned a series of monuments in the Penpont region which could be reached by a 'long, hard, single day's run', a fell run linked by his monuments (HE, 154).

None of the monuments, cairns, sheepfolds, walls or other permanent works would be signposted. Andy Goldsworthy figured that the people who knew about his stuff wouldn't require signs, but the works could still have an impact for those not in the know. It's part of a move, from the 1960s onwards, to avoid signing artworks, and let the pieces stand alone, and speak for themselves (along with titling every artwork *Untitled*). It was OK, though, Goldsworthy said, for his monuments to be marked on the map (Sh, 21). Again, Goldsworthy's acknowledgment of Ordnance Survey maps is part of the ethics of 1960s art, and land art in particular (land artists, including Goldsworthy, spend hours looking at maps).

EGYPTIAN INSTALLATIONS. The theme of the twisting serpent was especially pertinent to Andy Goldsworthy's installations in the Ancient Egyptian galleries of the British Museum and the Museo Egizo in Turin in 1994. Goldsworthy's large sculpture was made with local sand on the floors of the museums, snaking in between the exhibits of Egyptian artifacts. It was there for one day then dismantled (after being photographed, of course – the photographic record incorporated the themes of time and death just as piquantly as the sculpture itself, being *photographs*). Even if not explicitly like 'snakes', these sculptures evoked the Ancient Egyptian preoccupation with time, death, eternity and immortality. Goldsworthy spoke of the sand snake flowing

> through the room – touching the sculptures and incorporating them into its form to give a feeling of the underlying geological and cultural energies that flow through the sculptures. (TM)

The sweet chestnut leafworks which accompanied the sand serpent also evoked time – they were spiral shapes, set in an Ancient Egyptian sarcophagus and a libation bowl.[5] Of his serpentine form Goldsworthy commented in 1999: 'I have to stop making this form. It is becoming obsessive' (T, 167).

GRIZEDALE. Andy Goldsworthy's large-scale works, like James Turrell's, Nancy Holt's or Herbert Bayer's, are monumental works, which sprawl across the landscape. *Sidewinder* and *Seven Spires*, at Grizedale (a Forestry Commission site between Windermere and Coniston Water in Northern Britain), were trunks of trees stripped of their branches, and pinned together. In *Sidewinder*, the curved trunks were placed on the ground, to form a lengthy snake-like sculpture: the piece rests on the ground then curves into the air. The impression was of sliding, arching kinetic energy. In other words: a huge serpent slithering along the forest floor.

In *Seven Spires* the trees were pinned together to form tall spires. The result was a series of enormous edifices made of wood in amongst other trees. Andy Goldsworthy wanted to harness the sense of the 'almost desperate growth and energy driving upward' in the pine wood, and to evoke a cathedral-like atmosphere, with the spires stretching skyward with the brown gloom underneath.[6] It is, at first, not clear which is a tree and which is sculpture. Both, of course, are made of wood: Goldsworthy has simply drawn together the surrounding trees, it seems, but in doing so, he redefines the surrounding forest.

Seven Spires looks at first to be a gentle sculpture, blending in with the surrounding forest. 'In avoiding monumentality, however, Goldsworthy's sculptures do not forego grandeur', wrote art critic Andrew Causey.[7] Yet they do stand out, really, they are distinctly works of art, existing in a paradoxical relationship with the environment. A 'collaboration' is a polite way of saying what Goldsworthy's *Seven Spires* is about: a 'collaboration with nature', a phrase used about much of his art. Other spires, made around the same time, include *Bracken Spires* (1983) and *Stone Spire* (1983). Goldsworthy later reworked the spire form in the 2000s in San Francisco, in the Presidio Park (it's well worth visiting – aim for the golf house; it's nearby).

Andy Goldsworthy sometimes writes arrogantly about his art. For him, the human touch can improve on nature: combined with human culture and art, the natural world is made even more significant. It's not enough for nature to be existing on its own: it requires humans to make it complete. Or as Goldsworthy put it: '[i]f anything, I am giving nature a more powerful presence in the mass of earth, stone or wood that I use'.[8] In the *Sheepfolds* interview, Goldsworthy tried to deflate such claims: 'I'm not trying to compete with Nature. I'm not trying to improve it. I just need to work with it'

(Sh, 23).

SANDSTONE SHELTER/ STAIRCASE/ TOWER. Andy Goldsworthy's *Sandstone Shelter/ Staircase/ Tower* (1987) was a studio mock-up for a large hilltop monument (unbuilt so far). It was basically a spiral staircase, associated with the Scottish Iron Age round tower, called *brochs*. It recalled the viewing of mediæval Chinese gardens from platforms. Even in its scaled-down state, *Sandstone Shelter/ Staircase/ Tower* is 'heroic', said a critic.[9] It is a simple idea on a grand scale – if that equates with 'heroic', then so be it.

Slate stack at Stone Wood was another simple idea, on a grand scale: built next to (in 'partnership' with) a hollow tree, it consisted of a rectangular structure of flat pieces of slate.[10] The slate was set horizontally, but in the middle of the thick wall was a circle shape (actually a cylinder) made by placing the slate vertically. It looked a lot simpler than it sounded in a verbal description. Like many of Andy Goldsworthy's sculptures, the viewer gets the idea instantly. It is simple, but constructed on a 'monumental' scale.

For Andy Goldsworthy's large-scale works there are often drawings made, usually free, open drawings done in graphite, with heavy blacks. Goldsworthy's green romanticism comes over even in his choice of graphite as a drawing material: he likes the fact that graphite occurs 'naturally', is not manufactured, or bought in an art store. A connection was made, Goldsworthy said, with the 'source' (the Earth), by using graphite straight from a mountain. 'I am still drawing with earth', Goldsworthy said, pompously.[11] Well, what else could he be using except the 'earth' in some form or another? Everything comes from the Earth (except the odd meteorite). He could hardly be using stuff from a planet in a distant galaxy, could he? But he likes to think he's using 'the earth' in his drawings, just as he thinks he's drawing with 'real' snow or berries when he rubs 'em on a sheet of paper. 'The snowball will melt into a sheet of paper', Goldsworthy said, 'These drawings do not just represent the place – they *are* that place' (HE, 189). What does this statement mean? The berry or snow drawings 'are' a place? No. They are '*of* a place', '*from* a place', they are not the '*place itself*'. They are only someone's *interpretation* of a place, someone's *representation* or *simulation* of a place on a bit of paper. In the art statement "Touching North", Goldsworthy equated snow and stone, snow and sand, ice and slate. 'Snow is stone,' he asserted, but, plainly, it is not. 'Snow is like sand', he added, employing the key word, 'like'.[12] Snow may be *like* stone or sand, but snow is not sand or stone itself.[13]

ENTRANCE. In 1986 Andy Goldsworthy was commissioned by Common Ground (the New Milestones Project) to work at Hooke Park Wood near Beaminster, in West Dorset in Great Britain. He made *Woven beech*, a large arch that recalls his 'drawing in air' stick sculptures: a demi-circular arch provides an entrance point: but instead of shaping the branches above the arch, Goldsworthy allowed them to splay out in every direction. The inside of the arch is a rough half-circle, but the upper half of the arch is a tangle of branches and slender tree trunks.

For *Entrance* (also 1986), Andy Goldsworthy used the technique of strapping tree trunks and branches together that he employed in *Sidewinder* and *Seven Spires* at Grizedale. Aided by John Makepeace (of Parnham Trust in Dorset) and some students, Goldsworthy created a barrier or gateway to Hooke Park Wood from two circles of overlapping tree trunks. Drop-bar barriers were fixed on each standing circle, so they would cross in the middle, echoing Goldsworthy's icicle sculptures. Goldsworthy's concerns were that the sculptures would blend in with the environment, as well as being functional.

WALLS AND INSTALLATIONS. Other large-scale Andy Goldsworthy works include the installations *Slate Wall* and *Clay Wall* (1998, Edinburgh), *Clay Wall* (1996, San Francisco) and *Clay Wall* (2000, London). The installation work *Stone Sky* in Brussels (1992), comprised flat pieces of slate covering the entire floor of the large space, with a whitish circle in the centre, the white created by scratching the slate. The circle recalled Richard Long's slate circles, but the title, *Stone Sky*, referred directly to nature: the circle could be read as the sun, the moon, the sphere of the heavens, the orbits of planets, and so on. (*Pool of Light* was a form related to *Stone Sky,* and *Burnt Sticks*, below).

One or two of Andy Goldsworthy's works directly recall those of Richard Long: Andy Goldsworthy's *Burnt sticks* (1995), for example, is reminiscent of some of Long's and David Nash's installations which form circles from stone slabs on gallery floors. *Burnt sticks* consisted of sticks charred at one end, the blackened parts of the sticks were put together to form a circle on the gallery floor. The *Fall Creek* installation, at the Herbert F. Johnson Museum of Art at Cornell University (in 2000), comprised a group of low holed mounds fashioned from hundreds of branches on the floor. Goldsworthy has worked at Cornell a number of times: the university has a long history of land art links: one of the important land exhibitions, *Earth Art*, took place in 1969 (it featured Richard Long, Dennis Oppenheim, Roberts Smithson and Morris, and Michael Heizer).

POOL OF LIGHT was constructed in the Charente region of France (at Bioussac) in 2001, a private commission from Philippe and Libby d'Hémery. They wanted to use trees damaged and felled in a storm at the end of 1999. Andy Goldsworthy built a large rectilinear installation on the terrace at the back of the *château,* using chestnut logs laid in parallel on the ground. In a circular area in the centre of the installation Goldsworthy had the split logs laid at right angles to the others. The logs would catch the sunlight in different ways in the morning and the evening: 'a dark circle in the morning and the reverse in the evening. At midday, and on those days without sun, there is no circle at all' Goldsworthy explained (P, 88). For Goldsworthy, *Pool of Light* was 'an expression of the ability to survive storms and upheavals' (ib.).

NIGHT PATH (a.k.a. *Moonlit Path*, 2002) was constructed at Petworth Park in Sussex in Southern England (at the Leconfield Estate). It was a long path built from white chalk culled from the Sussex Downs that snaked through a wood. *Night Path* was meant to be experienced at night, though not necessarily a moonlit night (Andy Goldsworthy also said that the path could be visited at other times of the day, and perhaps a clear moonless night, or a full moon obscured by clouds would be better [P, 153]). The idea of walking along a path by moonlight might have appeared as too romantic, Goldsworthy said (P, 156). In the event, it wasn't: '[t]he sculpture has become a far darker piece, in all senses of the word' (ibid.). Much more significant than the path itself was the experience of being out in the trees at night. As Goldsworthy put it in *Passage*:

> A place is so different at night – it is like being somewhere else. Perception, feeling and senses are changed by darkness. A different range of emotions and senses is released. (P, 153)

Plenty of land artworks have been made specifically for the night, of course: James Turrell's sky-viewing spaces, for instance, or the walks that Hamish Fulton has undertaken throughout a whole night. Andy Goldsworthy's *Night Path* also recalls the spaces in Oriental gardens which were fashioned for contemplation in moonlight.

A work associated closely with *Night Path* was *Chalk Stones Trail*. This work comprised 14 chalk stone sculptures, each spherical or rounded, placed on a trial about five miles long (some of the stones weighed 14 tons). *Chalk Stones Trail* was situated at West Dean in West Sussex (North of Chichester), in England. Goldsworthy intended to produce a book featuring this work and others in Sussex.

LAMBTON EARTHWORK. Commissioned by Sustrans and Northern Arts, *Lambton Earthwork* (1988) was a quarter-mile long bank which coiled along the ground near Chester-le-Street in County Durham. The site was associated with railroads and heavy industry, but Andy Goldsworthy turned it into something wholly concerned with æsthetic and religious themes. The long spiralling banks of earth clearly derived from the earthwork sculptures of Robert Smithson and American earth art (Goldsworthy said he is wary of using the 'overblown spiral', the too-obvious spiral as a shape [HE, 163]. However, he hasn't yet been able to avoid using it entirely). Goldsworthy spoke of the serpentine shape as being like a river winding through a valley, or the root of a tree. [14]

Lambton Earthwork was seen by the artist as a 'river of earth', a response to the natural energies of the place (recall how Goldsworthy spoke of black holes and the energy in the Earth erupting from underneath). Certainly *Lambton Earthwork* was not about industrial archæology or nostalgic reminiscences of the bygone railroad era: it was a piece of land art which had powerful mythic overtones. For example, Lambton on the River Wear in Durham is associated with one of the great dragon legends of Britain: the Loathly Worm of Lambton.[15] Andy Goldsworthy has thus created a dragon – or a quarter-mile earthwork which corresponds with the Loathly Worm of Lambton.[16]

Passage was a show in early 2005 at Michael Hue-Williams' new Albion gallery in London (Andy Goldsworthy's UK art dealer). It was Goldsworthy's first major exhibition in the capital since 2000. Goldsworthy built some new installations for the exhibition: *Clay Stones* (most works are 2005) was the familiar Goldsworthy array of clay covered stones on the floor (this time wrapped in porcelain clay, with human hair and hay too). At an impressive 40 or so feet in length, *Root* comprised nine sections of chestnut branches set end-to-end and covered with Dumfriesshire clay mixed with hay and human hair. *Root* was an irregular, sandstone-hued continuous line, its smooth surface pitted with cracks.

Root led the visitor into *Stone Column*, an installation taking up a whole room, consisting of the familiar Andy Goldsworthy stones (17 of them) piled into a tower, 18 feet high, with a large boulder at the base, decreasing in size to a tiny pebble at the tip. The largest stone weighed one and a half tons. The stones were granite, from Glenluce Bay in Scotland, with sanded cavities to enable them to balance. Encasing the column was a dense wooden dome, with branches ten or fifteen feet long inter-laced – the 'stone houses' form that Goldsworthy has used most famously in North America (*Stone Houses*, 2004). *Stone Column* was lit by the available light coming from windows beyond the gallery, and the lighting in the *Root* room.

Finally, an enormous *Oak Cairn*, taking up another space, maybe twenty feet high, and built from stacked oak branches (from Gloucestershire, England). A group of leafworks (hollow serpentine forms and hollow holed globes) were displayed in glass-topped wooden boxes (six feet long) in another room. The leaves were sweet chestnut, pinned with thorns, as in Goldsworthy's leafworks of the 1980s. There were also photographs on show at Albion Gallery: a series of views of the Sussex *Night Path*; an icicle work; and a sequence of pictures of a *Sand Hole* (1999) made on the Aberdeenshire coast.

While there was nothing startling or 'new' at Andy Goldsworthy's 2005 London show (being variations on tried and tested forms), it was an important consolidation of Goldsworthy's art. It was a popular show too (visitors could be spotted taking pictures of the sculptures with their cel phones – which seems to be an essential act, another way of memorializing a gallery visit).

MAZE. The other Andy Goldsworthy earthwork at Durham (*Maze,* 1989, at Leadgate) also used ancient mythology and symbolism, this time the labyrinth (again, Robert Smithson, Richard Fleischner and Alice Aycock had created large earthwork mazes in the late 1960s/ early 1970s). Goldsworthy also designed an earthwork which was a curving ramp, exactly like Smithson's *Amarillo Ramp,* though on a much smaller scale.

Land artist Herman de Vries built a circular walled *Sanctuarium* (1997) in West-falen, Germany. Alan Sonfist planted a maze from oak trees at TICKON in 1993. In Dennis Oppenheim's *Maze* (1970), cattle are lab rats running after corn in a field (Oppenheim controlled the movement of the cows in his maze field with feed). Dan Graham combined hedges and mirrors in his *Two-Way Mirror Hedge Labyrinth* (1989). Chris Drury has produced circular mazes (some of which are reworked circular dew ponds). Drury also carved a maze from snow on a Sussex hill (1999). Bill Vazan has fashioned a number of earthworks on the ground, including a *Stone Maze* (1975-76, reminiscent of Richard Long's Connemara labyrinth). A number of (land) artists have made miniature labyrinths – maze models: Charles Simonds, Terry Fox and Patrick Ireland. Goldsworthy has drawn lines on sand, or stitched grass stalks pinned together, in swirling, spiralling shapes which echo the primæval forms of the snake, the spiral and the labyrinth.

Richard Fleischner created a *Sod Maze* in 1974, in the turf at Newport, Rhode Island, an enormous *Zig Zag* (1972) in grass (370 feet long) and a *Chain-Link Maze* (1978), 61 feet square. Michelangelo Pistoletto built an interior maze from large pieces of corrugated cardboard laid out across the whole gallery (*Labyrinth,* 1991). In *Monumental Ikebana* (1990), Hiroshi Teshigahara made a giant arched path from bamboo in a gallery space. For Vong Phaephanit's bamboo installation (*What Falls to the Ground Cannot Be Eaten,* 1991), a forest of bamboo sticks was hung from the ceiling of the London gallery, approached through a monumental black doorway.

Andy Goldsworthy's *Maze* can be seen as a part of the resurgence of interest in mazes which occurred in the 1980s (aligned, as ever, with green/ ecological/ occult/ New Age trends). Mazes were commissioned for country houses, zoos and theme parks. A maze became seen as one more feature for visitors to enjoy: apart from the country mansion or palace or museum interior and formal gardens, the public could visit a maze, and perhaps a children's play area. Some mazes were set beside adventure playgrounds, emphasizing the sense of play rather than ritual. At country houses such as Ragley Hall in Staffordshire (UK), the maze was part of the children's play area, and was conceived as something of a gym or assault course: there were walkways and bridges over some of the passages in the brick maze, which were climbed via ropes and ladders. Probably the most famous maze in Britain is at Hampton Court.

1991 was 'The Year of the Maze' in Blighty (largely orchestrated by maze designer Adrian Fisher of Minotaur Designs). Some modern mazes were conceived as part of civic architecture, such as the Bristol Water Maze, which took its design from a roof boss in nearby St Mary Redcliffe church. Some pavement mazes were made as part of new parks or new shopping centres (such as at Worksop). An underground maze was constructed at Leeds Castle in Kent. Old turf and hedge mazes were re-cut and restored (A. Fisher, 1991). At Symonds Yat in Herefordshire, the Jubilee Maze was made in 1977 by the brothers Lindsay and Edward Heyes. The way out of the maze led to a small Maze Museum, where the history of mazes was told via simple displays. The Symonds Yat Jubilee maze made a leisure outing of the maze: the maze is the centrepiece of the visit. This is unusual: mazes are more often add-ons to the theme park or country house.

The maze is a very satisfying motif or design: it is self-contained, like other geometric patterns; it can use almost any perimeter shape, from circles and squares to 'organic' shapes; it offers opportunities for games and play; it can be a visual device, for decorating floors or walls, or one of the main features of a garden; and it carries a sizable slice of symbolism, religion, paganism and history. The symbolism and history of the labyrinth can be happily ignored in favour of simply enjoying solving a maze as a puzzle. Unlike sacred sites such as churches and stone circles, which are loaded with religious significance, and generally demand some religious or intellectual response from the visitor, the maze can be consumed simply as an interesting structure. One doesn't need to know about mythology (such as Theseus and the Minotaur in the Greek myth) or religion (such as the ritual aspect in Christianity of walking a maze) to appreciate a maze.

Like *Lambton Earthwork* (but unlike most of Andy Goldsworthy's works), *Maze* was intended to be used by the general public. Both *Maze* and *Lambton Earthwork* were about responses to the energies in nature – thus the public was invited to explore similar things as they physically walked around the earthworks. The usual experiences of the maze were apparent in Goldsworthy's *Maze* – not being able to see the whole plan from above; being enclosed by high banks; a bewildering series of turns and paths. The interwoven series of embankments also recalled Iron Age forts (of which there are many in Britain), such as the complex (and enormous) array of defences at Maiden Castle in Dorset. The comparison between Goldsworthy's sculpture and Iron Age hillforts, though, is not quite fair: Iron Age earthworks were not made by bourgeois contemporary artists for the purposes of providing an interesting æsthetic experience, but were made to protect small, tough communities (Maiden Castle witnessed some bloody battles – especially when the Romans conquered the site).

One of the most important of Andy Goldsworthy's later commissions was the install-ation *Garden of Stone* (2003) at the Museum of Jewish Heritage in Lower Manhattan. *Garden of Stone: A Living Memorial* was a group of 18 hollowed Vermont granite glacial boulders, with an oak tree set inside (dwarf oaks, which only grow very slowly). The trees were planted at the top of each stone, with the hollow space below for the roots. The largest boulders weighed 13 tons. *Garden of Stone* was situated on the second floor garden, overlooking the river, with socio-political icons such as the Statue of Liberty and Ellis Island easily visible beyond. *Garden of Stone* cost a million dollars (the Public Art Fund collaborated with the museum), making it easily Golds-worthy's most expensive commission to date. Jacob Ehrenberg was project manager.

The glacial granite boulders were taken from Vermont (near Barre). They were then transported to a Connecticut quarry (Stony Creek) where Ed Monti, a guy in his seventies, hollowed them using a cutting torch. The bases were flattened so that the rocks would sit properly on the ground (Andy Goldsworthy said that in trimming the stones, he aimed to retain as much height to each stone as possible). Goldsworthy allowed the marks made on the boulders by their journeys and hollowing to remain. That was part of his preference for retaining evidence of the transformations materials under-go. It was part of the social project of Goldsworthy's art: it was important for the artist where the stones came from; the source was part of the overall sculpture. Hence the boulders were collected from fields and the landscape, rather than quarries (the more obvious place to shop for stones): 'how the sculpture is made and the journey of both the ideas and material are also important' (P, 65).

Andy Goldsworthy also wanted to maintain the integrity of his garden of trees and stones, and was concerned about the planting the Jewish Museum planned for the borders of the site. Goldsworthy said he hoped to retain the 'sense of barrenness' of just the stones and the trees, and the introduction of other plants would compromise his sculpture, as well as the look of the building (P, 69). Originally, Goldsworthy planned to have all of the stones roughly the same size, but the idea developed to having a range of sizes, with the larger ones acting as 'guardians or leaders in the group' (P, 67).

Garden of Stone was made as a memorial for the victims and survivors of the Holocaust. Andy Goldsworthy was an unusual choice, perhaps, for an artist to tackle such a massive political and ideological issue. Goldsworthy has not been known for addressing issues such as the Holocaust in his art. Certainly he could not be described as a high profile political artist. A Gentile he has also not had much of a connection with Jewish culture or history.

A group of Holocaust survivors were invited at the opening of the exhibit (Sept-ember 16, 2003) to plant the saplings in the stones. (Andy Goldsworthy's mother Muriel also planted a tree). *Garden of Stone* brought together two of Goldsworthy's favourite materials, trees and stones, and obvious (but no less noble) themes of change, growth, transformation, burial and rebirth.

Many Andy Goldsworthy's cairns are fabricated from slate (such as *Slate cone*, 1987, 1988); others from branches (*Oak branches*, 1990); or sandstone (*Sandstone*, 1990). Others are put into groups (such as the proposals for stone cone groups at Vassivière, Newcastle and Penpont). Later cairns include the commissions *Logie Cairn* (1999) in Aberdeenshire, *Penpont Cairn* (2000), *Three Cairns* (2002) in the U.S.A., and *Hollister Cairn* (1999) in California.

The first cairn that Andy Goldsworthy made (in Cumbria) he related to the natural rock formations in that part of North-West England (called the Nine Standards). For Goldsworthy, that pile of stones were guardians – and the idea of sentinels watching over the landscape has remained with the sculptor ever since, becoming the fundamental interpretation of all his cairns and cones. Part of the *Sheepfolds* project were the *Nine Pinfold Cones*, stone cones sited within pinfolds made in 'counterpoint and dialogue' with the Nine Standards. As well as 'sentinels', guardians of a place, the cairns were also memorials to a place, or a people (Goldsworthy has linked stone cairns to burial mounds [RA, 89]), or monuments that crown a summit.

The cairn/ cone form is also about the process of growth and energy. It is a form that celebrates for Andy Goldsworthy 'the fullness, vigour, heavy ripeness and power generated from a centre, deep inside' (S, 37). Like D.H. Lawrence and Friedrich Nietzsche, Goldsworthy here makes the age-old links between 'ripeness' in nature and femininity and pregnancy. The Goldsworthy cone, then, can be seen as another expression of female fecundity, in the Lawrencean manner, an equivalent for a pregnant woman (like the prehistoric "Stone Venuses", the squat, callipygous figurines): in short, stone Mother-Goddesses. Fullness, fruit, growth, ripeness ('ripeness is all' in *King Lear* [V, 2, 9]).

As the cairns were being constructed, Andy Goldsworthy explained, all sorts of irregularities would introduce themselves. Like many artists say of their works, Goldsworthy said when he completed a cairn, he only saw the mistakes. But it was precisely the accidents and mistakes which 'give the form a tension and energy' (RA, 101). The perfect artwork was a practical as well as philosophical impossibility. Goldsworthy said was often surprised by the final result: '[e]ach cairn is a shock, and not what I intended' (ibid.). Getting the belly of the cairn right was critical, Goldsworthy remarked, and the foundation and beginning was usually tricky, but the most important part was the top, the last three feet: '[t]he top draws the energy of the stone to a peak, just as the apex of an arch becomes a focus for its energy' (RA, 103).

Andy Goldsworthy often spoke of searching for the perfect form in his cairns. Every time he built a cairn he said he was looking for the ideal form, and tried to attain it, but always fell short. Goldsworthy seemed more anxious about the shape of his cairns than almost any of his other sculptures. 'I set myself an almost impossible task: to make the perfect form by eye and hand', Goldsworthy said in *Passage* (10). That's it: the artist started out with too high ideals, which could never be accomplished (he didn't begin most other works with the same high goals).

The anxiety perhaps also sprang from the fact that the cairns were built by hand

and judged by eye, not from architectural plans. They were intuitive forms, and the shape each cairn took was always being negotiated during construction. Thus, Andy Goldsworthy often talked about work starting slowly at first, about getting the foundation level, about working upwards to the belly, about wondering exactly when he should start working inwards, about putting particular stones in particular places, and feeling anxious again as the cairn approached completion.

In another passage in *Passage*, Andy Goldsworthy acknowledged that starting a work was always a somewhat anxious, uncertain time. Each big project tended to be different, with its own set of challenges and limitations, so that Goldsworthy always had to explore the possibilities of the project first for a few days before finding the right forms and methods. It wasn't a question of doing the same thing every time, with the same materials, in the same forms.

PENPONT CAIRN. The cairn Andy Goldsworthy built in 1999-2000 was commissioned by the village he had lived in since 1986: Penpont in Dumfriesshire. Goldsworthy acknowledged that he was nervous and self-conscious about making a work that was so close to his home, that he would have to live with, that he'd often see, that would be seen by locals and neighbours (P, 6). It was one sculpture he'd have to get right; if it went wrong, he'd be always reminded of his mistakes. Goldsworthy said he had 'given enormous thought to its making' (P, 6).

Penpont Cairn was sited on the summit of a low hill in a farmer's field. Its situation on the hill's brow meant that it would be visible from many spots in the neighbourhood. It was a location that was very open on all sides: 'I have never made a cairn in a place so open, not just to the view, but to the rising and setting sun', Andy Goldsworthy wrote in *Passage* (P, 8). Goldsworthy wondered if the siting of *Penpont Cairn* was perhaps a little *too* prominent; 'it might be too imposing and appear as if it were shouting for attention in a 'look at me' kind of way', Goldsworthy remarked (12). Silhouetting was particularly strong with the *Penpont Cairn*: because it was raised up from the ground on a large stone, the sky was always visible behind the sculpture. 'Although the making of a sculpture is obviously out of the ordinary, this particular work has a wonderful sense of the normal and everyday about it', Goldsworthy said during the construction of *Penpont Cairn* (P, 8).

In 1994-95 a new form appeared in Andy Goldsworthy's *œuvre*, the 'stone house', usually consisting of a hollow stick cairn or cone with a round or elliptical opening at the top. Sometimes the cairns or chambers were constructed from stones, like Goldsworthy's stone walls, but the basic structure was the same: an enclosed space, often with a hole to see in (and out), and often with an object (a boulder, a tree, or a balanced column of stones) sitting inside. (Chris Drury has made the shelter one of his primary forms). Examples of the 'stone house' include sculptures constructed at Digne les Bains and Mt. Kisco, New York (both 1995); the 'stone houses' built in New York were among the most prominent in Goldsworthy's *œuvre*. Like Drury, Goldsworthy has occasionally enclosed his cairns with other materials, such as the slabs of ice surrounding a stone cairn (1996), and the stone spire inside a stick cairn (1995). A *Stone House* built in Melbourne (Australia) in 1997 took the form of a rectangular wall with a circular opening and a boulder placed inside. 'Every stone that I place on a sculpture contains some of my own energy: the lifting, the cutting, the placing. Part of me stays with the stone, just as part of the stone stays with me', Goldsworthy said (P, 8).

STONE HOUSES. *Stone Houses* (2004) was a prestigious commission from the Metropolitan Museum of Art in Gotham, for its roof garden (Jeff Koons, Frank Stella, Ellsworth Kelly, Sol LeWitt and Roy Lichtenstein have also exhibited on the roof). The rocks were taken from Glenluce Bay in Scotland and transported to the U.S.A., but the wood (white cedar) for the *Stone Houses* was from New England. The roof garden overlooked Central Park and the formidable skyline of Manhattan, so the sculptures had plenty to contend with visually. This setting certainly wasn't the undulating hills around Penpont or the windswept beaches of Scotland or California, but one of the most famous cityscapes in the world.

The two columns of granite stones were about thirteen feet high. They were fashioned in the familiar Andy Goldsworthy form of a tapering column, decreasing in size so that the topmost stone was a pebble. Around the columns of stones Goldsworthy constructed an octagonal 'house' – basically a domed-shaped shelter structure which enclosed the columns (they were eighteen feet tall). The cedar wood had been split into rails, with each end overlapping.

Andy Goldsworthy continued his series of prestigious exhibitions in the United States of America with *Roof* (2005), at the National Gallery of Art in the nation's capital. *Roof* consisted of several slate domes which were basically very large versions of a form Goldsworthy had developed years ago: low, hollow domes of pieces of slate stacked on top of each other, with circular holes at the top. Goldsworthy related the dome shape of *Roof* to the famous domes of downtown Washington, including the West Building of the National Gallery, the U.S. Capitol, the National Museum of Natural History and the Jefferson Memorial. For the *Roof* project, Goldsworthy used stone (Buckingham slate) from the same source as the materials for the domes of the Smithsonian Castle and Ford's Theater. Goldsworthy had begun the commission by visiting Government Island, Stafford, Virginia, in 2003, where he made some ephemeral sculptures.

'Cone' is perhaps not quite the right term for an image or expression of fullness and ripeness: Andy Goldsworthy's 'cones' look more like fruit. The imagery of fruit would accord with Goldsworthy's 'ripeness' discourse. 'Cairn' is also not quite the right word either, though some of the 'cones' on rocky mountainsides (such as *Cone to mark day becoming night* at Glenleith Fell, and *Cone to mark night becoming day*, Scaur Glen [both 1991]) have affinities with natural cairns and outcrops of rock.

Some of the cairns were built at night, to be seen at night, as hymns to the night, or the dawn, or the sunset. Working on the Yorkshire *Ice hole* (1987), Andy Goldsworthy spoke of 'working with the moonlight' which was a 'very strange intense light'.[1] Working at night, Goldsworthy described approaching 'the most beautiful point, the point of greatest tension, as one moves towards daybreak'.[2] The *Clearing of Arches* installed at Goodwood sculpture park in Sussex, England (1995) were made to be viewed in moonlight.

In Australia Andy Goldsworthy constructed cairns 'for the moonlight', or 'for the day' (S, 43). Like the mulga tree branches edged with red sand to catch the setting sun, these stone cairns were made for particular lighting conditions: the orange-coloured stones fashioned into a cairn were associated with (and completed by) the setting sun. The stone cairns were the sculptural equivalent of lighting a fire in order to celebrate Midsummer or sunset; or erecting a little shrine for a minor deity. They were small-scale celebrations of the daily festivals of dawn, moonlight, noon and sunset, sacred moments that occur everyday, but which are no less holy for their common recurrence. Here Goldsworthy is working, like many a land artist, 'with the sky', with large-scale events such as nightfall and moonlight.

Also at Grizedale sculpture forest in England was a large circular enclosure made from wicker-work and larch posts, by Keir Smith (b. 1950). Like Andy Goldsworthy, Smith is sensitive to the work done by people in a landscape, to the sense of labour: thus, Smith included in the enclosure hints of human activity, such as stag antlers, which suggest human hunting, while a pair of shears allude to 'sheep-shearing and animal husbandry'.[3] Like Goldsworthy, Giuseppe Penone has made sculptures with trees, such as his *I Wove Together Three Trees* (1968), made in the Maritime Alps. Jan Dibbets produced a tree-work, *Construction of a Wood,* in 1969.

How different from Andy Goldsworthy's *Seven Spires* is another group of tree trunks tied together, Jackie Winsor's 1971 piece *30 to 1 Bound Trees.* Here, the binding of the trees, as in much of Winsor's work, relates to autobiographical, child-hood experiences, often painful, as well as the formal aspects of density, weight and repetition.[4] If Goldsworthy's works have similar autobiographical themes, they are hidden: the artist himself rarely talks in a personal, emotional manner (he doesn't make his own life the subject of his art, like Joseph Beuys or Mary Kelly).

Andy Goldsworthy does talk in autobiographical terms about his work, however, from time to time. For him, art and life cannot be easily separated (a common philo-sophy in modern art). One feeds the other, in a symbiotic relationship. One cannot say for certain where Goldsworthy's art ends and his life begins. He sees art as a continuation of life, where the feelings artists of the past had about nature (for example, J.M.W. Turner and John Constable and the British landscapists) feed on the same source as artists working today (that is, nature itself). Some people made their life their art (or was it the other way around?): Yves Klein, Joseph Beuys and Carolee Schneemann among artists, and personages such as Quentin Crisp and Anaïs Nin. Andy Goldsworthy is definitely not a larger than life personality like Anaïs Nin or Quentin Crisp (yet). He does, however, keep a diary, and carefully records the progress of his art, and the manufacture of each work. Around each sculpture, then, is an autobiographical residue, which is partly constructed from the title which includes details of the time and place of creation.

Three Cairns (2000-02) was an important large-scale commission to construct three stone cairns in the United States of America: one on the West Coast (in California), one on the East Coast (in New York state), and one in the Mid-West (at Des Moines, Iowa). *Three Cairns* was a collaboration with three cultural institutions: Des Moines Art Center, Neuberger Museum of Art, Purchase, New York, and La Jolla Museum in San Diego. In the event, Andy Goldsworthy built six cairns: apart from the three permanent pieces, there were three ephemeral sculptures: two were tidal, on the East and West coasts, and the third, in Iowa, was built on the prairie, which was set alight (with fire replacing water as the natural force which engulfed the sculpture. However, the stone cairn survived the fire).

The project had a conceptual basis, with the stone cairns linked up. They wouldn't be able to be viewed at the same time, in the same space, and thus part of *Three Cairns* 'will to an extent always exist only as an idea', as Andy Goldsworthy put it (P, 118). Goldsworthy defined the cairn for him again: '[t]he cairn is a marker to the flow of change, life, growth, decay, death and renewal of the prairie landscape' (P, 94).

The *Prairie Cairn* was constructed especially for the burn (the cairn and burn was managed in collaboration with Grinnell College and Faulconer Gallery). Andy Goldsworthy has often combined stones and heat – he's fired stones in stoves, for instance, and was fascinated by the process of hollowing out the glacial boulders for *Garden of Stones* with a cutting torch. In the event, the burning of *Prairie Cairn* was hot enough to melt part of Goldsworthy's camera, and he didn't get the shots he wanted of the prairie on fire around the cairn. Goldsworthy also failed to capture the collapse of the tidal cairn in the West, so the series of ephemeral U.S. cairns was in some way a failure. 'The series remains one of my strongest achievements and yet contains great failures' (P, 95).

The *West Coast Sea Cairn* was constructed at Half Moon Bay in California in August, 2001. The tidal process was central to the cairn, as with all of Andy Goldsworthy's sculptures made on the seaboard. It was built to collapse with the next tide, and, as ever, capturing the moment of the downfall photographically was crucial. It was a paradox that something as solid and enduring as stone could be so ephemeral. That was part of the conception of the stone cairns built on beaches: stone and water, the permanent and the impermanent, solidity and fragility.

As with his *Réfuges d'Art* sculptures in France's Digne, and the walls built at Clougha Pike in Lancashire (1999-2001), Andy Goldsworthy constructed some limestone walls with hollowed-out spaces, which surrounded the permanent *Midwest Cairn* at Des Moines Art Center. At Digne and Lancashire, Goldsworthy had built walls with vertical elliptical cavities, large enough for a person to stand in (there was a step just below the space to help the visitor up). In Iowa, Goldsworthy turned the elliptical hollows into cairn-shaped spaces. Now each wall had a recess in the middle of it shaped roughly like half an egg. The limestone walls were grouped around the central cairn in the familiar Goldsworthyan guise of guardians or sentinels

Each cairn-shaped cavity related directly to the exact shape of the three cairns, as if the cairns from the East and West coasts could be brought to Iowa and slotted into the walls, as if the coastal cairns had a womb-like resting place waiting for them in perpetuity in Iowa, as if the cairns on the coasts had travelled outwards, away from Iowa, and the Iowa walls were 'home'.

The *East Coast Cairn* (2001), built at the Neuberger Museum of Art, took on personal associations for Andy Goldsworthy, because his father had died recently (in October, 2001). The cairn, constructed under a large tree, became something of a memorial for his father (Goldsworthy also discussed the events of September 11, 2001 in relation to the work – *East Coast Cairn* was created a couple of months after the attacks on New York and Washington [P, 112, 115]).

The *West Coast Cairn* was built outside the Museum of Contemporary Art in San Diego in early 2002. The California cairn was constructed under another tree: Andy Goldsworthy spoke of the tree in his usual terms of sheltering and guardianship (P, 118). Scale was always an important consideration in siting a sculpture beside a tree: the tree shouldn't dominate the sculpture, and the sculpture should be able to assert itself.

Some of the poetic links artists make in the course of their work are sometimes obscure. Andy Goldsworthy liked the fact that the San Diego cairn was made of limestone, which was created, geologically, on the seabed, and the cairn was near the ocean (P, 117). It's a connection an artist can discover over time, because s/he's working on the piece for hours or days, but one wonders how many visitors to the Museum of Contemporary Art would make the link between limestone and the nearby Pacific Ocean.

11 : 9   WALLS

One of Andy Goldsworthy's favourite structures is the stone wall. The wall he built (his first) between his land and a neighbouring farmer's at Stone Wood, Penpont, in Scotland, was a snake-like sculpture (*The Wall*, 1989). *The Wall* was a 'monument to walls',[1] a neat way of creating, on Goldsworthy's side of the wall, a sculpture, and on the farmer's side, a sheepfold. Goldsworthy's walls have a dual purpose: practical, and æsthetic. The walls are boundaries or sheepfolds as well as artistic objects. Their æsthetic derives from their practical applications (S, 106). While later walls (such as *Room* or *The wall that went for a walk* or the *Storm King Wall*) did not have a 'practical' or agricultural function, Goldsworthy still related them to the practicalities of stonewalling. Goldsworthy spoke proudly and sentimentally of the practice of stonewalling: he talked in terms of 'tradition', 'history' and 'years of experience' (S, 106).

Another wall, related to the first, was made at Ile de Vassivière in France: *Two folds* (1992) comprised two curl-shapes, like two question marks, which mirrored each other, as in *The Wall*. The upper fold enclosed some trees, as in other Andy Goldsworthy wallworks, while the lower fold became flooded with water. This is a work that will decay, though: the lake will erode the wall, and the roots of the trees may alter the upper fold. The *Two folds* wall united three of Goldsworthy's favourite elements: water, stone and earth. The stone curves linked together the earth and the water, and both the seemingly 'weaker', more transient elements – water and trees – will change and even destroy the apparently 'stronger' element, the stone of the wall. For Goldsworthy, stone is hard and unyielding (the traditional view), but also 'flowing, changing, malleable', if, he adds, one is 'prepared to understand it in those ways' (Sh, 12).

The wall that went for a walk (1990, Grizedale) was a 150-yard long wall that literally snaked through the forest. The serpentine form of *The wall that went for a walk* related to *Lambton Earthwork* and *Sidewinder* (another Grizedale sculpture). *The wall that went for a walk* has no 'proper' function – i.e., no 'practical' function. It weaves between the trees and follows the lay of the land. Instead of ploughing through trees or rocks, Andy Goldsworthy's curving wall assiduously avoids them. 'The wall itself is an expression of movement; a line moving through the landscape', Goldsworthy said (Sh, 12). However, the wall doesn't need to be there in the first place (a notion that Goldsworthy cannot quite resolve: in the book *Stone* he related *The wall that went for a walk* to the old fields that were at Grizedale before the forest, but it's not a convincing argument).

Some of Andy Goldsworthy's wallworks are circular enclosures, derived mainly from agricultural sheepfolds. There is no direct agricultural function to these circular enclosures, however, so they must be regarded as, God forbid, 'decorative', as works of art. Though they are made with the assistance of traditional dry stone wallers such as Joe Smith and Steve Allen (who have built many of Goldsworthy's walls), the spectator can see immediately that these are not rural artifacts, used by farmers. Rather, Goldsworthy's circular enclosures, such as *Stone gathering* (Northumberland, 1993), *Rock fold* (Dumfriesshire, 1993), *Slate dome hole* (Edinburgh, 1990) and *Room* (Pennsylvania, 1992), are about creating shelters and particular spaces in an outdoor environment. 'The space is made quiet and intense by the containing wall, giving a sense of protection and care', says Goldsworthy (S, 106). Like the sheepfolds, Goldsworthy's circular enclosures are about marking a space separate from, yet a part of, the landscape, a sanctuary from the elements. Indeed, in *Stone gathering*, large boulders were placed inside the circular wall, just like cattle or sheep sheltering from the wind and rain. *Rock fold* encircled an excavated outcrop of rocks. *Slate dome hole*, in the Royal Botanic Gardens in Edinburgh, combined two Goldsworthyan motifs: the shallow dome with a hole at the summit, made from slate, and the circular dry stone wall. The central, sheltered rock in the Goldsworthy enclosure was compared by a critic to an altar or sacred centre.[2] Another Goldsworthy motif is to bury tree trunks and branches and boulders within his stone walls (as in New York state [1993], and at Storm King [1996]).

At 2,278 feet long, the *Storm King Wall* in the United States was not only Andy Goldsworthy's biggest wall, it was one of Goldsworthy's most significant works. Other artists who had worked at the Storm King Art Center in New York state included Richard Serra, Louise Nevelson, David Smith, Mark di Suvero, Isamu Noguchi, Alice

Aycock and Alexander Calder.

Another stone wall made by Joe Smith from Andy Goldsworthy's drawings was *Room*. This was a human-height stone wall situated in a wood of young, slender trees. It was another of those large-scale works, like those at Grizedale forest, which Goldsworthy enjoyed building under the trees, so it was always partially obscured by tree trunks. The circular enclosure of *Room* added to the already confined atmosphere of the forest. The use of five, not four, doors, indicated that this work was not about the four cardinal points and directions, like the snow circles at the North Pole: five is the symbolic number of magic, the occult pentacle, the human form (head and four limbs), and the cosmos.

11 : 10   SHEEPFOLDS (1996-)

In the mid-1990s, Andy Goldsworthy developed the *Sheepfolds* project: building and renewing a hundred sheepfolds in the North of England. The *100 Sheepfolds* project was funded by public money from Britain's National Lottery (who contributed a grant of £340,000 or about $545,000. A portion of the National Lottery ticket money went to arts projects). Steve Chettle, Public Arts Officer for Cumbria County Council, was chief shepherd of the project which included exhibitions in Cumbria, St Albans and London, TV documentaries, and books by Goldsworthy (*Sheepfolds* and *Arch*).

1996, the Year of the Visual Arts, was the launch of *Sheepfolds*; the completion date was later extended to 2003 and beyond. Initially, the *Sheepfolds* proposal was presented to local councils, environmental agencies, countryside agencies, educ-ational institutions, land owners and arts development boards. The *100 Sheepfolds* project was carried out in conjunction with all sorts of institutions, including town councils, district councils, parish councils, schools, tourist boards, art galleries, national parks, Cumbria College of Art & Design, East Cumbria Countryside Project, National Trust, Voluntary Action Cumbria, Northern Arts, Eden Arts, and the Arts Council.

Founded around building stone walls, the *Sheepfolds* project was a development of Andy Goldsworthy's love of stone walling. He had a deep respect for the wallers who built the sheepfolds, and employed traditional methods – such as using old walls to build new ones. The wallers took over from Goldsworthy, who didn't have quite the skill necessary for walling. Champion wall-builder Steve Allen led the building of Goldsworthy's later walls (such as the *Sheepfolds* project, and the *Storm King Wall*). The main materials involved in the *Sheepfolds* project would be stone, water, slate, hedges, wood, trees and grass.

The *Sheepfolds* project – Andy Goldsworthy's largest undertaking up until that time – revolved around sheep farming: the herding, washing, cleaning, branding, breeding, rearing, and shearing of sheep. Goldsworthy saw the *Sheepfolds* project as a 'monument to agriculture' (Sh, 16). The sense of time – of time past and time to come – was important in the walls and sheepfolds for Goldsworthy. 'Some people may consider the proposals for certain folds quite empty, and that is intentional because they are to be filled, in time, by the way people use them' (Sh, 15). Goldsworthy talked about embedding an earlier form inside a new one as 'like a memory within the wall' (Sh, 16).

The connection with the past was absolutely vital for all of the sheepfolds, pinfolds and washfolds in the *Sheepfolds* project. Andy Goldsworthy emphasized at every opportunity the link with the past, with the history of the area, with the social and industrial uses of the sites, with the many people who lived and farmed in Cumbria. The project wasn't about repeating the past, or about nostalgia (Sh, 14). Goldsworthy made one of the sheepfolds for his sister-in-law, who had recently died (Sh, 19).

There were six different variants of sheepfolds in the project; cairn folds (pinfolds), boulder folds, drove arch folds (folds rebuilt for the *Arch* project), restored folds, touchstone folds, which have works built into the walls, and the ephemeral pieces made on the Samuel Taylor Coleridge walk route. The sheepfolds containing cairns were built near the Nine Standards in Cumbria, rock formations which have long fascinated Goldsworthy.

Among the many proposals that Andy Goldsworthy submitted for the designs of the sheepfolds were circular structures, square structures, sheepfolds approached up steps (some set in the walls, some on the banks below the sheepfolds), sheepfolds containing enormous boulders, some with much smaller, low, flat boulders, spherical boulders in oval sheepfolds with a tree growing beside them (or enclosing the boulder with a ring of trees), square sheepfolds with walls featuring circular holes, boulders enveloped with a low circular wall inside a square sheepfold, a pyramid cone fashioned from small rocks and branches (another of rocks alone), a pyramid cone spreading nearly to the edges of an oval sheepfold, ringed by trees, a sentinel cone in a sheepfold, a tree growing out of a circular opening in a wall, a circular sheepfold surrounded by rocks heaped up to the height of the wall, a rectangular sheepfold with a tree growing in a smaller enclosure in each corner, a stream flowing under a sheepfold built into a pyramid cone, with trees growing out of the mound, an arch climbing into a square sheepfold, a rectangular sheepfold with vertical slate installed in the walls, half an arch up against a leaning pillar stone in a sheepfold, and a circular sheepfold with stone piled far above the walls.

Some of the sheepfolds will have water running through them (a favourite device in large-scale land art), which'll fall, to make a sound (some of the great gardens in history were designed to enhance the sound of water – the Mughal gardens, Hadrian's Villa at Tivoli, the Medici Renaissance gardens, Zen gardens and the paradise gardens of ancient Persia). It was an idea Andy Goldsworthy returned to in the Digne *Water Cairns*.

The idea of balance, of objects being held aloft, defying gravity, fascinates Andy Goldsworthy so much it becomes one of the central motifs of his work. He makes arches from thin pieces of slate (such as the *Slate Arch* [1985, Cumbria], and *Slate Arch* [Wales, 1982]), or has arches stretching up four steps (*Slate Arch*, 1990, Tarbes). *Over the stone* (1993) was a large arch made from loose stones found on the hillside at Scaur Glen: it was built over a large boulder, the internal form of the arch echoing the shape of the boulder. *Over the wall* (1993) was an arch that leapt over a stone wall; *Tree arch – river stones* (1993) was an arch of three components, leaning up against a tree of two trunks; *Between two trees* (1992, Pennsylvania) was a shallow arch wedged between some trees; *Out of the stones* (1993) was an arch leaning against the boulder that Goldsworthy used in *Over the stone*: it was two-thirds of an arch (these arches were made in the Winter of 1992-93 in Dumfriesshire [S, 98-99], apart from *Between two trees*).

In the children's 'space labs' and 'hands on' workshops at the Science Museum in London and in science museums around the world, visitors can learn how to construct an arch. One finds out how to build that key architectural form using large blocks of wood. The arch form, so simple yet so elegant, appears often in Andy Goldsworthy's art. Before he went to the North Pole, Goldsworthy constructed from stone a circular archway. *Touchstone North* (1990) was intended as a pointer to the Arctic from Goldsworthy's home in Scotland. It is a 'landmark that will orientate north', Goldsworthy wrote in his Arctic diary.[1]

Andy Goldsworthy has continued to build arches: it has become one of his most distinctive motifs. No other land artist had employed the arch so often as a key structure in their *œuvre*. Goldsworthy's arch sculptures include the offshoot of the *Sheepfolds* project, the *Arch* project of 1996-97; a number of 'herds' of stone arches (such as *Herd of Arches* and *A Clearing of Arches*); arches exhibited in Montréal (1998); a private commission made near the Storm King Art Center, *Eleven Arches* (1997); and some large commissioned arches: a stone arch sited in Montréal (1999) and Rainscombe Park, Oare, Wiltshire (2000), both constructed from red Scottish sandstone. Of the *Montréal Arch*, commissioned by Cirque du Soleil for its HQ, Goldsworthy remarked: '[t]he arch is heavy and strong, expressing permanence, but it is in fact about change, movement and journey' (T, 60).

The *Arch* project of Summer, 1997 (a.k.a. *Walking Arch* and *Drove Arch*) expressed many of Andy Goldsworthy's æsthetic concerns. It consisted of Goldsworthy and his team building a red sandstone arch at twenty-two key sites along the old tracks and roads where sheep and cattle were driven, between South-West Scotland and the North-West of England. The route was from Locharbriggs Quarry, North of Dumfries, via Longtown, Carlisle, Penrith and Shap, across Cumbria, to Kirkby Lonsdale. *Arch* was about ancient traditions, the history of the landscape, old economies, sheepfolds, and the contemporary landscapes of South-West Scotland and North-West England. Goldsworthy saw his art as just another layer of history on top on many layers of human history. 'I work in a landscape made rich by the people who have worked and farmed it. I can feel the presence of those who have gone before me' (T, 8). It wasn't simply nostalgia in reconstructing old agricultural buildings and structures either, Goldsworthy maintained, it was about finding new uses for them (RA, 107).

11 : 12   DIGNE (1995-)

In July, 1995, Andy Goldsworthy constructed a multi-layered cairn within sight of Mont St Vincent (in the River Bès valley in France). The cairn started out as a mound of yellow stones, on top of which Goldsworthy placed a different layer of material over a series of days: grey stones, different coloured stones (brown, yellow, white), then blue and yellow stones, then stalks with charred ends, then grey stones, then mud, which Goldsworthy wet, then a layer of sticks around the whole cairn, followed by more grey stones, and finally a 'house' of sticks with a large round hole. The form of the cairn echoed the mountain in the distance, while the changing state of the cairn each day evoked the constant processes of growth and decay in nature.

The stone cairn was built in South France, at Digne les Bains, which became one of Andy Goldsworthy's favourite spots (and he has returned to the region nearly every year since). The rocky, wooded hills and icy, rushing rivers of this beautiful area of South France became a kind of Mediterranean version of Goldsworthy's homeground of Dumfriesshire in Scotland: it had the rivers, the valleys, the forests and the hills which Goldsworthy loved, but lit by a Mediterranean light (and quite a bit warmer than Scotland, too – in fact, Goldsworthy found the heat a little uncomfortable, and took to working early in the morning and late in the afternoon. Keeping Mediterranean hours, in other words). And Digne offered a Southern, Mediterranean culture to Goldsworthy's usual stamping ground of Northern European culture.

Andy Goldsworthy was pleased to have cracked creating sculptures under the harsh, bright sun of South France (not usually liking direct, intense sunlight). One of his methods was to submerge stones in the Bès river (which he had tried once or twice before). 'I like the way that the water confuses the form of the stones, so you forget the stone and all you see is the colour', Goldsworthy commented (RA, 111).

Andy Goldsworthy found the Digne landscape very inspiring. As he put it, '[e]ach visit to Digne seems to have generated an idea, and a reason to come back again' (RA, 45). Goldsworthy's work in Digne developed into one of his major commissions: *Réfuges d'Art*, a series of works on a walking trail around the three river valleys in the Réserve Géologique. The nine 'refuges' were intended to be resting spots on a walking tour of the Réserve Géologique; they comprised existing buildings and structures which were given the Goldsworthy treatment. Some were for stopping overnight, others for shorter halts.

Probably the most intriguing refuge was the one built into the Chapelle Sainte-Madeleine in 2002: in a wall Andy Goldsworthy created an elliptical opening into a one-person-sized chamber, entered via a small step. One of the ideas of the refuges was to have the walker pause for a moment and look back at the landscape they had been traversing. In the case of the Thoard *Réfuge*, the rural region was framed by a vulval form (Goldsworthy likened it to an abstract figural form). The *Réfuge* was also about the traces of human presence (RA, 51). The pieces required people to visit them and use them, Goldsworthy maintained, building up layers of experience. The sculptures needed to have a social function; they weren't simply about nostalgia.

Part of Andy Goldsworthy's Digne works were the three *Sentinels* – very large stone cairns which marked the walking route in the three valleys. Another big commission was the five *Water Cairns*, built at the Réserve Géologique on the route to the car lot. These sculptures employed the sound of water flowing inside them (a common device in land and environmental art, but rare in Goldsworthy's *œuvre*). Also part of the Digne projects was the clay wall (*River of Earth*, 1999) constructed in the museum in Digne and filmed, to form a backdrop for Régine Chopinot and the Ballet Atlantique and their *Danse du Temps* (2000).

Andy Goldsworthy also made many other pieces in the Digne area, many of them in a favourite spot in the Bès valley, on the stony river. There were also exhibitions, and a book, of the Digne works. All told, the Digne projects developed into one of Goldsworthy's biggest undertakings to date; there are more permanent Goldsworthy works concentrated there than anywhere else.

Unusually, one of Andy Goldsworthy's Digne proposals had a political aspect, a link to the French Resistance, which had used a farmhouse at Draix. Goldsworthy recalled that he was keen to maintain the association with the Resistance, and talked about connecting the idea of a stone cairn occupying rooms in the upper and basement parts of the farmhouse with the Resistance being hidden and underground (RA, 89).

For the *Réfuges* in Digne, Andy Goldsworthy sketched out all sorts of proposals for interventions and adaptions to existing buildings and sites. Most of the ideas were variations on tried and tested Goldsworthy motifs: one had a giant spherical bundle of branches in a room. Another was a wall or screen of logs from floor to ceiling. Yet another was one of Goldsworthy's snakes climbing a wall. In another, a herd of arches. A pyramid cairn behind a low door, with the viewer sensing rather than seeing the rest of the cairn. A giant boulder nearly filling a room, with the bulk of it hidden behind a doorway. Many of Goldsworthy's proposals for sculptures at Digne were one form nestling inside or relating to another: squat rectangular structures with a large circular opening revealing a boulder, or a pyramid cairn; a holed cairn with a cone-shaped cairn inside it; a boulder sitting atop a low mound of stones.

12

Spirituality and Sculpture

Mysticism is emphasized in Andy Goldsworthy's writing, as also in the occasionally enigmatic statements of Robert Smithson, David Nash, Hamish Fulton and Walter de Maria.

> My art is unmistakably the work of a person [wrote Goldsworthy] – I would not want it otherwise – it celebrates my human nature and a need to be physically and spiritually bound to the earth. (*Stone*, 50)

Andy Goldsworthy's æsthetics are those of a neo-pagan, shamanic, Native American, Maori, pantheistic, nature worshipping kind, the sort of beliefs that some people call Goddess worship, and others kinda pagan or 'New Age'. Goldsworthy evoked the earth's energies and atmospheres. Goldsworthy explained:

> The energy and space around a material are as important as the energy and space within. The weather – rain, sun, snow, hail, mist, calm – is that external space made visible. When I touch a rock, I am touching and working the space around it. (RSS, 4)

This talk of 'earth energies' recalls ley lines, and the 'dragon lines' or *feng shui* of Chinese geomancy. Andy Goldsworthy has emphasized his notions of 'energy' in nature by 'drawing' around stones. He has stuck stalks together to form lines which he curves around rocks (see the photographs of rocks at Scaur Glen and Scaur Water in *Stone* [page 85]). These intertwining lines of stalks are meant to link up with the energy 'generated by the rock' (S, 83), not to tie it up or imprison it. In *Two River Stones* (2001), Goldsworthy enclosed some rocks on the edge of a river with bands of curved sticks. The continuous lines could be associated with the notions of 'aura' or the astral plane of occultism, the envelope of supernatural energy that surrounds objects and animals. The 'aura' or astral plane is another manifestation of primæval animism, associated with the concepts of *mana* and charisma.

Andy Goldsworthy's sculpture is very much about a primal animistic response to nature. Animism, the 'belief in spiritual beings', as anthropologists and psychoanalysts emphasize (in E.B. Tylor's definition), is the origin of all religion. There is an affinity, then, between Goldsworthy's (and any contemporary artist's or viewer's) response to rocks and sculptures and the so-called 'primitive' or ancient people's response to certain stones, or hilltops, or rivers, and statues, icons, totem poles, standing stones, and so on. For ancient peoples, rivers became goddesses and trees were spirits. Goldsworthy's continuous 'drawings' with grass stalks around mossy boulders in Dumfriesshire are not much different from the primæval response to the 'energies' in nature of ancient religions and cults. Goldsworthy's act of lacing the delicate grass stalks around the rocks in swirls and spirals valorizes the human-nature relationship, just as ancient tribes did by calling a river a Goddess, or regarding the buffalo as holy, or speaking of the Earth-Goddess Demeter and her daughter Persephone who was taken by Hades into the Underworld for half the year and relating it to the seasonal cycle of agriculture and crops.

One can see how Andy Goldsworthy has a 'sacred' relationship with particular objects – Scaur Water, boulders, leaves, cairns – which is often exactly like the shamanic, animistic relationship of ancient peoples. Goldsworthy goes around the world and makes art not out of places, or out of things, but out of his *relationship* with particular things and places. The continuous grass stalk lines around the boulders are like caresses – a way of, literally, 'touching nature'. Goldsworthy 'touches nature' in this literal manner by rubbing little stones into larger stones – the act of rubbing is like a lover's caress (the sculpture as fetishized, sexualized object). Goldsworthy speaks of wanting to explore the space in and around a stone 'with a touch that is a brief moment in its life' (S, 6). Goldsworthy admitted to a 'deep sense of spirituality', but said 'it doesn't manifest itself in any sort of religion'.[1]

One is reminded again of old John Cowper Powys who, on his morning walks, used to kiss certain stones and trees. In upstate New York in the 1930s, Powys went out walking every day and said his prayers and invocations to particular natural objects. He gave his beloved things names: there was the 'Dead Tree', the 'Skian Gates' (some stones), the 'Prometheus Stone', the 'Perdita Stone', 'the Flotsam', 'the Jetsam', the 'Unknown Stone', the '*Other* Unknown Stone', the 'Noble Wreck', the '*other* Apple Tree', the 'Thorn Bush' and the 'Sea Coal'.[2]

One doubts if Andy Goldsworthy kneels down and kisses the soil as he says his prayers, as John Cowper Powys did (Pope John Paul later made this act famous), but Goldsworthy's art is very much about this loving, holy relation with the natural world.

Andy Goldsworthy revisits certain stones, 'many times over' (S, 6), and gets very attached to places, which become like homes (HE, 58). He also admits 'I like touching stones touched many years ago.'[3] Like John Cowper Powys and the Romantic poets, like the archaic shaman, like Australian aborigines and 'primitive' peoples, Goldsworthy goes out into the landscape and communes with it,[4] knows every inch of it, knows this stone and that pool, this place for gathering strong grass stalks and that dramatic hilltop viewpoint. He says he likes revisiting old works, and sometimes includes photographs of revisits in his publications. 'I love the gathering of works, accumulated over time', he wrote in *Passage* (132).

The spiral and snake shape employed by so many cultures down the ages (in ancient Peru, or on the doors of Neolithic tombs, or in the Mid-West of America) is associated with Goddess cults and with the energies of life. The circles and spirals of Andy Goldsworthy, Alice Aycock, Dennis Oppenheim and Robert Smithson are also those of the Goddess, the ancient Earth Mother. In the eco-neo-pseudo-pagan view, land artists, then, make marks upon Mother Earth, upon the surface or skin of the Goddess. Goldsworthy inadvertently evoked phallic penetration when he said: 'I want to get under the surface… At its most successful, my 'touch' looks into the heart of nature' (WH). Land artists, then, penetrate or cut into nature. The Earth, which is regarded as feminine in this particular religious or pagan worldview, is penetrated – by Michael Heizer gouging vast chunks out of the American desert, by Walter de Maria thrusting a kilometre-long brass rod into the Earth (this must be art's biggest phallus, surely?), and Goldsworthy, seemingly so gentle, has cut trenches in the earth, or smashed slabs of slate or pebbles or leaves, to make lines of broken, shattered material on the earth. He has torn leaves apart to form a line, and has broken pebbles, making a line, like a fault line in continental structures (*Leaves Torn in Two*, 1986, *Broken Pebbles*, 1987 [AG]). These are violent gestures, destroying the organic make-up of the natural forms he so adores.

Sometimes the violence of a split-apart rock is emphasized by Andy Goldsworthy highlighting the rough edges of the crack with red – as in *Granite boulder found split open* (1990 [S, 76]). The red leaves stuck on the edges of the split make the jagged edge look like a wound. Another rock Goldsworthy marked out with red, the *Soft red stone* at Heysham Head in Lancashire (1991 [S, 82]), was chosen perhaps because it was a rock that had recently fallen from the cliff above. It was not smoothed by water and weather: its sheared-off edges and planes were exaggerated by the red colour. All land artists – all artists – must break up and reform materials, but these cracks and holes can look to the eco-friendly devotee like scars on the Earth.

Land artists often use circular forms, which hide the violence of their gestures. The spiral or circle is a kind, organic, even gentle shape, seemingly in tune with 'earth energies'. Circular structures (igloos, huts, stone circles, tombs, earthworks, pools) seem to be in harmony with nature, echoing the circle shapes of the planet itself, or suns, eyes, blood cells, orifices, orbits. The circular structures suggest primitive, archaic, more 'authentic' ethics, the 'back to nature' syndrome. There is, then, not only a mystical side to land art, to the art of Andy Goldsworthy, David Nash, Dennis Oppenheim and Mary Miss, but also a nostalgic element (nostalgia is a key element in any religion). Looking *back* to the land, land artists also look *back* to a former, even ancient era which was, patently, better (to a golden age which is and was imaginary, which never existed). This is the hidden utopian subtext in the writings of the land artists, this nostalgia for the better times of archaic cultures, when people lived 'in harmony' with the earth. This is, of course, a widespread nostalgia, but not backed up by the evidence, which is that for ancient and prehistoric peoples life was as hard, if not harder, than it is now.

Andy Goldsworthy's main visual motif is the circle, whether as a globe made of leaves, slate or snow, or a cone or cairn (often built from slate or snow), or circles from leaves half-frosted or stone rubbed with red powder, or circles cut into snow or leaves. The circle is 'such a fundamental form, one can never get away from it altogether', says Goldsworthy (HE, 19), though his circles are usually deliberately slightly irregular (he draws them by hand and eye) – he avoids the connotations of traditional symbolism.5 There are many 'negative' circles, made by the surrounding material, leaving the circle in the centre empty.

The 'feminine' quality of this primary circular symbol has already been mentioned. It sounds too obvious to say that Andy Goldsworthy's circles, globes, cones and rings should have 'feminine', maternal connotations, but it is precisely in this sort of simple world of equivalents and responses that Goldsworthy operates. The simplicity of the structures, such as a circle, cannot be improved upon, but no matter how 'natural' the circle is as a shape, it always looks humanmade in Goldsworthy's art. His circles of white leaves in amongst dark leaves (1981, Yorkshire) always stand out from the surroundings. The viewer is always aware that a human has made those marks, or arranged the leaves in that way.

The globe made from oak leaves (1985), for instance, is typical of Andy Goldsworthy's melding of the 'natural' and the human. Yes, the viewer has perhaps seen oak leaves many times, or any sort of tree leaves. Yes, the viewer has probably admired the multicoloured leaves of Fall. But Goldsworthy's sphere of leaves in the forest is not an object the viewer might expect to come across on a walk. The oak leaf globe asserts itself instantly as *art*, as a humanmade artifact. Yet how right these globes of ice, snow, slate and leaves can appear. The simplicity of the structure (the circle) makes these sculptures seem curiously 'obvious' and 'natural'. Like a really good pop song or film, one wonders: *why haven't they been made before?*

> The best of my work, sometimes the result of much struggle when made, appears so obvious that it is incredible I didn't see it before [Goldsworthy wrote]. It was there all the time.6

Some artworks seem so clear and 'obvious' (Leonardo da Vinci's scientific drawings, Giovanni Bellini's *Madonnas*, Johann Sebastian Bach's *B Minor Mass*), it's amazing that they weren't made centuries earlier. Even ancient stone circles, built *c.* 1000-500 BC, seem so 'obvious'. The stone circle seems such an obvious structure, marking off and enclosing a sacred space (Andy Goldsworthy, in his typical idiosyncratic manner, prefers ancient stone walls to stone circles [S, 106]).

Andy Goldsworthy's globe forms, whether fashioned from stacked rocks (Blaenau Ffestiniog, 1980), or snow (Lancashire, 1980), or from redwood sticks (California, 1995), seem so 'obvious' to the viewer. They look simultaneously 'out of place' and quite at home in their settings. Or maybe it's just that the viewer is so used to seeing the extraordinary structures humans make (New York City, a passenger jet, a television set, an oil refinery), that the sight of a snowball hanging in some trees or a globe made from stacked ice ain't that amazing. Some of the globes Goldsworthy constructed from branches got progressively bigger through his career, so they were eventually several yards across (as at Fondation Cartier in Paris [1998], *Oak Stack* at the Storm King Art Center [1999], and the Digne *Réfuge d'Art* proposal [2000]).

Other 'feminine' and labial imagery in Andy Goldsworthy's art includes the holes he's dug in the ground: sometimes he lines the edge of holes in the soil with grass stalks (in Cumbria, 1984). On the Isle of Wight (in 1987), Goldsworthy made a layered circular hole, and dusted the edges with red stone ground into a powder. The use of the colour red accentuated the æsthetic intention to investigate the energies of the Earth. If any colour is to be selected to heighten the livingness of things, it has to be red. 'Looking into a deep hole unnerves me. My concept of stability is questioned and I am made aware of the potent energies with the earth'.[7]

Andy Goldsworthy has created circular mounds out of leaves, slate, bracken and sticks which echo prehistoric monuments such as Silbury Hill, which have been interpreted as 'feminine' or womb images. Goldsworthy has made hollow snowballs – large snowballs, a few feet across, which are hollowed out like fruit: their hollowness is one of their central attributes. Goldsworthy cut a circular hole in them (at Blencathra, Cumbria, 1988 [AG]). Like Stone Age people who covered the white bones of the dead with red powder (red as the colour of life, of blood, passion, rage, warning, danger), Goldsworthy often uses red as a colour in his art. He has red leaves, stones rubbed with red stones, a boulder covered with red poppy leaves, sand dusted with red powder, petals wrapping a branch, and red rowan berries dropped into pinned-together iris blades.

13

Time In Andy Goldsworthy's Art

In the best landscapes we are fascinated by the mysterious shiftiness of the scene under our eyes; it shifts about as we watch it. And we realize, with a sort of transport, how intuitively true this is of landscape. It is not still. It has its own weird anima, and to our wide-eyed perception it changes like a living animal under our gaze.

D.H. Lawrence [1]

Andy Goldsworthy's snowball prints are the residue of snow melting on large pieces of paper. But it is the melting itself, the way the snow shifts and pours into the paper, that is really interesting. Similarly, with Yves Klein's 'body-paintings', the intriguing thing was the manufacture of the painting (other artists have printed directly with the body). In Yves Klein's case, this involved women (nude, of course) being doused with blue paint (International Klein Blue, naturally) and moving around on a huge canvas stretched on the floor. Klein's *Anthropometries of the Blue Period* were *avant garde*, self-conscious, ironic art happenings, accompanied by a string chamber orchestra (playing Klein's *Monotone Symphony*, naturally).[2] All very French, bohemian, cool, and guaranteed a mention in any book on Conceptual or performance art.

Andy Goldsworthy's snowball and rain shadow prints, then, are – like Yves Klein's *Anthropometries* – records of far more intriguing events that occurred elsewhere, during the artwork's manufacture. Goldsworthy produced a series of works in the 1980s which directly recall Klein's body paintings. Goldsworthy lay down on the ground when it was raining or snowing: the result was the outlines of his body left upon the ground. The title for each of these works (reproduced in different Andy Goldsworthy books) is: *Lay down as it started raining/ or snowing/ waited until the ground became wet or covered before getting up.*

Andy Goldsworthy 'prints' himself on the ground negatively, his body covers the dry earth, while around his body the earth (soil, stones) is darkened by the rain. Goldsworthy has also 'printed' his shadow on frosty grass in the early morning. Goldsworthy has made rain, frost and shadow prints at the Royal Museum of Scotland, Cornell University, Central Park in Gotham, Yorkshire, Cumbria, Holland, Japan, Angers (France), Australia, Denmark and Ciudad Real (Spain).

Kazuo Shiraga made works of art with his body, such as smearing mud on pieces of paper with his feet, or 'fighting' in the mud (1955). His body art was called 'the art of committing the whole self with the body'.[3] The Austrian performance painter who enacted 'symbolic 'self-mutilations' and sado-masochistic actions',[4] Günter Brus, said: '[m]y body is the intention, my body is the event, my body is the result'.[5] Andy Goldsworthy's 'ground-prints' and 'rain shadows' are spontaneous works; they cannot be planned; one has to be open to the weather, knowing it is just starting to rain or snow. One could never, in any country, plan such a work inside, then go outside and execute it. These works are always dependent on the weather, which is always unpredictable. For this reason, though they appear to be the most 'passive' of Goldsworthy's works – the easiest to produce (one just lies there) – Goldsworthy finds them challenging, because the conditions have to be just right. On many occasions, the rain is the wrong sort, or (as in New York City), though forecast, it doesn't come at all.

Yves Klein exhibited a gallery full of empty space – *Le Vide* (void) – and Andy Goldsworthy made his own version of Klein's non-sculpture in his *Hard earth.* The Conceptualism and New Realism of Klein and his contemporaries (Joseph Beuys, Bruce Nauman, Piero Manzoni, Victor Burgin, Yoko Ono) seems far removed from Goldsworthy's land art. Yet Goldsworthy cites Klein's dramatic (but faked) leap into the air as a powerful example of catching a moment in time: '[t]his amazing tension in the moment of suspense! It's like he's been there for ever, or he's gone in a moment. It's like one of my throws'.[6] For Goldsworthy, moments are intense precisely because they are only momentary: *pace* his icicle spiral sculpture of 1996, Goldsworthy said that 'intensity can only be shown for a short time. In fact, the moment is intense only because it lasts for a short time, and it would be wrong for such an intensity to last longer than that' (W, 10). In fact, it's difficult for the spectator, let alone the artist, to sustain that kind of æsthetic intensity.

In many of his photographs, Andy Goldsworthy documents artworks that last for a second or two. There are many photographs, for instance, which record 'throws', such as a ball of red earth being thrown into a river (July, 1992). Not just one photograph, but many, which were mounted in the 1994 exhibition side by side. These are large colour photographs. The red earth makes beautiful shapes as it hits the water in Goldsworthy's beloved Dumfriesshire. 'The first splash is white. It's the second I'm after. A red eruption from below', he says (ib.).

Andy Goldsworthy said that he is really working with time. 'If I had to describe in one word what I do, I'd say I work with *time*'.7 Although it seems, at first glance, to be all about space, about particular spaces and how materials react with certain locations, time is an important element in Goldsworthy's art. He spoke of adding another layer to preceding layers of 'human understanding and character' when he makes work in the landscape.8 He is conscious of the past and its layers of time on and in the landscape. 'The land is an expression of its past', he said (HE, 189). He investigates moments, the instant of a splash; then there are works that last a few minutes or hours: the soil drying after Goldsworthy's laid on it after rain; or days – the rocks covered in clay; then works that study seasons (Autumnal leaves, snow and ice works); and works that explore the slow, cosmic time of enduring media – stones, the sun, the sea. What counts, Goldsworthy commented, is not the duration of the work, but 'the experience of making.'9 'I've always been interested in the moment a work is made' (Sh, 15).

Many of the photographs in Andy Goldsworthy's exhibitions document very short occurrences: the red earth in the river, or mud being thrown in the shallows on a beach, or on a misty hillside: *Rainbow splashes* were made with a stick in Yorkshire (1980), *Slate throws* (Cumbria, 1988) consisted of throwing slate into the air, like *Hazel stick throws* (1980) and *Leaf throws* (Tayside, 1989); *Maple leaf throw* was made in Japan in 1990. In 1995, Goldsworthy had the Ballet Atlantique dance troupe throw sticks and soil into the air at once. In California (1994), Goldsworthy threw dust into the air against the sun, which he called *Breath of Earth* works.

It is the shapes the mud, earth and sticks make in the air that fascinate Andy Goldsworthy. He is seen in photos, throwing the mud and earth, his legs and arms raised high, caught in a moment of release. These photos are about time, about letting something go, and capturing the trajectory. Mud and earth is not 'alive', as a bird is, but Goldsworthy seems to throw the mud and earth as if he's releasing a bird. He wants the earth to fly. It doesn't: it arcs back to the ground, but these arcs are elegant, and become the subject of many photographs.

The 'throws' are also very dependent on particular lighting conditions. In the Lake Michigan photographs (1991), Andy Goldsworthy was photographed (by his wife Judith) against the light in a dusky sky, so that the trajectories of the wet sand in the air could be clearly seen. The *Rainbow splashes* required low side-lighting. The red mud throws at Scaur Water occurred against bright green foliage, which contrasts with the red. Colour contrasts are also central to the Mount Victor Station throws, which were made with red sand ejected into the clear blue Australian sky (1991). Goldsworthy has made fewer throws in later years, though they are still part of his repertoire (such as *Red river stones*, 1999).

The arcs or trajectories of the thrown earth become the artwork in itself. The curve of the earth against the sky actually *is* the sculpture. Similarly, Bruce Nauman (who is, like Yves Klein, another celebrated Conceptual artist), photographed himself as a water fountain (1966). Richard Long threw mud against walls, either in a curtain of mud, or in a circle. Kazuo Shiraga wallowed in mud and threw mudballs (*Making a Work With His Own Body*, 1955). Guo Qiang Cai created miniature explosions with gunpowder to evoke the mushroom clouds of nuclear explosions (1996). Bruce

McLean's *Splash Sculpture* and *Mud Sculpture* (both 1968) are precursors of Andy Goldsworthy's splashes and throws. Goldsworthy's throws offer plenty of ammunition to critics who dislike his work, because someone making splashes in a river with a stick or throwing sand or leaves in the air is the kind of art denigrated by the tabloid press in the Great Britain.

A set of four photographs, *Penpont Stone* (S, 22-23), made between 1991 and 1993 in (where else?) Dumfriesshire, crystallized the most explicit expression of Andy Goldsworthy's investigations of the cycle of the seasons. Like the Romantic poets (such as James Thomson, John Keats, Percy Bysshe Shelley and William Words-worth), who wrote of each season in turn, Goldsworthy produced four pictures of a stone in each of the four seasons. The Winter sculpture showed the boulder covered in dark brown wet ash leaves; the Spring photo revealed light green beech leaves; in Summer, dark green sycamore leaves; and in Autumn, the rock was covered with reddish brown hazel leaves.

It was not the rock and the leaves that were intriguing about this work, though, but the sequence of change in nature that was revealed. The background hills and the grass upon which the rock lay were just as interesting as the sculpture in the foreground. One saw the dead grass of Winter, the thick, lush grass of Spring, the taller, drier grass of Summer, and the shorter Autumnal grass. Andy Goldsworthy's photographs, in true modernist style, record Einsteinian periods of time and change, and the dynamics of chaos theory. 'My work decays, because nature decays', he asserted.[10] Goldsworthy loves the precariousness of (his) art, and encourages it.[11] He likes it when his arches collapse. On a dry boulder in the lake at Storm King (in October, 1997), Goldsworthy damped the surface with water, making a circle, and photographed it as it dried off (*Wall*, 66-67). Neil Hedges commented that 'each work evolves with the elements, reaches a peak at which point it is photographed, and then decays as would any other natural phenomenon' (66). Goldsworthy remarked:

> Sometimes a work is at its best when most threatened by the weather. A balanced rock is given enormous tension and force by a wind that might cause its collapse. I have worked with colourful leaves, delicate grasses and feathers made extra vivid by a dark, rain-laden sky that cast no shadow. (AG)

Andy Goldsworthy said he often returns to an outdoor work in order to watch it decay (RSS, 4). Decay, decline and collapse were central elements in Goldsworthy's art, especially, as he acknowledged, in his later works, which would be constructed with decay and change as 'an integral part of a work's purpose so that, if anything, it becomes stronger and more complete as it falls apart' (T, 7). That goes against traditional theory which valorizes things being whole, self-contained, complete, 'finished' and permanent; whereas post-Conceptual art emphasizes things being in process, continually changing, never static, never 'whole' and certainly never 'finished'. (Linked to *Penpont Stone* are works such as *Stick Hole* (1999) and *Dead Hazel Sticks* (1997), sculptures on the ground which the artist returned to a number of times to photograph – covered by frost, then grass, then ferns.)

Many of Andy Goldsworthy's sculptures are about a 'before' and an 'after', and the interval between, the difference, the changes. For instance, there are two photographs which depict a stick in a 'before' and 'after' setting (an early work, made in January, 1981 [in AG]). In the first photo, the sycamore branch is shown on top of snow; it's one of those images of contrast (black stick against white snow) which Goldsworthy likes so much. The second picture shows the stick with its bark now peeled off, so it looks white. Meanwhile the snow has melted, so the white shows up against the dark earth. Twenty years later Goldsworthy was fabricating the same sculptural idea: a fallen branch in a stream covered with powdery snow (2001), and branches wrapped with leaves in a Massachussetts brook (2001) or a Scottish stream (2003).

But there isn't a definite, immovable start – or finish – to these works, a moment when the work begins and another when it ends. Traditional philosophy would prefer an artwork to start at a certain time and finish at a certain time, to have quantifiable limits in space and time. But post-Conceptual art emphasizes flux, change, process.

> I have become aware of how nature is in a state of change and how that change is the key to understanding [said Goldsworthy]. I want my art to be sensitive and alert to changes in material, season and weather. (AG)

Sometimes the sense of change is not shown in Andy Goldsworthy's art, but is included in the work's title. For instance, one of Andy Goldsworthy's snow and ice sculptures, a wall made in Japan on Christmas Day, 1987, is described as 'a wall of frozen snow' which 'collapsed in the sunlight'. While it's obvious that any snow sculpture made outdoors will (eventually) melt and collapse, Goldsworthy feels the event is significant enough to include in the title of the work. All the time with Goldsworthy's sculpture one is reminded that he is using (as with Hans Haacke, Chris Drury, David Nash and Wolfgang Laib), materials that will not last: sand, snow, leaves, petals.

This notion of decay and entropy was an important element in Robert Smithson's earth art.[12] It's the same for Richard Long: 'my work is partly about change or disappearance, invisibility… all these strange states of matter'.[13] In his book *Stone,* as in the books *Andy Goldsworthy* and *Hand to Earth,* one finds photographs not only of sculptures that have toppled, but photographs of sculptures that are in the act of falling down. Goldsworthy loves to photograph works that have fallen to bits. 'I like to draw things out to a peak of intensity – hold them there – and let them go', he confessed.[14] So he has sculptures that are impossibly balanced. A line of rocks, for instance, placed on the slope of a quay that slopes into the sea (Wales, 1993). The photographs in the book *Stone* depict not only the artwork as it is 'meant' to be – a line of stones on a quay – but also the different stages of its collapse. The stones fell as the tide came in and the waves pushed them over. Other Cibachrome photographs of Goldsworthy's depict cairns or towers that fall over.

> Ice workshop. Made arch over a pile of sticks [Goldsworthy explained] – waited for it to freeze – temperature going up and down – thawing then freezing – managed to get out most of the sticks – lost concentration for a moment – all sticks lose but somehow knocked arch and caused its collapse.[15]

The moment when a sculpture topples is a moment of crisis, which Andy Golds-worthy believes is a key point in a work. Not only is it an exciting moment, when all that effort is gone in a flash, but it actualizes the cycles and times of change in the natural world which are at the heart of Goldsworthy's ethics. In his Arctic diary Golds-worthy noted:

The earth as a whole is probably in these cycles, going through different speeds and changing. Understanding those cycles is understanding the processes of nature' (HE, 158).

When a sculpture collapses, one of the many transformations of nature is made manifest, is valorized. The collapse is an expression of cyclical change. Andy Golds-worthy, ever the student of nature, knows that the collapse will soon be followed by another construction, one stone on top of the other. Similarly, when something dies in nature, another thing is born. The moment of collapse in Goldsworthy's photographs thus makes vivid the birth-death-rebirth cyclical quality in nature and in his art. 'A good work is the result of being in the right place at the right time with the right material', said Goldsworthy.[16]

Other balancing works in the Andy Goldsworthy *œuvre* include the two *Balanced Winstones*, *Balanced stone* and *Balanced rock*. *Balanced rock* (Cumbria, 1977) – like *Balanced stone* (Heysham Head, 1978) and *Balanced rocks* (High Nick Quarry, Northumberland, 1993) – is basically a 'logan stone', one of those rocks (there is a famous one at Treryn Dinas in West Penwith in Cornwall) which are balanced so delicately they can be rocked if pushed by hand. The 1987 *Balanced rocks* (Japan) was a group of three columns of four stones each, recalling Henry Moore or Barbara Hepworth sculptures. Another *Balanced rocks* piece (Cumbria, 1982) had four slabs teetering above and below a small spherical stone (AG). *Balanced rocks* at Bow Fell and Scafel Pike (Cumbria, 1977) explored problems usually associated with archi-tecture and engineering – the idea of counter-balancing and weight, for example (HE, 22-23). Goldsworthy's *Balanced rock* was shot against the sky, like so many of Golds-worthy's works, to bring out the fundamental point of the work: a rock which is carefully balanced.

Like Richard Serra and Eva Hesse, Andy Goldsworthy has made wall-standing sculptures, sculptures that require a wall to complete them (though both Serra and Hesse employ walls far more often than Goldsworthy). In the first *Balanced Winstone* (1988), the sculpture is, basically, two largish rocks, both with sharp ends, connected only at their points. One stands on top of the other, with the rest of the upper stone leaning against a studio wall. The second *Balanced Winstone* is the basic Goldsworthy cairn with a sharp-ended stone at the summit. On top of this balances another stone; the equivalent in large-scale would be a huge boulder the size of an apartment block storey on top of the Great Pyramid of Cheops.

Intensity is not perhaps a word one would apply to Andy Goldsworthy's sculpture. His art seems so soft, so tenderly 'in tune' with the natural world, so ecologically driven. Those delicate leafworks, they are not 'intense', surely? Yet the very nature of Goldsworthy's methodology, the way he goes out into the wilderness, to be alone, to work from dawn to dusk, suggests an intense, creative, determined personality. Further, those towers and arches which collapse are in fact very intense works. As Goldsworthy says, he likes to draw things out to an extreme point. In this he is intense, and is an archetypal Romantic modernist, someone who, like Mark Rothko or Jackson Pollock, knew one sometimes has to go to extremes, artistically, to get results. It's not the same way of working for everybody. But for some artists, this aspect of intensity is crucial, and is bound up with the utter importance of solitude, concentration, purity and depth of feeling.

Snow melts, and Andy Goldsworthy's sculptures exploit the precariousness and impermanence of snow as a material. He speaks of being frustrated in making snow sculptures, of snow crumbling before he could complete the piece. Yet his snowworks are some of his most exciting pieces: a snowball, for instance, caught in the branches of a tree (1980 and 1994). It looks impressive in the photographs, the ball of snow, so heavy and cold, floating, it seems, in the black, leafless branches of a tree. The viewer can only know such works through photographs: these snowballs held in the leafless branches in some seemingly remote forest are for an audience of one – the artist. Plus maybe his wife Judith Gregson, who sometimes takes photographs of Goldsworthy's work (or an assistant). The photos of Goldsworthy at work are usually taken by an assistant or Judith. Maybe one or two friends, or his children, or someone wandering off the beaten track, might see the remoter pieces, but not the 'general public'.

Andy Goldsworthy has, however, brought snow into the studio, most impressively in the series of large snowballs he brought from Craighall near Blairgowrie to Glasgow. Goldsworthy waited and waited for snow to fall during 1988-89. When it did, eventually, he made a series of snowballs which were exhibited in the Old Museum of Transport in Glasgow during the Summer of 1989 (a work re-staged on a much larger scale in London in 2000). The contrast of snowballs in Summer was part of the conception:

> Snowballs in summer [wrote Goldsworthy in the catalogue] is an exploration of snow and an expression of my understanding and feelings gathered over the years I have worked with it. It will bring together qualities of time, space, movement, noise, colour and texture forming often the unpredictable that makes up the character of snow.17

The lines of snowballs, in rows in the museum space, recall directly the Minimal exhibitions of the 1960s. Each snowball was roughly the same size, but, like Minimal artists such as Donald Judd with his stacks and cubes, Andy Goldsworthy made each one slightly different. Within each snowball, Goldsworthy rolled in different elements, most of which are favourite Goldsworthy materials: willowherb stalks, pine needles, pebbles, reeds, oak sticks, and so on. Each snowball, then, was not just a sphere of ice melting slowly in Summer, it was a container of natural materials, each with their own properties, which affected the melting of the snow. The melting of the snowballs itself was a natural process which the environment of a museum and London streets made highly visible. Each snowball melted in a different way. The inner stalks and pebbles became gradually more and more apparent, appearing on the outside of the snowball as it decreased in size. A pool of water formed around the snowball. Slowly, webs of stalks appeared, or a covering of old orange pine needles, looking like a cake decoration. Goldsworthy noted that:

> The elements of the melt will be best understood in the quiet stillness of an indoor space. The snowballs will speak louder having been made in the mountains yet melting in the city. (in ib.)

Each snowball became an alchemical vessel in which the arcane transmutations of the natural world were made visible. The secret processes of the natural world became apparent to all who visited the museum in Glasgow or the City of London's historical streets. Every stage of the melting transformation was captured on film – a record of alchemy. An early version of the 'snowballs in Summer' idea had been exhibited by Goldsworthy at Tatton Park in Cheshire in 1982 (in a group show with David Nash, Anthony Gormley, Paul Neagu and others). An associated snowwork, *Snow and mud layers* (1987), lasted two weeks: during the day the snow tower melted and slumped; during the night it refroze. Every day, in this cycle of freezing/ thawing, night/ day, the sculpted snow tower looked different (HE, 152-3).

Vision was not the only sense activated by *Snowballs in Summer*, because snow makes noises as it melts. There were other sounds, too: Andy Goldsworthy stuck large pebbles in the snowballs, so they clunked when they dropped off the melting snowball. These are noises that occur all the time in nature: dripping water, rocks falling, twigs cracking. To hear them in a museum context (with its quietly reverential atmosphere) makes one newly aware of the natural world. The alchemical trans- mutations of the snowballs renders nature's processes conscious; for, as always with Goldsworthy's art, the aim is a greater understanding of nature. It's not just the object itself that is important, Goldsworthy said, but also the processes going on inside and behind them that are valuable. Not a single object, but the processes of 'nature as a whole'.[18]

Aligned to the melting snowballs are the clay-covered rocks which Andy Golds- worthy exhibited in 1993 in San Francisco and Japan. The stones were covered in wet clay which was rubbed smooth: they looked like huge brown dinosaur eggs. As the clay dried, it cracked and fell off. The exhibits highlighted natural processes – such as the apparent randomness of nature (a bit of clay falling off the stone here, but not on that rock over there). Another installation using clay (at San Jose, California) consisted of hollowed clay spheres, with the characteristic Goldsworthy sharp interior edges. The series of globes dried out and shed chunks of clay. Later hollow spheres include *Sand stones*, built in Holland in 1999.

The enormous snowball set up outside the Andy Goldsworthy exhibition at Japan's Setagaya Art Museum in 1994 looked less like a contemporary sculpture than the kind of thing kids do every Winter. After snowball fights, rolling snowballs is a common activity among children (and adults) when it snows. Of course, the location of the snowball outside a modern art gallery inflected Goldsworthy's snowball with a differ- ent set of meanings from the snowballs one finds in fields in snowtime. Goldsworthy included some shots of the snowball in *Wood*, seen through the large windows of the Japanese museum, beyond the screen of horse chestnut leaf stalks.

Andy Goldsworthy tried different methods of actualizing or exploring the space around and within stones, the light and weather around them, the 'window' that's opened into their secret nature (HE, 167). Sometimes he covered a boulder completely in bark, or branches (as at Lake Tahoe in 1992 [S, 7-9]). A boulder wrapped in small sheets of ice became a kinetic sculpture as the ice melted and slipped off (S, 13).

In mid-September, 1991, Andy Goldsworthy made a sequence of stoneworks at the same site in Laumeier Sculpture Park, St Louis, Missouri: first he layered wet leaves, in the usual Goldsworthy colours (red, yellow and green), onto a large boulder which was partially buried in the river bank (the boulder was the focus of the work). The Autumnal colours recalled many of Goldsworthy's previous leafworks. Over the next few days Goldsworthy explored different ways of responding to the stone: he walled it in with flat rocks, photographing it when the river was empty, then with the tide coming in; a day or so later he wrapped wet green leaves around the rock, in the rain, with the river rising; Goldsworthy returned the following Summer, and enclosed the rock in a circle of sticks (S, 26-33).

Other methods of exploring the energies of a stone that Andy Goldsworthy employed included 'drawing' around the stone with continuous lines of grass stalks; rubbing red stones or dark peat into the stone; covering it with sheep and kangaroo bones; nesting it inside a circular stone wall; balancing one stone on top of another; and building an arch over a stone.

Time was central to Andy Goldsworthy's collaboration with a dance troupe. In 1995 the Ballet Atlantique-Régine Chopinot company put on a dance-based performance called *Végétal* at La Rochelle in France. *Végétal* consisted of five sections: earth, seed, root, branch and leaf. For the theatrical backdrop Goldsworthy made a wall drawing from ferns and bracken stuck on with rabbit skin glue in serpentine patterns. The ballet featured Goldsworthy's installations, which included sculptures (using stones, sticks, leaves and earth) that were both built and taken down by the dancers. Goldsworthy explained in the book *Wood* that collaborating on a dance work was quite natural for him, because the body plays such a large part in making sculpture: 'the body as the sculpture. I've always seen myself as an object in the work; that I'm nature too' (W, 7). Goldsworthy had already used the body directly in many works – the 'throws', for example, or the 'prints' and 'shadows' made by lying on the ground during rain or snow. (We've already seen earlier in this study how deep the links are between sculpture and performance, sculpture and dance).

Végétal evoked the favourite Andy Goldsworthyan themes of growth and decay, of change and cycles, of time, of boundaries and breathing. Régine Chopinot danced around the circumference of the stage, suggesting the passage of time. *Végétal* began with a black hole and red earth spread on the stage. The dancers next built a single stone column. The combination of column and hole inevitably had sexual connections: phallus and vagina, masculine and feminine, *yang* and *yin*, and so on. The context of the phallic column and womb-like hole in a dance all about growth and cycles enhanced the eroticism, as did having the dancers interact with each other in a 'germination dance'. This part of the dance was entitled 'Seed'. Feminists might criticize the insistence on heterosexual relationships and gender stereotypes in *Végétal,* the way the dancers, for example, were often put together in male and female couples.

Végétal continued in the 'Branch' section of the performance with ten dancers moving in circles around two dancers in the centre building a stick dome. This was then dismantled and the dancers made a large ring with the sticks. In the last part, 'Leaf', the dancers acted like leaves, spinning and falling. 'The tree is bare, loses its foliage, turns back within itself. Full cycle', wrote Goldsworthy (W, 11). A mound of leaves was placed centre-stage. The dancers performed Goldsworthyan 'leaf throws'. Another performance by the ballet group, *La Danse du Temps,* took place at La Roch-elle in France in November, 1999, and the Barbican Centre in London in September, 2000.

❈

Andy Goldsworthy can be expected to explore more collaborations, such as live performance, dance, maybe video, film or installations and the like. The Digne *Réfuges d'Art* and Cumbrian *100 Sheepfolds* projects are huge commitments, that will keep the sculptor busy for years. But the core of Goldsworthy's art, the spiritual heart and the essence of it, will continue to be his work within the landscape. That means working mainly on his own (as he has done throughout his career), and mainly in South-West Scotland (as he has done since the mid-1980s).

List of Works

Notes

Bibliography

List of Works

A list of some works cited in the text

ANDY GOLDSWORTHY

Slate Stack, 1988, Scaur Water Valley, Penpont, Dumfriesshire, Scotland; *Japanese maple leaves stitched together to make a floating chain*, Nov 21, 1987, Ouchiyama-mura, Japan; *Circular stalks in a lake*, April 29, 1987, Yorkshire Sculpture Park; *Autumn Horn*, Nov, 1986, chestnut leaves, Penpont, Dumfriesshire; *Dandelion Flowers*, May 1, 1987, 'flowers pinned to willowherb stalks laid in a ring held above bluebells with forked sticks', Yorkshire Sculpture Park, West Bretton; *Line and Carin,* May 31 & June 1, 1985, pebbles, St Abbs, the Borders; *Oak Globe*, Sept 15, 1985, branches and oak leaves, Jenny Noble's Gill, Dumfriesshire; *Slits cut into frozen snow*, Feb 12, 1988, Blencathra, Cumbria; *Snowball in Trees*, Feb, 1980, Robert Hall Wood, Lancashire; *Touching North*, April 24, 1989, North Pole; *Touching North*, Fabian Carlsson Gallery, London, 1989; *Leadgate and Lambton Earthworks*, 1989, County Durham; *Snow and Wind Damaged Pine Trees*, Spring, 1985, Grizedale forest; *Leaves torn in two*, Nov 2, 1986, Glasgow Green; *Broken Pebbles*, April 12, 1987, Scaur Water, Dumfriesshire; *Trench*, Aug 6-7, 1987, 'trench edged with clay supported by sticks', Yorkshire Sculpture Park, West Bretton; *Slate Crack Line*, Feb, 1988, Little Langdale, Cumbria; *Scaur Water Stone*, 1992, stone and iron ore and water, Grob Gallery, London; *Herd of Arches*, stone, 1994, London; *Stone*, 1994, Grob Gallery, London; *Wall*, 1998, Storm King Art Center, New York; *Sheepfolds*, 1996-, Cumbria; *Réfuges d'Art*, 1998-, Digne les Bains, France; *Arch*, 1998, Montréal; *Snowballs In Summer*, 2000, London; *Night Path*, 2002, Petworth Park, Sussex; *Garden of Stone*, 2003, Museum of Jewish Heritage, New York, NY; *Stone Houses*, 2004, Metropolitan Museum of Art, New York, NY.

OTHERS

Carl Andre: *Lead Piece (144 Lead Plates)*, Museum of Modern Art, New York; *Last Ladder*, 1959, Tate Gallery, London; *Cedar Piece*, 1959/64, Offentliche Kunstammlung Basel.
Alice Aycock: *One Thousand and One Nights in the Mansion of Bliss*, 1983, mixed media, private collection; *The Miraculous Machine in the Garden (Tower of the Winds)*, 1983, mixed media, 16 ft high, private collection.
Gianlorenzo Bernini: *David*, 1623, Galleria Borghese, Rome.
Joseph Beuys: *Lightning*, 1982-85, bronze, Anthony d'Offay Gallery, London.
Louise Bourgeois: *Nature Study,* 1984, bronze, Serpentine Gallery, London.
Constantin Brancusi: *Endless Column*, 1918, Museum of Modern Art, New York.
Alexander Calder: *Red Flock*, c.1949, hanging mobile, metal, 2.8 x 5.5ft, Phillips Collection, Washington, DC; *Thirteen Spines*, 1940, sheet steel, rods, wire and aluminium, 84 in, Wallraf-Richartz Museum, Cologne.
Canova: *Hercules and Lichas*, 1812-15, marble, 138in high, Gallery of Modern Art, Rome.
Benvenuto Cellini: *Perseus with the Head of Medusa*, 1554, bronze, Loggia dei Lanzi, Florence.
Christo: *Surrounded Islands, Biscoyne Bay, Greater Miami*, 1980-83, 6 million square feet of polypropylene fabric; *Valley Curtain*, synthetic fabric, 417m long, 1970-72, Grand Canyon, Colorado; *Running Fence*, 1972-76, steel poles, steel cables, woven

nylon, 18 ft high, 24.5 miles long, Sonoma & Marin Counties, CA.

Tony Cragg: *Instinctive Reactions*, 1987, 8 x 21 x 15ft, Lisson Gallery, London; *New Stones*, 1982, Marian Goodman Gallery, New York; *New Stones – Newton's Tones*, 1978, Arts Council, London; *Five Plates*, 1976, private collection, Belgium.

Richard Deacon: *Turning a Blind Eye No.2*, 1984-85, High Museum of Art, Atlanta, Georgia.

Donatello: *David, c.* 1440-42, bronze, Museo Nazionale, Florence.

Chris Drury: *River Vortex*, 1998; *Air Vessel*, 1994; *Wave Chamber*, 1996, Northumberland;*Basket Dewpond,* 1997, 1999, Sussex.

Mary Beth Edelson: *Great Goddess Series*, 1975, collection: the artist; *Blood Mysteries*, 1973, drawing, collection: the artist.

Helen Escobedo: *Snake,* 1980-81, painted steel, 49ft high, National University of Mexico Cultural Centre.

Barry Flanagan: *Soprano*, 1981, bronze, 80 x 66 x 57cm, Arts Council of Great Britain; *Hole In the Sea*, 1969.

Dan Flavin: *Untitled (to the "innovator" of Wheeling Peachblow)*, 1968, 96.5 x 96.5 x 5.7in, Museum of Modern Art, New York; *Untitled*, 1976, pink, blue, green fluorescent light, 96in high, Saatchi Collection, London.

Naum Gabo: *Kinetic Construction*, 1920, metal rod with electric vibrator, 24.2in high, Tate Gallery, London.

Henri Gaudier-Breska: *Red Stone Dancer*, 1914, waxed stone, 33.5in high, Tate Gallery, London.

Alberto Giacometti: *Spoon Woman*, 1926, bronze, 57.2in high, Kunsthaus, Zurich.

Nancy Graves: *Zaga*, 1983, Nelson-Atkins Museum of Art, Kansas City; M. Knoedler, New York.

Hans Haacke: *Fog Dripping From or Freezing On Exposed Surfaces*, 1971, Museum of Fine Arts, Boston, MA; *Sky Line*, 1967, Central Park, New York.

Tim Head: *State of the Art*, 1984, colour photograph, 183 x 274cm, collection: the artist.

Michael Heizer: *Double Negative*, 1969-70, 1,500 x 50 x 42 feet, Mormon Mesa, Nevada; *Displaced, Replaced Mass*, 1969, Silver Springs, Nevada.

Barbara Hepworth: *Forms in Movement*, 1956, Barbara Hepworth Museum and Sculpture Garden, St Ives, Cornwall; *Two Forms*, 1937, private collection.

Eva Hesse: *Contingent*, 1969, reinforced fibreglass and latex over cheesecloth, each of 8 units, 9.5-14 x 3-4ft, Australian National Gallery, Canberra; *Aught*, 1968, double sheets of latex rubber, polyethylene plastic inside, 4 units, each 78in high, collection: the artist; *Ice Piece*, 1969, fibreglass and wire, 62 x 1in, Xavier Fourcade Gallery, New York.

Nancy Holt: *Stone Enclosure: Rock Rings*, 1977-78, hand-quarried schist, outer ring 40 feet, inner ring 2 feet across, ring walls 10 feet high, Western Washington University, Bellingham; *Sun Tunnels*, 1973-76, concrete, each pipe 18 ft long, 9 ft high, Great Basin Desert, near Lucin, Utah; *Dark Star Park*, 1979-84, concrete, steel, water, earth, 0.67 of an acre, Rosslyn, Virginia.

Rebecca Horn; *Ballet of the Woodpecker,* 1986-87, room installation with mirrors, small hammers and a painting machine, Eric Franck Gallery, Geneva; *Peacock Machine*, 1982, installation at Documenta 7, Kassel.

Valerie Jaudon: *Caile*, 1985, oil on canvas, 48 x 40in, Sidney James Gallery, New York.

Donald Judd: *Untitled*, 1970, copper, private collection; *Untitled*, 1969, Norton Simon Museum of Art, Pasadena, CA; *Untitled*, 1978, Indiana University Art Museum, Bloomington, IN; *Untitled*, 1969, Hirshhorn Museum and Sculpture Garden, Washington, DC; *Untitled*, 1971, private collection; *Untitled*, 1968, Nelson A. Rockefeller Empire State Plaza Art Collection, New York.

Allan Kaprow: *Fluids*, 1967. Pasadena, CA.

Lila Katzen: *Guardian*, 1979, private collection, Saudi Collection.

Edward Kienholz: *Back Seat of a '38 Dodge*, 1964, the Kleiner Foundation, Los Angeles, CA.

Philip King: *Call*, 1967, fibreglass and painted steel, two pieces each 14.5 x 0.5 x 0.5ft, two pieces.

Joyce Kozloff: *New England Decorative Arts*, 1985, tile mural, 8 x 83 feet overall, Harvard Square subway station, Cambridge, MA.

Jannis Kounellis: *Cotton Sculpture*, 1967, steel and cotton, 3.9 x 3.9 x 4.9ft, collection: the artist.

Norbert Kricke: *Space Sculpture*, 1958-59, stainless steel, 9.4 ft high, Municipality Leverkusen, Germany.

Anish Kapoor: *Half*, 1984, polystyrene, cement, earth, acrylic medium and pigment, 5.6 x 3.1in, Barbara Gladstone Gallery, New York; *Six Secret Objects*, 1983, mixed media, 115 x 425 x 60cm, Lissom Gallery, London.

Wolfgang Laib: *Hazelnut Pollen*, Dokumenta 8, Kassel.

Sol LeWitt: *Untitled Cube*, 1968, 15.5 x 15.5 x 15.5in, Whitney Museum of Art, New York; *Open Modular Cube*, 1966, painted aluminium, 5ft cube, Art Gallery, Ontario, Canada.

Richard Long: *Untitled*, 1987, mud on paper, Anthony d'Offay Gallery, London; *Avon Mud Circle*, 1986, installation, Guggenheim Museum, New York; *Five, six, pick up sticks/ Seven, eight, lay them straight*, 1980, Anthony d'Offay Gallery, Sept, 1980.

Len Lye: *The Loop*, 1963, Art Institute, Chicago, IL; *Fountain II*, 1959, Howard Wise Gallery, New York.

Aristide Maillol: *Desire*, 1903-05, lead relief, Musée Nationale d'Art Moderne, Paris.

Agnes Martin: *Night Sea*, 1963, oil and gold leaf on canvas, 72 x 72in, Saatchi Collection, London; *Drift of Summer*, 1965, acrylic and graphite on canvas, 72 x 72in, Saatchi Collection, London; *Mountain II*, 1966, oil and pencil on canvas, 72 x 72in, collection: R. Solomon, New York.

John McCracken: *Untitled*, 1967, fibreglass and lacquer, 7.9 x 1.2 x 0.1 ft, Saatchi Collection, London.

Mary Miss: *Field Rotation*, 1981, wood, steel, gravel, earth, 5 acre site, central well 60 ft square and 7 feet deep, Governors' University, Park Forest South, IL.

Robert Morris: *Observatory*, 1971, earth, grass, wood, steel, granite, diameter *c.* 300 feet, Oosterlijk Flevoland, Holland; *Labyrinth*, 1974, painted masonite, plywood & two-by-fours, 96 x 360 in, Institute of Contemporary Art, University of Pennsylvania, Philadelphia, PA.

Henry Moore: *Reclining Figure*, 1945-46, elmwood, 75in long, collection: Humana Corp, Louisville; *Three Piece Reclining Figure: Draped*, 1975, bronze, 14ft 8in long, Henry Moore Foundation, Yorkshire.

David Nash: *Fletched Over Ash Dome*, 1977/9, Caen-y-Coed, Maentwrog, Wales; *Sea Hearth*, 1981, Isle of Bute, Scotland; *Slate Stove*, 1988, Blaenau Ffestiniog, Wales; *Wood Stove*, 1979, Maentwrog, Wales; *Snow Stove*, 1982, Kotoku, Japan; *Wooden Boulder*, 1978, oak, Maentwrog, Wales.

Louise Nevelson: *Royal Tide IV*, 1960, Ludwig Museum, Cologne; *Sky Cathedral – Moon Garden Plus One*, 1957-60, collection: A. & M. Glimcher, New York.

Barnett Newman: *Broken Obelisk*, 1963-67, Cor-Ten steel, 26 ft high, Institute of Religion and Human Development, Houston, TX.

Isamu Noguchi: *Red Cube*, 1969, 140, Broadway, New York.

Dennis Oppenheim: *Annual Rings*, 1968, 150 x 200 feet, Fort Kent, Maine and Clair, New Brunswick, NJ; *Branded Mountain*, 1969, 30 ft diameter, San Pablo, CA; *Whirlpool Eye of Storm*, 1973, El Mirage Dry Lake, CA.

Roger Partridge: *Arch*, 1983, Portland stone, 77 x 91.5 x 20cm, private collection.

Anne & Patrick Poirier: *Archæological Model*, 1986, Bath International Festival, Somerset.

Beverly Pepper: *Sand Dunes*, 1985, Mylar over wood, approximately 100 ft long, temporary installation for the Atlantic Center for the Arts, New Smyrna Beach, FL.

Gio Pomodoro: *Tensione*, 1959, black fibreglass, 5.9 x 4.2 x 1.9 ft, David Anderson Gallery, Buffalo, CO.

George Rickey: *Peristyle III*, 1966, stainless steel, 40.5 x 102.5 x 60.2in, Corcoran Gallery of Art, Washington, DC.

Robert Ryman: *Department*, 1981, oil on aluminium, 60 x 60in, collection: Rhona J. Hoffman, Chicago, IL.

Lucas Samaras: *Book 4*, 1962,5.5 x 8.8 x 11.5in, Museum of Modern Art, New York.

Niki de Sant-Phalle: *Black Venus*, 1967, painted polyester, 110 x 35 x 24in, Whitney Museum of American Art, New York; *Pink Childbirth*, 1964, painted relief, 86.24in high, Moderner Museet, Stockholm; *Un Ensemble de "Les Nanas"*, 1965, Archives Galerie Alexandre Iolas, New York.

Kurt Schwitters: *Picture*, 1925, Sammlung Janlet, Brussels.

Richard Serra: *Clara-Clara*, 1983, Cor-Ten steel, installation, Jardin des Tuileries, Paris; *Prop*, 1968, 96in high, sheet 60 x 60in, Whitney Museum of American Art, New York.

David Smith: *Cubi XXVII*, 1965, stainless steel, 9.2ft high, Guggenheim Museum, New York.

Tony Smith: *Die*, 1962, 72 x 72 x 72in, Paula Cooper Gallery, New York.

Robert Smithson: *Spiral Jetty*, 1969-70, rock, salt crystal and earth, 1,500 feet long, Great Salt Lake, Utah; *Closed Mirror Square*, 1969, rock salt, mirrors and glass, Blum Helman Gallery, New York; *Amarillo Ramp*, 1973, red sandstone shale, 1800 in diameter, estate of the artist; *Floor Piece*, 1964, 17 x 17 x 288 in, Green Gallery, New York.

Frank Stella: *Ophir*, 1960-61, copper oil paint on canvas, 250.2 x 210.2cm, private collection.

George Sugarman: *Bardana*, 1962-63, polychromed woof, 8 x 12 x 5.1ft, Galerie Renee Ziegler, Zurich.

James Turrell: *Roden Crater*, 1977-, Flagstaff, Arizona; *Space That Sees*, 1992, Jerusalem; *Heavy Water*, 1992, Poitier, France; *Razor*, 1991, London.

Andrea del Verrocchio: *David*, c. 1475, bronze, Museo Nazionale, Florence.

Alison Wilding: *Bare*, 1989-90, Newlyn Art Gallery, *Into the Dark*, 1986, Newlyn Art Gallery. Cornwall; *Hemlock III*, 1986, Karsten Schubert, London; *Blueblack*, 1984, collection: the artist.

Jackie Winsor: *Burnt Piece*, 1977-78, concrete, wire and burnt wood, 36in cube, Paula Cooper Gallery, New York.

Bill Woodrow: *Winter Jacket*, 1986, mixed media, collection: Anne MacDonald Walker, San Francisco, CA.

Notes

INTRODUCTION

1. R. Krauss, 1979.

CHAPTER 1 • ANDY GOLDSWORTHY: LIFE AND WORK

1 : 1 LIFE

1. For an excellent exploration of the influence of the art school system on British popular culture, see S. Frith & H. Horne, *Art into Pop*, Methuen, London, 1987.
2. A. Goldsworthy, *Sheepfolds*, 11.

1 : 2 WORKS

1. Many of the big names in British sculpture have exhibited works at Goodwood, including Elisabeth Frink, David Mach, Phillip King, David Nash, Eduardo Paolozzi, Bill Woodrow, Tony Cragg, Ian Hamilton Finlay, Stephen Dilworth, Anthony Caro and Anthony Gormley.
2. For Simon Schama, Goldsworthy's art is

   at least as conceptually rich as Smithson's; his compressions and space and water as metaphysically suggestive as the sculpture of Anish Kapoor; his use of found materials as inflected with past use and future alterations as the wood pieces of his friend David Nash; and his meditations on decay, mortality, and generation as smart as Damien Hirst's. (*The New Yorker*, Sept 22, 2003)

1 : 3 CRITICS OF ANDY GOLDSWORTHY'S ART

1. J. Jones, "Something nasty in the woods", *The Guardian*, Mch 4, 2000.

CHAPTER 2 • ANDY GOLDSWORTHY AND SCULPTURE IN THE MODERN ERA

2 : 1 ANDY GOLDSWORTHY AND WOMEN SCULPTORS

1. B. Hepworth, quoted in A.M. Hammacher, 1968, 99.
2. R. Long, 1985, 2, 21.
3. Other artists who have worked in postmodern, feminist modes include Cindy Sherman, Mary Kelly, Marie Yates, Yves Lomax, Martha Rosler, Sutapa Biswas, Mitra Tabrizian, Zarina Bhimji, Mona Hatoum, Lubaina Himid, Barbara Kruger, Jenny Holzer, Rose Garrard, Susan Hiller, Nancy Spero, Rosa Lee and Rachel Whiteread.
4. In C. Nemser, 62.
5. See B. Barrette, *Eva Hesse's Sculpture: Catalogue Raisonné,* New York, NY, 1989; R. Krauss & E. Hesse, 1979; C. Nemser, 1973, 12-13.
6. A. Chave, in H. Cooper, ed. *Eva Hesse*, Yale University Press, New Haven, CT, 1992, 100f.
7. In L. Lippard, 1976.
8. Quoted in L. Lippard, ib., 6.
9. D. Wheeler, 1991, 323.
10. See M. Roustayi, "Getting Under the Skin: Rebecca Horn's Sensibility Machines", *Arts*, May, 1989; M. Kimmelman, "A Sculptural Circus of Whips and Suspense",

New York Times, Sept 23, 1988.

11. In A. Hammacher, op.cit., 98.
12. B. Hepworth, in W. Forma, 1965.
13. See H. Gresty, 1993; G. Hilty, 1991; A. Wilding, 1994.
14. See L. Cooke, 1985; L. Biggs, 1986; W. Beckett, 116; T. Neff, 43-45.
15. In W. Beckett, 116.
16. In T. Neff, 45.
17. See D. Bourdon, 1987; J. Mock, *Niki de Sant-Phalle: Exposition Retrospective*, CGP, 1980.
18. See A. Berman, "Nancy Graves", *Art News*, Feb, 1986; D. Bricker Balken and L. Nochlin, *Nancy Graves: Painting, Sculpture, Drawing 1980-85*, Vassar College Art Gallery, Poughkeepsie, 1986; E.A. Carmean *et al*, *The Sculpture of Nancy Graves*, Fort Worth, TX, 1987; A. Collins and B. Collins, "The Sum of the Parts [Nancy Graves]", *Art in America*, 1988; L. Cathcart: *Nancy Graves: A Survey, 1969-1980*, Albright-Knox Gallery, Buffalo, New York, NY, catalogue, 1981.
19. D. Wheeler, 1991, 303.
20. L. Tickner, "Body Politic", op.cit., 239.
21. See T. Gouma-Peterson & P. Matthews, "The feminist critique of art history", *The Art Bulletin*, LXIX, 1987, 326-57.
22. See Carolee Schneemann, *Interior Scroll*, 1975; *More Than Meat Joy: Complete Performance Works and Selected Writings*, ed. B. MacPherson, Documentext, New York, NY, 1979
23. C. Carr, "Unspeakable Practices, Unnatural Acts", *Village Voice*, June 24, 1986.
24. See A. Adler, "Dangerous Woman: Karen Finley", *Chicago Reader*, Oct 26, 1990; R. Lacayo, "Talented Toiletmouth", *Time*, June 4, 1990; M. Joseph, "Further Finley", *The Drama Review*, Winter, 1990, 13; K. Larson, "Censor Deprivation", *New York Times*, Aug 6, 1990; C. Schuler, "Spectator Response and Comprehensions: The Problems of Karen Finley's *Constant State of Desire*", *The Drama Review*, Spring, 1990, 131-145; C. Barnes, "Finley's Fury", *New York Post*, July 24, 1990; T. Page, "Karen Finley's Tantrum, Amid Chocolate", *New York Newsday*, July 24, 1990.
25. M. Duffy, *Cutting the Ties That Bind*, 1987; *Stories of a Body*, 1990; see H. Robinson, "The Subtle Abyss: Sexuality and Body Image in Contemporary Feminist Art", unpublished dissertation, RCA, London, 1987; M. Duffy, "Cutting the Ties that Bind", *Feminist Art News*, 2, 10, 1989, 6-7; M. Duffy, "Redressing the Balance", *Feminist Art News*, 3, 8, 1991.
26. J. Spence and T. Sheard, *Narratives of Disease*; see J. Spence, *Putting Myself in the Picture: A Political, Personal and Photographic Autobiography*, Camden Press, London, 1986; P. Holland, J. Spence and S. Watney, eds. *Photography/ Politics: Two*, Commedia, London, 1986; D. Grigsby, "Dilemmas of Visibility: Contemporary Women Artists' Representations of Female Bodies", *Michigan Quarterly Review*, 29, 4, Autumn, 1990, 584-618.
27. C. Elwes, "Floating femininity: a look at performance art by women", in S. Kent & J. Morreau, eds. *Women's Images of Men*, Pandora Press, London, 1985, 172.
28. C. Elwes, ib., 182.
29. Quoted in I. Lippard, 219; see also L. Lippard, 1980, 122.
30. *Rosarium Philosophorum*, quoted in A. Mann, 87.

2 : 2 SIXTIES MINIMAL AND POSTMINIMAL ART

1. R. Morris, 1966, 20-23; P. Patton, 1983.
2. B. Rose, 1964, 41.
3. See I. Sandler, *American Art*, 245f; L. Lippard, 1966b, 62; R. Morris, "Notes on Sculpture", op.cit.; K. McShine, 1966; R. Lund, 1986.
4. P. Fuller, 1993, xxxv.

5. L. Lippard, 1966a, 50.
6. A. Warhol, in K. Stiles, 340.
7. D. Judd, "Questions to Stella and Judd", in G. Battock, 1995, 159.
8. J. Mellow, "New York Letter", *Art International*, April 20, 1966, 89.
9. B. Rose, 1965a, 34.
10. H. Kramer, "Display of Judd Art Defines an Attitude", *The New York Times*, May 14, 1971, D48.
11. B. Haskell, *Donald Judd*, 72.
12. In K. McShine, 1966.
13. R. Mangold, in F. Colpitt, 121.
14. R. Rosenblum, "Notes on Sol LeWitt", in *Sol LeWitt*, Museum of Modern Art, New York, NY, 1978, 15-16.
15. D. Judd, 1965, 82.
16. Rosalind Krauss wrote in *Passages in Modern Sculpture:*

The art of [Rodin and Brancusi] represented a relocation of the point of origin of the body's meaning – from its inner core to its surface – a radical act of decentring that would include the space to which the body appeared and the time of its appearing. What I have been arguing is that the sculpture of our time continues this project of decentring through a vocabulary of form that is radically abstract. The abstractness of Minimalism makes it less easy to recognize the human body in those works and therefore less easy to project ourselves into the space of that sculpture with all of our settled prejudices left intact. Yet our bodies and our experience of our bodies continue to be the subject of this sculpture – even when a work is made of several hundred tons of earth. (1977, 279)

2 : 3 CONSTANTIN BRANCUSI, ANDY GOLDSWORTHY AND CONTEMPORARY SCULPTURE

1. H. Moore, in *The Listener*, 1937, quoted in H. Chipp, 595.
2. B. Flanagan, quoted in the catalogue of *Entre el Objeto y la Imagen: Escultura britanica contemporanea*, Palacio de Velasquez, Madrid, 1986, 233.

2 : 4 SUGARMAN, NOGUCHI, POMODORO, SAMARAS

1. I. Noguchi, *A Sculptor's World,* Harper & Row, New York, NY, 1968, 38.

2 : 5 KINETIC SCULPTURE

1. Norbert Kricke, *Space Sculpture*, 1958-59, Municipality, Leverkusen, Germany.

2 : 6 LIGHT AND SPACE

1. Quoted in J. Butterfield, 161.

CHAPTER 3 • ANDY GOLDSWORTHY AND LAND ART

3 : 1 SPIRIT OF PLACE: LAND ART

1. A. Goldsworthy, in N. Hedges, 69.
2. H. Moore, "The Sculptor Speaks" in *The Listener*, Aug, 1937, quoted in H. Chipp, 595.
3. David Nash wrote:

The term "landscape" is like "portrait". It is an expression of a distancing: here I am and there it is. But what has been happening in the last twenty years or so is that artists have been getting right in there. Saying no, it is not out there. It is here. We want to make our images with what is here – here. That is why it is called land art rather than landscape art, "scape" denoting distancing. (D. Nash, in B. Redhead, 24-25)

4. D. Nash, in B. Redhead, 22.
5. S. Ross, 1993, 161.
6. S. Ross, 1998, 23.
7. S. Bann, in M. Mosser & G. Teyssot, eds., *The History of Garden Design*, Thames & Hudson, London, 1991, 495.
8. R. Smithson, paraphrased by Lucy Lippard (1983).

3 : 2 THE POLLEN PATH

1. J. Campbell, *Power*, 118.
2. J. Campbell, ib., 230.
3. On the 'pollen path', see J. Campbell, *The Power of Myth,* 230; on Australian 'dreamtime', see P. Devereux, *The Dreamtime Earth and Avebury's Open Secrets*, Gothic Image, Glastonbury, 1992, 7-12.
4. Alfred Watkins published *The Old Straight Track* and his theory of 'leys' in 1925.
5. See J. Cowan, *The Mysteries of the Dream-Time*, Prism Press, 1989; B. Chatwin, *The Songlines*, Picador, London, 1988; L. Levy-Bruhl, *Primitive Mythology,* University of Queensland Press, 1983.
6. Rilke wrote in the *Sonnets to Orpheus*: 'Gesang ist Dasein. Für ein Gott ein Leichtes. / Wann aber *sind* wir?' ('Song is Being. It's easy for a god. But when shall we *be*?').
7. B. Flanagan, in G. Baro, 1969.
8. J. Turrell, 1987.
9. G. Celant, 1969.
10. P. Redgrove, in J. Robinson, *Here Comes the Flood: The Poetry of Peter Redgrove*, Crescent Moon, 2008.
11. J.C. Powys, *In Defence of Sensuality*, Gollancz, London, 1930, 104.
12. From *The Countess of Pembroke's Arcadia,* in G. Miller, ed. *Poems of the Elizabethan Age*, Methuen, London, 1977, 215.
13. L. Durrell, 1971, 156.

3 : 3 THE ALCHEMY OF MATTER

1. "David Smith Makes a Sculpture", 1951, in D. Smith, 149.
2. R.W. Emerson, *Nature*, 1836, in H. Hugo, 386-7.
3. Wolfgang Goethe, *The Sorrows of Young Werther,* tr. M. Hulse, Penguin, London, 1989, 44.
4. E. Burke wrote, '[t]he passion caused by the great and sublime in *nature*, when those causes operate most powerfully, is astonishment: and astonishment is that state of the soul in which all its motions are suspended, with some degree of horror'. (E. Burke, in *The Philosophy of Edmund Burke*, University of Michigan Press, Ann Arbor, MI, 1967, 256.)
5. C. Greenberg, "Abstract, Representational, and so forth", in 1961, 133.
6. There is eroticism in Tony Cragg's steel vessels, or Anne and Patrick Poirier's long, elegant *Archæological Model*, or Jannis Kounellis' *Cotton Sculpture*, a mass of cotton stuffed into a large steel container – a sculpture of contrasts between the softness of the cotton and the rigidity of the steel, or Jackie Winsor's *Burnt Piece*,

a 3 ft cube made of concrete, wire and burnt wood. Tony Cragg has spoken of having 'an erotic response to the external world', something which, it seems, all artists have, or have to have, to be truly great artists (quoted in D. Wheeler, 1991, 324). See also T. Neff, 1967; B. Jones, 1977, 16; L. Ponti, 50-51; I. Lamaitre, 1985, 7-11; G. Celant, 40-46.

7. Quoted in N. Lynton, 1982, 2.
8. M. Eliade, "The Sacred and the Modern Artist", *Criterion*, 4, 1965, and in M. Eliade, 1988.
9. In A. Benjamin, 91.

3 : 4 THE ECONOMICS OF LAND ART

1. A. Henri, *Total Art*, 81-82.
2. Richard Long, quoted in S. Gablik, *Has Modernism Failed?*, Thames & Hudson, London, 1984, 44.
3. 'I make art in the capitalist system which in itself is a political statement (selling art for the next walk)', remarked Hamish Fulton (1995).
4. In A. Haden-Guest, 40.
5. If the Christos' artworks cost a lot, this is chickenfeed next to scientific and military experiments, which cost billions of dollars. Just one nuclear submarine costs the same amount. In the mid-1980s, 1,000,000 dollars per minute were spent on the arms industry (1982 figures). That's $16,500 per second. Cheap, eh?

3 : 5 THE OBJECT IN LAND ART AND MINIMAL ART

1. On Minimalism, see M. Tuchman, 1967; F. Tuten, "American Sculpture of the Sixties", *Arts Magazine*, 41, 7, May, 1967; I. Sandler, 1965; R. Wollheim, "Minimal Art", *Arts Magazine*, 39, 4, Jan, 1965; D. Mayhall, 1979; R. Krauss, 1973; B. Reise, 1969; P. Tuchman, 1988.
2. See C. Robins, 1966; M. Fried, "Art and Objecthood", 1967.
3. B. Rose, "ABC Art", 1965, 66.
4. M. Bochner, "Systematic", 1966, 40.
5. F. Stella, "The Pratt Lecture", 1960, in B. Richardson, *Frank Stella: The Black Paintings*, Baltimore Museum of Art, Baltimore, MD, 1976, 78.
6. W. Tucker, 1969, 12-13.
7. C. Andre, 1978, 31).
8. R. Morris, 1966, in G. Battock, 1995, 224.
9. R. Morris, 1966, 20-23. See also: P. Patton, 1983.
10. D. Oppenheim, 1992.

3 : 6 LAND ART AND CONCEPTUAL ART

1. "Mel Bochner on Malevich", interview with J. Coplans, *Artforum*, June, 1974, 62.
2. R. Serra, in *Richard Serra, Interviews,* Hudson River Museum, New York, NY, 1980, 37.
3. D. Oppenheim, in 1992.
4. L. Weiner, in E. Lucie-Smith, 1987, 117.
5. R. Long, 1985, 2, 24.

3 : 7 LAND ART AND PHOTOGRAPHY

1. S. Mills, "Special Kaye [Tony Kaye]", *Sunday Times Magazine*, June 12, 1994, 55.
2. D. Smith, *c.* 1953-54, in D. Smith, 158.
3. In N. Hedges, 77.

4. E. Hesse, in *Eva Hesse*, Guggenheim Museum, New York, NY, 1972.
5. J. Dibbets, 1970.
5. R. Long, FE.
6. R. Long, in W. Malpas, 1995.
7. R. Long, 1985, 1, 1.
8. Jasper Johns explained why he used 'real objects' stuck onto his paintings:

    My thinking is perhaps dependent on a realization of a thing as being the real thing… I like what I see to be real, or to be my idea of what is real. And I think I have a kind of resentment against illusion when I can recognize it. Also, a large part of my work has been involved with the painting as object, as real thing in itself. And in the face of that 'tragedy,' so far, my general development… has moved in the direction of using real things as painting. That is to say I find it more interesting to use a real fork as painting than it is to use painting as a real fork. (Quoted in D. Sylvester, op. cit., 15-16)

9. R. Smithson, in C. Robins, 1984, 78.

3 : 8 INTERIOR AND EXTERIOR ART

1. In M. Heizer, 1970.
2. D. Oppenheim, 1992.
3. In A. McPherson, 30.
4. Robert Smithson reckoned that a 'work of art when placed in a gallery loses its charge and becomes a portable object or surface disengaged from the outside world' (RS, 132).
5. In M. Heizer, 1970.
6. D. Nash, in B. Nemitz, 98.
7. L. Weiner, in *Avalanche*, Spring, 1972, 67.

3 : 9 LAND ART AND CHANGE

1. J. Beuys, in *Documenta 7*, 2, Documenta, Kassel, 1982.
2. See J. Burnham, 1971.
3. Quoted in G. Baro, 1969, 122; see C. Harrison, 1968, 266-8; J. Kirshner, "Barry Flanagan", *Artforum*, 23, 10, Summer, 1985, 112.

3 : 10 LAND ART AND RELIGION

1. M. Basho, *The Narrow Road to the Deep North and Other Travel Sketches*, tr. N. Yuasa, Penguin, London, 1966, 33.
2. M. Ueda, *Matsuo Basho*, Twayne, New York, NY, 1970, 167.
3. C. Andre, in *Carl Andre: Sculpture*, 1984.
4. M. Heizer, 1970.
5. Chuang-tzu, *Basic Writings*, tr. B. Watson, Columbia University Press, New York, NY, 44.
6. J. White, 67-69.
7. A. Goldsworthy, *Hand to Earth*, 101-2.
8. R. Long, 1985, 1, 14.
9. P. Redgrove, in J. Robinson, *Here Comes the Flood*, op. cit., 2008.
10. R. Long, interview with R. Cork, in D. Sylvester.
11. 'I think the sexual energy or the energy of creativity or the adrenalin energy you get from being on a mountain, sometimes they are all very close'). (R. Long, 1985, 2, 22).

12. M. Eliade, 1984, 136.
13. M. Fried, "Art And Objecthood", 1967, in G. Battock, 1995, 28.
14. M. Eliade, 1984, 185.
15. M. Eliade, "Sacred Architecture and Symbolism", in *Eliade*, ed. C. Tacou, L'Herne, Paris, 1978, and in M. Eliade, 1988, 107.
16. M. Eliade, 1988, 107.
17. P. Fuller, 1993, xxxvi-xxxvii.

3 : 11 CIRCLES

1. See M. Berger, 1989.
2. Quoted in L. Lippard, 1967c, 26.
3. The allusions to prehistory would be quite different if Richard Long had stuck a picture of the Cerne Giant next to himself instead of the Wilmington Man. The Cerne Giant has the biggest penis in public (or any) art (at least in the United Kingdom).
4. R. Long, 1972, in *Fragments of a Conversation I-VI*, in *Walking in Circles*, 38.

3 : 12 GENDER AND SCALE IN LAND ART

1. D. Judd, 1975, 200f.
2. Mark Rothko wrote of his intentions with regard to scale thus:

    I paint very large pictures... The reason I paint them... is precisely because I want to be very intimate and human. To paint a small picture is to place yourself outside your experience, to look upon an experience as a stereopticon view or with a reducing glass. However you paint the larger picture, you are in it. It isn't something you command. (1951)

3. "Donald Judd", *The New York Times*, Apl 1, 1977, C20.
4. L. Lippard, 1968, 42.
5. L. Lippard, 1979, 88.
6. See L. Anderson, 1973; *Mary Miss: Interior Works*, Bell Gallery, University of Rhode Island, Autumn, 1981.
7. See N. Holt, 1975, 1977; T. Castle, 1982.
8. See D. Judd, 1975; W. Agee, 1975, 40-49; P. Carlson, 1984, 114-8; D. Kuspitt, "Donald Judd", 1985; B. Haskell, 1988; B. Smith, 1975.
9. Such as Tony Smith, *Die*, 1962, 72 x 72 x 72 in, Paula Cooper Gallery, New York, NY. See L. Lippard, 1972a; G. Baro, 1967; E. Greene, "Morphology of Tony Smith's Work", *Artforum*, April, 1974.
10. Such as Dan Flavin, *Untitled (to the "innovator" of Wheeling Peach-blow)*, 1968, Museum of Modern Art, New York, NY; *Untitled*, 1976, pink, blue, green fluorescent light, Saatchi Collection, London. See I. Licht, 1968; W. Wilson, "Dan Flavin: Fiat Lux", *Art News*, Jan, 1970; J. Burnham, 1969.
11. Such as Richard Serra, *Clara-Clara*, 1983, Cor-Ten steel, installation, Jardin des Tuileries, Paris; *Prop*, 1968, 96 in high, sheet 60 x 60 in, Whitney Museum of Art, New York, NY. See R. Krauss, 1972; D. Crimp, "Richard Serra: Sculpture Exceeded", *October*, Fall, 1981.
12. See K. Baker, 1980, 88-94; D. Waldman, Oct, 1970, 60-62, 75-79; P. Tuchman, 1978, 29-33; E. Develing, 1969.

3 : 13 LAND ART AND BRITISH SCULPTURE

1. D. Lee, "Wimbledon Sculpture", in G. Hughes, 1989, 25.
2. P. Fuller, "Likely Prospects: A British Art Questionnaire", *Artscribe*, 50, Jan, 1985; "Onward Christian Soldiers", *Artscribe*, 52, July, 1985.
3. P. Fuller, "Black cloud over the Hayward", *Art Monthly*, 70, Oct, 1983; "Lee Grand-Jean and Glynn Williams", *Art Monthly*, 51, Nov, 1981.
4. J. Roberts, 1990, 111f.
5. T. Cragg, in E. Lucie-Smith, 1987, 130.

3 : 14 THE BRITISH LANDSCAPE TRADITION

1. R. Long, 1985, 2, 9.
2. R. Rosenblum, 1988, 7.
3. C. Andre, quoted in A. Causey, 1977, 126.
4. In the 19th century, landscape painting and garden design began to diverge, with only one-off exceptions, such as Monet's Giverny garden, merging the two disciplines.
5. Goldsworthy made a direct connection with the Romantics when he produced *Coleridge's Walk* (1997), a series of ephemeral pieces along a route the poet traversed in the Lakes.
6. T. Hughes, 1969, 79-80.

CHAPTER 4 • LAND ARTISTS IN BRITAIN, EUROPE AND AMERICA

4 : 1 ROBERT SMITHSON

1. In C. Robins, 78.
2. R. Hobbs, 12.
3. J.G. Ballard, in R. Smithson, 1997.
4. Smithson labelled pre-existing sites land artworks, non-sites, such as the pipes, boxes and walkways of an industrial zone in *Monuments of Passaic* (1967)
5. R. Smithson, "A Sedimentation of the Mind: Earth Projects", in RS, 85.
6. J.G. Ballard, in R. Smithson, 1997.
7. R. Smithson, "Discussion with Heizer, Oppenheim, Smithson", *Avalanche*, 1970, and in E. Johnson, 1982, 182.
8. In *Flow of Earth*, 1992.
9. J. Kounellis, in W. Sharp: "Structure and Sensibility", *Avalanche*, 5, Summer, 1972.
10. C. Robins, 1984, 82.
11. See M. Gimbutas, *The Language of the Goddess*, Thames & Hudson, London, 1989
12. R. Smithson, "The Spiral Jetty", unpublished MS, quoted in R. Krauss, 282. See R. Hobbs, 1981.
13. I. Sandler, 1990, 60.
14. A. Goldsworthy, interview, Dec 9, 1987, in HE, 163.
15. In R. Hobbs, 212.
16. J. Coplans, "Robert Smithson: The Amarillo Ramp", in R. Hobbs, 53.

4 : 2 DENNIS OPPENHEIM

1. In D. Oppenheim, 1992.
2. L. Lippard, 1983, 52.
2. In M. Heizer, 1970.
3. D. Oppenheim, in M. Heizer, 1970.

4. In D. Oppenheim, 1978.

4 : 3 ROBERT MORRIS

1. J. Perreault, 1995, 259.
2. R. Morris, quoted in M. Fried, 1967, in G. Battock, 1995, 126.
3. M. Friedman, 1966, 23.
4. D. Factor, 1966, 13.
5. In M. Compton, 1971, 16.
6. R. Morris, "Notes on Sculpture", 4, 51.
7. In D. Wheeler, 1991, 221.
8. D. Sylvester, 1996, 243.
9. In M. Compton, 1971, 19.

4 : 4 CARL ANDRE

1. And Clement Greenberg, Michael Fried, Lawrence Alloway, Bruce Glaser, Mel Bochner, David Bourdon, Lucy Lippard and Harold Rosenberg among art critics.
2. C. Andre, quoted in D. Bourdon, "The Razed Sites of Carl Andre", in G. Battock, 1995, 103.
3. L. Lippard, 1973, 157.
4. Ib., 104.
5. C. Andre, in *Carl Andre: Sculpture*, 1984.
6. L. Lippard, 1965, 58.
7. C. Andre, 1970, 61.
8. D. Bourdon, 1978, 56. See M. Bochner, 1967, 39-43.
9. D. Bourdon, in G. Battock, 1995, 107.
10. R. Krauss, 1977, 271f.
11. D. Bochner, in G. Battock, 1995, 94.
12. C. Andre, in L. Lippard, 1970, 7.
13. Carl Andre, *Joint*, 1968, 183 units, each 14 x 18 x 36 in, installation at Windham College, Putney, Vermont.
14. C. Andre, quoted in D. Bourdon, in G. Battock, 1995, 108.
15. T. Smith, quoted in M. Fried, 1967, in G. Battock, 1995, 131.
16. David Lee said that 'Andre repeats one thing in each piece; Smithson repeats one thing but increases its size' (1967, 44).

4 : 5 MICHAEL HEIZER

1. See A. Sonfist, 1983; J. Beardsley, 1984. Sol LeWitt was sceptical of enormity: '[i]f it's so big that you can't really comprehend it except by its emotive force then I don't want it' (in F. Colpitt, 77). And Robert Morris wrote that 'beyond a certain size the object can overwhelm and the gigantic scale becomes the loaded term' (1966, 21).
2. See J. Brown, 1984; G. Müller, 42-45.
3. In H. Smagula, 1983, 286.
4. M. Heizer, in J. Bell, "Positive and Negative", *Arts Magazine*, Nov, 1974, 55.
5. R. Hughes, 1997, 571.
6. M. Heizer, 1970.
7. R. Hughes, 1991, 386.

4 : 6 JAMES TURRELL

1. Dia Foundation, the McArthur Foundation, the National Endowment for the Arts, the

Lannan Foundation, the Canon Company, the Bohen Foundation, the Martin Bucks-baum Family Foundation, Count Guiseppe Panza di Buimo, Dr Pentti Kouri, Jean Stein, plus other donors.
2. J. Turrell, in A. Benjamin, 47.
3. J. Turrell, 1987.

4 : 7 NANCY HOLT

1. N. Holt, "Sun Tunnels", 1977, 34.
2. In T. Castle, 1982, 88.
3. See N. Holt, 1975, 1977; T. Castle, 1982.
4. C. Robins, 1984, 10.
5. On the North Star, shamanism, ascension, flight, tent poles and Cosmic Trees, see M. Eliade, 1975, 64f.

4 : 8 ALICE AYCOCK

1. H. Risatti, 37.
2. A. Aycock, quoted in E. Johnson, 1982, 223.
3. Aycock, quoted in N. Rosen, "A Sense of Place: Five American Artists", *International Sculpture*, Merriewold West, 1975.
4. R. Smith, 1975, 68.
5. W. Johnson, 1982, 221.
6. A. Aycock, 1977.

4 : 9 MARY MISS

1. R. Onoratio, 1978, 32. See also R. Onoratio, 1979; K. Linker, "Mary Miss", *Mary Miss*, ICA, 1983.
2. See L. Anderson, 1973; M. Miss, 1981.

4 : 10 WALTER DE MARIA

1. De Maria proposed another shaft, *Olympic Mountain Project* (1970) – never made – which would have been 400 feet deep and three feet wide.
3. Quoted in H. Smagula, 289.
4. R. Smith, 1978, 104.
5. H. Rosenberg, 1972, 36.
5. K. Baker, 1988, 125-7.
6. See D. Bourdon, 1968, 39-43, 72; M. Winton, 1970, 18-19; R. Smith, 1978, 102-5.
7. W. de Maria, 1980.
8. See P. Redgrove, *The Black Goddess and the Sixth Sense*, Bloomsbury, London, 1987; *The Cyclopean Mistress*, Bloodaxe, Newcastle, 1993. In many poems, Peter Redgrove wrote of the sensualism of nature, thunderstorms being particular favourite natural phenomena. This is from the poem 'The Pale Brows of Lightning':

And lightning opens its shutter but an instant,
When it catches you burn like a candle,
What is that lambent shadow fluttering into the woods
In its own blue light that illuminates primrose
The ripped tree's flesh?
(P. Redgrove, *The Man Named East and other new poems*, Routledge & Kegan Paul, London, 1985.)

9. H. Smagula, 290. De Maria himself thought that a lightning strike is a 'false climax' to the work, which really needs to be seen over a period of time to appreciate its qualities.
10. The Large Hadron Collider (built 1998-2008), is a 17-mile tunnel deep underground in Switzerland. These particle accelerators go far beyond most land art in creating sheer astonishment. Not the least amazing aspect about these circular tunnels is that they are so large, using gigantic machines set in caverns. The ironic thing is that such massive scientific equipment is being used to explore... the tiniest, invisible objects, the most mysterious things in the New Physics: atoms, quarks, strangeness, charms, Higgs' bosons, neutrons and protons. The Large Hadron Collider, for instance, cost $1.5 billion.
11. R. McKie, "Why we are so positive", *The Observer*, May 1, 1994.

4 : 11 OTHER AMERICAN EARTH ARTISTS

1. G. Matta-Clark, "Interview With *Avalanche*", *Avalanche*, Dec, 1974.
2. See L. Lippard, 1983, 49.
3. T. Murak. in B. Nemitz, 94.
4. D. Hollis, in B. Oakes, 107.

4 : 12 CHRISTO

1. J. Marck, *Wrapped Museum*, Museum of Contemporary Art, Chicago, IL, 1969.
2. Christo, quoted in E. Johnson, 1982, 198.
3. See W. Spies, *The Running Fence Project, Christo*, Abrams, New York, NY, 1977.
4. Christo, in A. Haden-Guest, 40.

4 : 13 HANS HAACKE

1. H. Haacke, in J. Burnham, 1967.
2. H. Haacke, in ib.

4 : 14 RICHARD LONG

1. H. Thoreau. in *Walking*, 1861, in *The Portable Thoreau*, ed. C. Bode, Viking, New York, NY, 1980, 592.
2. A. Seymour, "Walking in Circles", 1.
3. R. Long, in *Walking In Circles*, 23.
4. R. Long, in W. Maplas, 1995.
5. *Old World, New World*, 54.
6. H. Fulton, in M. Auping, in *Common Ground*, John & Mable Ringling Museum of Art, Sarasota, 1982.
7. R. Long, in *Walking In Circles*, 1986, 23.
8. R. Long, in ib., 224.
9. D. Reason, "Echo and Reflections", in S. Bann, 1991, 169.
10. R. Long, interview, Santa Fe, 1993, 236.
11. A. Goldsworthy, in N. Hedges, 77.
12. R. Long, in *An Interview With Richard Long*, R. Cork, in R. Long, *Walking In Circles*, 20.
13. J. Augoyard, *Pas a Pas. Essai sur le cheminement quotidien en milieu urbain*, Paris, 1979; C. Norberg-Schultz, *Existence, Space and Architecture*, London, 1971.
14. Kate Blacker, discussing Richard Long, Finlay and Willats wrote:

I don't think Long ...reversed anything. They just weren't concerned with the same things as their predecessors were. Long went to St Martin's and was introduced to a very strict set of self-perpetuating rules. He seems to have spent no time considering what [Anthony] Caro or [Philip] King had to say. Instead he placed himself in another British tradition: that of landscape. Regardless of the format of how to display the sculpture, he was the first British artist to bring landscape indoors. It's no longer a framed picture, a window onto the landscape, as it was in Constable or the Norfolk School. He brings the sense of scale, the whole sensibility of that tradition, into three dimensions. (K. Blacker, in P. de Monchaux, 1983, 92.)

15. R. Long, 1985, 2, 24.
16. R. Long, 1985, 1, 17.
17. In R. Long, interview, Santa Fe, 1993, 236.
18. R. Long, interview with G. Lobacheff, 1994, 6.
19. R. Long, interview, Santa Fe, 1993, 236.
20. Richard Long wrote:

   Even though it is necessary to get a good photograph, the photographs should be as simple as possible… the photographs have got to be fairly simple and straight-forward, so that the feeling of the work somehow accurately comes through. (R. Long, in *An Interview With Richard Long*, R. Cork, in R. Long, *Walking In Circles*, 24)

21. R. Long, interview, Santa Fe, 1993, 236.
22. *An Interview with Richard Long*, Santa Fe.
23. R. Long, interview with G. Lobacheff, 1994, 8.
24. R. Long, 1985, 1, 12.

4 : 15 DAVID NASH

1. See A. McPherson, 1978; H. Adams, 1979; D. Nash, 1980.
2. H. Adams, 1979, 46-47.
3. D. Nash, *Sea Hearth*, 1981, Isle of Bute, Scotland, *Wood Stove*, 1979, Maentwrog, Wales, *Slate Stove*, 1981, Blaenau Ffestiniog, Wales, *Snow Stove*, 1982, Kotoku, Japan.
4. At the University of Colorado, 1991.
5. D. Nash, in R. Martin, 1990, 66.
6. H. de Vries, in M. Gooding, 2002, 69.
7. D. Nash, *Fletched Over Ash Dome*, planted 1979, Caen-y-Coed, Maentwrog, Wales.
8. D. Nash, in Welsh Sculpture Trust, 120.
9. In A. Causey, 1980.

4 : 16 CHRIS DRURY

1. C. Drury, 2002, 72, 76.
2. C. Drury, 1998, 12.
3. C. Drury, 2002, 79.
4. C. Drury, 2002, 76, 84.
5. Quoted in *Andy Goldsworthy*, 1999.
6. Statement, on Drury's website.
7. C. Drury, in 1998, 6.
8. C. Drury, 1998, 7.

4 : 17 HAMISH FULTON

1. H. Fulton, in D. Beal, 2000.

2. H. Fulton, 1995.
3. Michael Archer, comparing the art of Long and Fulton, reckoned that Fulton 'offers possibilities', while Long 'designates'. Long's art was 'intentional in ways which Fulton's is not', and 'Fulton's art is conceptual in ways which Long's is not' (Archer, 1991).
4. H. Fulton, in 1999.
5. H. Fulton, in M. Auping, 1990.

4 : 18 OTHER BRITISH LAND ARTISTS

1. R. Harris, quoted in D. Petherbridge, "Public commissions and the new concerns in sculpture", in P. de Monchaux, 136.
2. R. Martin, 31.
3. B. Nemitz, 78.
4. N. Pope, quoted in W. Strachan, 70.

CHAPTER 5 • ANDY GOLDSWORTHY: WHOLE EARTH ARTIST

1. J. Dibbets, in D. Ashton, ed. *20th Century Artists on Art*, Pantheon, New York, NY, 1985, 174.
2. A. Goldsworthy, in A. Causey, 1980.
3. A. Goldsworthy, in *Aspects*, 1986.
4. A. Goldsworthy, ib., HE, 165.
5. K. Bloomert, 34; see also J. Gibson, 1966.
6. The Christmas 2003 stamps, valued at 20p, 38p, 53p, 68p and £1.12, comprised *Ice Spiral, Icicle Star, Wall of Frozen Snow, Ice Ball, Ice Hole, Snow Pyramids*. They were designed by Dick Davis from Goldsworthy's photographs. The stamps were also featured as Smilers™ stamps, personalized stamps in photobooths, and also part of the gamecard promotion with a first prize of £1 million.
7. Interview with T. Friedman, *Third Ear*, June, 1989 in HE, 166.
8. D.H. Lawrence, *The Rainbow*, Penguin, London, 1981, 244.

CHAPTER 7 • ANDY GOLDSWORTHY'S ART AND DECORATIVE ART

7 : 1 ANDY GOLDSWORTHY'S ART AND DECORATIVE ART

1. R. Long, in W. Malpas, 1995.
2. In D. Wheeler, 1991, 285.
3. C. King, "Feminist Arts", in F. Bonner *et al*, eds. *Imagining Women Cultural Representations and Gender*, Polity Press, Cambridge, 1992, 185.
4. A. Goldsworthy, *Mountains and Coast, Autumn into Winter*, 1988, HE, 163.
5. A. Goldsworthy, sketchbook no. 13, and in N. Sinden.
6. K. Carter, "*Stone*", *New Welsh Review*, 27, Winter, 1994-95, 100.
7. A. Goldsworthy, *Wall*, 68-69.
8. 'My strongest work is so rooted in place that it cannot be separated from where it is made', Goldsworthy wrote in *Stone* (6).
9. J.C. Powys, 1955, 926.
10. J.C. Powys, 1937, 353.

7 : 2 COLOUR IN ANDY GOLDSWORTHY'S ART

1. H. Voegls, "Haarlemmerhout", in HE, 54.

2. 1985, HE, 59.
3. Robert Rosenblum wrote:

There's a German artist Wolfgang Laib who does something of this sort too. He spends a lot of time in the woods gathering such things as pollen and collecting it and forming minimal geometric patterns out of gossamer and natural materials such as honey or dust of various kinds. It is some kind of ecological last gasp of communion with some pure beautiful stuff of nature. I guess this attitude is expiring even though it may, as in the case of Richard Long, still produce some marvellous artists. (R. Rosenblum, 1988, 11)

4. Quoted in P. Nesbitt, "Leafworks", in HE, 108.
5. In N. Hedges, 68.
6. Goldsworthy produced a special version of the leafworks display case for a collector in California in 1996.
7. Quoted in *Leaves*, Natural History Museum, London, 1989, 18.
8. *Leaves*, op.cit., 18.
9. Yet, after a few minutes, one'll experience something extraordinary. Or at least, it would be extraordinary to an 18th century landscape painter if s/he had ventured thus far into the mountains with her/ his sketchbook. It will come upon one *very* quickly. A deafening roar right over one's head, as a military jet screams over the rise of the hill in front. Within ten seconds, the plane has banked away to the North, veering East. One listens to the sound of the engines booming and echoing all around the valleys and peaks. This is how humanity alters the landscape. It's incredible. That jet appearing from nowhere in Britain's wildernesses might be regarded by prehistoric people as an amazing event (perhaps incomprehensible). For Western, First Worlders, in the early 21st century, it's all so 'normal'.
10. In A. Papadakis, 1991, 250.
11. In J. Beardsley, 1984, 134.

CHAPTER 8 • TREES, TIDES, PLANTS AND HOLES

8 : 1 LIVING PLANTS

1. J. Koons, in A. Muthesiues, ed. *Jeff Koons*, Cologne, 1992.

8 : 2 TREES

1. Writers on the symbolic and religious aspects of trees include Mircea Eliade (*Patterns of Comparative Religion*), Robert Graves (*The White Goddess*), James G. Frazer (*The Golden Bough*), and J.R.R. Tolkien, among others.
2. A. Goldsworthy, *Sheepfolds* website.
3. Film director John Boorman's phrase.

8 : 3 THE BLACK HOLE

1. C. Koelb, "Castration Envy", in P.J. Burgard, ed. *Nietzsche and the Feminine*, University Press of Virginia, Charlottesville, VI, 1994, 79.
2. A. Papadakis, 1991, 249.
3. Ib., 250.

CHAPTER 9 • ANDY GOLDSWORTHY THE SNOWMAN

9 : 1 ANDY GOLDSWORTHY AND SNOW

1. In *Andy Goldsworthy*.
2. A. Goldsworthy, interview, Dec 9, 1987, in HE, 163.
3. 'Urban living has always tended to produce a sentimental view of nature' wrote John Berger (*The White Bird: Writings by John Berger*, London, 1988, 7).
4. 'Nature for me is the clearest path to discover – *uncluttered by personalities* or associations – *it just is*', says Goldsworthy in a telling statement (my emphasis, sketchbook no. 19, 1988, HE, 150).
5. A. Goldsworthy, sketchbook, Jan 22, 1983, HE, 146.
6. 'Working in Britain means working close to change: a clear day soon clouds over, snow melts quickly, a calm morning turns windy. These qualities give urgency and energy to what I do' (AG).

9 : 2 TOUCHING NORTH

1. A. Goldsworthy, *Touching North*, 1989, and in HE, 75.

CHAPTER 10 • ANDY GOLDSWORTHY THE GREEN MAN

1. A. Goldsworthy, HE, 163.
2. P. Nesbitt, "A Landscape Touched by Gold", in G. Hughes, 1990, 49.
3. G. Evans, "Sculpture and Reality", *Studio International*, 177, no. 908, Feb, 1969, 62.
4. A. Goldsworthy, *Andy Goldsworthy*, Viking, London, 1990, no page numbers; and in N. Hedges, 67; HE, 160-1.
5. A. Causey, "Environmental Sculptures", in HE, 128.
6. A. Goldsworthy, *Third Ear*, BBC Radio 3, June 30, 1989, in HE, 168.
7. A. Goldsworthy, *Mountain and Coast, Autumn into Winter*, 1988, in HE, 163 (my italics).
8. *Artists in National Parks*, Victoria & Albert Museum, London, 1988, and in HE, 73.
9. AG; WH; and HE, 162.
10. D. Judd, "Specific Objects", in G. de Vries, 1974, 128.
11. A. Goldsworthy, *Touching North*, 1989.

CHAPTER 11 • INSTALLATIONS AND LARGE-SCALE WORKS

11 : 3 LARGE-SCALE WORKS AND INSTALLATIONS

1. R. Long, in *Words After the Fact*, in R. Fuchs, 1986, 236.
2. 'Goldsworthy's pieces dig at the roots of our relationship with nature, he is conducting an interrogative process with the fundamentals of our world – water, stone, earth, growing things and – latterly, in his work with volcanic rock and 'fired' stones – fire' (P. Whitaker, 1995, 109).
3. In B. Redhead, 19.
4. 'Some works have qualities of snaking but are not snakes. The form is shaped through a similar response to environment' commented Goldsworthy (AG).
5. Goldsworthy wrote that a 'work made with leaves is a celebration of growth, yet cannot work without expressing some anticipation of death, in a way that understands that death is a part of growth. The sarcophagi are not just containers of death, they are containers of life, in that out of death comes life' (TM). Goldsworthy

had also made snaking sand sculptures in Australia (*Sand / brought to an edge / to catch the morning light,* in 1991).

6. In R. Davies, 1984, 151.
7. A. Causey, 1990, 128.
8. N. Hedges, 71.
9. T. Friedman, "Monuments", HE, 154.
10. In HE, 147, 189.
11. A. Goldsworthy, sketchbook no. 19, March 3, 1988, HE, 154.
12. A. Goldsworthy, Arctic diary, April, 1989, in *Touching North*, HE, 158.
13. Chris Drury has also written that a 'stick is a forest, a stone a mountain' (1998, 58).
14. A. Goldsworthy, unpublished notes, 1988, in HE, 134-5.
15. J. & C. Bord, *Mysterious Britain*, Paladin, London, 1974, 240-1.
16. Goldsworthy said he heard about the dragon legend after he had made *Lambton Earthwork* (HE, 135).

11 : 6 CAIRNS

1. 1987, HE, 147.
2. In Y. Baginsky, 1989.
3. In W. Strachan, 179.
4. See R. Parker, 1987, 316; L. Lippard, 1976, 203.

11 : 8 WALLS

1. A. Goldsworthy, quoted in T. Friedman, "Monuments", in HE, 154.
2. A. Causey, 140.
3. R. Harris, quoted in D. Petherbridge, "Public commissions and the new concerns in sculpture", in P. de Monchaux, 136.

11: 10 ARCHES

1. A. Goldsworthy, April 8, 1989, in *Touching North*, 1989, and in HE, 158.

CHAPTER 12 • SPIRITUALITY AND SCULPTURE

1. A. Papadakis, 1991, 250.
2. J.C. Powys, *Petrushka and the Dancer: The Diaries of John Cowper Powys, 1929-1939*, Carcanet/ Alyscamps, 1995, 98, 136.
2. A. Goldsworthy, sketchbook no. 22, 1988, HE, 150.
3. 'My days are defined by my work which leaves a trail that marks out my life', said Goldsworthy (S, 82).
4. Goldsworthy dislikes geometry being 'imposed upon nature' (HE, 162), though all his sculpture (like all art) can be seen as something 'imposed upon nature'. Even the most ephemeral and minuscule of Goldsworthy sculptures, such as the tiny flower or leafworks, are impositions and additions to the natural world. They are events which do not happen 'naturally'.
5. *Winter Harvest*; HE, 162.
6. 1984, in AG.

1. D.H. Lawrence, "Introduction To His Paintings", in *Selected Essays*, Penguin, London, 1950, 342.
2. See D. de Menil *et al*, *Yves Klein: 1958-62: A Retrospective*, Institute for the Arts, Rice University, Houston, TX, 1982.
3. See J. Yoshihara, in B. Bertozzi & K. Wolbert, *Gutai: Japanese Avant-Garde*, Darmstadt, 1991.
4. In K. Stiles, 755.
5. G. Brus, in *Günter Brus*, Whitechapel Gallery, London, 1980.
6. Quoted in M. Church.
7. In M. Church; and S, 120.
8. A. Goldsworthy, sketchbook no. 19, Feb, 1988. HE, 150.
9. A. Goldsworthy, *Rain sun snow hail mist calm*, 4.
10. Interview, HE, 168.
11. 'Each work grows, stays, decays – integral parts of a cycle which the photograph shows at its height, marking the moment when the work is most alive' (AG).
12. R. Smithson, *Writings*, 56-57; C. Robins, 1984, 80.
13. R. Long, 1986, 1, 9.
14. In M. Church.
15. A. Goldsworthy, 1985, quoted in S. Clifford & A. King, "Hampstead Heath and Hooke Park Wood, 1985-86", in HE, 57.
16. *Snowballs in Summer Installation*, 1989.
17. J. Beardsley, 1984, 134.
18. In N. Sinden, 1988, 28.

Bibliography

ANDY GOLDSWORTHY

Andy Goldsworthy, Alan Rankle, Nigel Jepson, Brampton Banks, Cumbria, 1982
Rain sun snow hail mist calm: Photoworks by Andy Goldsworthy, Henry Moore Centre
   for the Study of Sculpture, Leeds, Yorkshire, 1985
Land Matters, Blackfriars Arts Centre, Reed Press, 1986
"Hampstead Heath", *Aspects*, 32, Spring, 1986
& J. Fowles. *Winter Harvest*, Scottish Arts Council, 1987
Mountain and Coast: Autumn Into Winter: Japan 1987, Art Data, 1988
Parkland, Yorkshire Sculpture Park, West Bretton, 1988
Touching North, Fabian Carlsson, London, 1989
Snowballs in Summer Installation, Old Museum of Transport, Glasgow, 1989
Garden Mountain, Centre d'Art Contemporain, Castres, 1989
Leaves, Common Ground, London, 1989
Singular Visions, University of Warwick, 1989
Andy Goldsworthy, Viking, London, 1990
Hand to Earth: Andy Goldsworthy, Sculpture, 1976-1990, Henry Moore Centre for Sculpt-
   ure, Leeds, Yorkshire, 1990
interview, *Third Ear*, BBC Radio 3, June 30, 1989, in 1990 (HE)
"Geometry and Nature", interview, *Art & Design*, in A. Papadakis, 1991
Sand Leaves, Arts Club of Chicago, IL, 1991
Ice and Snow Drawings, Fruitmarket Gallery, Edinburgh, 1992
Andy Goldsworthy: Breakdown, Rose Art Museum, 1992
Andy Goldsworthy: Futatsu no aki, Tochigi Kenritsu Bijutsukan, Tokyo, 1993
"Andy Goldsworthy: an artist's diary", *Arts Review*, 45, Sept, 1993
"Andy Goldsworthy", *Art & Design,* 9, 5/6, May/ June 1994
Stone, Viking, London, 1994
Black Stones, Red Pools, Pro Arte Foundation, 1995
Wood, Viking, London, 1996
Sheepfolds, with S. Chettle, P. Nesbitt, A. Humphries, Michael Hue-Williams Gallery,
   London, 1996
Végètal, Ballet Atlantique-Régine Chopinot, La Rochelle, France, 1996
Alaska Works, Anchorage Museum of History and Art, Anchorage, AK, 1996
Andy Goldsworthy: A Collaboration With Nature, Abrams, New York, NY, 1996
Andy Goldsworthy: Jack's Fold, ed. J. Glasman, University of Hertfordshire, St Albans,
   Hertfordshire, 1996
Hand to Earth: Andy Goldsworthy Sculpture, T. Friedman, Thames and Hudson, London,
   1997 & 2004
Cairns, Musée départemental de Digne, Reserve Geologique de haute Provence, 1997
Andy Goldsworthy, Musée d'art contemporain de Montréal, Canada, 1998
Arch, with D. Craig, Thames & Hudson, London, 1999
Andy Goldsworthy, with M. Kuipers & T. Karreman, Province Noord-Holland aan Staats-
   bosbeheer, 1999
Wall, intr. K. Baker, Thames & Hudson, London, 2000
Time, Thames & Hudson, London, 2000
Midsummer Snowballs, intr. J. Collins, Thames & Hudson, London, 2001
Andy Goldsworthy – Réfuges d'Art, Editions Artha, 2002
Passage, Thames & Hudson, London, 2004
Enclosure, Thames & Hudson, London, 2007

OTHERS

H. Adams. "The Woodman", *Art and Artists*, 13, Apl, 1979
—. "Fabian Carlsson Gallery: London: Exhibit", *New Art Examiner*, 15, May, 1988
C. Adcock. *James Turrell*, University of California Press, Berkeley, CA, 1990
W.C. Agee. *Don Judd*, Whitney Museum of American Art, New York, NY, 1968
—. "Unit, Series, Site: A Judd Lexicon", *Art in America*, May, 1975
—. *The Sculpture of Donald Judd*, Art Museum of South Texas, Corpus Christi, TX, 1977
D. Alberge. "Making an impression with the elements", *The Independent*, Feb 18, 1989
L. Aldrich. *Cool Art: 1967*, Museum of Contemporary Art, 1968
P. Allison *et al. Beyond the Minimal,* Architectural Association Publications, London, 1998
L. Alloway. "The American Sublime", *Living Arts*, 1, 2, June, 1963
—. *Systematic Painting*, New York, NY, 1966
—. *Christo*, Abrams, New York, NY, 1969
—. "Robert Smithson's Development", *Artforum*, Nov, 1972
—. "Residual Sign Systems in Abstract Expressionism", *Artforum*, Nov, 1973
L. Anderson. "Mary Miss", *Artforum*, Nov, 1973
W. Anderson. *American Sculpture in Process, 1930/ 1970*, New York Graphics Society, Boston, MA, 1975
C. Andre. "Frank Stella: Preface to Stripe Painting", in D. Miller, 1959
—. "An Interview with Carl Andre", P. Tuchman, *Artforum*, 8, 10, June, 1970
—. *Carl Andre, Sculpture, 1958-1974*, Kunsthalle, Bern, 1975
—. "Object v Phenomenon", *Sculpture Today*, The International Sculpture Center, Toronto, 1978
—. *Carl Andre: Sculpture*, State University of New York Press, Albany, NY, 1984
—. *Carl Andre: works on land*, Exhibitions International, 2001
C. Andreae. "Art shaped by the weather", *Christian Science Monitor,* Sept 21, 1987
—. "Fire and ice", *Art News*, 89, 7, Sept, 1990
J. Andrews. *The Sculpture of David Nash*, Lund Humphries, London, 1999
M. Andrews. *Landscape and Western Art,* Oxford Paperbacks, Oxford, 1999
E. de Antonio & Mitch Tuchman. *Painters Painting*, Abbeville Press, New York, NY, 1984
"Andy Goldsworthy", *Rambler Magazine*, 16, Summer, 2003
M. Archer. "A Walk In the Endless Summer From Duncansby Head To the Place of the Camel Droppinh", *Art Monthly*, Sept, 1991
—. *Art Since 1960*, Thames & Hudson, London, 1997
D. Archibald. "Art forms fashioned with the help of mother nature", *Dumfries and Galloway Standard*, Nov 18, 1988
—. "Andy's unique view of nature takes him round the world", *Dumfries and Galloway Standard*, Feb 3, 1988
D. Ashton. *American Art Since 1945*, Thames & Hudson, London, 1982
—. *Modern American Sculpture*, Abrams, New York, NY, 1968
M. Auping. *Common Ground*, John and Mable Ringling Museum of Art, Sarasota, 1982
—. "Hamish Fulton", *Art in America*, 71, Feb, 1983
A. Aycock. "Work", "Maze", 1975, in A. Sondheim, 1977
J. Baal-Teshuva, ed. *Christo: The Reichstag and Urban Projects,* Prestel Verlag, Munich, 1993
Y. Baginsky. "Sculptor for whom success snowballs", *Scotland on Sunday*, Jan 15, 1989
M. Bailey. "Carve a name in ice", *The Observer*, June 11, 1989
E. Baker: "Judd the Obscure", *Art News*, 67, 2, 1968

K. Baker. "Andre in Retrospect", *Art in America*, Apl, 1980a

—. "Reckoning with Notation: The Drawings of Pollock, Newman, and Louis", *Artforum*, 18, 10, Summer, 1980b

—. *Minimalism: Art of Circumstance*, Abbeville, New York, NY, 1988

—. "Andy Goldsworthy: Haines", *Art News*, 91, 8, Oct. 1992

—. "Goldsworthy's natural approach", *San Francisco Chronicle*, June 1, 1994

—. "An earthy show", *San Francisco Sunday Examiner*, Feb 19, 1995

—. "Setting the record straight on Yves Klein", *San Francisco Chronicle*, June 11, 1995

—. "Art that knocks and sculpts and rearranges wood", *San Francisco Chronicle*, Oct 20, 1996

—. "A welcome complexity in new shows", *San Francisco Examiner*, Dec 13, 1996

—. "Feat of Clay in the (Un)making: many reverberations in cracking wall at Haines", *San Francisco Chronicle*, Dec 11, 1996

—. "Searching for the window into nature's soul", *Smithsonian*, Feb, 1997

S. Bann & W. Allen, eds. *Interpreting Contemporary Art*, Reaktion Books, London, 1991

—. "Shrines, Gardens, Utopias", *New Literary History*, 24, 4, Autumn, 1994a

—. "The Map As Index of the Real: Land Art and the Authentication of Travel", *Imago Mundi*, 46, British Library, London, 1994b

G. Baro. "Toward Speculation in Pure Form", *Art International*, Summer, 1967

—. "American Sculpture", *Studio International*, 172, 896, 1968

—. "Sculpture made visible: Barry Flanagan in discussion with Gene Baro", *Studio International*, 178, 915, Oct, 1969

M. Bartlett. "A tribe of one: Andy Goldsworthy at Haines Gallery", *ArtWeek*, 23, 19, July 9, 1992

G. Battock, ed. *The New Art*, Dutton, New York, NY, 1966

—. *Idea Art*, Dutton, New York, NY, 1973

—. "Art in America: Confusions", *Domus*, Mch, 1975

—. ed. *New Artists Video*, Dutton, New York, NY, 1978

—. ed. *The Art of Performance*, Dutton, New York, NY, 1984

—. ed. *Minimal Art: A Critical Anthology*, University of California Press, Berkeley, CA, 1995

G. Beal. "Richard Long: "the simplicity of walking, the simplicity of stones"", in T. Neff, 1987

—. ed. *Art In the Landscape*, Chinati Foundation, Texas, 2000

J. Beardsley. *Probing the Earth: Contemporary Land Projects,* Smithsonian Press, Washington, DC, 1977

—. *Art in Public Spaces*, Partners For Liveable Places, Washington, DC, 1981

—. *Earthworks and Beyond: Contemporary Art in the Landscape*, Abbeville Press, New York, NY, 1984/ 1998

M.R. Beaumont. "Romantic Sculpture", in A. Papadakis, 1988

—. "Fabian Carlsson Gallery: London: Exhibit", *Arts Review,* 40, Mch 11, 1988

—. "Andy Goldsworthy", *Arts Review*, 41, July 14, 1989

M. Beeren. *Century in Sculpture*, Stedelijk Museum, Amsterdam, 1992

A. Benjamin, ed. *Installation Art, Art & Design*, 30, 1993

L. Bennett. *The Life and Work of Andy Goldsworthy*, Heinemann, London, 2005

N. Bennett, ed. *The British Art Show: Old Allegiances and New Directions, 1979-1984*, Arts Council/ Orbis, London, 1984

M. Berger. *Labyrinths: Robert Morris, Minimalism and the 1960s,* Harper & Row, New York, NY, 1989

—. *Minimal Politics*, University of Maryland, Fine Arts Gallery

S. Bérubé. "Goldsworthy et Singer: l'art de jouer avec la nature", *La Presse*, Apl 25, 1998

R. Bevan. "A snake in the British Museum", *Art Newspaper*. 5, 43, Dec 1994

L. Biggs: *Between Object and Image*, British Council, London, 1986

W. Bishop. "A corporate collection", *British Journal of Photography*, June 12, 1987
M. Bloem, ed. *Lawrence Weiner*, Stedelijk Museum, Amsterdam, 1989
K.C. Bloomert & C.W. Moore. *Body, Memory and Architecture*, New Haven, CT, 1977
Eugen Blume *et al. Richard Long: Berlin Circle*, 2011
M. Bochner. "Art in Process – Structures", *Arts Magazine*, 40, 9, 1966a
—. "Primary Structures", *Arts*, June, 1966b
—. "Systematic", *Arts Magazine*, 41, 1, Nov, 1966c
—. "Serial Art Systems: Solipsism", *Arts Magazine*, 41, 8, Summer, 1967
S. Boettger. *Earthworks*, University of California Press, Berkeley, CA, 2002
Y. Bois. *Donald Judd*, Galerie Lelong, Paris, 1991
D. Bonetti, David. "Facing Eden: 100 years of landscape art in the Bay Area, is a show that limns a strong tradition", *San Francisco Examiner*, June 25, 1995
A. Bonnano. "Andy Goldsworthy", *Art and Design*, 9, 5/6, May/ June 1994
C. Borland *et al. The Cauldron,* Henry Moore Institute, Leeds, Yorkshire, 1996
D. Bourdon. "Walter de Maria: The Singular Experience", *Art International*, Dec 20, 1968
—. *Christo*, Abrams, New York, NY, 1971
—"The Mini-Conceptual Age", *Village Voice*, Oct 17, 1974
—. "You Can't Tell a Painter By His Colors", *Village Voice*, Mch 24, 1975
—. *Carl Andre: Sculpture, 1959-1977*, Jaap Rietman, New York, NY, 1978
—. *et al: Niki de Sant-Phalle: Fantastic Vision*, Nassau County Museum of Fine Art, Rosyln, New York, NY, 1987
—. "Andy Goldsworthy at Lelong", *Art in America*. 81, 11, Nov, 1993
—. *Designing the Earth*, Abrams, New York, NY, 1995
C. Brown. "Natural arts", *The Magazine,* July, 1987
D. Brown. "New British sculpture in Normandy", *Arts Review*, Feb 10, 1989
I. Brown. "From urban nightmare to primal scream: Chopinot/ Goldsworthy at the Playhouse", *Electronic Telegraph*, 820, Aug, 23, 1997
J. Brown *et al. Michael Heizer: Sculpture in Reverse*, see M. Heizer, 1984
—. ed. *Occluding Front: James Turrell*, Lapis Press, Larkspur Landing, CA, 1985
D. Bruckner. "Earth works", *New York Times Book Review*, Jan, 1996
P. Buchanan. "The Nature of Goldsworthy", *The Architectural Review*, Feb, 1988
J. Burnham. "Hans Haacke: Wind and Water Sculpture", 1967, in A. Sonfist, 1983
—. *Beyond Modern Sculpture*, Braziller, New York, NY, 1968
—. "A Dan Flavin Retrospective in Ottawa", *Artforum*, 8, 4, Dec, 1969
—. "Robert Morris", *Artforum*, 8, 7, 1970
—. "Haacke's Cancelled Show at the Guggenheim", *Artforum*, June, 1971
—. *Great Western Salt Works*, Brazillier, New York, NY, 1974
K. Bussman & F. Matzner, eds. *Hans Haacke*, Cantz, Stuttgart, 1993
J. Butterfield. *The Art of Light and Space*, Abbeville Press, New York, NY, 1993
D. Cameron. "When is a door not a door?", *XLIII esposizione Internazionale d'Arte La Biennale di Venezia*, Edizioni La Biennale, Venice, 1988
—. "Art for the new year: who's worth catching?", *Art & Auction*, Jan, 1994
J. Campbell. *The Power of Myth*, with B. Moyers, ed. B.S. Flowers, Doubleday, New York, NY, 1988
—. *The Hero With a Thousand Faces,* Paladin, London, 1988
—. *An Open Life*, Larson Publications, New York, NY, 1988
—. *The Hero's Journey: Joseph Campbell On his Life and Work,* ed. P. Cousineau, Harper & Row, San Francisco, CA, 1990
P. Carlson. "Donald Judd's Equivocal Objects", *Art in America*, Jan, 1984
K. Carter: "*Stone*", *New Welsh Review*, 27, Winter, 1994-95
T. Castle. "Nancy Holt, Siteseer", *Art in America*, Mch, 1982
A. Causey. *Nature as Material: An Exhibition of Sculpture and Photographs Purchased For the Arts Council Collection,* Arts Council, London, 1980
—. "Environmental Sculptures", in A. Goldsworthy, 1990

—. "Space and Time in British Land Art", *Studio International*, 193, 98, Feb, 1977
G. Celant. "Introduction", *Arte Povera*, Praeger, New York, NY, 1969
—. *Conceptual Art, Arte Povera, Land Art*, Galeria Civica d'Arte Moderna, Turin, 1970
—. "Tony Cragg and Industrial Platonism", *Artforum*, 20, 3, Nov, 1981
—. *Dennis Oppenheim*, Edizioni Charta Srl, 1997
A. Chave: "Minimalism and the Rhetoric of Power", *Arts*, Jan, 1990
C. Chandler. *The Ultimate Seduction*, Quartet, London, 1984
H.B. Chipp, ed. *Theories of Modern Art*, University Press of California, Los Angeles, CA, 1968
A. Christian. "Art of a craftsman: the sculptures of Andy Goldsworthy reflect a deep passion for the natural world", *Resurgence Magazine*, Feb, 1998
B. Christian. "Scottsdale Center present "nature oriented" shows", *Scottsdale Life*, Aug 18, 1994
M. Church. "A shower of stones, a flash in the river", *Sunday Telegraph*, Apl 10, 1994
A. Clabburn. "A sanctuary in the city", *The Age*, Oct, 22, 1997
F. Colpitt. *Minimal Art: The Critical Perspective*, University of Washington Press, Seattle, WA, 1990
B. Commoner. *The Closing Circle: Nature, Man and Technology*, Knopf, New York, NY, 1975
M. Compton & D. Sylvester. *Robert Morris*, Tate Gallery, London, 1971
—. *Some Notes on the Work of Richard Long*, British Council, London, 1976
Concept Art, Minimal Art, Land Art, Edition Cantz, Stuttgart, 1990
L. Cooke. "Richard Long replies to a critic", *Art Monthly*, 68, July, 1983
—. *Alison Wilding*, Serpentine Gallery, London, 1985
J. Coplans. "Serial Imagery", *Artforum*, 7, 2, Oct, 1968
—. *Donald Judd*, Pasadena Art Museum, CA, 1971
—. "Robert Smithson", *Artforum,* Apl, 1974
R. Cork. "Paying the price", *Listener Guide*, Dec 9, 1985
—. "Burnished in bush country", *The Times*, May 28, 1993
—. "Andy Goldsworthy", *The Times*, Apl 23, 1994
D. Cosgrove, ed. *Mappings*, London, 1999
T. Cragg. *Writings*, Editions Isy Brachot, Brussels, 1992
—. *Sculptures on the Page*, Henry Moore Institute, Leeds, Yorkshire, 1997
M. Craig-Martin. *Minimalism*, Tate Gallery, Liverpool, 1989
D. Crane. *The Transformation of the Avant Garde: The New York Art World, 1940-1985*, University of Chicago Press, Chicago, IL, 1987
M. Crichton. *Jasper Johns*, Thames & Hudson, London, 1977
P. Crowther, ed. *The Contemporary Sublime, Art & Design*, 40, 1995
P. Curtis. *Modern British Sculpture from the Collection*, Tate Gallery, Liverpool, 1988
C. Dal Canto. "As nature dictates", *Casa Vogue*, 248, Feb, 1993
—. "Stones", *Casa Vogue*, 266, 1994
G. Danto. "A clearing in the woods", *Art News*, 93, 2, Feb, 1994
P. Davey. "Delight", *Architectural Review*, 193, Apl, 1993
A. Davies. "Richard Long and Hamish Fulton", *Art Monthly*, 25, Apl, 1979
R. Davies & T. Knipe, eds. *A Sense of Place: Sculpture in Landscape*, 1984
R. Deakin. "Zen and the art of Andy Goldsworthy", *Modern Painters*, 10, 1, Spring, 1997
W. de Maria. "The Lightning Field", *Artforum*, 18, 8, Apl, 1980
Amy Dempsey. *Destination Art: Land Art: Site-Specific Art: Sculpture Parks*, 2011
P. de Monchaux, *et al*, eds. *The Sculpture Show*, Arts Council of Great Britain, London, 1983
N. de Oliveira *et al*. *Installation Art*, Thames & Hudson, London, 1994
—. *et al. Installation Art in the New Millennium*, Thames & Hudson, London, 2003
M. Derby. "Fleeting moments: Andy Goldsworthy at Karekare", *Art New Zealand*, 63, Winter 1992

R. Deutsche *et al. Hans Haacke*, MIT Press, Cambridge, MA, 1986
E. Develing. *Carl Andre*, Gemeentenmeuseum, The Hague, 1969
—. & L. Lippard. *Minimal Art*, Stadtische Kunsthalle, Dusseldorf, 1969
J. Dibbets, in L. Bear & W. Sharp: "DIBBETTS", *Avalanche*, 1, Autumn, 1970.
M. Dobson. "Breath of fresh air", *The New Statesman*, Jan 10, 1986
—. "Shared sentiments", *BBC Wildlife*, Jan, 1987
R. Donnell. *Double Vision: Perspectives On Gender and the Visual Arts*, Farleigh
   Dickinson University Press, Rutherford, NJ, 1995
M. Donovan. *The Andy Goldsworthy Project*, Thames & Hudson, London, 2010
L. Dougherty. "Art in nature: a new site for sculpture in Denmark", *Maquette*, Sept,
   1994
M. Drabble. "Andy Goldsworthy", *Modern Painters*, 2, 3, Autumn, 1989
C. Drury. *Shelters and Baskets*, Orchard Gallery, 1988
—. *Vessel: Sculpture 1990-95*, Towner Art Gallery, 1995
—. *Stones and Bundles*, Rebecca Hossack Gallery, London, 1995
—. *Silent Spaces*, Thames & Hudson, London, 1998/ 2004
—. *Journeys On Paper*, Stephen Lacey Gallery, London, 2000
—. interview with W. Furlong, in M. Gooding, 2002
—. *Defying Gravity*, North Carolina Museum of Art, NC, 2003
—. *Heart of Stone*, Aberystwyth Art Gallery, Wales, 2003
A. Dumas. "Andy Goldsworthy at Fabian Carlson Gallery", *Art in America*, May, 1988
M. Duncan. "On site: straddling the great divide", *Art in America*. 83, 3, Mch, 1995
—. "Live from the Getty", *Art in America,* 86, 5, May, 1998
R. Durand. "Andy Goldsworthy", *Le printemps de Cahors: catalogue des expositions,*
   Marval, Paris, 1996
L. Durrell. *Justine*, Faber, London, 1963
—. *Spirit of Place*, Faber, London, 1971
A. Dyson. *Richard Long: Sao Paulo Biennial 1994,* The British Council, 1994
J.C. Eade, ed. *Projecting the Landscape*, Humanities Research Centre, Canberra, 1987
D. Ebony. "Goldsworthy's Living Memorial", *Art in America*, Nov, 2003
M. Eliade. *Patterns in Comparative Religion*, Sheed & Ward, London, 1958
—. *Shamanism: Archaic Techniques of Ecstasy*, Princeton University Press, Princeton,
   NJ, 1972
—. *Myths, Dreams and Mysteries*, Harper & Row, New York, NY, 1975
—. *From Primitives to Zen: A Sourcebook*, Collins, London, 1977
—. *A History of Religious Ideas*, I, Collins, London, 1979
—. *Ordeal by Labyrinth*, University of Chicago Press, Chicago, IL, 1984
—. *Symbolism, the Sacred and the Arts*, Crossroad, New York, NY, 1988
Patrick Elliott. *Richard Long: Walking and Marking*, 2007
G. Evans. "Sculpture and Reality", *Studio International*, 177, 908, Feb, 1969
Ulrike Ezika. *Ready-made und Landschaft: Zur künstlerischen Verwendung der Natur bei
   Andy Goldsworthy*, 2010
J. Fabricus. *Alchemy: The Medieval Alchemists and Their Royal Art*, Aquarian Press,
   Northamptonshire, 1989
D. Factor. "Los Angeles", *Artforum*, 4, 9, May, 1966
S. Farr. "Andy Goldsworthy: stone works in America", *Reflex*, 8, 6, Dec, 1995
R. Ferguson *et al*, eds. *Discourses: Conversations in Postmodern Art and Culture*, MIT
   Press, Cambridge, MA, 1990
S. Field. "Touching the Earth", *Art and Artists*, 8, Apl, 1973
J. Fineberg: "Robert Morris Looking Back", *Arts Magazine*, 55, 1, 1980
—. *Art Since 1940: Strategies of Being*, Laurence King, London, 2000
A. Fisher & J. Saward. *The British Maze Guide*, Minotaur Designs, 1991
—. & D. Kingham. *Mazes,* Shire Publications, 1991
J. Fisher. "Richard Long", *Aspects*, 14, Spring, 1981

S. Foley. *Unitary Forms: Minimal Structures by Carl Andre, Donald Judd, John McCracken, Tony Smith*, Museum of Modern Art, San Francisco, CA, 1970

N. Foote. "Long Walks", *Artforum*, 18, Summer, 1980

W. Forma. *Five British Sculptors*, New York, NY, 1965

P. Frank & M. McKenzie. *New, Used and Improved: Art For the '80s*, Abbeville Press, New York, NY, 1987

D. Frankel. "Andy Goldsworthy", *Artforum*, Oct, 2000

M. Fried. "Shape as Form: Frank Stella's New Paintings", *Artforum*, 5, 3, Nov, 1966

—. "Art and Objecthood", *Artforum*, 5, Summer, 1967

M. Friedman. "Robert Morris: Polemics and Cubes", *Art International*, 10, 10, Dec, 1966

—. *14 Sculptors*, Walker Art Center, Minneapolis, MN, 1969

E. Fry. *Alice Aycock*, University of South Florida Art Galleries, Tampa, FL, 1981

—. "The Poetic Machines of Alice Aycock", *Portfolio*, Nov, 1981

—. et al. *Robert Morris*, Museum of Contemporary Art, Chicago, IL, 1986

R.H. Fuchs. "Memories of Passing: A Note on Richard Long", *Studio International*, 187, 965, Apl, 1974

—. *Carl Andre*, Van Abenmuseum, Eindhoven, 1978

—. *Richard Long*, text, in R. Long, 1986

P. Fuller. *Peter Fuller's Modern Painters: Reflections on British Art*, ed. J. McDonald, Methuen, London, 1993

H. Fulton. *Hamish Fulton: Selected Walks, 1969-89*, Albright-Knox Art Gallery, Buffalo, New York, NY, 1990

—. *Richard Long*, Thames & Hudson, London, 1991

—. *One Hundred Walks*, Haags Gemeetemuseum, The Hague, 1991

—. "Into a Walk Into Nature", *Thirty One Horrors*, Lenbachhaus, Munich, 1995

—. *Walking Artist*, Annely Juda, London, 1998

—. *Wild Life*, Pocketbooks, Edinburgh, 2000

—. *Walking Artist*, Richter Verlag, Düsseldorf, 2001

—. "Specific Places and Particular Events", in B. Tufnell, 2002

S. Gardiner. "Their medium is nature", *Landscape Architecture*, 80, Feb, 1990

M. Garlake. "Andy Goldsworthy", *Art Monthly*, 93, Feb, 1986

J. Gear. "Andy Goldsworthy", *Review*, Dec. 1, 1996

L. Gendron. "Le sculpteur d'éphémère", *L'actualité*, 22, 12, Aug, 1997

Gokce Gerekli. *Land Art on the Border between Topology and Atopology*, 2009

J. Gibson. *The Senses Considered as a Perceptual System*, Houghton Mifflin, Boston, MA, 1966

A. Gide. *The Counterfeiters*, tr. D. Bussy, Penguin, London, 1966

J. Giovannini. *Mary Miss*, Architectural Association, London, 1987

P. Giquel. "Andy Goldsworthy: Centre d'art contemporain Midi-Pyrénées", *Art Press*, 158, May, 1991

T. Godfrey. "Richard Wilson's watertable, Andy Goldsworthy", *Burlington Magazine*, 136, 1096, July, 1994

—. *Conceptual Art*, Phaidon, London, 1998

E. Goheen. *Wrapped Walk Ways*, Abrams, New York, NY, 1978

R. Goldberg. *Performance: Live Art Since the 60s*, Thames & Hudson, London, 1998

A. Goldstein, ed. *Reconsidering the Object of Art: 1965-1975*, Museum of Contemporary Art, L.A., CA, 1995

M. Gooding & W. Furlong. *Song of the Earth*, Thames and Hudson, London, 2002

A. Gopnik. "Basic Stuff: Robert Smithson, Myth, Science and Primitivism", *Art Magazine*, Mch, 1983

A. Graham-Dixon. "Turning over an old leaf", *The Independent*, Feb 3, 1988

—. "Cutting Ice", *The Independent*, June, 24, 1989

—. "An artist does the strand", *The Independent*, Aug 5, 1989

—. "Great Britain: neo, no: still faithful to the old guard", *Art News*, 88, 7, Sept, 1989

J. Grande. *Balance: art and nature*, Black Rose Books, Montréal, 1994
—. "Back to nature?", *Sculpture*, 13, 4, July/ Aug, 1994
—. *Art Nature Dialogues*, State University of New York Press, NY, 2004
N. Graydon. "Magic in the field", *Ritz*, 133, 1989
B. Graziani. "Robert Smithson's Picturable Situation", *Critical Inquiry*, 20, 3, Spring, 1994
C. Greenberg. *Art and Culture*, Beacon Press, Boston, MA, 1961
H. Gresty & D. Reason. *Landscape*, Kettle's Yard, Cambridge, 1986
—. *Bare: Alison Wilding: Sculptures, 1982-1993*, Newlyn Art Gallery, Cornwall, 1993
G. Greig. "Circular Tours In the Name of Art", *Sunday Times*, June 16, 1991
C. Grout. "Andy Goldsworthy: une esthétique pragmatique", *Art Press*, 192, May, 1994
H. Haacke. *Framing and Being Framed*, New York University Press, New York, NY, 1975
A. Haden-Guest. "The King of Wrap", *The Sunday Times Magazine*, Jan, 1994
C. Hagen. "Art in review", *New York Times*, 1993
J. Haldane. *A Road From the Past To the Future*, Crawford Arts Centre, St Andrews, 1997
—. "Images After the Fact", *Modern Painters*, 11, 3, Fall, 1998
—. "Back To the Land", *Art Monthly*, June, 1999
O. Hahn & P. Restany. *Christo*, Editioni Apollinaire, Milan, 1966
C. Hall. "Shared earth", *Arts Review*, 43, June 14, 1991
—. "Site lines", *Arts Review*, 46, Oct, 1994
J. Hamlin. "Andy Goldsworthy: artist lets nature take its course", *San Francisco Chronicle*, May 4, 1994
A.M. Hammacher. *The Sculpture of Barbara Hepworth*, Abrams, New York, NY, 1968
C. Harrison. "Barry Flanagan's Sculpture", *Studio International*, 175, 900, May, 1968
—. "Sculpture's Recent Past", in T. Neff, 1987
B. Haskell. *BLAM! The Explosion of Pop, Minimalism, and Performance, 1958-64*, Whitney Museum of American Art, New York, NY, 1984
—. *Donald Judd*, Whitney Museum of American Art, New York, NY, 1988
J. Hattam. "Restoration art focussing on nature's power to reclaim [Andy Goldsworthy]", *Sierra*, May-June, 2003
M. Hayde. "Nature is his studio: Great Britain's Andy Goldsworthy, master of the ephemeral "earth sculpture", will give a free lecture at Stanford", *Palo Alto Weekly*, Jan 27, 1995
N. Hedges. "Growth, decay and the movement of change", *World Magazine*, 45, Jan, 1991
M. Heizer, D. Oppenheim & R. Smithson. "Discussion", *Avalanche*, 1, Autumn, 1970
—. *Sculpture in Reverse*, Museum of Contemporary Art, Los Angeles, CA, 1984
A. Henri. *Environments and Happenings*, Thames & Hudson, London, 1974
—. *Total Art*, Praeger, New York, NY, 1974
C. Henry. "Lumps of the Landscape", *The World of Interiors*, Oct, 1987
—. "A style with natural life", *Glasgow Herald*, Aug 21, 1987
—. "Artist in love with nature puts down roots", *Glasgow Herald*, July 19, 1988
—. "Goldsworthy at Work or Paving the Way", *Artline*, 14, 33, Nov, 1988
—. "Royal Botanic Garden: Edinburgh: Exhibit", *Arts Review*, 40, July 15, 1988
—. "Melting moments", *Glasgow Herald*, July 28, 1989
—. "Natural History Museum: London: Exhibit", *Arts Review*, 41, Oct 6, 1989
—. "Andy Goldsworthy: Stone shapes a life", *The Herald*, Apl 22, 1994
—. "Only branching out", *The Herald*, Jan, 18, 1997
A. Hess. "Technology Exposed", *Landscape Architecture*, May, 1992
T. Hess. *Barnett Newman*, Walker, New York, NY, 1969
—. & L. Nochlin. *Woman as Sex Object: Studies in Erotic Art*, Newsweek, New York, NY, 1972
—. & E. Baker. *Art and Sexual Politics*, Art New Series, Macmillan, New York, NY, 1973
Galerie Max Hetzler. *Carl Andre, Gunther Forg, Hubert Kiecol, Richard Long, Meuser,*

Reinhard Mucha, Bruce Nauman and Ulrich Ruckreim, Cologne, 1985
P. Hill. "Sjoerd Buisman", *Alba*, 11, Spring 1989
R. Hill. "Ice and snow drawings", *Crafts*, 119, Nov/ Dec, 1992
E. Hilliard. "In tribute to the wild bunch", *The Independent*, June 22, 1988
G. Hilty. *Recent British Sculpture*, Arts Council, London, 1993
—. *Alison Wilding: Immersion/ Exposure*, Tate Gallery, Liverpool, 1991
A. Hindry. "Sculpture anglaise: le clavier de l'imagination", *Art Press*, 214, June, 1996
R.C. Hobbs. *Robert Smithson: Sculpture,* Cornell University Press, Ithaca, NY, 1981
—. "Earthworks", *Art Journal*, 42, Fall, 1982
N. Hodges ed. *Art and the Natural Environment, Art & Design,* 36, 1994
—. ed. *The Contemporary Sublime, Art & Design,* 40, 1995
N. Holt. "Amarillo Ramp", *Avalanche*, Fall, 1973
—. "Hydra's Head", *Arts Magazine*, Jan, 1975
—. "Sun Tunnels", *Artforum*, Apl, 1977
P. Hovdenakk. *Christo: Complete Editions*, Schellman & Klüser, Munich, 1982
S. Howell. "Kingdom of the ice man", *Observer Magazine*, June 28, 1987
—. "Goldsworthy: the ice-man cometh", *World of Interiors*, July/ Aug, 1989
S. Hubbard & R. Sandall. "Peter Gabriel's *US*: the artists' boxes project: artists'
    statements", *Contemporary Art*, 1, 2, Winter, 1992
—. intr. *Sculpture At Goodwood: A Vision For 21st Century British Sculpture*, Sculpture
    At Goodwood, Sussex, 2002
S. Huchet. "Un exercise de la terre: le travail d'Andy Goldsworthy", *Ligeia*, 11/12, Dec,
    1992
G. Hughes. "Artists in parks", *Arts Review*, 40, July 15, 1988
—. ed. *Arts Review Yearbook, 1989,* Arts Review Magazine, London, 1989
—. *Arts Review Yearbook, 1990*, Arts Review Magazine, London, 1990
R. Hughes. *Nothing If Not Critical: Selected Essays on Art and Artists*, Collins Harvill,
    London, 1990
—. *The Shock of the New*, Thames & Hudson, London, 1991
—. *American Visions: The Epic History of Art In America*, Knopf, New York, NY, 1997
T. Hughes. *Poetry in the Making*, Faber, London, 1969
—. *New Selected Poems, 1957-1994*, Faber, London, 1995
H.E. Hugo, ed. *The Portable Romantic Reader,* Viking Press, New York, NY, 1957
L. Hull. "In residence: Grizedale Forest sculpture park", *Maquette*, May/ June 1993
S. Hunter, ed. *An American Renaissance: Painting and Sculpture Since 1940*, Abbeville
    Press, New York, NY, 1986
M. Hutchinson. "So follow him, follow him, down to the hollow", *Hampstead and
    Highate Express*, Dec 13, 1985
L. Iizawa. "Earth work", *Studio Voice*, Mch, 1988
P. Inch. "Andy Goldsworthy", *Arts Review*, 42, July 13, 1990
R. Ingleby. "Visual arts: Andy Goldsworthy", *The Independent*, Nov 8, 1996
In Praise of Trees, Salisbury Festival, Wilts., 2002
D. Isaac. "When leaves turn to gold", *Echoes*, Mch 24, 1992
Y. Ishii. "Creating beauty from nature", *Chubu Yomiuri Shimbun*, 21, Feb 2, 1988
W. Januszczak. "The Heath Robinson", *The Guardian*, Jan, 5, 1986
—. "The magic of icicle works", *The Guardian*, July 7, 1987
G. Jeppson. *Richard Long*, Harvard College, Cambridge, MA, 1980
E.H. Johnson. *Modern Art and the Object*, Harper & Row, New York, NY, 1976
—. ed. *American Artist on Art*, Harper & Row, New York, NY, 1982
W. Johnson. *Riding the Ox Home: A History of Meditation from Shamanism to Science*,
    Rider, London, 1982
J. Johnston. "Walling into Art", *Art in America*, 75, 4, Apl, 1987
B. Jones. "A New Wave in Sculpture", *Artscribe*, 8, Sept, 1977
C. Joyce. "Walling into History", *Flash Art*, Summer, 1989

D. Judd. "Frank Stella", *Arts Magazine,* 36, Sept, 1962
—. "In the Galleries", *Arts Magazine,* 37, 10, Sept, 1963
—. "Local History", *Arts Yearbook 7,* 1964
—. "Black, White and Gray", *Arts Magazine,* 38, 6, Mch, 1964
—. "Specific Objects", *Arts Yearbook,* 8, Art Digest, New York, NY, 1965
—. "Barnett Newman", *Studio International,* 179, 919, Feb, 1970
—. *Complete Writings, 1959-1975,* Nova Scotia College of Art and Design, Halifax, Canada, 1975
—. *Complete Writings, 1975-1986,* Van Abbemuseum, Netherlands, 1987
E. Juncosa. "Landscape as experience", *Lapiz,* 61 Oct, 1989
Philip Kaiser & Miwon Kwon. *Ends of the Earth: Art of the Land to 1974,* 2012
D. Karshan. *Conceptual Art and Conceptual Aspects,* Farleigh Dickinson University, 1970
J. Kastner, ed. *Land and Environmental Art,* Phaidon, London, 1998
R. Katz. *Naked By the Window: The Fatal Marriage of Carl Andre and Ana Mendieta,* Atlantic Monthly Press, New York, NY, 1990
B. Kedar & R. Werblowsky, eds. *Sacred Space: Shrine, City, Land,* New York University Press, Albany, NY, 1998
S. Kemal & I. Gaskell, eds. *Landscape, natural beauty and the arts,* Cambridge University Press, Cambridge, 1993
M. Kemp. "Doing what comes naturally: morphogenesis and the limits of the genetic code", *Art Journal,* 55, 1, Spring 1996
G. Kepes, ed. *Arts of the Environment,* Brazillier, New York, NY, 1972
N. Khan. "Beating nature", *Art Express,* 25, Mch, 1986
P. King *et al.* "Colour in Sculpture", *Studio International,* 177, 907, 1969
C. Kino. "Andy Goldsworthy: Galerie Lelong", *Art News,* 95, 10, Nov, 1996
M. Kirby. *Happenings,* Dutton, New York, NY, 1966
C. Knight: *Art of the Sixties and Seventies: The Panza Collection,* Rizzoli, New York, NY, 1987
N. Konstam: *Sculpture: The Art and the Practice,* Collins, London, 1984
D. Kozinska. "Stones in motion: show of Andy Goldsworthy's work gives a preview of colossal rock arch coming here soon across the Atlantic", *The Gazette,* Apl 18, 1998
R. Kostelanetz. *The Theatre of Mixed Means,* Dial, New York, NY, 1968
—. *On Innovative Performance(s),* McFarland, Jefferson, NC, 1994
R.E. Krauss. "Richard Serra: Sculpture Redrawn", *Artforum,* May, 1972
—. "Sense and Sensibility: Reflection on Post '60s Sculpture", *Artforum,* 12, Nov, 1973
—. *Passages in Modern Sculpture,* Thames & Hudson, London, 1977
—. "Sculpture in the Expanded Field", *October,* 8, Spring, 1979
—. *Eva Hesse,* Whitechapel Art Gallery, London, 1979
—. *et al. Robert Morris,* Abrams, New York, NY, 1994
Z. Kraus, ed. *From Nature to Art, From Art to Nature,* Venice Biennale, Milan, 1978
D. Krug. "Ecological Design: Andy Goldsworthy, Ballet Atlantique", ArtsEdNet, Getty Education Institute for the Arts, 1997
D. Kuspitt. "Sol LeWitt", *Art in America,* 63, 5, 1975
—. "Authoritarian Abstraction", *Journal of Aesthetics and Art Criticism,* 36, 1, Autumn, 1977
—. "Robert Smithson's Drunken Boat", *Arts Magazine,* Oct, 1981
—. "Aycock's Dream Houses", *Art in America,* Sept, 1985
—. "Donald Judd", *Artforum,* 23, 5, Feb, 1985
J. Kutner. "Brice Marden, David Novros, Mark Rothko: The Urge to Communicate through Non-Imagistic Painting", *Arts Magazine,* 50, 1, Sept, 1975
S. Lacey. "Putting yin and yang into the landscape", *Electronic Telegraph,* 549, Nov 23, 1996
I. Lamaitre. "Interview with Tony Cragg", *Artefactum,* 2, Dec, 1985

T. Lang. "News from the imagination", *Issues in Architecture, Art & Design*, 3, 1, 1993
Land Marks, Edith C. Blum Art Institute, Bard College, Annadale-on-Hudson, 1984
D. Laporte. *Christo*, Pantheon Books, New York, NY, 1985
F. Laughlin. "Andy Goldsworthy, the geometrician", *Landscape Architecture,* Dec, 1997
B. Laws. "Where Art and Nature Meet", *The Telegraph Weekly*, Nov 12, 1988
C. Lebowitz. "Andy Goldsworthy", *Art in America*, Oct, 2000
D. Lee. "Serial Rights", *Art News*, 66, 8, Dec, 1967
—. "London Ecology Centre, Exhibit", *Arts Review*, 38, Jan 17, 1986
—. "Great art of the outdoors: bio-degrading sculptures", *Country Life*, 181, 35, Aug 27, 1987
—. "Pure, ephemeral spires", *The Times*, June 26, 1989
—. "Opinion: Richard Long and Hamish Fulton", *Arts Review*, July 26, 1991
—. "In profile: Goldsworthy", *Arts Review*, 47, Feb 1995
A. Legg, ed. *Sol LeWitt*, Museum of Modern Art, New York, NY, 1978
P. Leider. "For Robert Smithson", *Art in America*, Nov, 1973
B. Le Messurier. *Dartmoor Artists*, Halsgrove, Tiverton, Devon, 2002
K. Levin. "Robert Smithson", *Art News*, Sept, 1982
—. "Reflections on Robert Smithson's *Spiral Jetty*", *Arts Magazine*, May, 1978
G. Lewis. "No sculpture like snow sculpture", *This is London*, 1709, July 7, 1989
F. Licht. *Sculpture, 19th and 20th Centuries*, Michael Joseph, London, 1967
—. "Dan Flavin", *Artscanada*, Dec, 1968
D. Lillington. "Andy Goldsworthy: organic chemistry", *Time Out*, Apl 13, 1994
L. Lippard. "New York Letter: Apl-June, 1965", *Art International*, 9, 6, 1965
—. "New York Letter: Recent Sculpture as Escape", *Art International*, Feb, 1966a
—. "An Impure Situation", *Art International*, May 20, 1966b
—. *Ad Reinhardt*, Jewish Museum, New York, NY, 1966c
—. *Pop Art*, Oxford University Press, New York, NY, 1966d
—. "The Silent Art", *Art in America*, 55, 1, Jan-Feb, 1967a
—. "Sol LeWitt: Non-Visual Structures", *Artforum*, Apl, 1967b
—. "Tony Smith", *Art International*, Summer, 1967c
—. "Rebelliously Romantic?", *New York Times*, June 4, 1967d
—. "Escalataion in Washington", *Art International*, 12, 1, Jan, 1968
—. ed. *Surrealists on Art*, Prentice-Hall, Englewood Cliffs, NJ, 1970
—. *Tony Smith*, Thames & Hudson, London, 1972a
—. *Grids*, Philadelphia Institute of Contemporary Art, PA, 1972b
—. *Six Years: The Dematerialization of the Art Object from 1966 to 1972*, Praeger, New York, NY, 1973
—. *From the Center: feminist essays on women's art*, Dutton, New York, NY, 1976
—. *Eva Hesse*, New York University Press, New York, NY, 1976
—. et al. *Sol LeWitt*, Museum of Modern Art, New York, NY, 1978
—. "Complexities: Architectural Sculpture in Nature", *Art in America*, Feb, 1979
—. "Dinner Party", *Art in America*, Apl, 1980
—. *Ad Reinhardt*, Abrams, New York, NY, 1981
—. *Overlay*, Pantheon, New York, NY, 1983
C. Loeffier, ed. *Performance Anthology*, Contemporary Art Press, San Francisco, CA, 1979
R. Long. *Richard Long: In Conversation*, Parts 1 & 2, MW Press, Noordwijk, Holland, 1985-86
—. *Richard Long*, text by R.H. Fuchs, Thames & Hudson, London, 1986
—. *Old World New World*, Anthony d'Offay, London, 1988
—. *Richard Long: Walking in Circles*, Hayward Gallery/ Thames & Hudson, London, 1992
—. *Kicking Stones*, Anthony d'Offay Gallery, London, 1990
—. *Mountains and Water*, Anthony d'Offay, London, 1992

—. *From Time to Time*, DAP, 1997
—. *Richard Long*, Hatje Cantz, Stuttgart, 1997
—. *A Walk Across England*, Thames & Hudson, London, 1997
—. *Mirage*, Phaidon, London, 1998
—. *Selected Walks, 1979-1996*, Morning Star Press, 1999
—. *Richard Long: a Moving World,* Tate Publishing, London, 2002
—. *Richard Long – Walking the Line,* Thames and Hudson, London, 2002
M. Lothian. "Distant thunder", *Arts Review*, 40, Sept 9, 1988
O. Lowenstein. "Natural Time and Human Experience", *Sculpture*, 22, 5, June, 2003
E. Lucie-Smith. *Sculpture Since 1945*, Phaidon, London, 1987
A. Lund. "Landskab og skultur", *Landskab*, Dec, 1989
R. Lund. "Why Isn't Minimal Art Boring?", *Journal of Aesthetics and Art Criticism*, 45, 2, Winter, 1986
N. Lynton. introduction to *Tony Cragg*, Fifth Triennale India, British Council, 1982
—. *David Nash: Sculpture, 1971-90*, Serpentine Gallery, London, 1990
R. Mabey. "Art and ecology", *Modern Painters*, 3, 4, Winter, 1990
C. Maclay. "Grounds for exploration", *San Jose Mercury News*, Feb 5, 1995
D. Macmillan. "David Nash: Brancusi Joins the Garden Gang", *Art Monthly*, 65, Apl, 1983
L. MacRitchie. "Ancient Egypt", *Financial Times*, Dec 12, 1994
—. "Residency on earth", *Art in America*, 83, 4, Apl, 1995
S. Madoff. "Andy Goldsworthy", *Garden Design*, 13, June, 1994
W. Malpas. *Richard Long: The Art of Walking*, Crescent Moon, 1995/ 1998
—. *Land Art, Earthworks, Installations, Environments, Sculpture*, Crescent Moon, 1996/ 1998/ 2004
A.T. Mann. *Sacred Architecture*, Element Books, Shaftesbury, Dorset, 1993
J. van der Marck. *Wrapped Museum*, Museum of Contemporary Art, Chicago, IL, 1969
—. *Herbert Bayer*, Dartmouth College Museum, Hanover, NH, 1977
M. Marmer. "James Turrell", *Art in America*, 69, May, 1981
R. Martin. "Andy Goldsworthy: Fabian Carlsson, London", *Flash Art,* 140, May/ June, 1988
—. *The Sculpted Forest: Sculpture in the Forest of Dean*, Redcliff, Bristol, 1990
B. Matilsky. *Fragile Economies*, Rizzoli, New York, NY, 1992
D. Matless & G. Revill. "A solo ecology: the erratic art of Andy Goldsworthy", *Ecumene*, 2, 4, 1995
K. Matsui. "Column people", *Asahi Shimbun*, Feb 2, 1988
J. May. "Landscape Fired by Ice", *Landscape*, Dec, 1987
D. Mayhall. *The Minimal Tradition*, The Aldrich Museum of Contemporary Art, Ridgefield, CT, 1979
D. Marzona & E. Carlini. *Minimal Art*, Taschen, Cologne, 2004
B. McAvera. "Public art: site sensitivities", *Art Monthly*, 215, Apl, 1998
A. McGill. "Portrait of the artist as a bent twig", *London Standard*, Jan 22, 1984
D. McKinney. *Yves Klein, Brice Marden, Sigmar Polke*, Hirschl & Alder Modern, New York, NY, 1989
A. McPherson. "David Nash: interviewed by Allan McPherson", *Artscribe*, 12, June, 1978
K. McShine. *Primary Structures*, Jewish Museum, New York, NY, 1966
—. *Information*, Museum of Modern Art, New York, NY, 1970
—. *An International Survey of Recent Painting and Sculpture*, MOMA, New York, NY, 1984
W. Messer. "A tale of two festivals: Printemps de Cahors: Les rencontres d'Arles", *Art World*, 12, Winter, 1997
L. Metrick. "Disjunctions In Nature and Culture: Andy Goldsworthy", *Sculpture*, 22, 5, June, 2003

J. Meyer, ed. *Minimalism*, Phaidon, London, 2000

U. Meyer. *Conceptual Art*, Dutton, New York, NY, 1972

R. Millard. "The sculptor Andy Goldsworthy is turning part of Cumbria into a sculpture park", *The Independent*, Mch 25, 1996

D.C. Miller, ed. *Sixteen Americans*, Museum of Modern Art, New York, NY, 1959

M. Miller. *The Garden as an Art*, State University of New York Press, Albany, NY, 1993

M. Miss. *Mary Miss: Interior Works*, Bell Gallery, University of Rhode Island, Autumn, 1981

T. Mizutani. "Conversation with nature", *Bijutsu Techo,* Mch, 1988

—. "Close relation with nature", *Mainichi Shimbun*, Jan 29, 1988

R.C. Morgan. "Richard Long's Poststructural Encounters", *Arts*, 61, 6, Feb, 1987

—. *Art Into Ideas*, Cambridge, 1996

J. Morland. *New Milestones: Sculpture, Community and the Land*, Common Ground, London, 1988

H. Morphy & M. Boles, eds. *Art from the Land*, University of Washington Press, 2000

R. Morris. "Notes on Sculpture", *Artforum*, Feb, 1966, Oct, 1966, June, 1967, Apl, 1969

—. "Aligned with Nazca", *Artforum*, Oct, 1975

—. *Robert Morris: Mirror Works, 1961-1978*, Leo Castelli Gallery, New York, NY, 1979

—. *et al. Earthworks*, Seattle Art Museum, Seattle, WA, 1979

—. *Selected Works*, Contemporary Arts Museum, Houston, TX, 1981

—. *Continuous Project Altered Daily*, MIT Press, Cambridge, MA, 1993

S. Morris. "A Rhetoric of Silence: Redefinitions of Sculpture in the 1960s and 1970s", in S. Nairne, 1981

J. Morrison. "Landmatters", *British Journal of Photography*, 133, June 6, 1986

A. Morgan. "Maze and labyrinth", *Sculpture*, 14, 4, July/ Aug, 1995

D. Morse. "At Runnymede Farm, the crop is sculptures", *San Francisco Examiner*, May 2, 1997

G. Müller. "Michael Heizer", *Arts Magazine*, Dec, 1969

—. "The Earth, Subjected To Cataclysms, Is a Cruel Master", *Arts Magazine*, Nov, 1971

A. Murphey. "White magic", *The Observer*, Dec, 1996

S. Nairne & N. Serota. *British Sculpture in the Twentieth Century*, Whitechapel Art Gallery, London, 1981

H. Nakamura. "Andy Goldsworthy and Anthony Green", *Ikebana Ryusei*, 38, Apl, 1988

D. Nash. *Fletched Over Ash*, AIR Gallery, 1978

—. "David Nash", *Aspects*, 10, Spring, 1980

—. *Stoves and Hearths*, Duke Street Gallery, London, 1982

T.A. Neff, ed. *A Quiet Revolution: British Sculpture Since 1965*, Thames & Hudson, London, 1987

B. Nemitz. *Trans Plant: Living Vegetation in Contemporary Art*, Hatje Cantz, Stuttgart, 2000

C. Nemser. "An interview with Eva Hesse", *Artforum*, May, 1970

—. "My Memories of Eva Hesse", *Feminist Art Journal*, Winter, 1973

P. Nesbitt. "At Home with Nature: Andy Goldsworthy in Scotland", *Alba*, Spring, 1989

—. "A Landscape Touched by Gold", in G. Hughes, 1990

E. Newhall. "Andy Goldsworthy", *New York Magazine*, Sept 13, 1993

M. Newman. "New Sculpture in Britain", *Art in America*, Sept, 1982

R. Nilsen. "Show only a nibble of Goldsworthy art", *Arizona Republic*, Sept 25, 1994

M. Nixon. *Eva Hesse*, MIT Press, Cambridge, MA, 2002

P. Noever. *Donald Judd: Architecture*, Hatje Cantz, Stuttgart, 2003

I. Noguchi. *A Sculptor's World,* Harper & Row, New York, NY, 1968

J. Norrie. "Andy Goldsworthy", *Arts Review*, July 3, 1987

B. Oakes, ed. *Sculpting the Environment*, Van Nostrand Reinhold, New York, NY, 1995

P. Oakes. "The Incomparable Andy Goldsworthy", *Country Living*, 48, Dec, 1989

S. Oksenhorn. "Art, naturally", *The Aspen Times*, 116, 50, Dec 9, 1995

W. Oliver. "A natural at work", *Yorkshire Post*, Feb 24, 1986
R. Onoratio. "Illusive Spaces: The Art of Mary Miss", *Artforum*, Dec, 1978
—. *Mary Miss – Perimeters/ Pavilions/ Decoys*, Nassau County Museum, 1979
D. Oppenheim. *Dennis Oppenheim*, Musée d'Art Contemporain, Montréal, 1978
—. *Selected Works, 1967-1990*, Abrams, New York, NY, 1992
E. Osaka. *Andy Goldsworthy: Mountain and Coast: Autumn Into Winter*, Gallery Takagi, Nagoya, 1987
P. Osborne, ed. *Conceptual Art*, Phaidon, London, 2002
W. Packer. "Andy Goldsworthy's Transient Touch", *Sculpture*, July, 1989
—. "Sculpture from the countryside", *Financial Times*, July 7, 1987
T. Padon. "New York, New York", *Sculpture*, 13, 1, Jan/ Feb, 1994
A.C. Papadakis, ed. *British and American Art: The Uneasy Dialectic*, Art & Design, 3, 9/1, Academy Group, London, 1987
—. ed. *Abstract Art and the Rediscovery of the Spiritual*, Art & Design, 3, 5/6, Academy Group, London, 1987
—. ed. *The New Romantics*, Art & Design, 4, 11/12, Academy Group, London, 1988
—. *et al*, eds. *New Art*, Academy Group, London, 1991
R. Parker & G. Pollock. *Old Mistresses: Women, Art an Ideology*, Routledge & Kegan Paul, London, 1981
—. *Framing Feminism*, Pandora Press, London, 1987
D. Parr. "City focus: St. Louis: 'a different kind of energy'", *Art News*, 95, 3, Mch, 1996
J. Partridge. "Forest work", *Craft*, 81, July/ Aug, 1986
T. Passes. "Rain sun snow hail mist calm", *Venue Magazine*, Sept 11, 1986
A. Patrizio. "Cube garden: sculpture at the Edinburgh Festival 1990", *Arts Review*, 42, July 27, 1990
P. Patton. "Robert Morris and the Fire Next Time", *Art News*, 82, 10, Dec, 1983
E. Pavese, ed. *Christo: Surrounded Islands*, Abrams, New York, NY, 1986
N. Pennick. *Mazes and Labyrinths*, Hale, London, 1990
C. Peres. "Arte: collaborare con la natura, *Casa Vogue*, 228, Mch, 1991
J. Perreault. "A Minimal Future? Union-Made: Report on a Phenomenon", *Arts Magazine*, 41, Mch, 1967
J. Perrone. "Seeing Through Boxes", *Artforum*, 15, Nov, 1976
K. Petersen & J.J. Wilson: *Women Artists: Recognition and Reappraisal from the Early Middle Ages to the Twentieth Century*, Women's Press, London, 1978
C. Peterson. "Inside the Goldsworthy installation", *Aspen Times*, Dec 16, 1995
P. Piguet. "Vassivière: une île pour la sculpture: an island for the sculpture", *Cimaise*, 41, 228, Jan, 1994
R. Pincus-Witten. *Postminimalism*, Out of London Press, New York, NY, 1977
—. *Entries: Maximalism*, Out of London Press, London, 1983
—. *Post-Minimalism into Maximalism*, UMI Research Press, Ann Arbor, MI, 1987
J. Poetter. *Donald Judd*, Cantz, Stuttgart, 1989
G. Pollock. *Vision and Difference: femininity, feminism and histories of art*, Routledge, London, 1988
L. Ponti. "Tony Cragg", *Domus*, 611, Nov, 1980
F. Popper. *Art, Action and Participation*, New York University Press, New York, NY, 1975
J.C. Powys. *Maiden Castle*, Cassell, London, 1937
—. *A Glastonbury Romance*, Macdonald, London, 1955
—. *Wolf Solent*, Penguin, London, 1964
—. *Autobiography*, Macdonald, London, 1967
A. Price. "A Conversation With Alice Aycock", *Architectural Design*, Apl, 1980
G. Prince. "With mud on their hands, growth, decay and the movement of change", *World Magazine*, Jan, 1991
J. Prinz. *Art Discourse*, Rutgers University Press, New Brunswick, NJ, 1991
S. Prokopoff: *A Romantic Minimalism*, Institute of Contemporary Art, Philadelphia, PA,

1967
J. Prown *et al. Discovered Lands, Invented Pasts*, Yale University Press, New Haven, CT, 1992
E. Rankin. "Popularising public sculpture in Britain: from landscape gardens to forest trails", *de Arte*, 53, Apl, 1996
C. Ratcliff. *In the Realm of the Monochrome*, Renaissance Society, University of Chicago, Chicago, IL, 1979
—. "The Compleat Smithson", *Art in America*, Jan, 1980
—. *Out of the Box*, Allworth Press, London, 2001
B. Redhead. *The Inspiration of Landscape: Artists in National Parks*, Phaidon, London, 1989
M. Regimbald. "L'homme qui plantait des arches [The man who planted arches]", *Espace*, 45, Autumn, 1998
W. Reh & C. Steenbergen. *Architecture and Landscape,* Prestel Publishing, 1996
K.J. Reiger, ed. *The Spiritual Image in Modern Art,* Theosophical Publishing House, Wheaton, IL, 1987
B. Reise. "'Untitled 1969': A Footnote on Art and Minimal Stylehood", *Studio International*, 179, 910, Apl, 1969
T. Rettig. "Contextualizing the work of Reinhard Reitzenstein", *Espace*, 25, Sept, 1993
N. Reynolds. "Lottery aid elevates sheep pens to fine art", *Electronic Telegraph*, 436, July 26, 1996
H. Risatti. "The Sculpture of Alice Aycock", *Woman's Art Journal*, Summer, 1985
A.C. Ritchie: *Sculpture in the Twentieth Century*, MOMA, New York, NY, 1952
J. Roberts. *Postmodernism, Politics and Art,* Manchester University Press, Manchester, 1990
C. Robins. "Object, Structure or Sculpture: Where Are We?", *Arts Magazine*, 40, 9, 1966
—. "Empty Paintings", *SoHo Weekly News*, Apl 22, 1976
—. *The Pluralist Era: American Art, 1968-1981*, Harper & Row, New York, NY, 1984
P. Rodaway. *Sensuous Geographies*, Routledge, London, 1994
Dieter Roelstraete. R*ichard Long (One Work) (Afterall)*, 2010
B. Rose. "New York Letter", *Art International*, Feb 15, 1964
—. "Looking at American Sculpture", *Artforum*, 3, Feb, 1965a
—. "ABC Art", *Art in America*, 53, 5, Nov, 1965b
—. *A New Aesthetic*, Washington Gallery of Modern Art, Washington, DC, 1967
—. *American Art Since 1900*, Thames & Hudson, London, 1967
—. *American Painting*, Skira/ Rizzoli International, New York, NY, 1986
—. *Robert Morris*, Corcoran Gallery, Washington, DC, 1990
H. Rosenberg. *The De-Definition of Art*, Horizon Press, New York, NY, 1972
R. Rosenblum. "Notes on Sol LeWitt", in A. Legg, 1978
—. *Modern Painting and the Northern Romantic Tradition*, Thames & Hudson, London, 1978
—. "Romanticism and Retrospective: An Interview with Robert Rosenblum", in A. Papadakis, 1988
—. "A postscript: some recent neo-romantic mutations", *Art Journal*, 52, 2, Summer, 1993
C. Ross. *Star Axis*, University of New Mexico Press, Albuqerque, NM, 1992
S. Ross. "Gardens, earthworks, and environmental art", in S. Kemal, 1993
—. *What Gardens Mean*, University of Chicago Press, Chicago, IL, 1998
M. Roth. "Robert Smithson on Duchamp", *Artforum*, Oct, 1969
—. ed. *The Amazing Decade: Women and Performance Art in America 1970-80*, Astro Artz, Los Angeles, CA, 1983
M. Rothko. *Mark Rothko in New York*, Guggenheim Museum, New York, NY, 1994
R. Rubinstein. "Andy Goldsworthy: Galerie Lelong", *Art News*, 92, 10, Dec, 1993
M. Ryan, ed. *Gravity and Grace: The Changing Condition of Sculpture, 1965-1975*, Hay-

ward Gallery, London, 1993

A. Saalfield. *Mary Miss*, Fogg Art Museum, Cambridge, MA, 1980

T. Sakurai. "Here comes the gold light'. *Ikebana Ryusei*, 10, Jan, 1988

—. "Goldsworthy with snow", *Ikebana Ryusei*, 10, Feb, 1988

I. Sandler. *American Art of the 1960s,* Harper & Row, New York, NY, 1988

—. *Art of the Postmodern Era: From the 1960s to the Early 1990s*, Harper-Collins, London, 1997

P. Schjeldahl. *Art in Our Time: The Saatchi Collection*, Lund Humphries, London, 1984

P. Schuck. "Interview: Earth, Water, Wind", *Contemporanea*, Apl, 1990

W. Scott. "In the gallery", *New York Post,* Dec 21, 1996

P. Selz. *Directions in Kinetic Sculpture*, University of California Press, Berkeley, CA, 1966

—. *Art in Our Times: A Pictorial History 1890-1980*, Thames & Hudson, London, 1982

A. Seymour. *The New Art*, Hayward Gallery, London, 1972

—. "Walking in Circles", in R. Long, *Walking in Circles*

—. "Old World New World", in R. Long, *Old World New World*

E. Shanes: *Constantin Brancusi*, Abbeville, New York, NY, 1989

G. Shapiro. *Earthworks: Robert Smithson and After Babel*, University of California Press, Berkeley, CA, 1995

W. Sharp *et al. Earth Art*, Andrew Dickson White Museum of Art, Cornell University, Ithaca, NY, 1969

A. Sherman. "Bound to earth", *Metro*, Feb 23, 1995

N. Shulman. "Monday at the North Pole", *Arts Review*, June 2, 1989

N. Sinden. "Interview: Art in Nature: Andy Goldsworthy", *Resurgence*, 129, Aug, 1988

H.J. Smagula. *Currents: Contemporary Directions in the Visual Arts*, Prentice-Hall, Englewood Cliffs, NJ, 1983

B. Smith. *Fluorescent Light, etc, from Dan Flavin*, National Gallery of Canada, Ottawa, 1969

—. *Donald Judd*, National Gallery of Canada, Ottawa, 1975

D. Smith. *Sculpture and Drawings*, ed. J. Merkert, Prestel-Verlag, Munich, 1986

R. Smith. "Sol LeWitt", *Artforum*, Jan, 1975

—. "Review", *Artforum*, Dec, 1975

—. "De Maria: Elements", *Art in America*, May, 1978

—. review, *New York Times*, Sept, 2004

R. Smithson. "Entropy and the New Monuments", *Artforum*, 4, 10, June, 1966

—. "Incidents of Mirror-Travel in the Yucatan", *Artforum*, Sept, 1967

—. The Monuments of Passaic", *Artforum*, Dec, 1967

—. "Toward the Development of an Air Terminal Site", *Artforum*, Summer, 1967

—. "A Museum of Language in the Vicinity of Art", *Art International*, 12, 3, Mch, 1968

—. *The Writings of Robert Smithson*, ed. N. Holt, New York University Press, New York, NY, 1979

—. *Robert Smithson*, ed. J. Flam, University of California Press, Berkeley, CA, 1996

—. *Robert Smithson: A Collection of Writings*, Pierogi Galery New York, NY, 1997

T. Sokolowski *et al. Robert Morris*, New York University Press, New York, NY, 1989

A. Sondheim, ed. *Post-Movement Art in America*, Dutton, New York, NY, 1977

A. Sonfist. *Alan Sonfist*, Neuberger Museum, New York, NY, 1978

—. ed. *Art in the Land: A Critical Anthology of Environmental Art*, Dutton, New York, NY, 1983

W. Spies. *The Running Fence Project, Christo*, Abrams, New York, NY, 1977

N. Stapen. "Bringing nature inside the museum", *Boston Sunday Globe*, Mch 29, 1992

J. Stathatos. "Andy Goldsworthy's Evidences", *Creative Camera*, 255, Mch, 1986

J. Steele. "In a natural mould", *Farmers Weekly*, May 13, 1988

F. Stella. *Working Space*, Harvard University Press, Cambridge, MA, 1986

N. Stewart. "Richard Long, Lines of Thought: A Conversation with Nick Stewart", *Circa*,

Nov, 1984

K. Stiles & P. Selz, eds. *Theories & Documents of Contemporary Art: A Sourcebook of Artists' Writings*, University of California Press, Berkeley, CA, 1996

S.L. Stoops. *Andy Goldsworthy: Breakdown*, Rose Art Museum, 1992

W.J. Strachan. *Open Air Sculpture in Britain*, Zwemmer, London, 1984

Roy Strong *et al. Close: Landscape Design and Land Art in Scotland*, 2010

E. Suderburg, ed. *Space, Site, Intervention*, University of Minnesota Press, Minneapolis, MN, 2000

T. Sultan. *Inability To Endure or Deny the World: Representation and Text In the Work of Robert Morris*, Corcoran Gallery, Washington, DC, 1990

G. Sutton. "Land art", *Landskab*, Dec, 1989

D. Sylvester. *About Modern Art*, Chatto & Windus, London, 1996

L. Talbot. "Fleeting beauty from the elements forger", *Hampstead and Highgate Express*, Feb 12, 1988

H. Teague. "Good as Goldsworthy", *Aspen Magazine*, 1996

M. Thomas. "Monkeys and guerrillas", *Photofile*, 35, May, 1992

J. Thym. "An artist by nature" *Oakland Tribune*, Feb 8, 1995

G. Tiberghien. *Land Art*, Art Data, London, 1995

S. Tillim. "Earthworks and the New Picturesque", *Artforum*, Dec, 1968

C. Tomkins. *Post- to Neo-: The Art World of the 1980s*, Penguin, London, 1989

M. Treib. "Frame, moment and sequence: the photographic book and the designed landscape", *Journal of Garden History*, 15, 2, Summer, 1995

M. Tromble. "A conversation with Andy Goldsworthy", *ArtWeek*, 23, 19, July 9, 1992

—. "A conversation with Robin Lasser", *ArtWeek*, 24, 20, Oct 21, 1993

E. Tsai. *Robert Smithson Unearthed*, Columbia University Press, New York, NY, 1991

M. Tuchman. *American Sculpture of the Sixties*, Los Angeles County Museum of Art, 1967

P. Tuchman. "Minimalism and Critical Response", *Artforum*, 15, 9, May, 1977

—. "Background of a Minimalist: Carl Andre", *Artforum*, Mch, 1978

—. "Minimalism", *Three Decades: The Oliver-Hoffmann Collection*, Museum of Contemporary Art, Chicago, IL, 1988

M. Tucker. *Robert Morris*, New York, NY, 1970

W. Tucker. *The Language of Sculpture*, Thames & Hudson, London, 1974

B. Tufnell & A. Wilson. *Hamish Fulton: Walking Journey*, Tate Publishing, London, 2002

C. Turnbull. "Beautiful Behaviour: The Photoworks of Andy Goldsworthy", *The Green Book*, 2, 6, 1987

J. Turrell. *Mapping Spaces*, Peter Blum, New York, NY, 1987.

—. interview, in B. Oakes, 1995

G. de Vries, ed. *On Art: Artists' Writings on the Changed Notion of Art After 1965*, Cologne, 1974

A.M. Wagner. *Three Artists (Three Women): Modernism and the Art of Hesse, Krasner and O'Keeffe*, University of California Press, Berkeley, CA, 1996

D. Waldman. *Carl Andre*, Guggenheim Museum, New York, NY, 1970a

—. "Holding the Floor", *Art News*, Oct, 1970b

—. *Robert Ryman*, Guggenheim Museum, New York, NY, 1972

Clarrie Wallis. *Richard Long: Heaven and Earth*, Tate, London, 2009

J. Watkins. "In the artist's studio: Andy Goldsworthy: Touching North", *Art International*, 9 Winter, 1989

M. Webster. "Andy Goldsworthy at San Jose Museum of Art", *ArtWeek*, 26, 4, Apl, 1995

S. Webster. "Art in the Woods [Andy Goldsworthy]", *Arts & Activities*, Sept, 2000

U. Weilacher *et al. Between Landscape Architecture and Land Art,* Birkhauser Verlag AG, 1999

L. Weiner. *Lawrence Weiner, Works*, Anatol AV und Filmproduktion Hamburg, 1977

Welsh Sculpture Trust. *Sculpture in a Country Park*, Welsh Sculpture Trust, 1983

C. West. "From genesis to box", *Modern Painters*, 5, 4, Winter, 1992

D. Wheeler. *Art Since Mid-Century: 1945 to the Present*, Thames & Hudson, London, 1991

P. Whitaker. "Andy Goldsworthy", *London Magazine*, 34, 10, Jan, 1995

J. White. *The Birth and Rebirth of Pictorial Space*, Faber, London, 1981

O. Wick *et al. James Turrell*, Turske & Turske Gallery, Zurich, 1990

G. Widdicombe. "Andy Goldsworthy: between a rock and a hard place", *The Independent*, Apl 13, 1994

A. Wildermuth. *Richard Long*, Galerie Buchmann, Basel, 1985

A. Wilding: *Alison Wilding*, with M. Tooby, Tate Gallery, St Ives, Cornwall, 1994

R. Williams. *After Modern Sculpture: Art in the United States and Europe 1965-70*, Manchester University Press, Manchester, 2000

A. Windsor, ed. *British Sculptors of the 20th Century*, Ashgate, Aldershot, Hants., 2003

C. van Winkel. "The Crooked Path, Patterns of Kinetic Energy", *Parkett*, 33, 1992

R. Wishart. "Andy Goldsworthy: art without additives", *Scotsman*, Apl 16, 1994

K. Withers. "Is it art?", *Venue Magazine*, Dec, 1989

G. Woods *et al*, eds. *Art Without Boundaries*, Thames & Hudson, London, 1972

M. Wortz. *Light and Space*, Whitney Museum of American Art, New York, NY, 1980

S. Wrede & W. Adams. *Denatured Visions: Landscape and Culture in the 20th Century*, Abrams, New York, NY, 1991

S. Yard. *Christo: Oceanfront*, Princeton University Press, Princeton, NJ, 1975

—. *Sitings*, La Jolla Museum of Contemporary Art, La Jolla, CA, 1986

M. Yule. "Andy Goldsworthy, a Lake District photowork", *National Art-Collections Fund Review*, 88, 1992

WEBSITES

Andy Goldsworthy, Sheepfolds site: <www.sheepfolds.org> <sheepfoldscumbria.co.uk>
Striding Arches <stridingarches.com>
Andy Goldsworthy, *Rivers and Tides* DVD <www.skyline.uk.com/riversandtides>
Andy Goldsworthy Digital Catalogue <goldsworthy.cc.gla.ac.uk>
Crescent Moon Publishing: <www.crmoon.com>
Earthworks <www.earthworks.org>
The Artists: <www.the-artists.org>
Sculpture at Goodwood, CASS: <www.sculpture.org.uk>
Robert Smithson <www.robertsmithson.com>
Walter de Maria <www.lightningfield.org>
Christo <www.christojeanneclaude.net>
James Turrell <www.rodencrater.org>
Mary Miss <www.marymiss.com>
Hamish Fulton <www.hamish-fulton.com>
Chris Drury <www.chrisdrury.co.uk>
Donald Judd <www.chinati.org>
Richard Long <www.richardlong.org>
Richard Long Newsletter <therichardlongnewsletter.org>

CRESCENT MOON PUBLISHING

ARTS, PAINTING, SCULPTURE

The Art of Andy Goldsworthy
Andy Goldsworthy: Touching Nature
Andy Goldsworthy in Close-Up
Andy Goldsworthy: Pocket Guide
Andy Goldsworthy In America
Land Art: A Complete Guide
The Art of Richard Long
Richard Long: Pocket Guide
Land Art In the UK
Land Art in Close-Up
Land Art In the U.S.A.
Land Art: Pocket Guide
Installation Art in Close-Up
Minimal Art and Artists In the 1960s and After
Colourfield Painting
Land Art DVD, TV documentary
Andy Goldsworthy DVD, TV documentary
The Erotic Object: Sexuality in Sculpture From Prehistory to the Present Day
Sex in Art: Pornography and Pleasure in Painting and Sculpture
Postwar Art
Sacred Gardens: The Garden in Myth, Religion and Art
Glorification: Religious Abstraction in Renaissance and 20th Century Art
Early Netherlandish Painting
Leonardo da Vinci
Piero della Francesca
Giovanni Bellini
Fra Angelico: Art and Religion in the Renaissance
Mark Rothko: The Art of Transcendence
Frank Stella: American Abstract Artist
Jasper Johns
Brice Marden
Alison Wilding: The Embrace of Sculpture
Vincent van Gogh: Visionary Landscapes
Eric Gill: Nuptials of God
Constantin Brancusi: Sculpting the Essence of Things
Max Beckmann
Caravaggio
Gustave Moreau
Egon Schiele: Sex and Death In Purple Stockings
Delizioso Fotografico Fervore: Works In Process 1
Sacro Cuore: Works In Process 2
The Light Eternal: J.M.W. Turner
The Madonna Glorified: Karen Arthurs

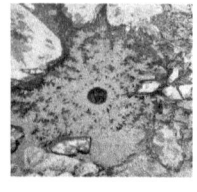
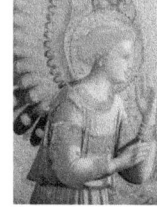

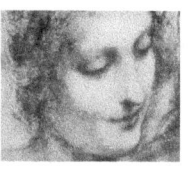
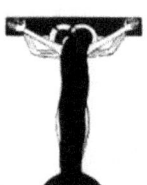
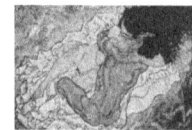

LITERATURE

J.R.R. Tolkien: The Books, The Films, The Whole Cultural Phenomenon
J.R.R. Tolkien: Pocket Guide
Tolkien's Heroic Quest
The *Earthsea* Books of Ursula Le Guin
Beauties, Beasts and Enchantment: Classic French Fairy Tales
German Popular Stories by the Brothers Grimm
Philip Pullman and *His Dark Materials*
Sexing Hardy: Thomas Hardy and Feminism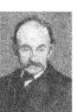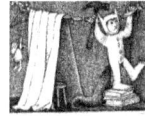
Thomas Hardy's *Tess of the d'Urbervilles*
Thomas Hardy's *Jude the Obscure*
Thomas Hardy: The Tragic Novels
Love and Tragedy: Thomas Hardy
The Poetry of Landscape in Hardy
Wessex Revisited: Thomas Hardy and John Cowper Powys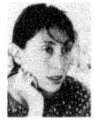
Wolfgang Iser: Essays and Interviews
Petrarch, Dante and the Troubadours
Maurice Sendak and the Art of Children's Book Illustration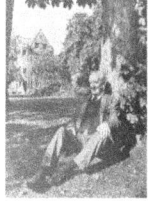
Andrea Dworkin
Cixous, Irigaray, Kristeva: The *Jouissance* of French Feminism
Julia Kristeva: Art, Love, Melancholy, Philosophy, Semiotics and Psychoanalysis
Hélene Cixous I Love You: The *Jouissance* of Writing
Luce Irigaray: Lips, Kissing, and the Politics of Sexual Difference
Peter Redgrove: Here Comes the Flood
Peter Redgrove: Sex-Magic-Poetry-Cornwall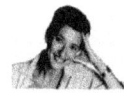
Lawrence Durrell: Between Love and Death, East and West
Love, Culture & Poetry: Lawrence Durrell
Cavafy: Anatomy of a Soul
German Romantic Poetry: Goethe, Novalis, Heine, Hölderlin
Feminism and Shakespeare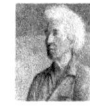
Shakespeare: Love, Poetry & Magic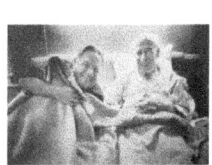
The Passion of D.H. Lawrence
D.H. Lawrence: Symbolic Landscapes
D.H. Lawrence: Infinite Sensual Violence
Rimbaud: Arthur Rimbaud and the Magic of Poetry
The Ecstasies of John Cowper Powys
Sensualism and Mythology: The Wessex Novels of John Cowper Powys
Amorous Life: John Cowper Powys and the Manifestation of Affectivity (H.W. Fawkner)
Postmodern Powys: New Essays on John Cowper Powys (Joe Boulter)
Rethinking Powys: Critical Essays on John Cowper Powys
Paul Bowles & Bernardo Bertolucci
Rainer Maria Rilke
Joseph Conrad: *Heart of Darkness*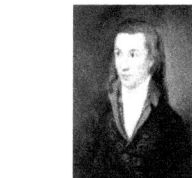
In the Dim Void: Samuel Beckett
Samuel Beckett Goes into the Silence
André Gide: Fiction and Fervour
Jackie Collins and the Blockbuster Novel
Blinded By Her Light: The Love-Poetry of Robert Graves
The Passion of Colours: Travels In Mediterranean Lands
Poetic Forms

POETRY

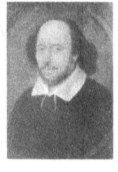
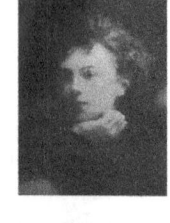

Ursula Le Guin: Walking In Cornwall
Peter Redgrove: Here Comes The Flood
Peter Redgrove: Sex-Magic-Poetry-Cornwall
Dante: Selections From the Vita Nuova
Petrarch, Dante and the Troubadours
William Shakespeare: Sonnets
William Shakespeare: Complete Poems
Blinded By Her Light: The Love-Poetry of Robert Graves
Emily Dickinson: Selected Poems
Emily Brontë: Poems
Thomas Hardy: Selected Poems

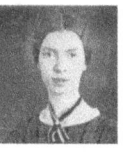
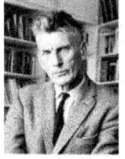
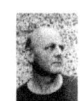

Percy Bysshe Shelley: Poems
John Keats: Selected Poems
Joh n Keats: Poems of 1820
D.H. Lawrence: Selected Poems
Edmund Spenser: Poems
Edmund Spenser: Amoretti
John Donne: Poems
Henry Vaughan: Poems
Sir Thomas Wyatt: Poems
Robert Herrick: Selected Poems

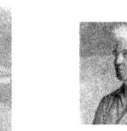
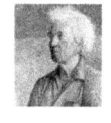
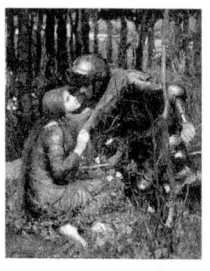

Rilke: Space, Essence and Angels in the Poetry of Rainer Maria Rilke
Rainer Maria Rilke: Selected Poems
Friedrich Hölderlin: Selected Poems
Arseny Tarkovsky: Selected Poems
Arthur Rimbaud: Selected Poems
Arthur Rimbaud: A Season in Hell
Arthur Rimbaud and the Magic of Poetry
Novalis: Hymns To the Night
German Romantic Poetry
Paul Verlaine: Selected Poems
Elizaethan Sonnet Cycles

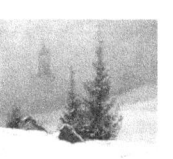
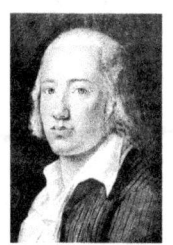

D.J. Enright: By-Blows
Jeremy Reed: Brigitte's Blue Heart
Jeremy Reed: Claudia Schiffer's Red Shoes
Gorgeous Little Orpheus
Radiance: New Poems

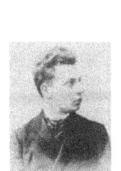
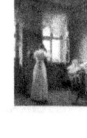

Crescent Moon Book of Nature Poetry
Crescent Moon Book of Love Poetry
Crescent Moon Book of Mystical Poetry
Crescent Moon Book of Elizabethan Love Poetry
Crescent Moon Book of Metaphysical Poetry
Crescent Moon Book of Romantic Poetry
Pagan America: New American Poetry

J.R.R. Tolkien: The Books, The Films, The Whole Cultural Phenomenon
J.R.R. Tolkien: Pocket Guide
The *Lord of the Rings* Movies: Pocket Guide
The Cinema of Hayao Miyazaki
Hayao Miyazaki: *Princess Mononoke*: Pocket Movie Guide
Hayao Miyazaki: *Spirited Away*: Pocket Movie Guide
Tim Burton
Ken Russell
Ken Russell: *Tommy*: Pocket Movie Guide
The Ghost Dance: The Origins of Religion
The Peyote Cult
Cixous, Irigaray, Kristeva: The *Jouissance* of French Feminism
Julia Kristeva: Art, Love, Melancholy, Philosophy, Semiotics and Psychoanalysis
Luce Irigaray: Lips, Kissing, and the Politics of Sexual Difference
Hélene Cixous I Love You: The *Jouissance* of Writing
Andrea Dworkin
'Cosmo Woman': The World of Women's Magazines
Women in Pop Music
Discovering the Goddess (Geoffrey Ashe)
The Poetry of Cinema
The Sacred Cinema of Andrei Tarkovsky
Andrei Tarkovsky: Pocket Guide
Andrei Tarkovsky: *Mirror*: Pocket Movie Guide
Andrei Tarkovsky: *The Sacrifice*: Pocket Movie Guide
Walerian Borowczyk: Cinema of Erotic Dreams
Jean-Luc Godard: The Passion of Cinema
Jean-Luc Godard: *Hail Mary*: Pocket Movie Guide
Jean-Luc Godard: *Contempt*: Pocket Movie Guide
Jean-Luc Godard: *Pierrot le Fou*: Pocket Movie Guide
John Hughes and Eighties Cinema
Ferris Bueller's Day Off: Pocket Movie Guide
Jean-Luc Godard: Pocket Guide
The Cinema of Richard Linklater
Liv Tyler: Star In Ascendance
Blade Runner and the Films of Philip K. Dick
Paul Bowles and Bernardo Bertolucci
Media Hell: Radio, TV and the Press
An Open Letter to the BBC
Detonation Britain: Nuclear War in the UK
Feminism and Shakespeare
Wild Zones: Pornography, Art and Feminism
Sex in Art: Pornography and Pleasure in Painting and Sculpture
Sexing Hardy: Thomas Hardy and Feminism

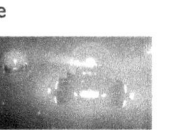
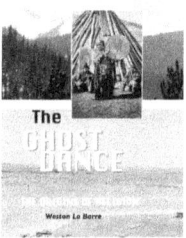

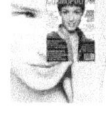
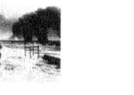
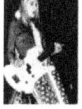
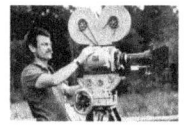
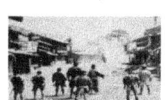
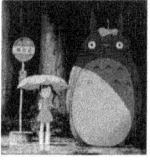
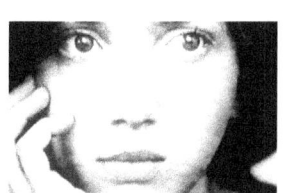

In my view The *Light Eternal* is among the very best of all the material I read on Turner. (Douglas Graham, director of the Turner Museum, Denver, Colorado)

The *Light Eternal* is a model monograph, an exemplary job. The subject matter of the book is beautifully organised and dead on beam. (Lawrence Durrell)

It is amazing for me to see my work treated with such passion and respect. (Andrea Dworkin)

CRESCENT MOON PUBLISHING
P.O. Box 1312, Maidstone, Kent, ME14 5XU, Great Britain. www.crmoon.com